# Cross Game

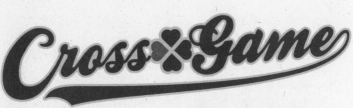

## Volume 4

Mitsuru Adachi

# Contents Volume 4

# 8

Story & Art by
**Mitsuru Adachi**

## Story Wrap-Up

First-year high school student Ko Kitamura is the only child of the family that runs Kitamura Sporting Goods. Down the street is a family of four sisters, whose second daughter Wakaba tragically drowned when she and Ko were in the fifth grade.

In high school, Ko starts playing baseball with Akaishi and friends, but coldhearted coach Daimon banishes them to a prefab portable shack. The Portables lose their first game to Varsity but manage to pull off a victory in a heated rematch. As a result of the loss, Coach Daimon and most of the first stringers leave Seishu, but the big slugger Yuhei Azuma decides to stay and join Ko and the rest of the team. Now in April, Ko is in his second year of high school, and Aoba Tsukishima is in her first year. Also, an "early bird" has entered the picture to complicate things a bit.

# CHAPTER 61
# MIZUKI ASAMI

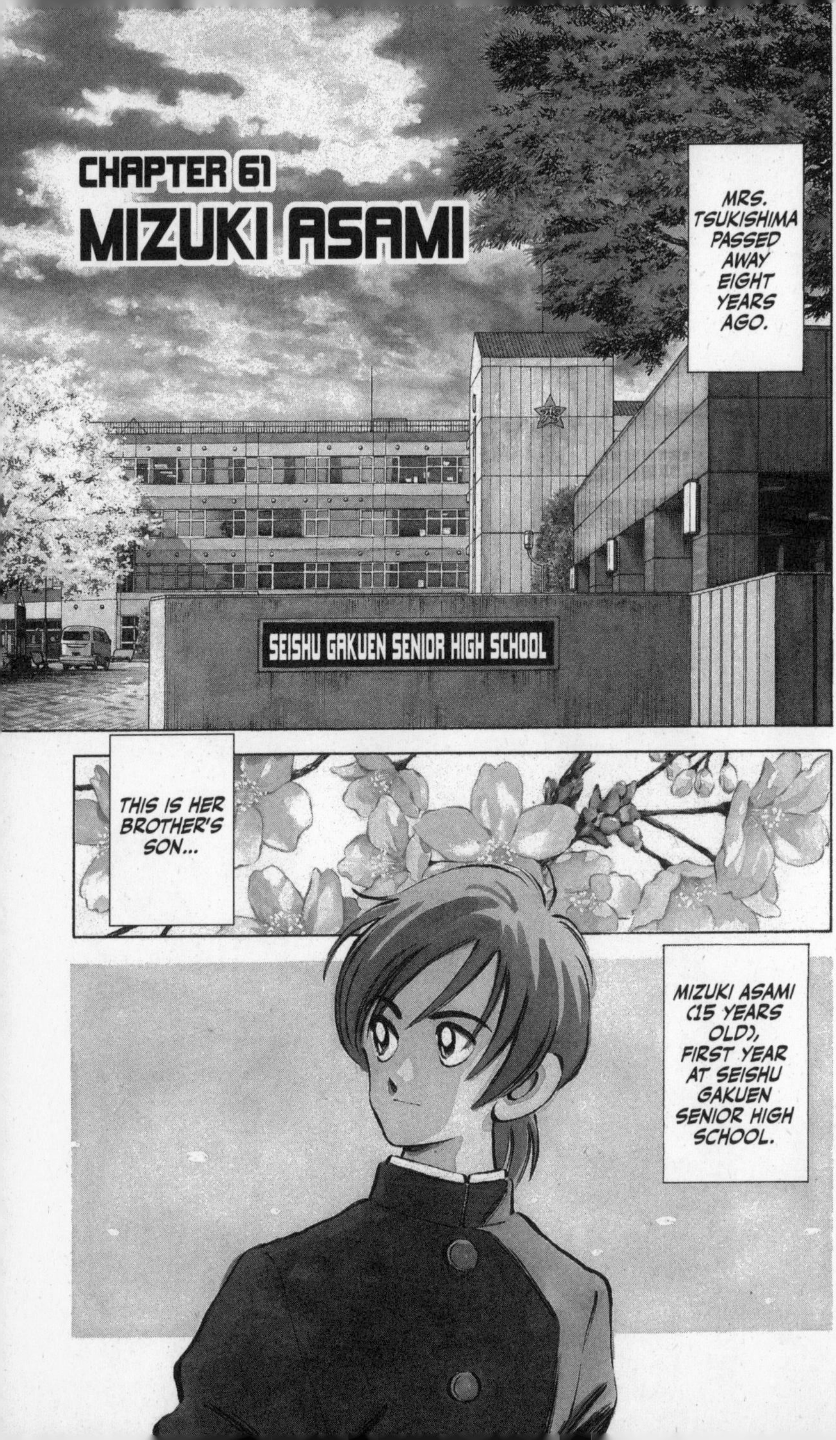
MRS. TSUKISHIMA PASSED AWAY EIGHT YEARS AGO.
SEISHU GAKUEN SENIOR HIGH SCHOOL
THIS IS HER BROTHER'S SON...
MIZUKI ASAMI (15 YEARS OLD), FIRST YEAR AT SEISHU GAKUEN SENIOR HIGH SCHOOL.

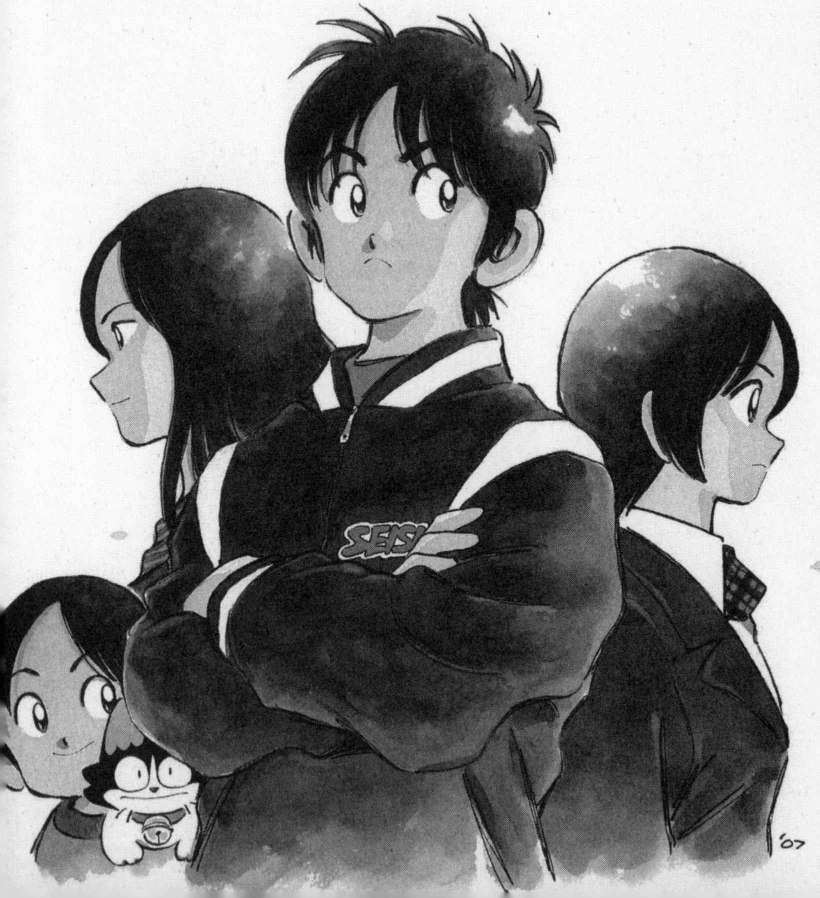

# CHAPTER 61
# MIZUKI ASAMI

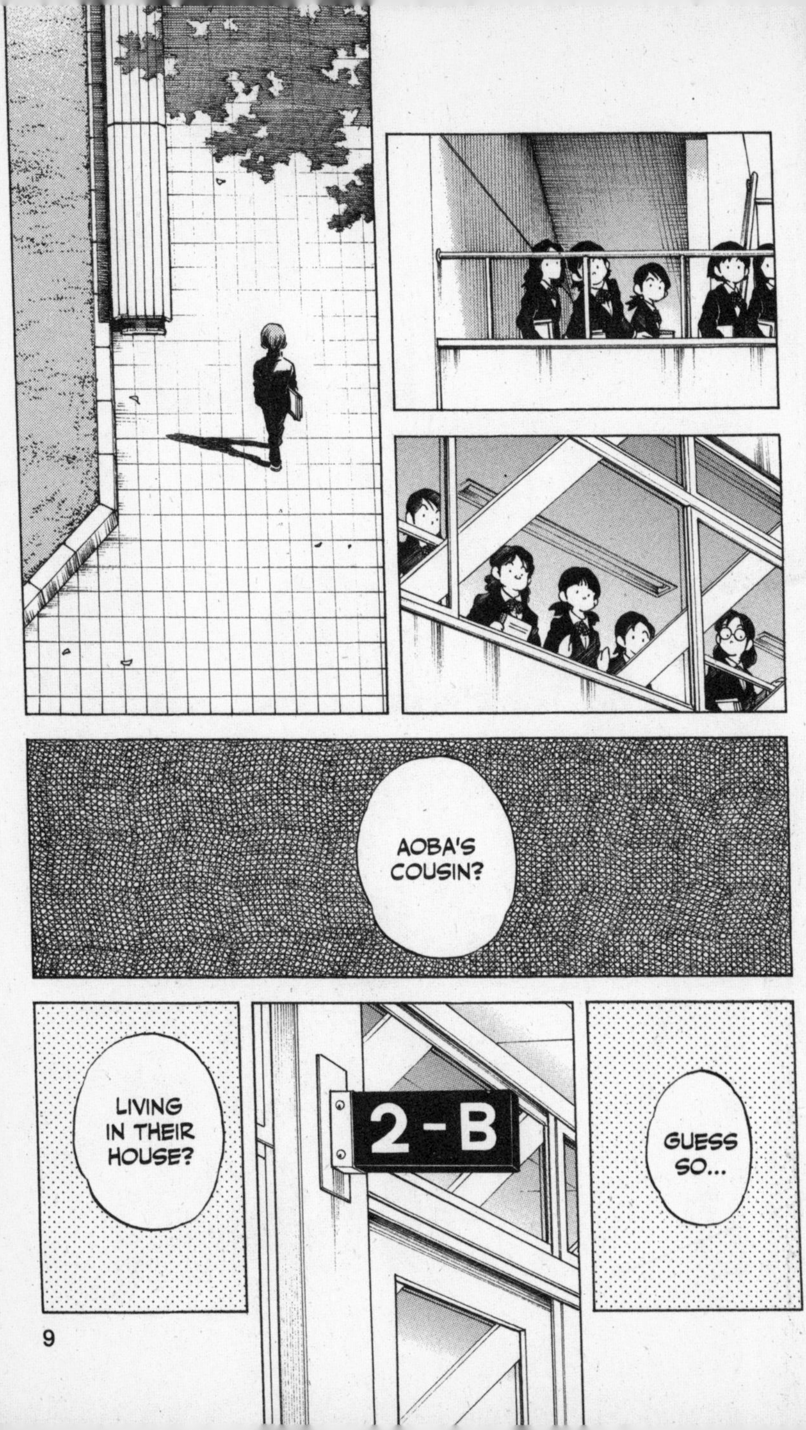
AOBA'S COUSIN?
GUESS SO...
2-B
LIVING IN THEIR HOUSE?

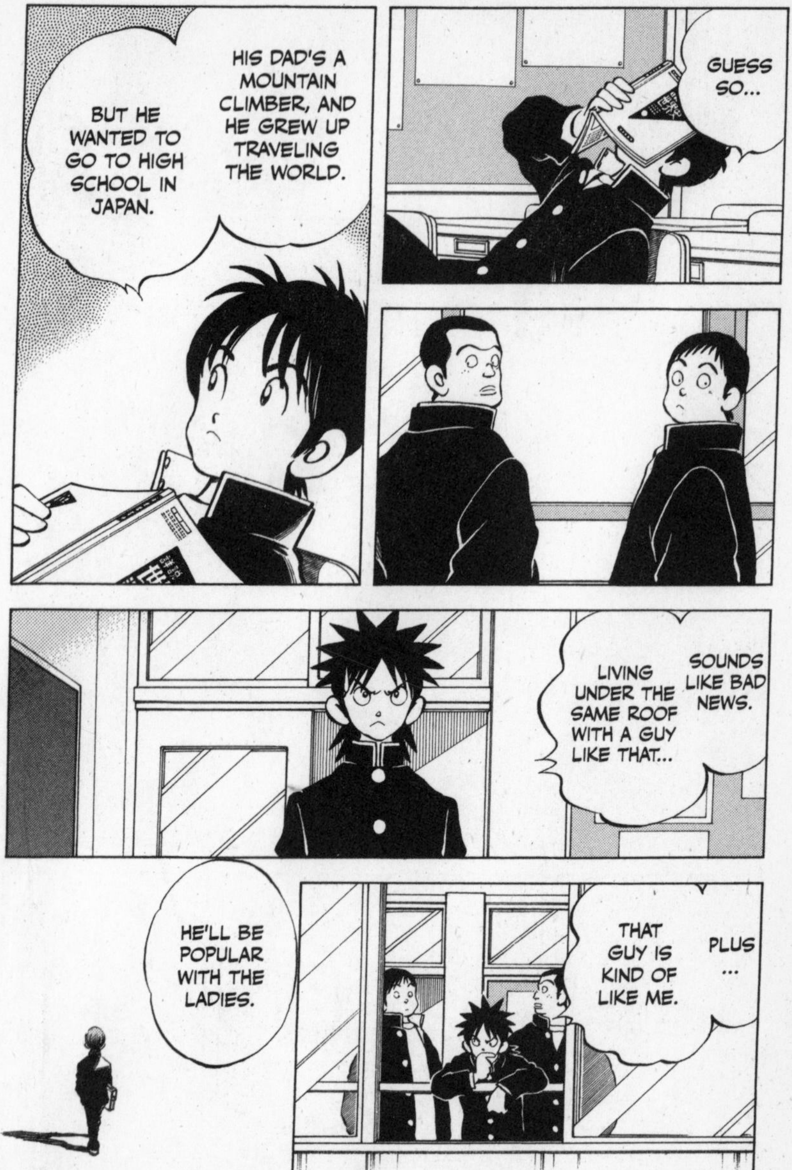
GUESS SO...
HIS DAD'S A MOUNTAIN CLIMBER, AND HE GREW UP TRAVELING THE WORLD.
BUT HE WANTED TO GO TO HIGH SCHOOL IN JAPAN.
SOUNDS LIKE BAD NEWS.
LIVING UNDER THE SAME ROOF WITH A GUY LIKE THAT...
PLUS ...
THAT GUY IS KIND OF LIKE ME.
HE'LL BE POPULAR WITH THE LADIES.

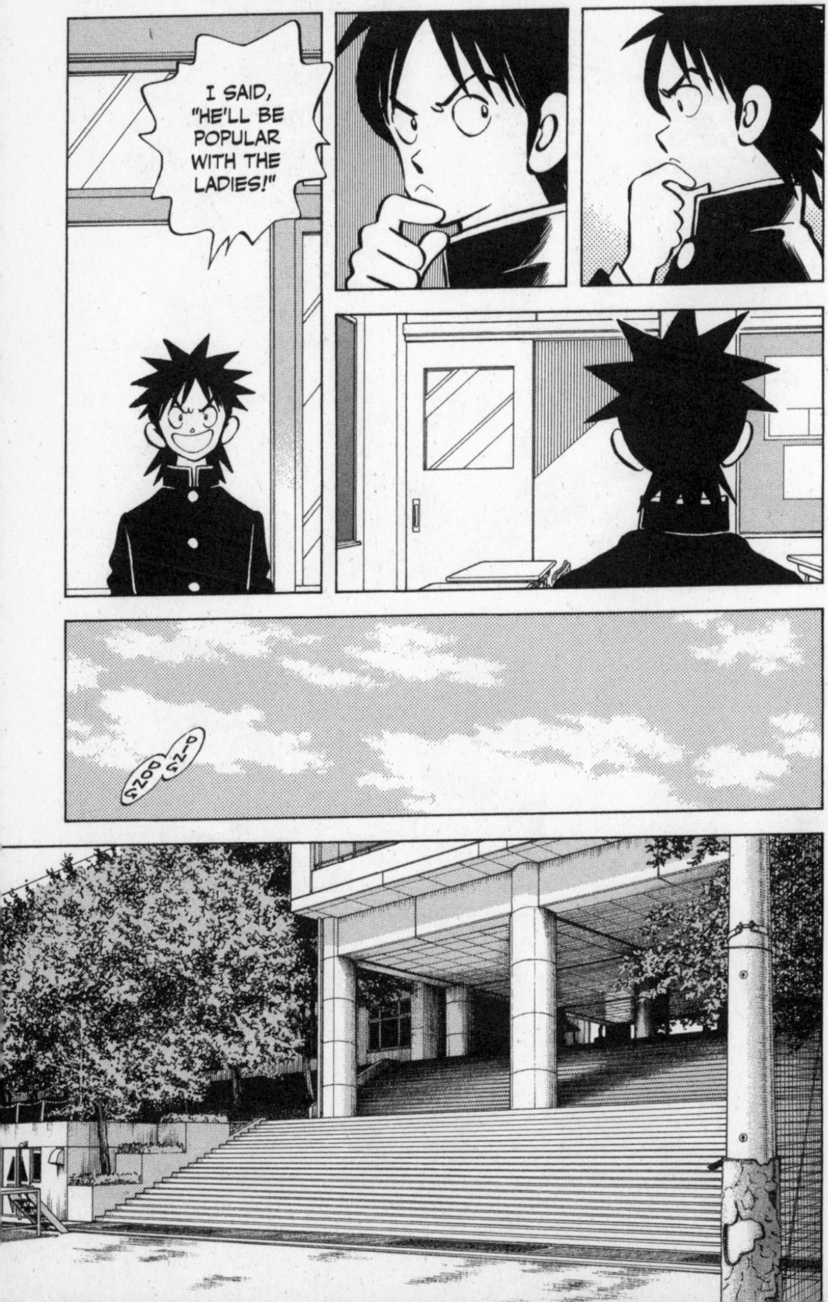
I SAID, "HE'LL BE POPULAR WITH THE LADIES!"
DING DONG

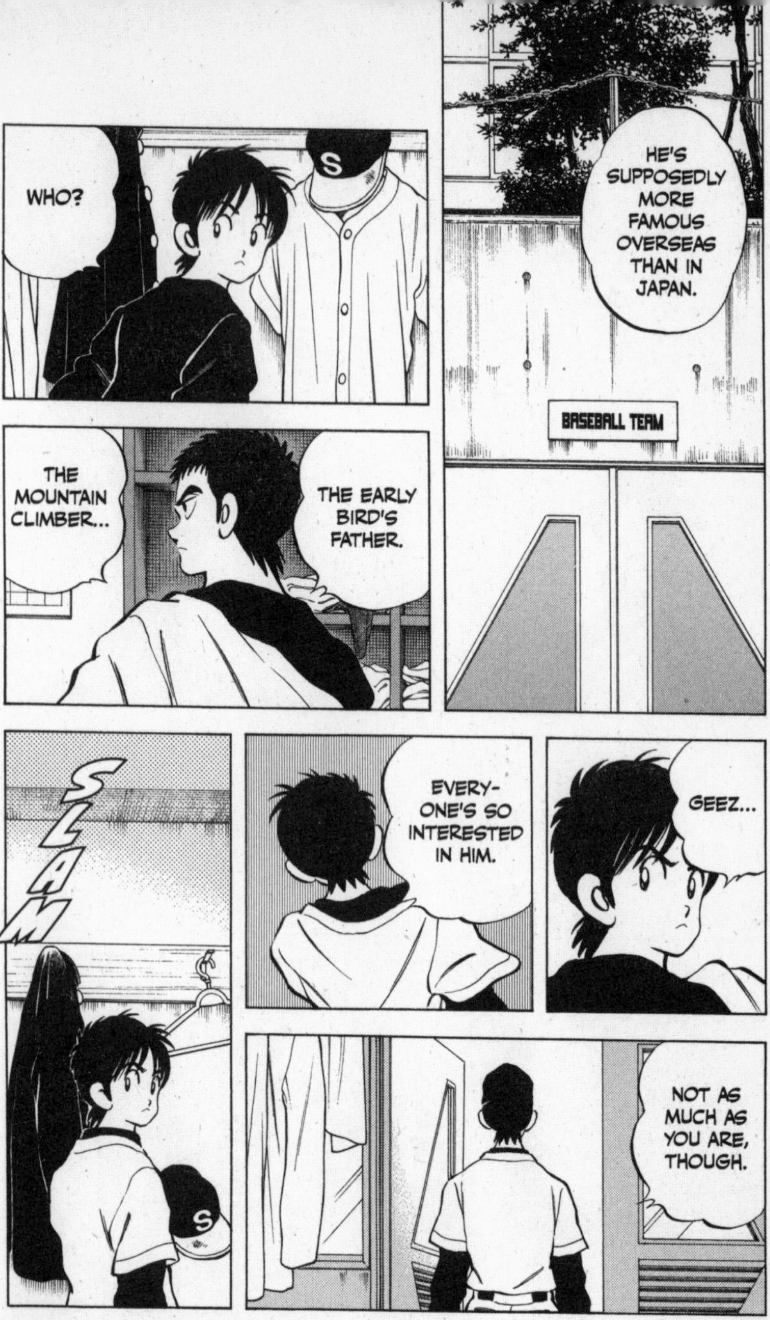
HE'S SUPPOSEDLY MORE FAMOUS OVERSEAS THAN IN JAPAN.
BASEBALL TEAM
WHO?
THE EARLY BIRD'S FATHER.
THE MOUNTAIN CLIMBER...
GEEZ...
EVERY-ONE'S SO INTERESTED IN HIM.
NOT AS MUCH AS YOU ARE, THOUGH.
SLAM

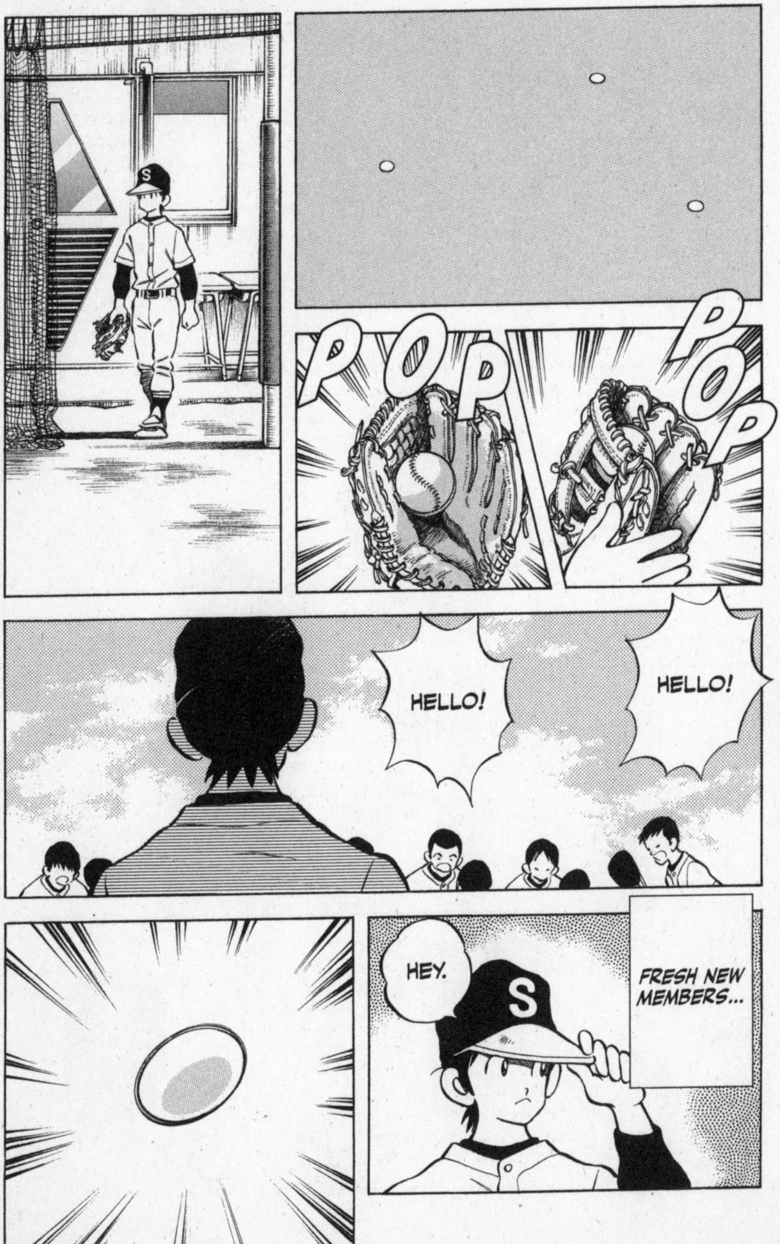
POP
POP
HELLO!
HELLO!
FRESH NEW MEMBERS...
HEY.

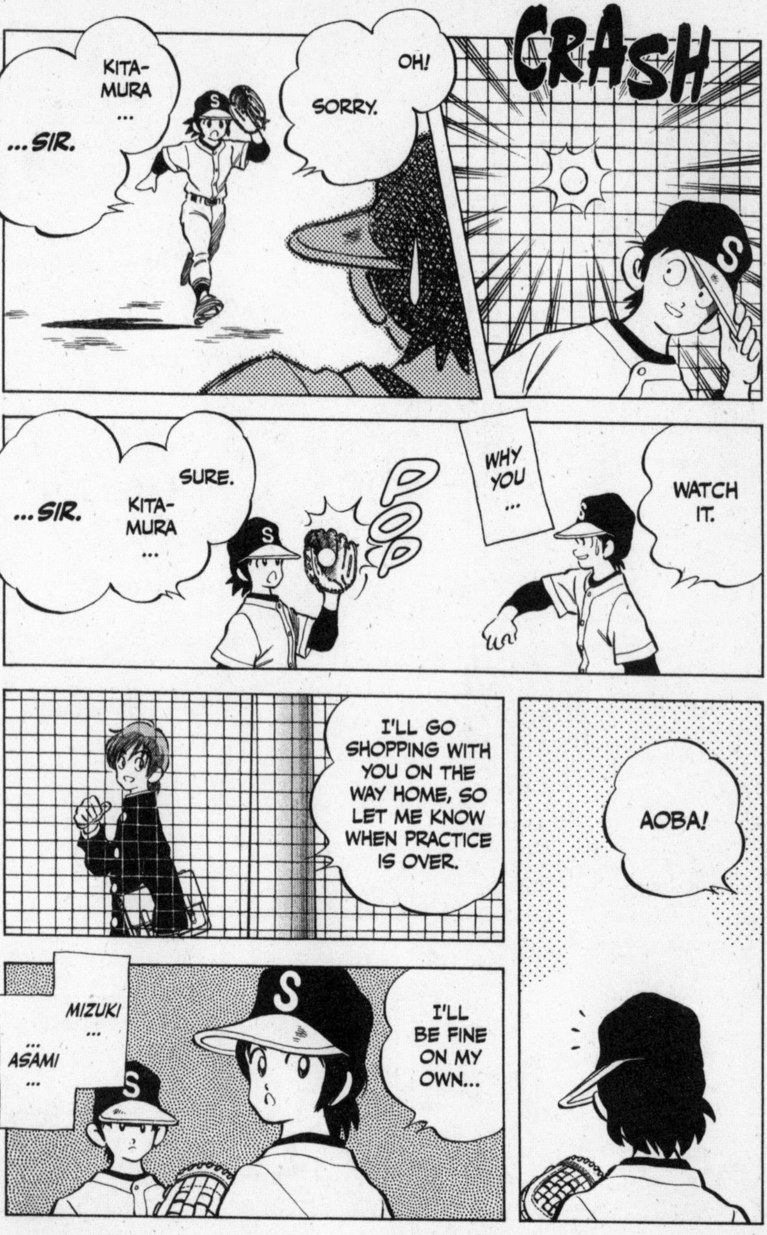
CRASH
OH!
SORRY.
KITA-MURA...
...SIR.
WATCH IT.
WHY YOU...
POP
SURE.
KITA-MURA...
...SIR.
AOBA!
I'LL GO SHOPPING WITH YOU ON THE WAY HOME, SO LET ME KNOW WHEN PRACTICE IS OVER.
I'LL BE FINE ON MY OWN...
MIZUKI...
...ASAMI...

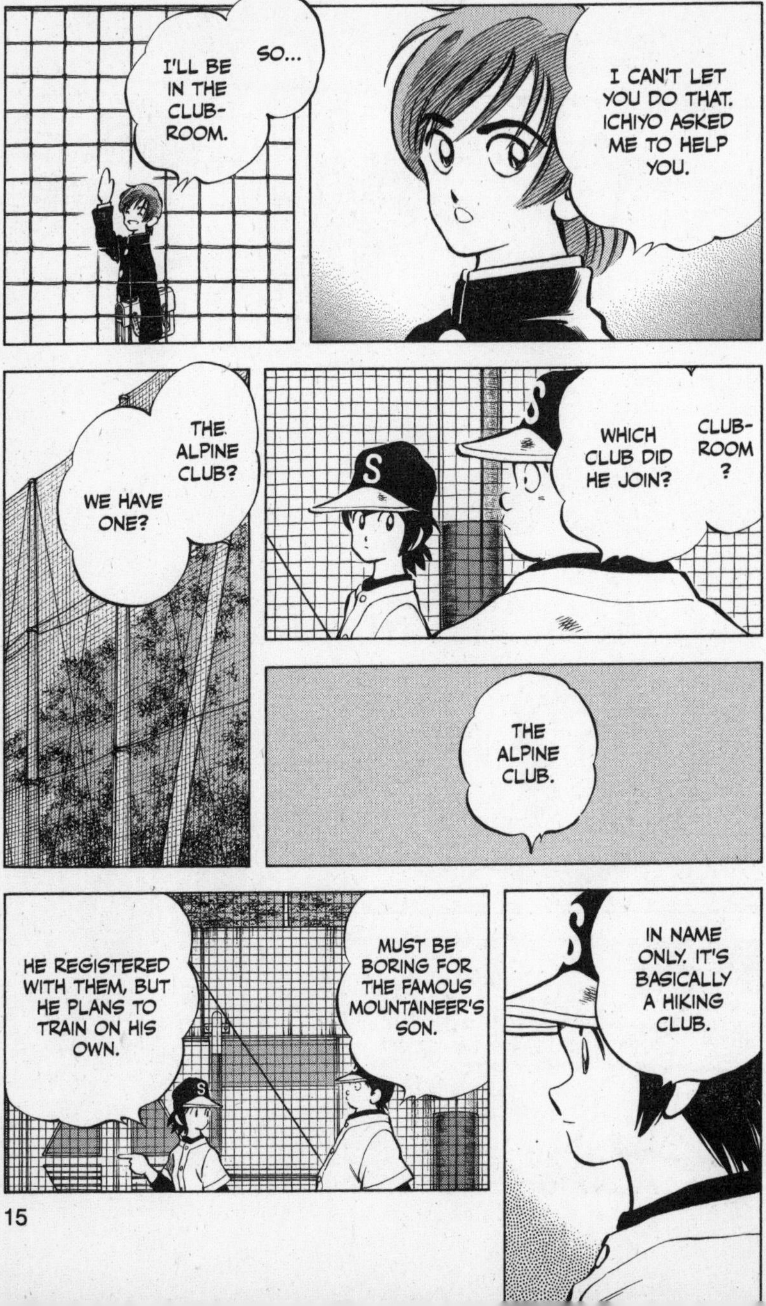
I CAN'T LET YOU DO THAT. ICHIYO ASKED ME TO HELP YOU.
SO...
I'LL BE IN THE CLUB-ROOM.
CLUB-ROOM?
WHICH CLUB DID HE JOIN?
THE ALPINE CLUB.
THE ALPINE CLUB?
WE HAVE ONE?
IN NAME ONLY. IT'S BASICALLY A HIKING CLUB.
MUST BE BORING FOR THE FAMOUS MOUNTAINEER'S SON.
HE REGISTERED WITH THEM, BUT HE PLANS TO TRAIN ON HIS OWN.

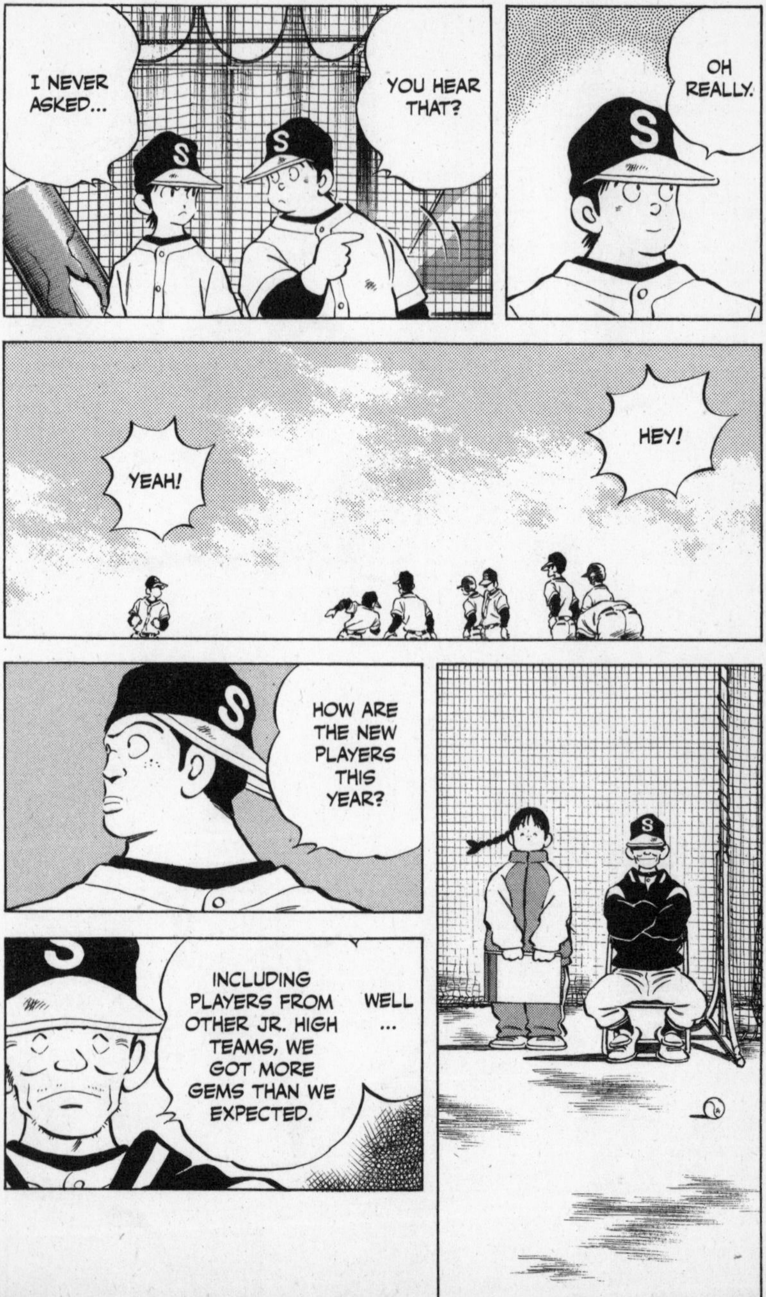
OH REALLY.
YOU HEAR THAT?
I NEVER ASKED...
HEY!
YEAH!
HOW ARE THE NEW PLAYERS THIS YEAR?
WELL ...
INCLUDING PLAYERS FROM OTHER JR. HIGH TEAMS, WE GOT MORE GEMS THAN WE EXPECTED.

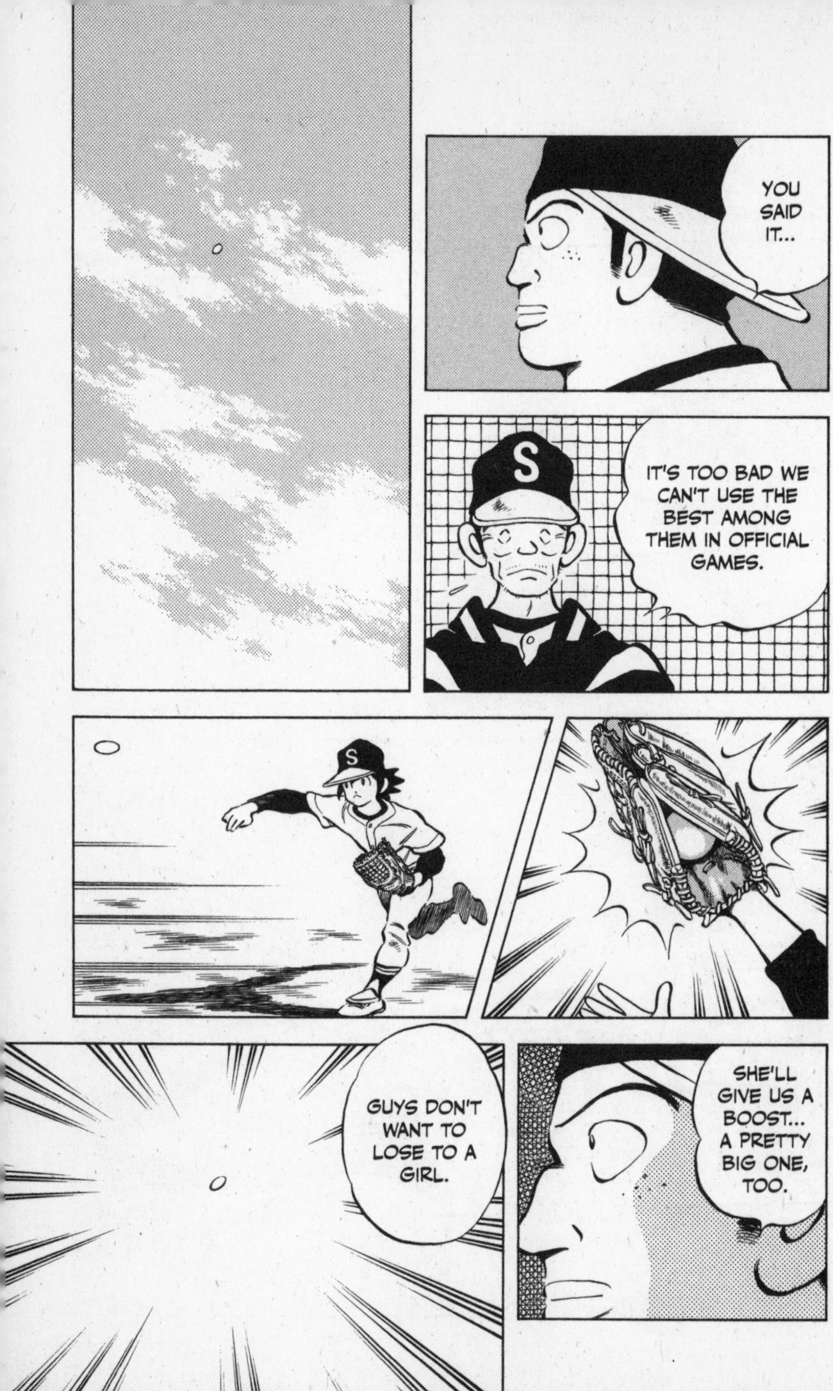
YOU SAID IT...
IT'S TOO BAD WE CAN'T USE THE BEST AMONG THEM IN OFFICIAL GAMES.
SHE'LL GIVE US A BOOST... A PRETTY BIG ONE, TOO.
GUYS DON'T WANT TO LOSE TO A GIRL.

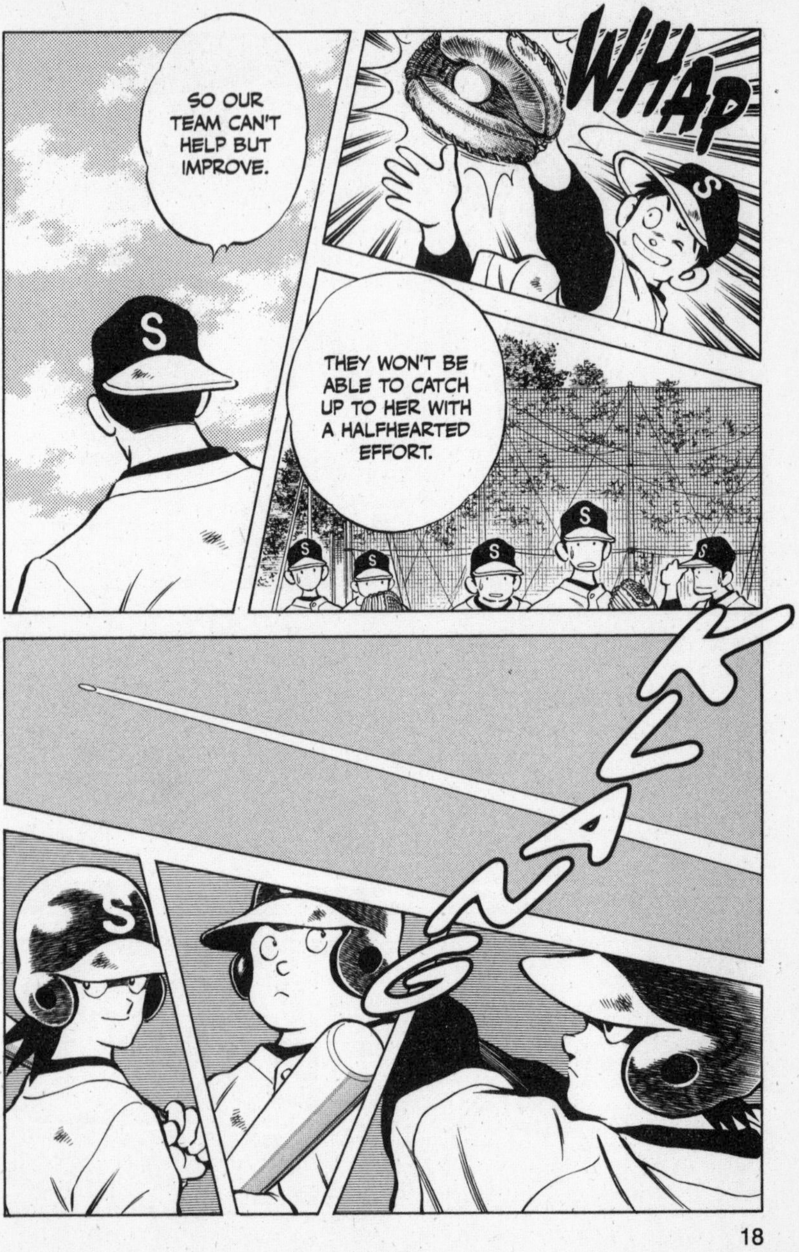
WHAP
THEY WON'T BE ABLE TO CATCH UP TO HER WITH A HALFHEARTED EFFORT.
SO OUR TEAM CAN'T HELP BUT IMPROVE.
KLANG

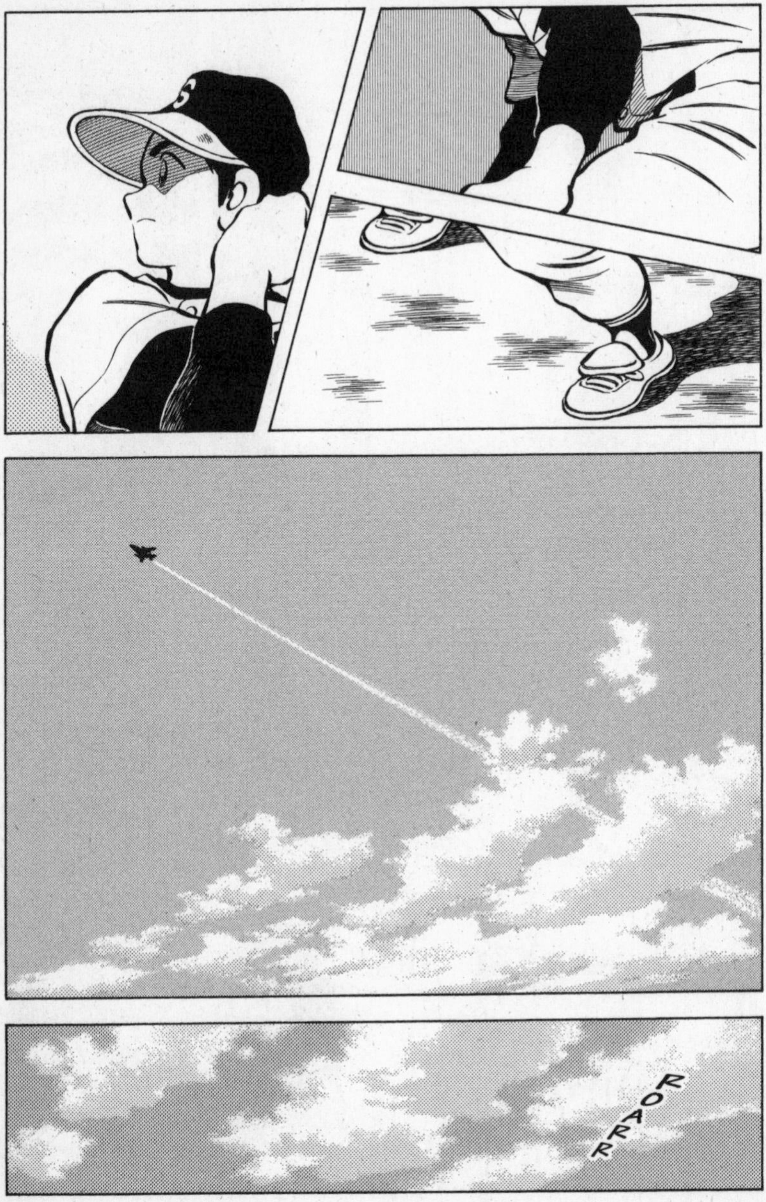
ROARR

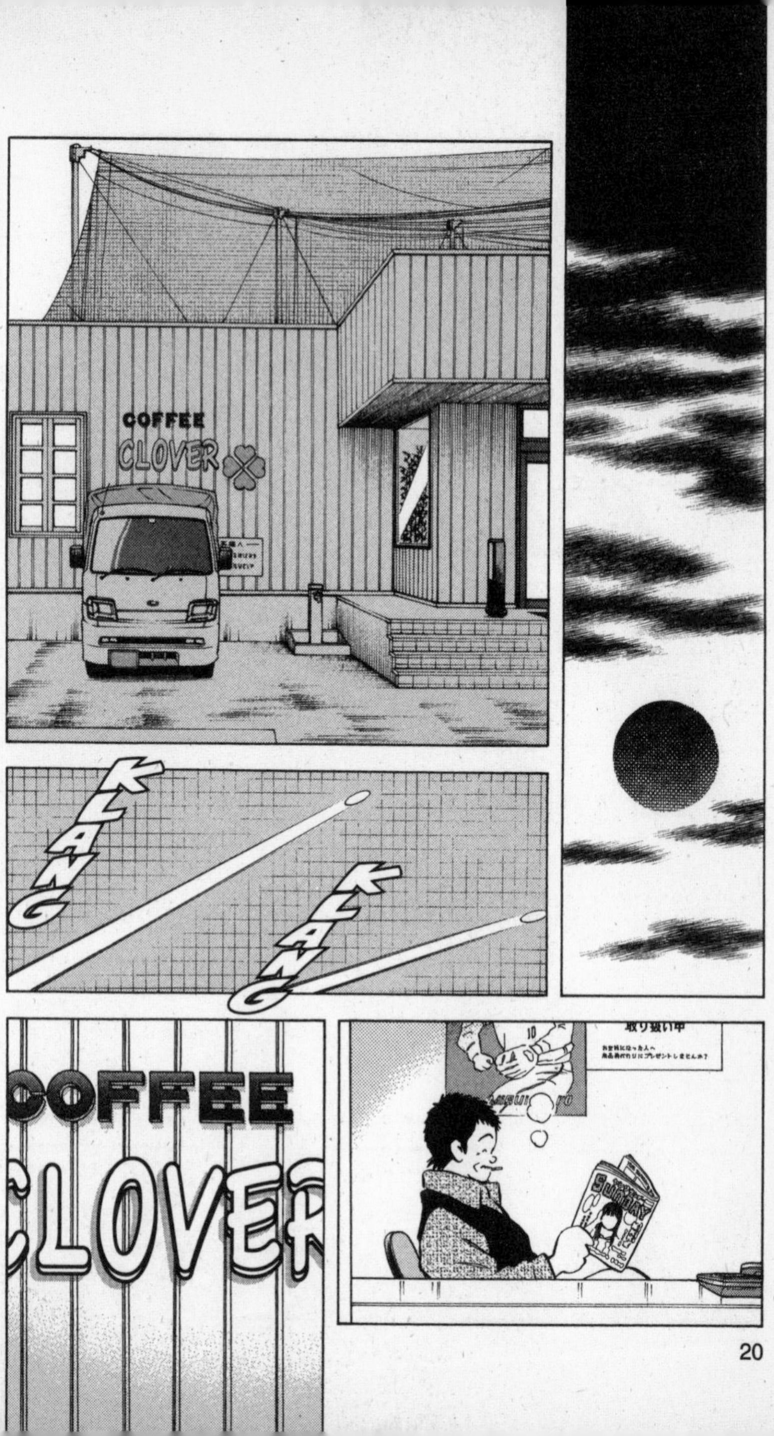

COFFEE
CLOVER
KLANG
KLANG
取り扱い中
COFFEE
CLOVER

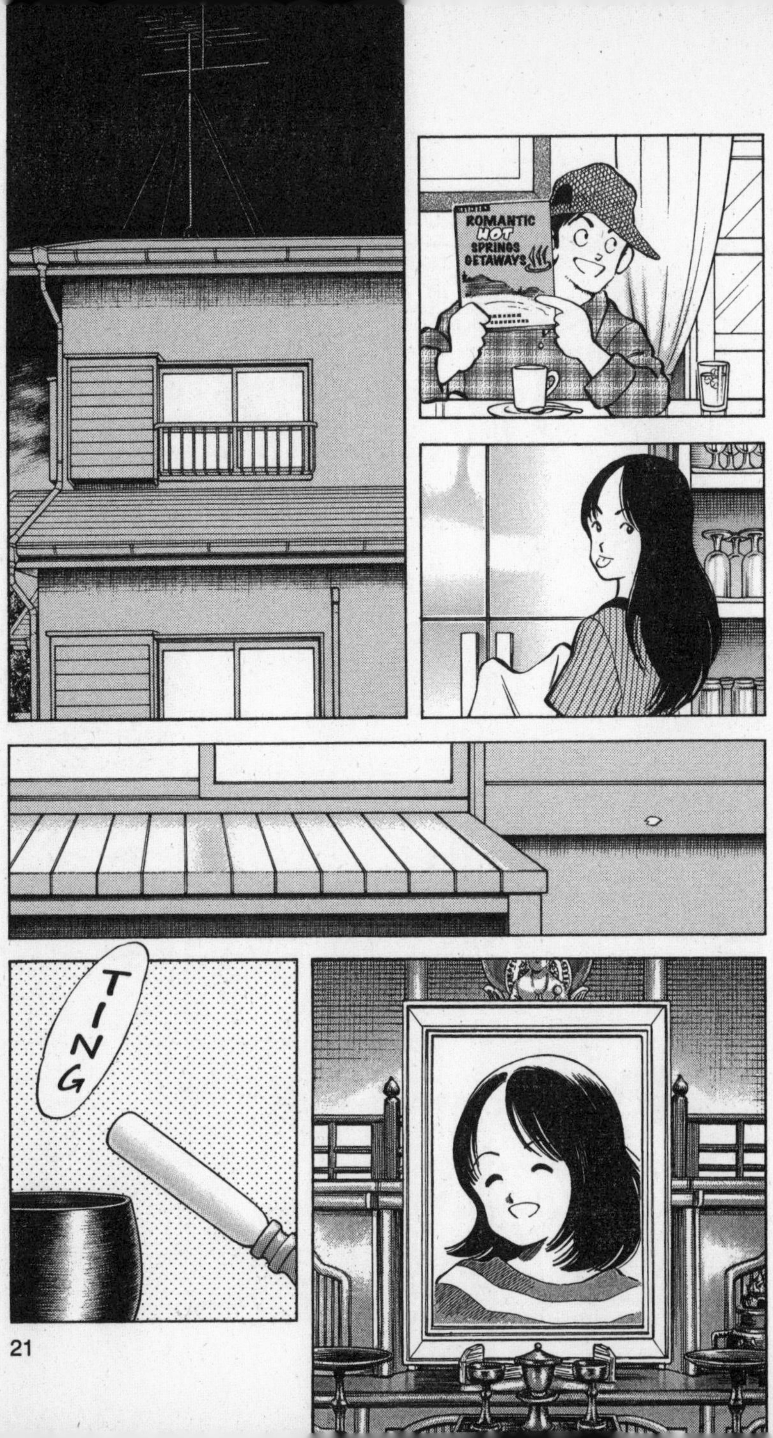
ROMANTIC HOT SPRINGS GETAWAYS
TING

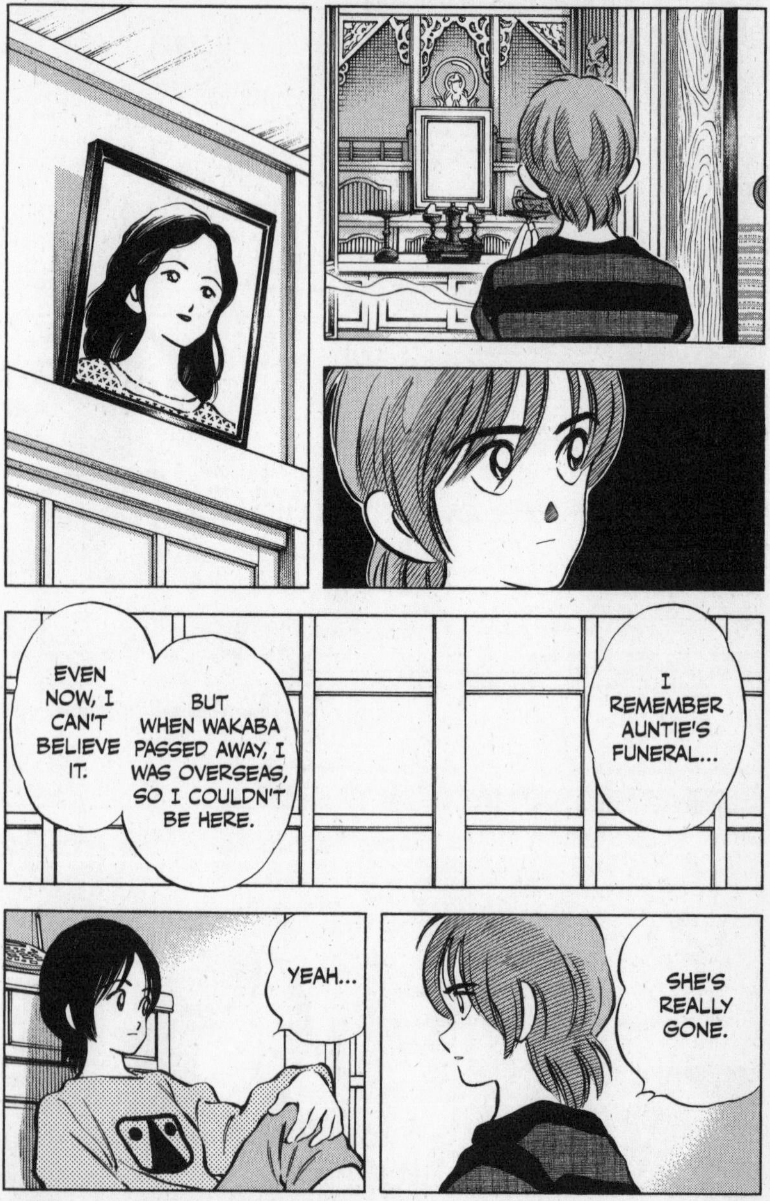
I REMEMBER AUNTIE'S FUNERAL...
BUT WHEN WAKABA PASSED AWAY, I WAS OVERSEAS, SO I COULDN'T BE HERE.
EVEN NOW, I CAN'T BELIEVE IT.
SHE'S REALLY GONE.
YEAH...

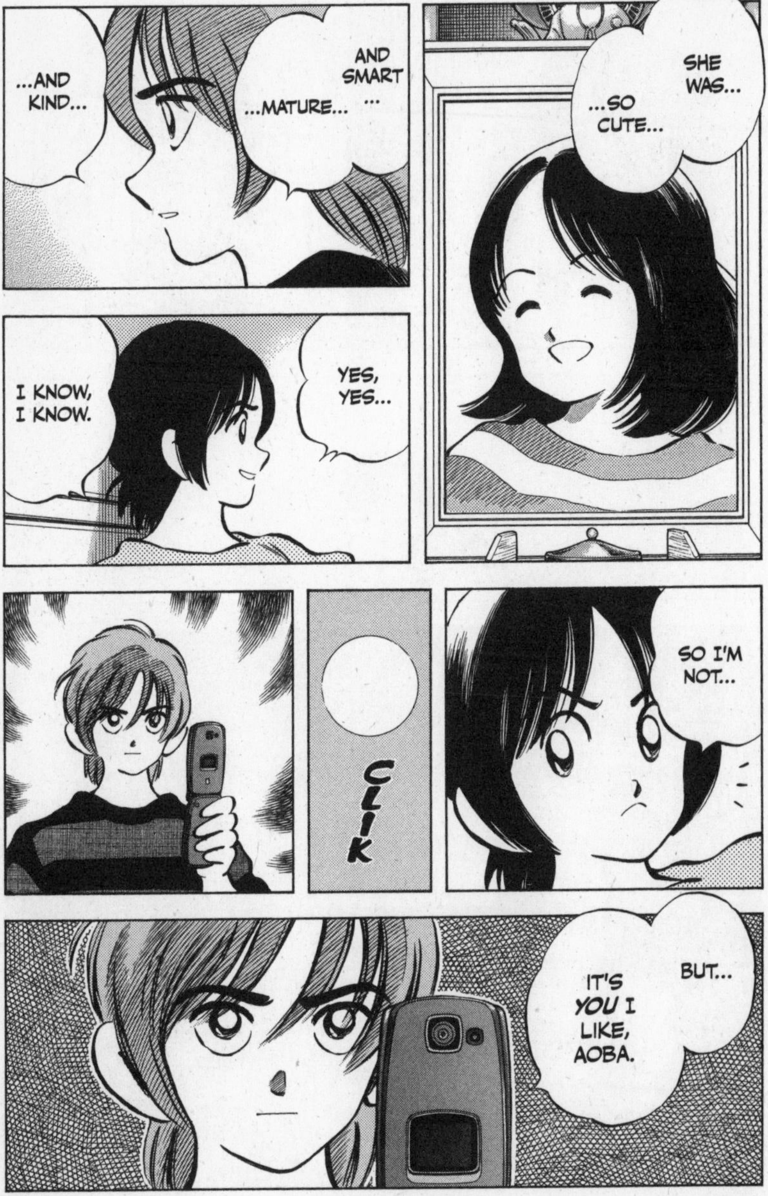
SHE WAS... ...SO CUTE...
...MATURE... AND SMART...
...AND KIND...
YES, YES...
I KNOW, I KNOW.
SO I'M NOT...
CLIK
BUT... IT'S *YOU* I LIKE, AOBA.

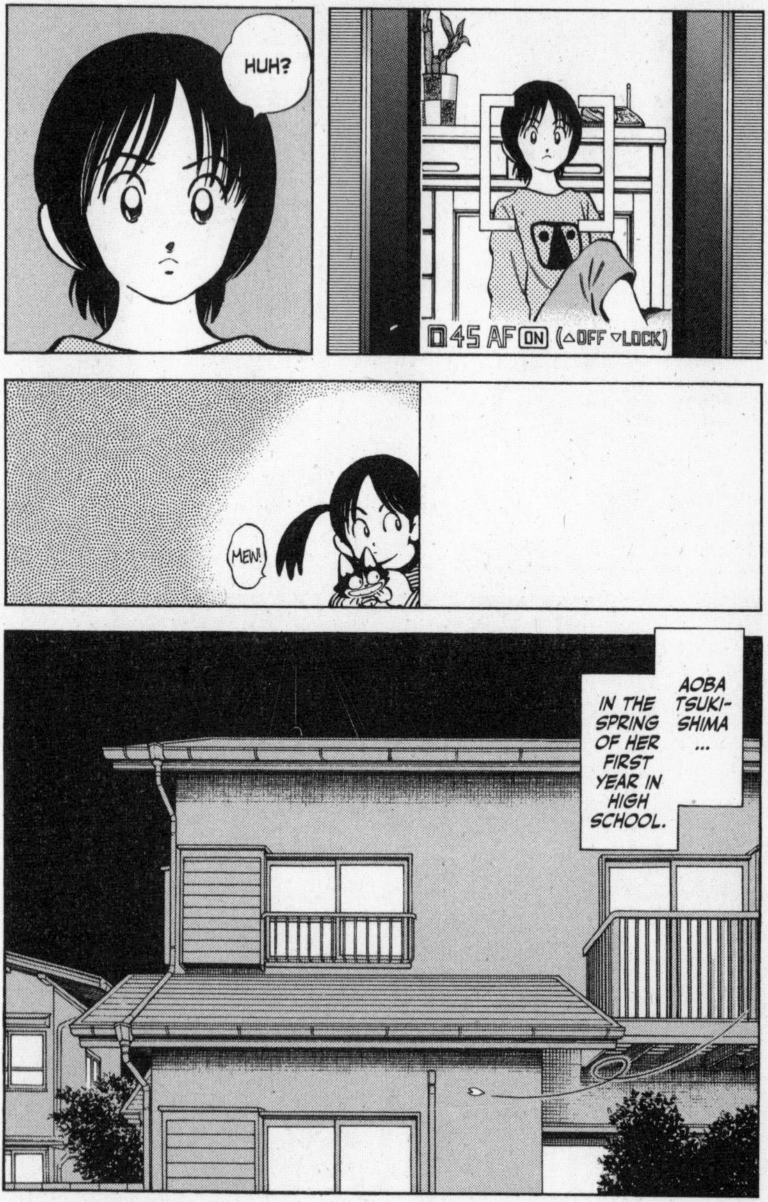
45 AF ON (△OFF ▽LOCK)
HUH?
MEW!
AOBA TSUKISHIMA...
IN THE SPRING OF HER FIRST YEAR IN HIGH SCHOOL.

# CHAPTER 62
# FOR REAL?

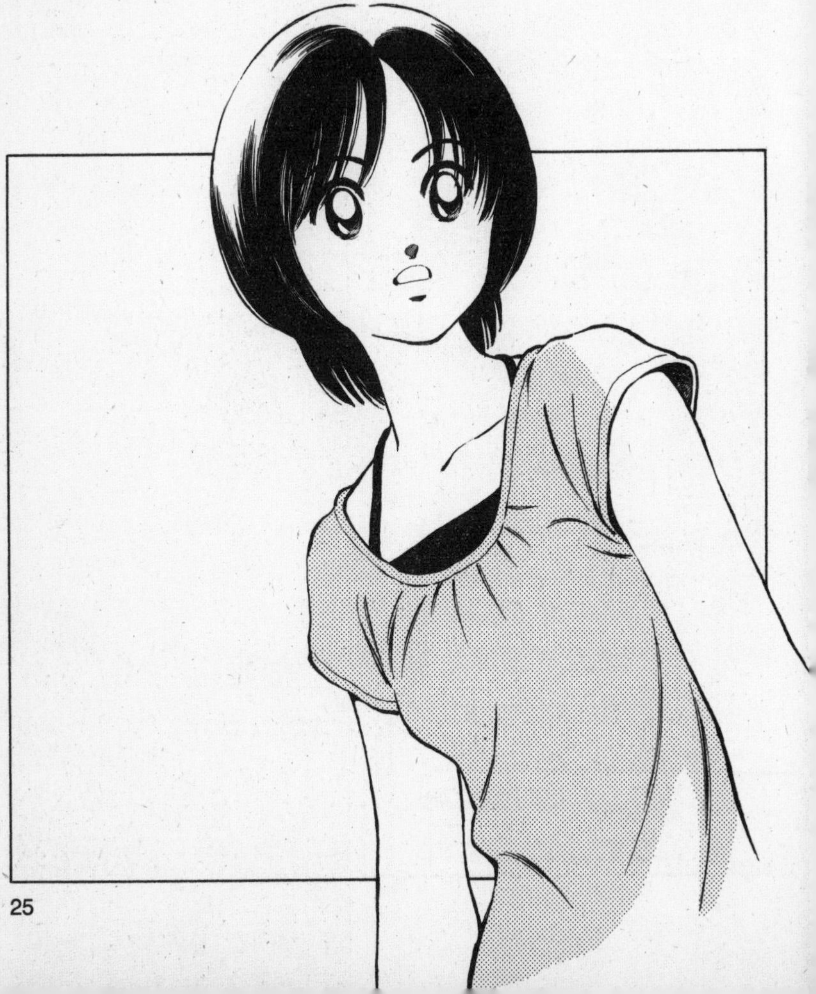

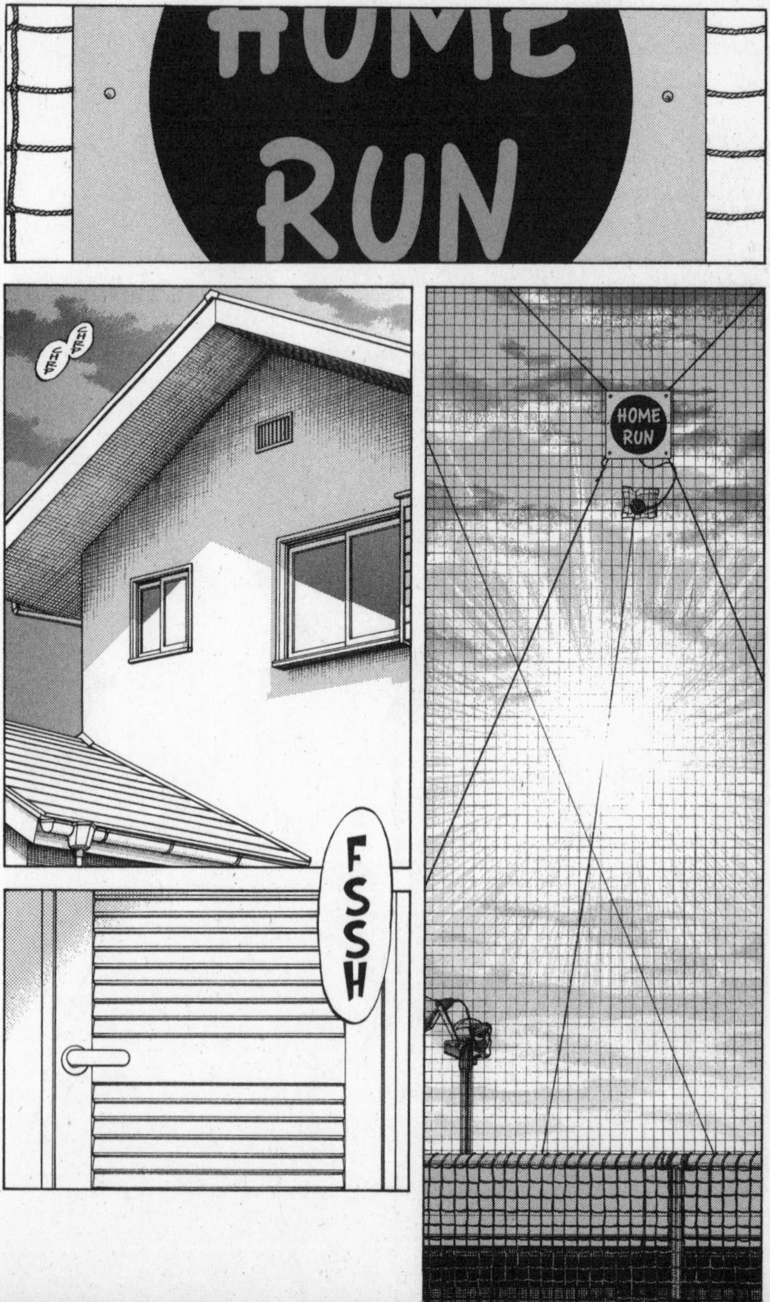
HOME RUN
HOME RUN
CHEP CHEP
FSSH

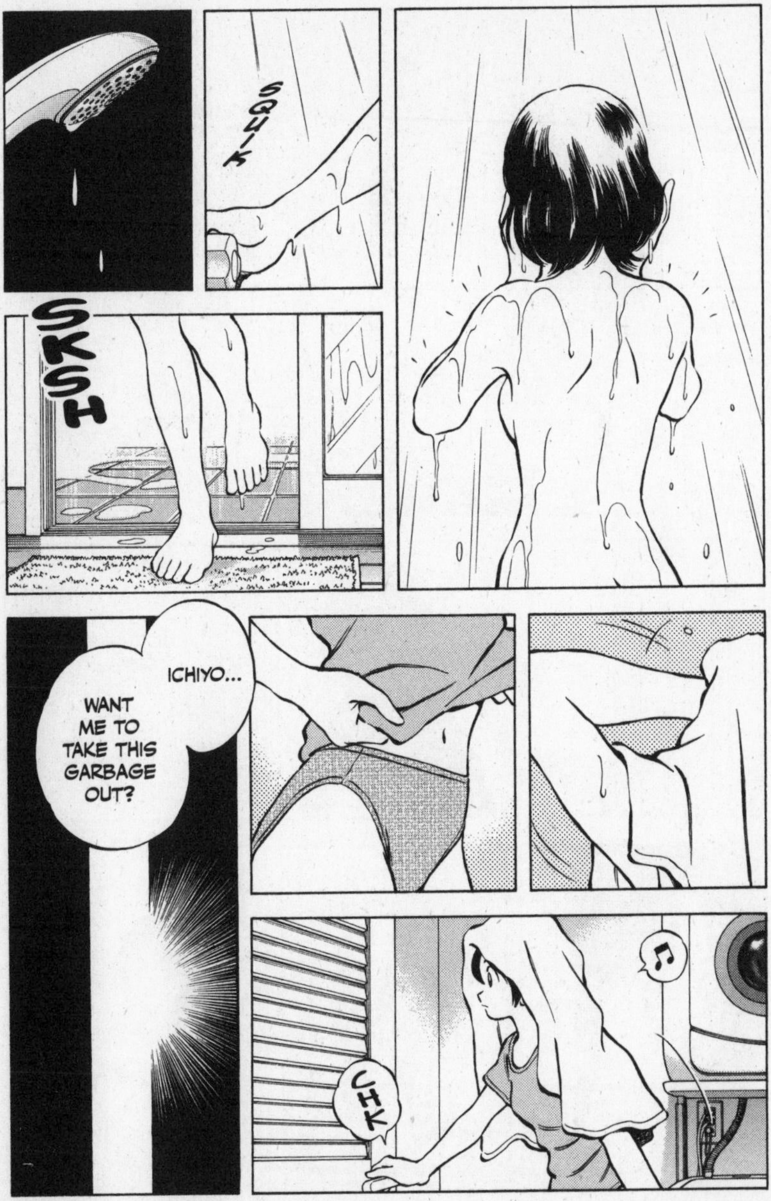
SQUIK
SKSH
♪
CHK
ICHIYO... WANT ME TO TAKE THIS GARBAGE OUT?

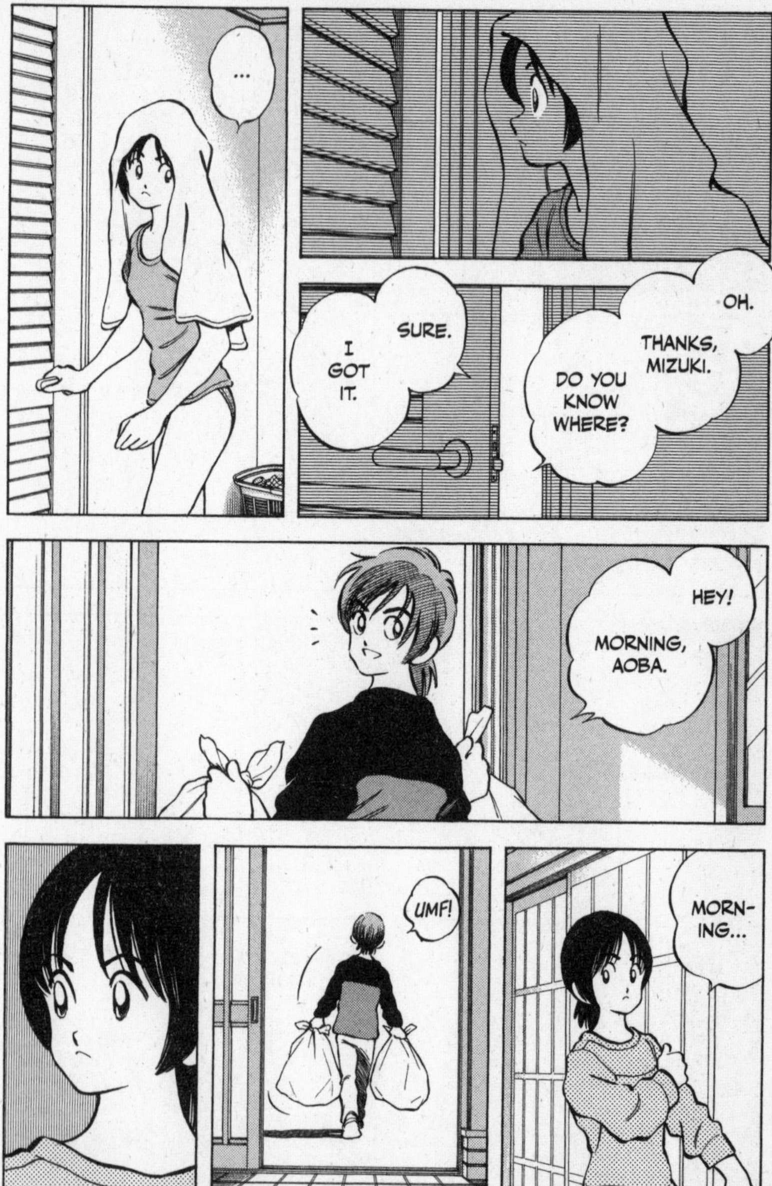
OH.
THANKS, MIZUKI.
DO YOU KNOW WHERE?
SURE.
I GOT IT.
...
HEY!
MORNING, AOBA.
MORN- ING...
UMF!

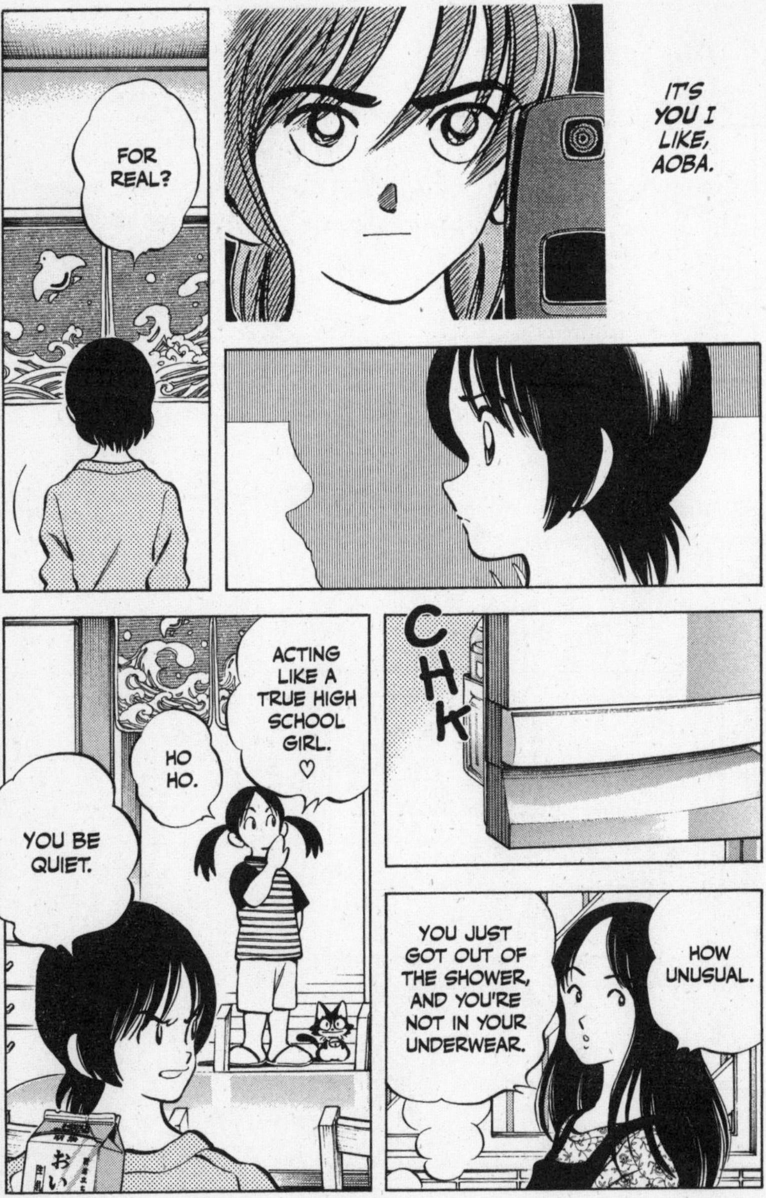
IT'S YOU I LIKE, AOBA.
FOR REAL?
CHK
HOW UNUSUAL.
YOU JUST GOT OUT OF THE SHOWER, AND YOU'RE NOT IN YOUR UNDERWEAR.
ACTING LIKE A TRUE HIGH SCHOOL GIRL. ♡
HO HO.
YOU BE QUIET.

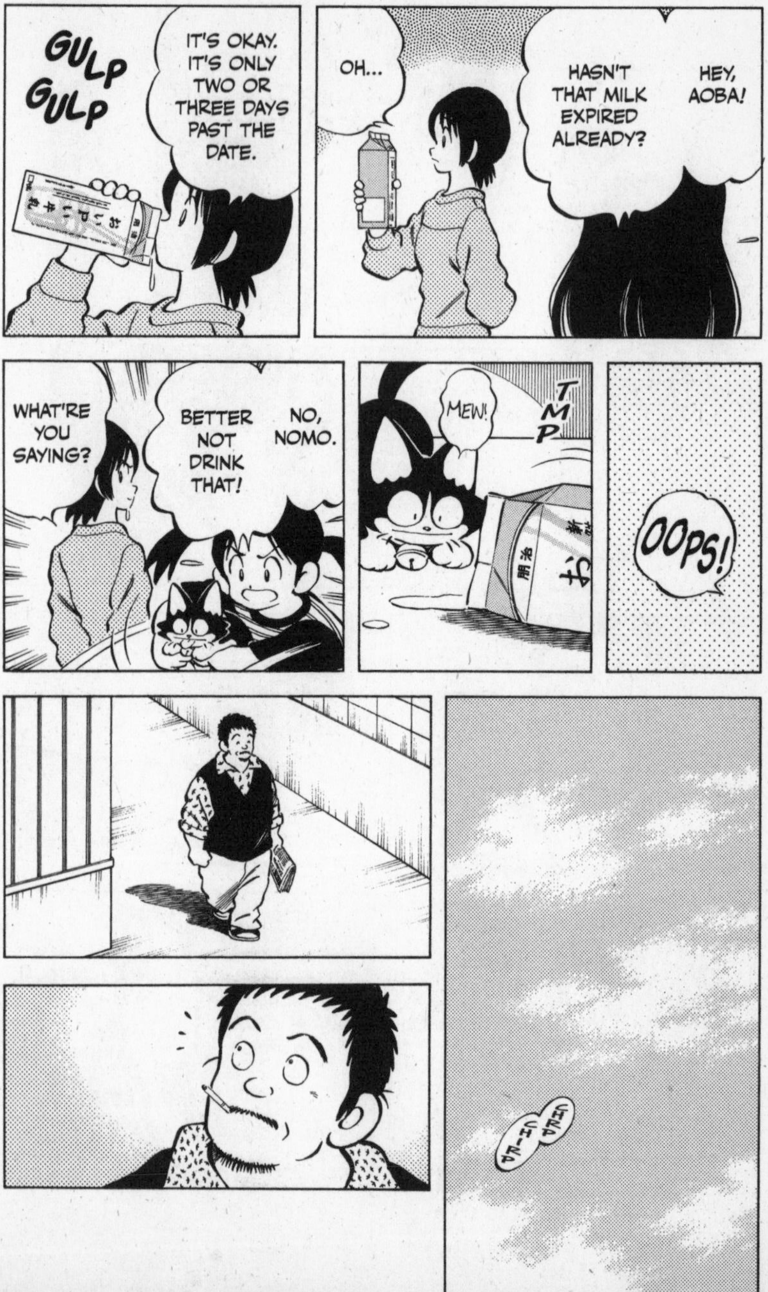
HEY, AOBA!
HASN'T THAT MILK EXPIRED ALREADY?
OH...
IT'S OKAY. IT'S ONLY TWO OR THREE DAYS PAST THE DATE.
GULP GULP
OOPS!
TMP
MEW!
NO, NOMO.
BETTER NOT DRINK THAT!
WHAT'RE YOU SAYING?
CHIRP CHIRP

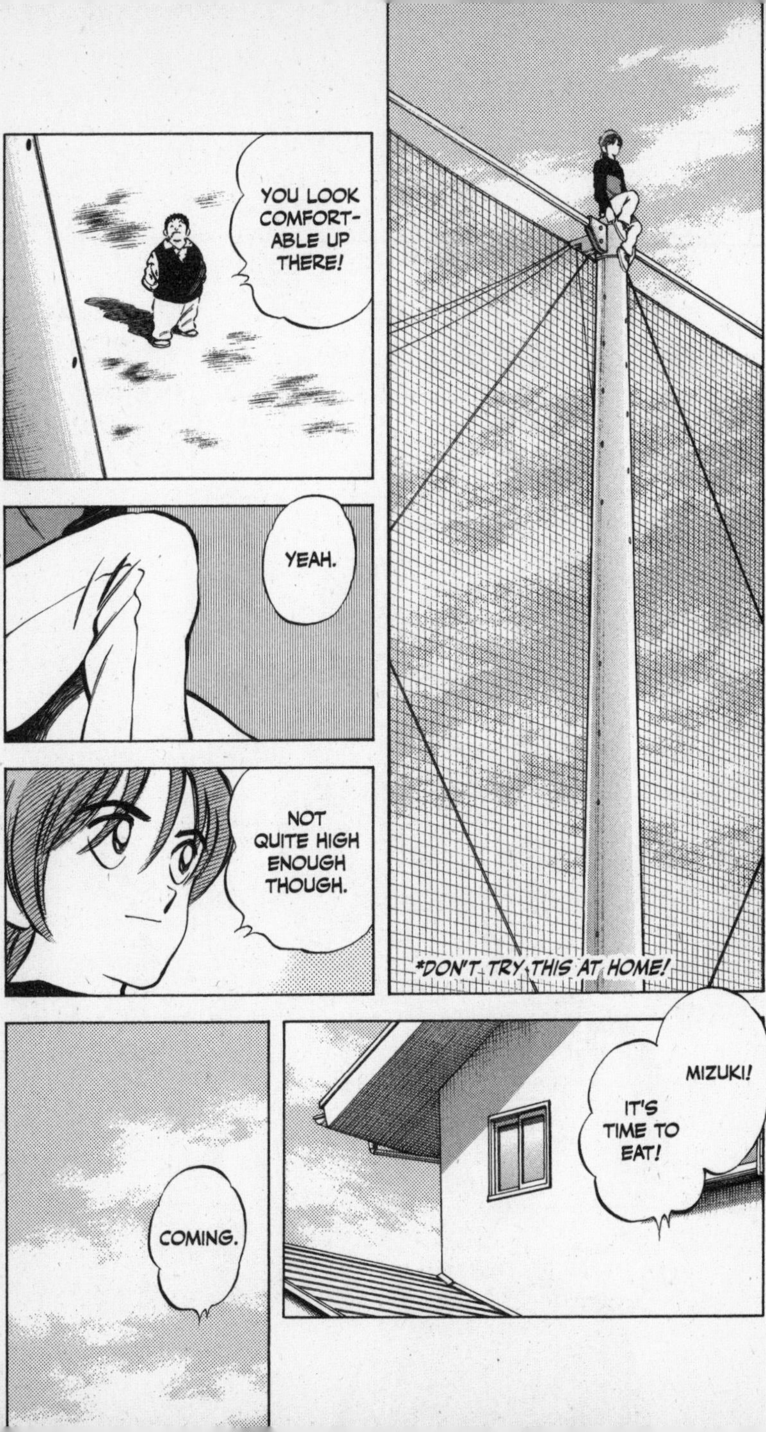
*DON'T TRY THIS AT HOME!
YOU LOOK COMFORT-ABLE UP THERE!
YEAH.
NOT QUITE HIGH ENOUGH THOUGH.
MIZUKI!
IT'S TIME TO EAT!
COMING.

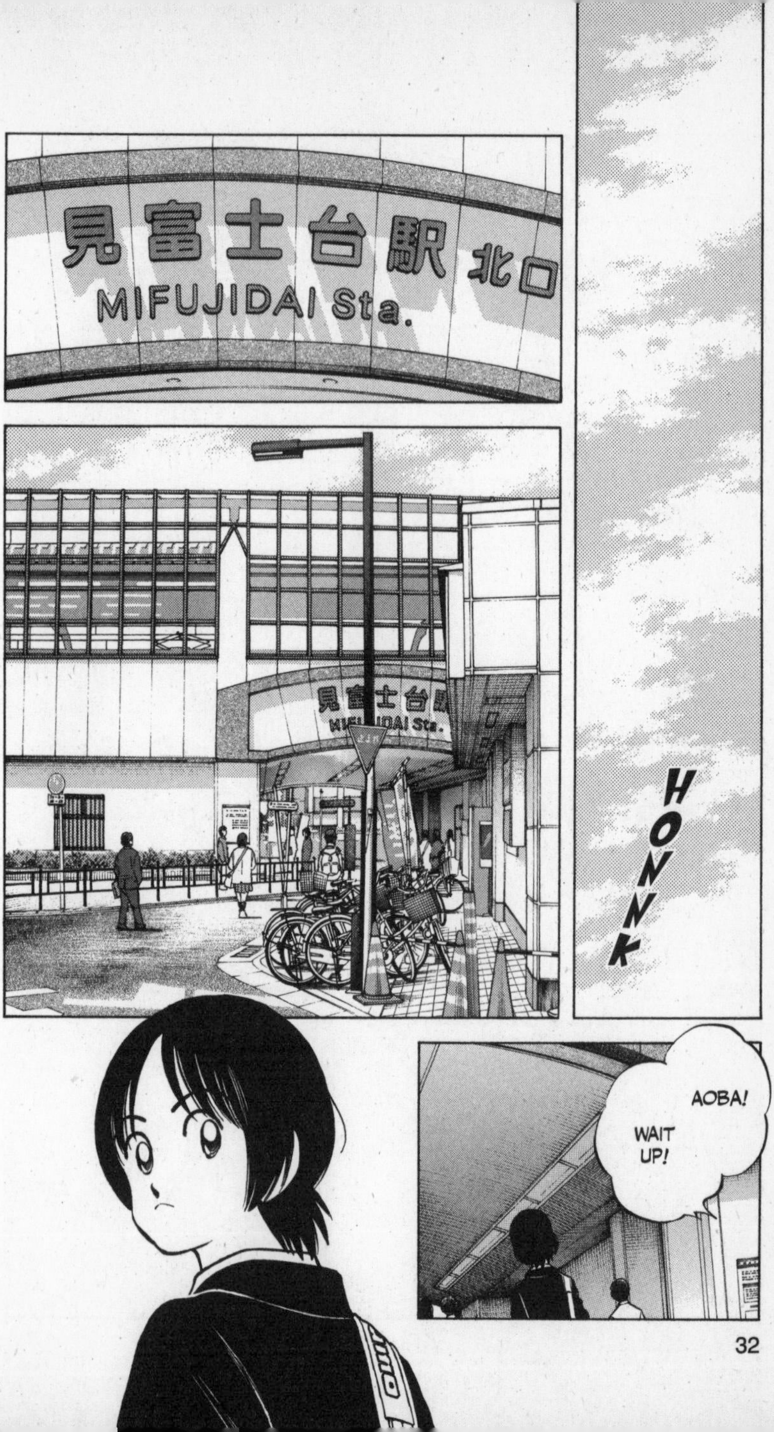
HONNK
見富士台駅
北口
MIFUJIDAI Sta.
見富士台駅
MIFUJIDAI Sta.
AOBA!
WAIT UP!

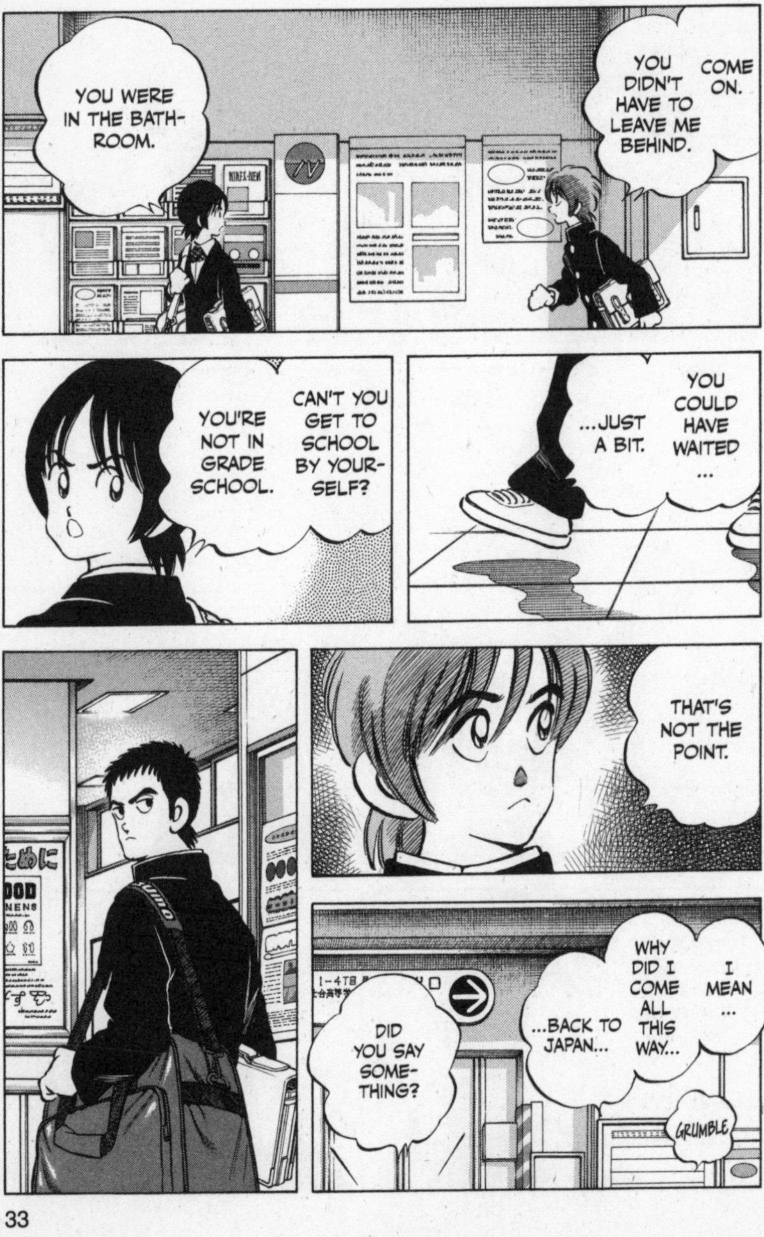
COME ON.
YOU DIDN'T HAVE TO LEAVE ME BEHIND.
YOU WERE IN THE BATH-ROOM.
YOU COULD HAVE WAITED...
...JUST A BIT.
CAN'T YOU GET TO SCHOOL BY YOUR-SELF?
YOU'RE NOT IN GRADE SCHOOL.
THAT'S NOT THE POINT.
I MEAN...
WHY DID I COME ALL THIS WAY...
...BACK TO JAPAN...
GRUMBLE
DID YOU SAY SOME-THING?

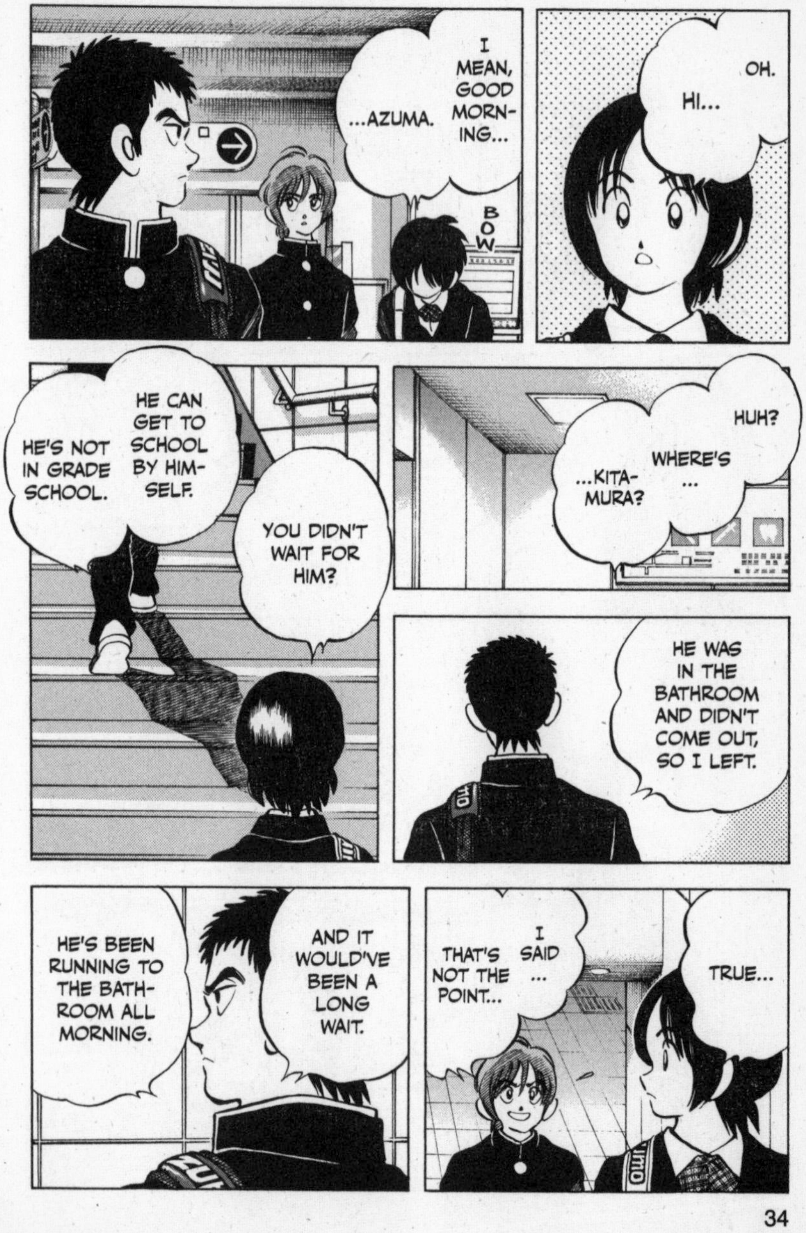
OH.
HI...
I MEAN, GOOD MORNING...
...AZUMA.
BOW
HUH?
WHERE'S ...
...KITAMURA?
HE WAS IN THE BATHROOM AND DIDN'T COME OUT, SO I LEFT.
HE CAN GET TO SCHOOL BY HIMSELF.
HE'S NOT IN GRADE SCHOOL.
YOU DIDN'T WAIT FOR HIM?
TRUE...
I SAID ...
THAT'S NOT THE POINT...
AND IT WOULD'VE BEEN A LONG WAIT.
HE'S BEEN RUNNING TO THE BATHROOM ALL MORNING.

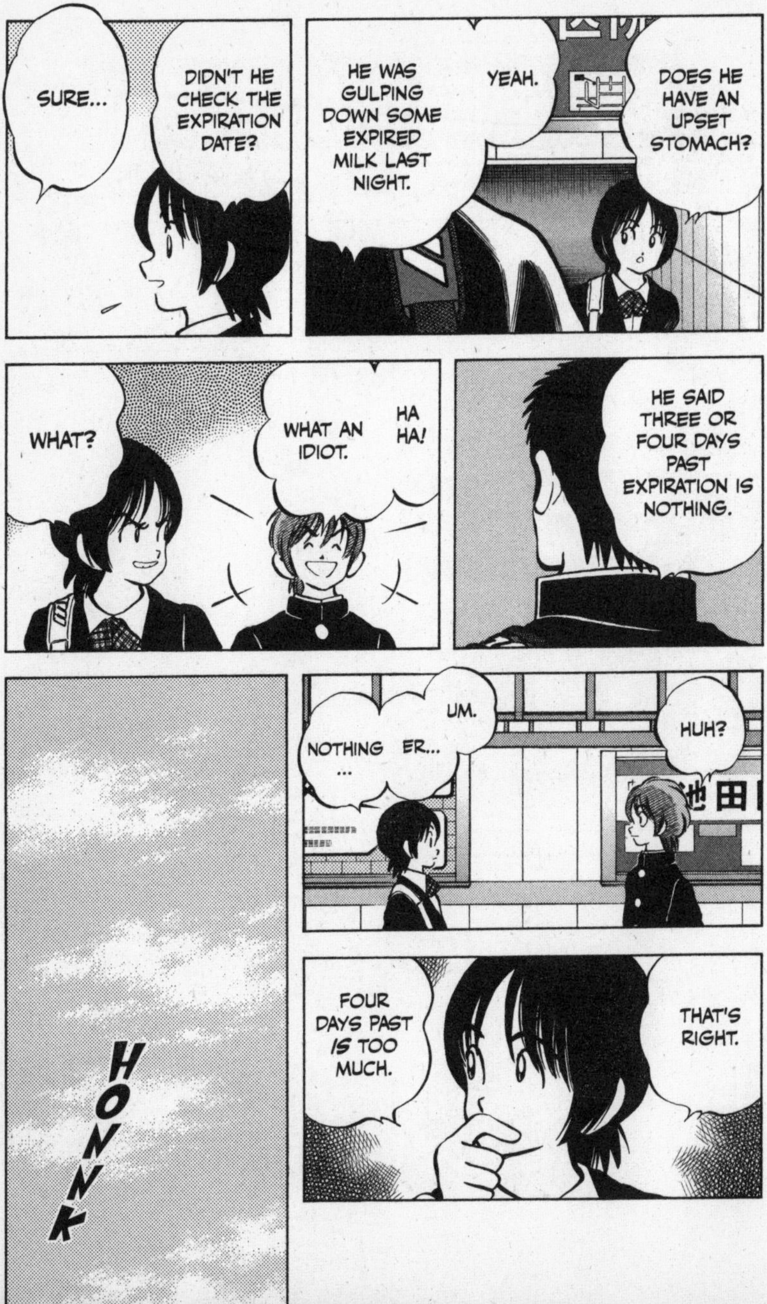
DOES HE HAVE AN UPSET STOMACH?
YEAH.
HE WAS GULPING DOWN SOME EXPIRED MILK LAST NIGHT.
DIDN'T HE CHECK THE EXPIRATION DATE?
SURE...
HE SAID THREE OR FOUR DAYS PAST EXPIRATION IS NOTHING.
HA HA!
WHAT AN IDIOT.
WHAT?
HUH?
UM.
ER...
NOTHING...
THAT'S RIGHT.
FOUR DAYS PAST *IS* TOO MUCH.
HONNK

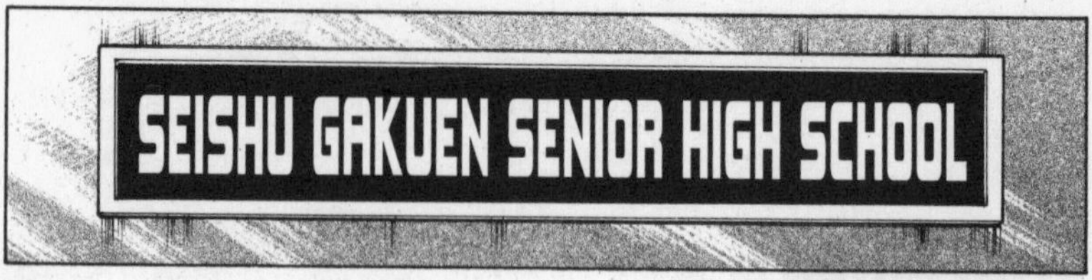
SEISHU GAKUEN SENIOR HIGH SCHOOL

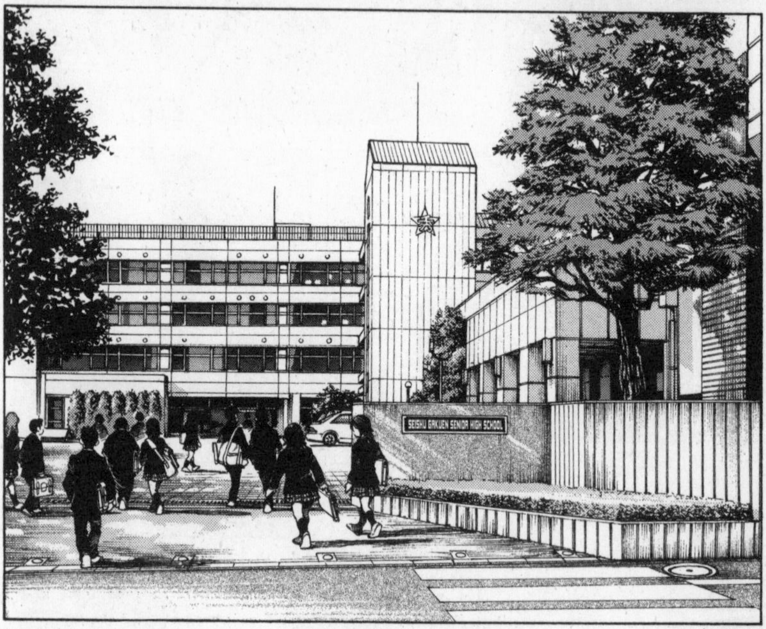
SEISHU GAKUEN SENIOR HIGH SCHOOL

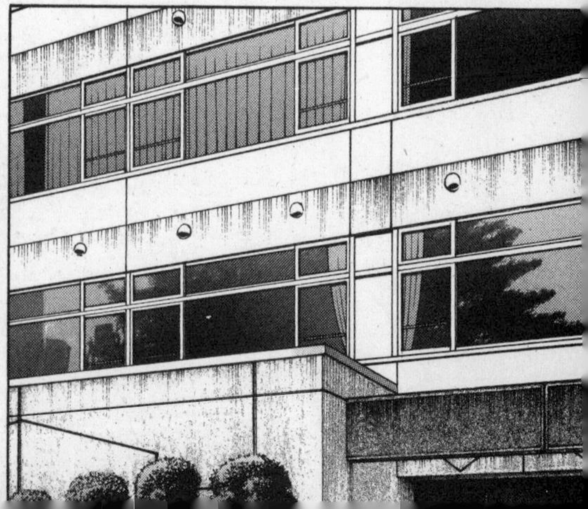

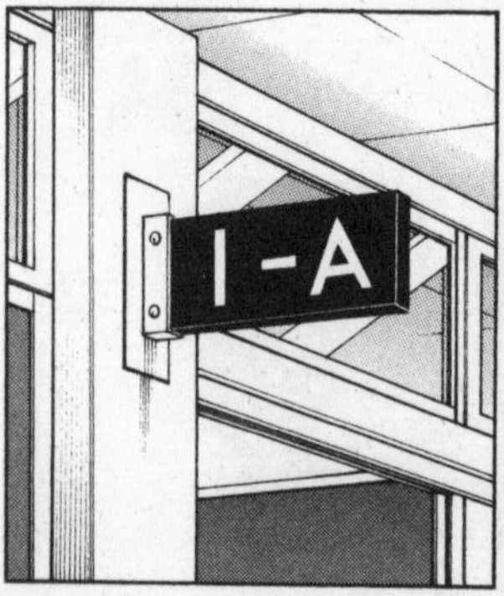
1-A

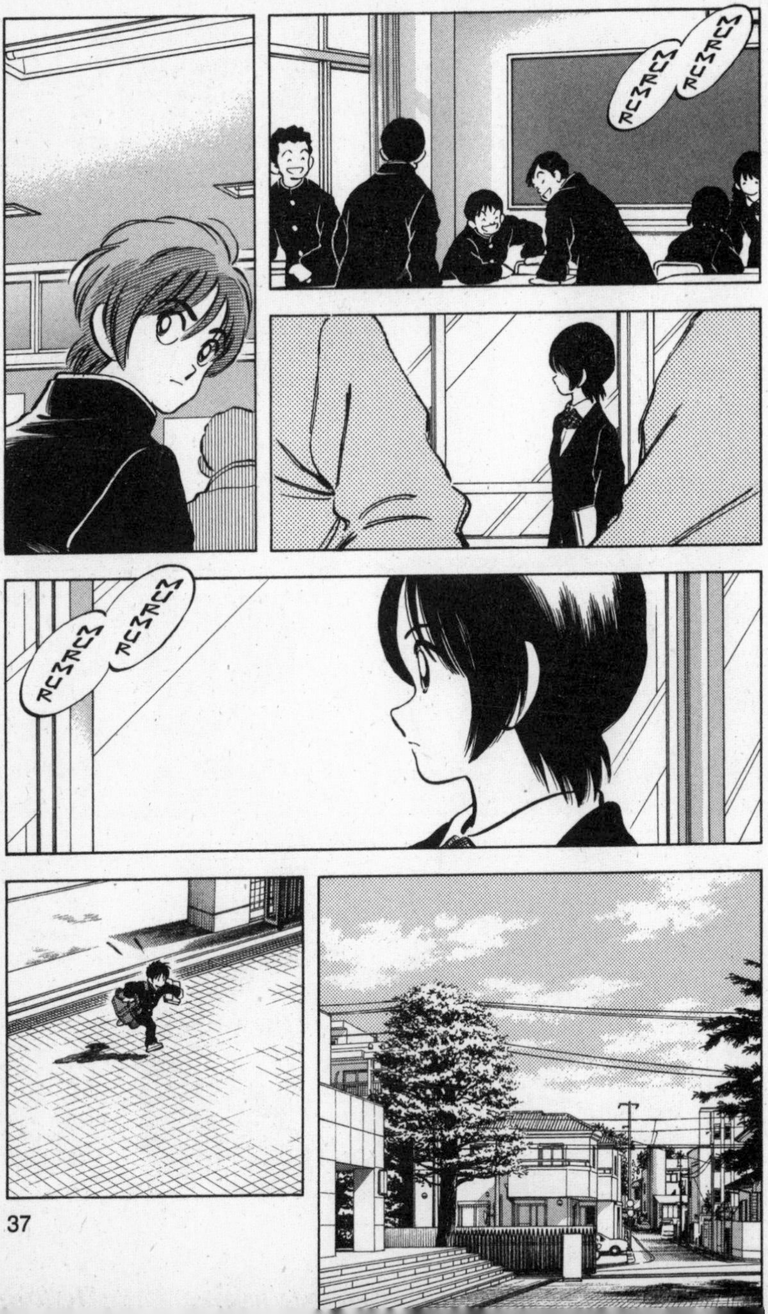
MURMUR
MURMUR
MURMUR
MURMUR

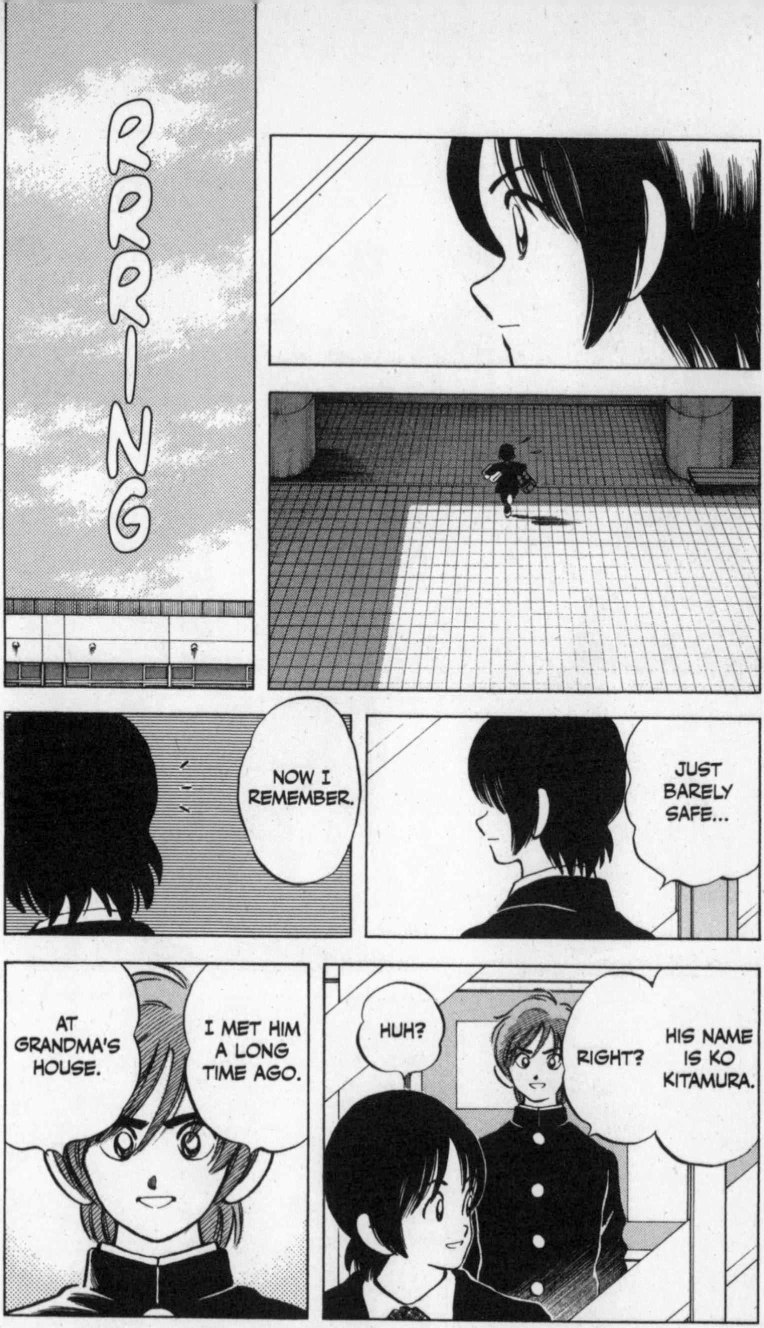
RRRING
JUST BARELY SAFE...
NOW I REMEMBER.
HIS NAME IS KO KITAMURA.
RIGHT?
HUH?
I MET HIM A LONG TIME AGO.
AT GRANDMA'S HOUSE.

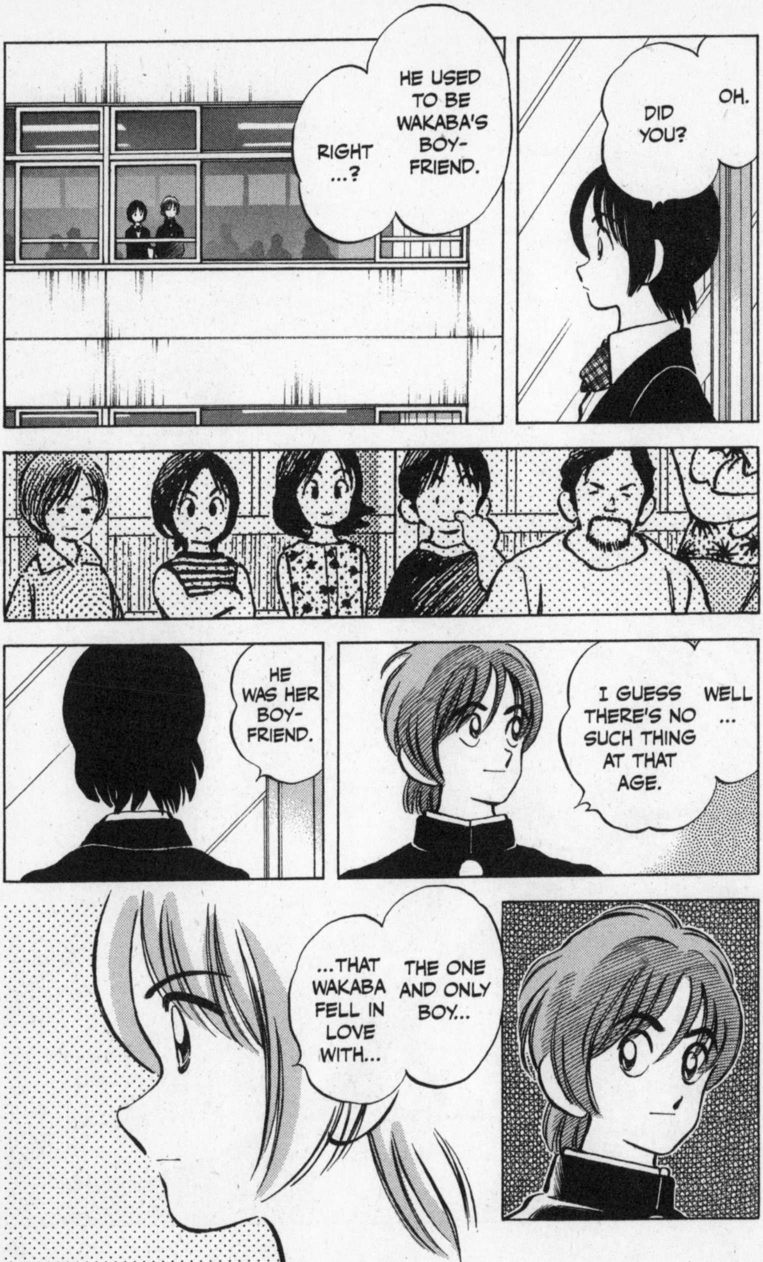
OH.
DID YOU?
HE USED TO BE WAKABA'S BOY-FRIEND.
RIGHT ...?
WELL ...
I GUESS THERE'S NO SUCH THING AT THAT AGE.
HE WAS HER BOY-FRIEND.
THE ONE AND ONLY BOY...
...THAT WAKABA FELL IN LOVE WITH...

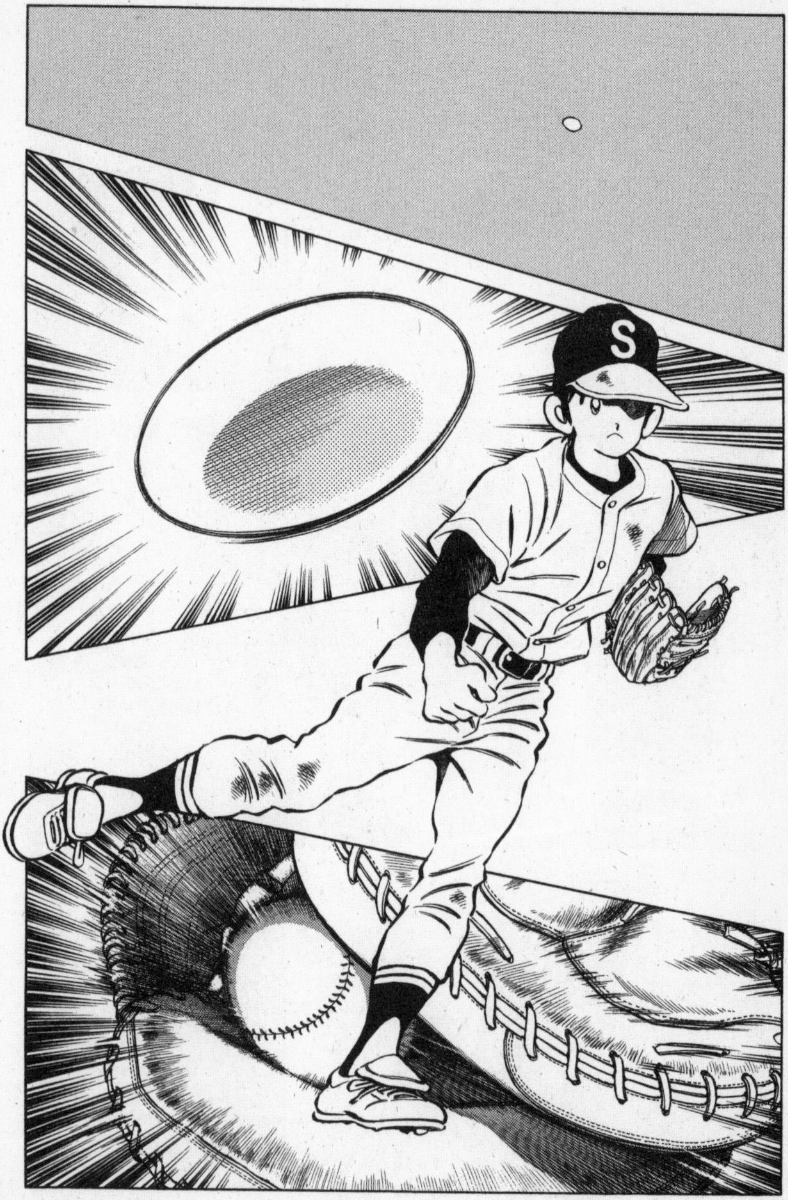

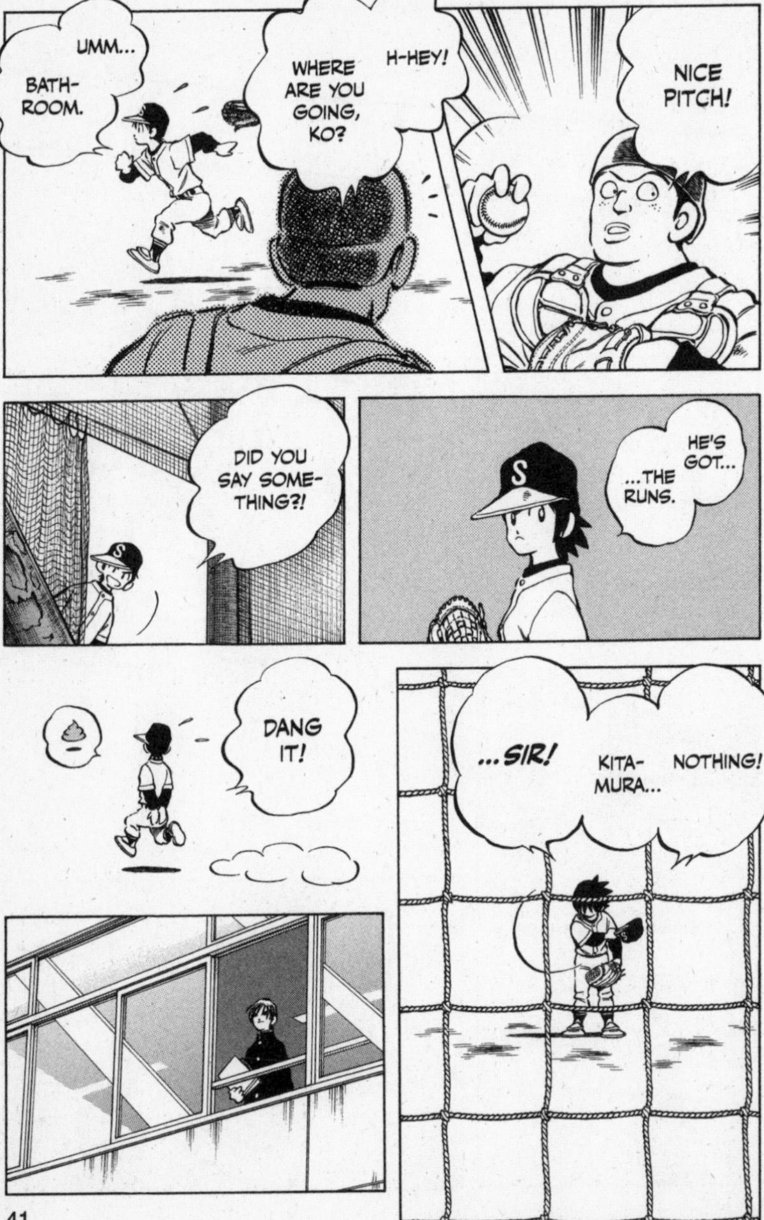
NICE PITCH!
H-HEY!
WHERE ARE YOU GOING, KO?
UMM...
BATH-ROOM.
HE'S GOT...
...THE RUNS.
DID YOU SAY SOME-THING?!
NOTHING!
KITA-MURA...
...SIR!
DANG IT!

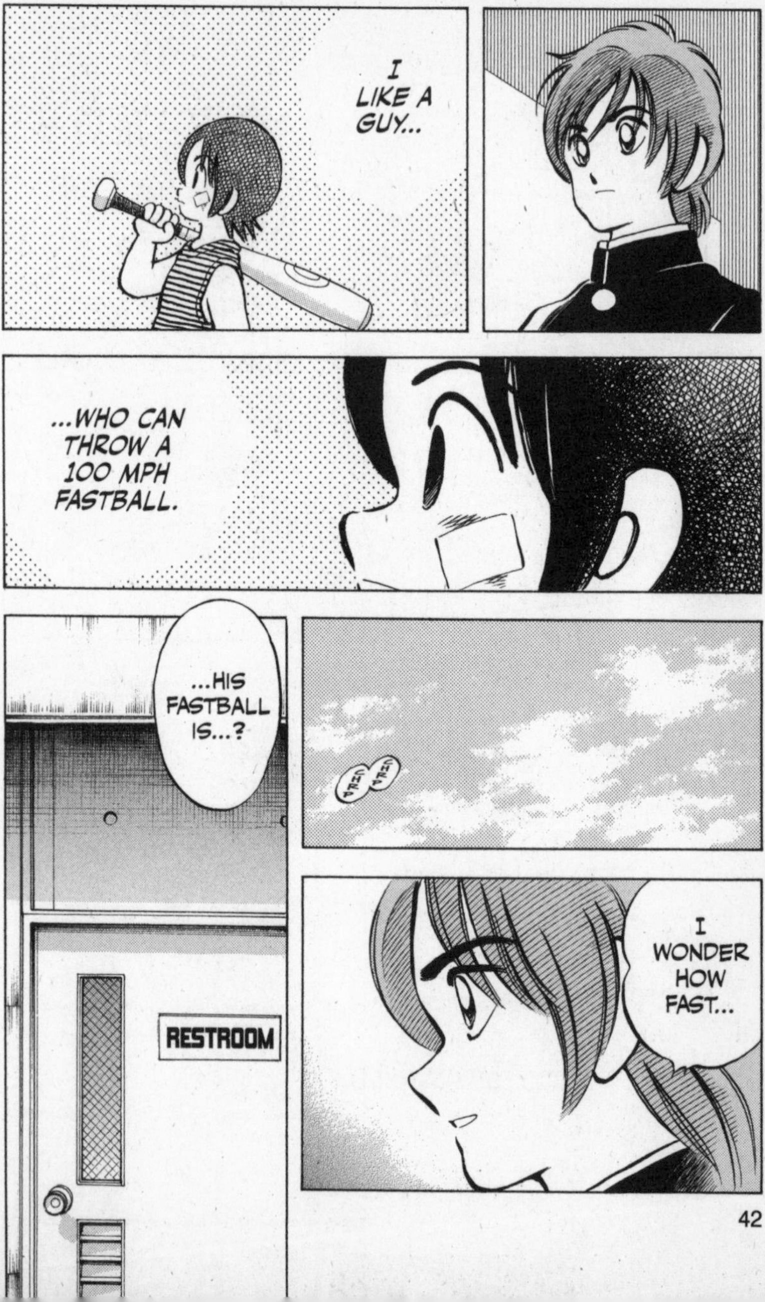
I LIKE A GUY...
...WHO CAN THROW A 100 MPH FASTBALL.
CHRP
CHRP
I WONDER HOW FAST...
...HIS FASTBALL IS...?
RESTROOM

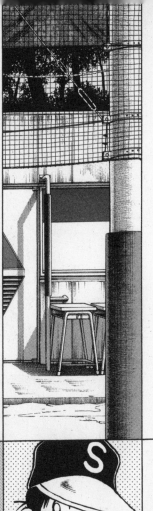

# CHAPTER 63
# YES, THEY CAN

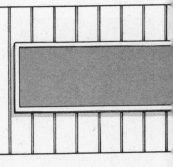

COFFEE
CLOVER

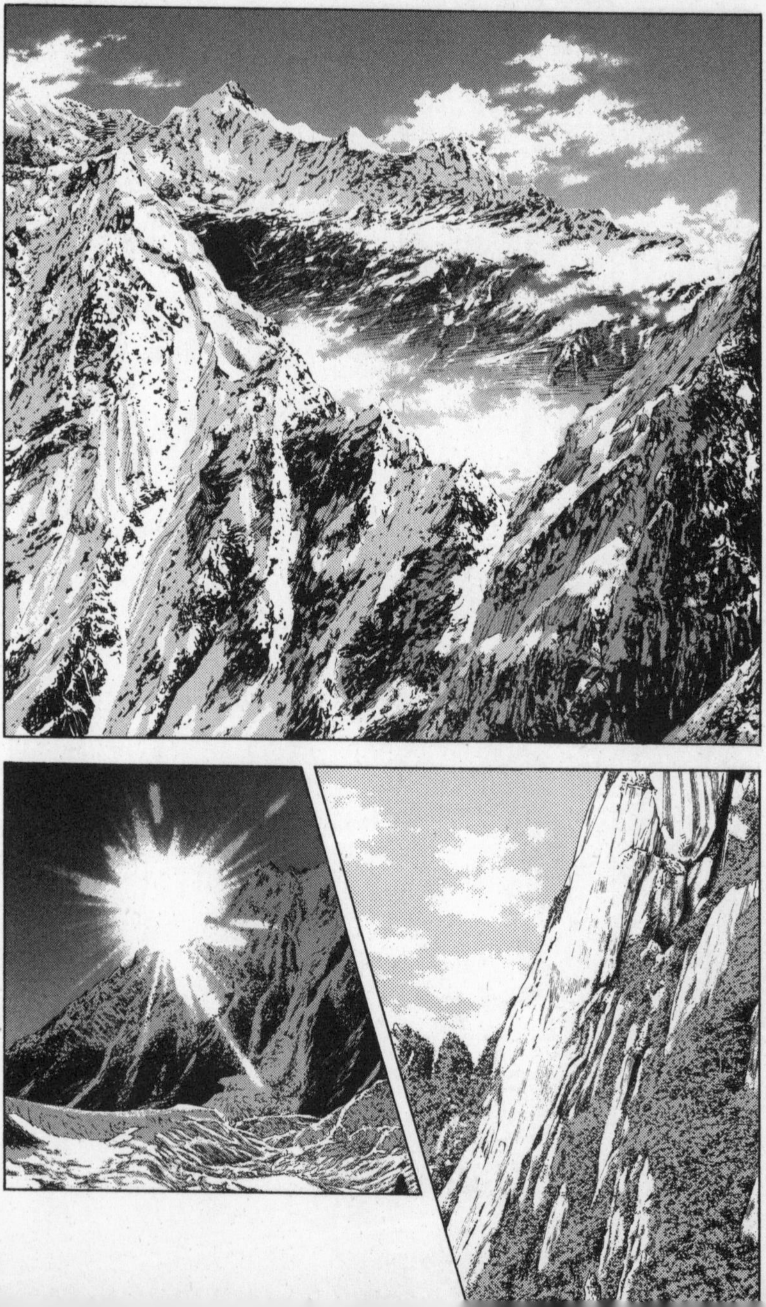

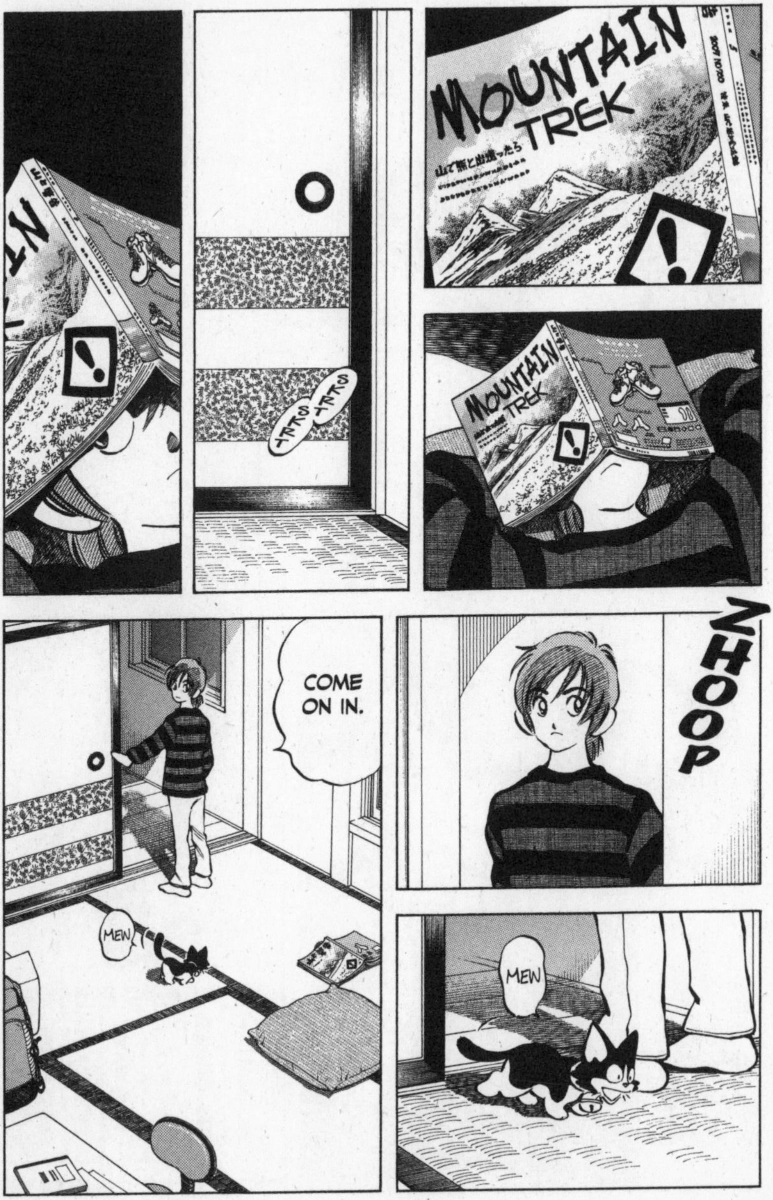
MOUNTAIN TREK
MOUNTAIN TREK
SKRT SKRT
ZHOOP
MEW
COME ON IN.
MEW

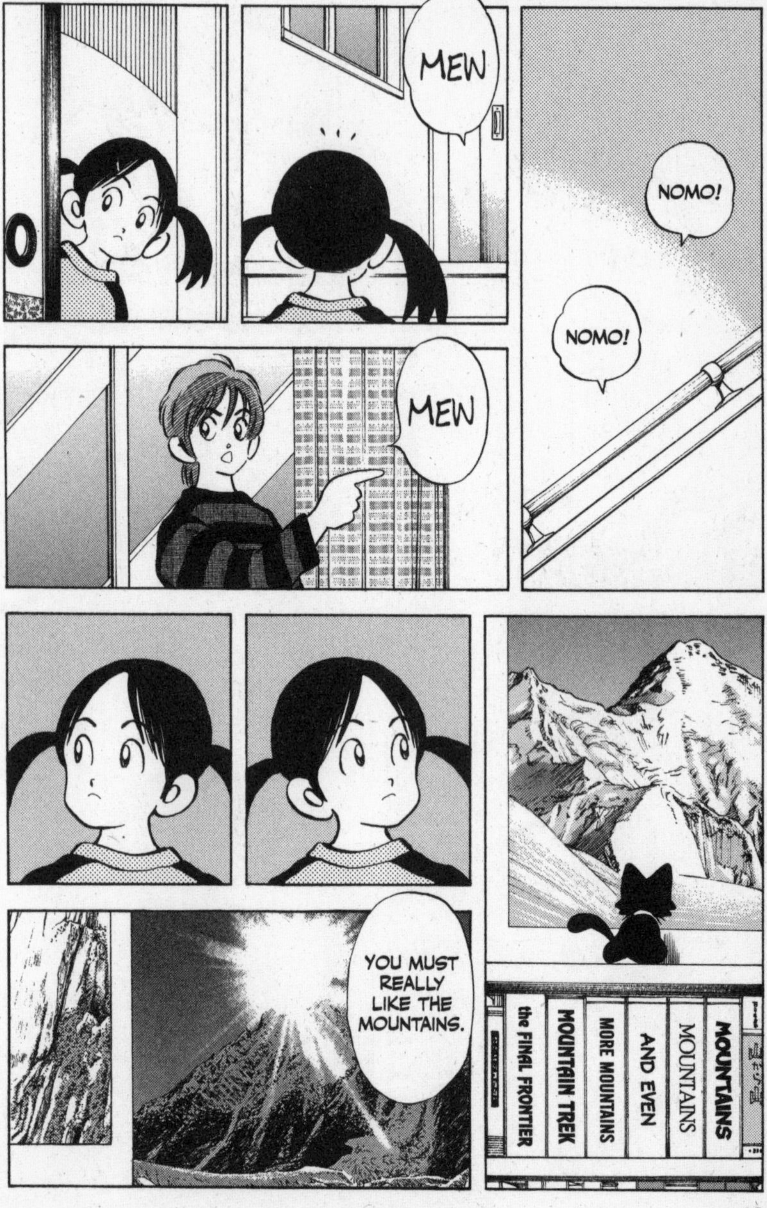
NOMO!
NOMO!
MEW
MEW
MOUNTAINS
MOUNTAINS
AND EVEN
MORE MOUNTAINS
MOUNTAIN TREK
the FINAL FRONTIER
YOU MUST REALLY LIKE THE MOUNTAINS.

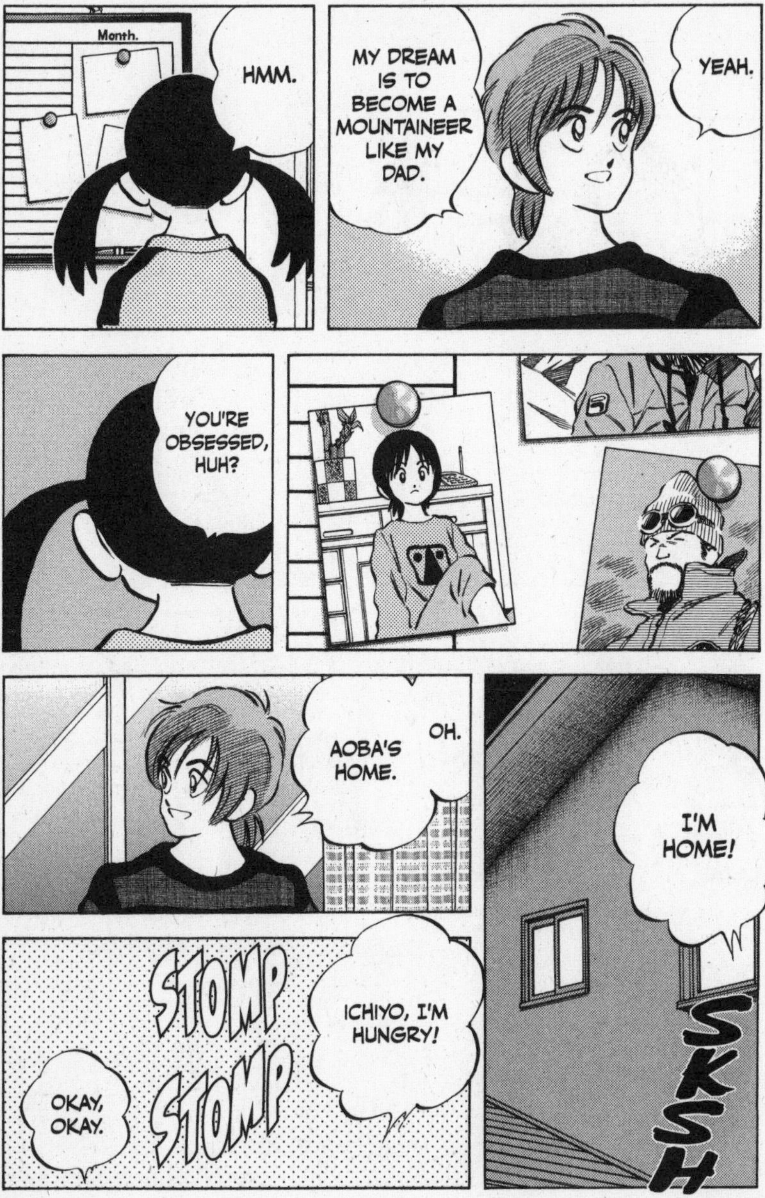
YEAH.
MY DREAM IS TO BECOME A MOUNTAINEER LIKE MY DAD.
HMM.
Month.
YOU'RE OBSESSED, HUH?
I'M HOME!
SKSH
OH.
AOBA'S HOME.
ICHIYO, I'M HUNGRY!
STOMP STOMP
OKAY, OKAY.

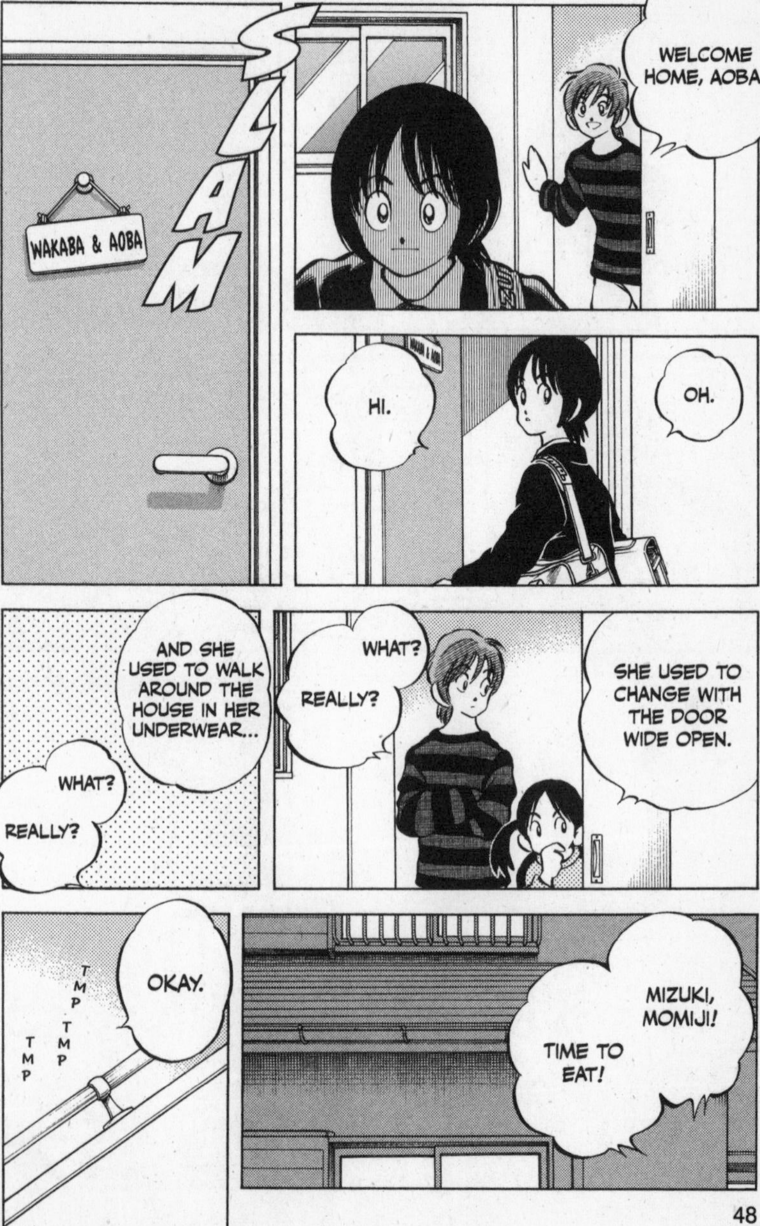
WELCOME HOME, AOBA!
OH.
HI.
SLAM
WAKABA & AOBA
SHE USED TO CHANGE WITH THE DOOR WIDE OPEN.
WHAT?
REALLY?
AND SHE USED TO WALK AROUND THE HOUSE IN HER UNDERWEAR...
WHAT?
REALLY?
MIZUKI, MOMIJI!
TIME TO EAT!
OKAY.
TMP TMP TMP

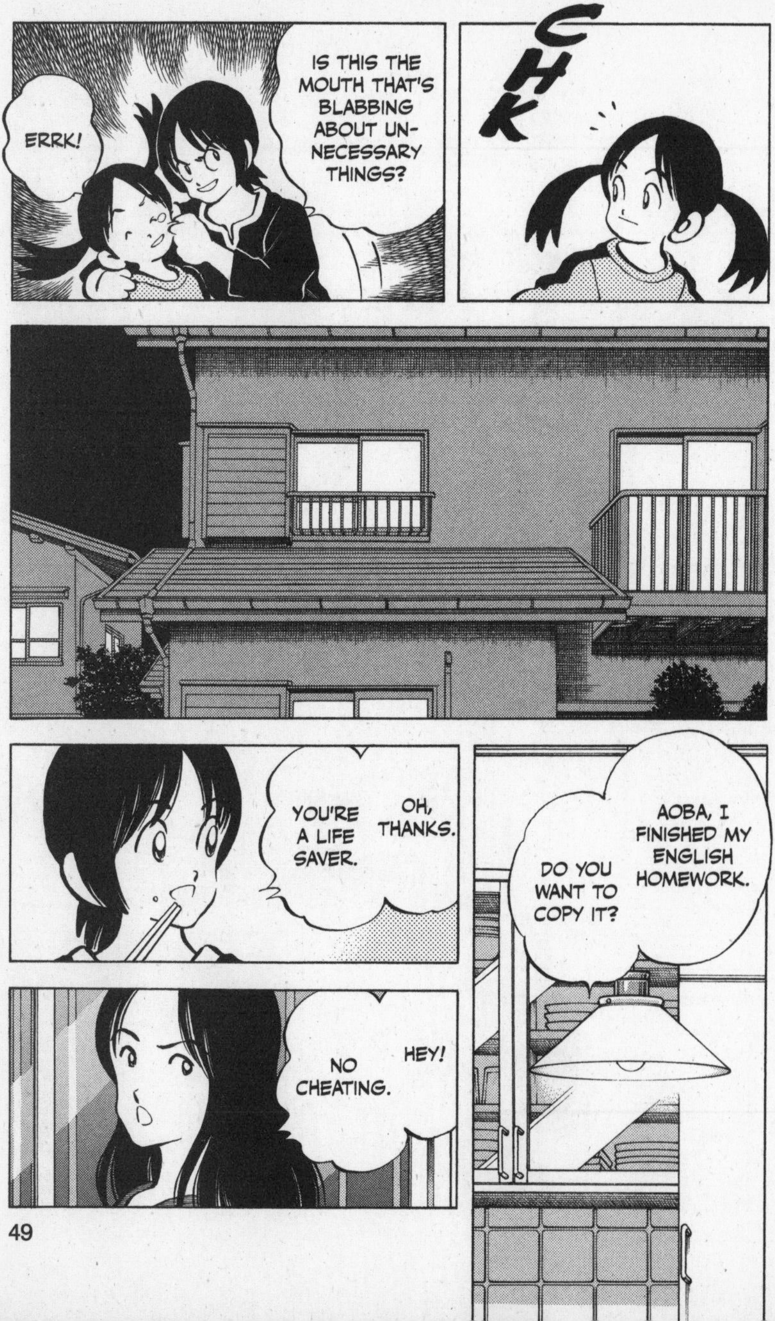
CHK
IS THIS THE MOUTH THAT'S BLABBING ABOUT UN-NECESSARY THINGS?
ERRK!
AOBA, I FINISHED MY ENGLISH HOMEWORK.
DO YOU WANT TO COPY IT?
OH, THANKS.
YOU'RE A LIFE SAVER.
HEY!
NO CHEATING.

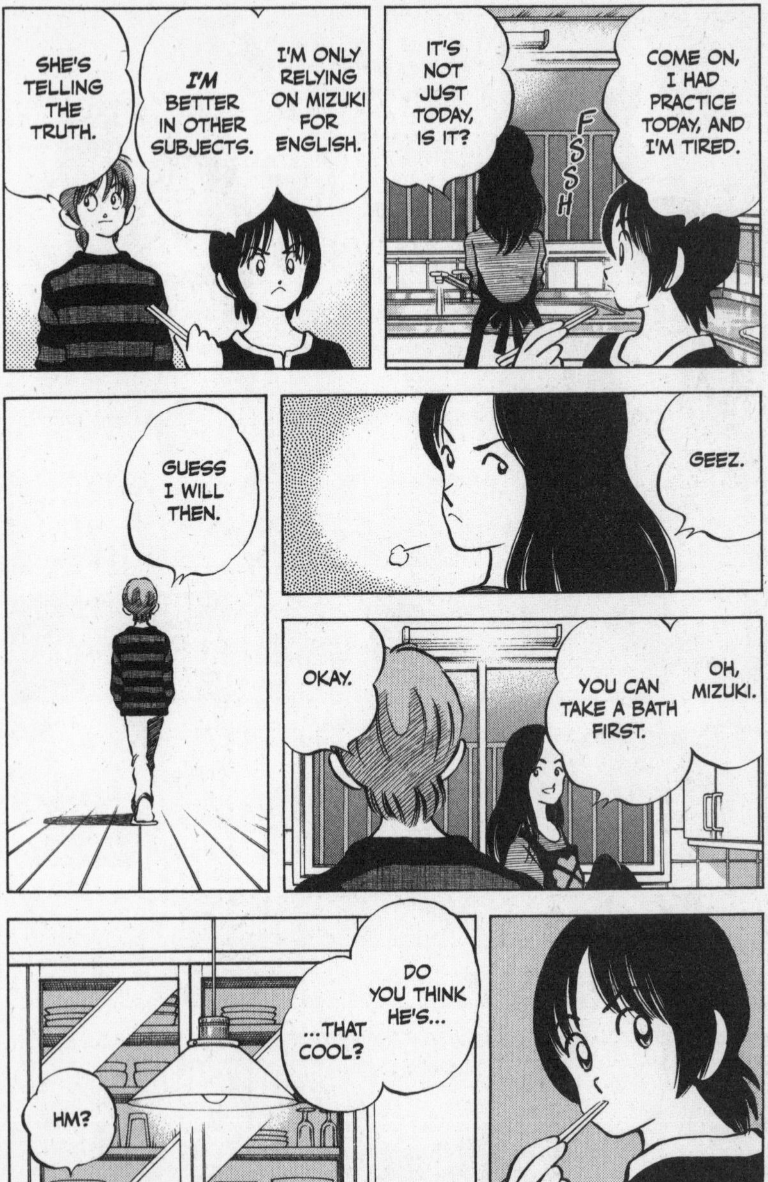
COME ON, I HAD PRACTICE TODAY, AND I'M TIRED.
FSSH
IT'S NOT JUST TODAY, IS IT?
I'M ONLY RELYING ON MIZUKI FOR ENGLISH.
*I'M* BETTER IN OTHER SUBJECTS.
SHE'S TELLING THE TRUTH.
GEEZ.
OH, MIZUKI.
YOU CAN TAKE A BATH FIRST.
OKAY.
GUESS I WILL THEN.
DO YOU THINK HE'S...
...THAT COOL?
HM?

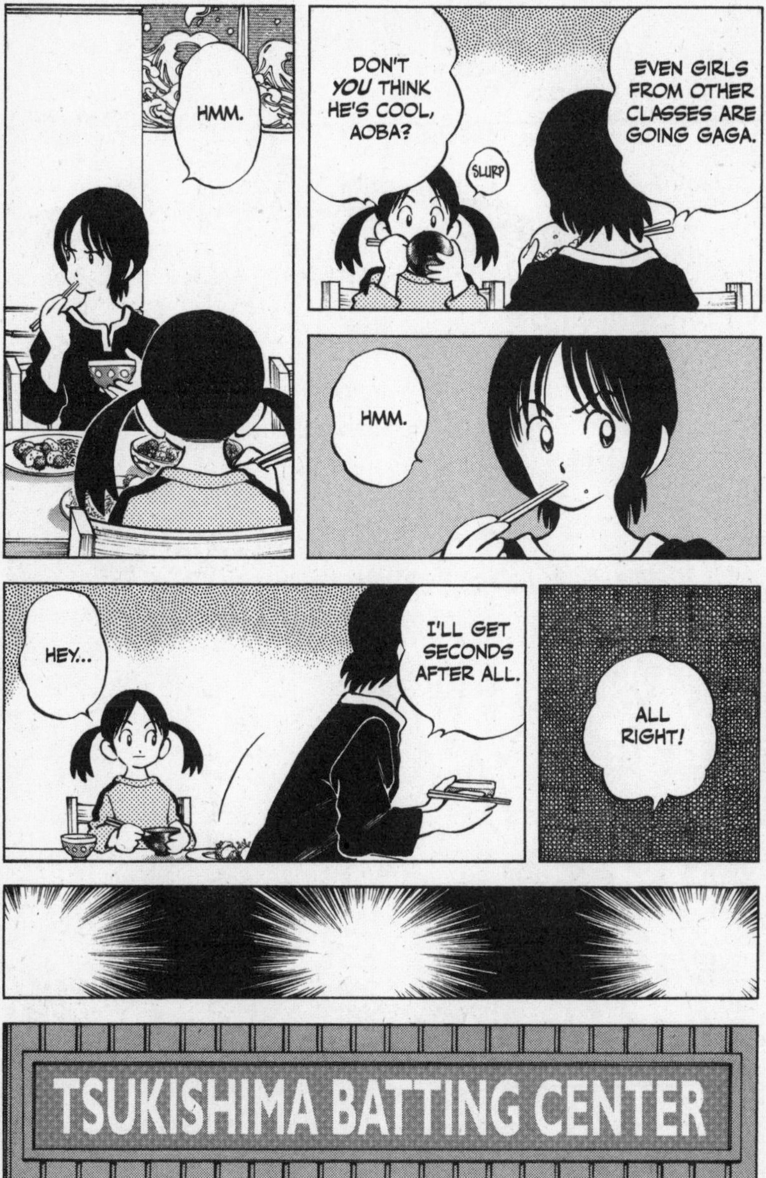
EVEN GIRLS FROM OTHER CLASSES ARE GOING GAGA.
DON'T *YOU* THINK HE'S COOL, AOBA?
SLURP
HMM.
HMM.
ALL RIGHT!
I'LL GET SECONDS AFTER ALL.
HEY...
TSUKISHIMA BATTING CENTER

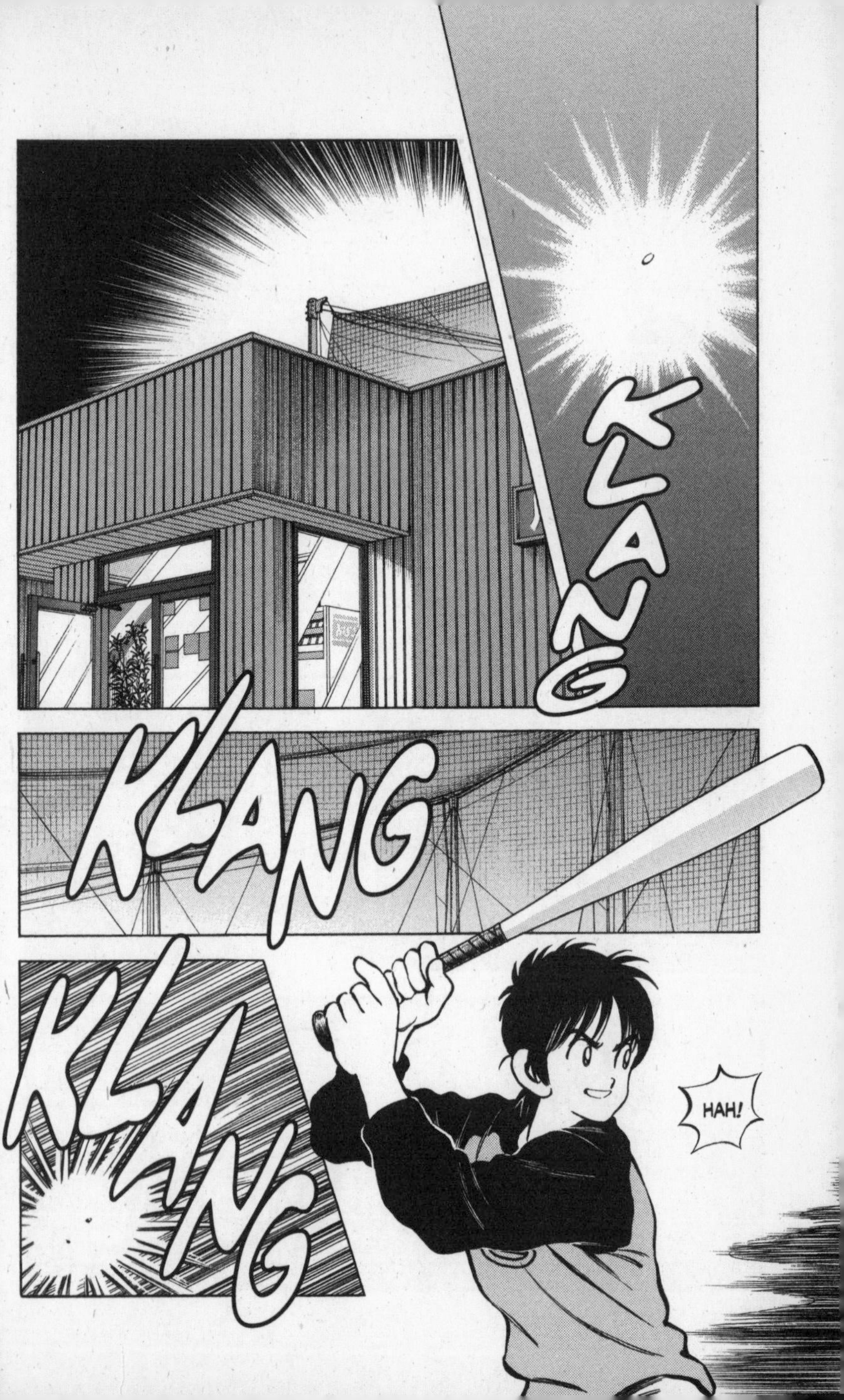
KLANG
KLANG
HAH!
KLANG

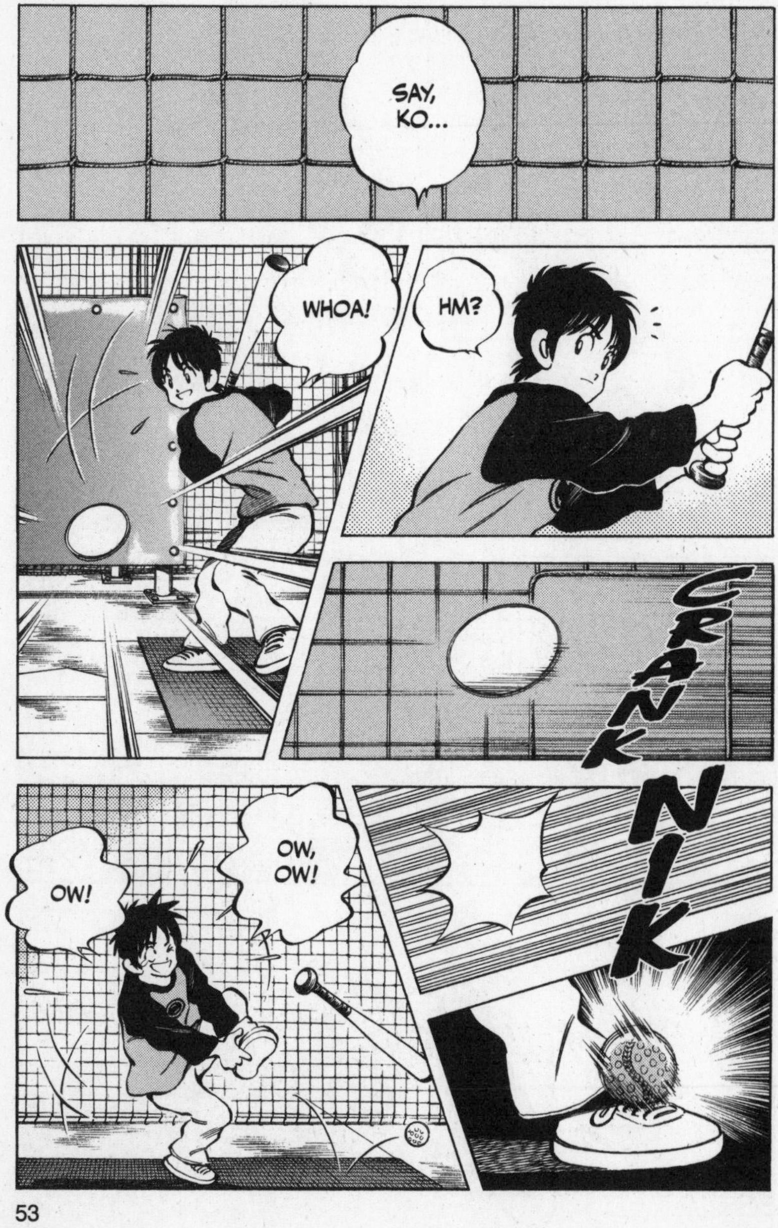
SAY, KO...
HM?
CRANK
WHOA!
NIK
OW, OW!
OW!

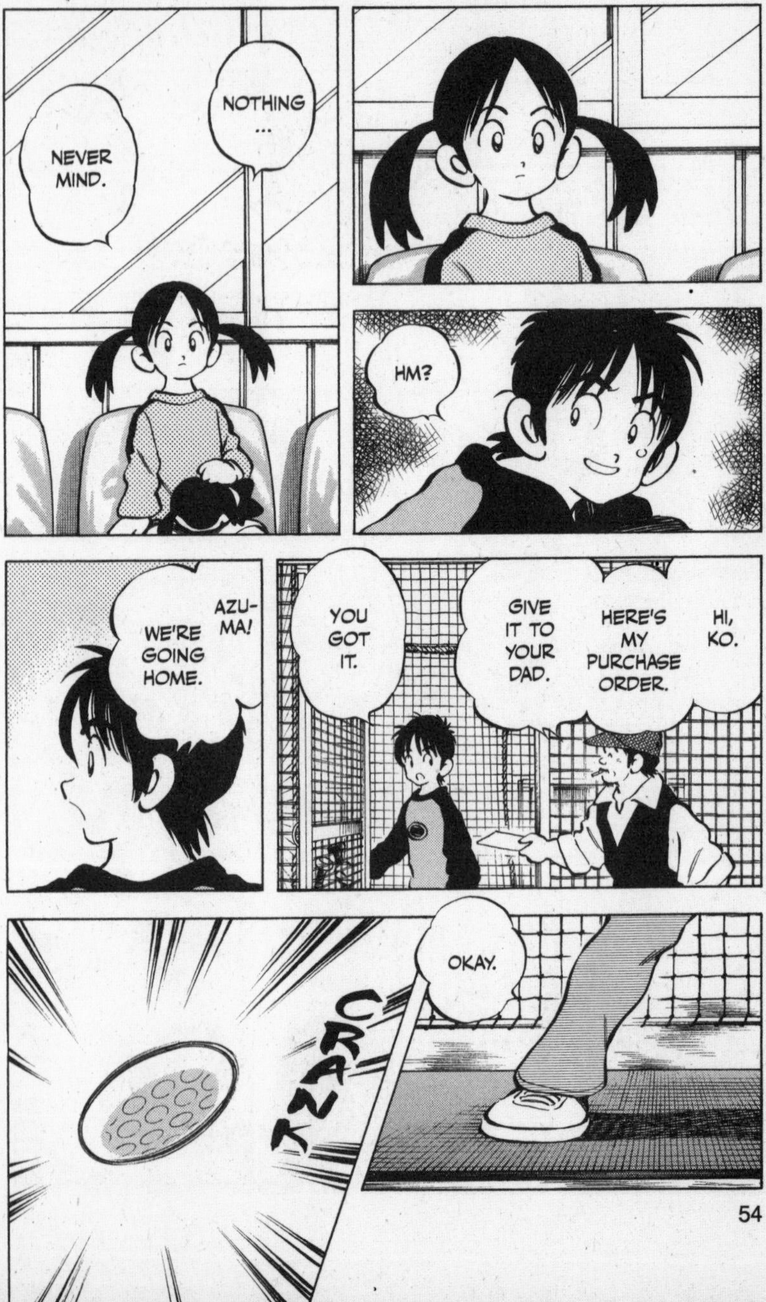
NOTHING ...
NEVER MIND.
HM?
HI, KO.
HERE'S MY PURCHASE ORDER.
GIVE IT TO YOUR DAD.
YOU GOT IT.
AZUMA!
WE'RE GOING HOME.
OKAY.
CRANK

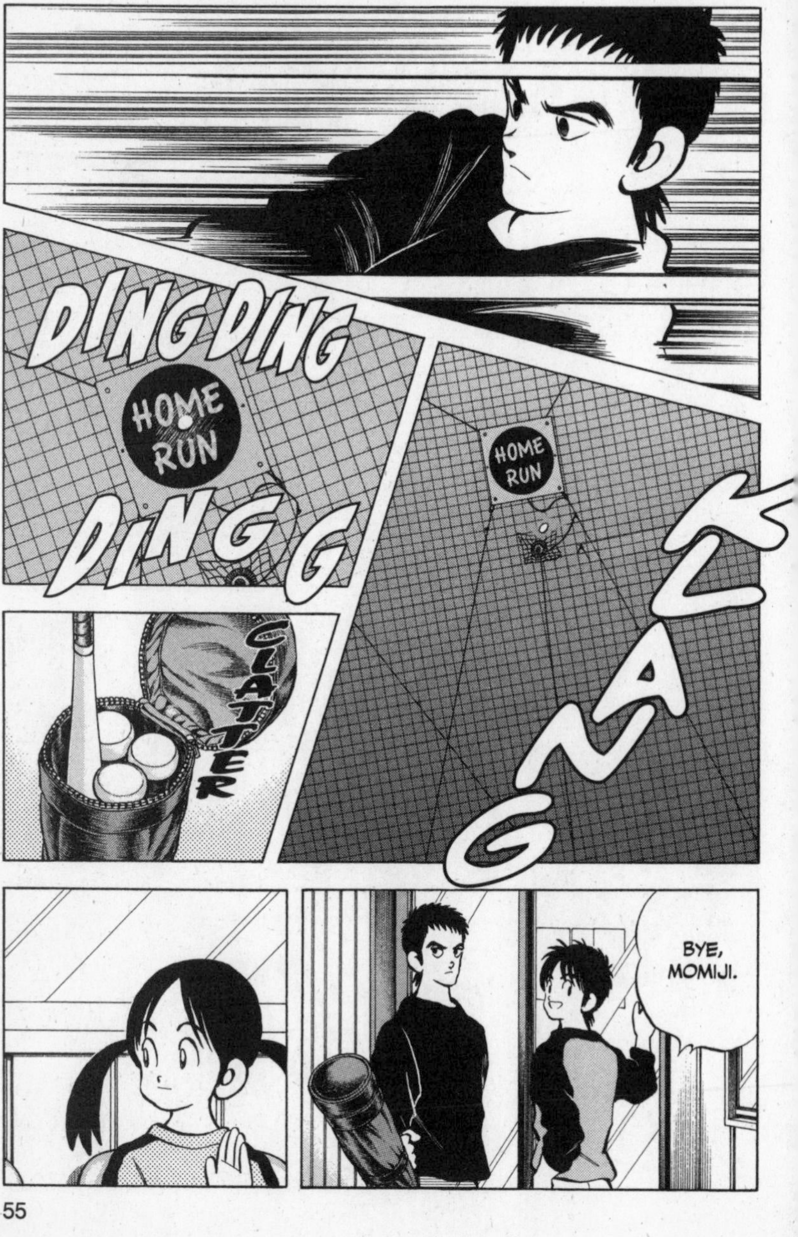

DING DING
HOME RUN
DING G
HOME RUN
KLANNG
CLATTER
BYE, MOMIJI.

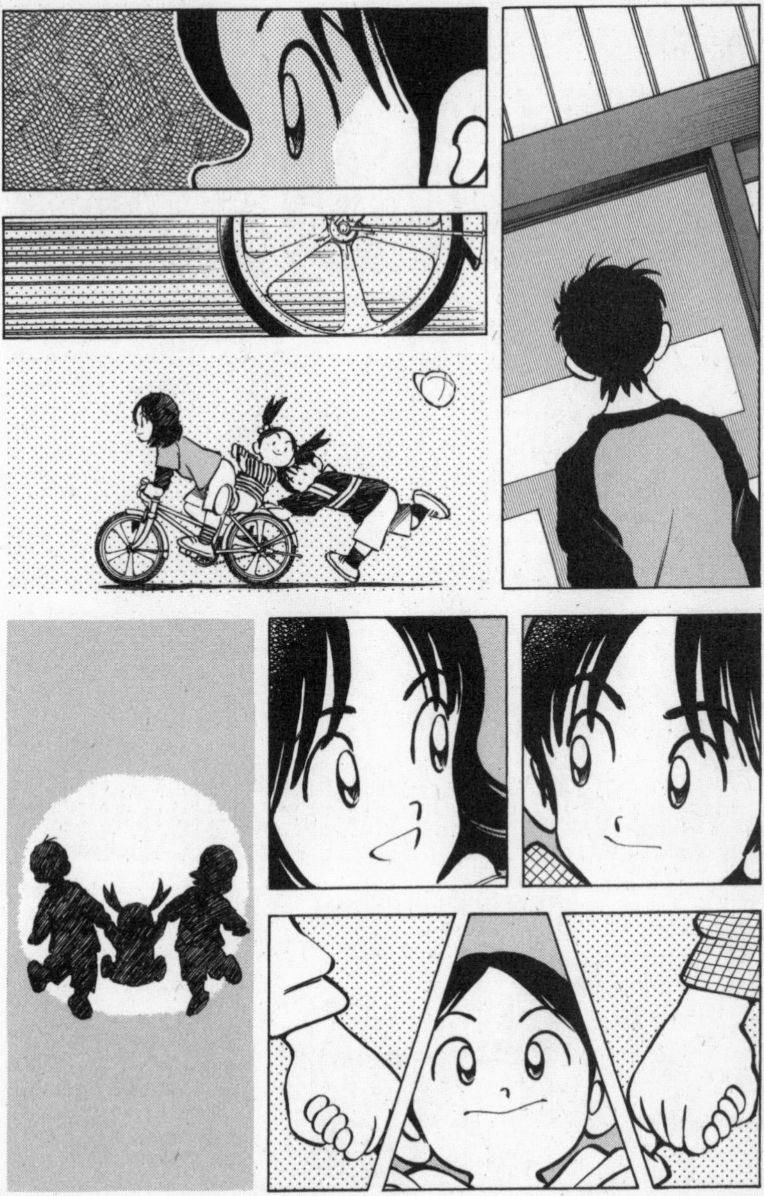

SORRY...

WAKA.

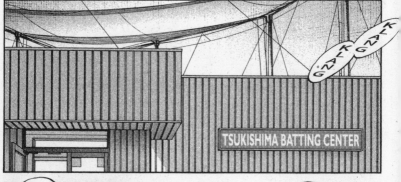

TSUKISHIMA BATTING CENTER

KAN G

KAN G

KITTY CORNER!

STRAIGHT!

RIGHT!

I TOLD YOU!

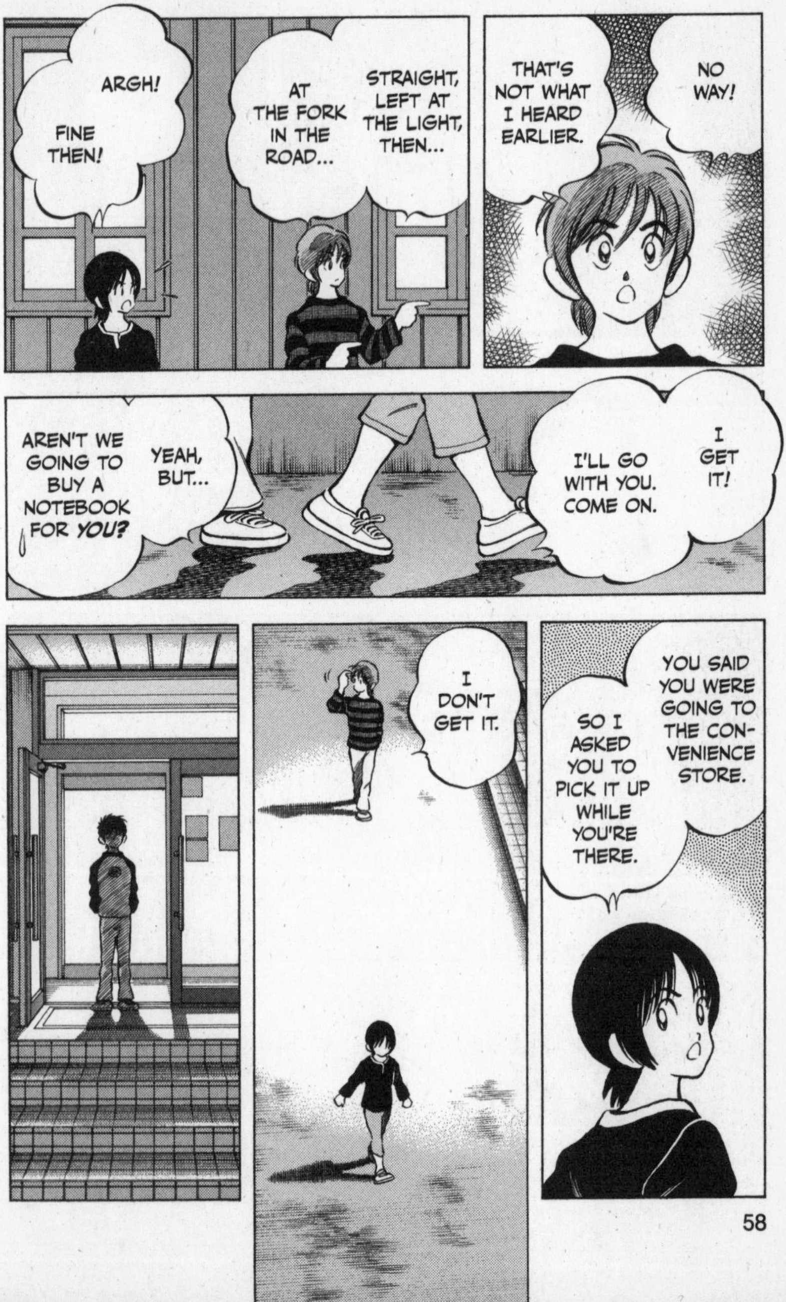
NO WAY!
THAT'S NOT WHAT I HEARD EARLIER.
STRAIGHT, LEFT AT THE LIGHT, THEN...
AT THE FORK IN THE ROAD...
ARGH!
FINE THEN!
I GET IT!
I'LL GO WITH YOU. COME ON.
YEAH, BUT...
AREN'T WE GOING TO BUY A NOTEBOOK FOR *YOU?*
YOU SAID YOU WERE GOING TO THE CON-VENIENCE STORE.
SO I ASKED YOU TO PICK IT UP WHILE YOU'RE THERE.
I DON'T GET IT.

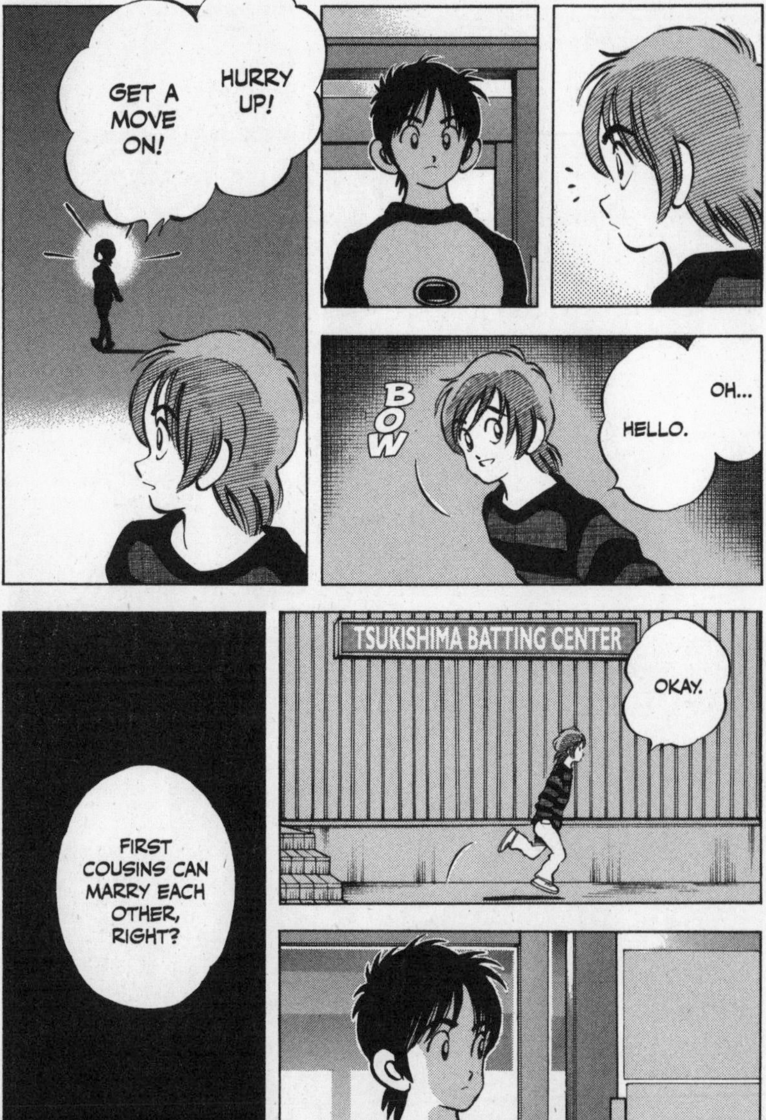

B O W
OH... HELLO.
HURRY UP!
GET A MOVE ON!
TSUKISHIMA BATTING CENTER
OKAY.
FIRST COUSINS CAN MARRY EACH OTHER, RIGHT?

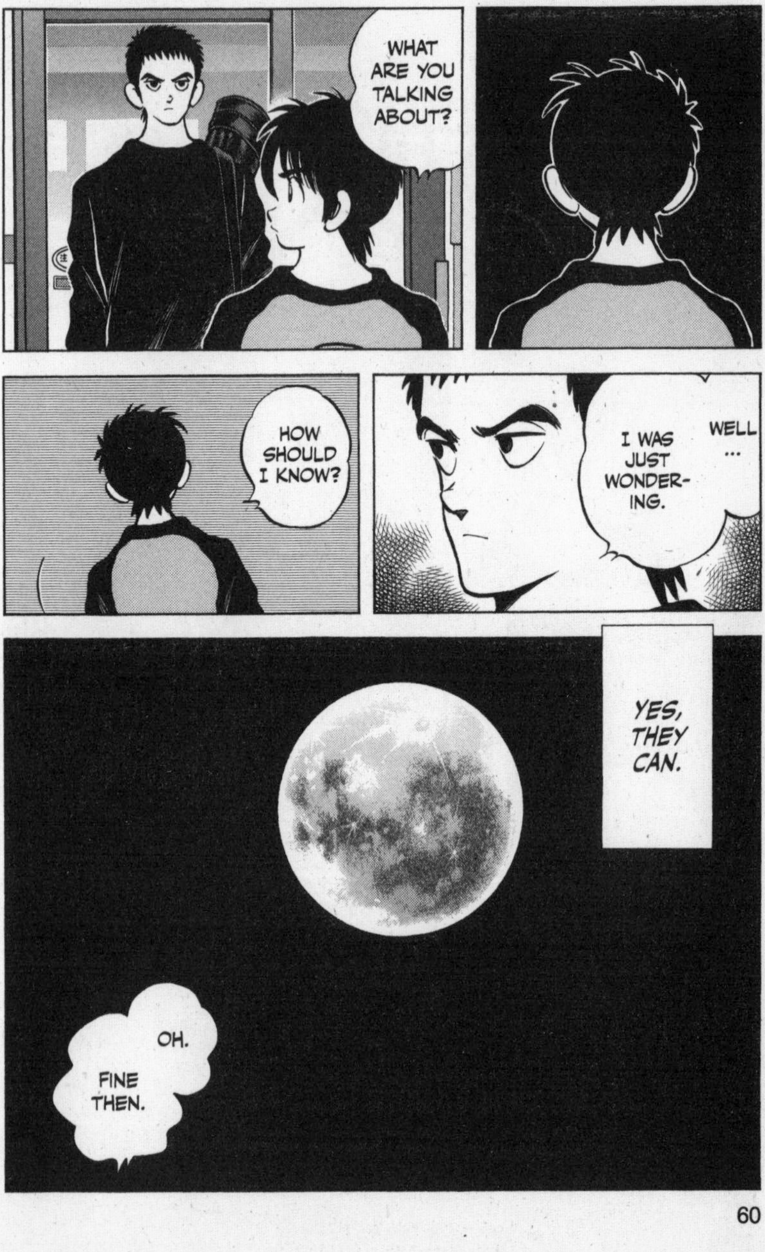
WHAT ARE YOU TALKING ABOUT?
WELL ...
I WAS JUST WONDER-ING.
HOW SHOULD I KNOW?
YES, THEY CAN.
OH.
FINE THEN.

## CHAPTER 64

# THAT'S A FALSE RUMOR

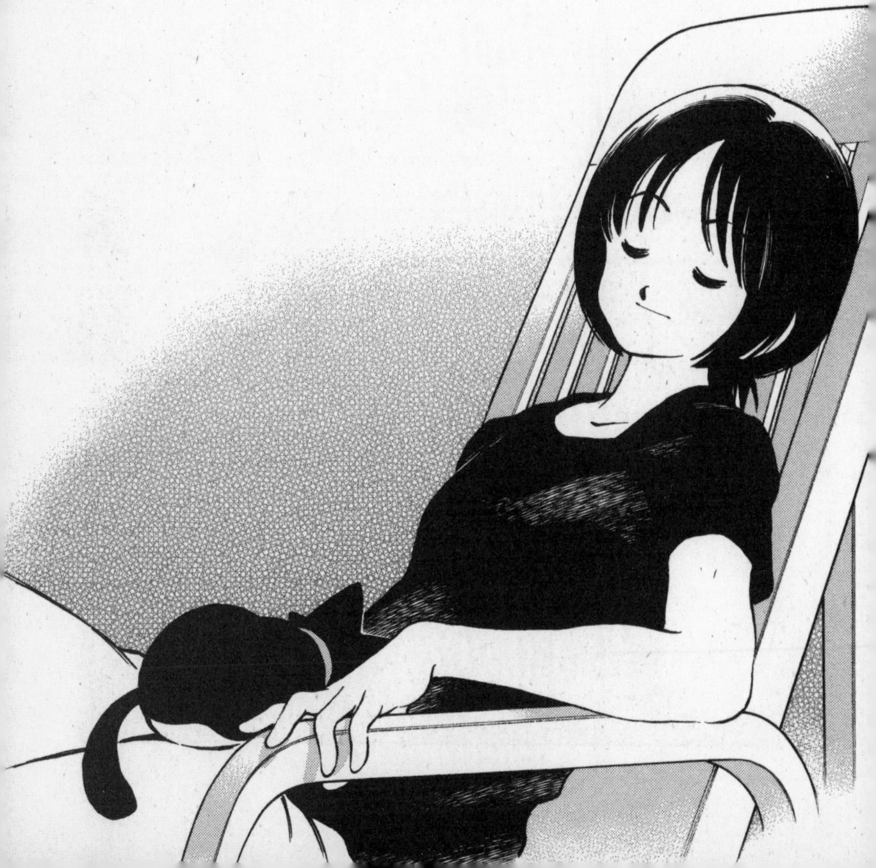

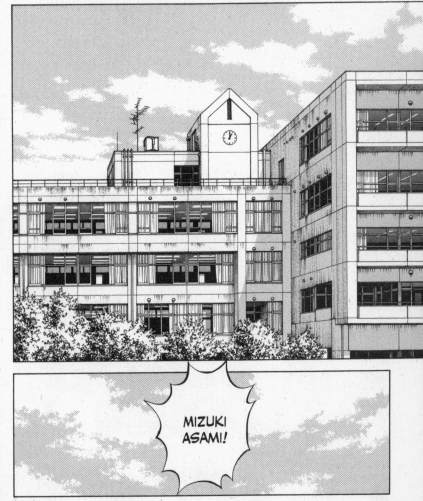

SEISHU GAKUEN SENIOR HIGH SCHOOL

MIZUKI ASAMI!

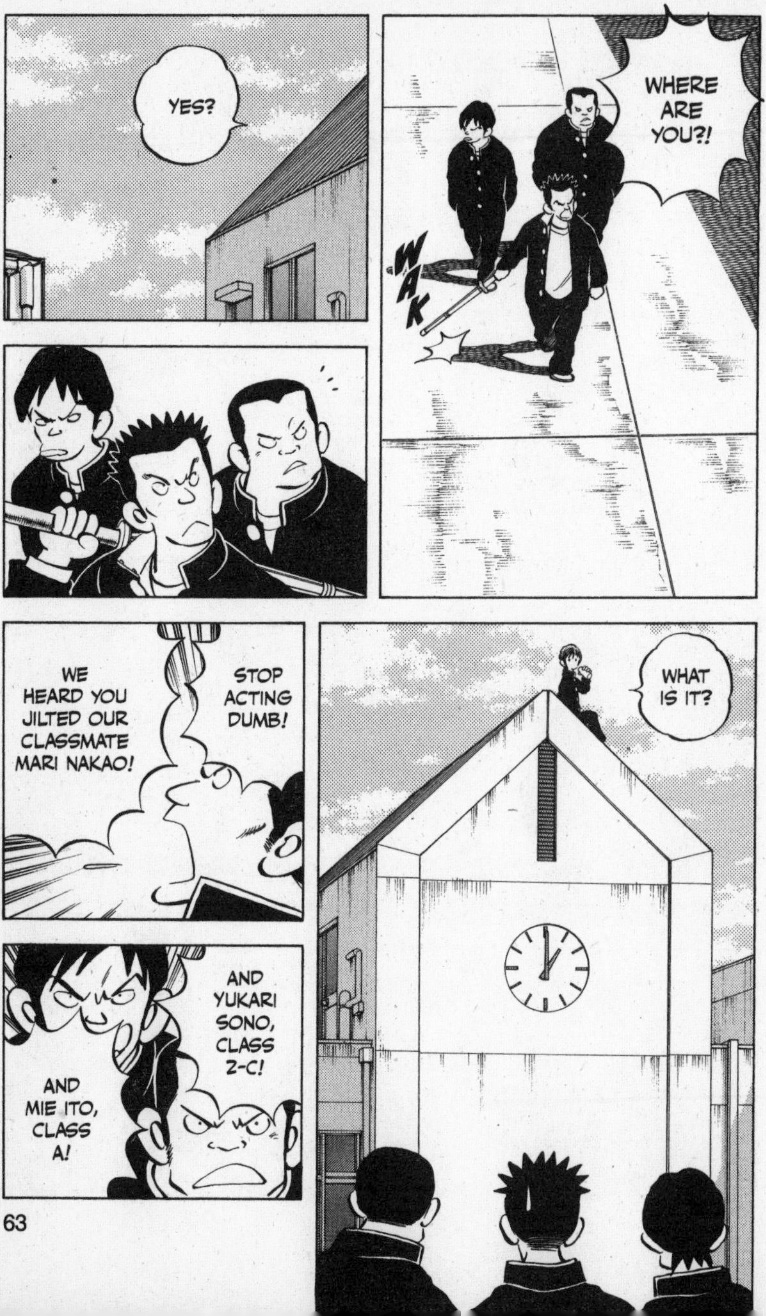
WHERE ARE YOU?!
WAK
YES?
WHAT IS IT?
STOP ACTING DUMB!
WE HEARD YOU JILTED OUR CLASSMATE MARI NAKAO!
AND YUKARI SONO, CLASS 2-C!
AND MIE ITO, CLASS A!

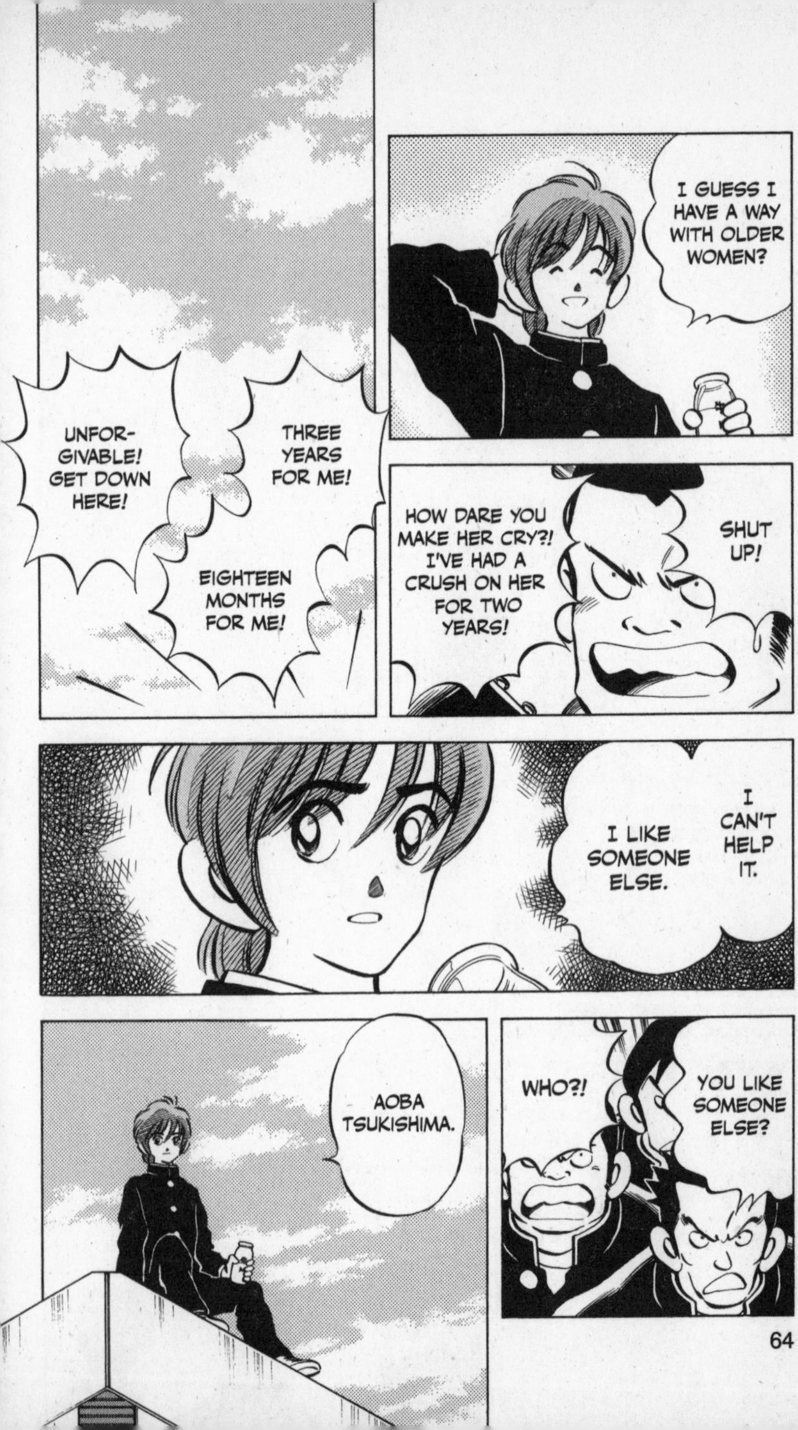
I GUESS I HAVE A WAY WITH OLDER WOMEN?
SHUT UP!
HOW DARE YOU MAKE HER CRY?! I'VE HAD A CRUSH ON HER FOR TWO YEARS!
THREE YEARS FOR ME!
UNFOR-GIVABLE! GET DOWN HERE!
EIGHTEEN MONTHS FOR ME!
I CAN'T HELP IT.
I LIKE SOMEONE ELSE.
YOU LIKE SOMEONE ELSE?
WHO?!
AOBA TSUKISHIMA.

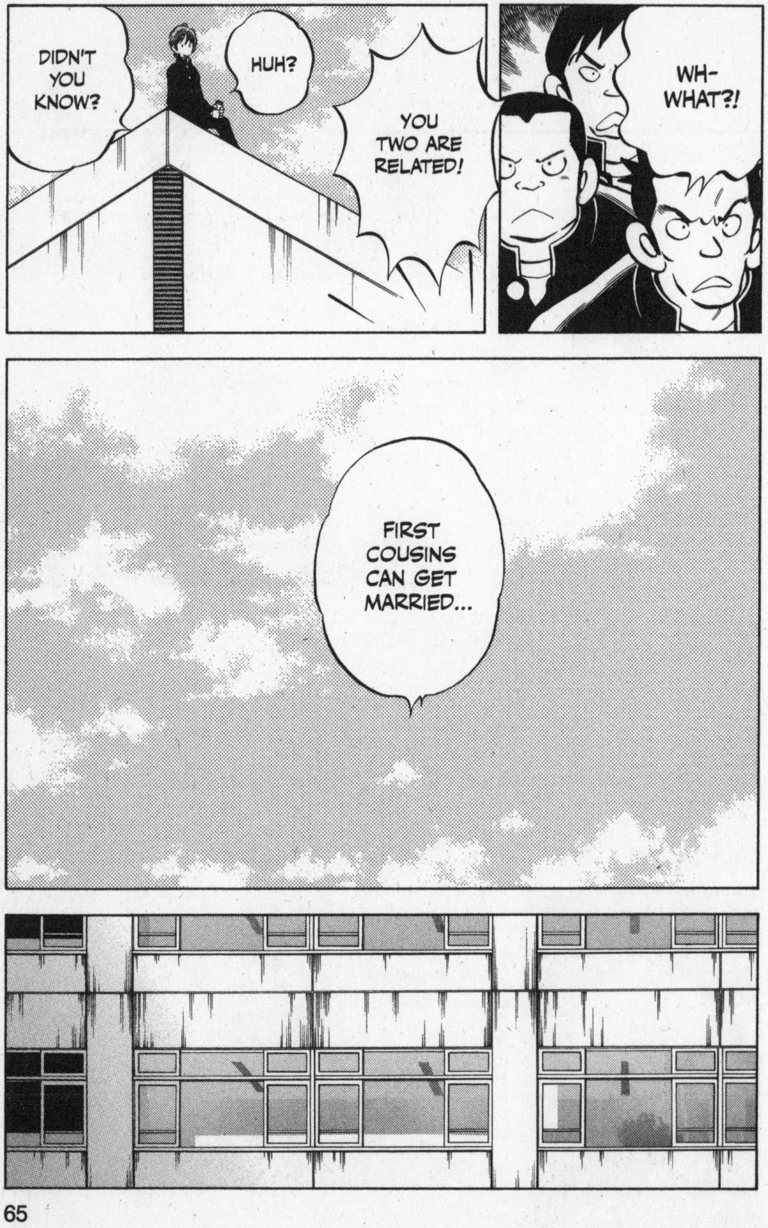
WH-WHAT?!
YOU TWO ARE RELATED!
HUH?
DIDN'T YOU KNOW?
FIRST COUSINS CAN GET MARRIED...

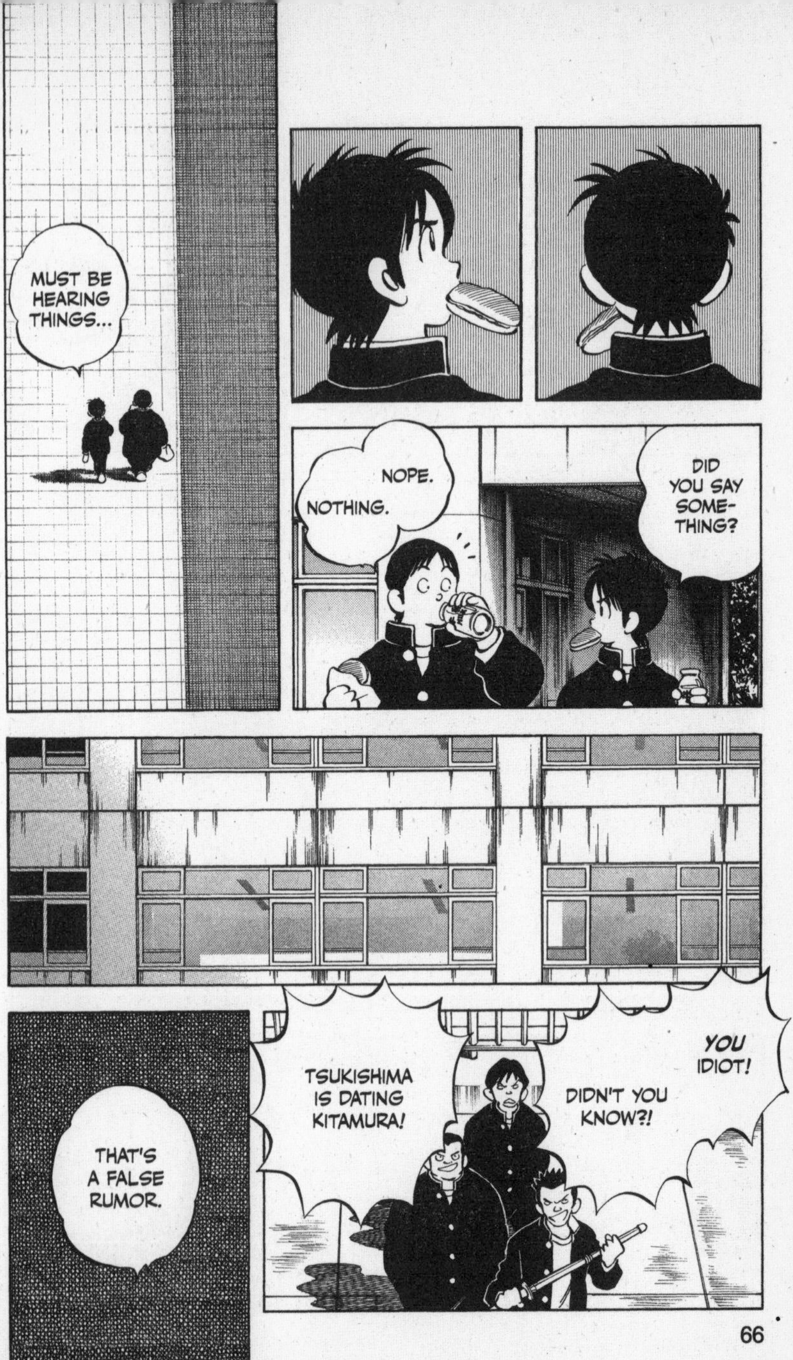
DID YOU SAY SOME-THING?
NOPE. NOTHING.
MUST BE HEARING THINGS...
YOU IDIOT!
DIDN'T YOU KNOW?!
TSUKISHIMA IS DATING KITAMURA!
THAT'S A FALSE RUMOR.

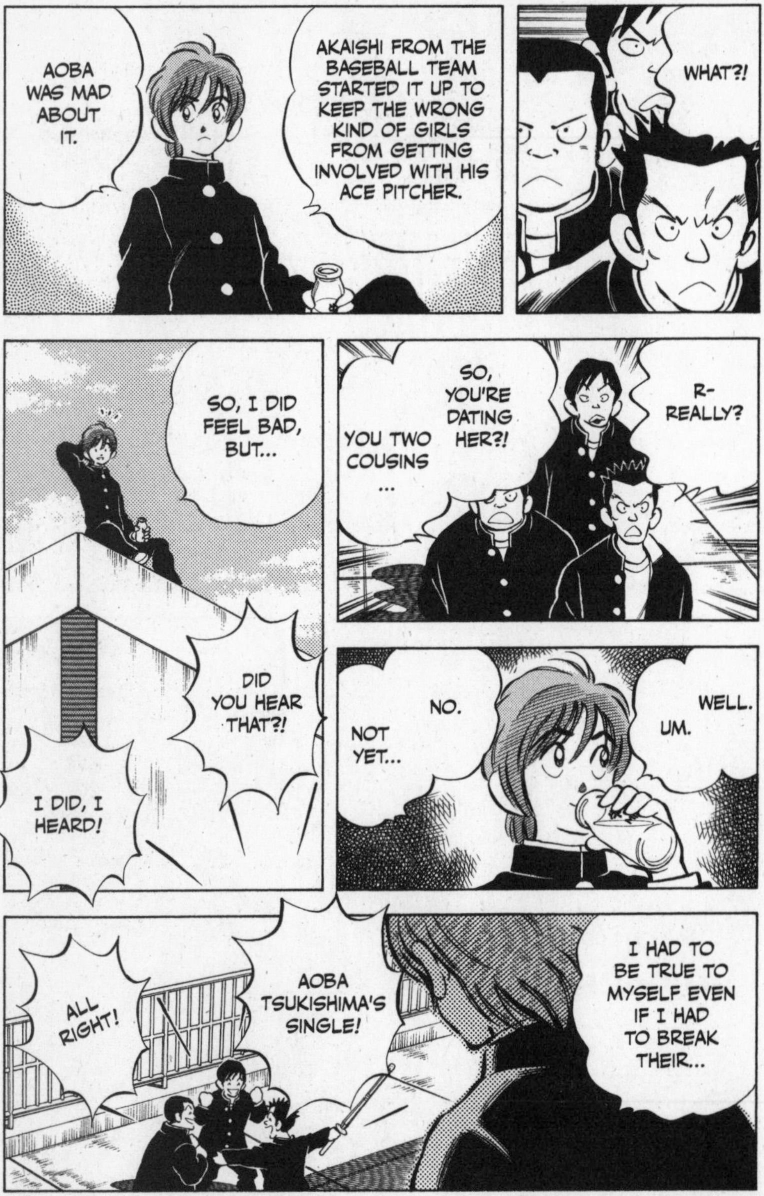

WHAT?!
AKAISHI FROM THE BASEBALL TEAM STARTED IT UP TO KEEP THE WRONG KIND OF GIRLS FROM GETTING INVOLVED WITH HIS ACE PITCHER.
AOBA WAS MAD ABOUT IT.
R-REALLY?
SO, YOU'RE DATING HER?!
YOU TWO COUSINS ...
WELL. UM.
NO. NOT YET...
SO, I DID FEEL BAD, BUT...
DID YOU HEAR THAT?!
I DID, I HEARD!
I HAD TO BE TRUE TO MYSELF EVEN IF I HAD TO BREAK THEIR...
AOBA TSUKISHIMA'S SINGLE!
ALL RIGHT!

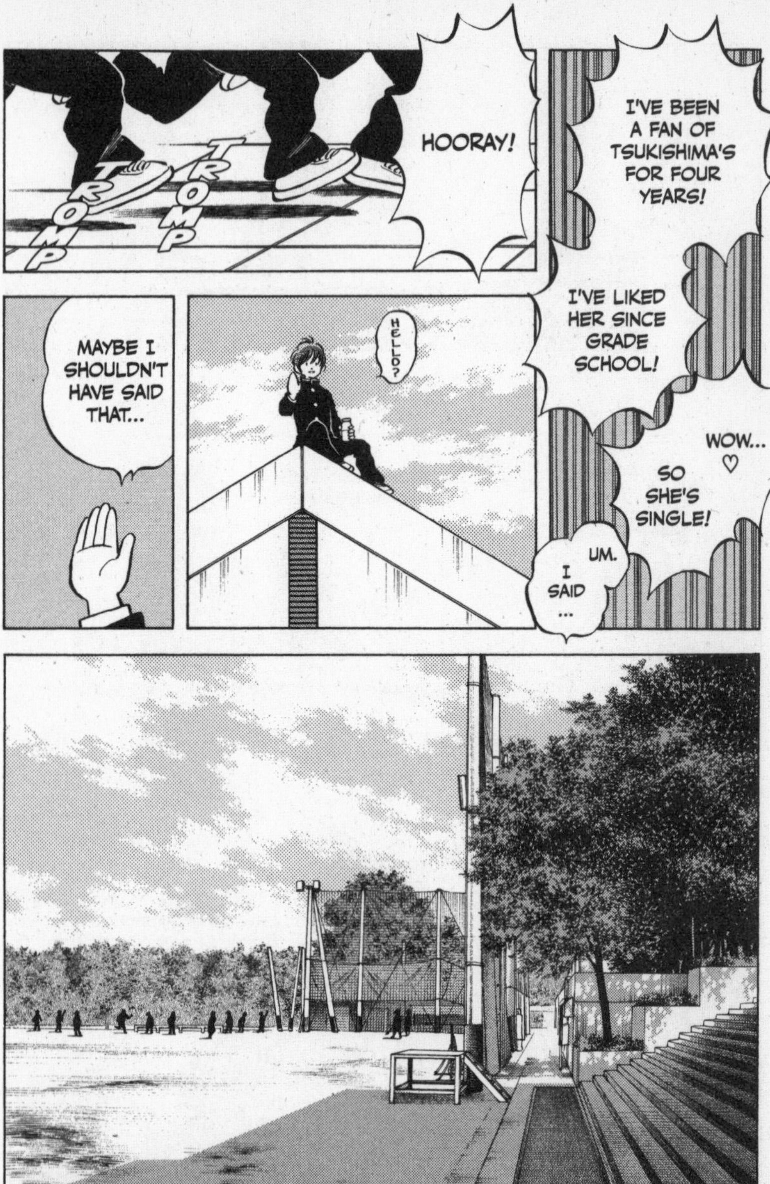

I'VE BEEN A FAN OF TSUKISHIMA'S FOR FOUR YEARS!
I'VE LIKED HER SINCE GRADE SCHOOL!
WOW... ♡
SO SHE'S SINGLE!
UM. I SAID ...
HOORAY!
TROMP
TROMP
HELLO?
MAYBE I SHOULDN'T HAVE SAID THAT...

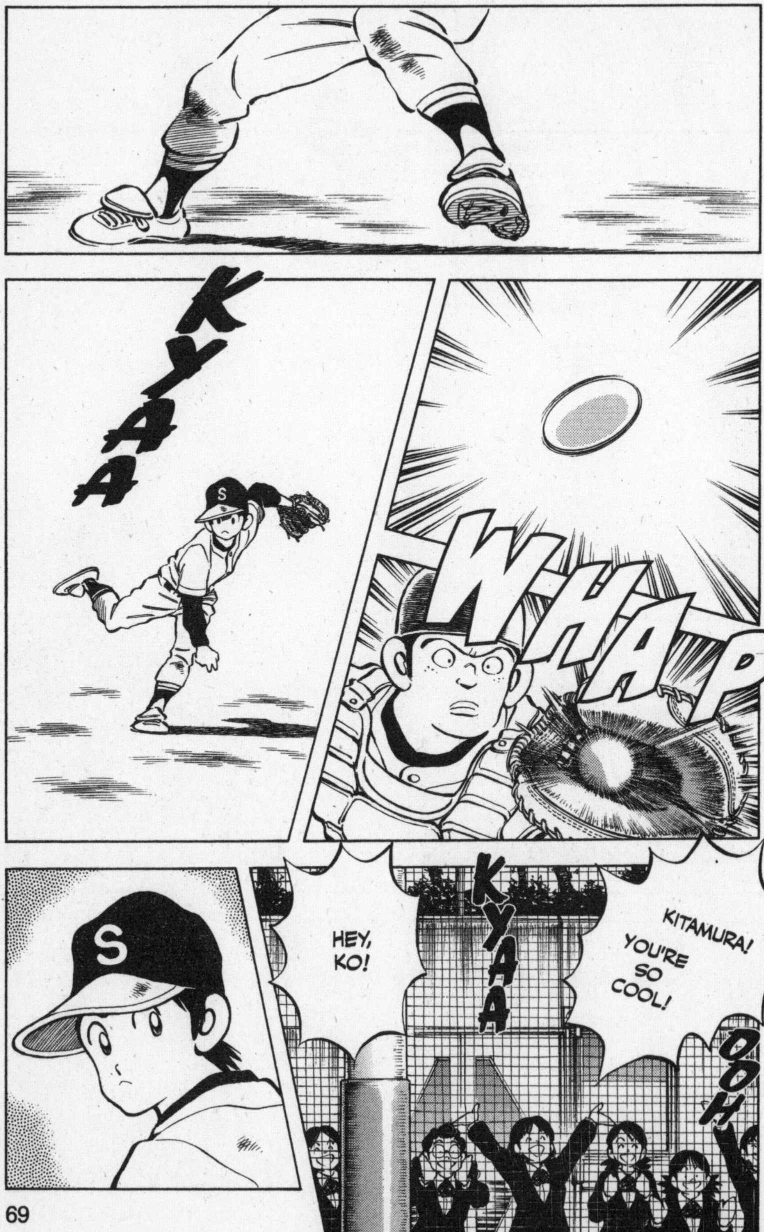
WHAP
KYAAA
KITAMURA! YOU'RE SO COOL!
KYAA
HEY, KO!
OOH

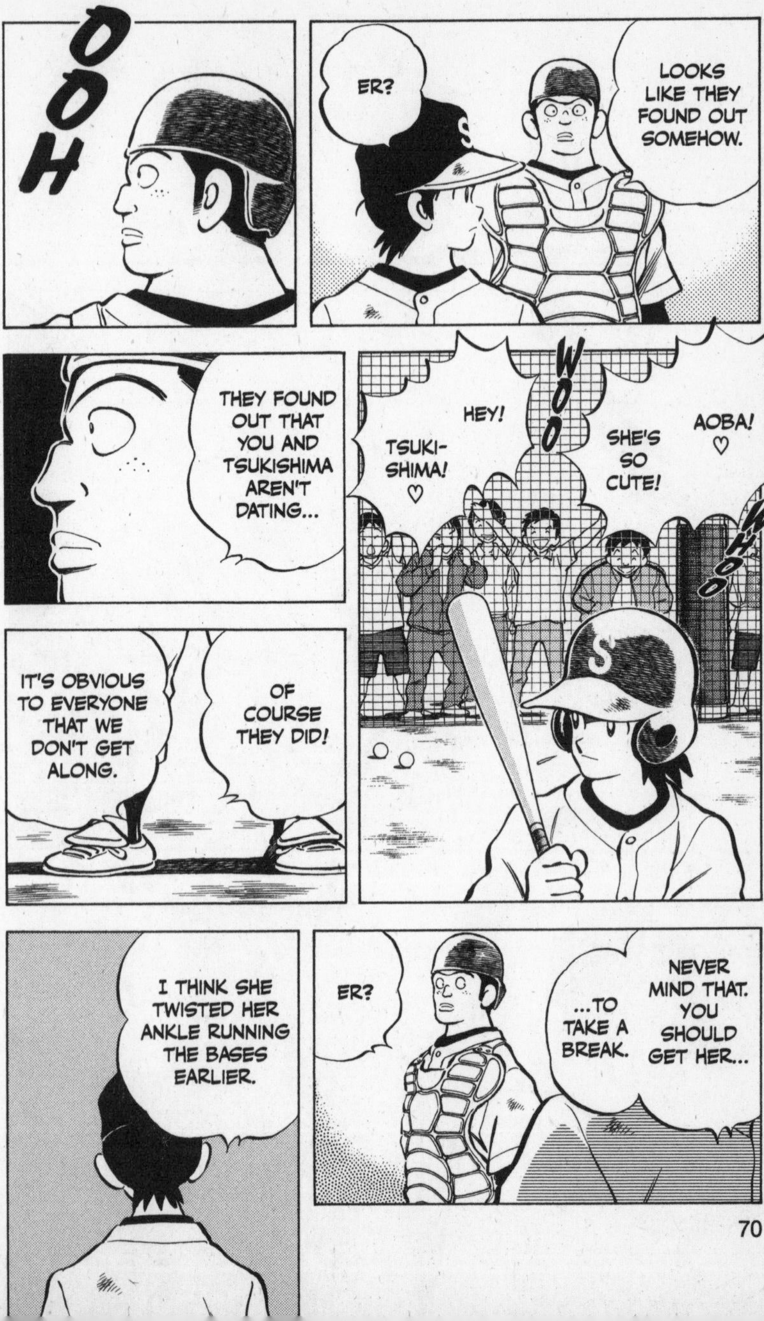

LOOKS LIKE THEY FOUND OUT SOMEHOW.
ER?
OOOH
WOOO
AOBA! ♡
SHE'S SO CUTE!
HEY!
TSUKI-SHIMA! ♡
WHOOO
THEY FOUND OUT THAT YOU AND TSUKISHIMA AREN'T DATING...
OF COURSE THEY DID!
IT'S OBVIOUS TO EVERYONE THAT WE DON'T GET ALONG.
NEVER MIND THAT. YOU SHOULD GET HER...
...TO TAKE A BREAK.
ER?
I THINK SHE TWISTED HER ANKLE RUNNING THE BASES EARLIER.

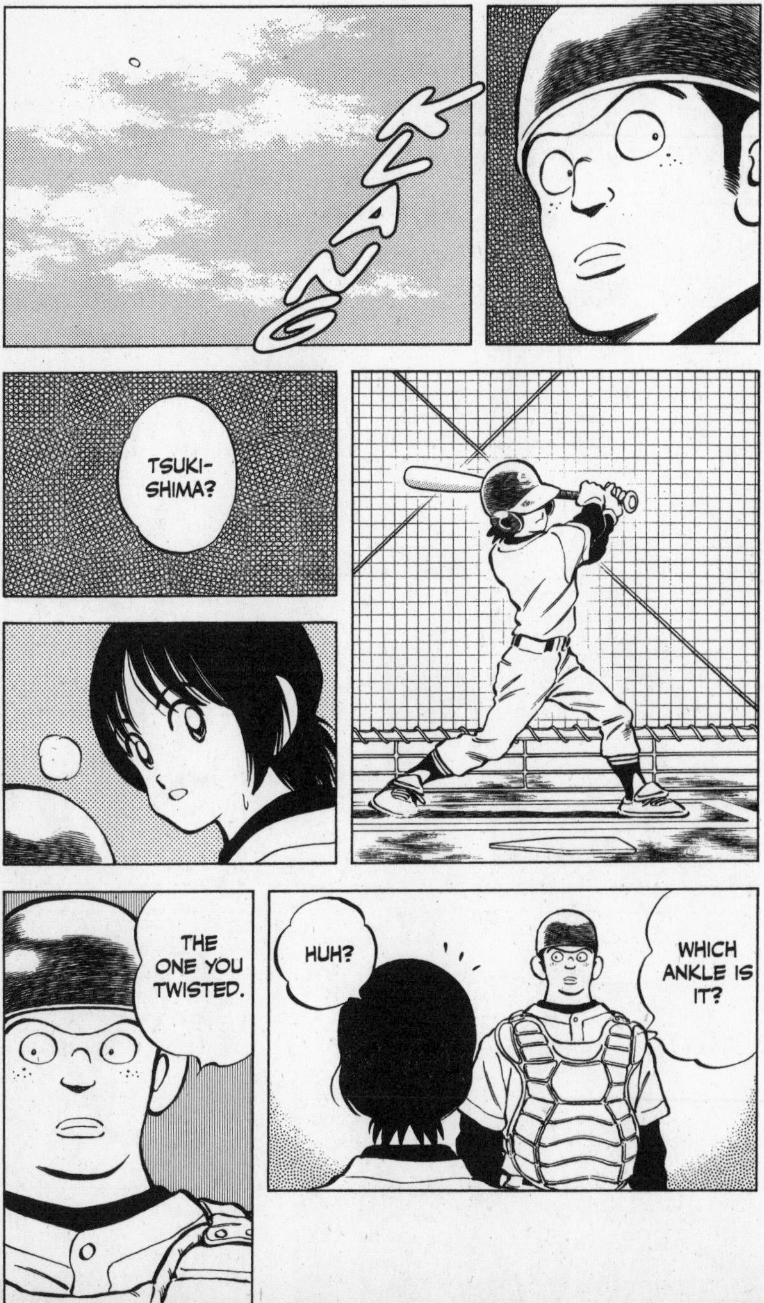
KLANG
TSUKI-SHIMA?
WHICH ANKLE IS IT?
HUH?
THE ONE YOU TWISTED.

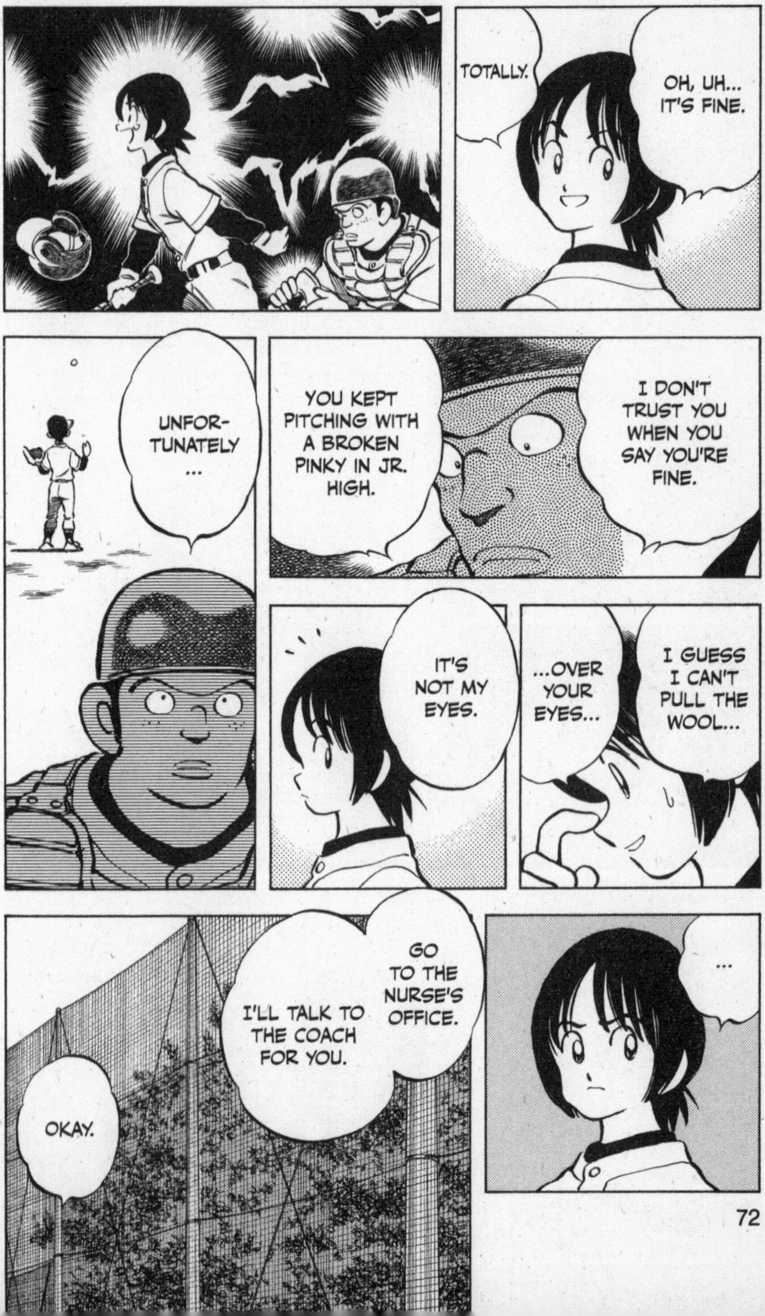
OH, UH... IT'S FINE.
TOTALLY.
I DON'T TRUST YOU WHEN YOU SAY YOU'RE FINE.
YOU KEPT PITCHING WITH A BROKEN PINKY IN JR. HIGH.
I GUESS I CAN'T PULL THE WOOL...
...OVER YOUR EYES...
IT'S NOT MY EYES.
UNFOR-TUNATELY ...
...
GO TO THE NURSE'S OFFICE.
I'LL TALK TO THE COACH FOR YOU.
OKAY.

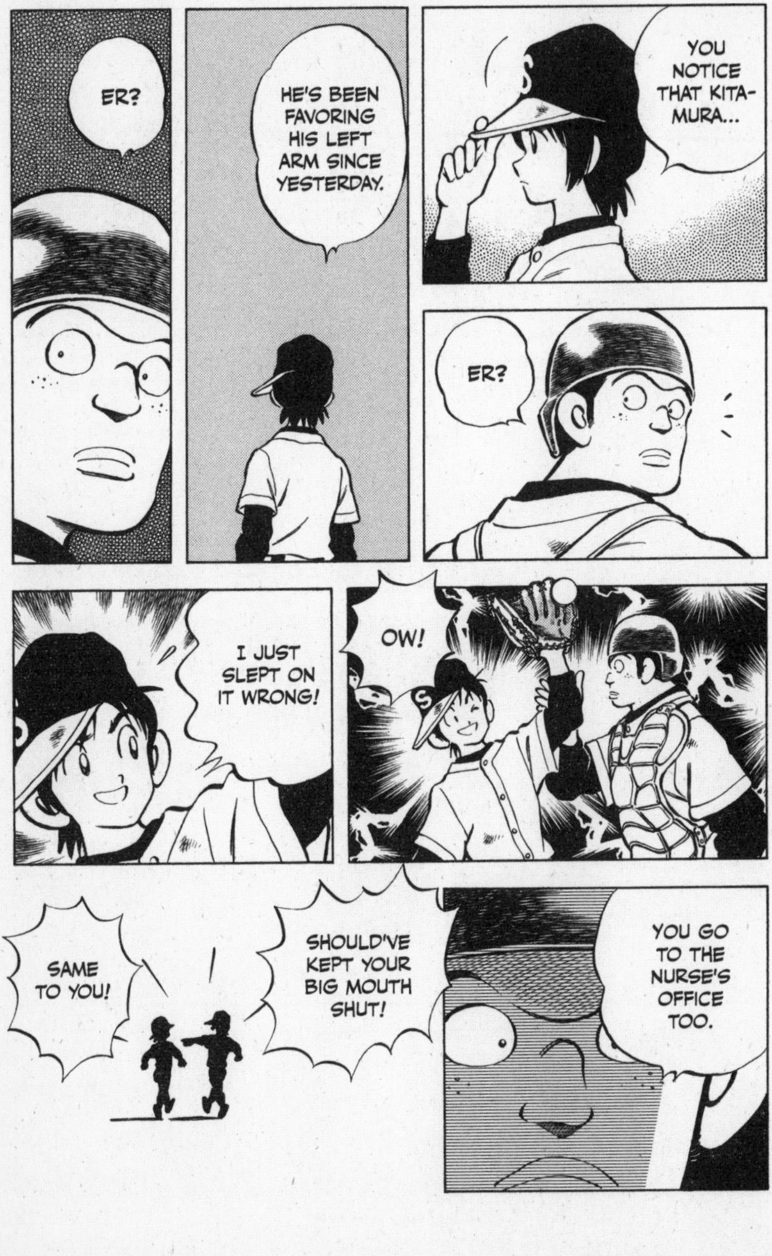
YOU NOTICE THAT KITA-MURA...
ER?
HE'S BEEN FAVORING HIS LEFT ARM SINCE YESTERDAY.
ER?
OW!
I JUST SLEPT ON IT WRONG!
YOU GO TO THE NURSE'S OFFICE TOO.
SHOULD'VE KEPT YOUR BIG MOUTH SHUT!
SAME TO YOU!

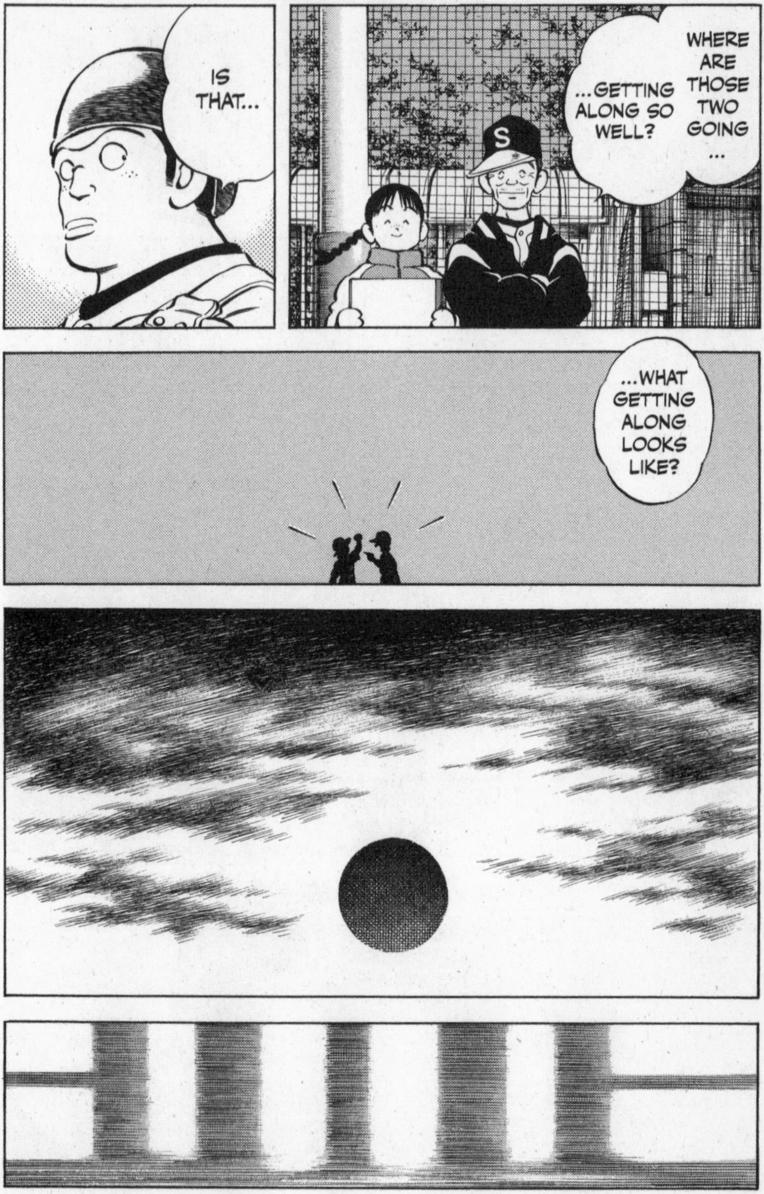
WHERE ARE THOSE TWO GOING...
...GETTING ALONG SO WELL?
IS THAT...
...WHAT GETTING ALONG LOOKS LIKE?

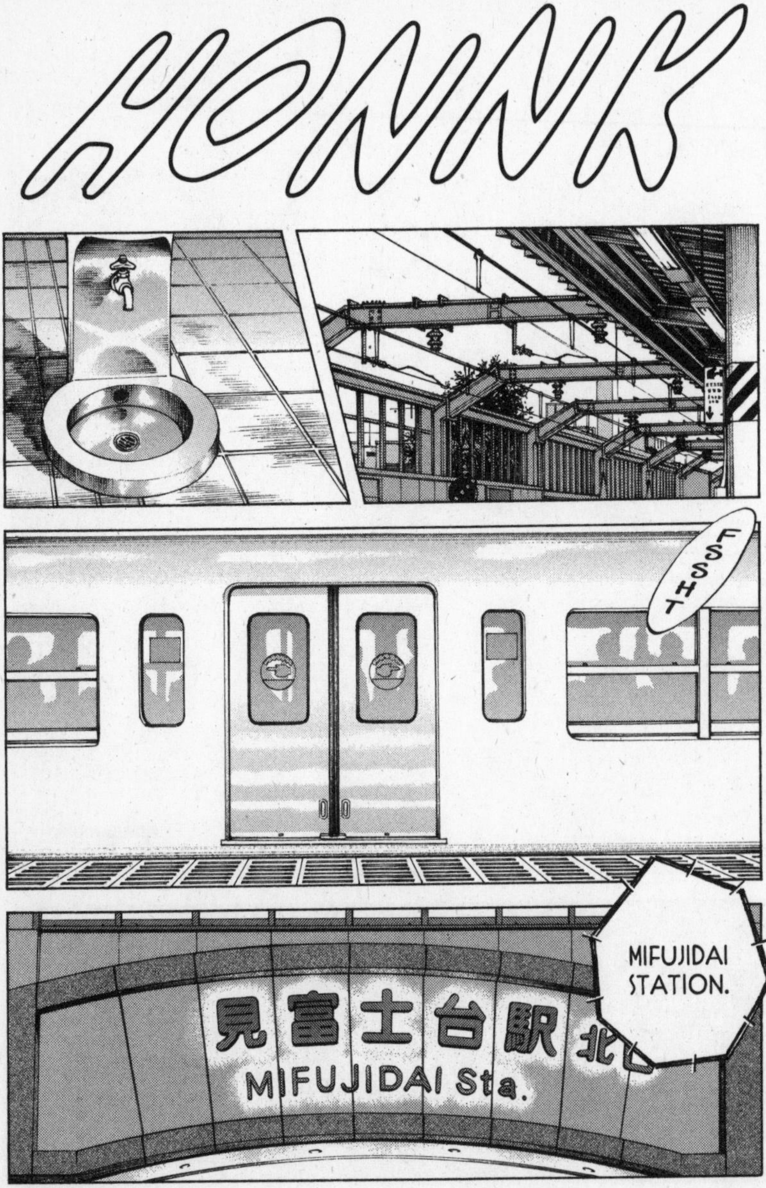
HONK
FSSHT
MIFUJIDAI STATION.
見富士台駅
北口
MIFUJIDAI Sta.

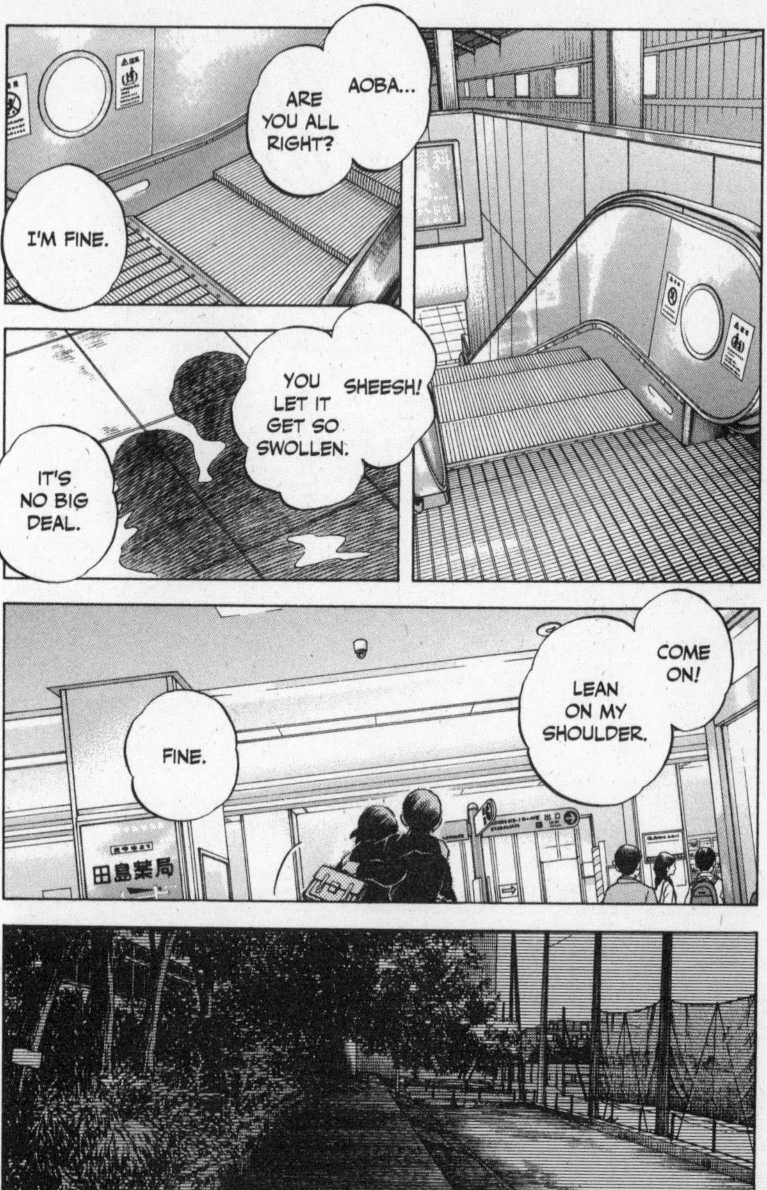
AOBA... ARE YOU ALL RIGHT?
I'M FINE.
SHEESH! YOU LET IT GET SO SWOLLEN.
IT'S NO BIG DEAL.
COME ON! LEAN ON MY SHOULDER.
FINE.

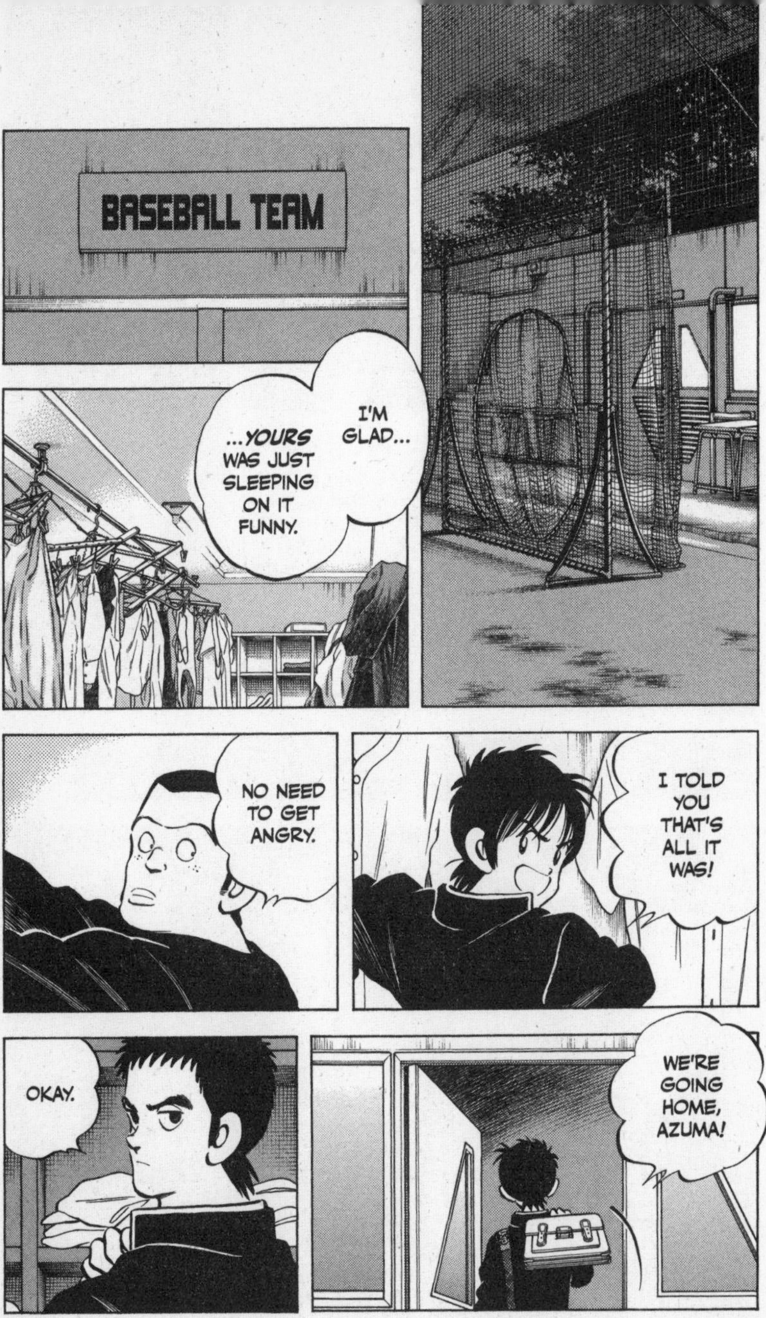
BASEBALL TEAM
I'M GLAD...
...YOURS WAS JUST SLEEPING ON IT FUNNY.
I TOLD YOU THAT'S ALL IT WAS!
NO NEED TO GET ANGRY.
WE'RE GOING HOME, AZUMA!
OKAY.

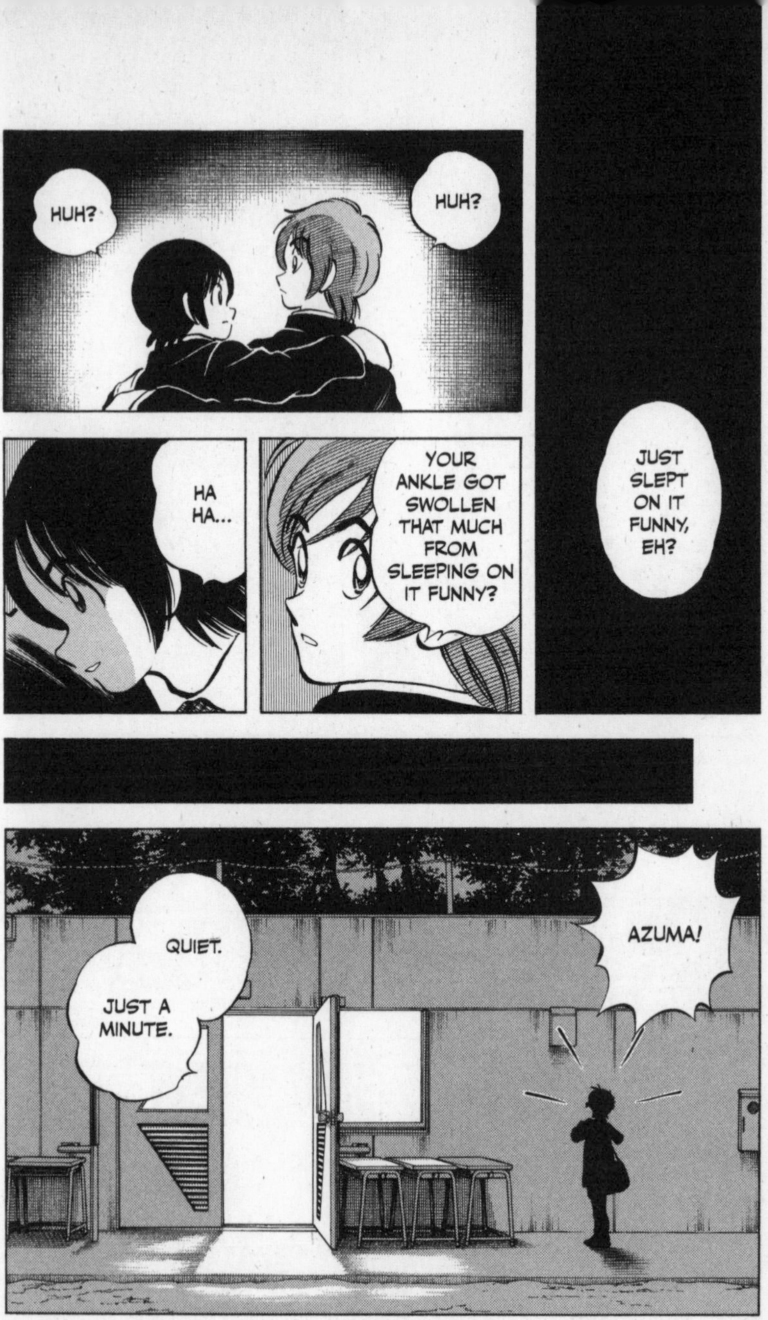
JUST SLEPT ON IT FUNNY, EH?
HUH?
HUH?
YOUR ANKLE GOT SWOLLEN THAT MUCH FROM SLEEPING ON IT FUNNY?
HA HA...
AZUMA!
QUIET.
JUST A MINUTE.

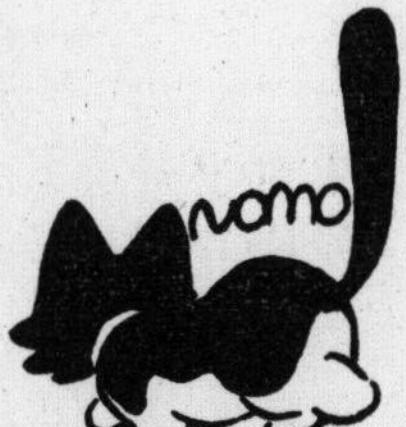
nono

# CHAPTER 65
# HUSTLE!

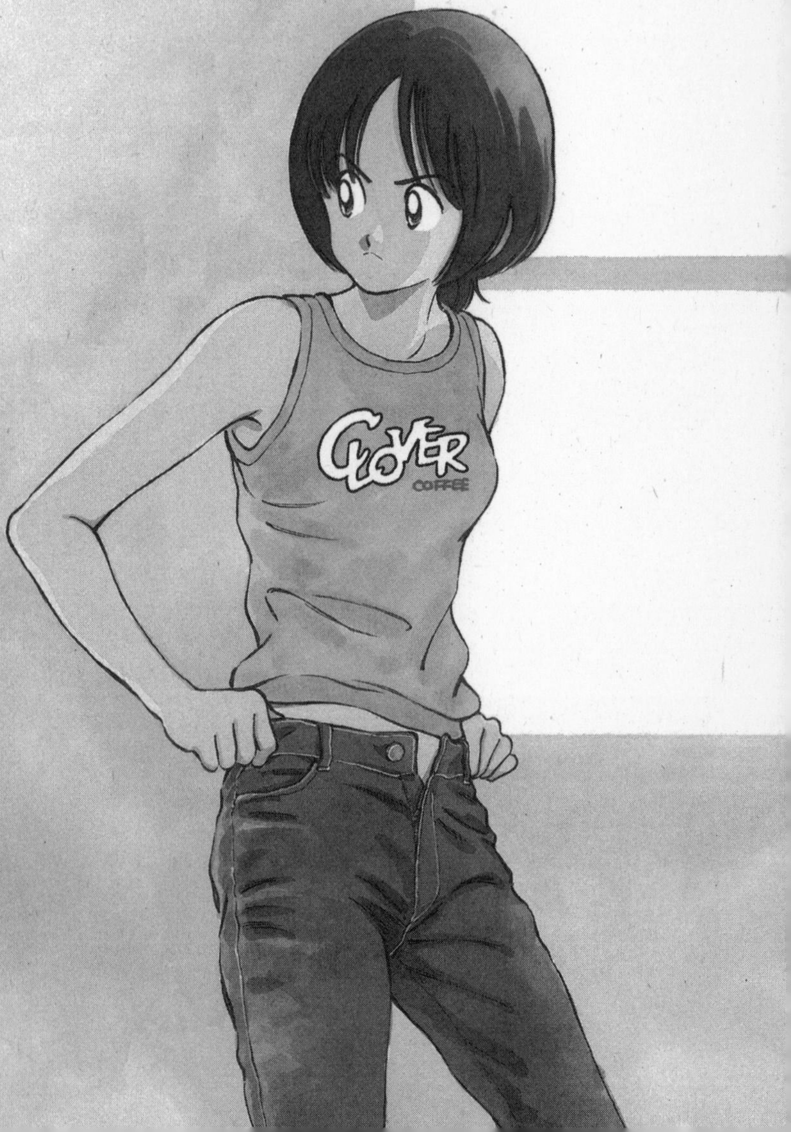
CLOVER
COFFEE

THE NEW
SEISHU
BASEBALL
TEAM.

| TEAM | 1 | 2 | 3 | 4 | 5 | 6 | 7 | | 9 |
|---|---|---|---|---|---|---|---|---|---|
| SEISHU | 2 | 0 | 1 | 0 | | | | | |
| WHOEVER | 0 | 0 | 0 | 0 | | | | | |

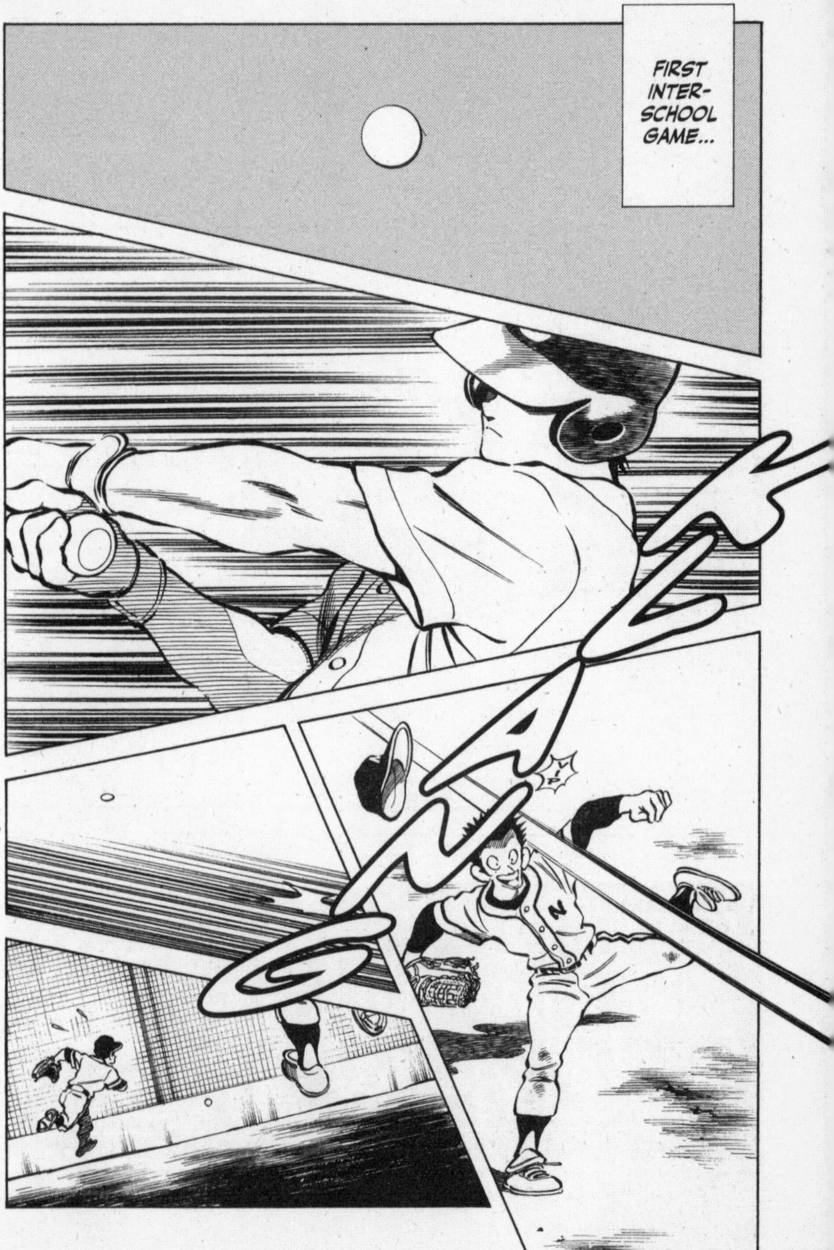
FIRST INTER-SCHOOL GAME...
VIP

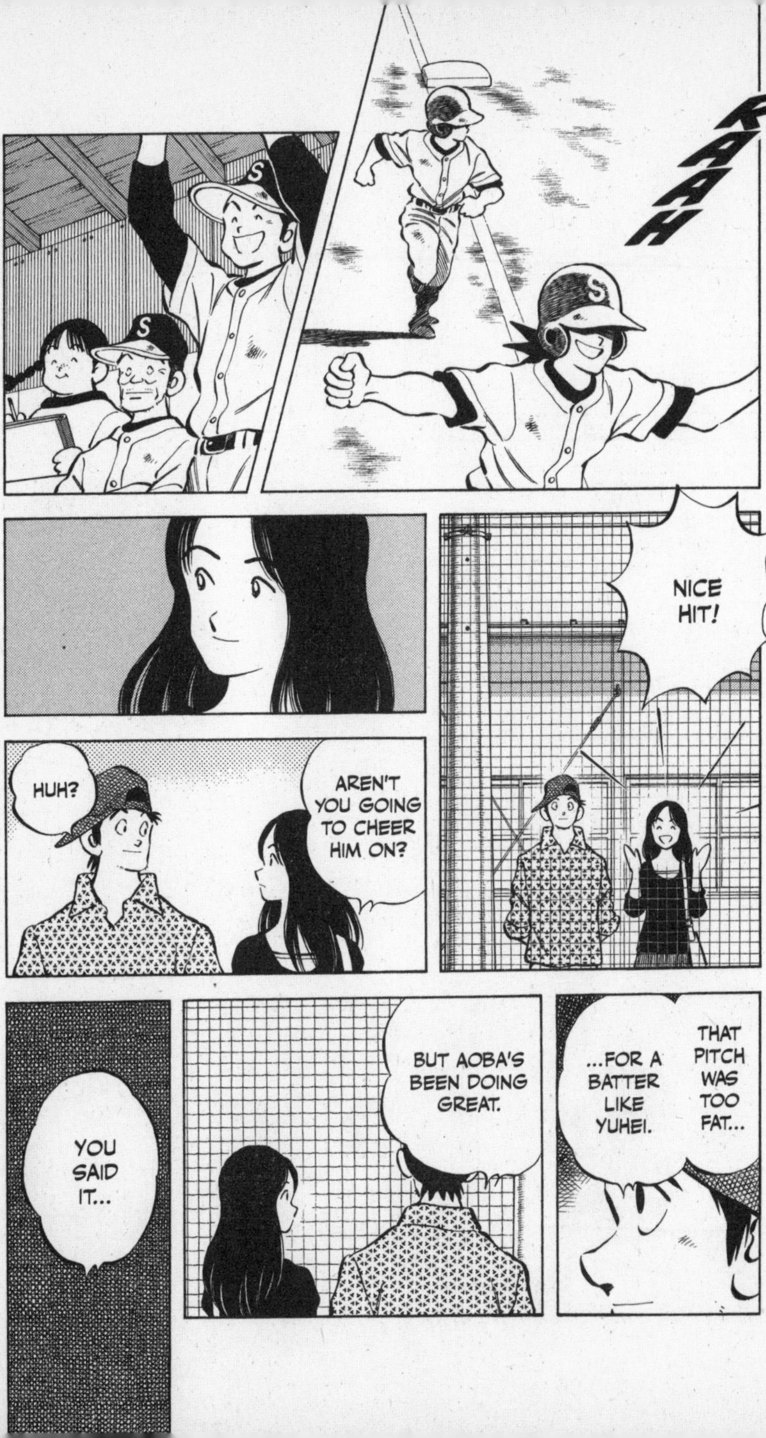
RAAAH
NICE HIT!
AREN'T YOU GOING TO CHEER HIM ON?
HUH?
THAT PITCH WAS TOO FAT...
...FOR A BATTER LIKE YUHEI.
BUT AOBA'S BEEN DOING GREAT.
YOU SAID IT...

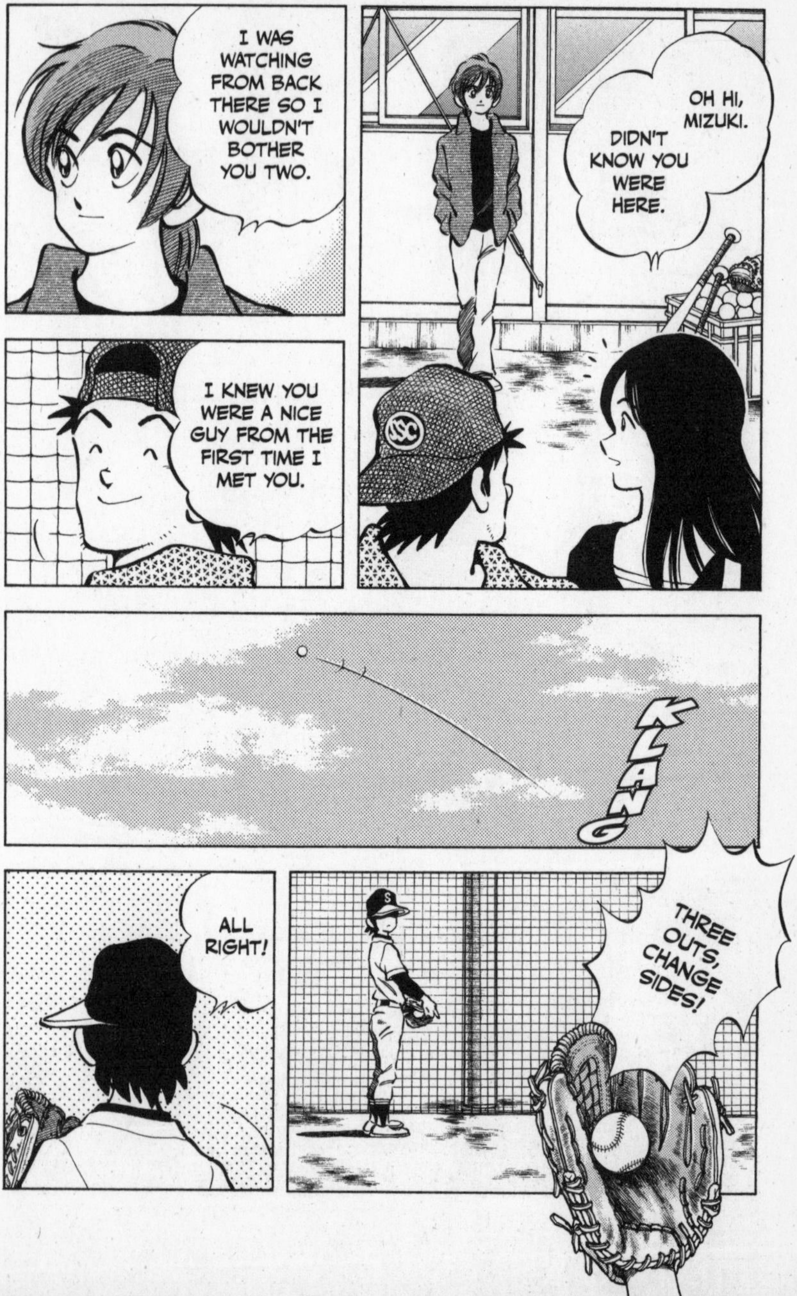
OH HI, MIZUKI.
DIDN'T KNOW YOU WERE HERE.
I WAS WATCHING FROM BACK THERE SO I WOULDN'T BOTHER YOU TWO.
I KNEW YOU WERE A NICE GUY FROM THE FIRST TIME I MET YOU.
KLANG
THREE OUTS, CHANGE SIDES!
ALL RIGHT!

HOW LONG DO YOU PLAN TO KEEP TSUKISHIMA PITCHING? THE GAME'S GOING TO END.

PROMISED HER SHE COULD PITCH UNTIL THEY GET A RUN OFF OF HER. I CAN'T HELP IT.

WHO CARES ABOUT THAT!

GET OUT TO YOUR POSITION! CENTER FIELD.

FEH! HUSTLE!

ARGH!

| TEAM | 1 | 2 | 3 | 4 | 5 | 6 | 7 | 8 | 9 | T |
|------|---|---|---|---|---|---|---|---|---|---|
| SEISHU | 2 | 0 | 1 | 0 | 2 | | | | | |
| WHOEVER | 0 | 0 | 0 | | | | | | | |

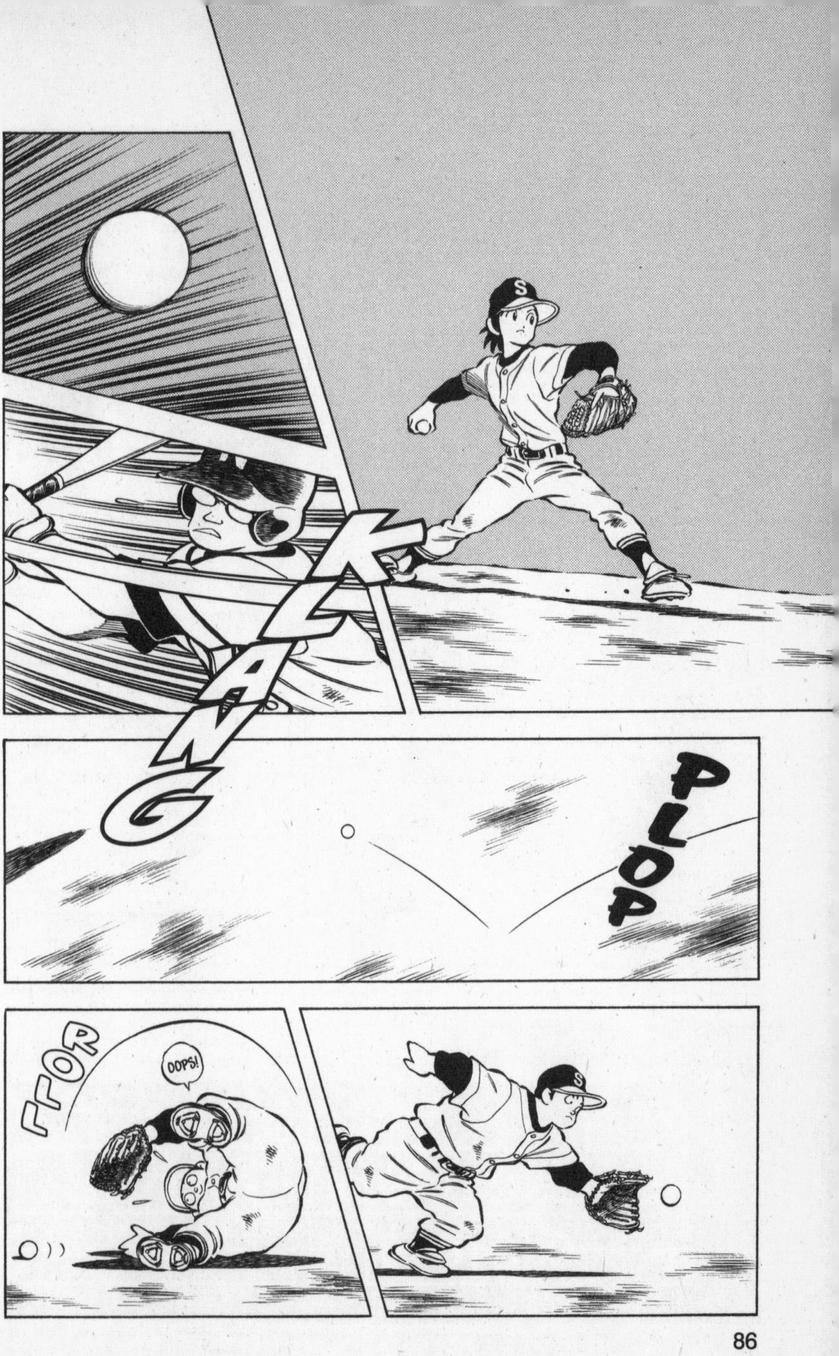
KLANG
PLOP
LLOR
OOPS!

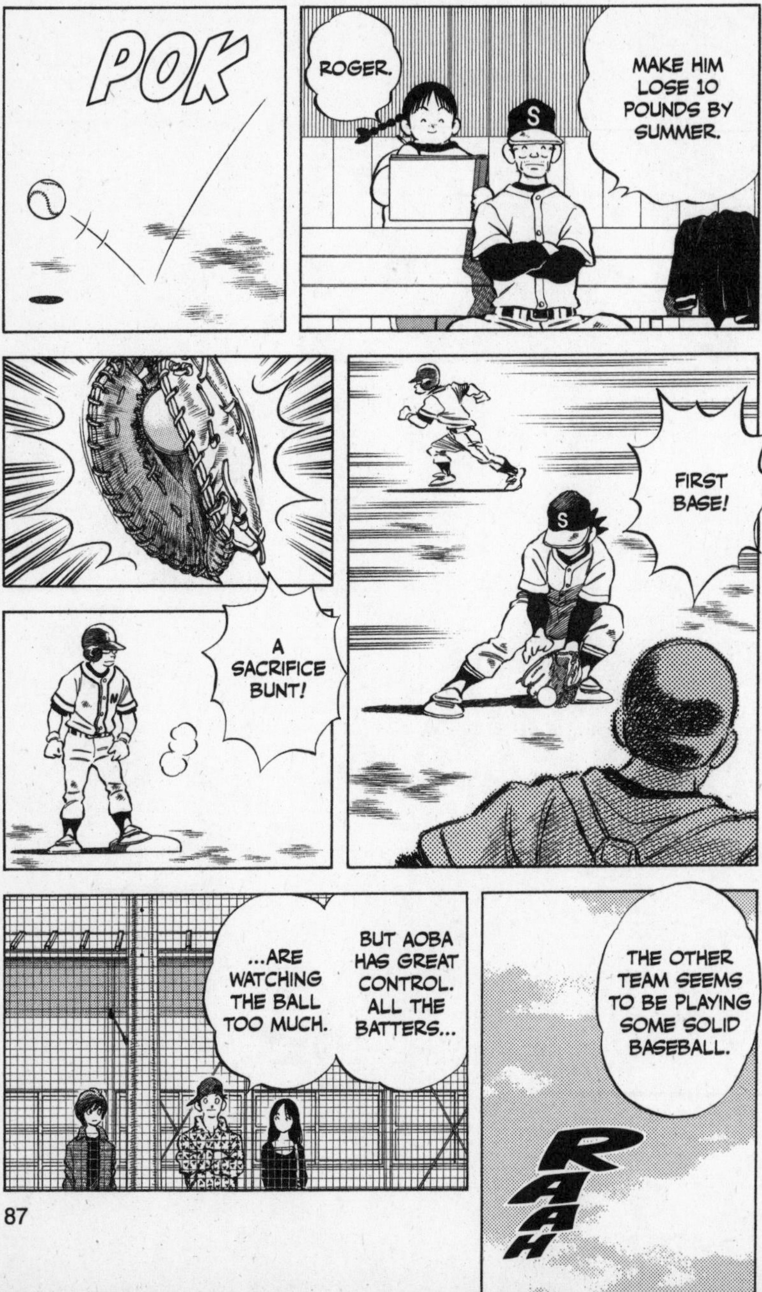
MAKE HIM LOSE 10 POUNDS BY SUMMER.
ROGER.
POK
FIRST BASE!
A SACRIFICE BUNT!
THE OTHER TEAM SEEMS TO BE PLAYING SOME SOLID BASEBALL.
RAAAH
BUT AOBA HAS GREAT CONTROL. ALL THE BATTERS...
...ARE WATCHING THE BALL TOO MUCH.

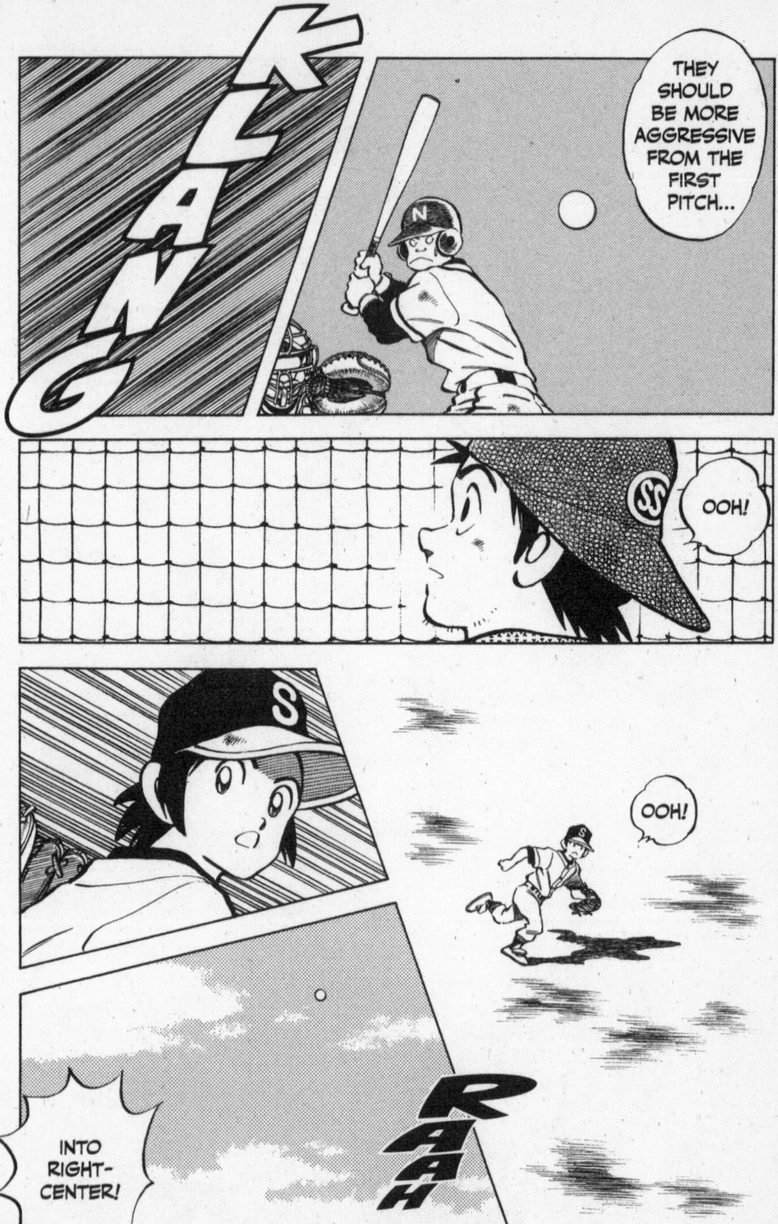
THEY SHOULD BE MORE AGGRESSIVE FROM THE FIRST PITCH...
KLANG
OOH!
OOH!
RAAH
INTO RIGHT-CENTER!

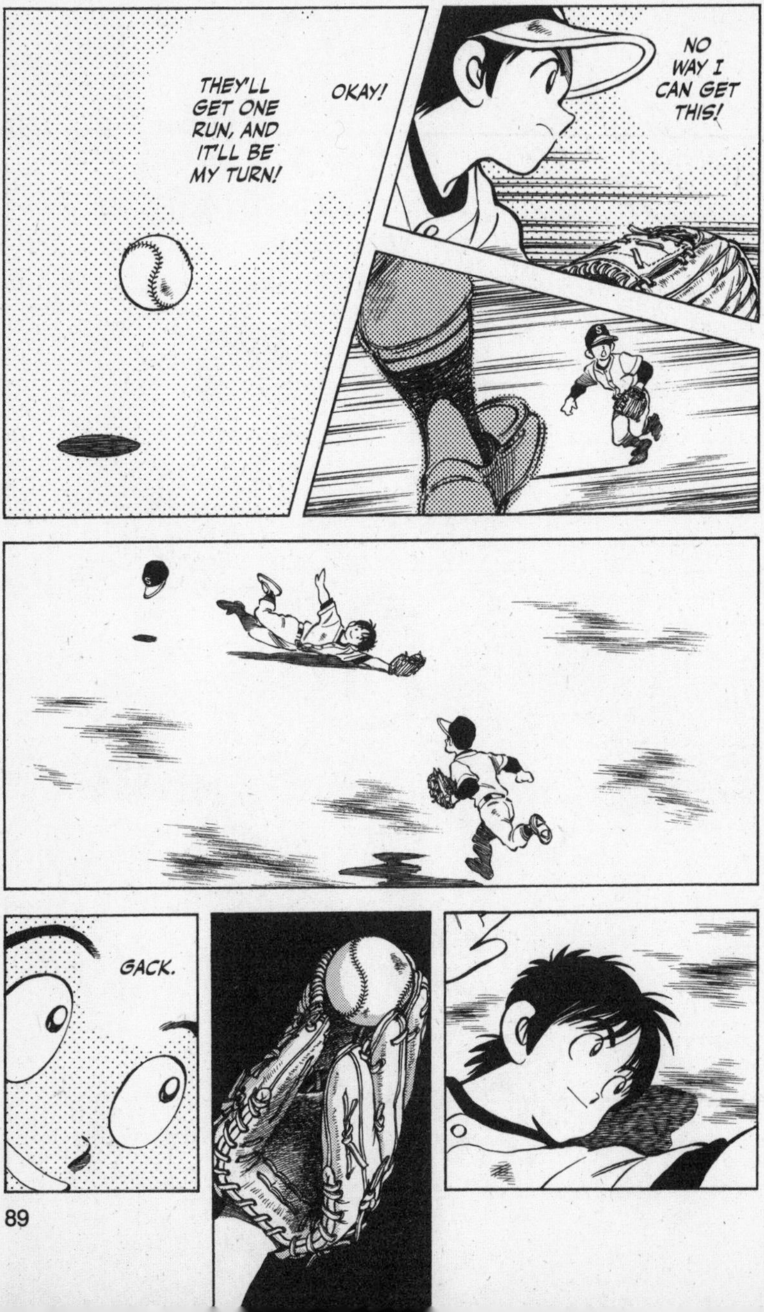
NO WAY I CAN GET THIS!
OKAY!
THEY'LL GET ONE RUN, AND IT'LL BE MY TURN!
GACK.

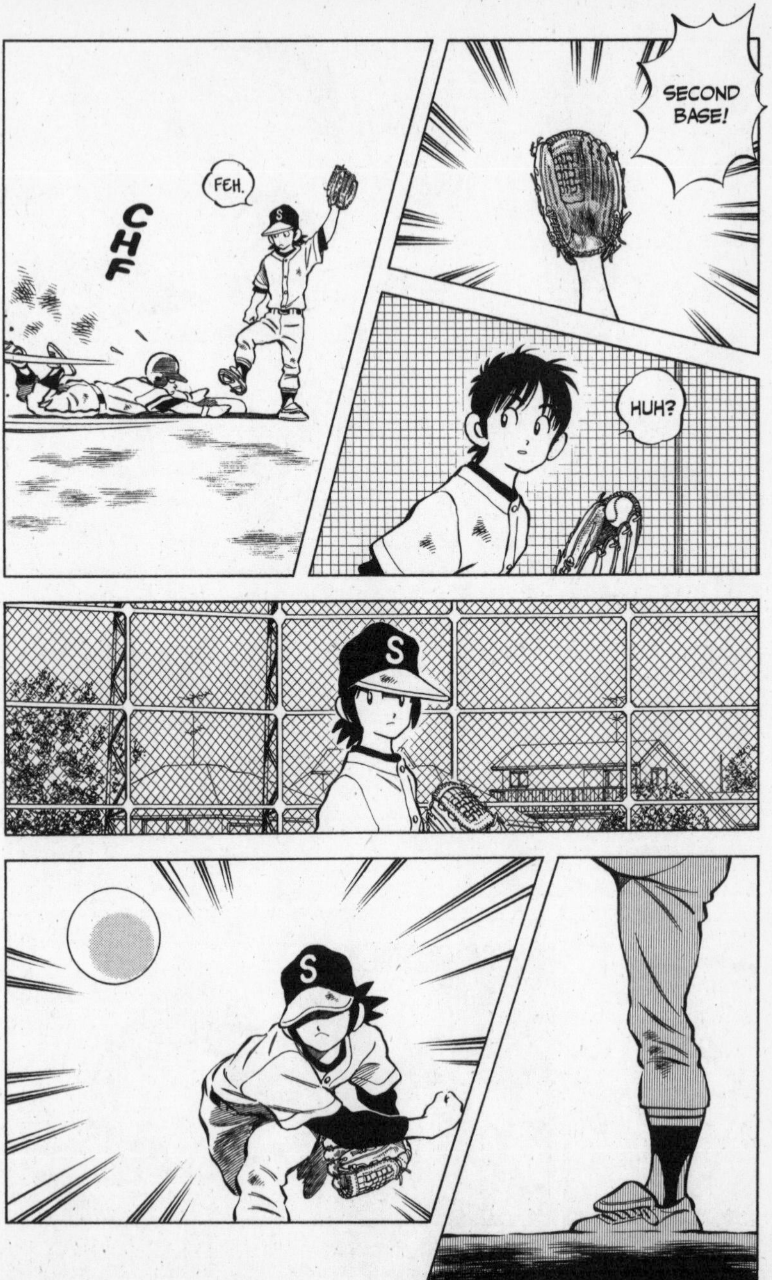
SECOND BASE!
HUH?
FEH.
CHF

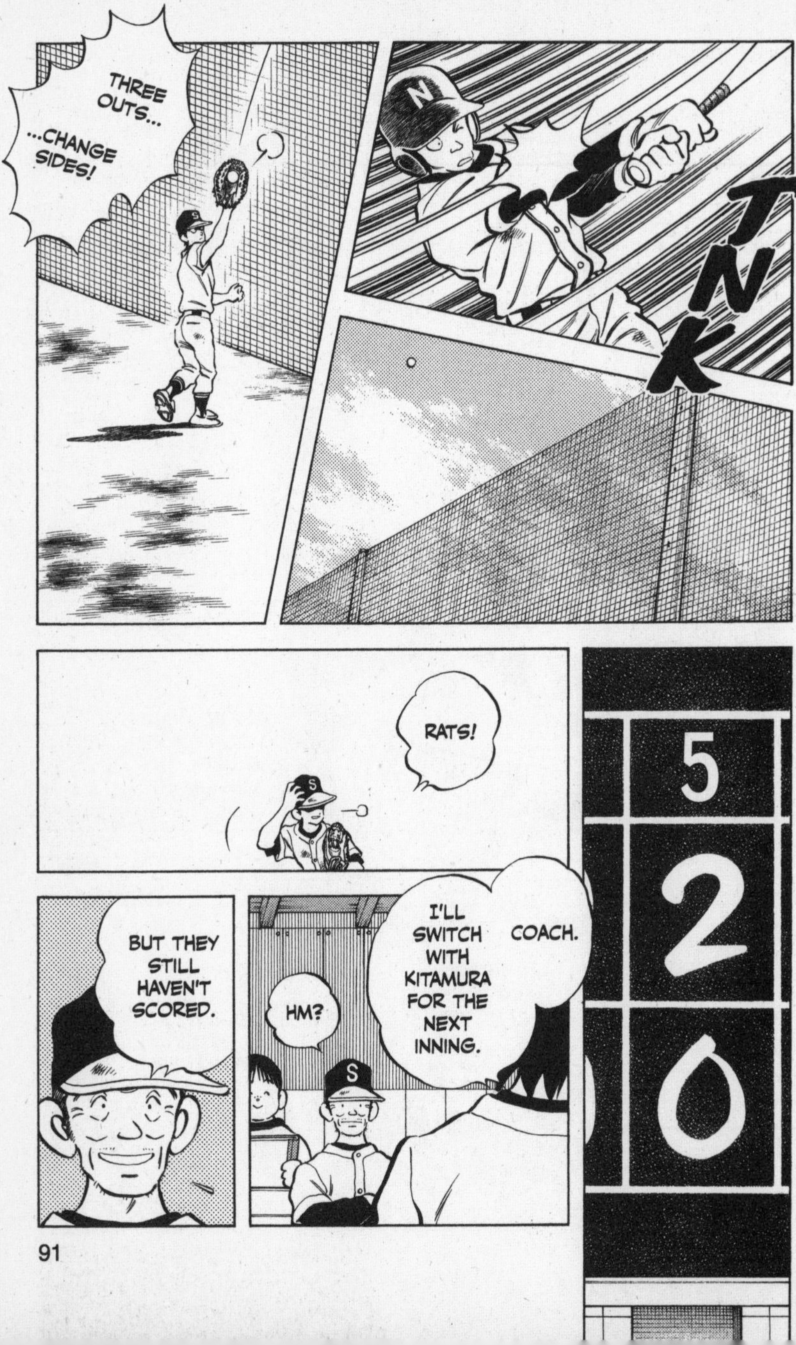
TINK
THREE OUTS... ...CHANGE SIDES!
5
2
0
RATS!
COACH.
I'LL SWITCH WITH KITAMURA FOR THE NEXT INNING.
HM?
BUT THEY STILL HAVEN'T SCORED.

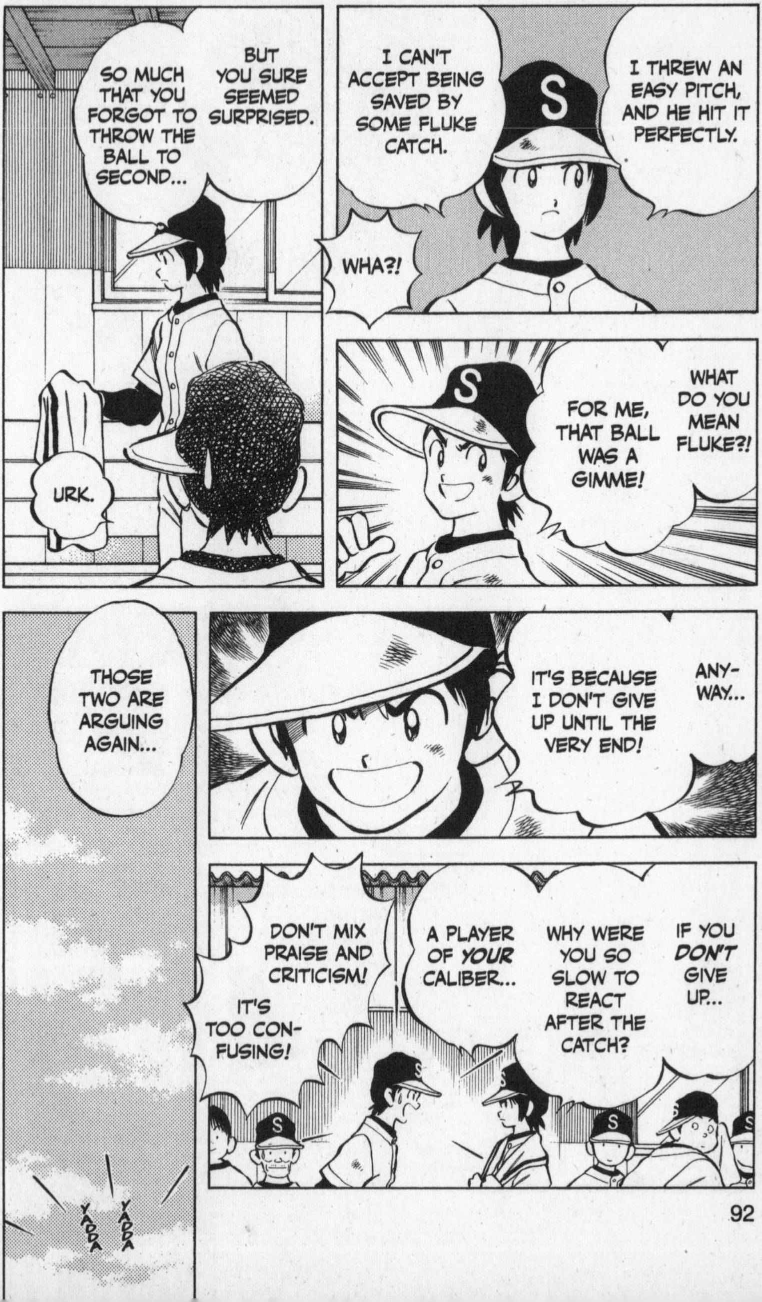
I THREW AN EASY PITCH, AND HE HIT IT PERFECTLY.
I CAN'T ACCEPT BEING SAVED BY SOME FLUKE CATCH.
WHA?!
WHAT DO YOU MEAN FLUKE?!
FOR ME, THAT BALL WAS A GIMME!
BUT YOU SURE SEEMED SURPRISED.
SO MUCH THAT YOU FORGOT TO THROW THE BALL TO SECOND...
URK.
ANY-WAY...
IT'S BECAUSE I DON'T GIVE UP UNTIL THE VERY END!
IF YOU *DON'T* GIVE UP...
WHY WERE YOU SO SLOW TO REACT AFTER THE CATCH?
A PLAYER OF *YOUR* CALIBER...
DON'T MIX PRAISE AND CRITICISM!
IT'S TOO CON-FUSING!
THOSE TWO ARE ARGUING AGAIN...
YADDA
YADDA

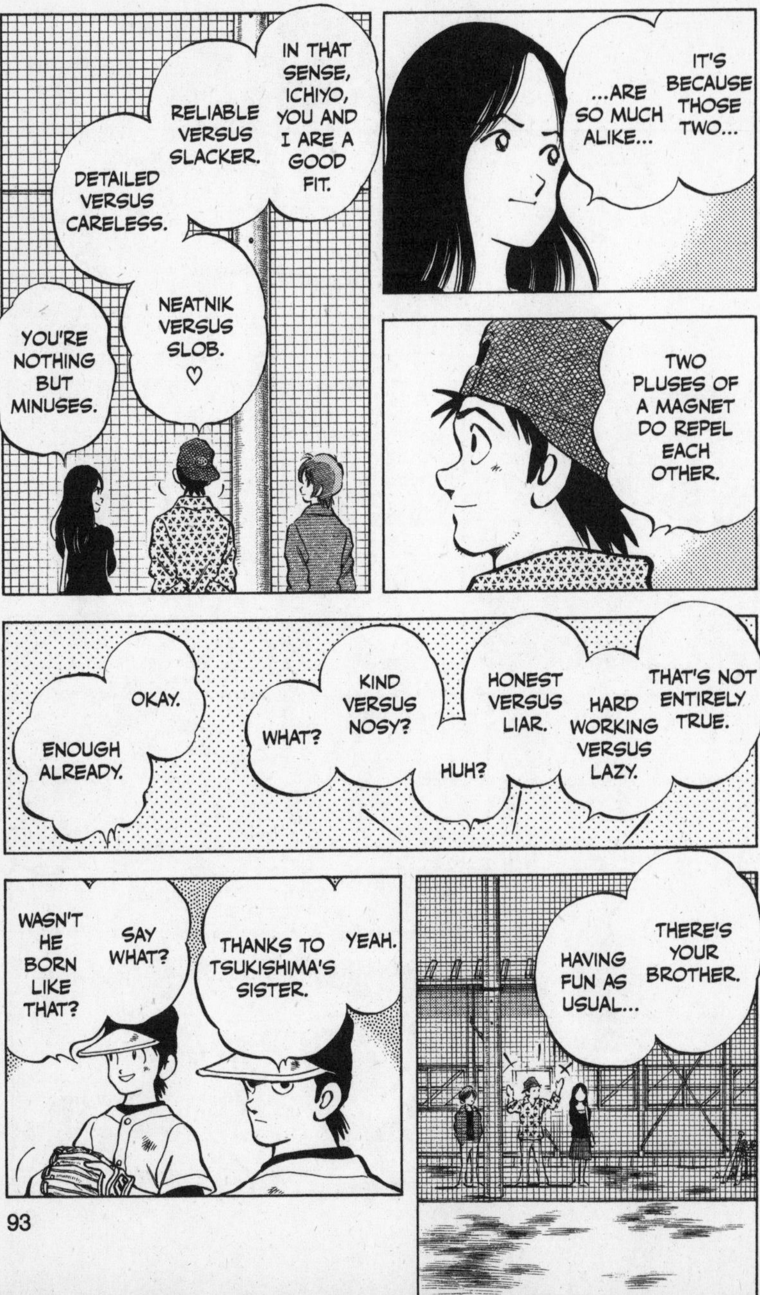
IT'S BECAUSE THOSE TWO...
...ARE SO MUCH ALIKE...
TWO PLUSES OF A MAGNET DO REPEL EACH OTHER.
IN THAT SENSE, ICHIYO, YOU AND I ARE A GOOD FIT.
RELIABLE VERSUS SLACKER.
DETAILED VERSUS CARELESS.
NEATNIK VERSUS SLOB. ♡
YOU'RE NOTHING BUT MINUSES.
THAT'S NOT ENTIRELY TRUE.
HARD WORKING VERSUS LAZY.
HONEST VERSUS LIAR.
HUH?
KIND VERSUS NOSY?
WHAT?
OKAY.
ENOUGH ALREADY.
THERE'S YOUR BROTHER.
HAVING FUN AS USUAL...
YEAH.
THANKS TO TSUKISHIMA'S SISTER.
SAY WHAT?
WASN'T HE BORN LIKE THAT?

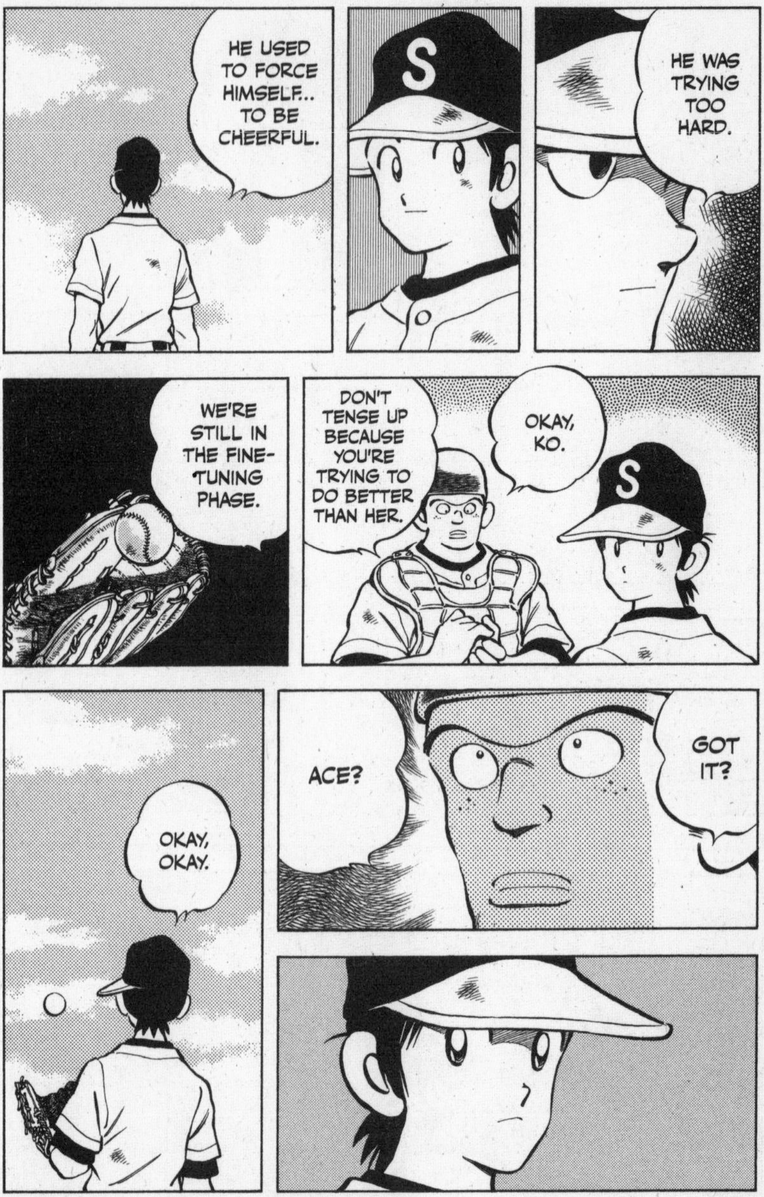
HE WAS TRYING TOO HARD.
HE USED TO FORCE HIMSELF... TO BE CHEERFUL.
OKAY, KO.
DON'T TENSE UP BECAUSE YOU'RE TRYING TO DO BETTER THAN HER.
WE'RE STILL IN THE FINE-TUNING PHASE.
GOT IT?
ACE?
OKAY, OKAY.

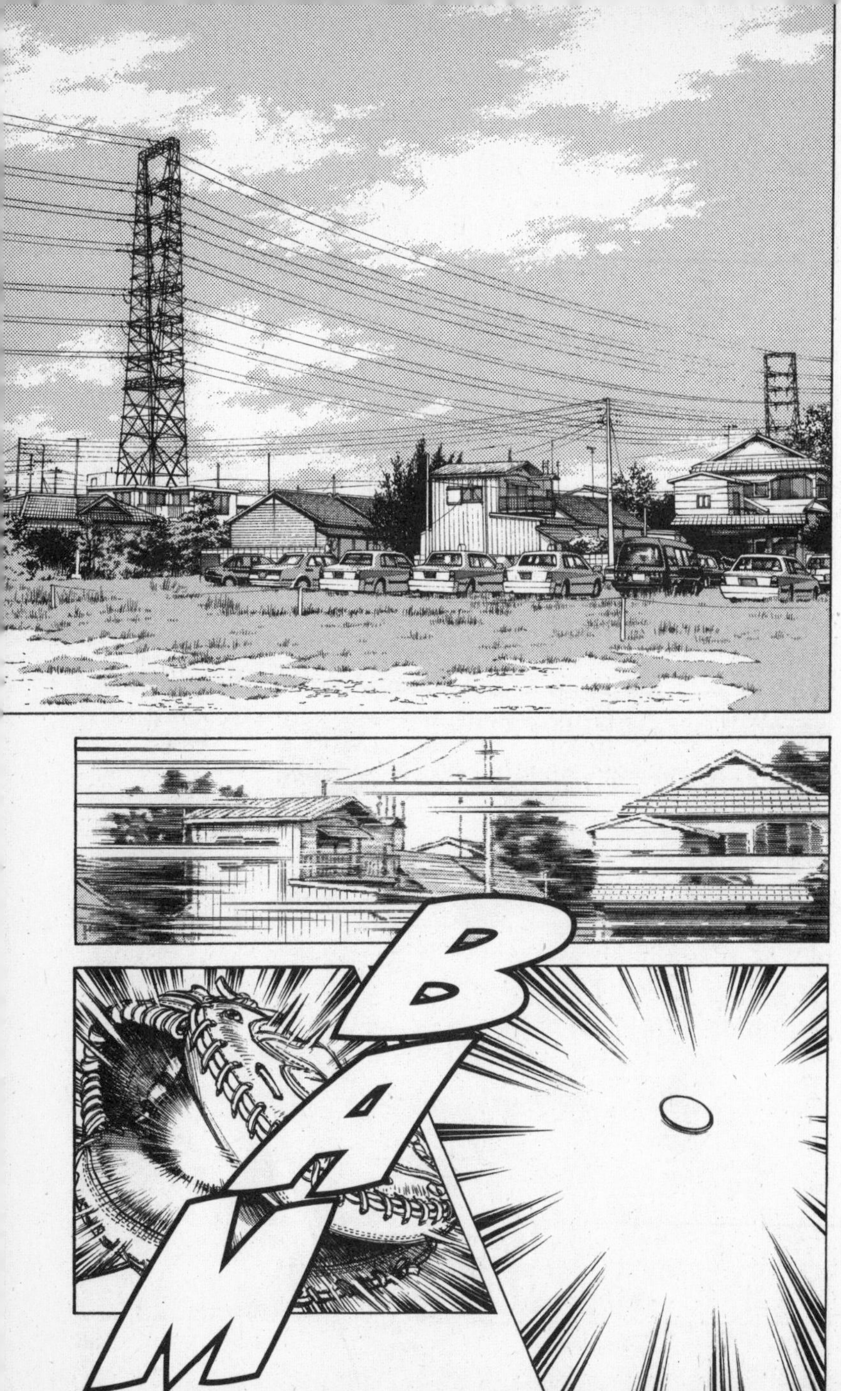
BAM

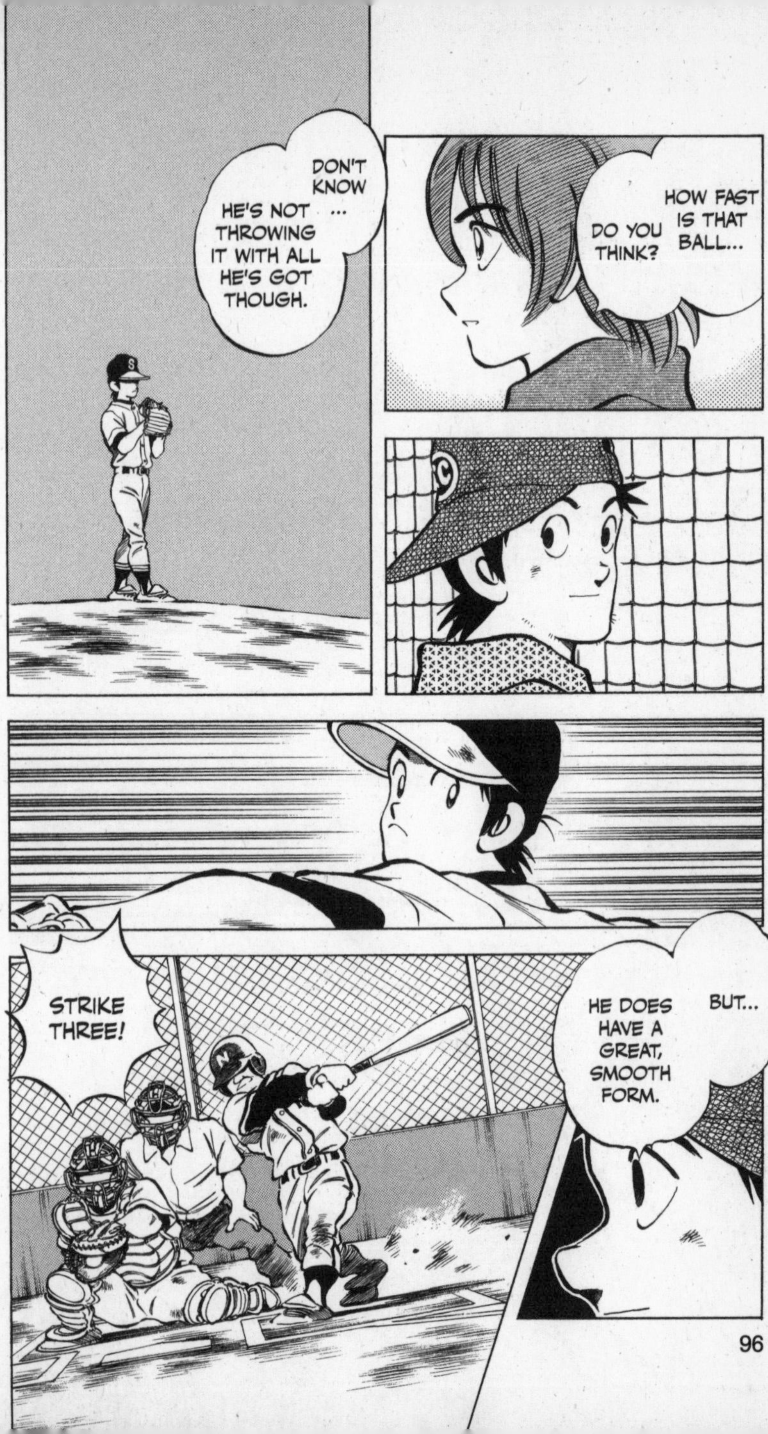
HOW FAST IS THAT BALL... DO YOU THINK?
DON'T KNOW ...
HE'S NOT THROWING IT WITH ALL HE'S GOT THOUGH.
BUT...
HE DOES HAVE A GREAT, SMOOTH FORM.
STRIKE THREE!

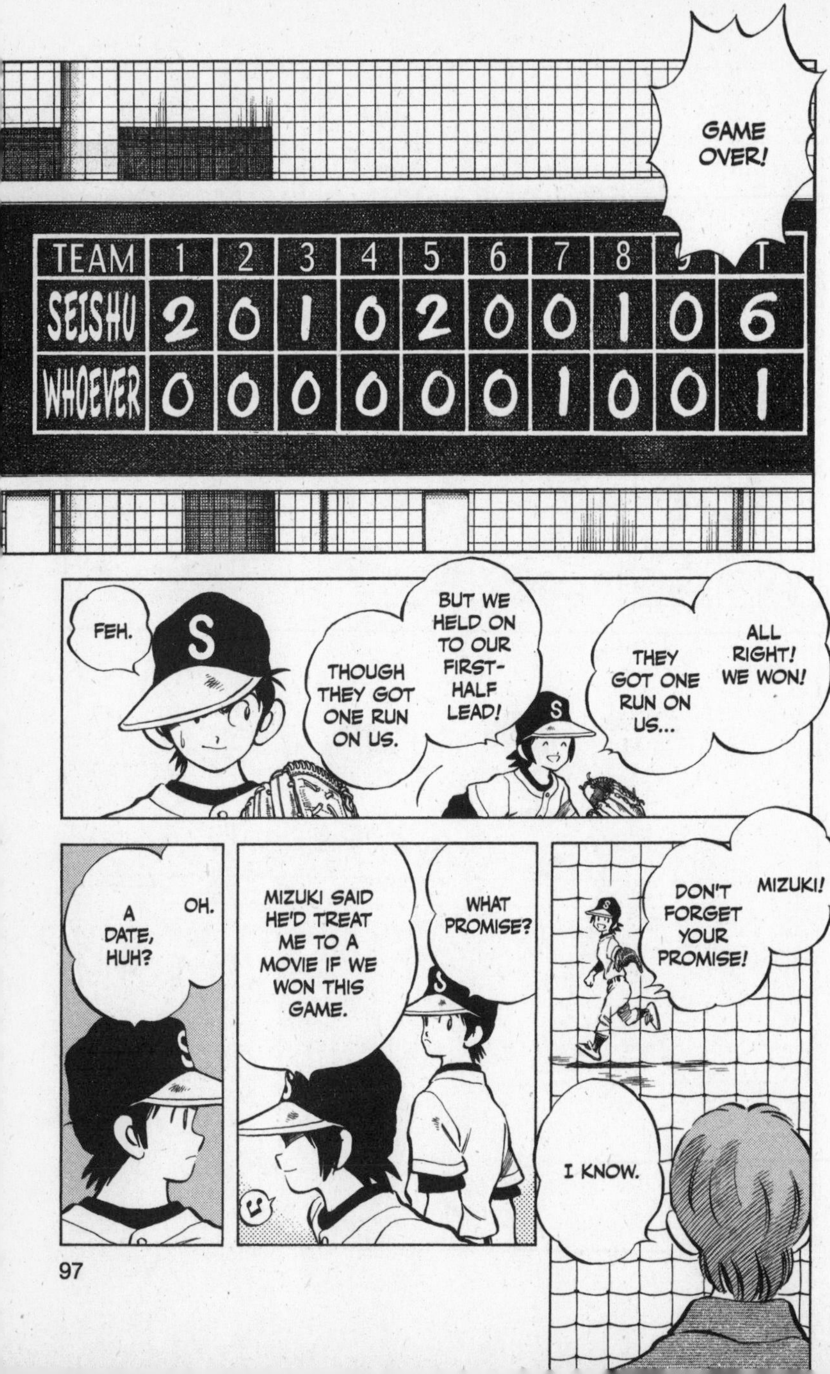
GAME OVER!
TEAM 1 2 3 4 5 6 7 8 9 T
SEISHU 2 0 1 0 2 0 0 1 0 6
WHOEVER 0 0 0 0 0 0 1 0 0 1
ALL RIGHT! WE WON!
THEY GOT ONE RUN ON US...
BUT WE HELD ON TO OUR FIRST-HALF LEAD!
THOUGH THEY GOT ONE RUN ON US.
FEH.
MIZUKI!
DON'T FORGET YOUR PROMISE!
I KNOW.
WHAT PROMISE?
MIZUKI SAID HE'D TREAT ME TO A MOVIE IF WE WON THIS GAME.
OH.
A DATE, HUH?

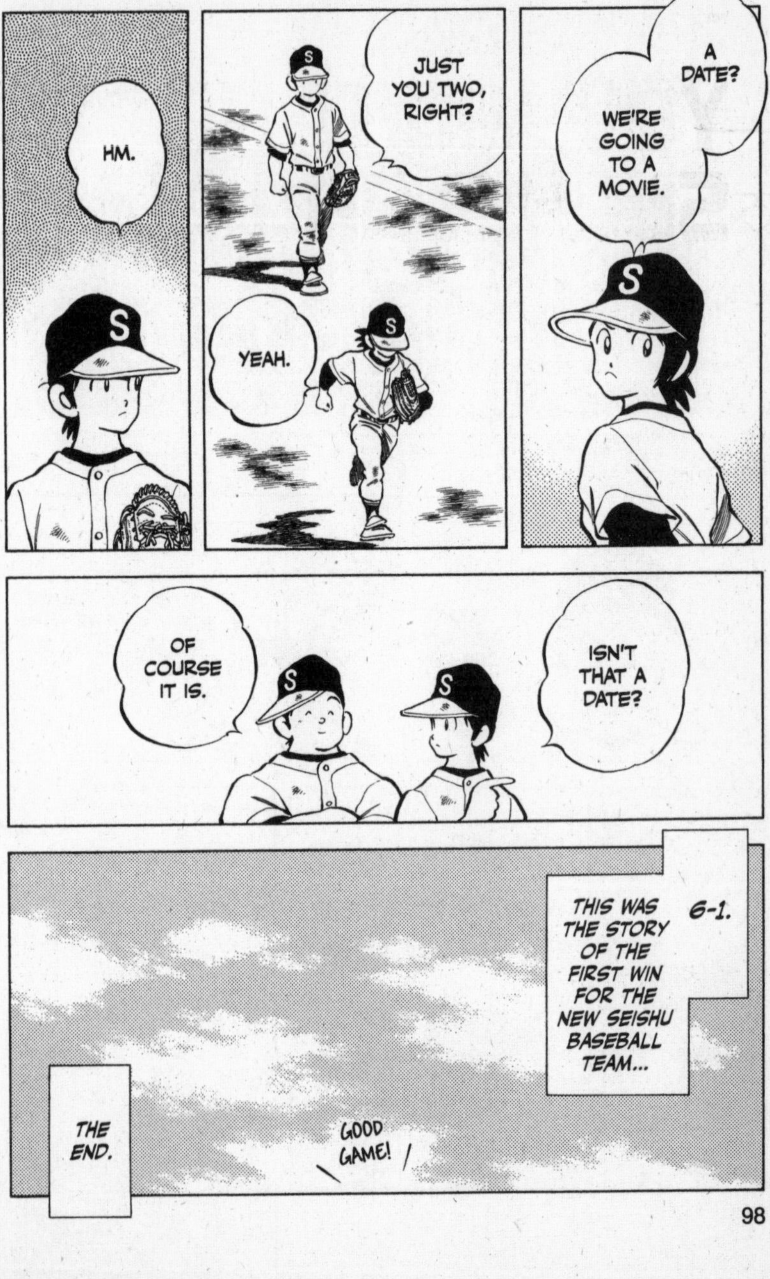
A DATE?
WE'RE GOING TO A MOVIE.
JUST YOU TWO, RIGHT?
YEAH.
HM.
ISN'T THAT A DATE?
OF COURSE IT IS.
6-1.
THIS WAS THE STORY OF THE FIRST WIN FOR THE NEW SEISHU BASEBALL TEAM...
GOOD GAME!
THE END.

# CHAPTER 66
# YOU MIGHT NOT BE SUCH A BAD GUY

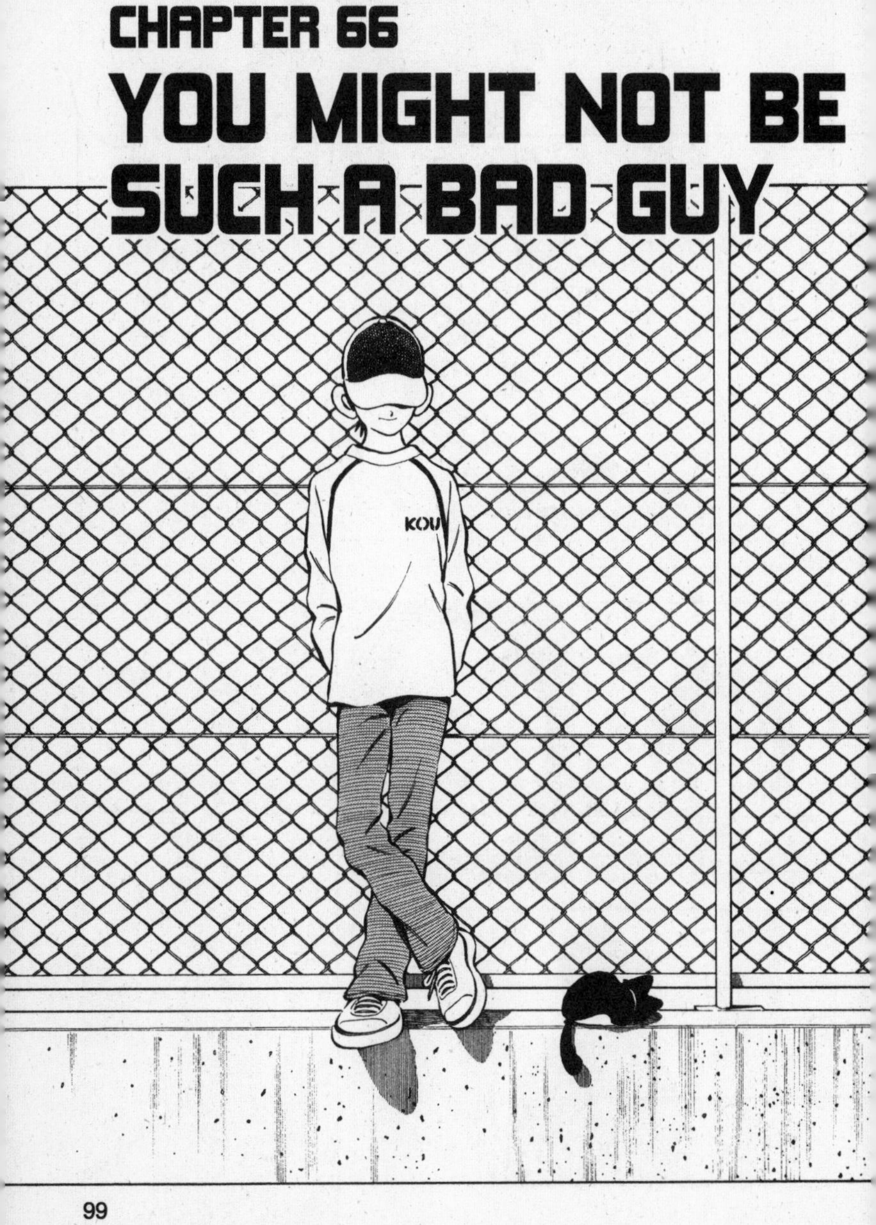
KOU

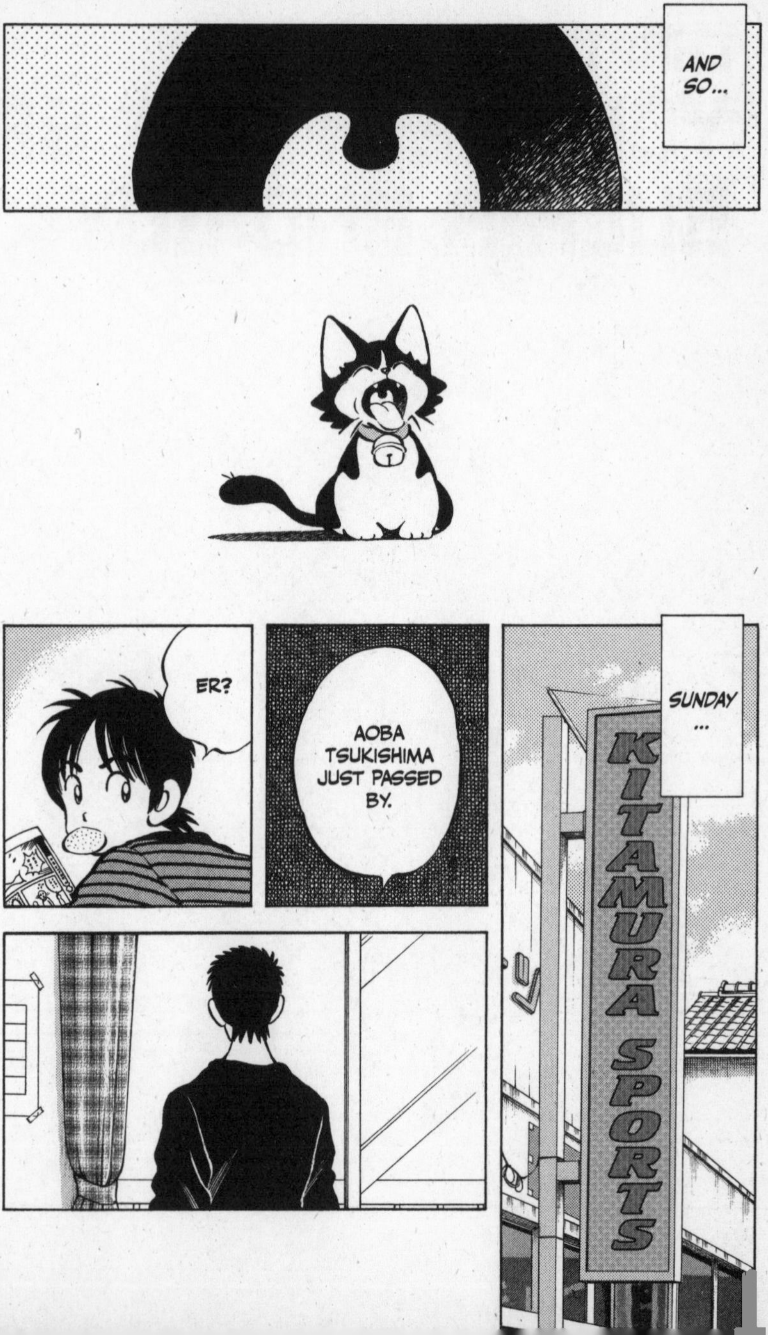
AND SO...
SUNDAY ...
KITAMURA SPORTS
AOBA TSUKISHIMA JUST PASSED BY.
ER?

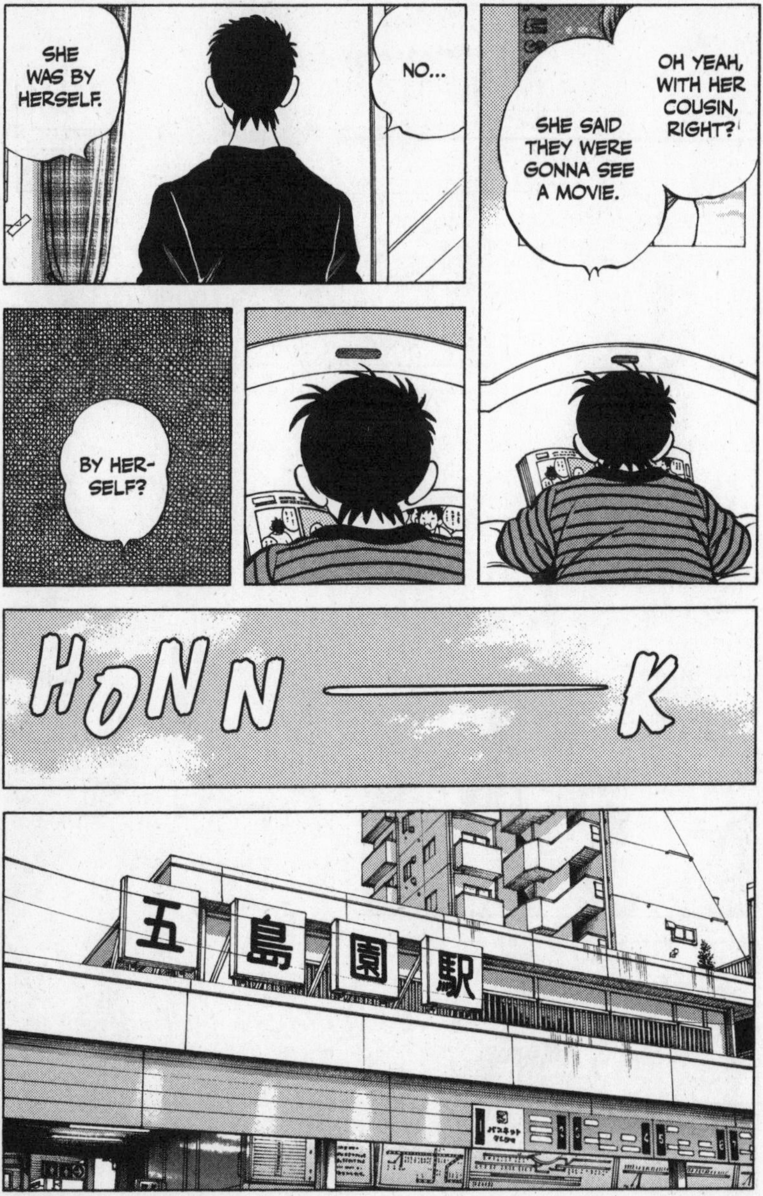
OH YEAH, WITH HER COUSIN, RIGHT?
SHE SAID THEY WERE GONNA SEE A MOVIE.
NO...
SHE WAS BY HERSELF.
BY HER-SELF?
HONN——K
五島園駅

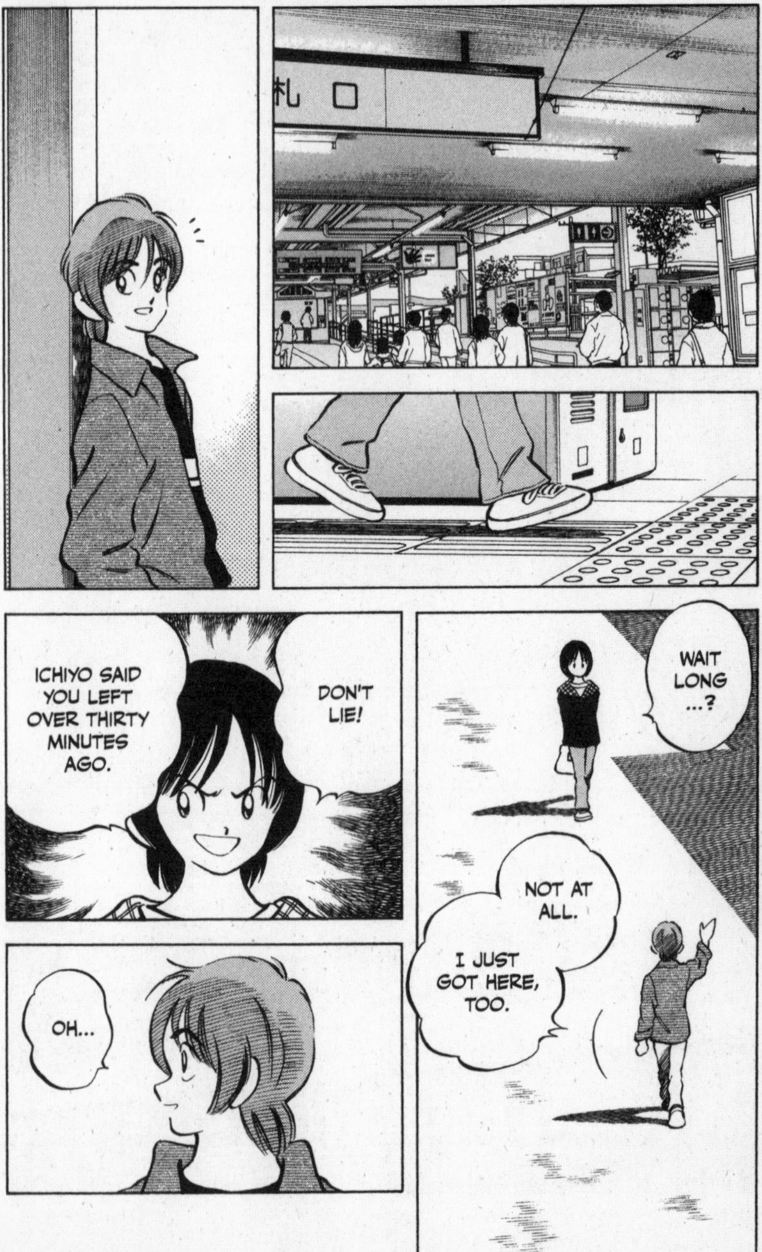
WAIT LONG ...?
NOT AT ALL.
I JUST GOT HERE, TOO.
DON'T LIE!
ICHIYO SAID YOU LEFT OVER THIRTY MINUTES AGO.
OH...

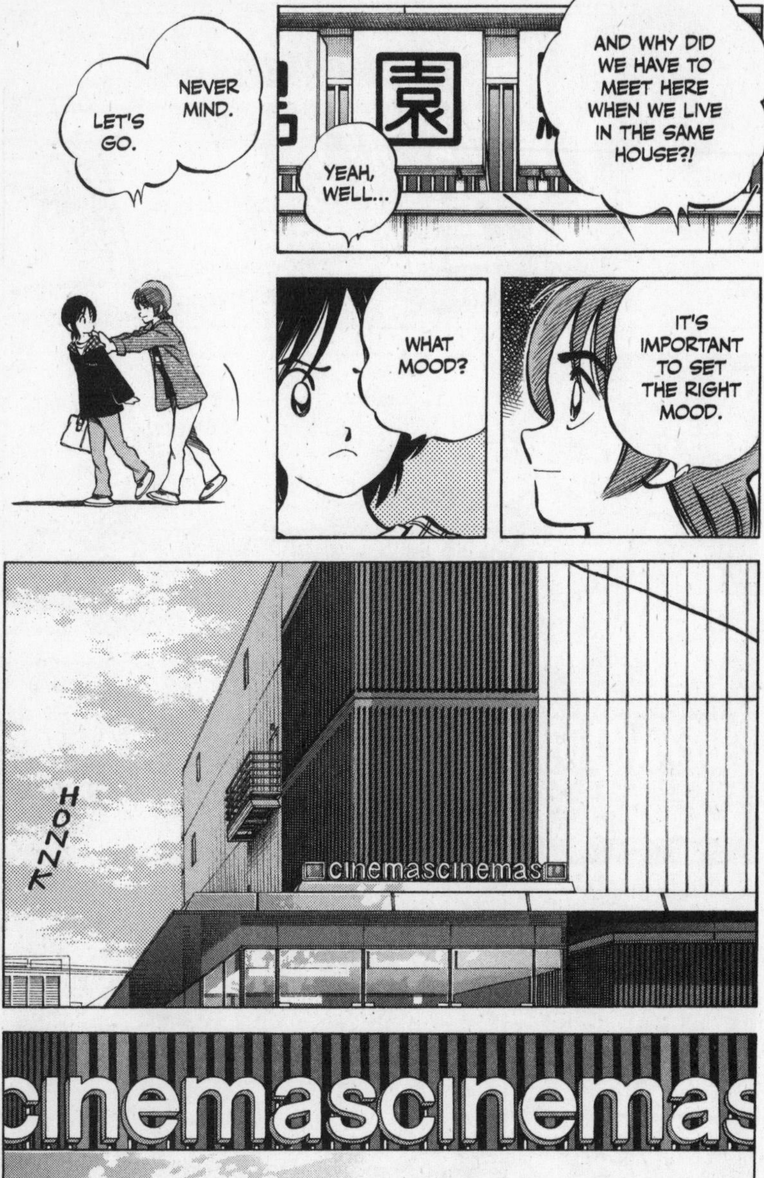
AND WHY DID WE HAVE TO MEET HERE WHEN WE LIVE IN THE SAME HOUSE?!
YEAH, WELL...
IT'S IMPORTANT TO SET THE RIGHT MOOD.
WHAT MOOD?
NEVER MIND.
LET'S GO.
HONNK
cinemascinemas
cinemascinemas

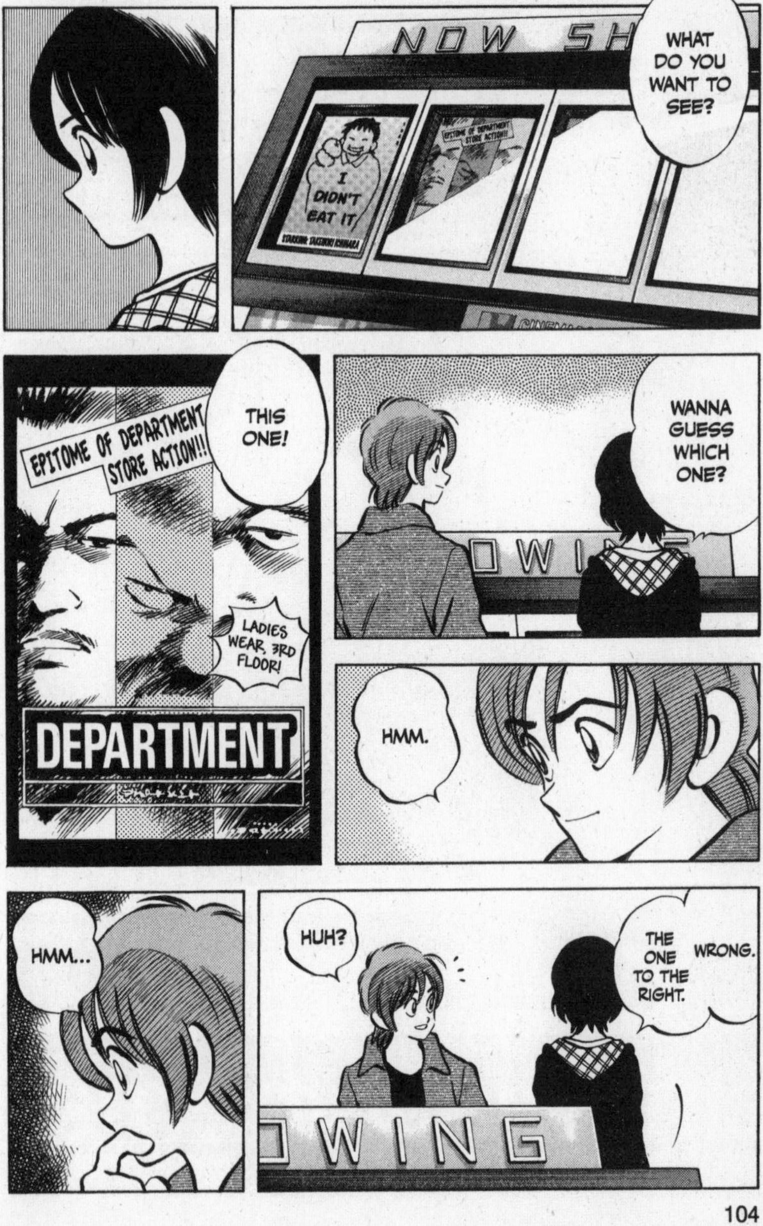
NOW SH
WHAT DO YOU WANT TO SEE?
I DIDN'T EAT IT
EPITOME OF DEPARTMENT STORE ACTION!!
WANNA GUESS WHICH ONE?
OWIN
HMM.
THIS ONE!
EPITOME OF DEPARTMENT STORE ACTION!!
LADIES WEAR, 3RD FLOOR!
DEPARTMENT
WRONG.
THE ONE TO THE RIGHT.
HUH?
OWING
HMM...

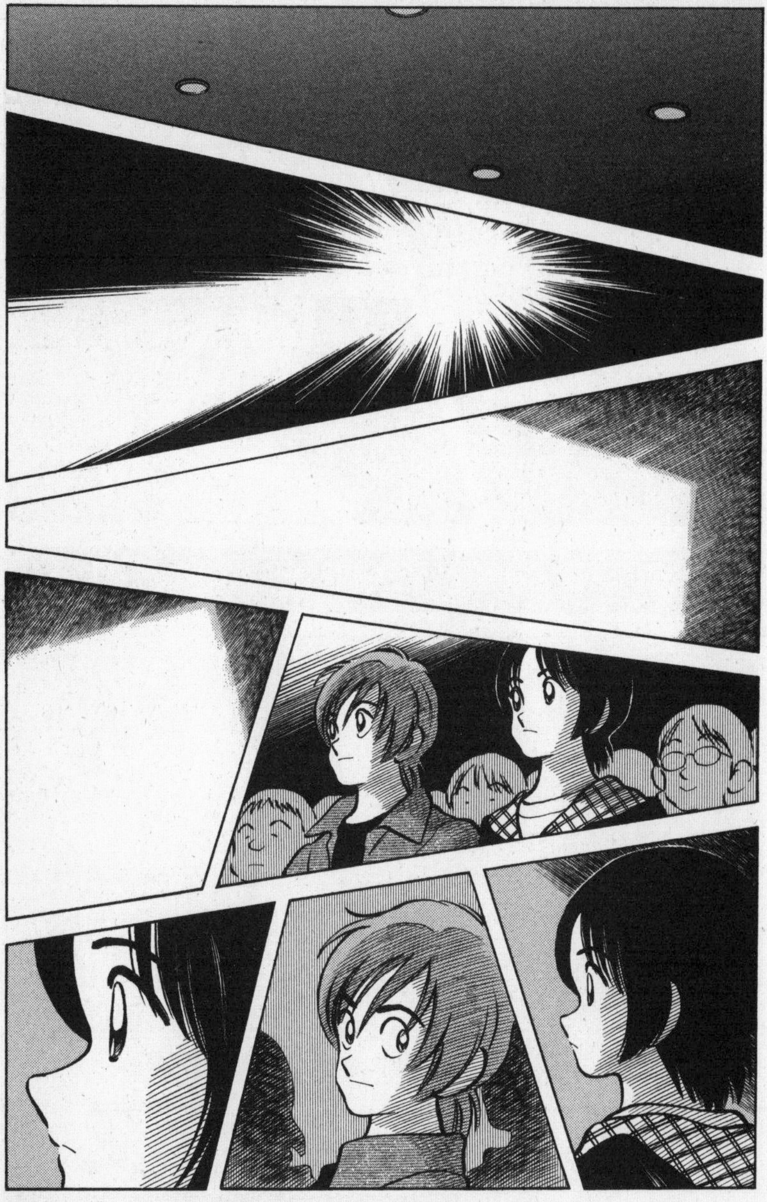

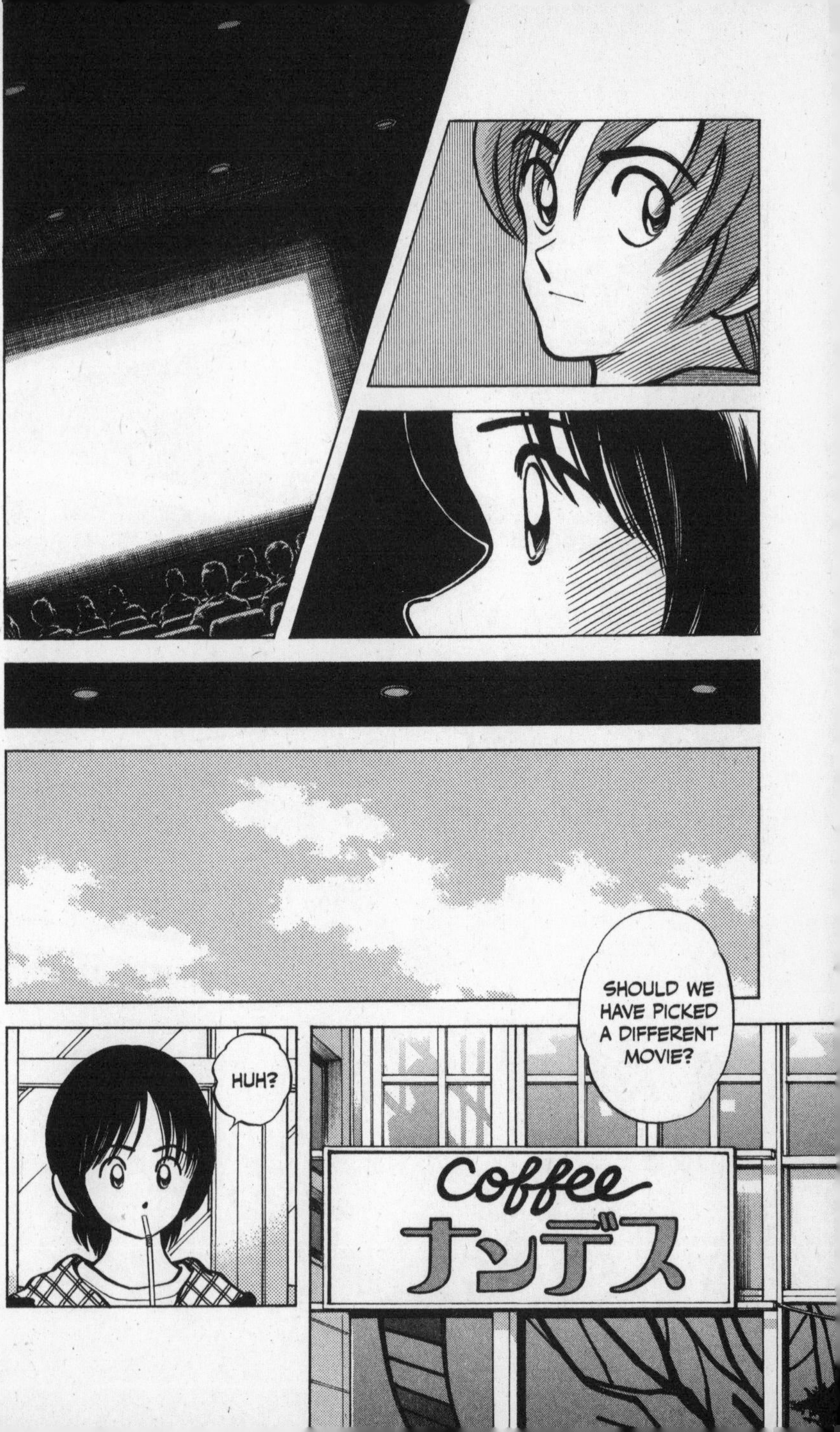
SHOULD WE HAVE PICKED A DIFFERENT MOVIE?
Coffee
ナンデス
HUH?

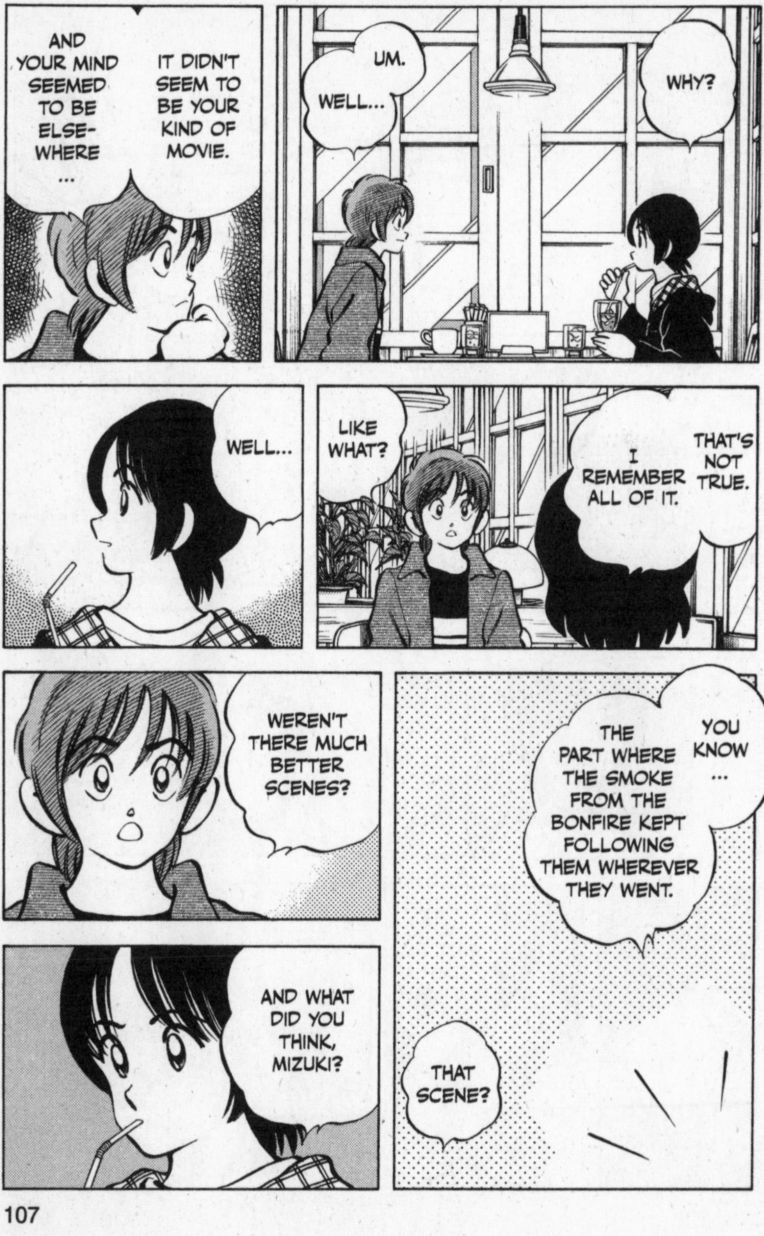
WHY?
UM.
WELL...
IT DIDN'T SEEM TO BE YOUR KIND OF MOVIE.
AND YOUR MIND SEEMED TO BE ELSE-WHERE ...
THAT'S NOT TRUE.
I REMEMBER ALL OF IT.
LIKE WHAT?
WELL...
YOU KNOW ...
THE PART WHERE THE SMOKE FROM THE BONFIRE KEPT FOLLOWING THEM WHEREVER THEY WENT.
THAT SCENE?
WEREN'T THERE MUCH BETTER SCENES?
AND WHAT DID YOU THINK, MIZUKI?

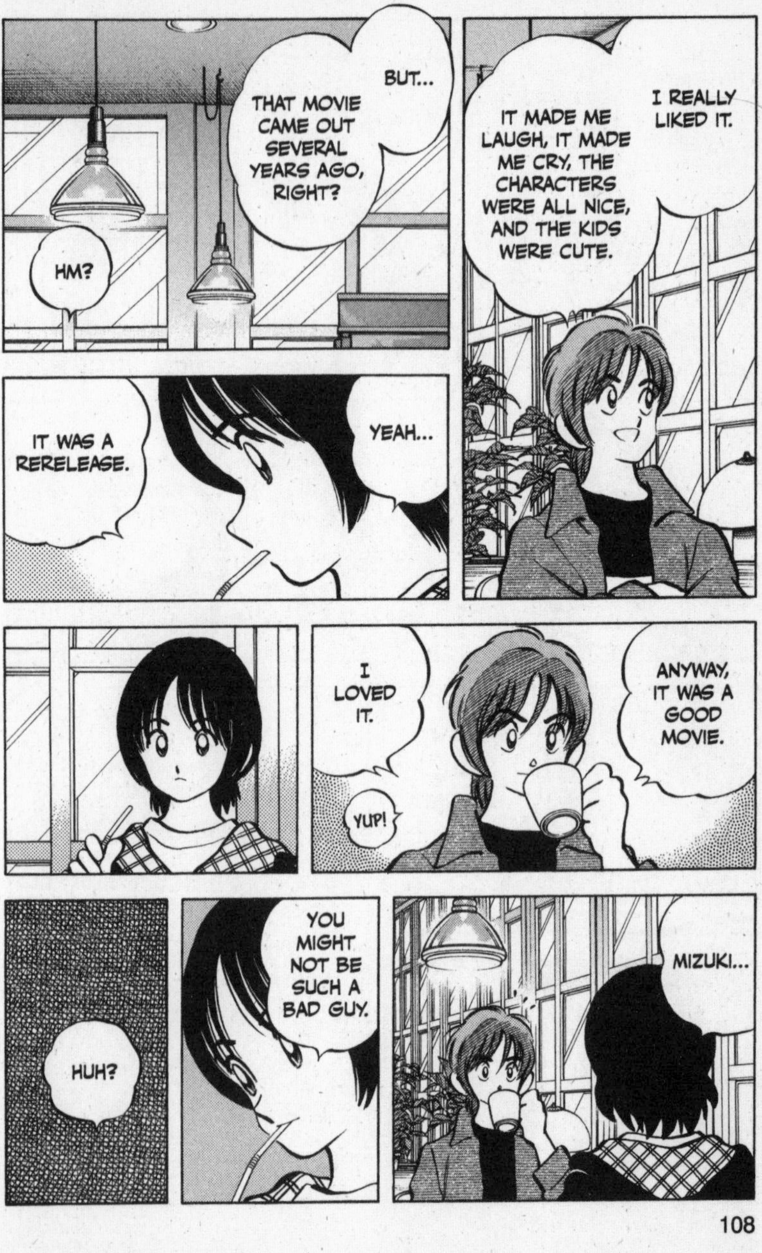
I REALLY LIKED IT.
IT MADE ME LAUGH, IT MADE ME CRY, THE CHARACTERS WERE ALL NICE, AND THE KIDS WERE CUTE.
BUT...
THAT MOVIE CAME OUT SEVERAL YEARS AGO, RIGHT?
HM?
YEAH...
IT WAS A RERELEASE.
ANYWAY, IT WAS A GOOD MOVIE.
I LOVED IT.
YUP!
MIZUKI...
YOU MIGHT NOT BE SUCH A BAD GUY.
HUH?

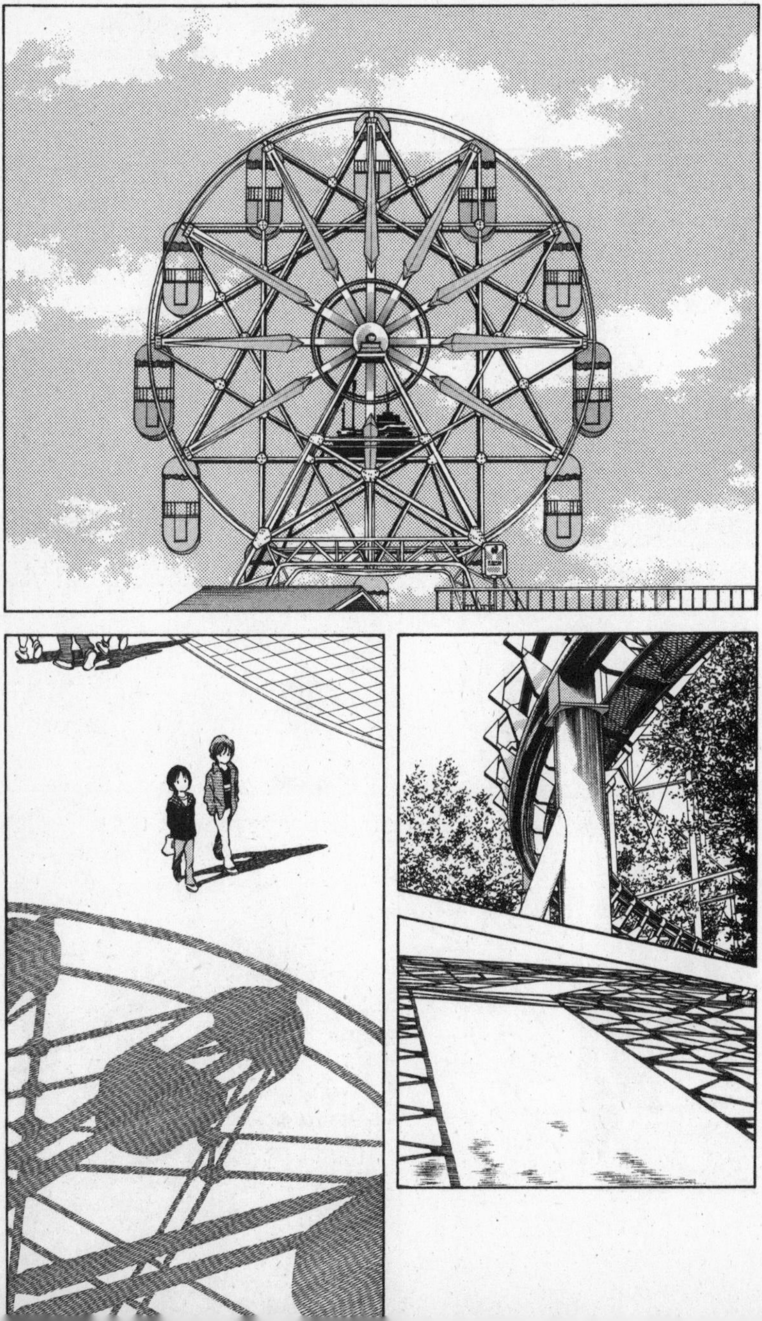

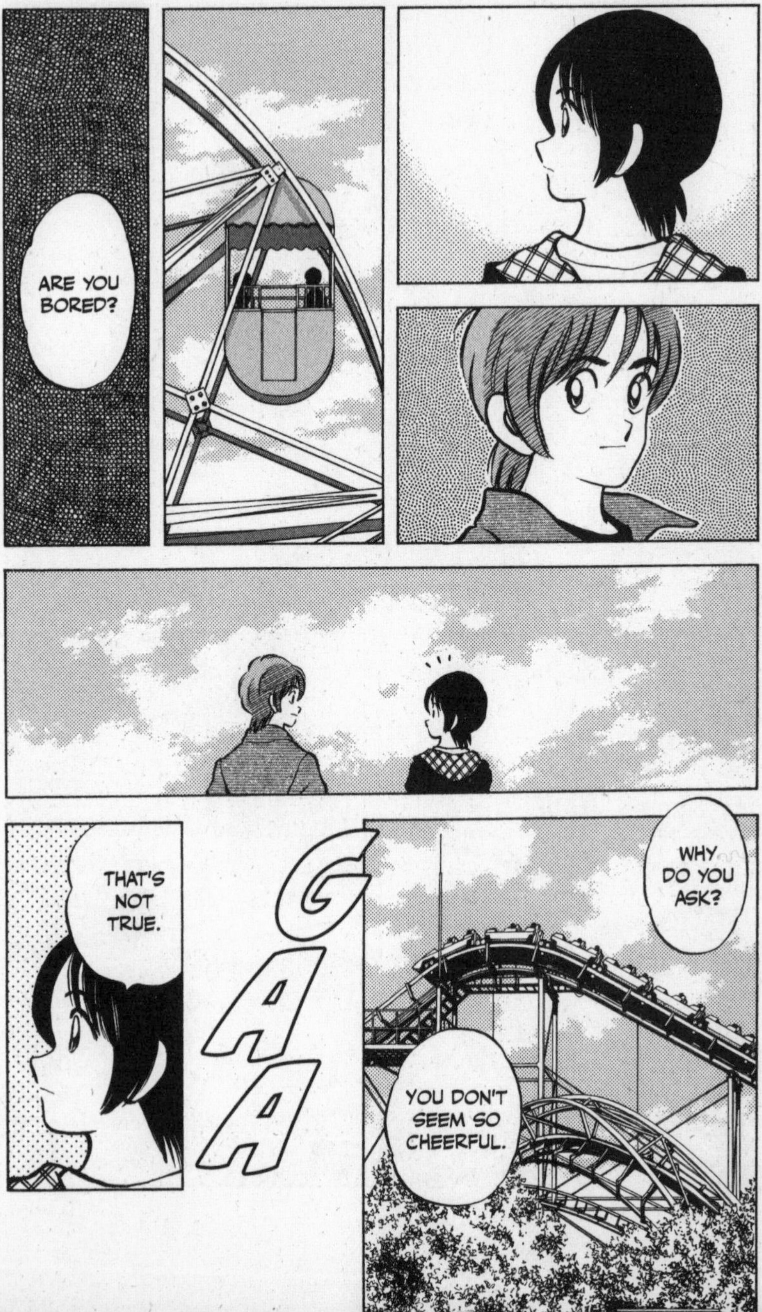
ARE YOU BORED?
WHY DO YOU ASK?
YOU DON'T SEEM SO CHEERFUL.
GAAA
THAT'S NOT TRUE.

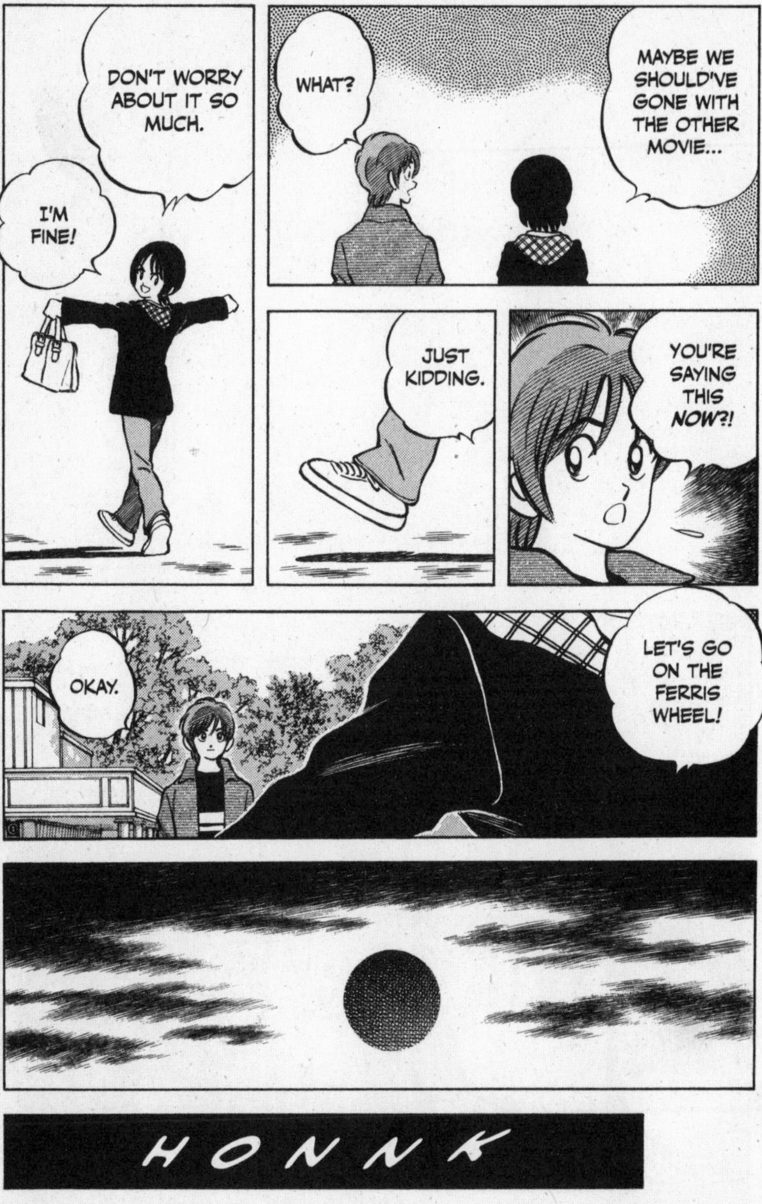
MAYBE WE SHOULD'VE GONE WITH THE OTHER MOVIE...
WHAT?
YOU'RE SAYING THIS *NOW*?!
JUST KIDDING.
DON'T WORRY ABOUT IT SO MUCH.
I'M FINE!
LET'S GO ON THE FERRIS WHEEL!
OKAY.
HONNK

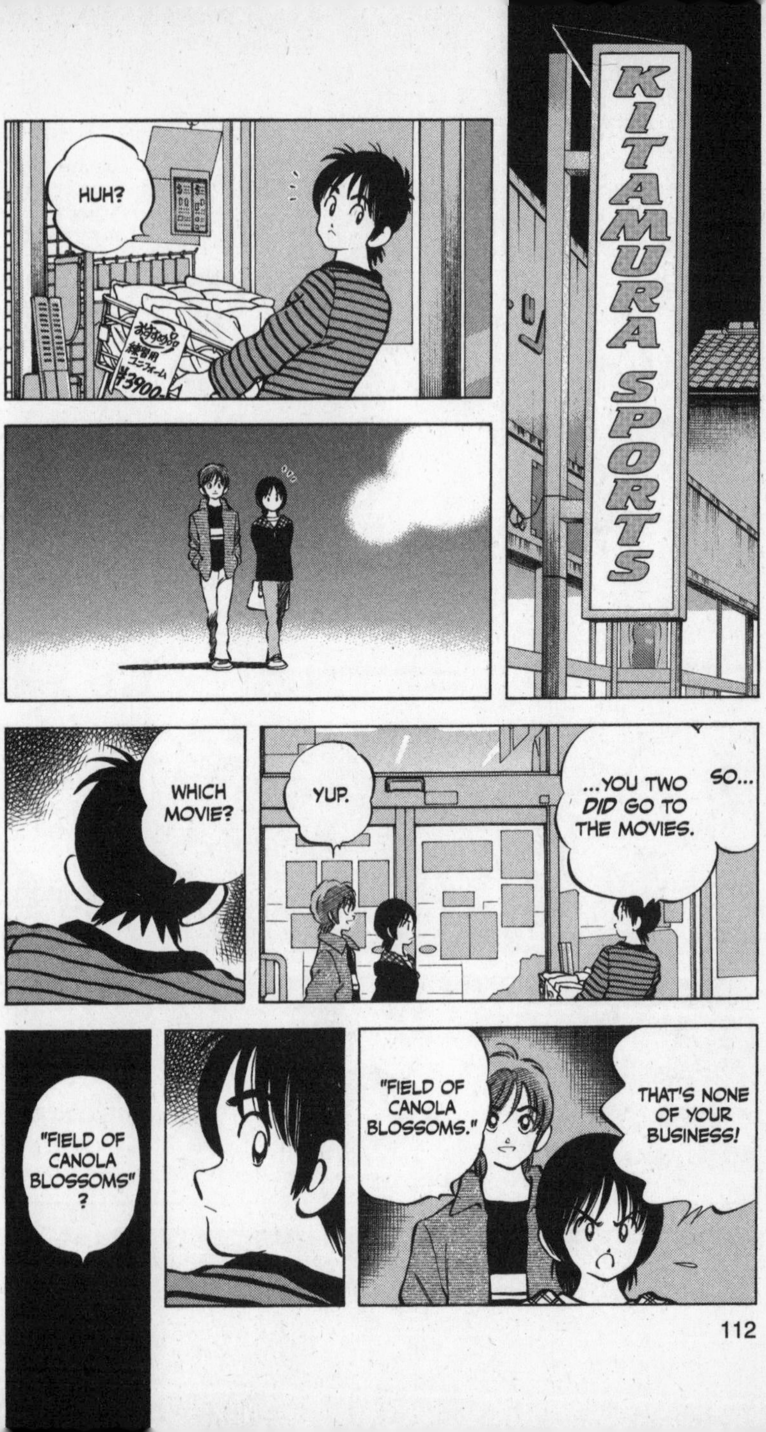
KITAMURA SPORTS
HUH?
SO...
...YOU TWO *DID* GO TO THE MOVIES.
YUP.
WHICH MOVIE?
THAT'S NONE OF YOUR BUSINESS!
"FIELD OF CANOLA BLOSSOMS."
"FIELD OF CANOLA BLOSSOMS"?

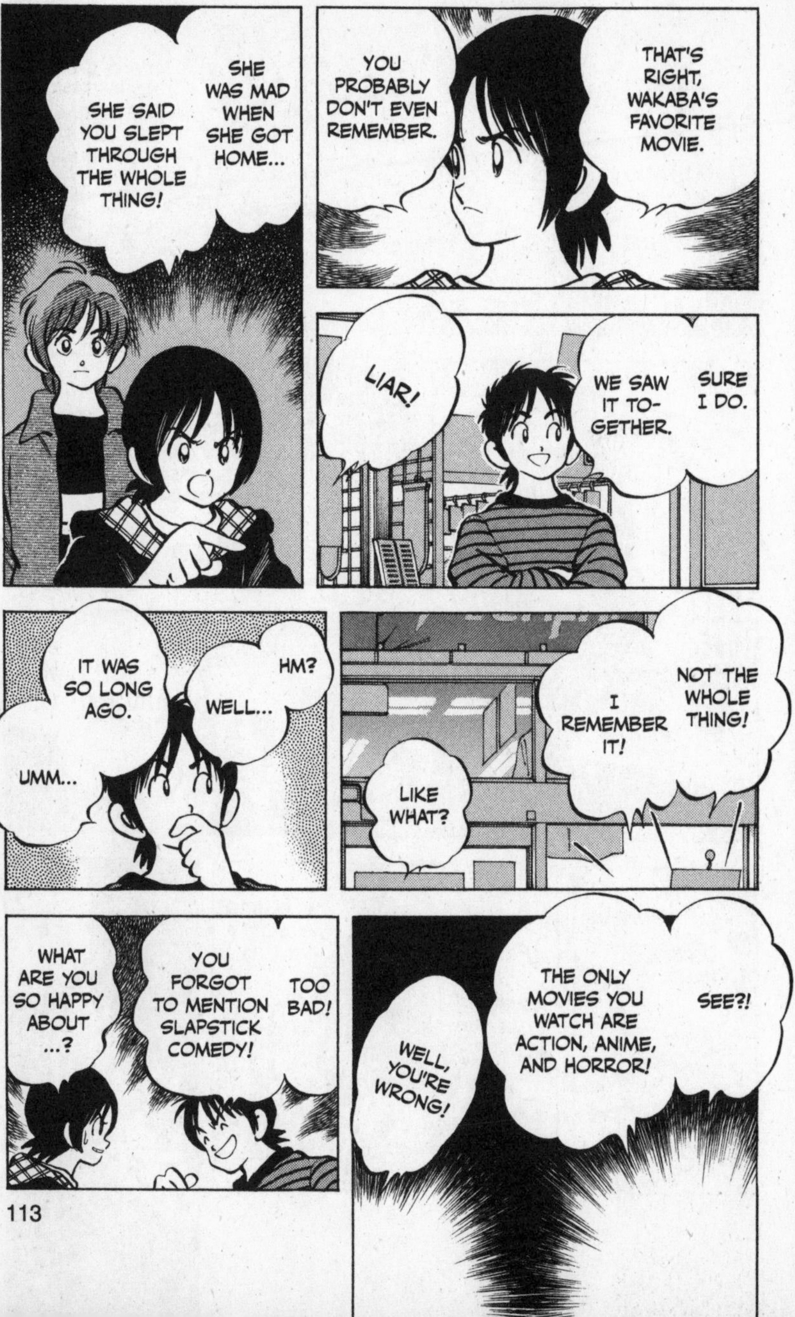
THAT'S RIGHT, WAKABA'S FAVORITE MOVIE.
YOU PROBABLY DON'T EVEN REMEMBER.
SURE I DO.
WE SAW IT TO-GETHER.
LIAR!
SHE WAS MAD WHEN SHE GOT HOME...
SHE SAID YOU SLEPT THROUGH THE WHOLE THING!
NOT THE WHOLE THING!
I REMEMBER IT!
LIKE WHAT?
HM?
WELL...
IT WAS SO LONG AGO.
UMM...
SEE?!
THE ONLY MOVIES YOU WATCH ARE ACTION, ANIME, AND HORROR!
WELL, YOU'RE WRONG!
TOO BAD!
YOU FORGOT TO MENTION SLAPSTICK COMEDY!
WHAT ARE YOU SO HAPPY ABOUT ...?

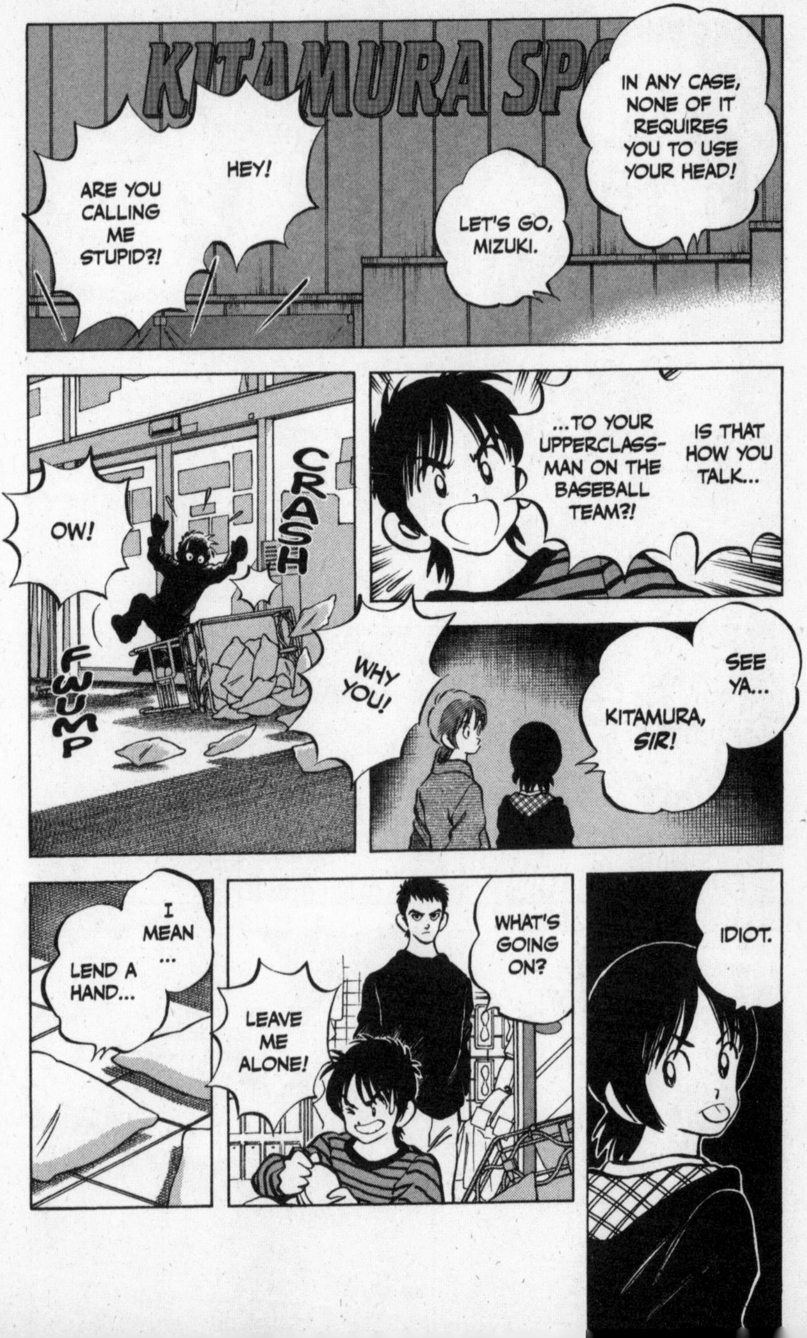
IN ANY CASE, NONE OF IT REQUIRES YOU TO USE YOUR HEAD!
LET'S GO, MIZUKI.
HEY!
ARE YOU CALLING ME STUPID?!
IS THAT HOW YOU TALK...
...TO YOUR UPPERCLASSMAN ON THE BASEBALL TEAM?!
SEE YA... KITAMURA, *SIR*!
WHY YOU!
CRASH
OW!
FWUMP
IDIOT.
WHAT'S GOING ON?
LEAVE ME ALONE!
I MEAN... LEND A HAND...

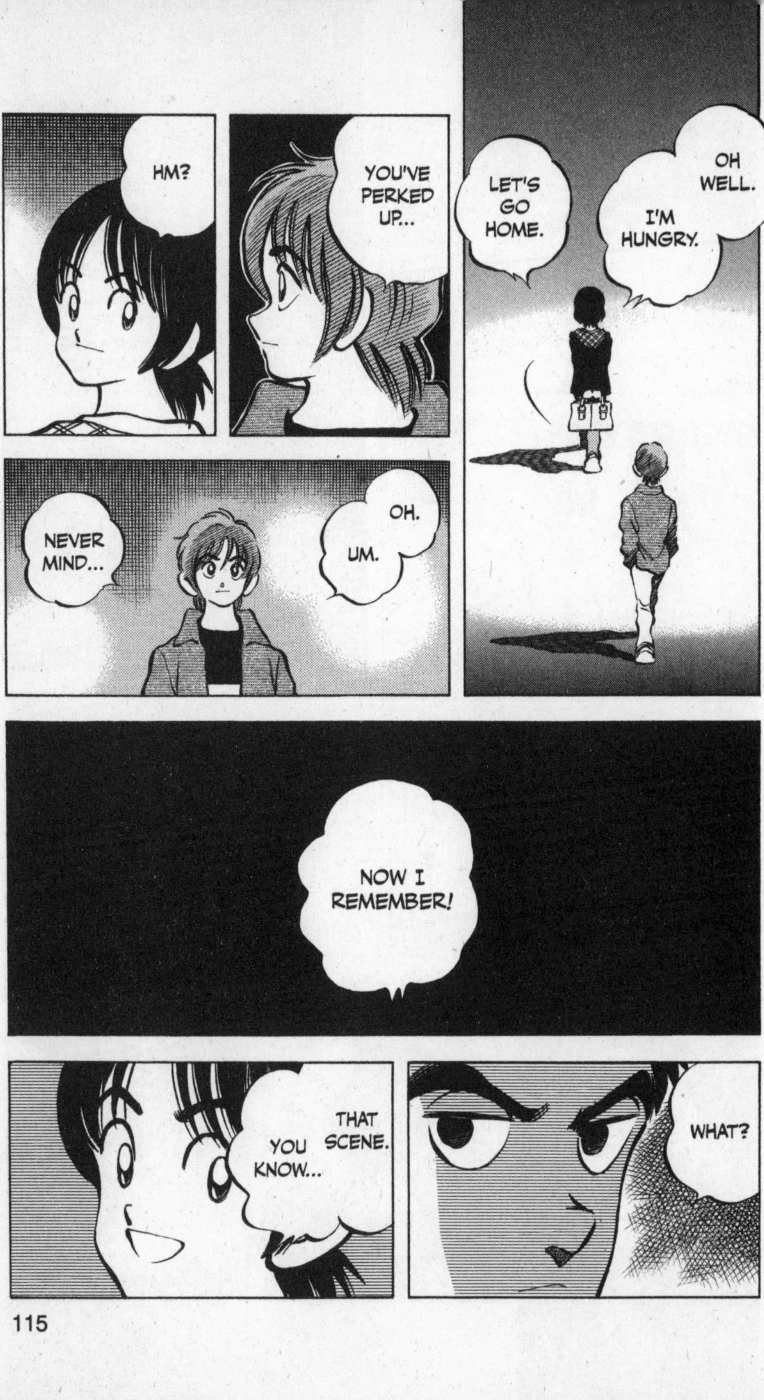
OH WELL.
I'M HUNGRY.
LET'S GO HOME.
YOU'VE PERKED UP...
HM?
OH.
UM.
NEVER MIND...
NOW I REMEMBER!
WHAT?
THAT SCENE.
YOU KNOW...

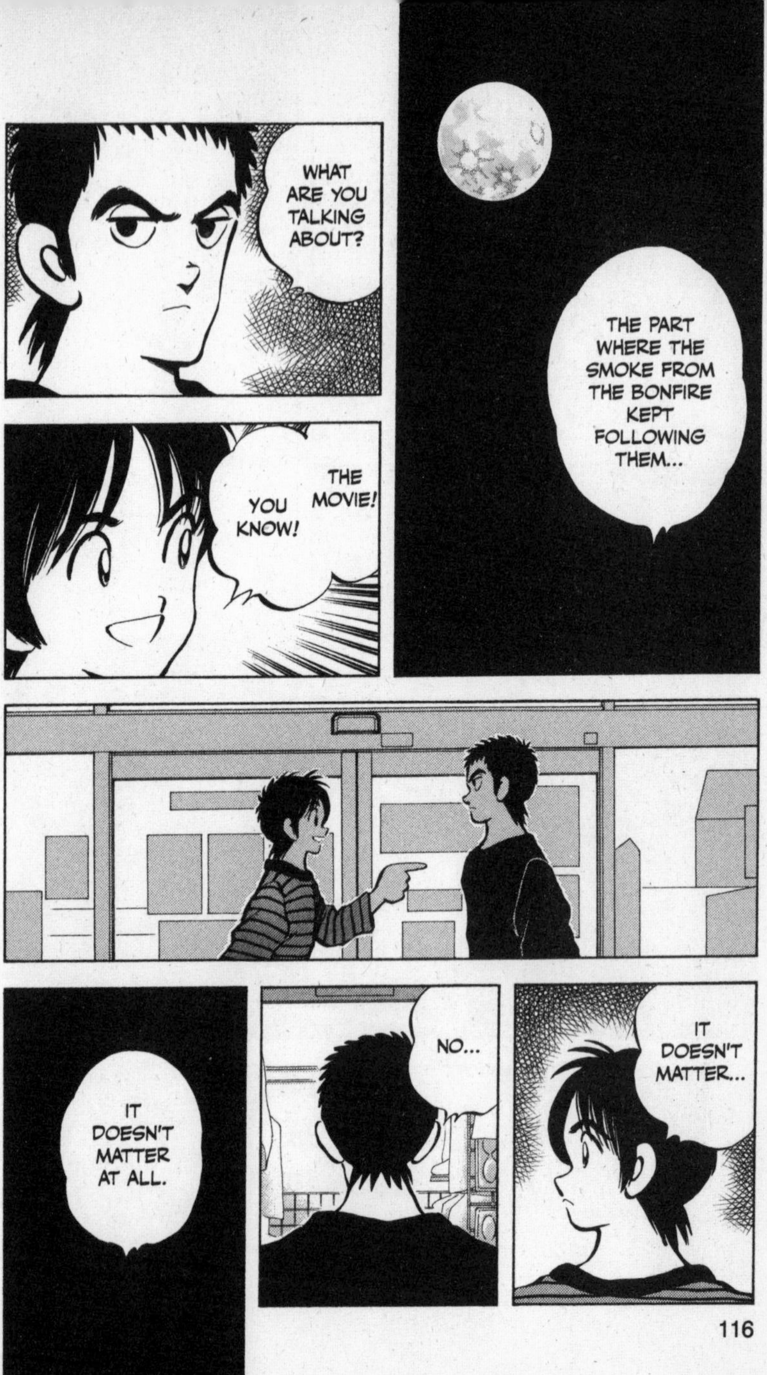
THE PART WHERE THE SMOKE FROM THE BONFIRE KEPT FOLLOWING THEM...
WHAT ARE YOU TALKING ABOUT?
THE MOVIE!
YOU KNOW!
IT DOESN'T MATTER...
NO...
IT DOESN'T MATTER AT ALL.

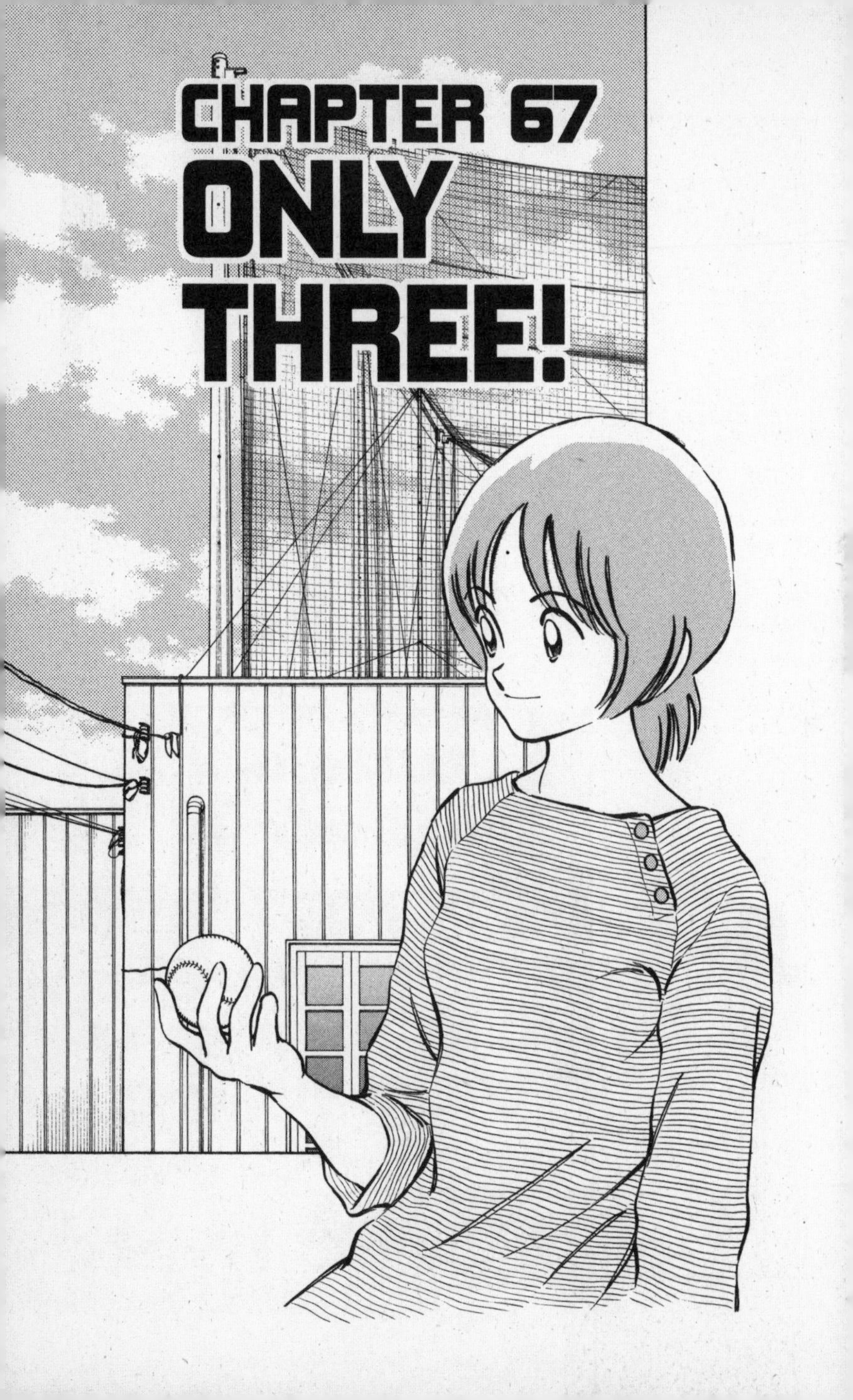
CHAPTER 67
ONLY THREE!

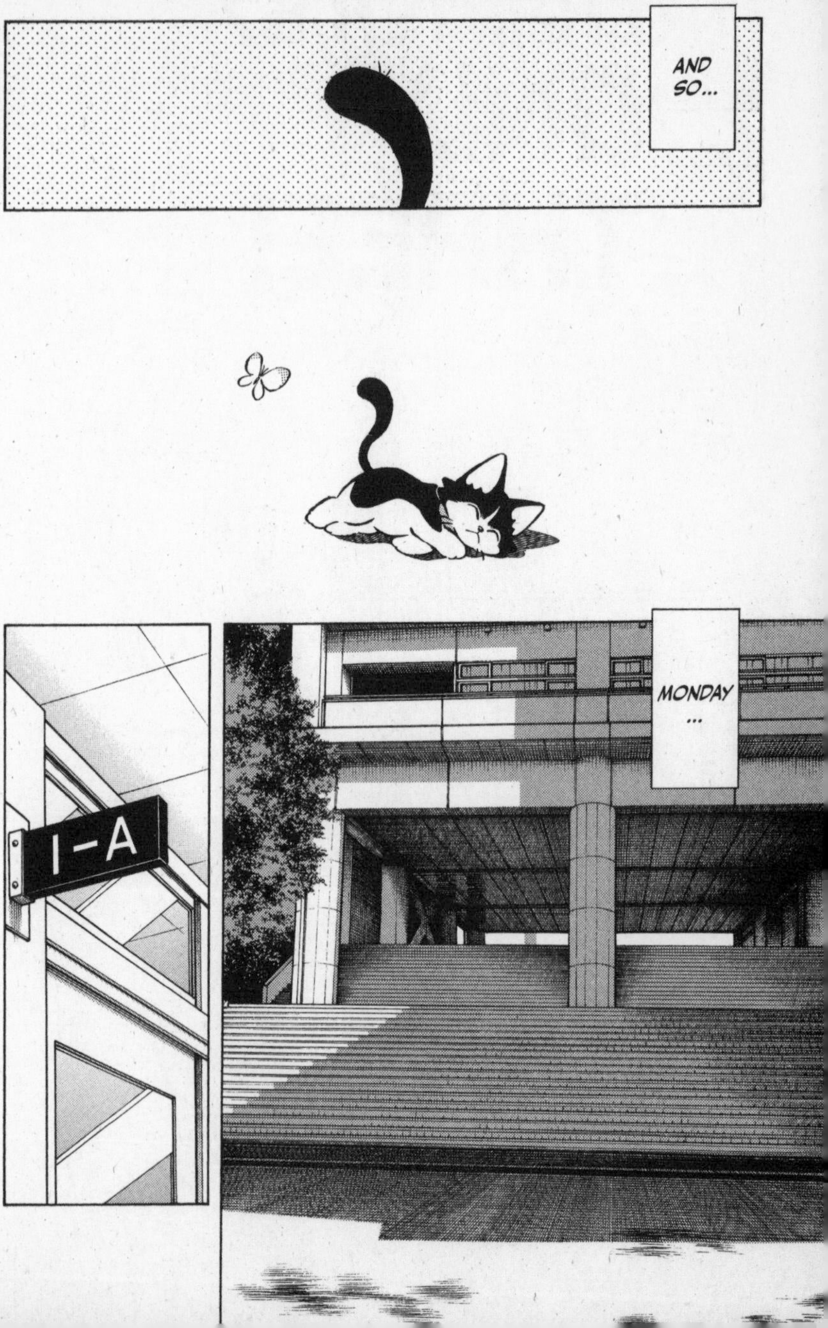
AND SO...
MONDAY ...
I-A

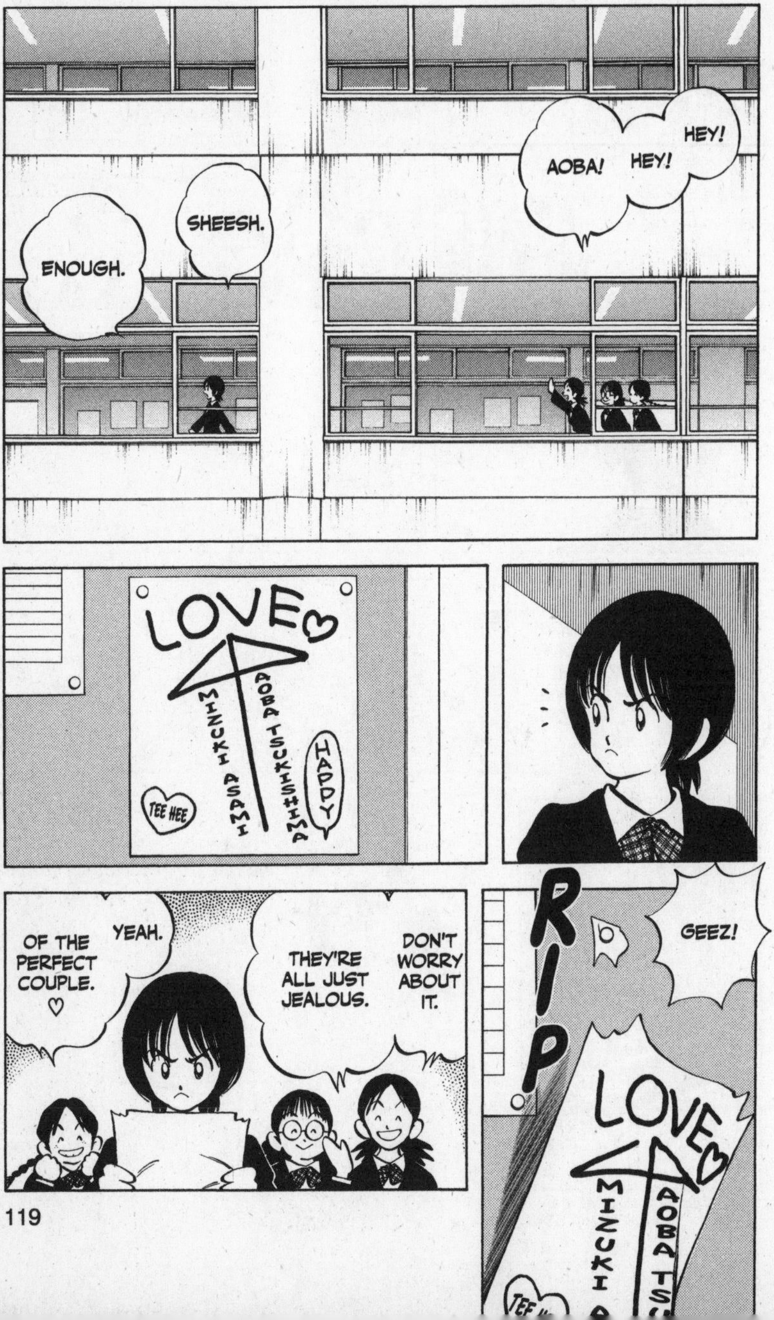
AOBA! HEY! HEY!
SHEESH.
ENOUGH.
LOVE ♡
MIZUKI ASAMI
AOBA TSUKISHIMA
HAPPY
TEE HEE
GEEZ!
RIP
LOVE
DON'T WORRY ABOUT IT.
THEY'RE ALL JUST JEALOUS.
YEAH.
OF THE PERFECT COUPLE. ♡

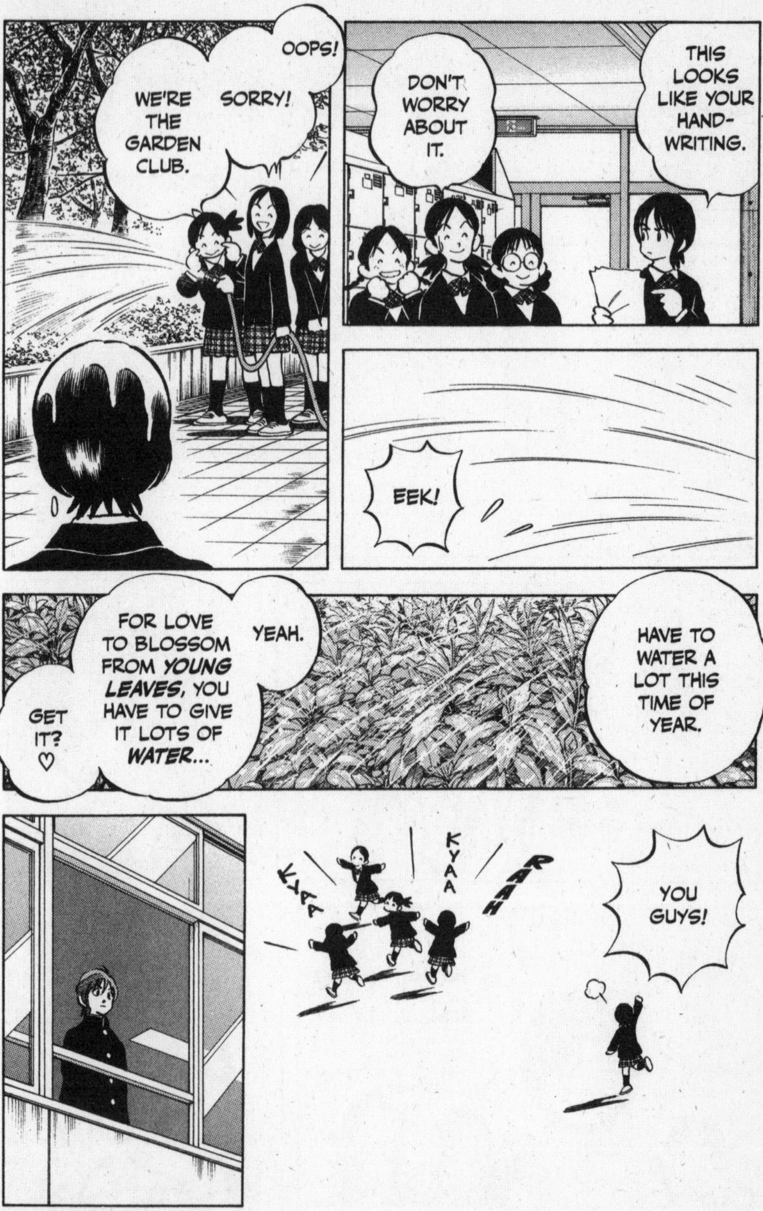
THIS LOOKS LIKE YOUR HAND-WRITING.
DON'T WORRY ABOUT IT.
EEK!
OOPS!
SORRY!
WE'RE THE GARDEN CLUB.
HAVE TO WATER A LOT THIS TIME OF YEAR.
YEAH.
FOR LOVE TO BLOSSOM FROM *YOUNG LEAVES*, YOU HAVE TO GIVE IT LOTS OF *WATER*...
GET IT? ♡
YOU GUYS!
RAAH
KYAA
KYAA

* AOBA MEANS YOUNG LEAVES.
THE MIZU IN MIZUKI MEANS WATER.

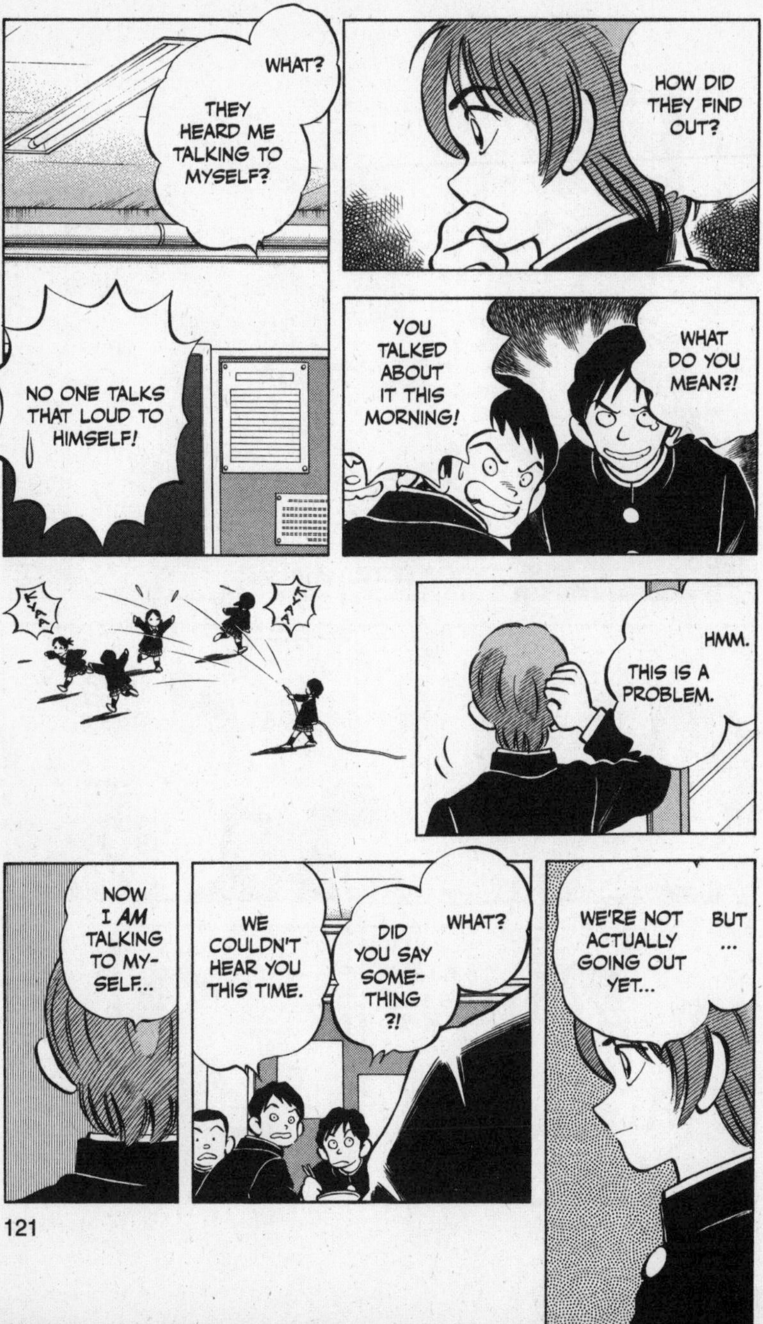
HOW DID THEY FIND OUT?
WHAT?
THEY HEARD ME TALKING TO MYSELF?
WHAT DO YOU MEAN?!
YOU TALKED ABOUT IT THIS MORNING!
NO ONE TALKS THAT LOUD TO HIMSELF!
HMM.
THIS IS A PROBLEM.
BUT...
WE'RE NOT ACTUALLY GOING OUT YET...
WHAT?
DID YOU SAY SOMETHING?!
WE COULDN'T HEAR YOU THIS TIME.
NOW I AM TALKING TO MYSELF...

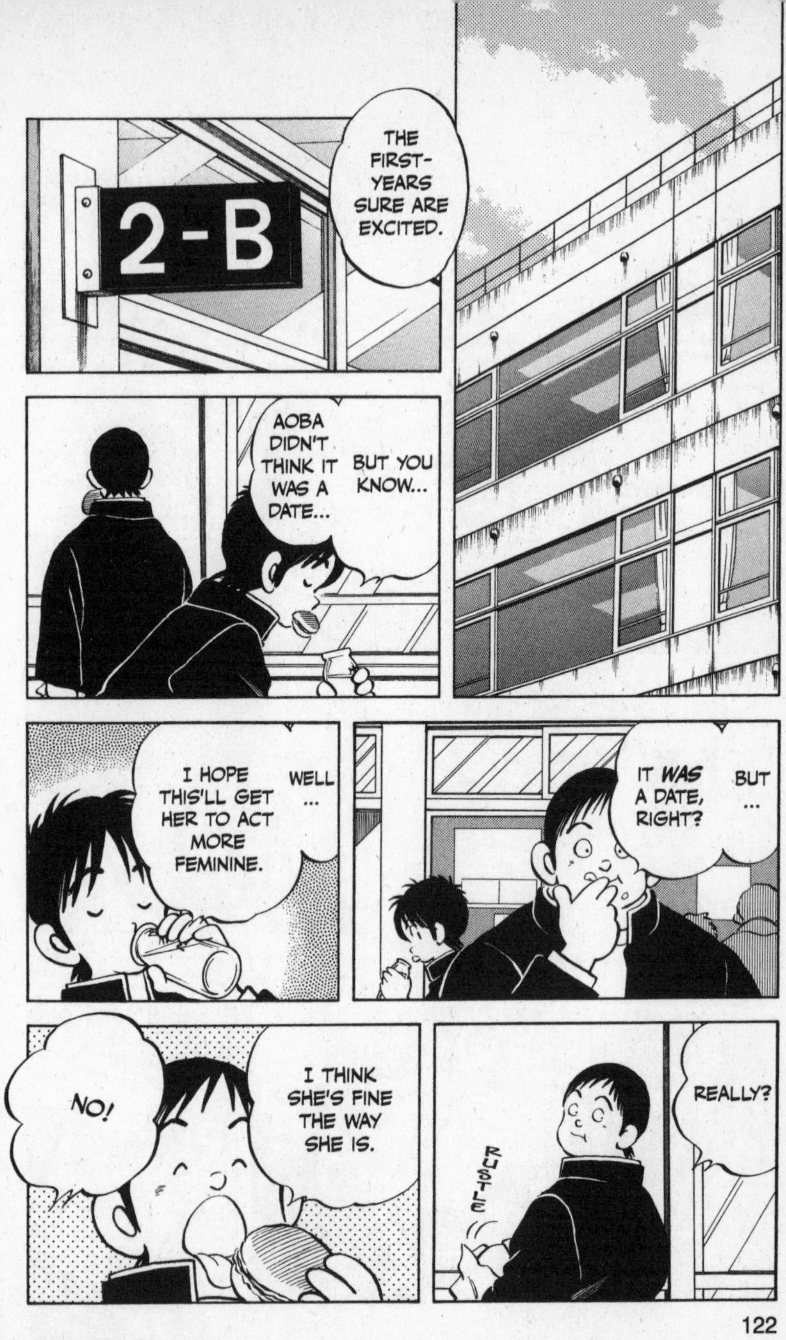
2-B
THE FIRST-YEARS SURE ARE EXCITED.
BUT YOU KNOW...
AOBA DIDN'T THINK IT WAS A DATE...
BUT...
IT *WAS* A DATE, RIGHT?
WELL...
I HOPE THIS'LL GET HER TO ACT MORE FEMININE.
REALLY?
RUSTLE
I THINK SHE'S FINE THE WAY SHE IS.
NO!

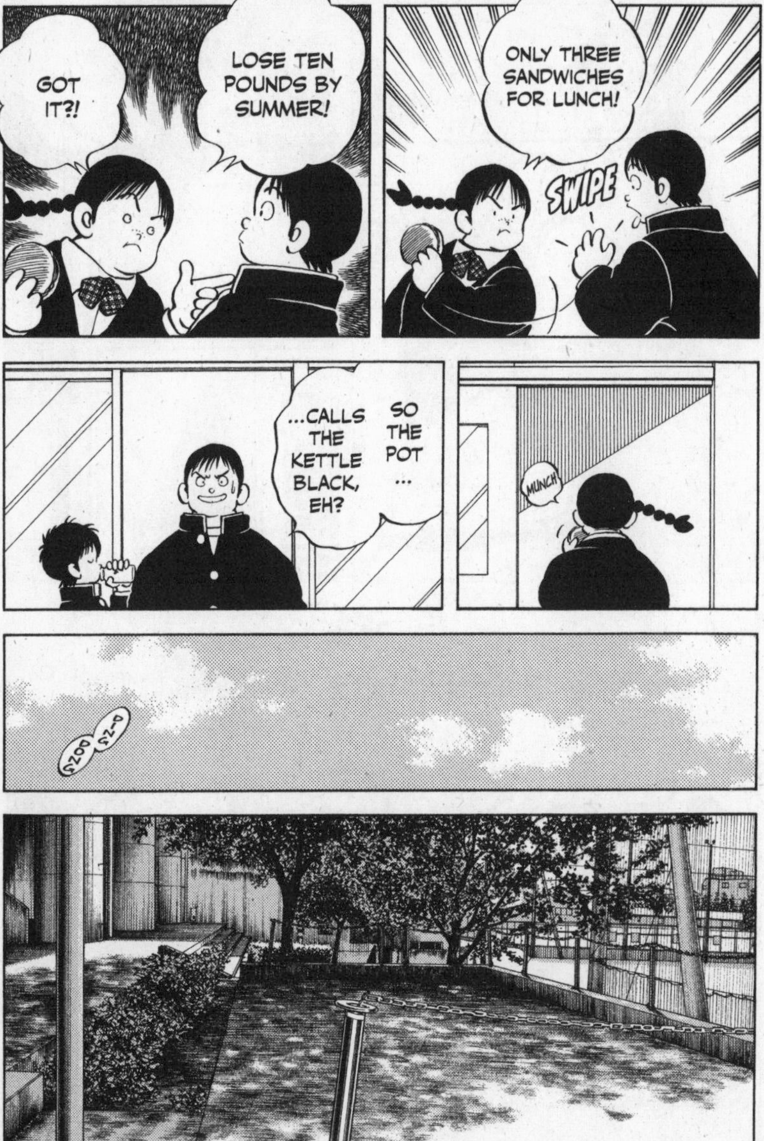
ONLY THREE SANDWICHES FOR LUNCH!
SWIPE
LOSE TEN POUNDS BY SUMMER!
GOT IT?!
MUNCH
SO THE POT ...
...CALLS THE KETTLE BLACK, EH?
DING
DONG

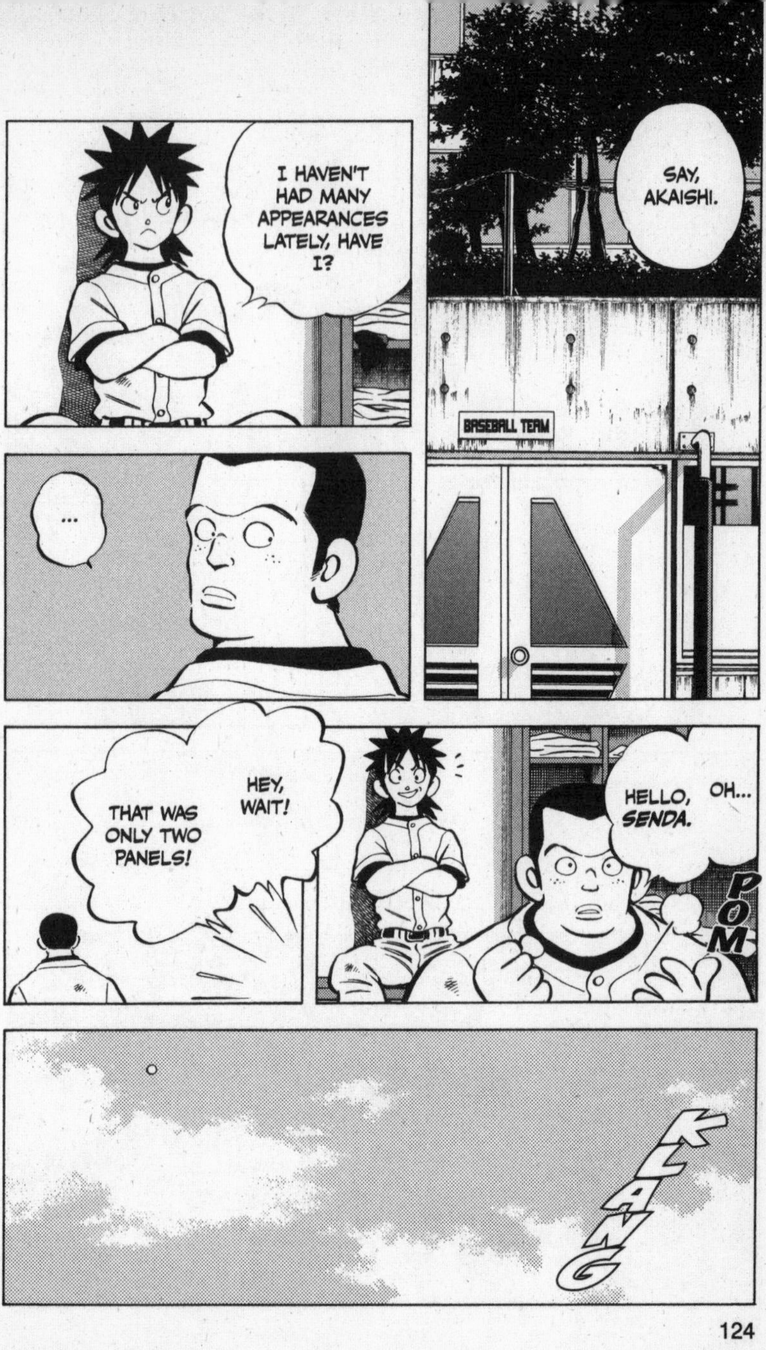
SAY, AKAISHI.
I HAVEN'T HAD MANY APPEARANCES LATELY, HAVE I?
BASEBALL TEAM
...
OH...
HELLO, SENDA.
POM
HEY, WAIT!
THAT WAS ONLY TWO PANELS!
KLANG

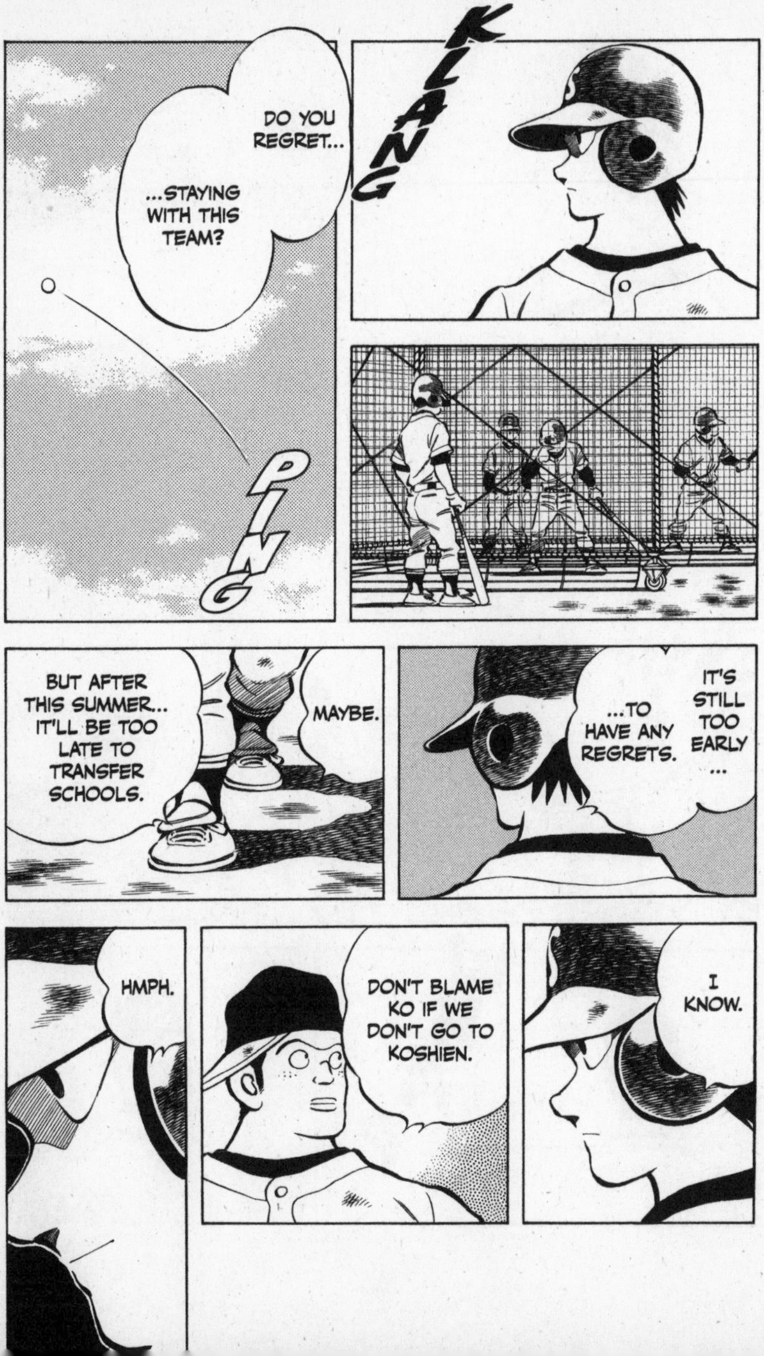
KLANG
DO YOU REGRET...
...STAYING WITH THIS TEAM?
PING
IT'S STILL TOO EARLY...
...TO HAVE ANY REGRETS.
MAYBE.
BUT AFTER THIS SUMMER... IT'LL BE TOO LATE TO TRANSFER SCHOOLS.
I KNOW.
DON'T BLAME KO IF WE DON'T GO TO KOSHIEN.
HMPH.

WITH ME AND KITAMURA ON THE TEAM, IF WE DON'T GET TO KOSHIEN...

...THEN *YOU GUYS* ARE TO BLAME.

AKAISHI!

WHIFF

WHIFF

HUH?

I GOTTA PRACTICE MY SWING.

SORRY.

WHAP

HEY!

126

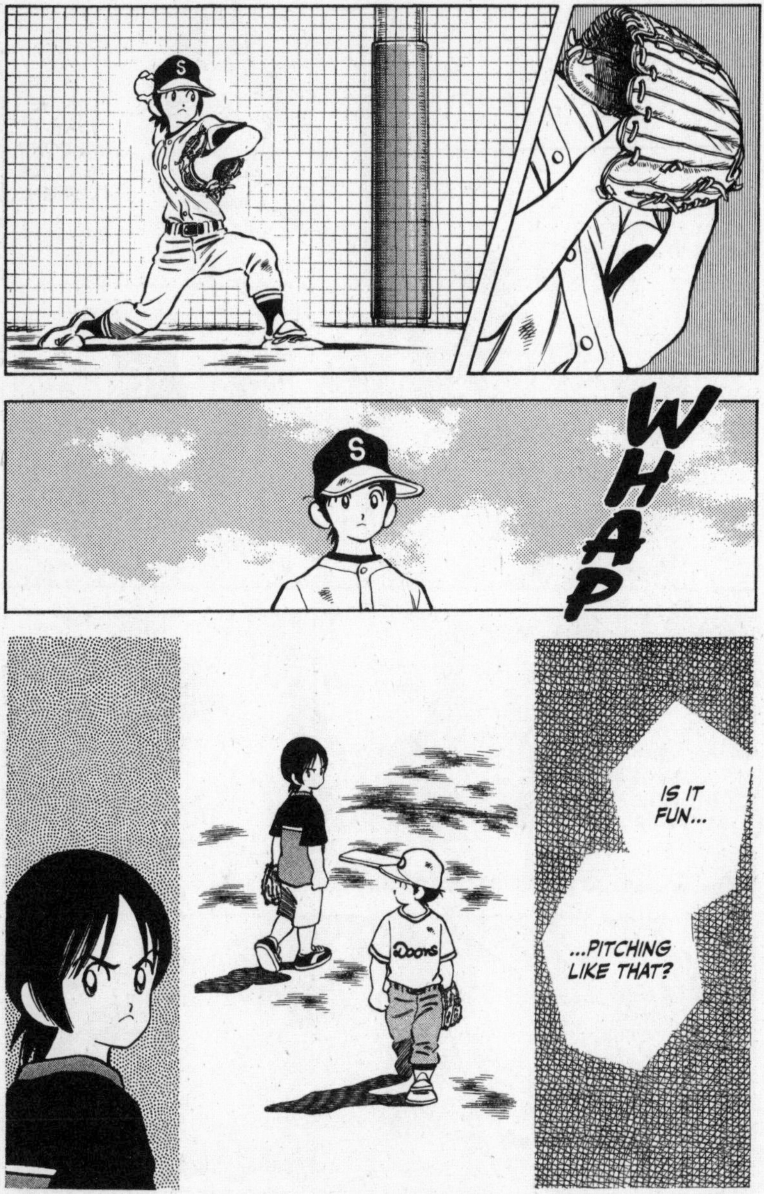
WHAP
IS IT FUN...
...PITCHING LIKE THAT?
Doors

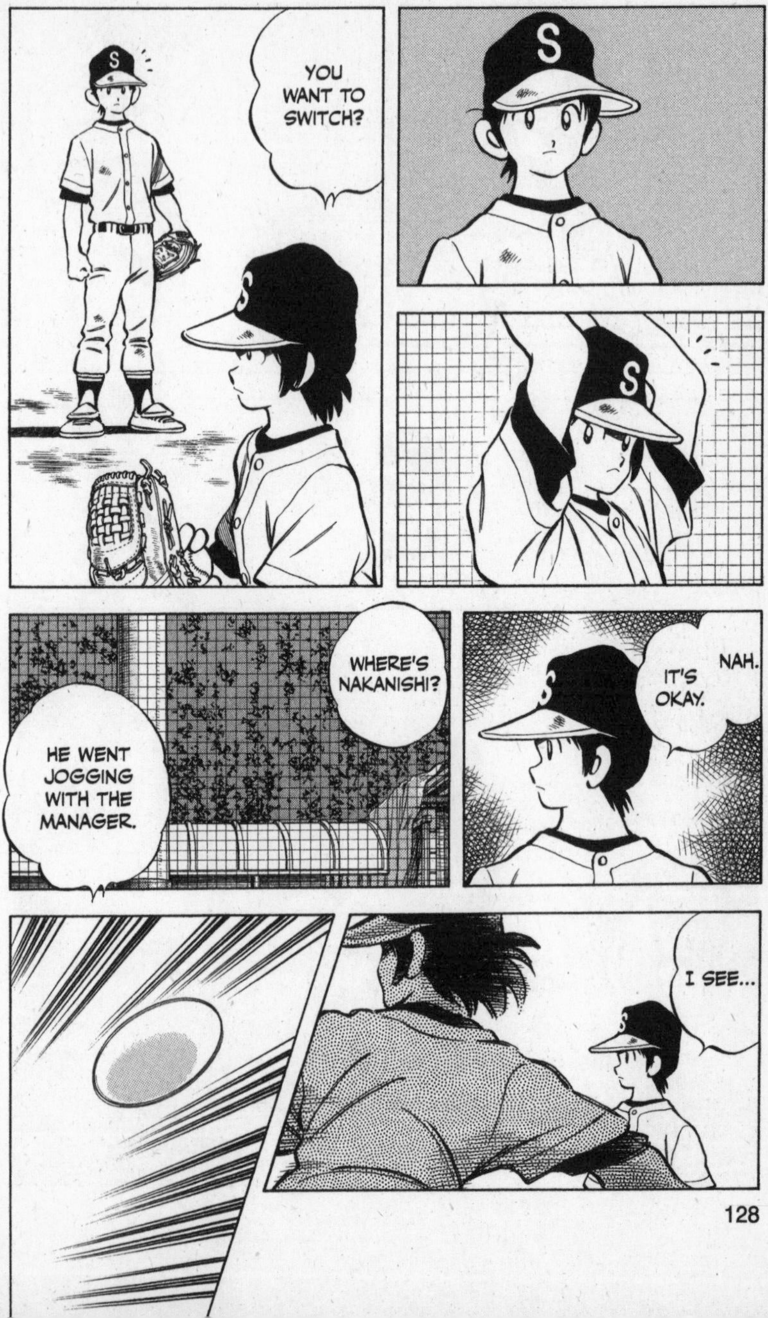
YOU WANT TO SWITCH?
NAH. IT'S OKAY.
WHERE'S NAKANISHI?
HE WENT JOGGING WITH THE MANAGER.
I SEE...

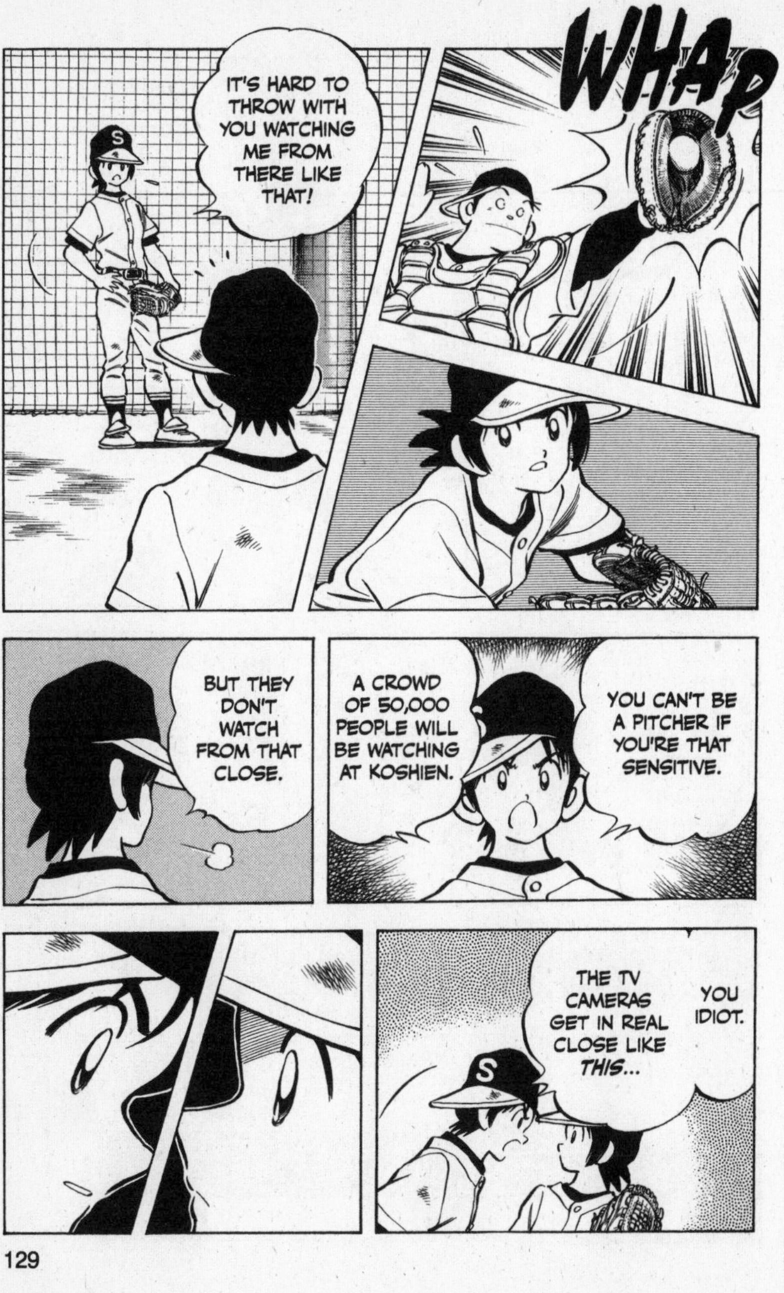
WHAP
IT'S HARD TO THROW WITH YOU WATCHING ME FROM THERE LIKE THAT!
YOU CAN'T BE A PITCHER IF YOU'RE THAT SENSITIVE.
A CROWD OF 50,000 PEOPLE WILL BE WATCHING AT KOSHIEN.
BUT THEY DON'T WATCH FROM THAT CLOSE.
YOU IDIOT.
THE TV CAMERAS GET IN REAL CLOSE LIKE *THIS*...

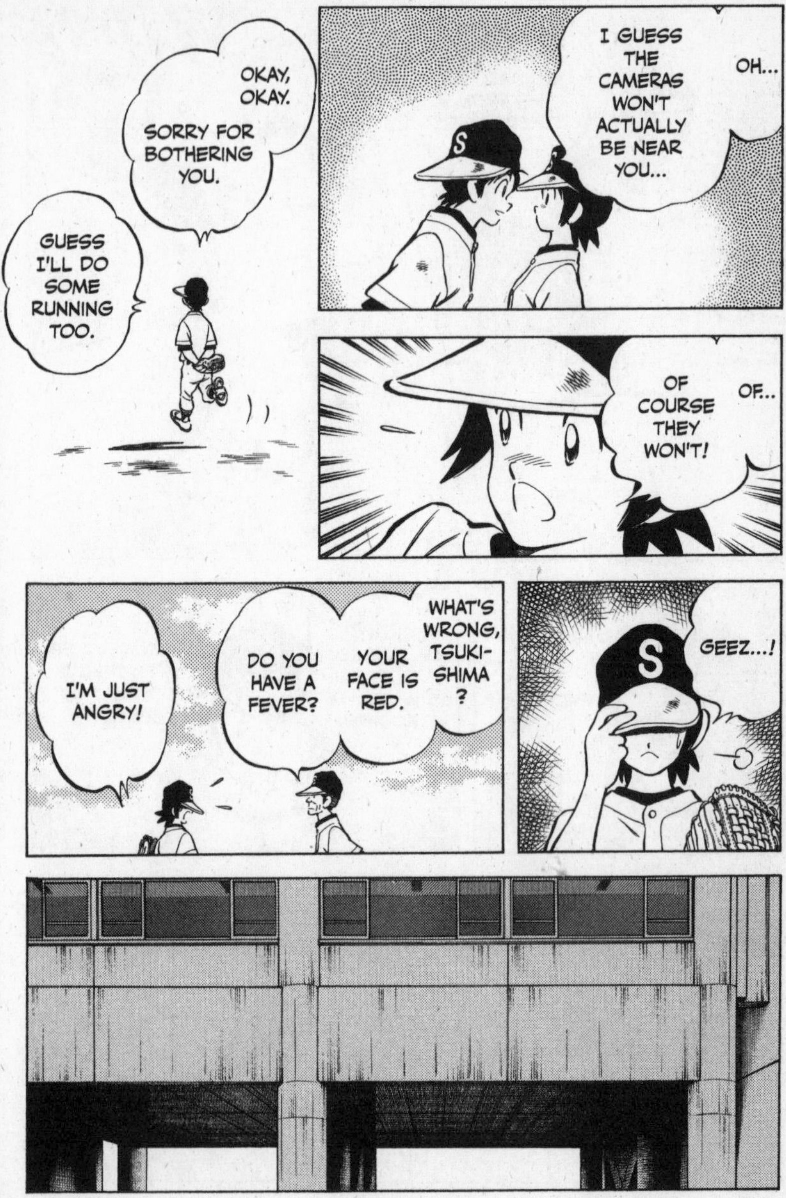
OH...
I GUESS THE CAMERAS WON'T ACTUALLY BE NEAR YOU...
OF...
OF COURSE THEY WON'T!
OKAY, OKAY.
SORRY FOR BOTHERING YOU.
GUESS I'LL DO SOME RUNNING TOO.
GEEZ...!
WHAT'S WRONG, TSUKISHIMA?
YOUR FACE IS RED.
DO YOU HAVE A FEVER?
I'M JUST ANGRY!

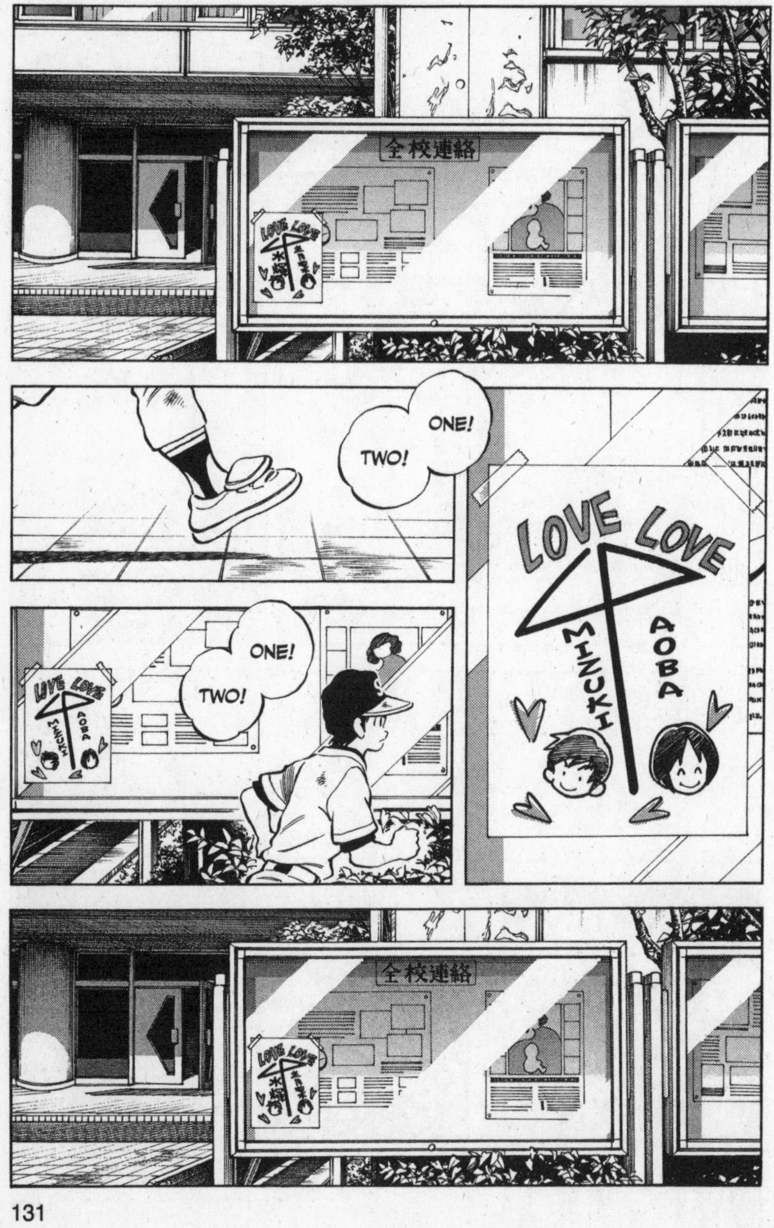
全校連絡
LOVE LOVE
LOVE LOVE
MIZUKI
AOBA
ONE!
TWO!
ONE!
TWO!
LOVE LOVE
MIZUKI
AOBA
全校連絡
LOVE LOVE

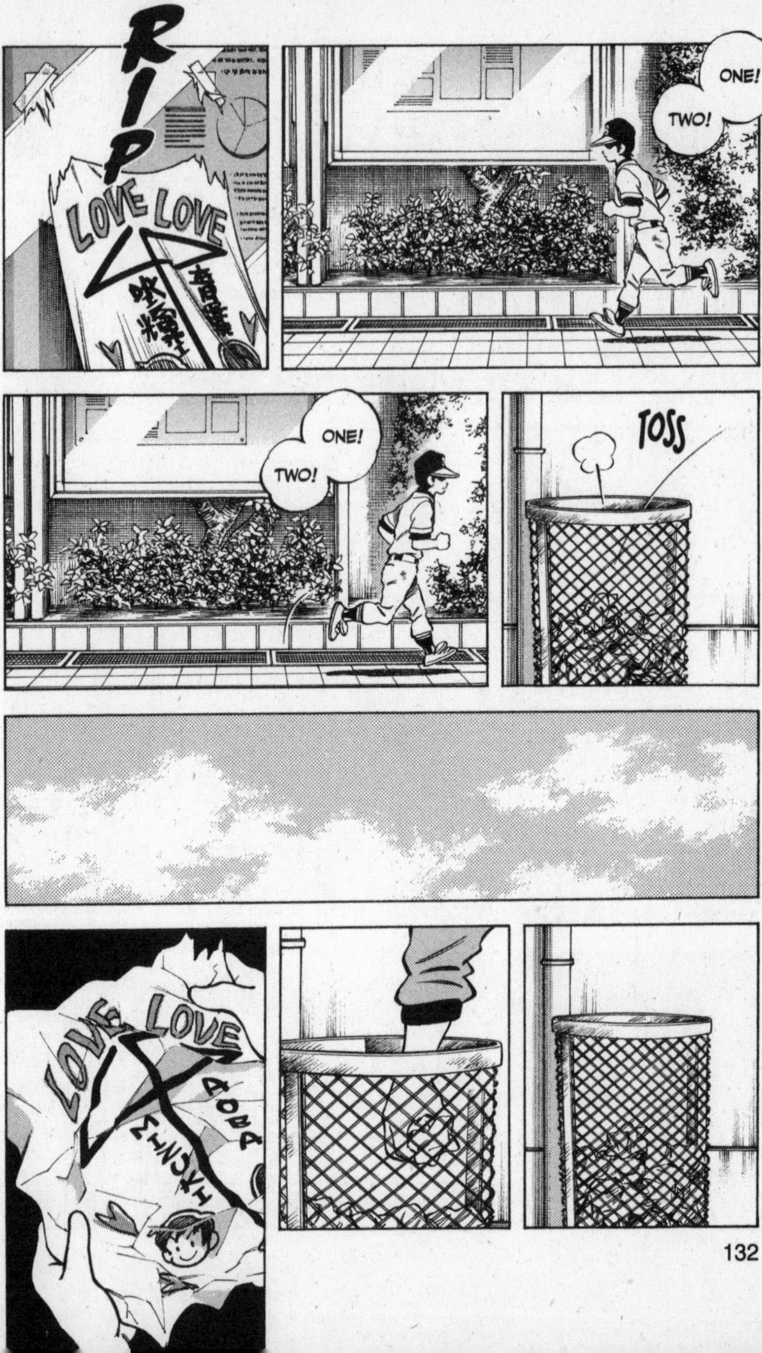
ONE!
TWO!
RIP
LOVE LOVE
TOSS
ONE!
TWO!
LOVE LOVE
AOBA

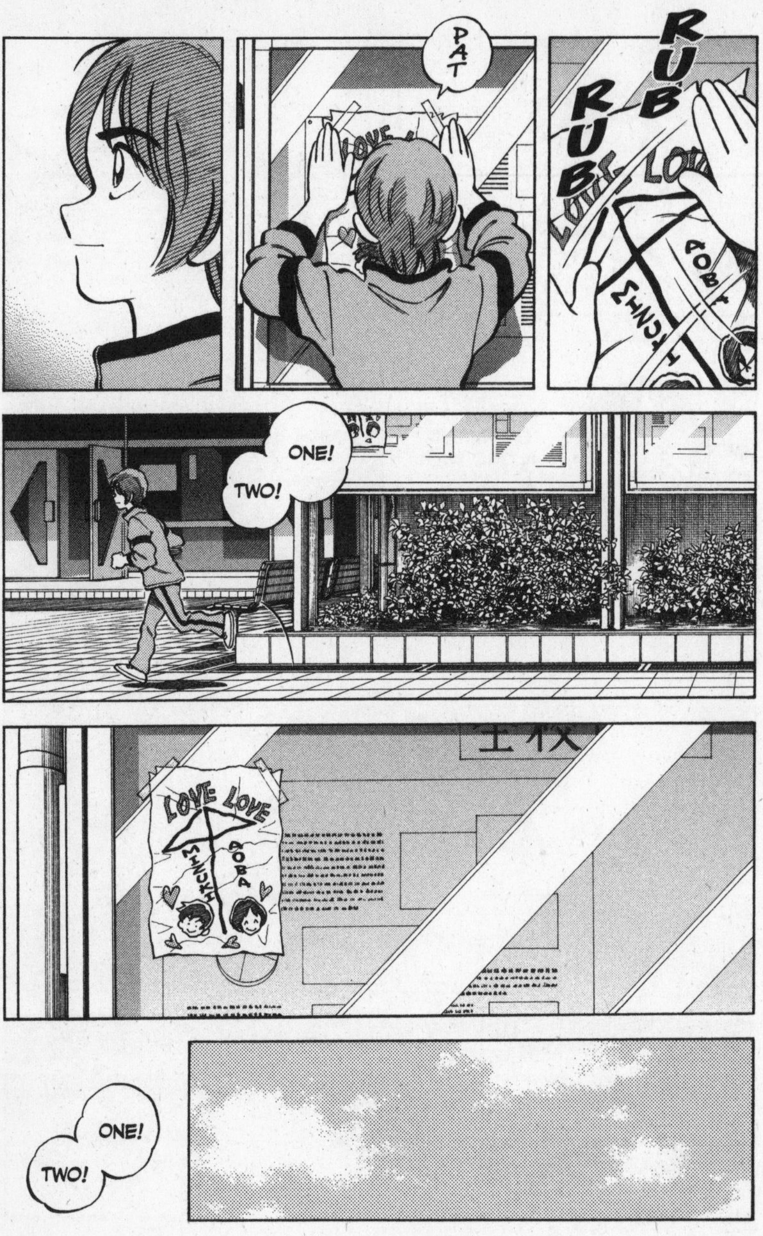
RUB
RUB
RUB
RUB
PAT
ONE!
TWO!
LOVE LOVE
MIZUKI
AOBA
ONE!
TWO!

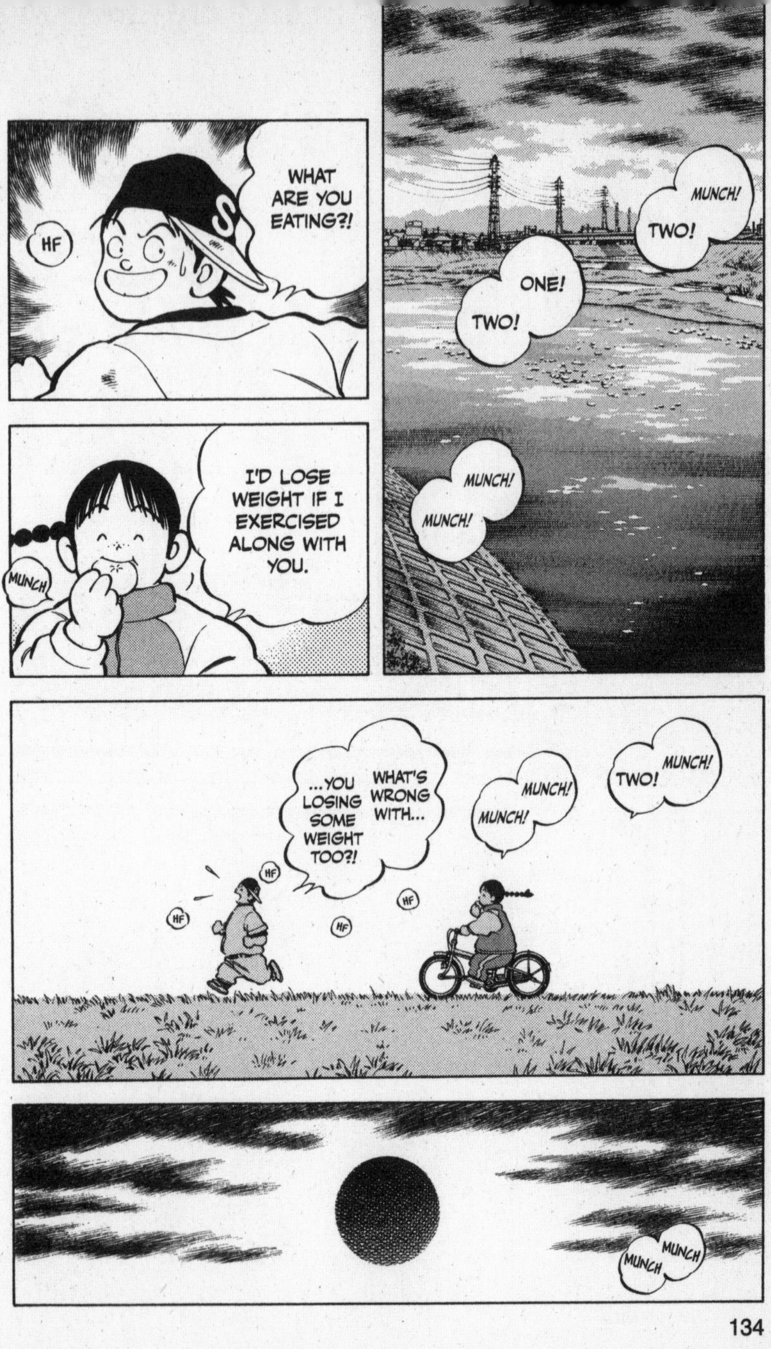
MUNCH!
TWO!
ONE!
TWO!
MUNCH!
MUNCH!
WHAT ARE YOU EATING?!
HF
I'D LOSE WEIGHT IF I EXERCISED ALONG WITH YOU.
MUNCH
MUNCH!
TWO!
MUNCH!
MUNCH!
WHAT'S WRONG WITH...
...YOU LOSING SOME WEIGHT TOO?!
HF
HF
HF
HF
MUNCH
MUNCH

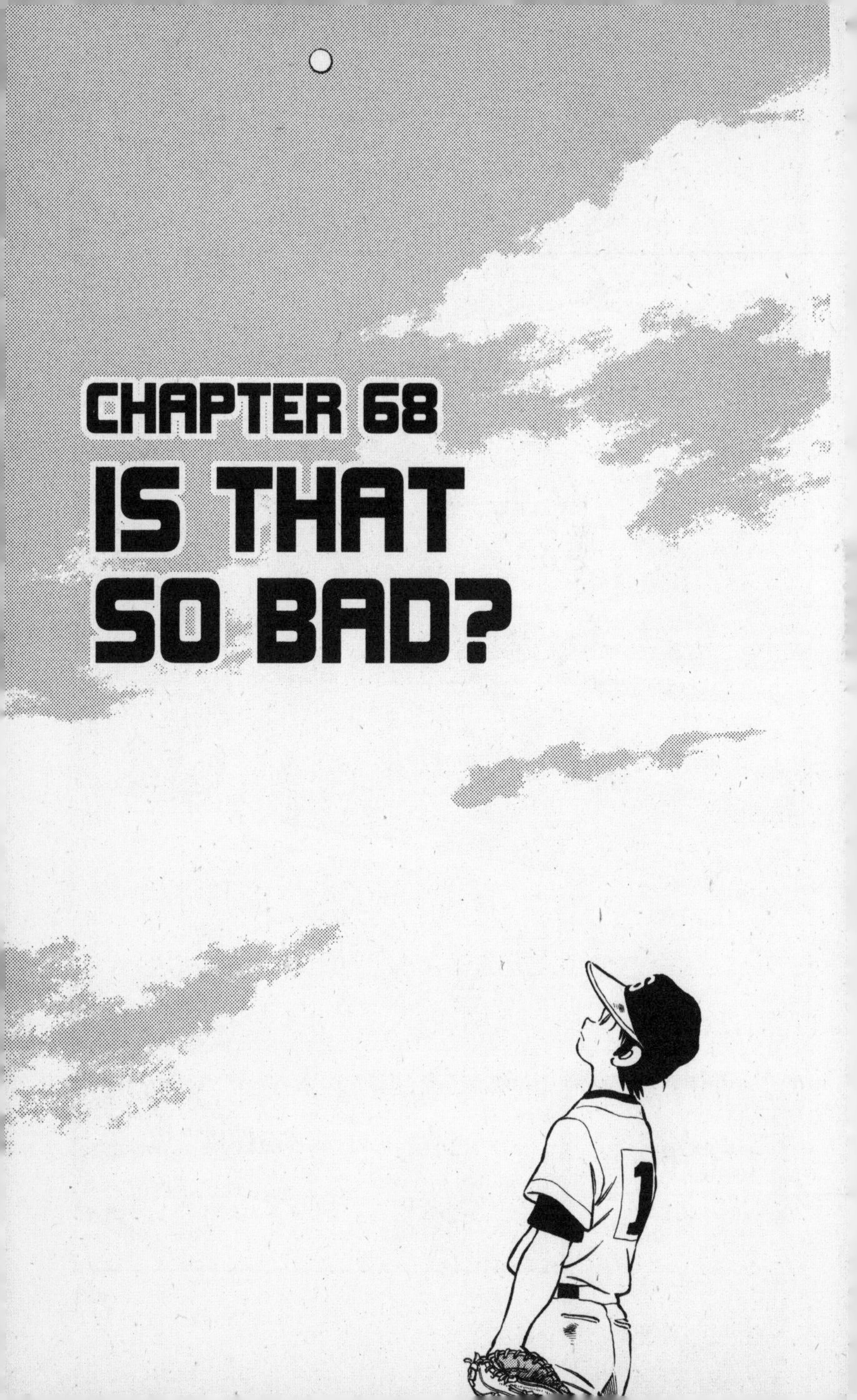
CHAPTER 68
IS THAT SO BAD?

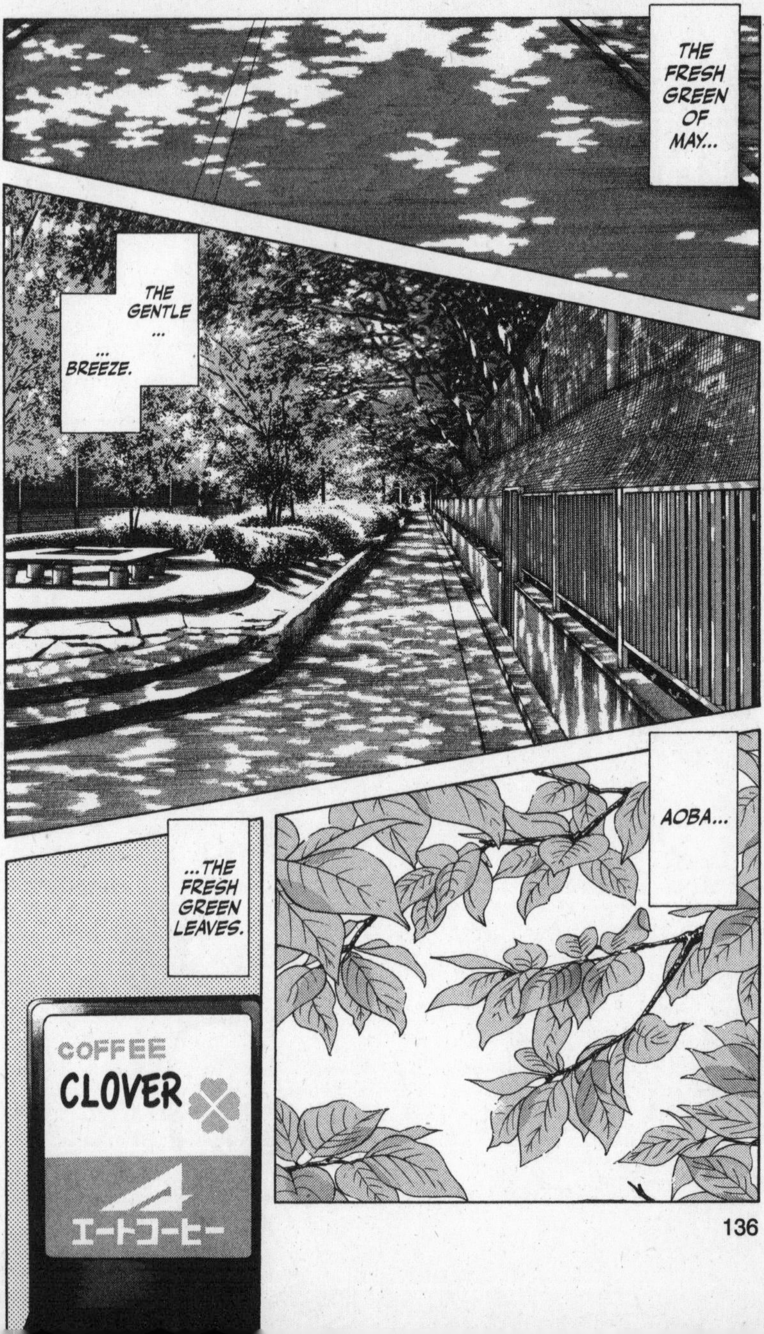
THE FRESH GREEN OF MAY...
THE GENTLE ... ... BREEZE.
AOBA...
...THE FRESH GREEN LEAVES.
COFFEE
CLOVER
エートコーヒー

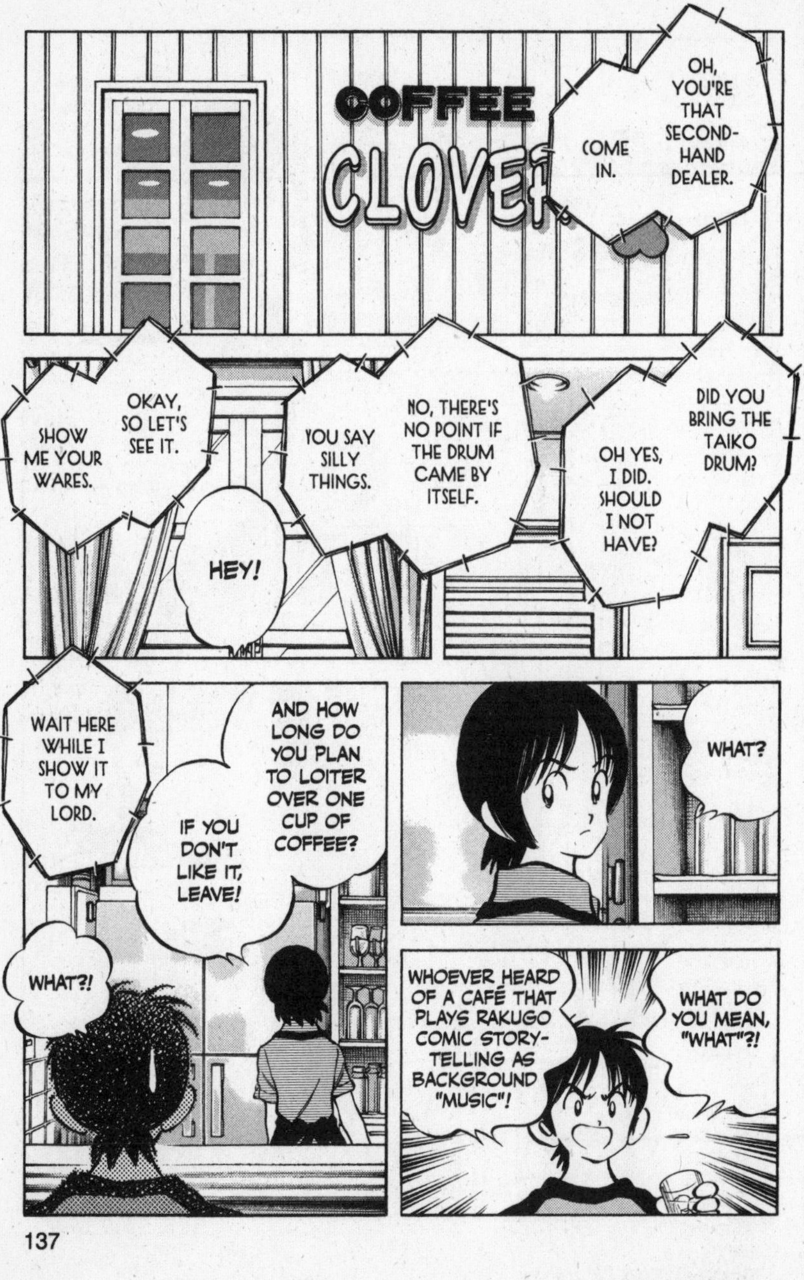
COFFEE
OH, YOU'RE THAT SECOND-HAND DEALER.
COME IN.
DID YOU BRING THE TAIKO DRUM?
OH YES, I DID. SHOULD I NOT HAVE?
NO, THERE'S NO POINT IF THE DRUM CAME BY ITSELF.
YOU SAY SILLY THINGS.
HEY!
OKAY, SO LET'S SEE IT.
SHOW ME YOUR WARES.
WHAT?
WHAT DO YOU MEAN, "WHAT"?!
WHOEVER HEARD OF A CAFÉ THAT PLAYS RAKUGO COMIC STORY-TELLING AS BACKGROUND "MUSIC"!
AND HOW LONG DO YOU PLAN TO LOITER OVER ONE CUP OF COFFEE?
IF YOU DON'T LIKE IT, LEAVE!
WAIT HERE WHILE I SHOW IT TO MY LORD.
WHAT?!

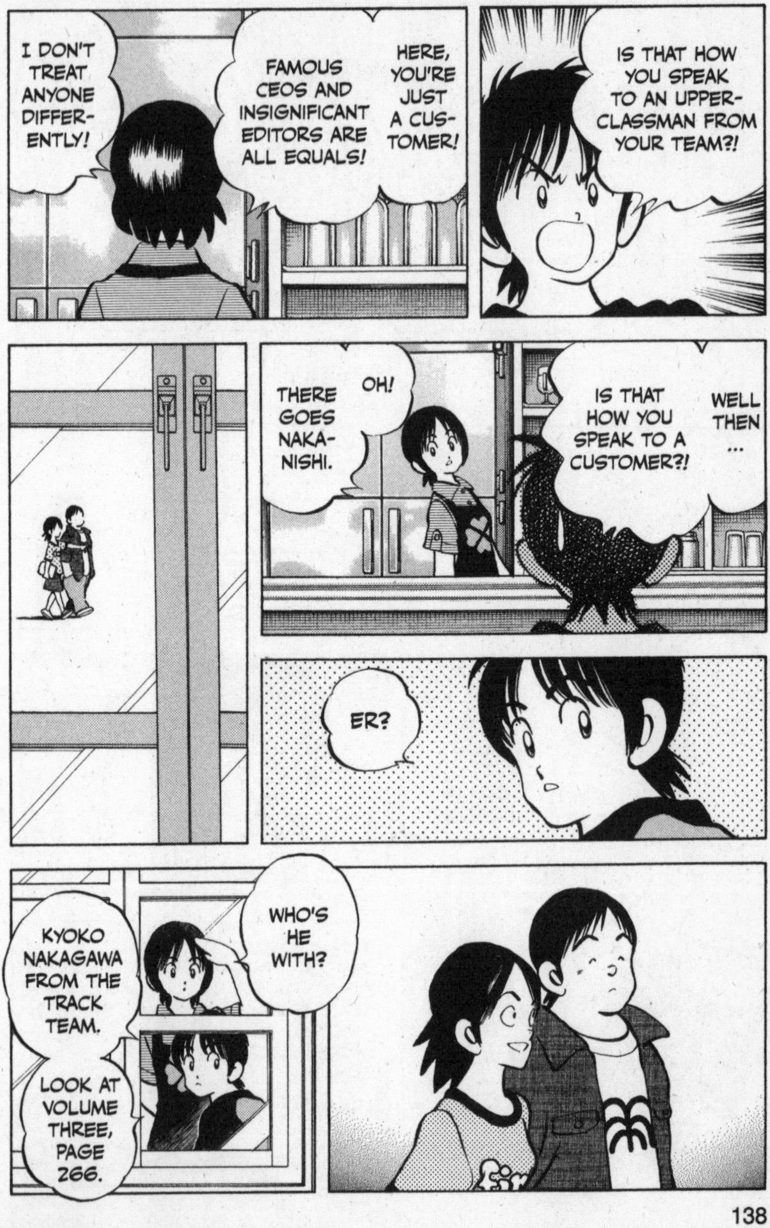
IS THAT HOW YOU SPEAK TO AN UPPER-CLASSMAN FROM YOUR TEAM?!
HERE, YOU'RE JUST A CUS-TOMER!
FAMOUS CEOS AND INSIGNIFICANT EDITORS ARE ALL EQUALS!
I DON'T TREAT ANYONE DIFFER-ENTLY!
WELL THEN ...
IS THAT HOW YOU SPEAK TO A CUSTOMER?!
OH!
THERE GOES NAKA-NISHI.
ER?
WHO'S HE WITH?
KYOKO NAKAGAWA FROM THE TRACK TEAM.
LOOK AT VOLUME THREE, PAGE 266.

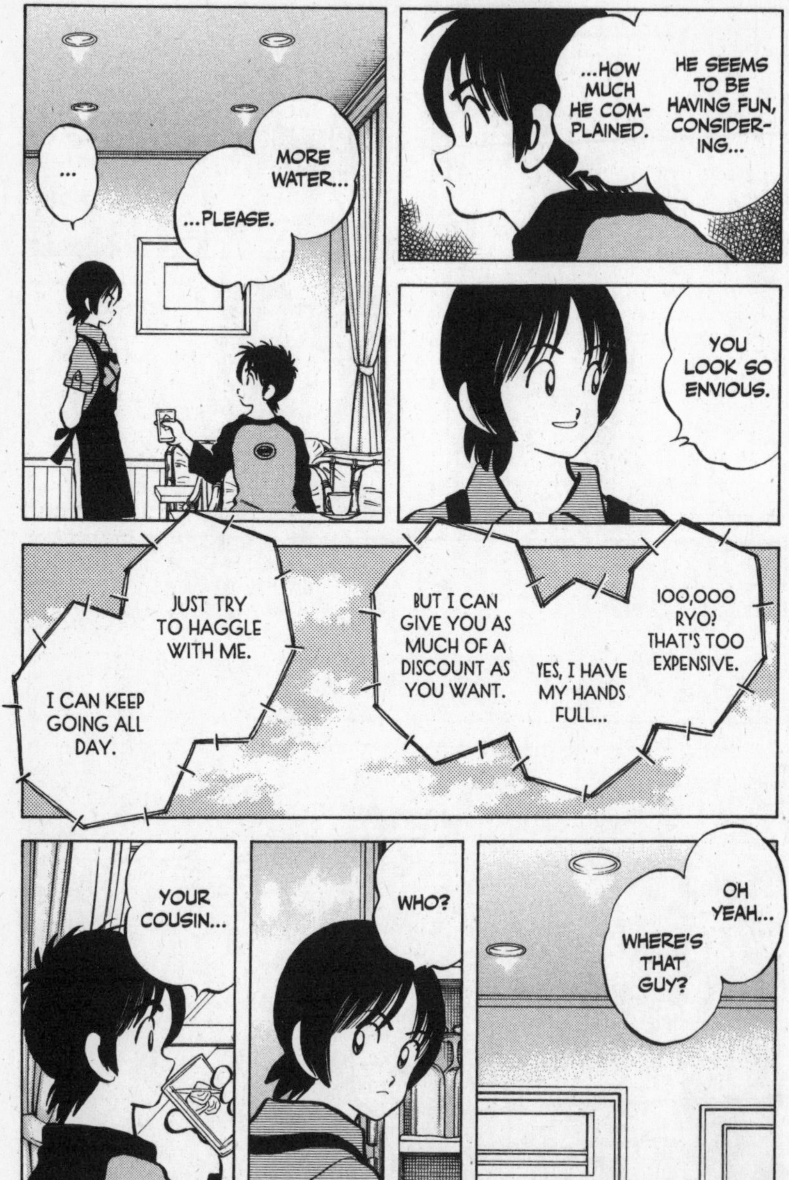
HE SEEMS TO BE HAVING FUN, CONSIDERING...
...HOW MUCH HE COMPLAINED.
YOU LOOK SO ENVIOUS.
MORE WATER...
...PLEASE.
...
100,000 RYO? THAT'S TOO EXPENSIVE.
YES, I HAVE MY HANDS FULL...
BUT I CAN GIVE YOU AS MUCH OF A DISCOUNT AS YOU WANT.
JUST TRY TO HAGGLE WITH ME.
I CAN KEEP GOING ALL DAY.
OH YEAH...
WHERE'S THAT GUY?
WHO?
YOUR COUSIN...

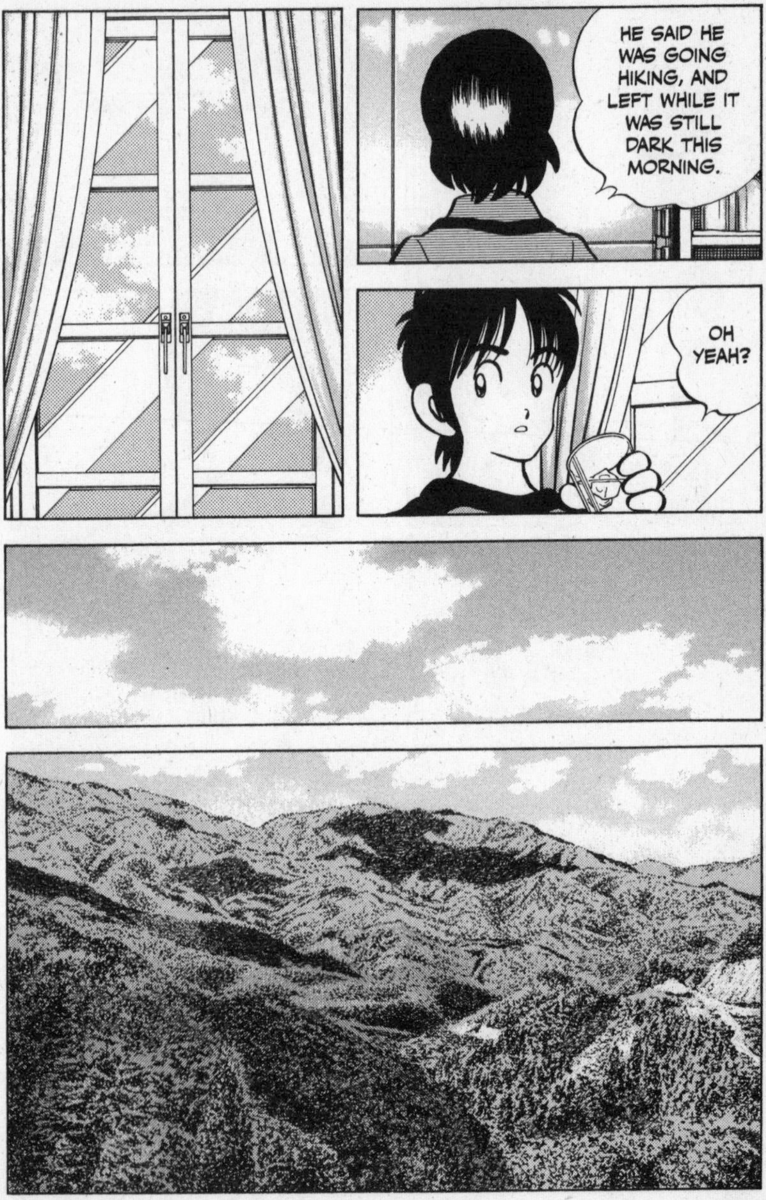
HE SAID HE WAS GOING HIKING, AND LEFT WHILE IT WAS STILL DARK THIS MORNING.
OH YEAH?

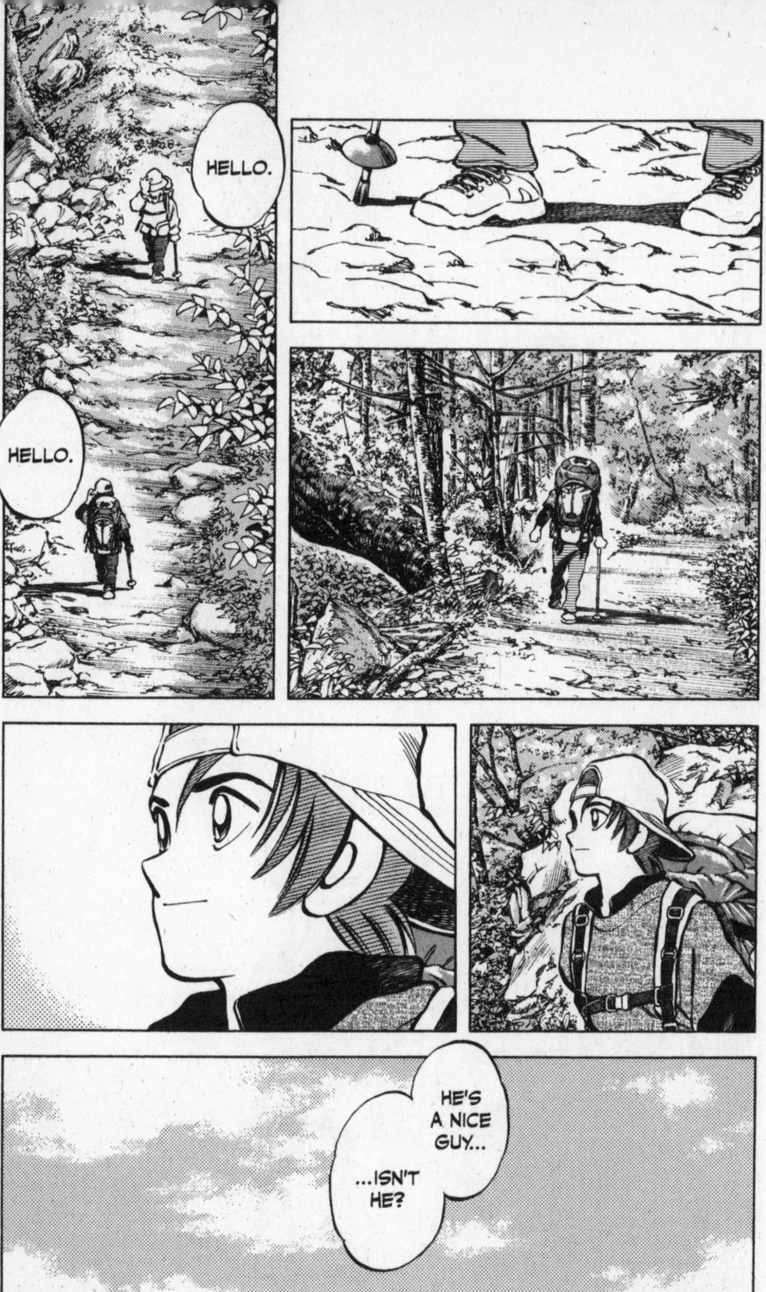
HELLO.
HELLO.
HE'S A NICE GUY...
...ISN'T HE?

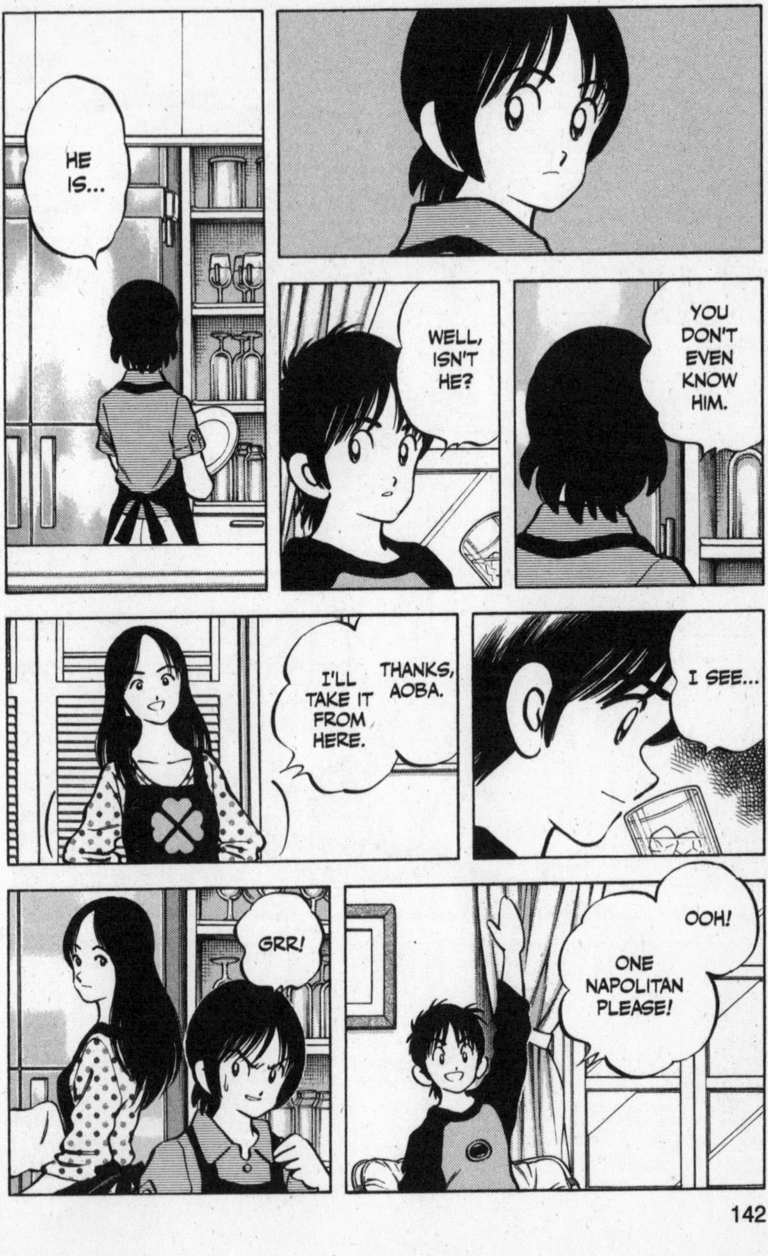
YOU DON'T EVEN KNOW HIM.
WELL, ISN'T HE?
HE IS...
I SEE...
THANKS, AOBA.
I'LL TAKE IT FROM HERE.
OOH!
ONE NAPOLITAN PLEASE!
GRR!

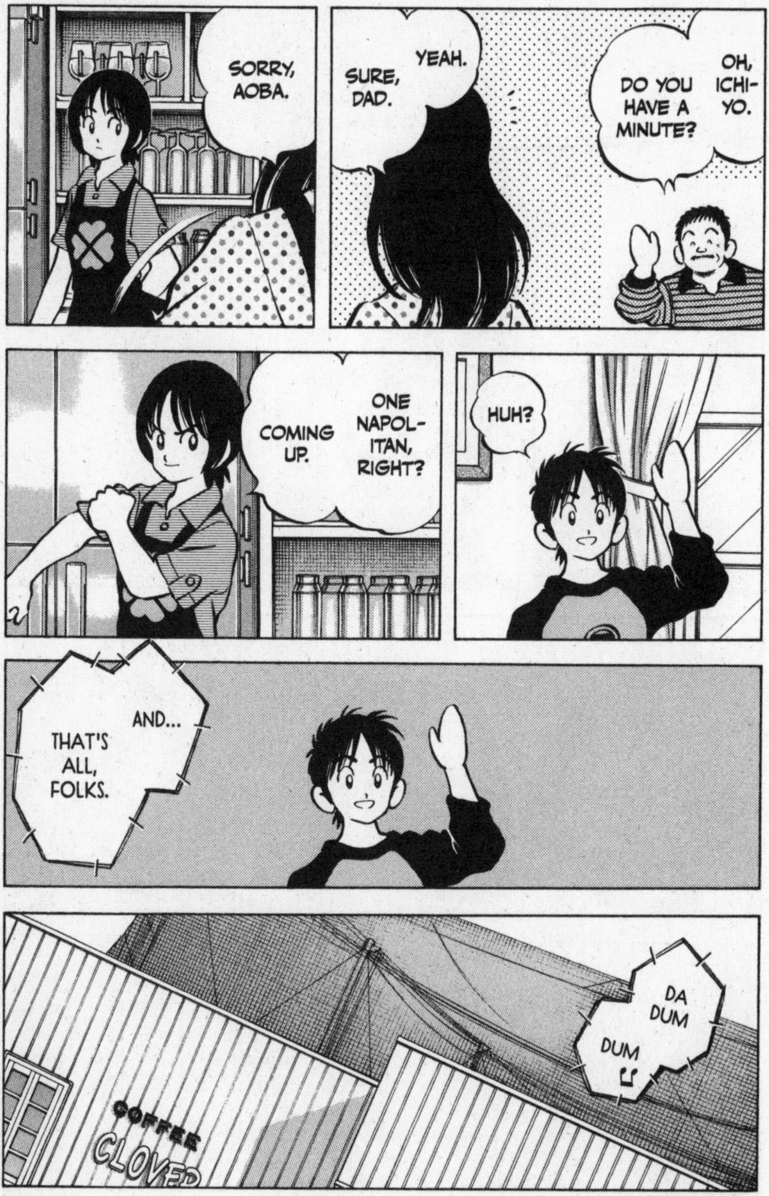
OH, ICHI-YO. DO YOU HAVE A MINUTE?
YEAH.
SURE, DAD.
SORRY, AOBA.
HUH?
ONE NAPOL-ITAN, RIGHT?
COMING UP.
AND...
THAT'S ALL, FOLKS.
DA DUM
DUM
COFFEE

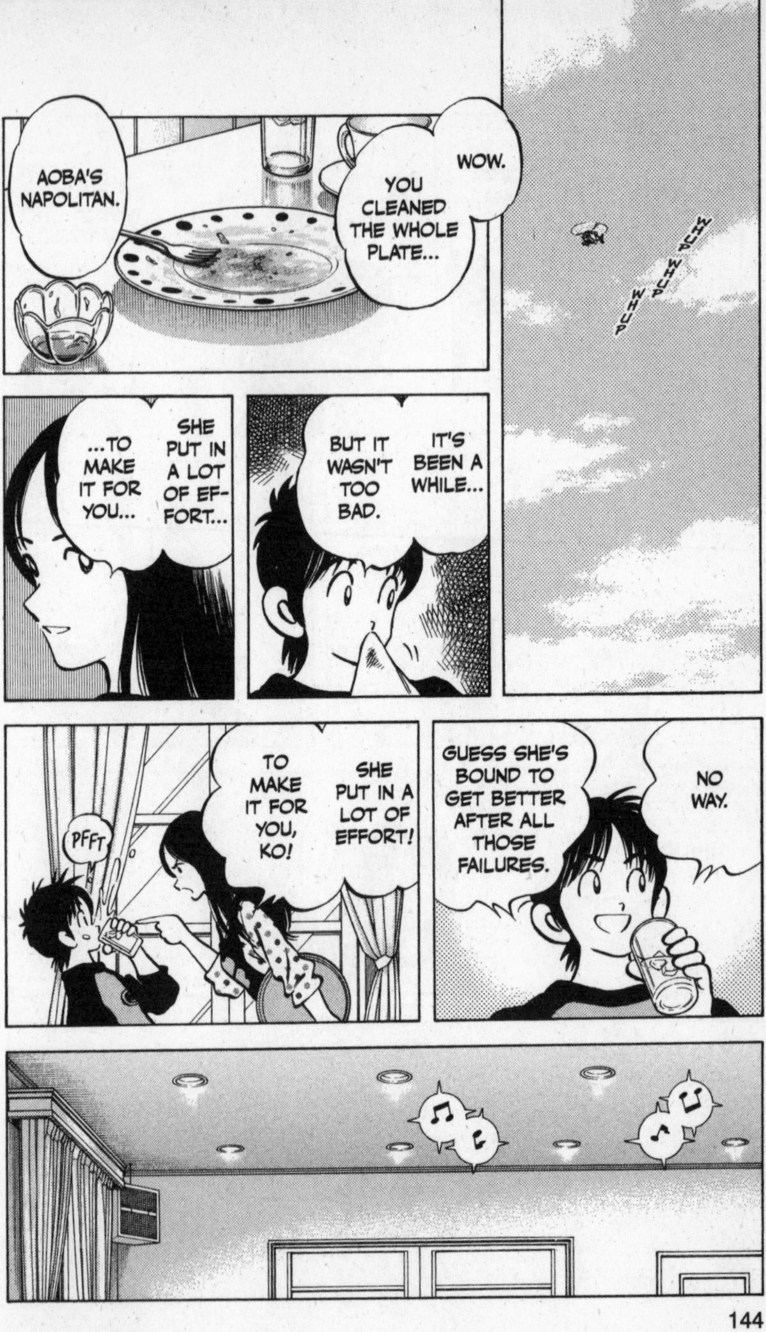
WHUP WHUP WHUP
WOW. YOU CLEANED THE WHOLE PLATE...
AOBA'S NAPOLITAN.
IT'S BEEN A WHILE... BUT IT WASN'T TOO BAD.
SHE PUT IN A LOT OF EF-FORT... ...TO MAKE IT FOR YOU...
NO WAY.
GUESS SHE'S BOUND TO GET BETTER AFTER ALL THOSE FAILURES.
SHE PUT IN A LOT OF EFFORT! TO MAKE IT FOR YOU, KO!
PFFT

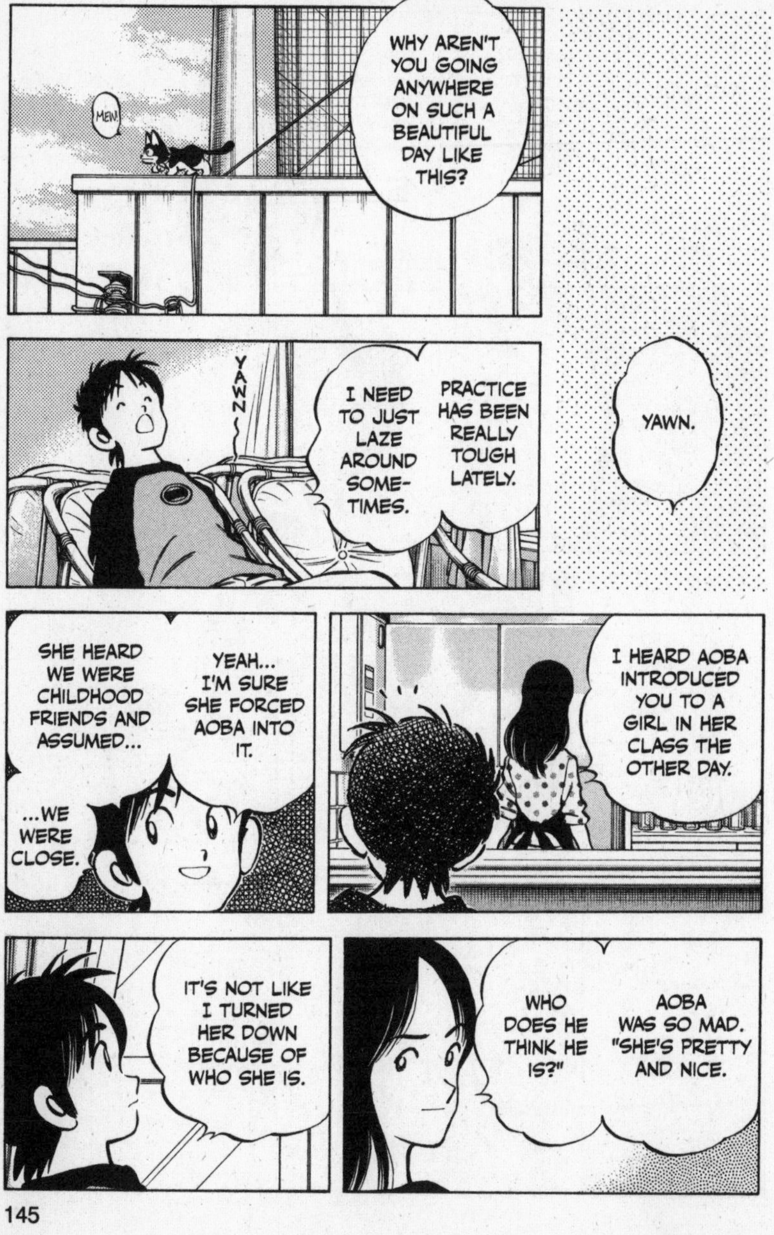
YAWN.
MEW!
WHY AREN'T YOU GOING ANYWHERE ON SUCH A BEAUTIFUL DAY LIKE THIS?
YAWN~
PRACTICE HAS BEEN REALLY TOUGH LATELY.
I NEED TO JUST LAZE AROUND SOME-TIMES.
I HEARD AOBA INTRODUCED YOU TO A GIRL IN HER CLASS THE OTHER DAY.
YEAH... I'M SURE SHE FORCED AOBA INTO IT.
SHE HEARD WE WERE CHILDHOOD FRIENDS AND ASSUMED...
...WE WERE CLOSE.
AOBA WAS SO MAD. "SHE'S PRETTY AND NICE.
WHO DOES HE THINK HE IS?"
IT'S NOT LIKE I TURNED HER DOWN BECAUSE OF WHO SHE IS.

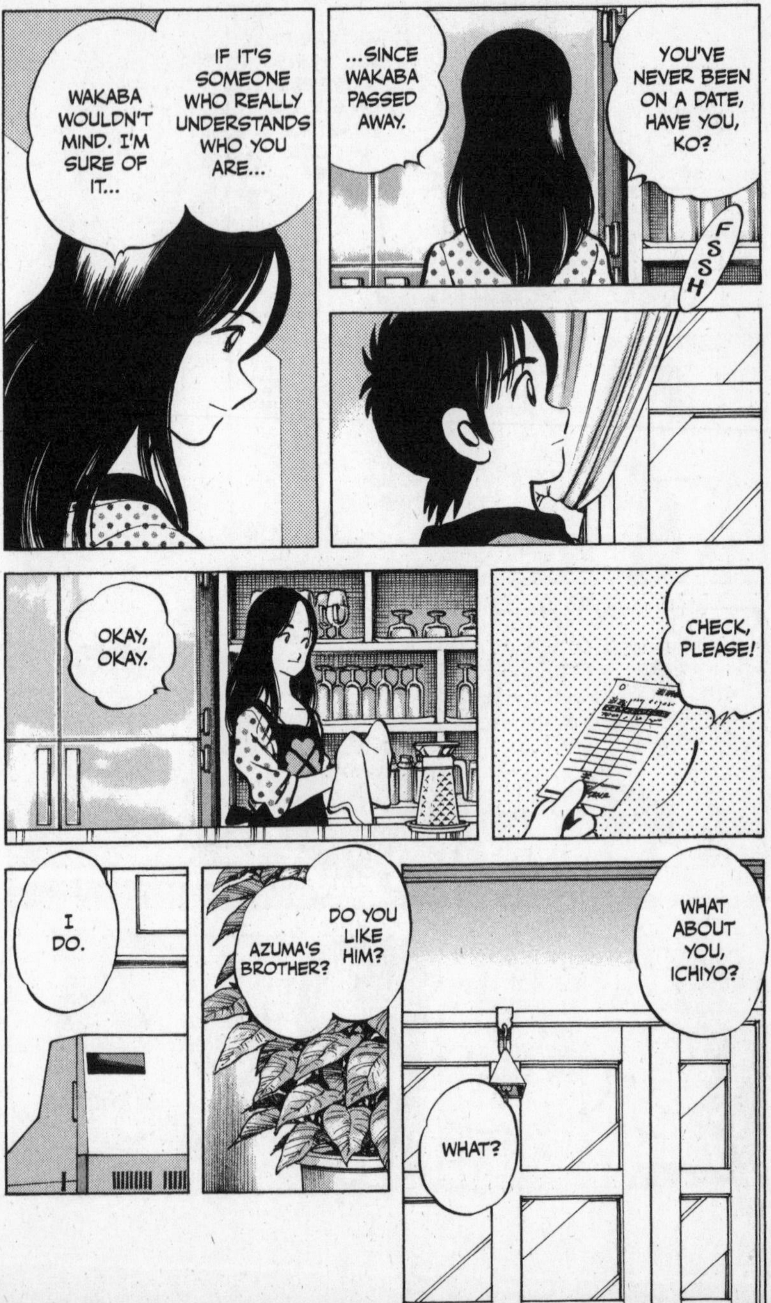
YOU'VE NEVER BEEN ON A DATE, HAVE YOU, KO?
...SINCE WAKABA PASSED AWAY.
FSSH
IF IT'S SOMEONE WHO REALLY UNDERSTANDS WHO YOU ARE...
WAKABA WOULDN'T MIND. I'M SURE OF IT...
CHECK, PLEASE!
OKAY, OKAY.
WHAT ABOUT YOU, ICHIYO?
WHAT?
DO YOU LIKE HIM?
AZUMA'S BROTHER?
I DO.

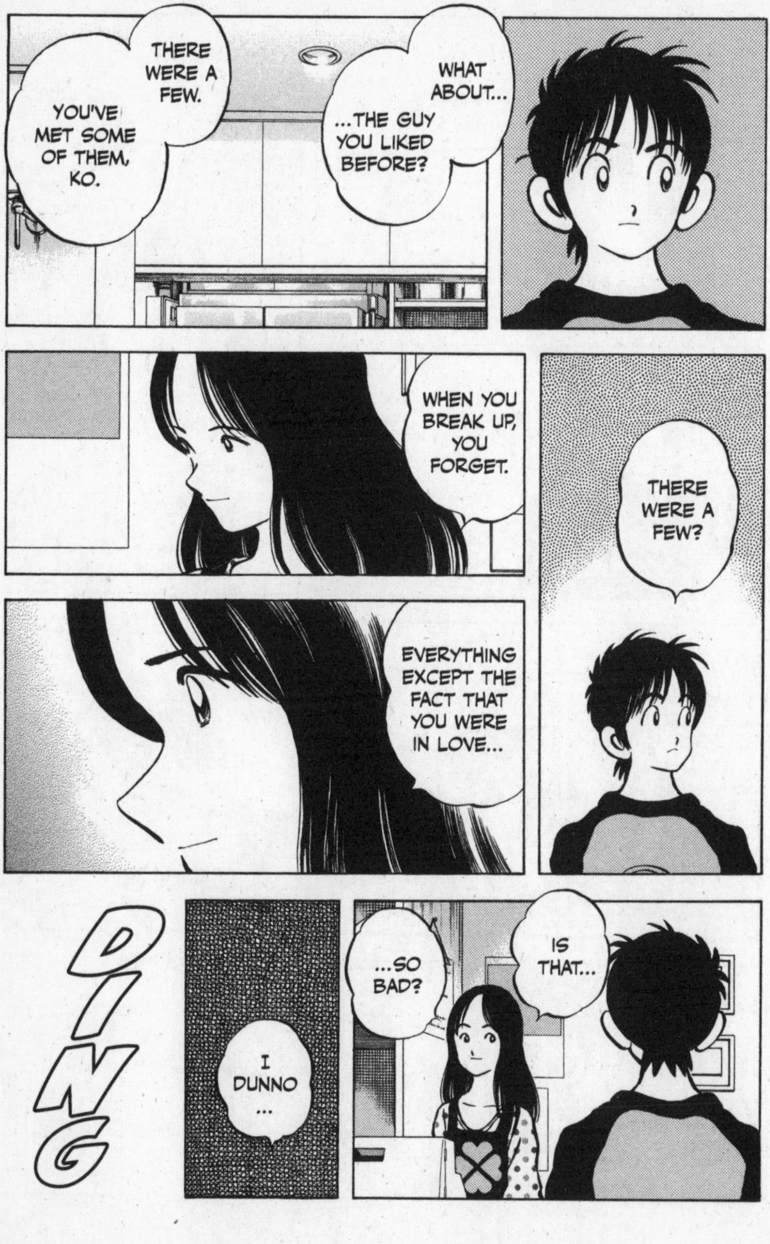
WHAT ABOUT...
...THE GUY YOU LIKED BEFORE?
THERE WERE A FEW.
YOU'VE MET SOME OF THEM, KO.
THERE WERE A FEW?
WHEN YOU BREAK UP, YOU FORGET.
EVERYTHING EXCEPT THE FACT THAT YOU WERE IN LOVE...
IS THAT...
...SO BAD?
I DUNNO ...
DING

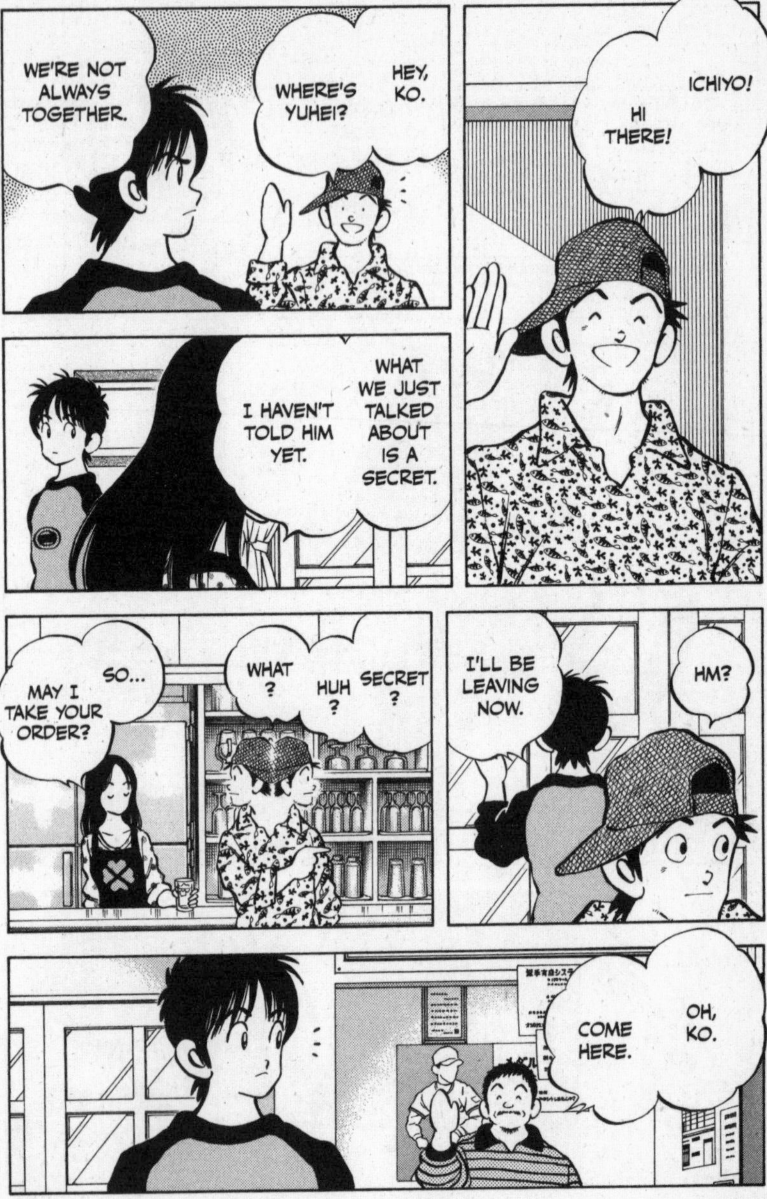
ICHIYO! HI THERE!
HEY, KO. WHERE'S YUHEI?
WE'RE NOT ALWAYS TOGETHER.
WHAT WE JUST TALKED ABOUT IS A SECRET. I HAVEN'T TOLD HIM YET.
HM?
I'LL BE LEAVING NOW.
SECRET? HUH? WHAT?
SO... MAY I TAKE YOUR ORDER?
OH, KO. COME HERE.

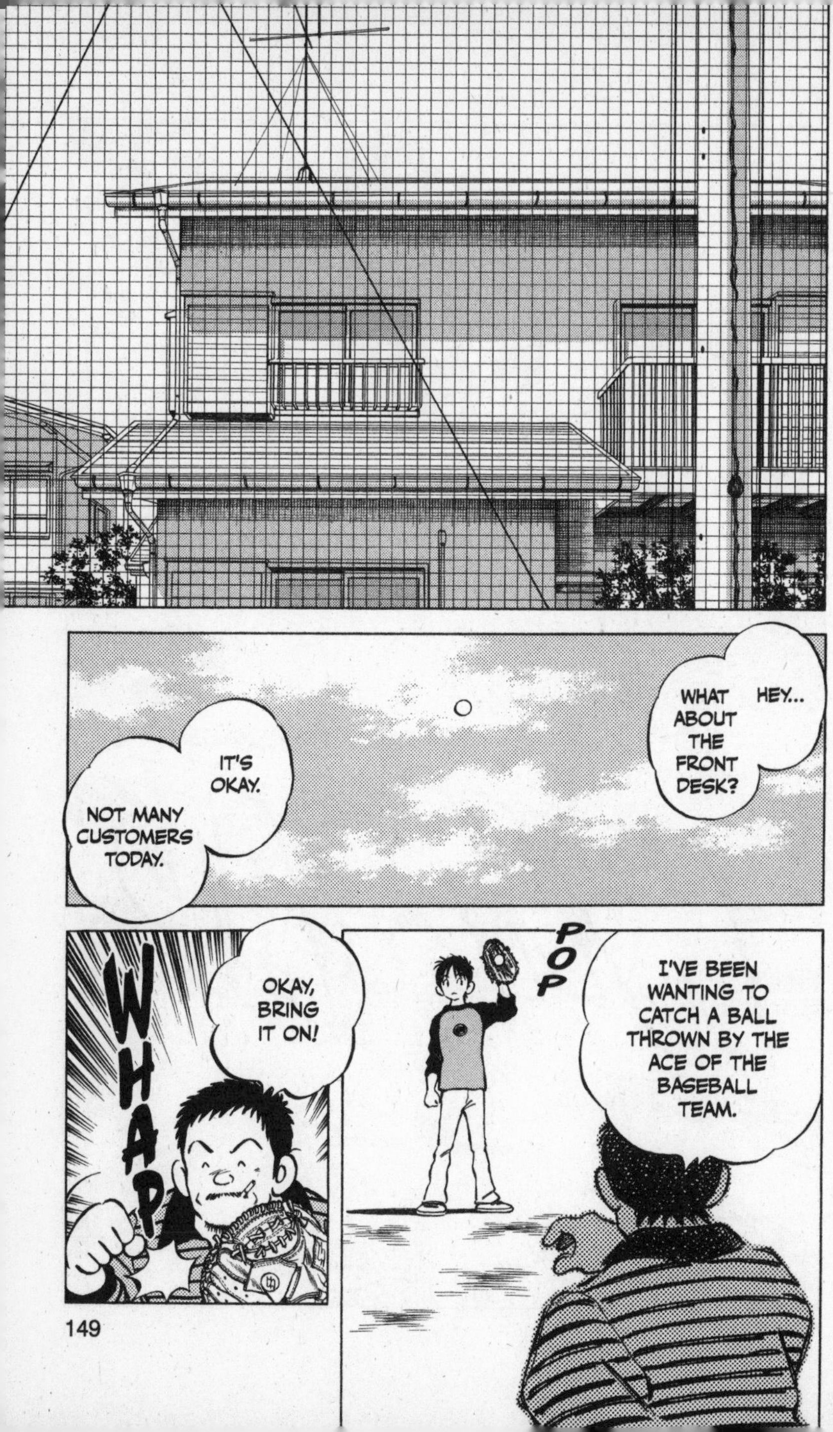
HEY...
WHAT ABOUT THE FRONT DESK?
IT'S OKAY.
NOT MANY CUSTOMERS TODAY.
POP
I'VE BEEN WANTING TO CATCH A BALL THROWN BY THE ACE OF THE BASEBALL TEAM.
OKAY, BRING IT ON!
WHAP

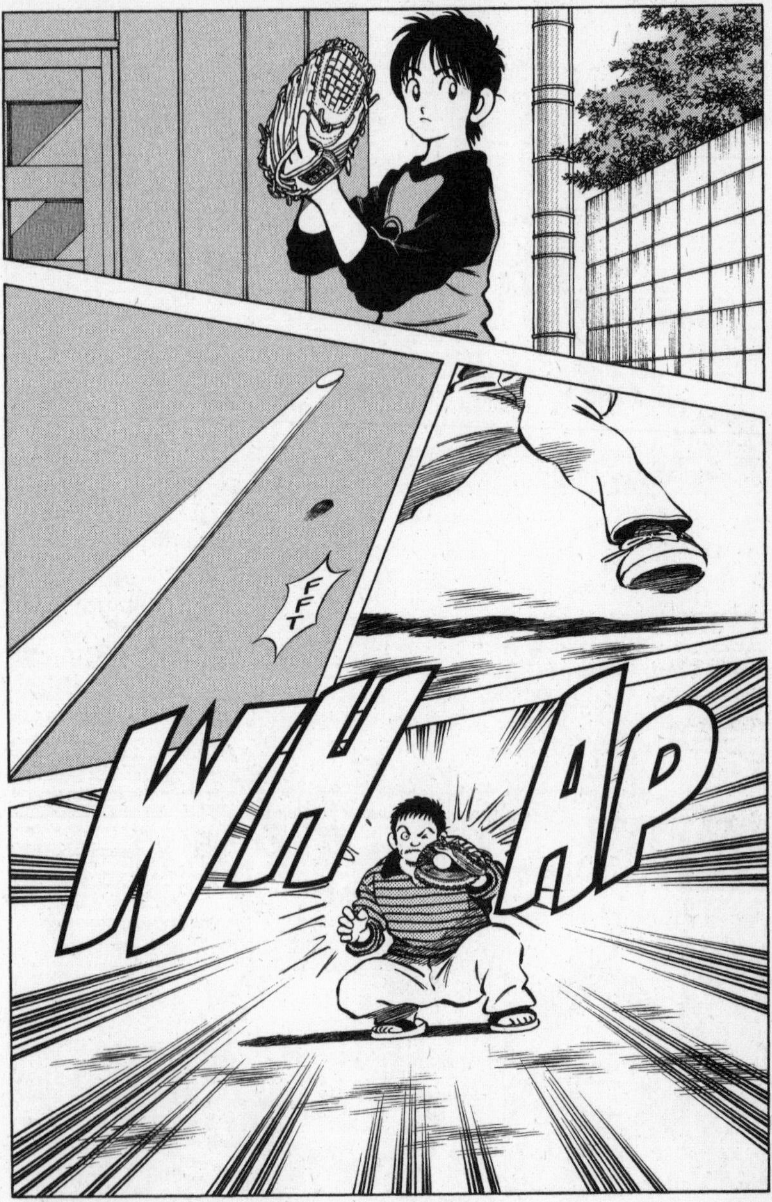
FFT
WHAP

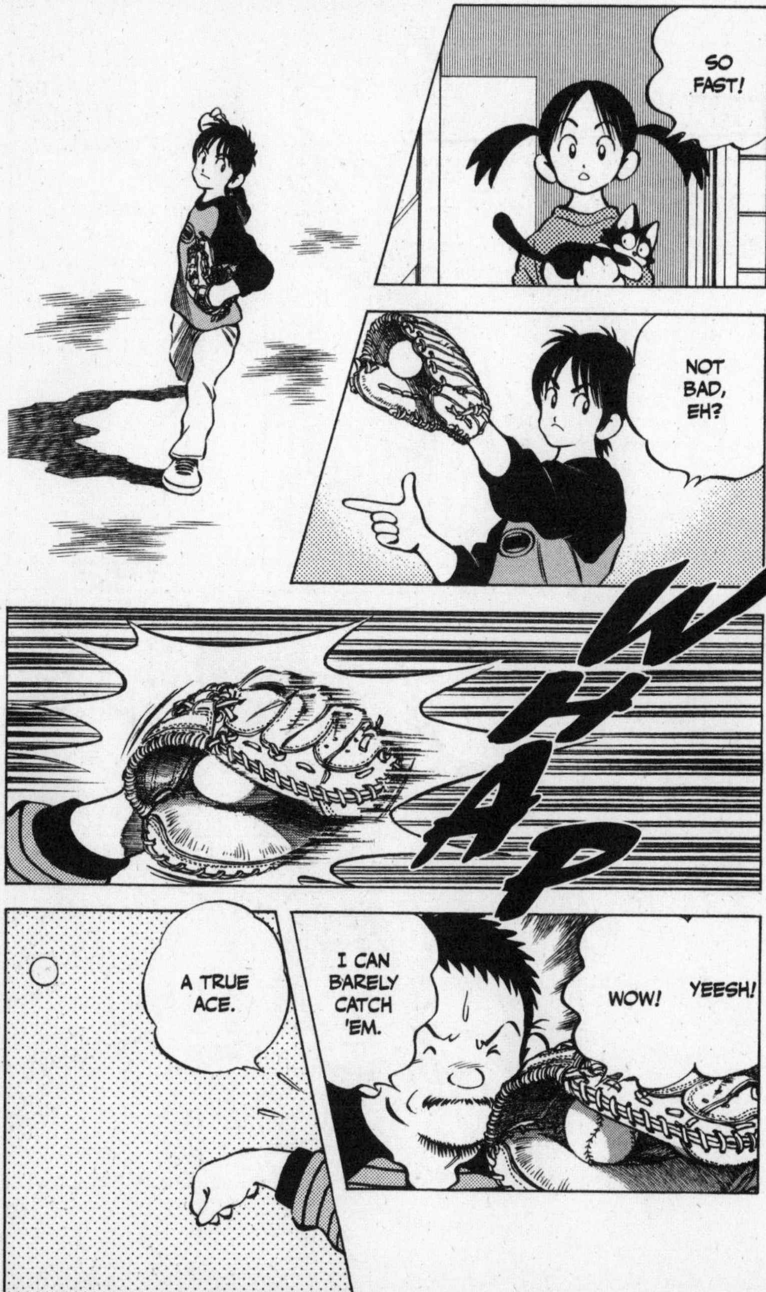
SO FAST!
NOT BAD, EH?
WHAP
WOW! YEESH!
I CAN BARELY CATCH 'EM.
A TRUE ACE.

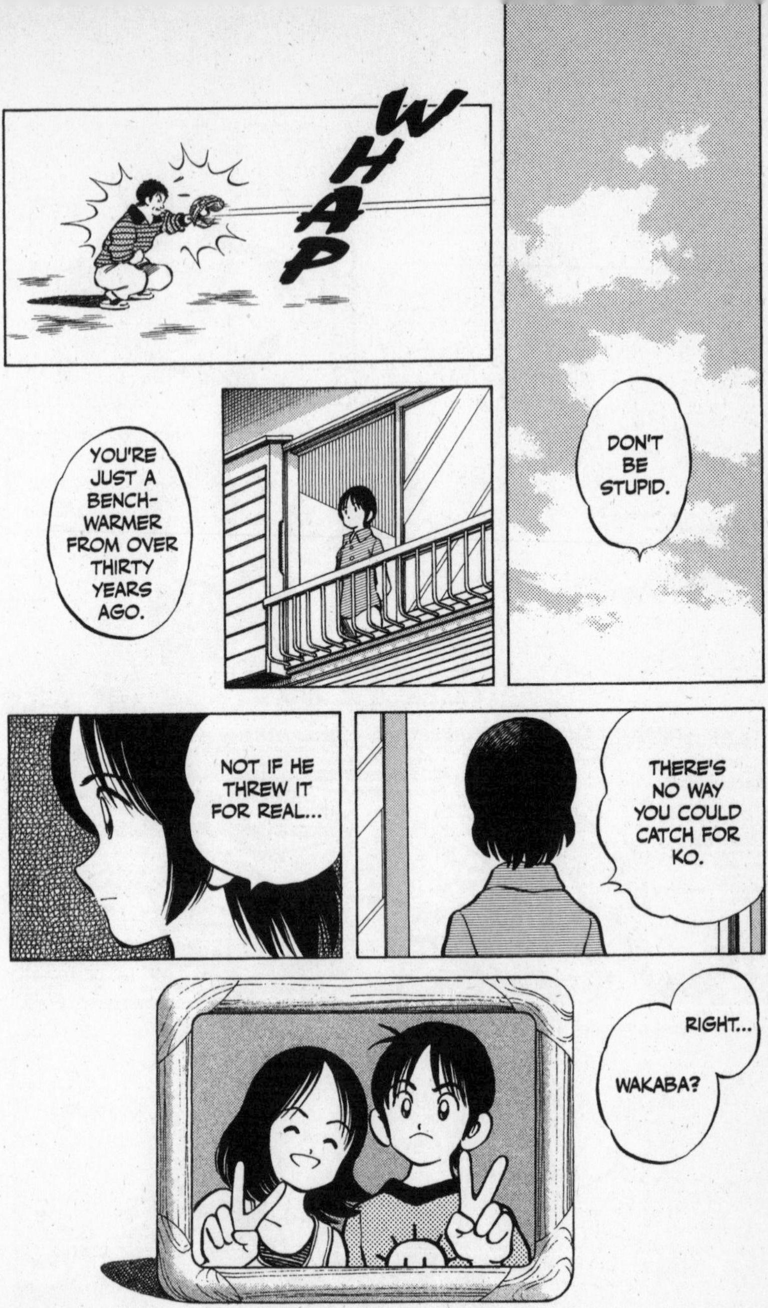
DON'T BE STUPID.
WHAP
YOU'RE JUST A BENCH-WARMER FROM OVER THIRTY YEARS AGO.
THERE'S NO WAY YOU COULD CATCH FOR KO.
NOT IF HE THREW IT FOR REAL...
RIGHT...
WAKABA?

# CHAPTER 69
# WHO'S THAT GUY AGAIN?

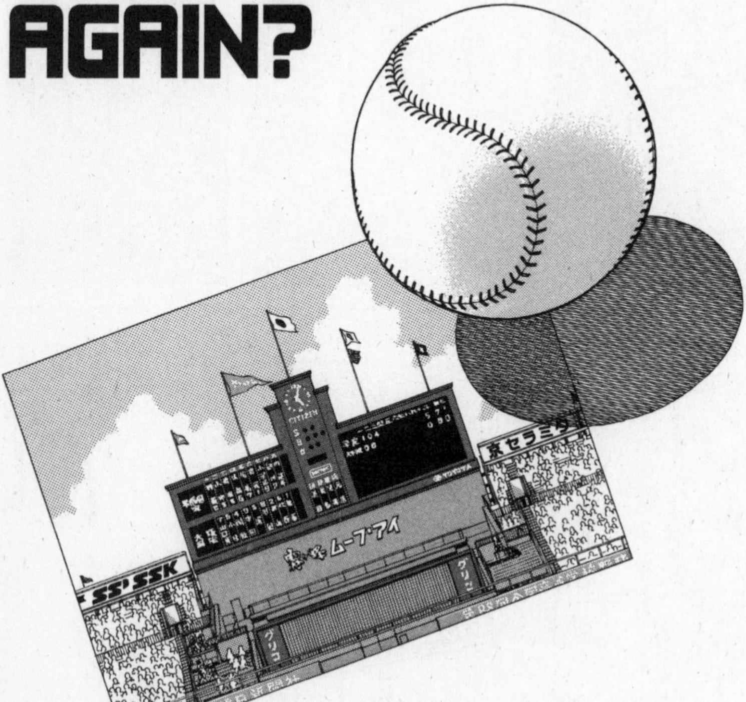
京セラミタ
SS' SSK
グリコ

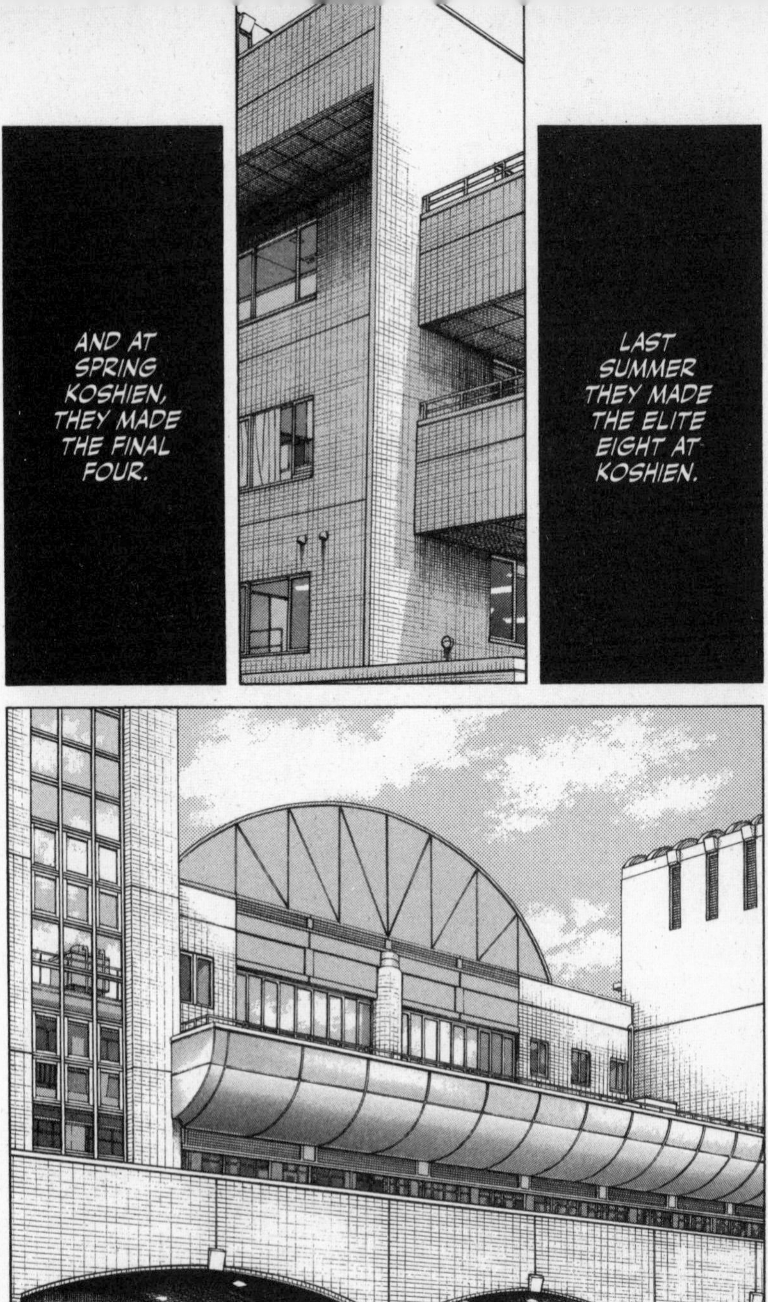
LAST SUMMER THEY MADE THE ELITE EIGHT AT KOSHIEN.
AND AT SPRING KOSHIEN, THEY MADE THE FINAL FOUR.

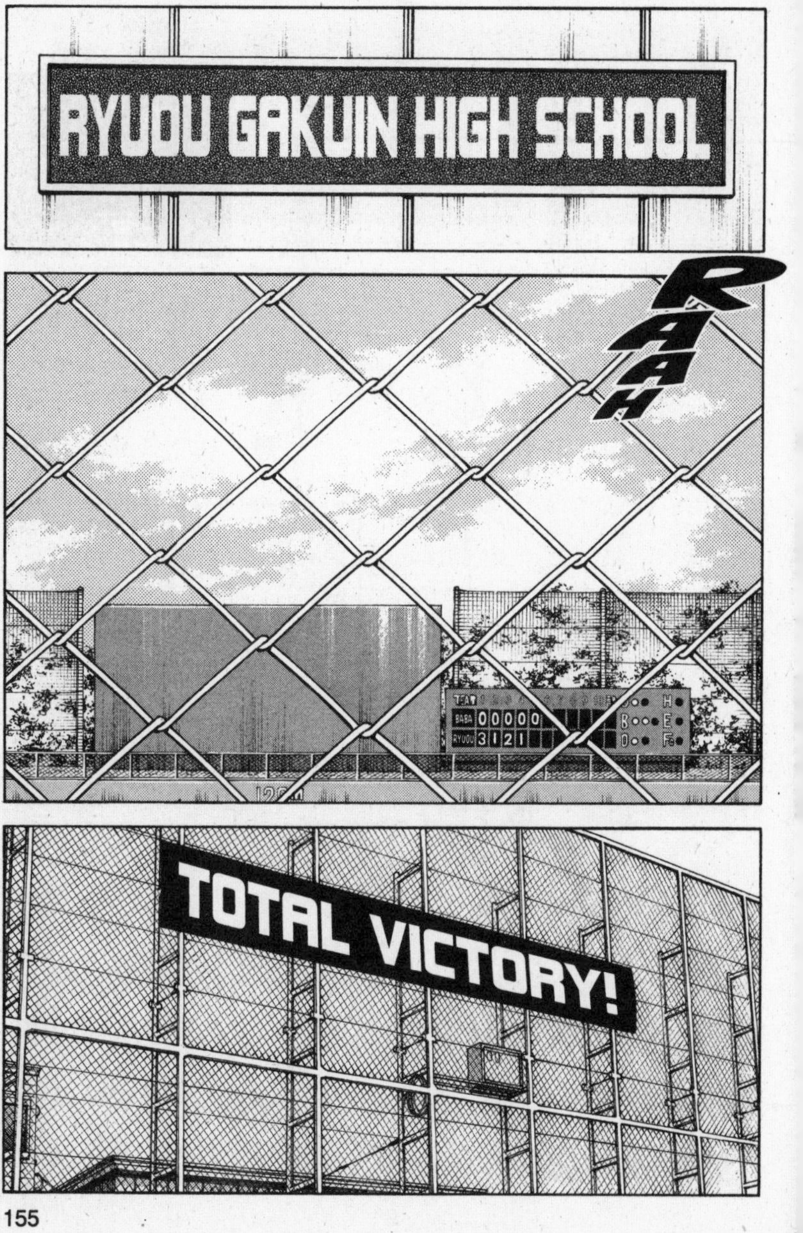
RYUOU GAKUIN HIGH SCHOOL
RAAAH
TOTAL VICTORY!

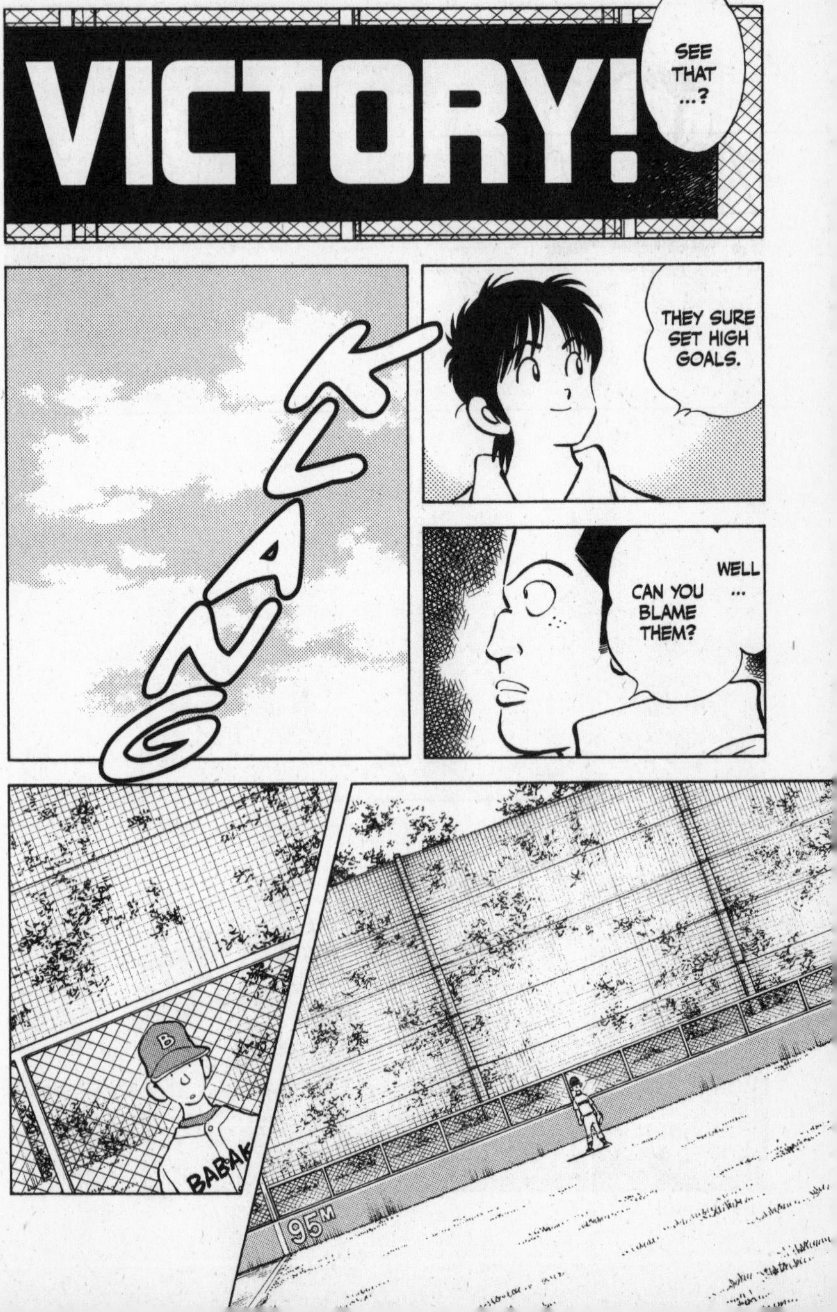

SEE THAT ...?
VICTORY!
THEY SURE SET HIGH GOALS.
WELL ...
CAN YOU BLAME THEM?
KLANG
95M
BABAK

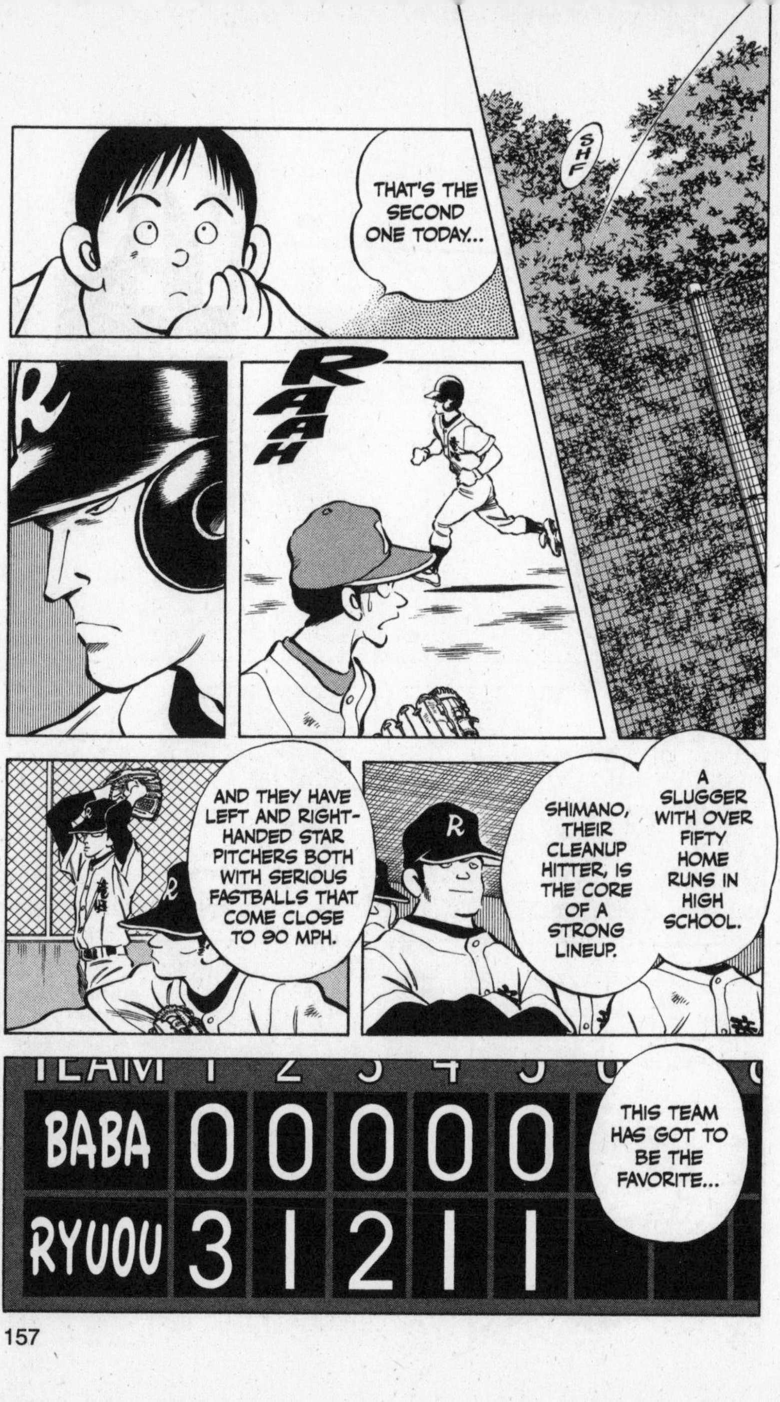
SHF
THAT'S THE SECOND ONE TODAY...
RAAH
A SLUGGER WITH OVER FIFTY HOME RUNS IN HIGH SCHOOL.
SHIMANO, THEIR CLEANUP HITTER, IS THE CORE OF A STRONG LINEUP.
AND THEY HAVE LEFT AND RIGHT-HANDED STAR PITCHERS BOTH WITH SERIOUS FASTBALLS THAT COME CLOSE TO 90 MPH.
TEAM 1 2 3 4 5
BABA 0 0 0 0 0
RYUOU 3 1 2 1 1
THIS TEAM HAS GOT TO BE THE FAVORITE...

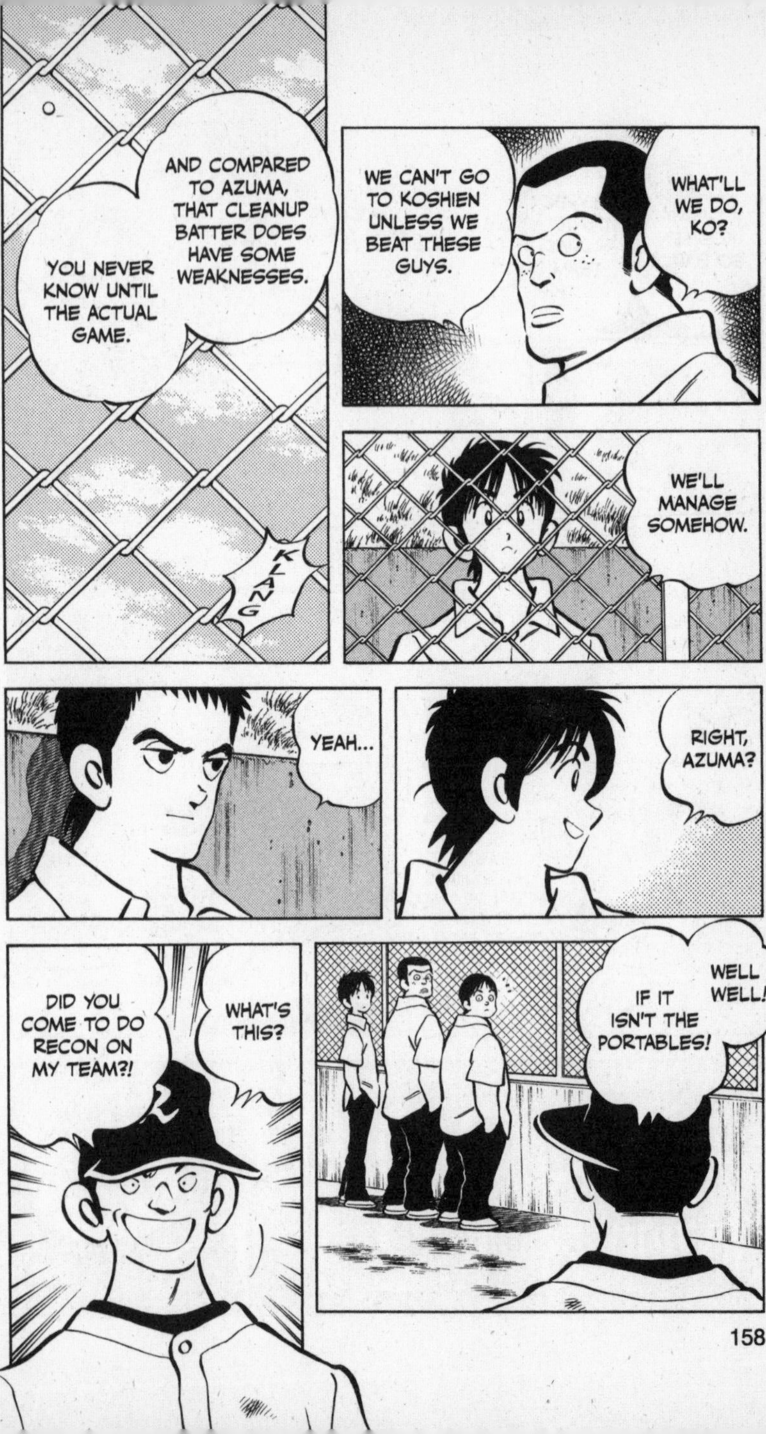
WHAT'LL WE DO, KO?
WE CAN'T GO TO KOSHIEN UNLESS WE BEAT THESE GUYS.
WE'LL MANAGE SOMEHOW.
AND COMPARED TO AZUMA, THAT CLEANUP BATTER DOES HAVE SOME WEAKNESSES.
YOU NEVER KNOW UNTIL THE ACTUAL GAME.
KLANG
RIGHT, AZUMA?
YEAH...
WELL WELL!
IF IT ISN'T THE PORTABLES!
WHAT'S THIS?
DID YOU COME TO DO RECON ON MY TEAM?!

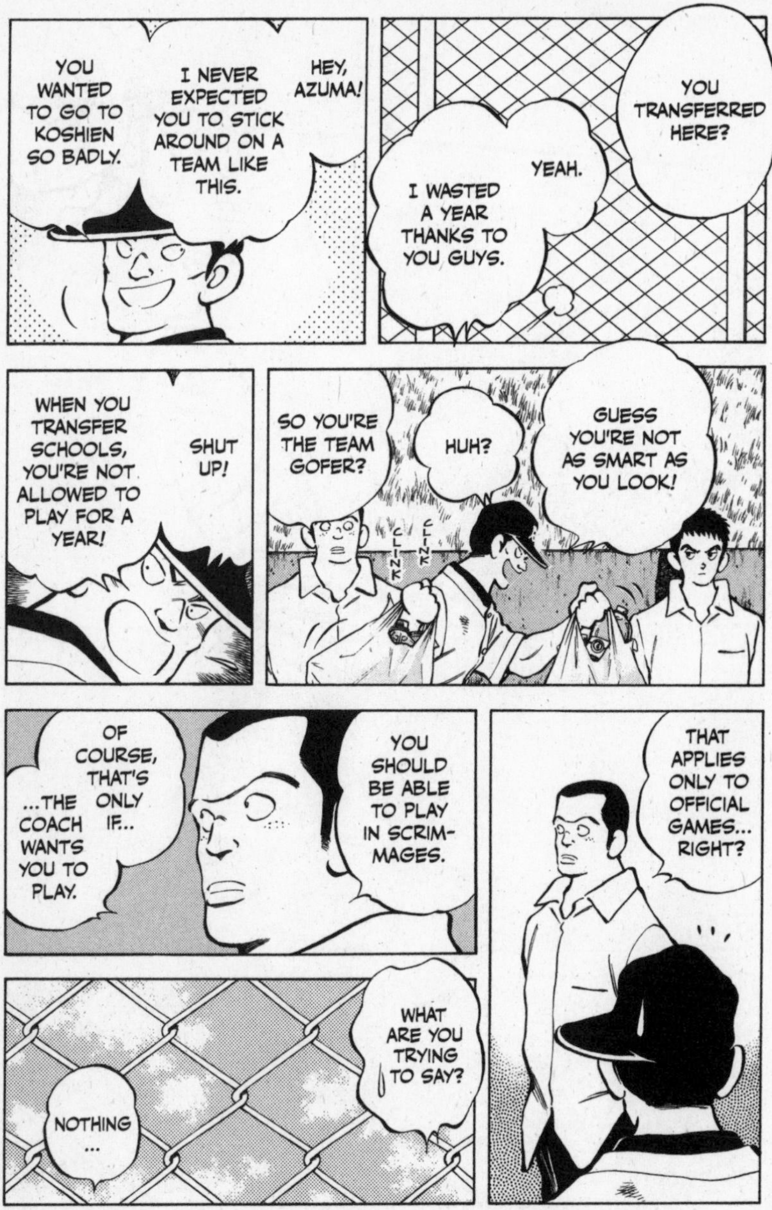
YOU TRANSFERRED HERE?
YEAH.
I WASTED A YEAR THANKS TO YOU GUYS.
HEY, AZUMA!
I NEVER EXPECTED YOU TO STICK AROUND ON A TEAM LIKE THIS.
YOU WANTED TO GO TO KOSHIEN SO BADLY.
GUESS YOU'RE NOT AS SMART AS YOU LOOK!
HUH?
SO YOU'RE THE TEAM GOFER?
CLINK
CLINK
SHUT UP!
WHEN YOU TRANSFER SCHOOLS, YOU'RE NOT ALLOWED TO PLAY FOR A YEAR!
THAT APPLIES ONLY TO OFFICIAL GAMES... RIGHT?
YOU SHOULD BE ABLE TO PLAY IN SCRIM-MAGES.
OF COURSE, THAT'S ONLY IF...
...THE COACH WANTS YOU TO PLAY.
WHAT ARE YOU TRYING TO SAY?
NOTHING ...

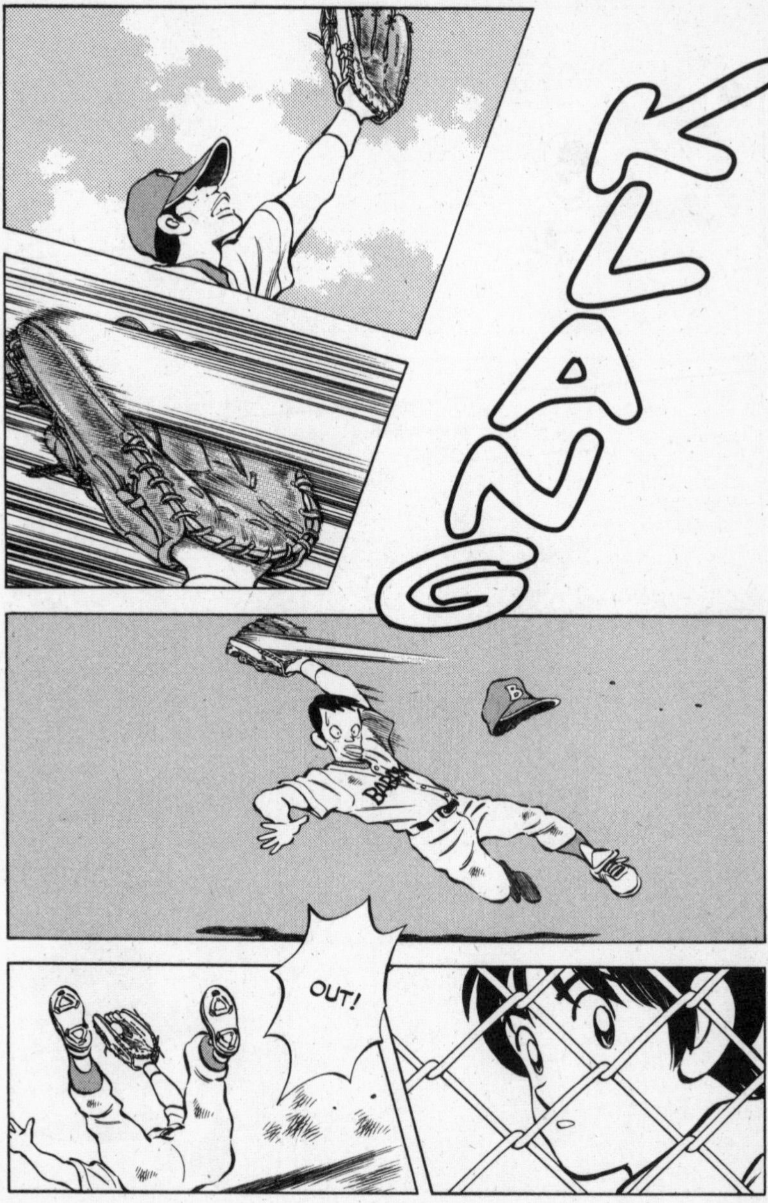
KLANG
OUT!

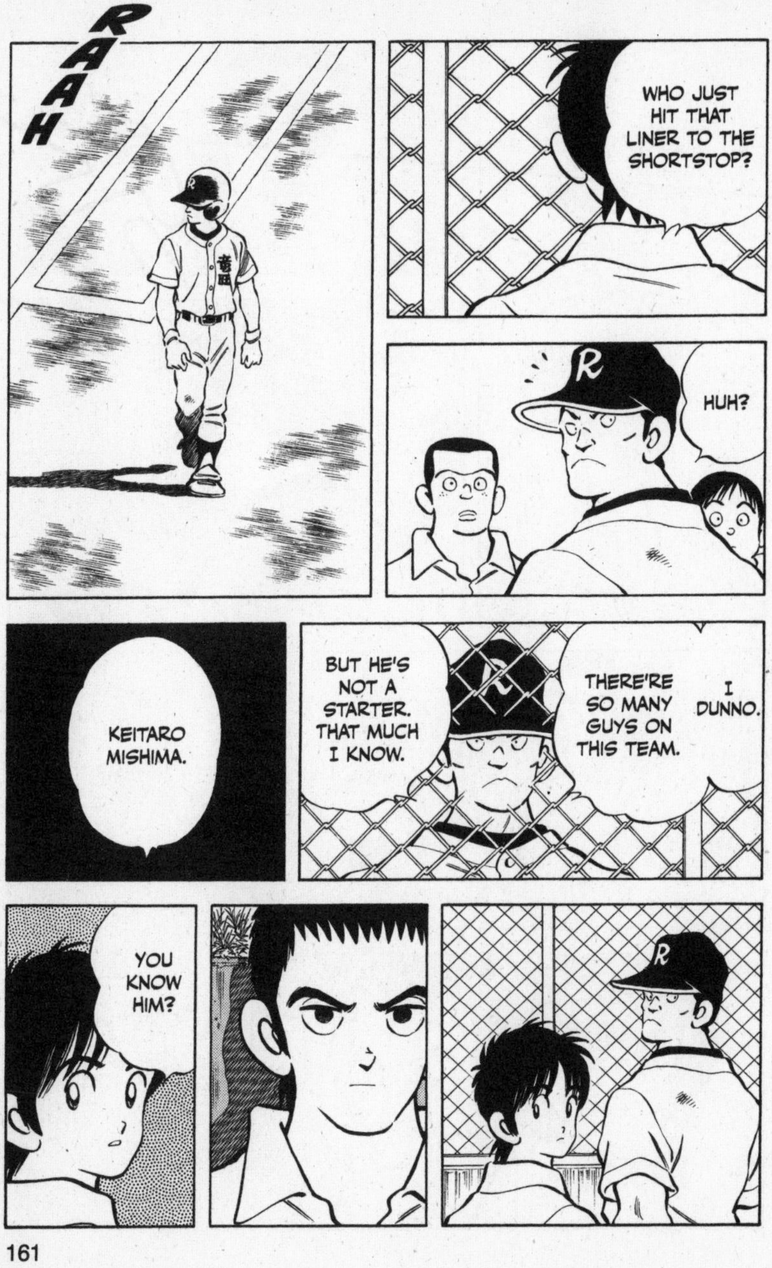
WHO JUST HIT THAT LINER TO THE SHORTSTOP?
HUH?
RAAAH
I DUNNO.
THERE'RE SO MANY GUYS ON THIS TEAM.
BUT HE'S NOT A STARTER. THAT MUCH I KNOW.
KEITARO MISHIMA.
YOU KNOW HIM?

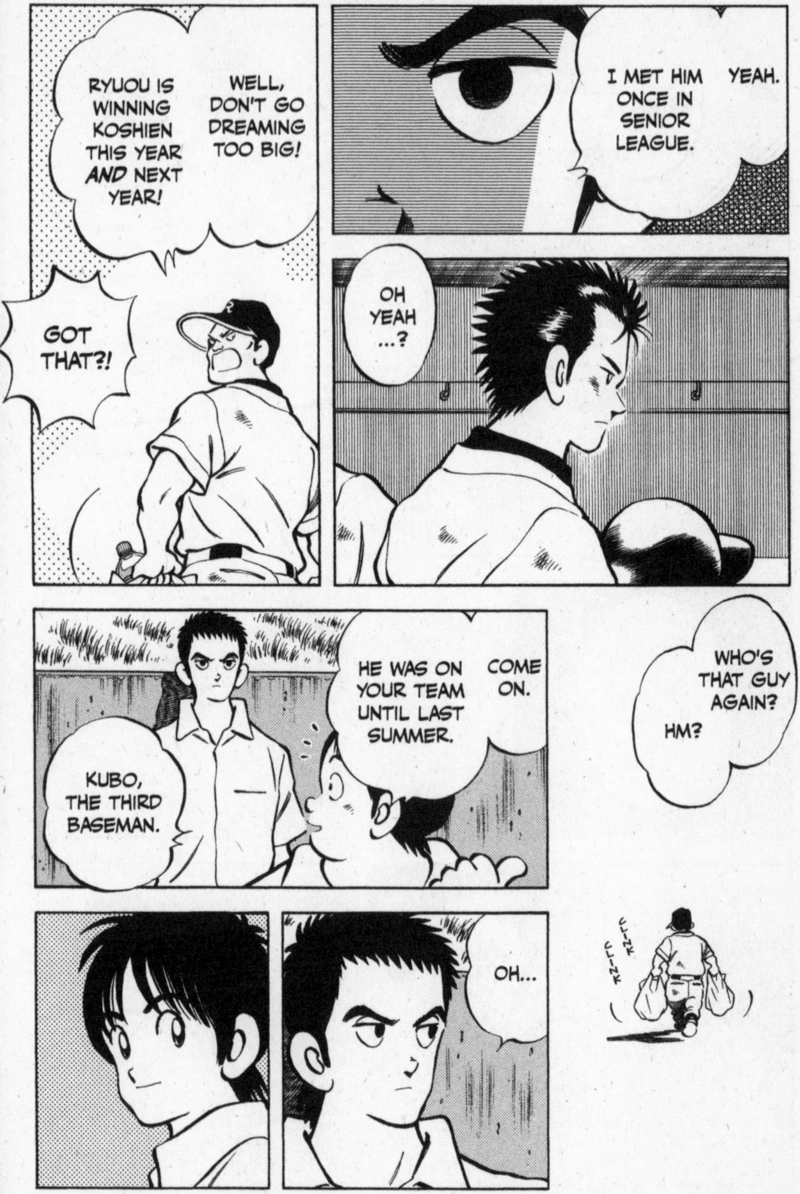
YEAH.
I MET HIM ONCE IN SENIOR LEAGUE.
OH YEAH ...?
WELL, DON'T GO DREAMING TOO BIG!
RYUOU IS WINNING KOSHIEN THIS YEAR *AND* NEXT YEAR!
GOT THAT?!
WHO'S THAT GUY AGAIN?
HM?
COME ON.
HE WAS ON YOUR TEAM UNTIL LAST SUMMER.
KUBO, THE THIRD BASEMAN.
CLINK
CLINK
OH...

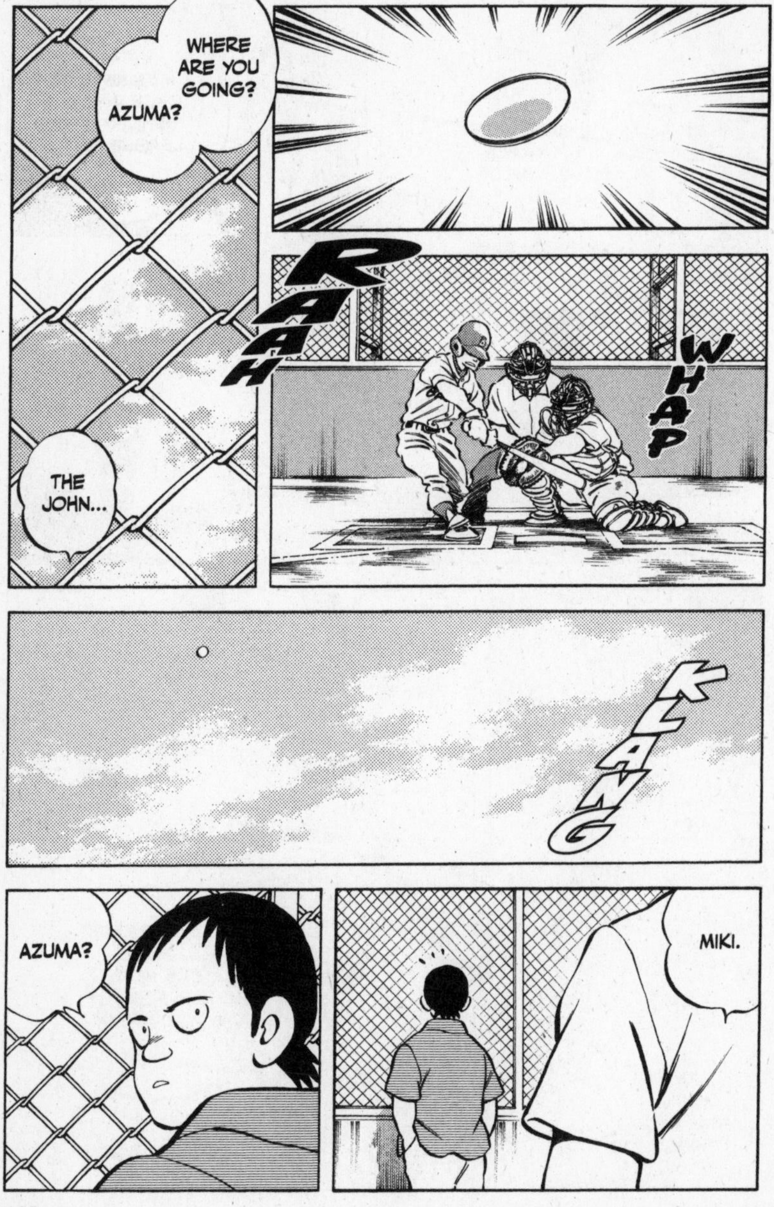
RAAAH
WHAP
WHERE ARE YOU GOING? AZUMA?
THE JOHN...
KLANG
MIKI.
AZUMA?

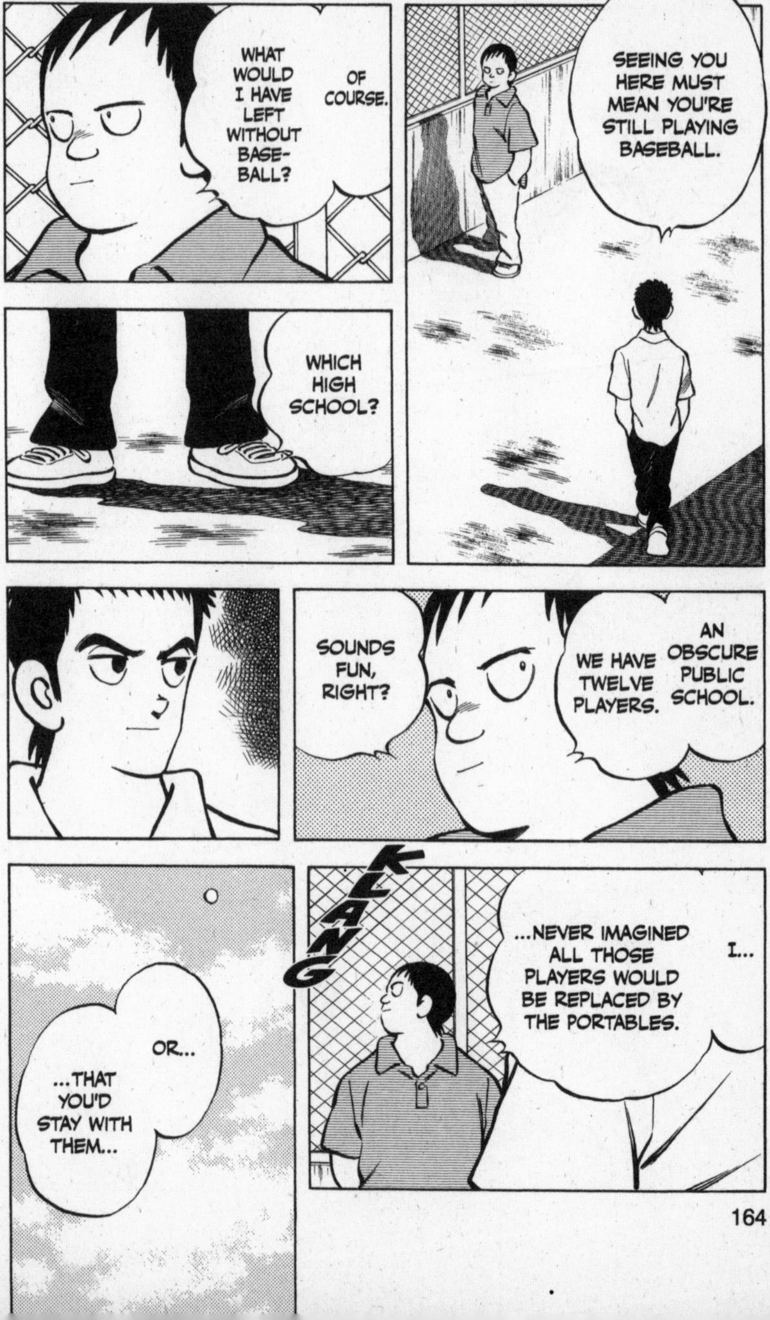
SEEING YOU HERE MUST MEAN YOU'RE STILL PLAYING BASEBALL.
OF COURSE.
WHAT WOULD I HAVE LEFT WITHOUT BASE-BALL?
WHICH HIGH SCHOOL?
AN OBSCURE PUBLIC SCHOOL.
WE HAVE TWELVE PLAYERS.
SOUNDS FUN, RIGHT?
I...
...NEVER IMAGINED ALL THOSE PLAYERS WOULD BE REPLACED BY THE PORTABLES.
KLANG
OR...
...THAT YOU'D STAY WITH THEM...

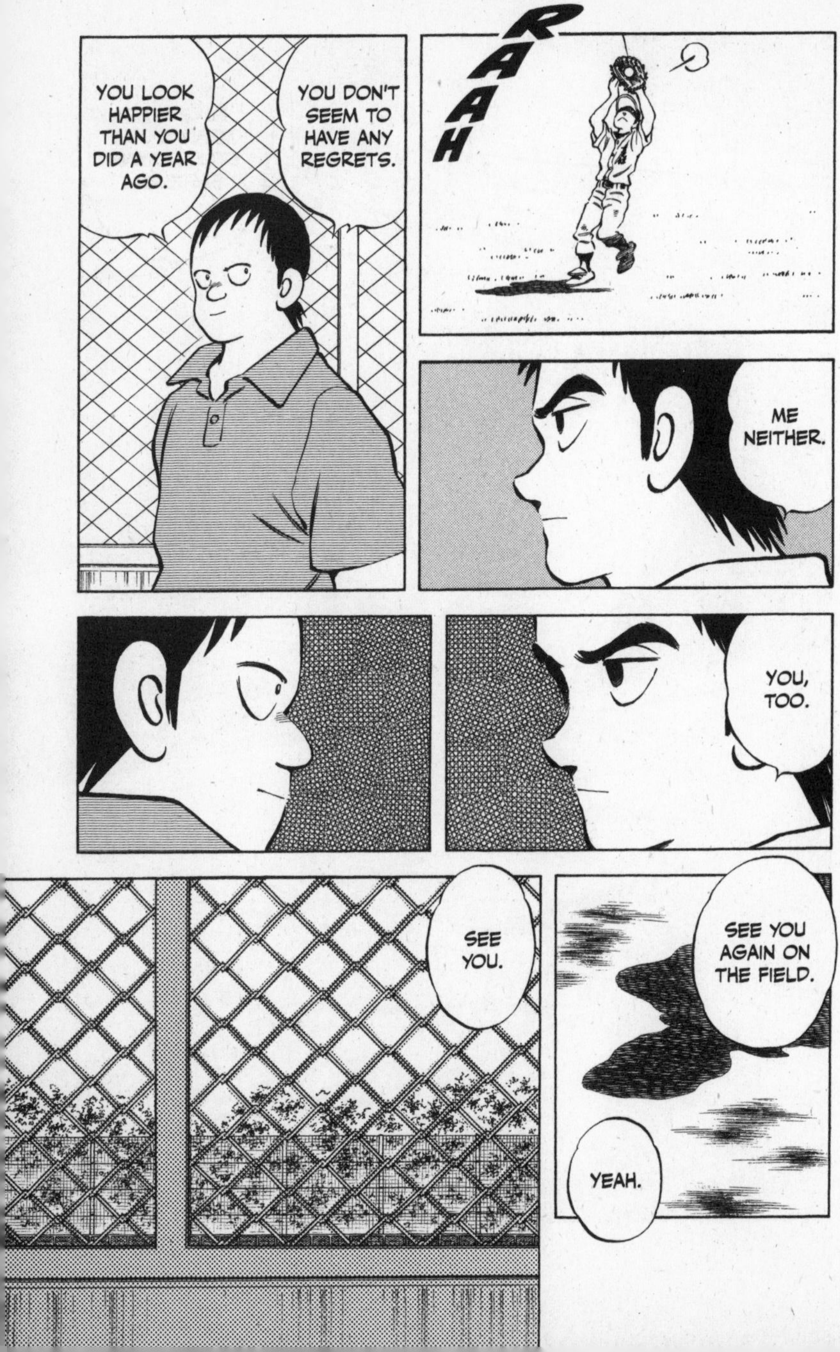
RAAH
ME NEITHER.
YOU DON'T SEEM TO HAVE ANY REGRETS.
YOU LOOK HAPPIER THAN YOU DID A YEAR AGO.
YOU, TOO.
SEE YOU AGAIN ON THE FIELD.
YEAH.
SEE YOU.

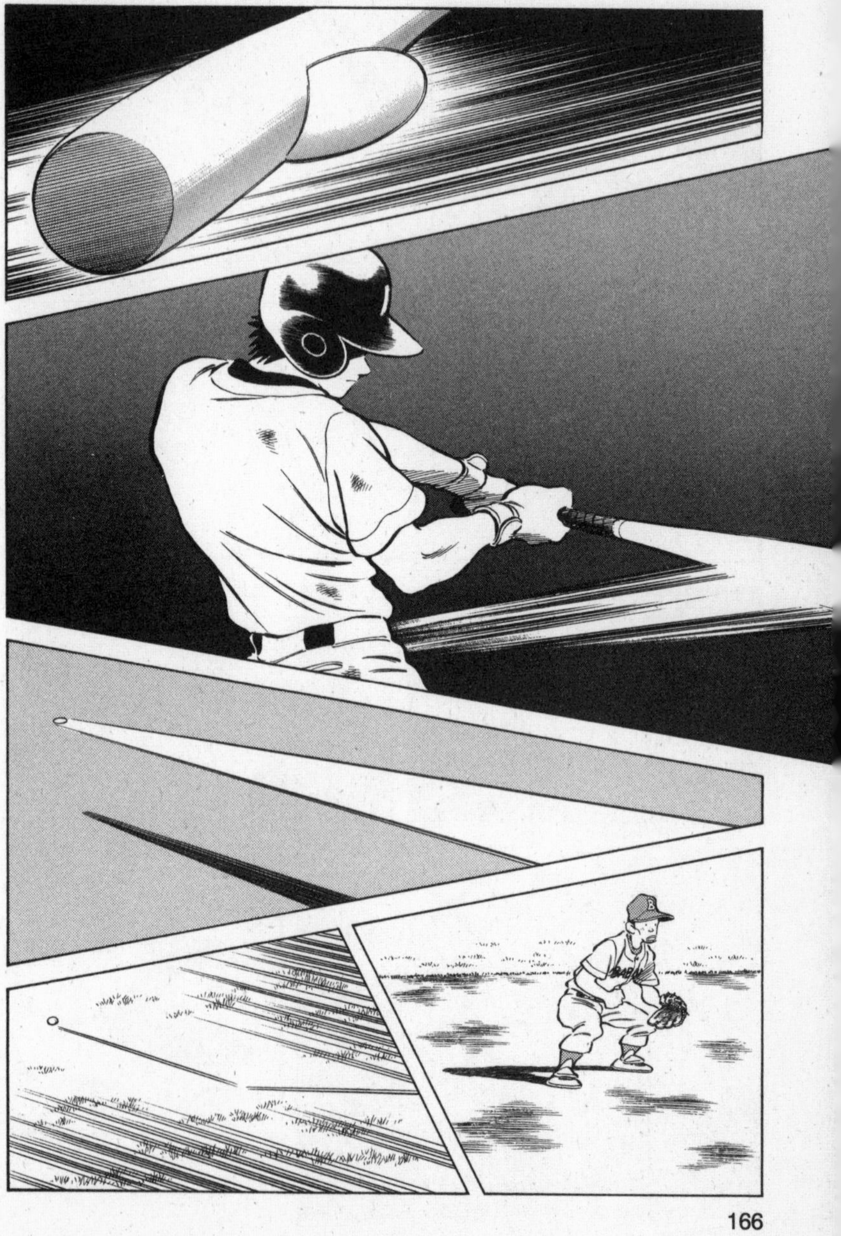

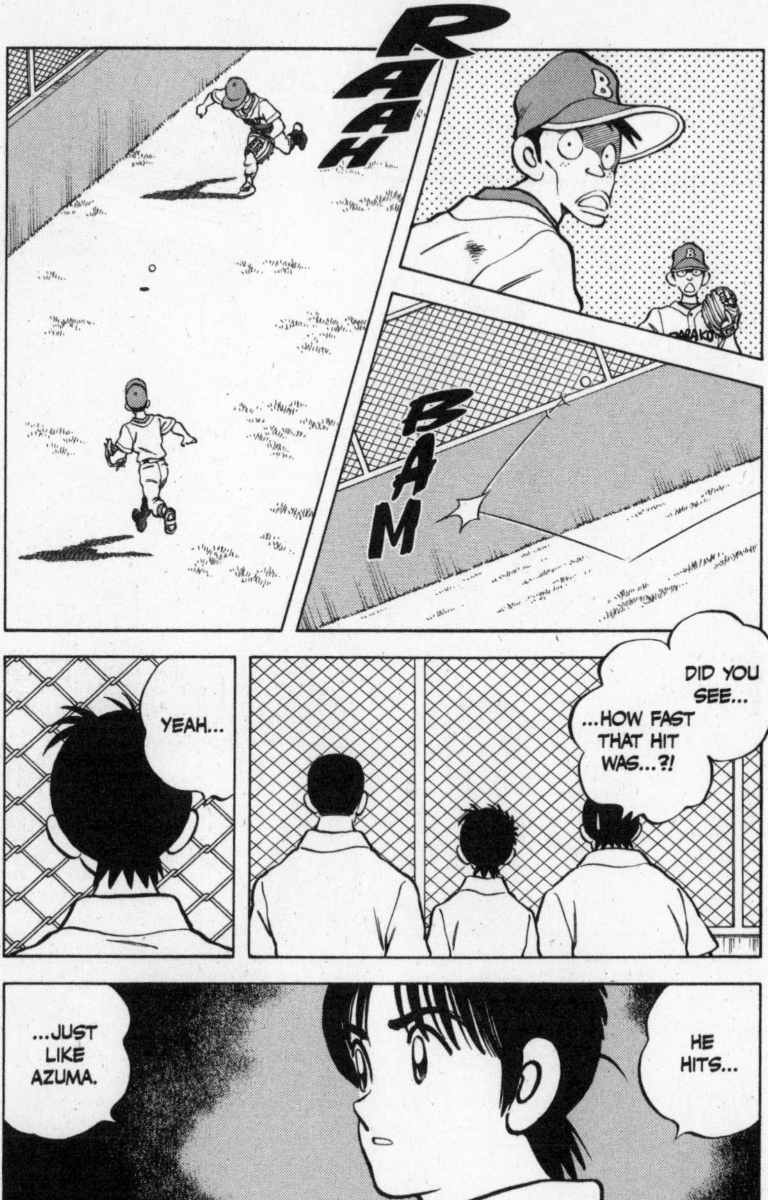
RAAAH
BAM
DID YOU SEE...
...HOW FAST THAT HIT WAS...?!
YEAH...
HE HITS...
...JUST LIKE AZUMA.

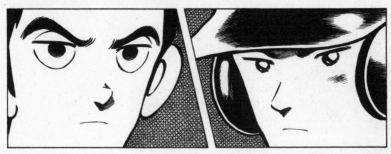

AZUMA REMEM-BERED HIS NAME...

...AFTER MEETING HIM JUST ONCE...

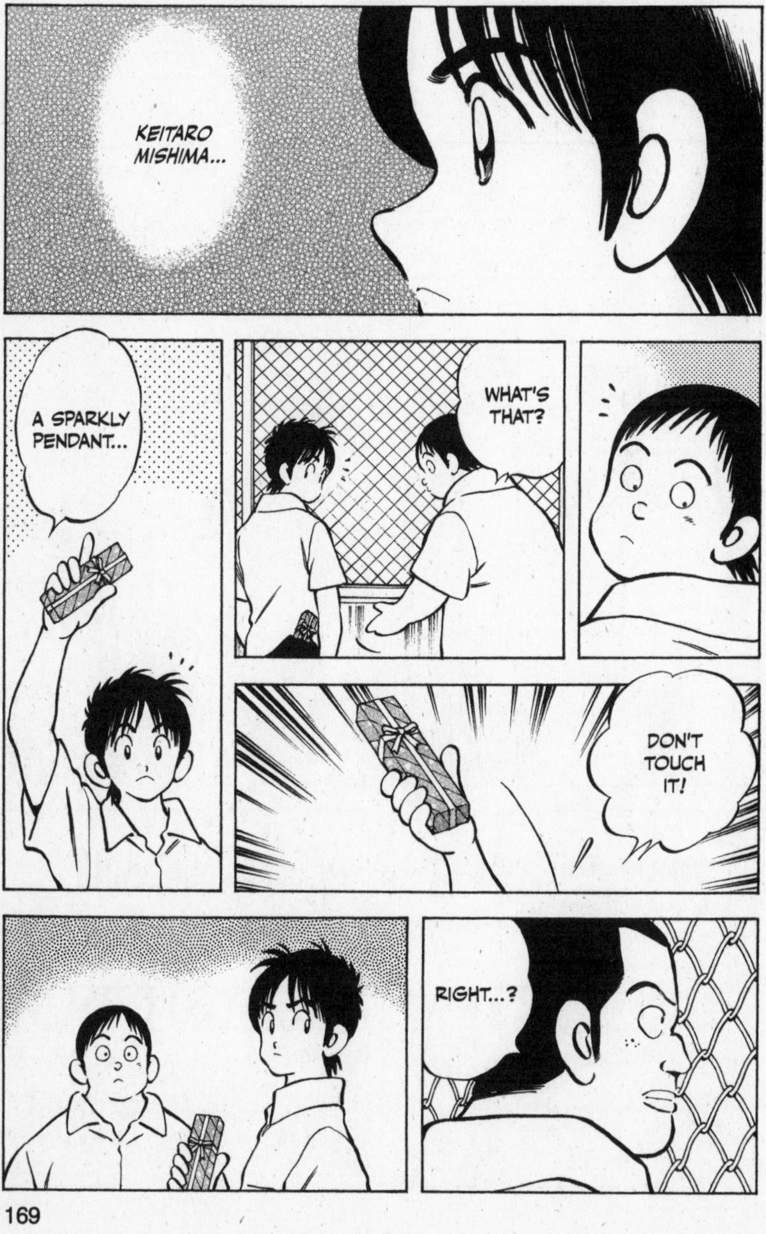
KEITARO MISHIMA...
WHAT'S THAT?
DON'T TOUCH IT!
A SPARKLY PENDANT...
RIGHT...?

ALMOST THE RAINY SEASON ...

JUNE 10.

SAY WHAT?

KITAMURA SPORTS

KITAMURA SPORTS

Ttenphi

OPEN

KO KITAMURA'S 17TH BIRTHDAY...

WAKABA TSUKISHIMA

BIRTHDAY PRESENT LIST

| | | | |
|---|---|---|---|
| 12th | CUTE PJ'S | 17th | SPARKLY PENDANT |
| 13th | CUTE SANDALS | 18th | SOMEWHAT PRICEY EARRINGS |
| 14th | CUTE PURSE | 19th | PRICIER NECKLACE |
| 15th | STUFFED MONKEY | 20th | ENGAGEMENT RING |
| 16th | CAT TEAPOT FROM "BARACAN" | | TO BE CONTINUED |

WAKABA TSUKISHIMA

PRESENT LIST

| | |
|---|---|
| 17th | SPARKLY PENDANT |

# CHAPTER 70
# AT ANY RATE

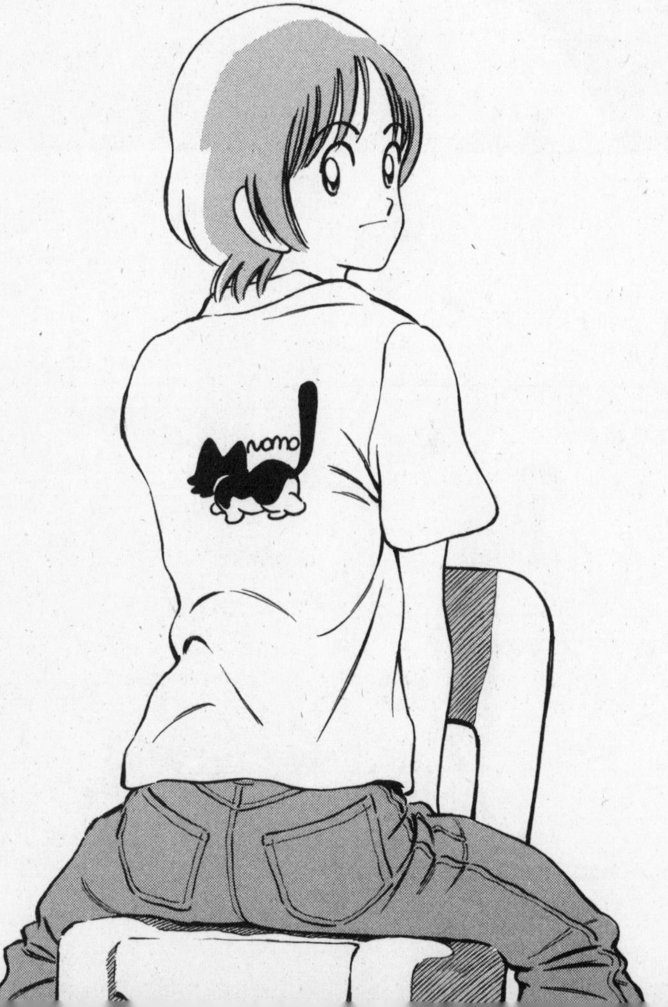

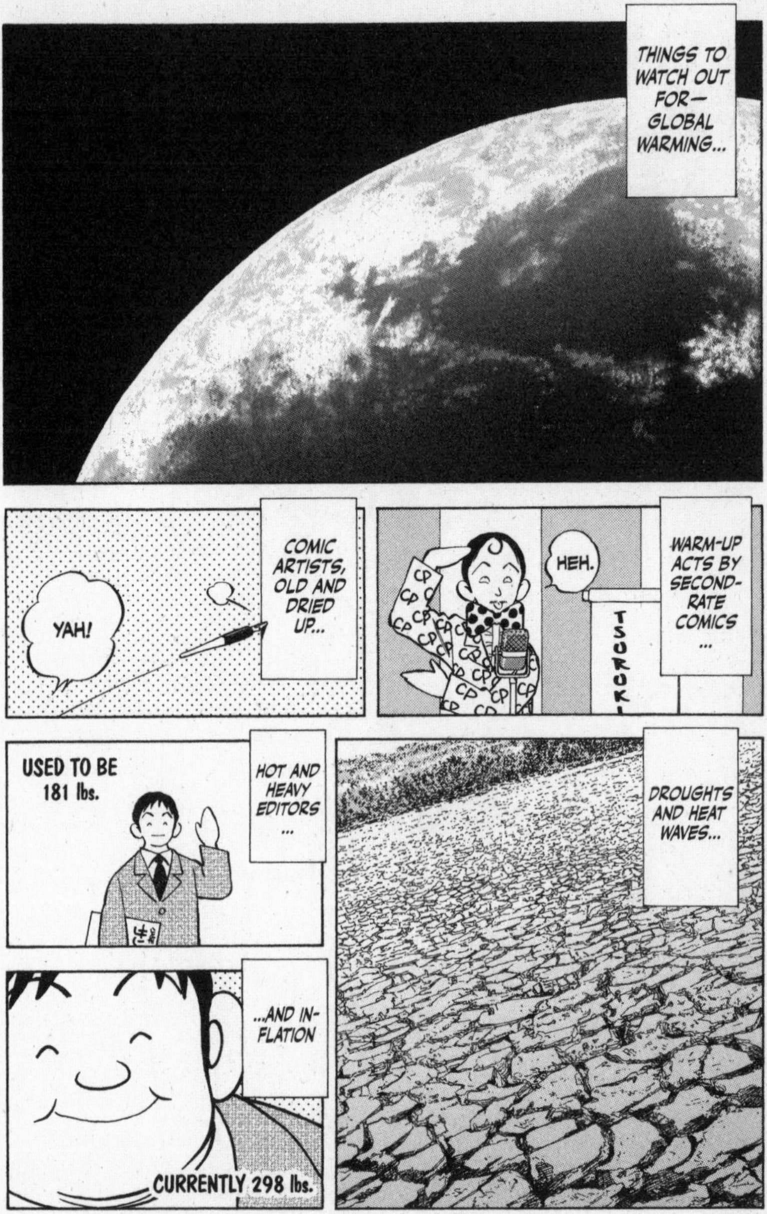

THINGS TO WATCH OUT FOR— GLOBAL WARMING...
WARM-UP ACTS BY SECOND-RATE COMICS ...
HEH.
TSURUKI
COMIC ARTISTS, OLD AND DRIED UP...
YAH!
DROUGHTS AND HEAT WAVES...
HOT AND HEAVY EDITORS ...
USED TO BE 181 lbs.
...AND IN-FLATION
CURRENTLY 298 lbs.

RIBBIT

RIBBIT

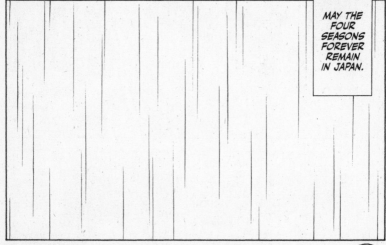

MAY THE FOUR SEASONS FOREVER REMAIN IN JAPAN.

OKAY...

THAT'S ALL FOR TODAY.

DING

DONG

I-A

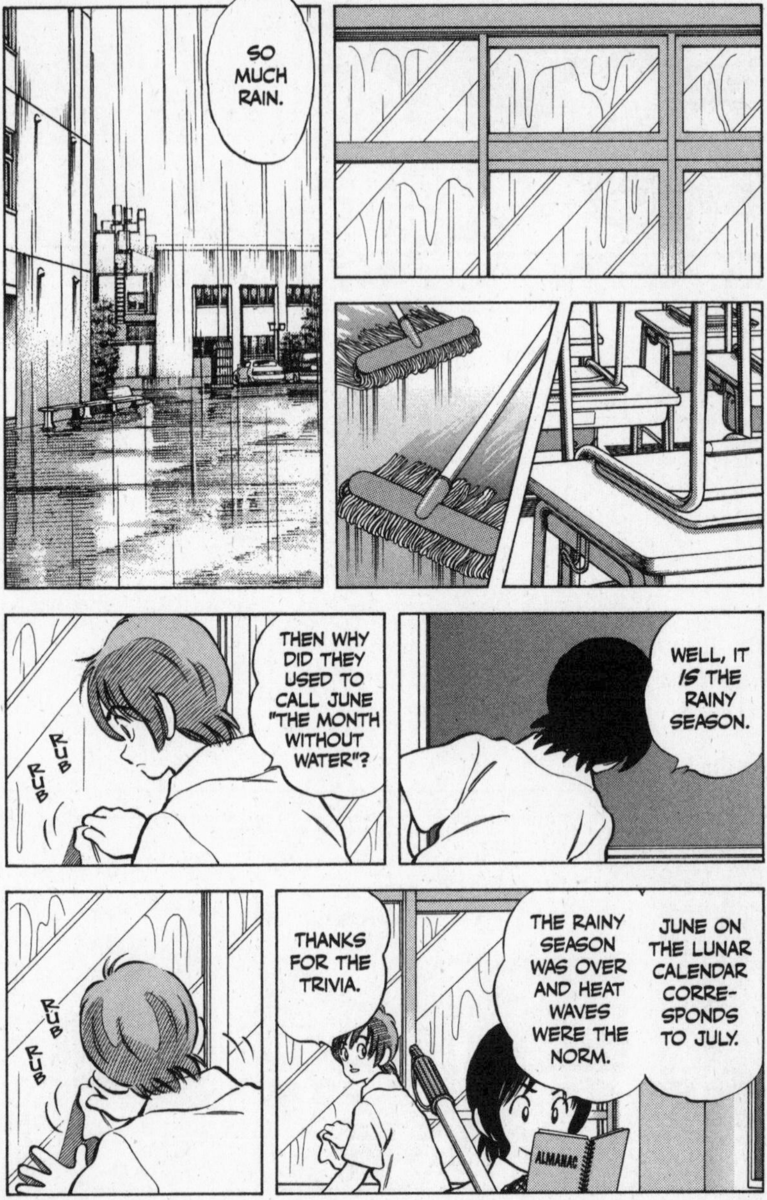
SO MUCH RAIN.
WELL, IT *IS* THE RAINY SEASON.
THEN WHY DID THEY USED TO CALL JUNE "THE MONTH WITHOUT WATER"?
RUB RUB
JUNE ON THE LUNAR CALENDAR CORRE-SPONDS TO JULY.
THE RAINY SEASON WAS OVER AND HEAT WAVES WERE THE NORM.
THANKS FOR THE TRIVIA.
ALMANAC
RUB RUB

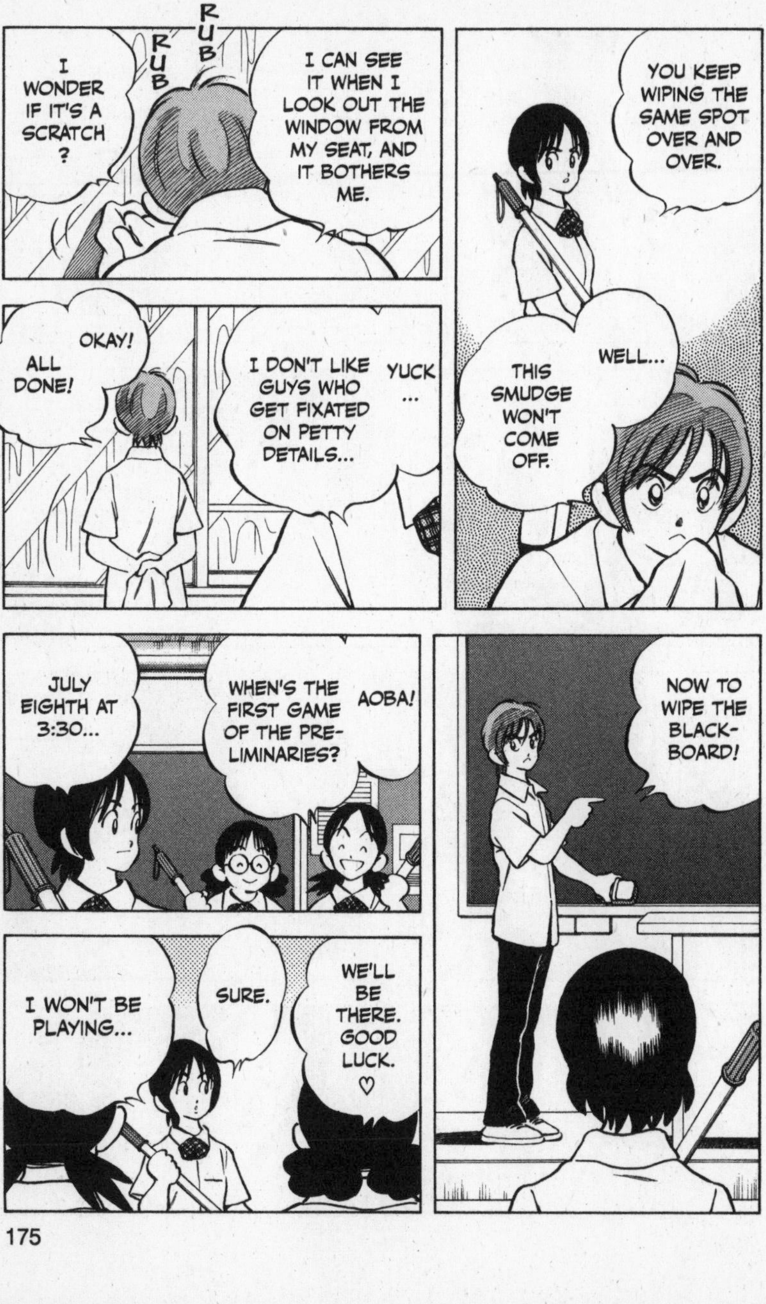
YOU KEEP WIPING THE SAME SPOT OVER AND OVER.
WELL... THIS SMUDGE WON'T COME OFF.
RUB RUB
I CAN SEE IT WHEN I LOOK OUT THE WINDOW FROM MY SEAT, AND IT BOTHERS ME.
I WONDER IF IT'S A SCRATCH?
YUCK...
I DON'T LIKE GUYS WHO GET FIXATED ON PETTY DETAILS...
OKAY! ALL DONE!
NOW TO WIPE THE BLACK-BOARD!
AOBA!
WHEN'S THE FIRST GAME OF THE PRE-LIMINARIES?
JULY EIGHTH AT 3:30...
WE'LL BE THERE. GOOD LUCK. ♡
SURE.
I WON'T BE PLAYING...

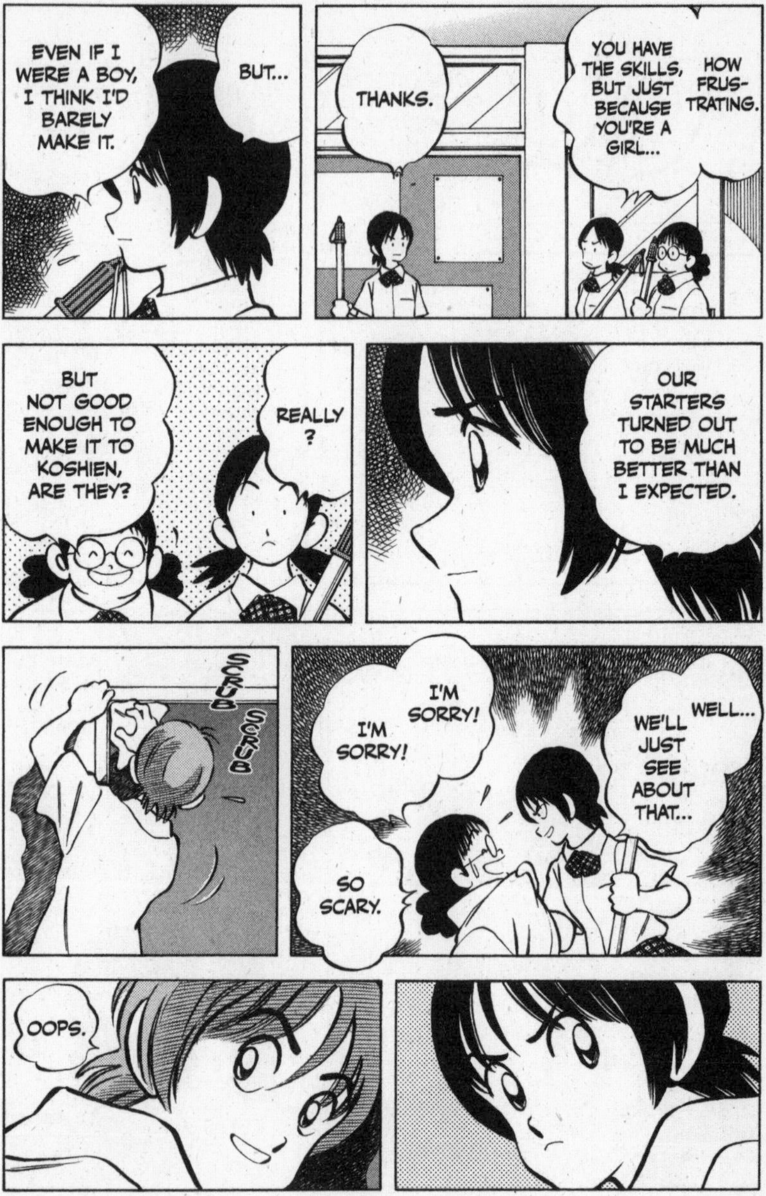
YOU HAVE THE SKILLS, BUT JUST BECAUSE YOU'RE A GIRL...
HOW FRUS-TRATING.
THANKS.
BUT...
EVEN IF I WERE A BOY, I THINK I'D BARELY MAKE IT.
OUR STARTERS TURNED OUT TO BE MUCH BETTER THAN I EXPECTED.
REALLY?
BUT NOT GOOD ENOUGH TO MAKE IT TO KOSHIEN, ARE THEY?
WELL...
WE'LL JUST SEE ABOUT THAT...
I'M SORRY!
I'M SORRY!
SO SCARY.
SCRUB
SCRUB
OOPS.

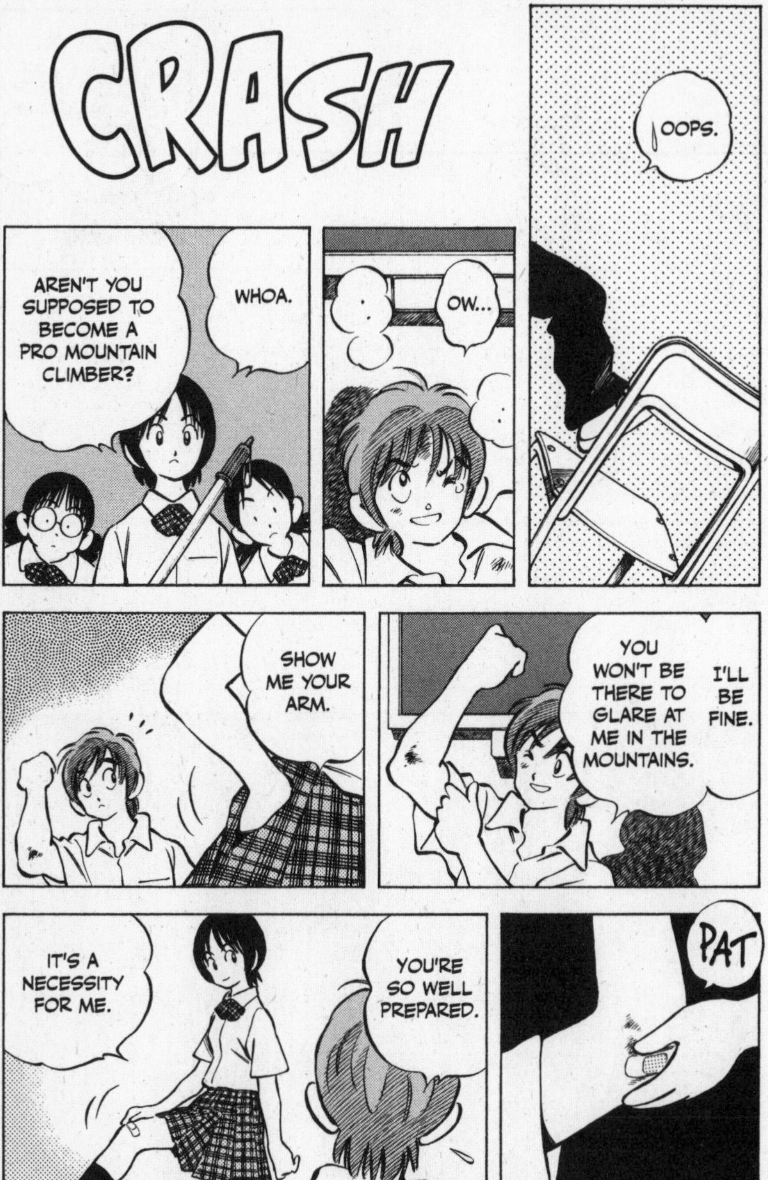
OOPS.
CRASH
OW...
WHOA.
AREN'T YOU SUPPOSED TO BECOME A PRO MOUNTAIN CLIMBER?
I'LL BE FINE.
YOU WON'T BE THERE TO GLARE AT ME IN THE MOUNTAINS.
SHOW ME YOUR ARM.
PAT
YOU'RE SO WELL PREPARED.
IT'S A NECESSITY FOR ME.

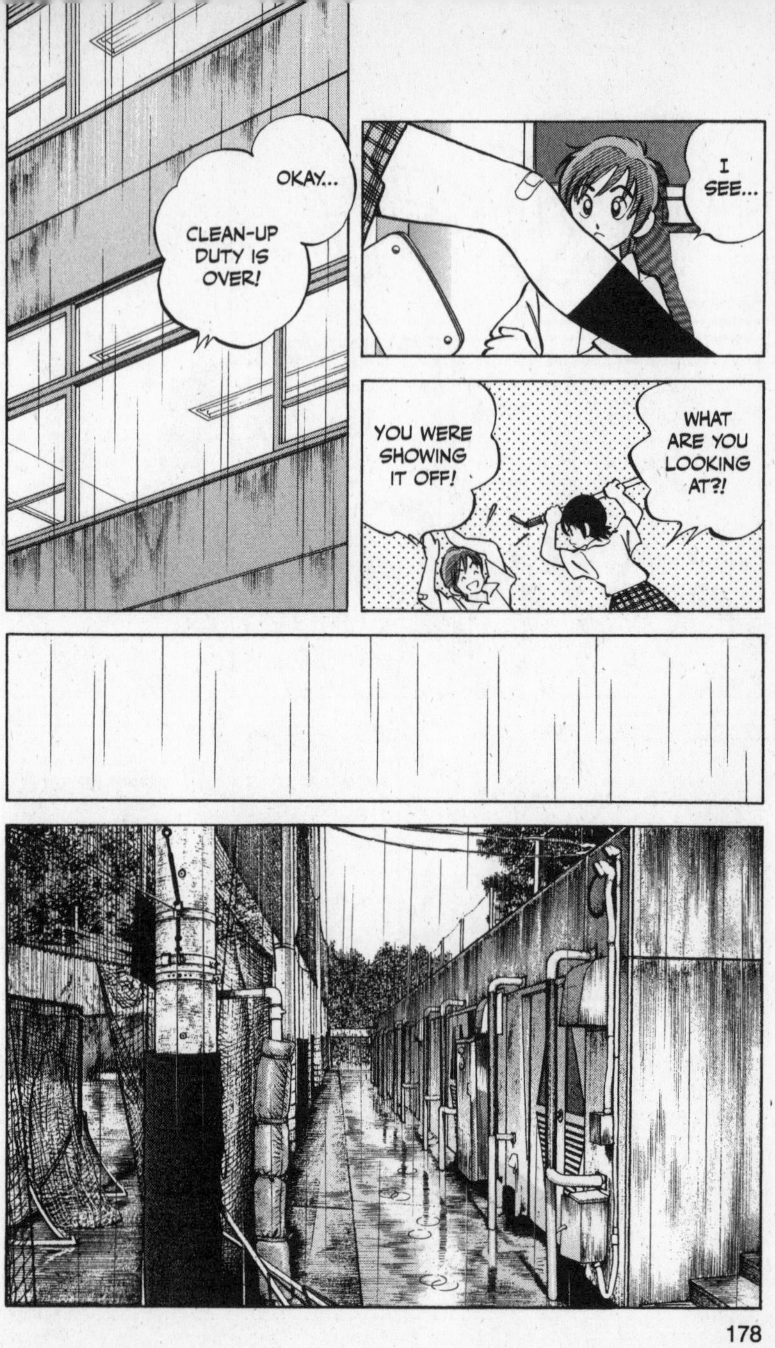
I SEE...
WHAT ARE YOU LOOKING AT?!
YOU WERE SHOWING IT OFF!
OKAY...
CLEAN-UP DUTY IS OVER!

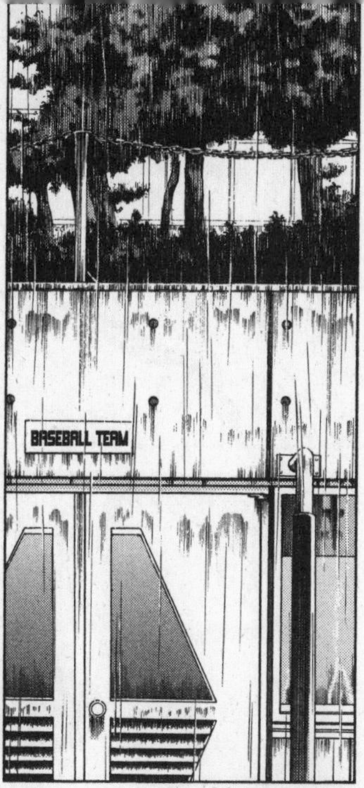
BASEBALL TEAM

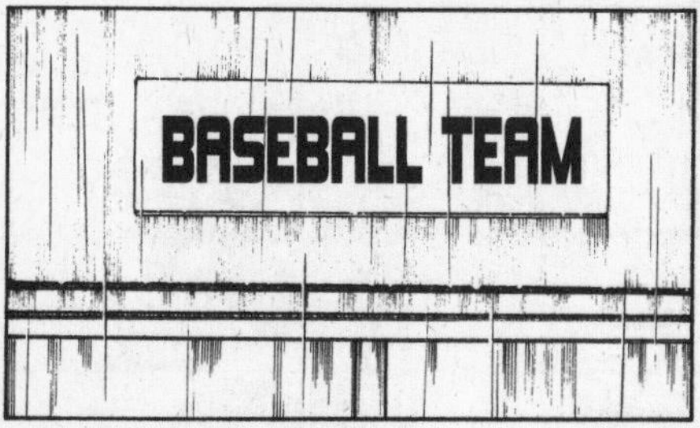
BASEBALL TEAM

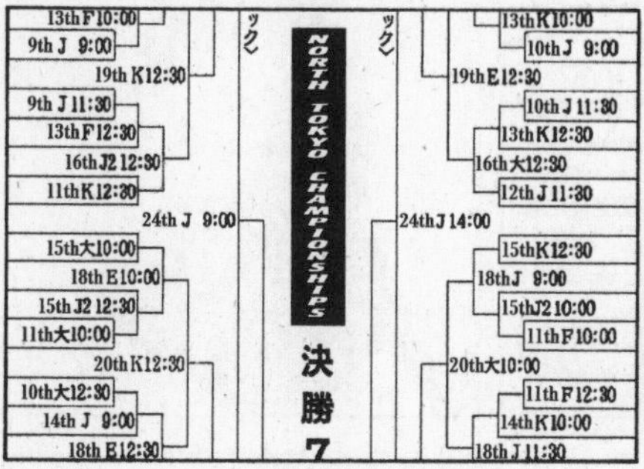
NORTH TOKYO CHAMPIONSHIPS
決勝
13th F 10:00
9th J 9:00
19th K 12:30
9th J 11:30
13th F 12:30
16th J2 12:30
11th K 12:30
24th J 9:00
15th 大 10:00
18th E 10:00
15th J2 12:30
11th 大 10:00
20th K 12:30
10th 大 12:30
14th J 9:00
18th E 12:30
13th K 10:00
10th J 9:00
19th E 12:30
10th J 11:30
13th K 12:30
16th 大 12:30
12th J 11:30
24th J 14:00
15th K 12:30
18th J 9:00
15th J2 10:00
11th F 10:00
20th 大 10:00
11th F 12:30
14th K 10:00
18th J 11:30

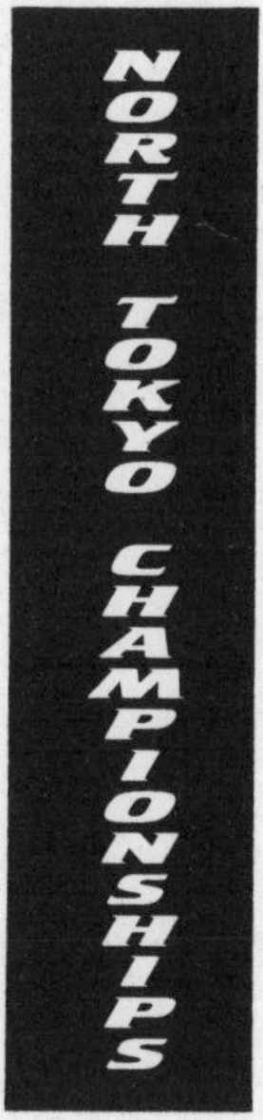
NORTH TOKYO CHAMPIONSHIPS

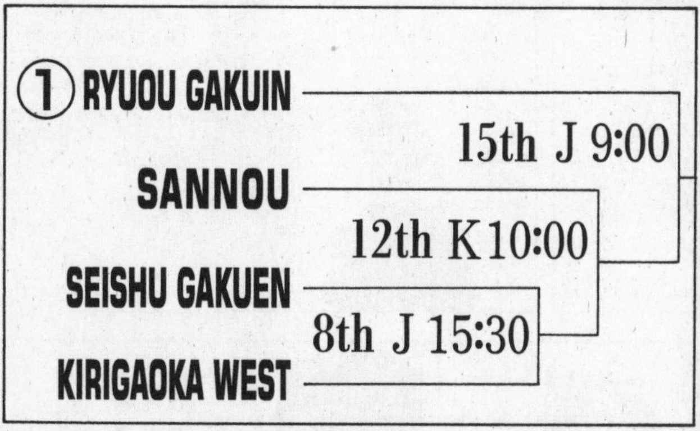
① RYUOU GAKUIN
15th J 9:00
SANNOU
12th K 10:00
SEISHU GAKUEN
8th J 15:30
KIRIGAOKA WEST

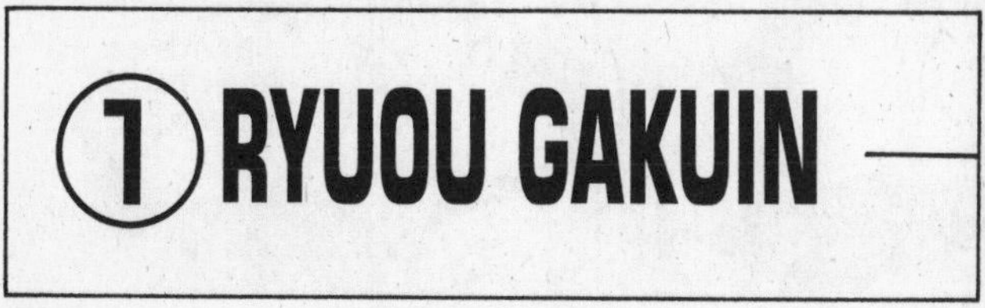
① RYUOU GAKUIN

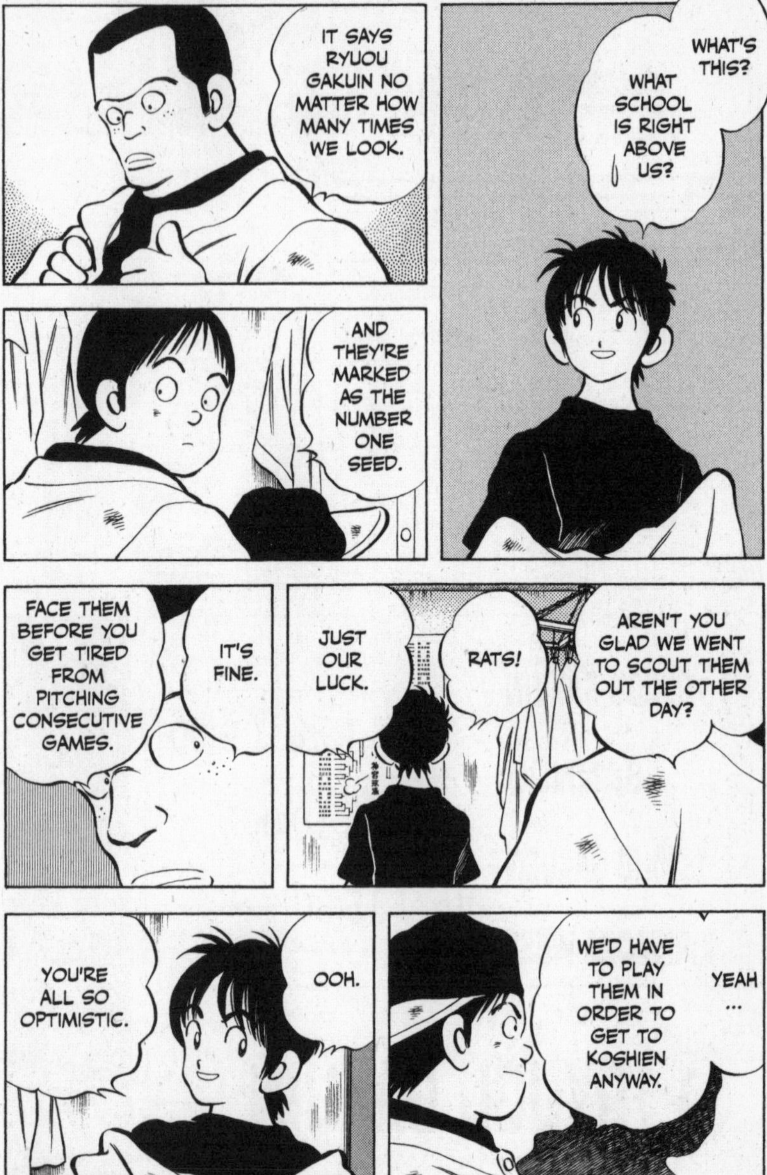
WHAT'S THIS?
WHAT SCHOOL IS RIGHT ABOVE US?
IT SAYS RYUOU GAKUIN NO MATTER HOW MANY TIMES WE LOOK.
AND THEY'RE MARKED AS THE NUMBER ONE SEED.
AREN'T YOU GLAD WE WENT TO SCOUT THEM OUT THE OTHER DAY?
RATS!
JUST OUR LUCK.
IT'S FINE.
FACE THEM BEFORE YOU GET TIRED FROM PITCHING CONSECUTIVE GAMES.
YEAH ...
WE'D HAVE TO PLAY THEM IN ORDER TO GET TO KOSHIEN ANYWAY.
OOH.
YOU'RE ALL SO OPTIMISTIC.

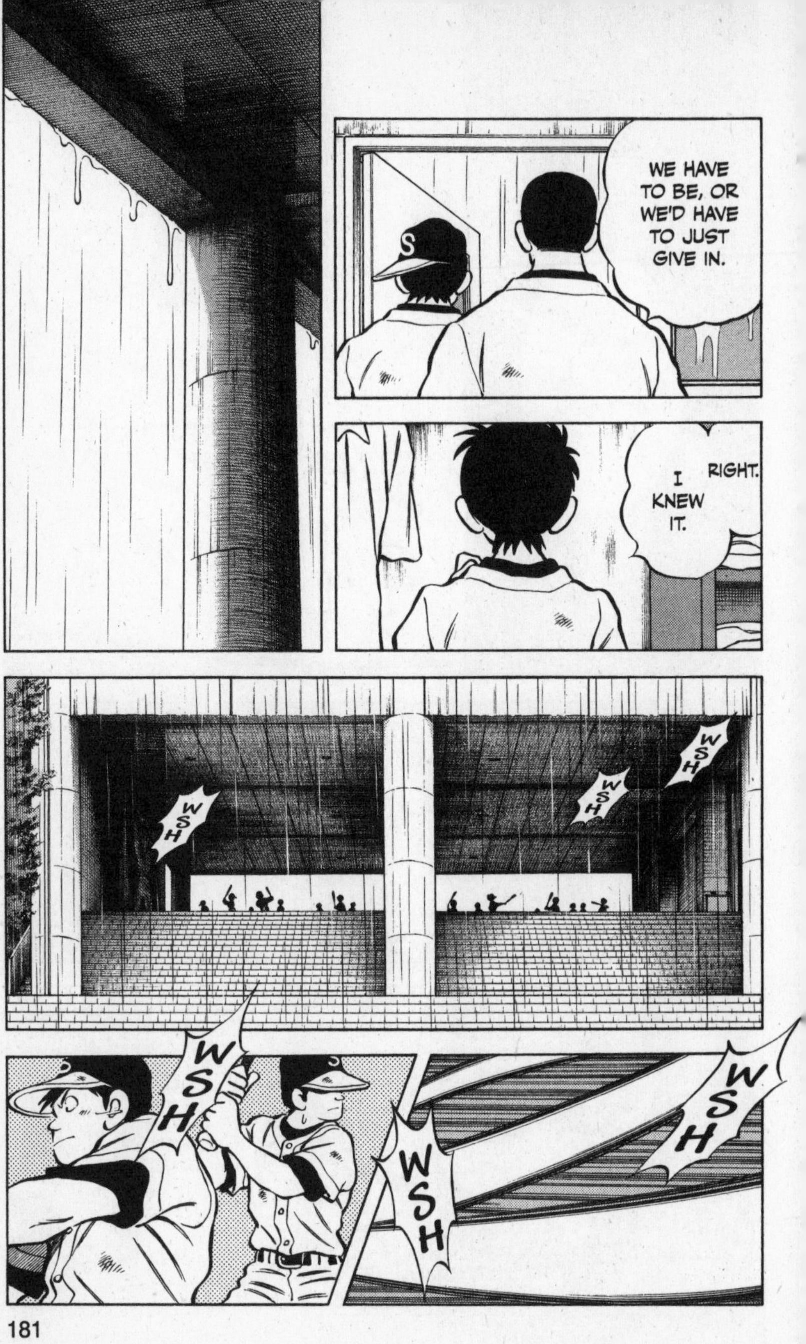
WE HAVE TO BE, OR WE'D HAVE TO JUST GIVE IN.
RIGHT. I KNEW IT.
WSH
WSH
WSH
WSH
WSH
WSH

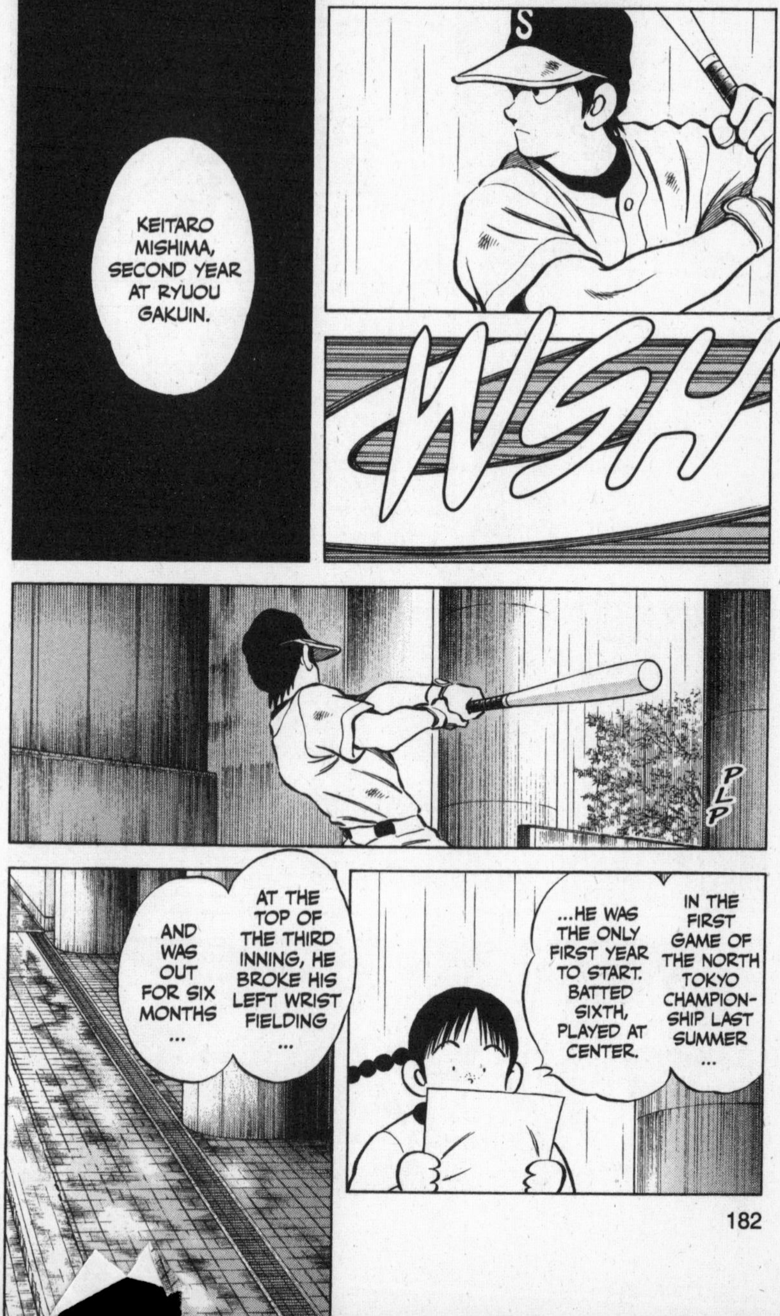
WSH
KEITARO MISHIMA, SECOND YEAR AT RYUOU GAKUIN.
PLP
IN THE FIRST GAME OF THE NORTH TOKYO CHAMPIONSHIP LAST SUMMER ...
...HE WAS THE ONLY FIRST YEAR TO START. BATTED SIXTH, PLAYED AT CENTER.
AT THE TOP OF THE THIRD INNING, HE BROKE HIS LEFT WRIST FIELDING ...
AND WAS OUT FOR SIX MONTHS ...

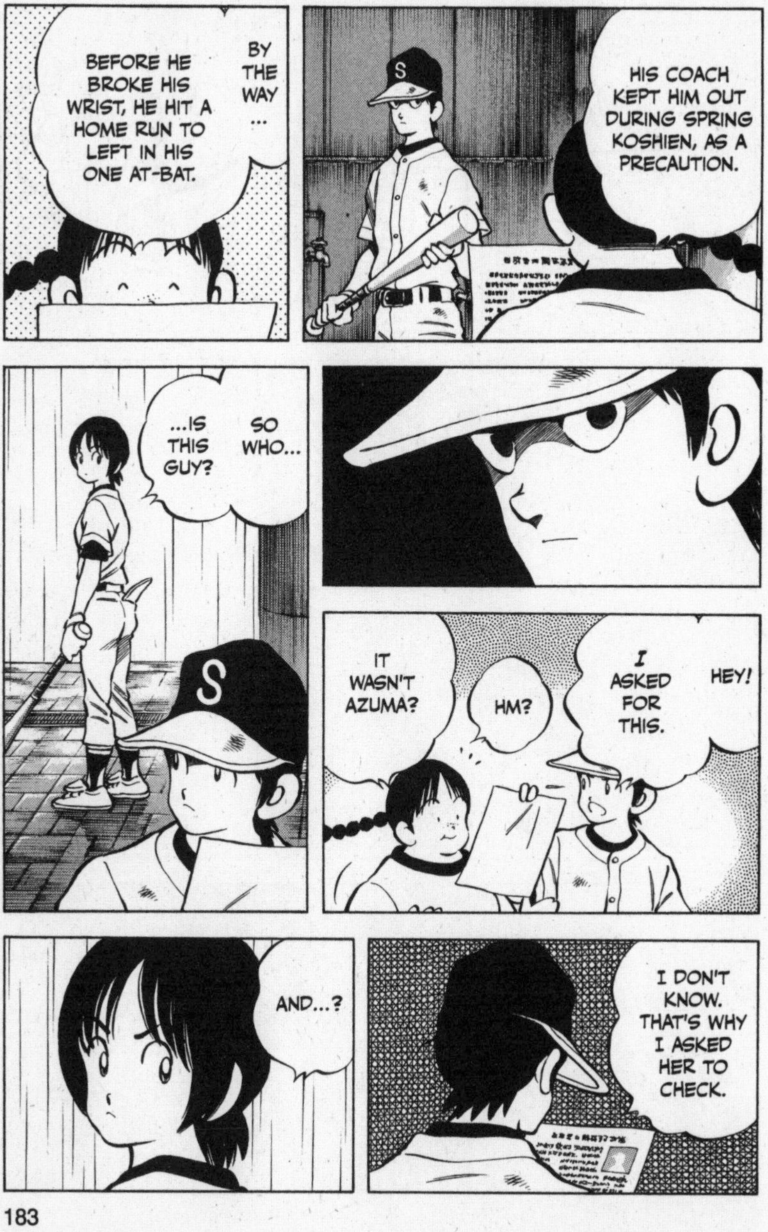
HIS COACH KEPT HIM OUT DURING SPRING KOSHIEN, AS A PRECAUTION.
BY THE WAY ...
BEFORE HE BROKE HIS WRIST, HE HIT A HOME RUN TO LEFT IN HIS ONE AT-BAT.
HEY!
*I* ASKED FOR THIS.
HM?
IT WASN'T AZUMA?
SO WHO...
...IS THIS GUY?
I DON'T KNOW. THAT'S WHY I ASKED HER TO CHECK.
AND...?

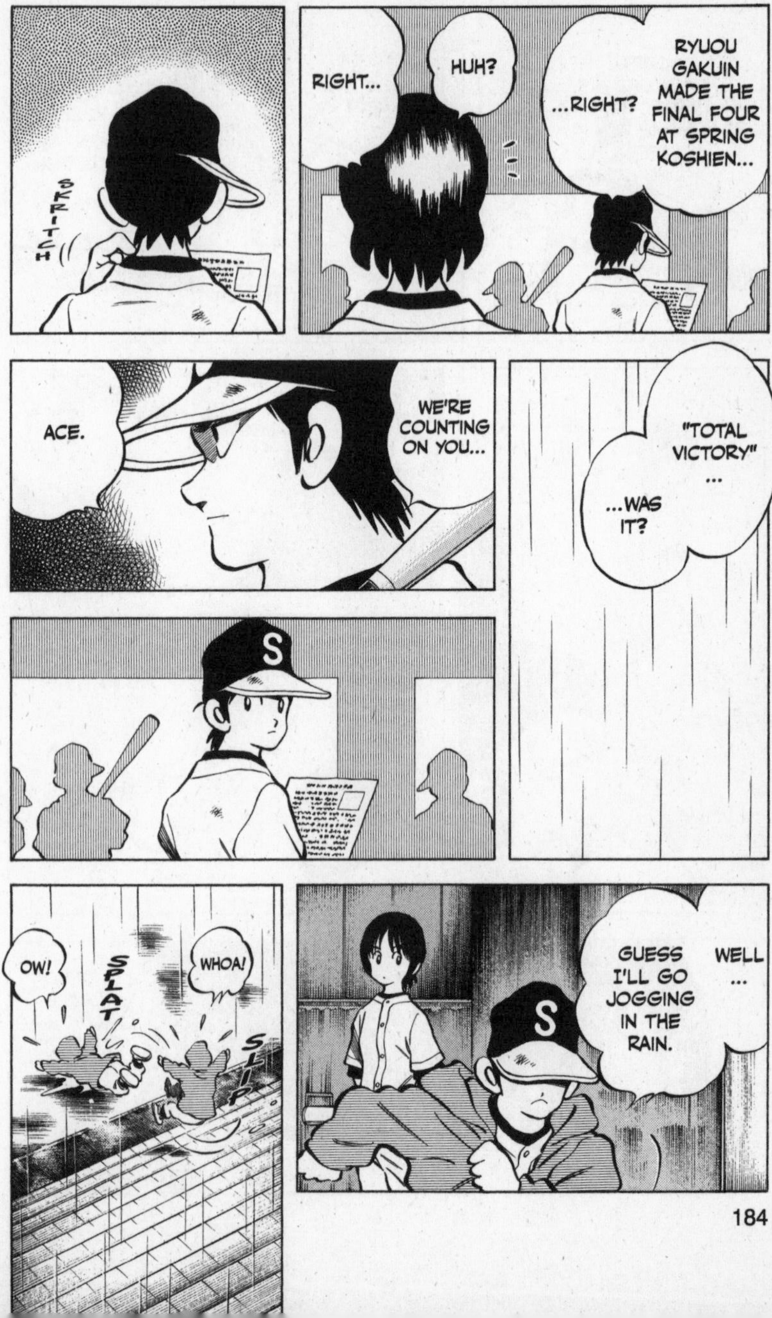
RYUOU GAKUIN MADE THE FINAL FOUR AT SPRING KOSHIEN...
...RIGHT?
HUH?
RIGHT...
SKRITCH
"TOTAL VICTORY" ...
...WAS IT?
WE'RE COUNTING ON YOU...
ACE.
WELL ...
GUESS I'LL GO JOGGING IN THE RAIN.
WHOA!
SLIP
SPLAT
OW!

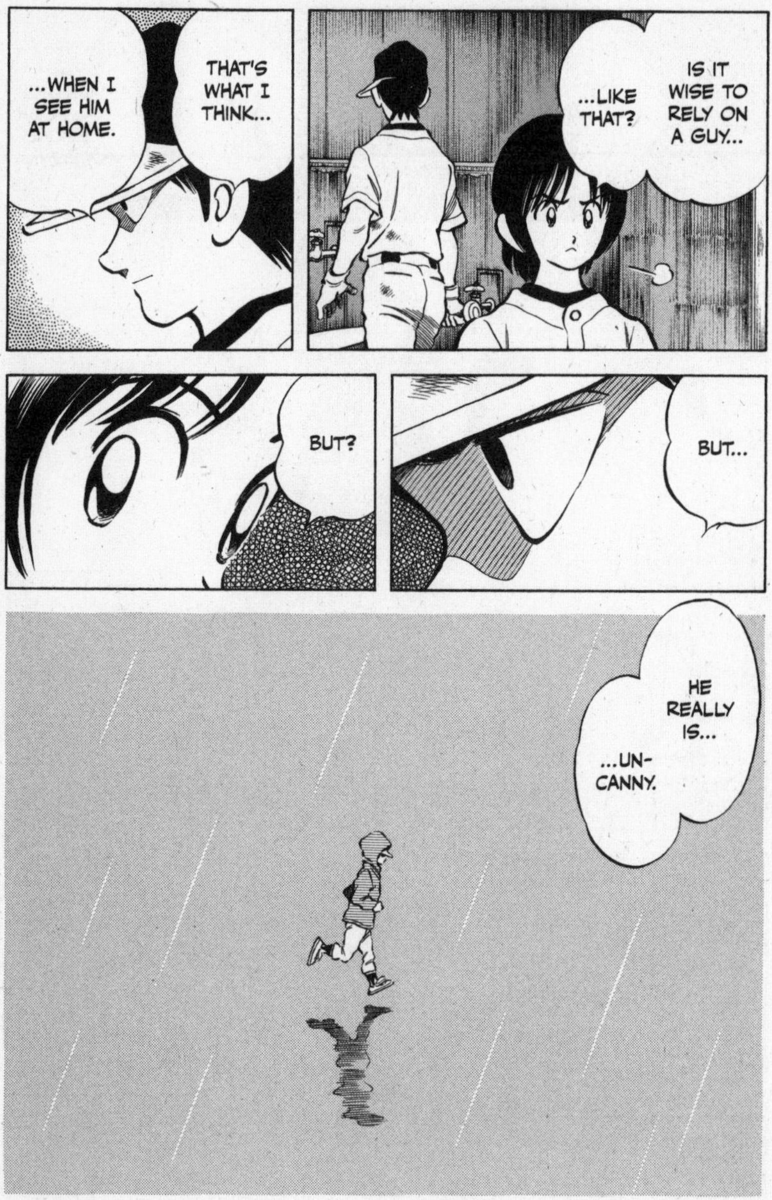
IS IT WISE TO RELY ON A GUY...
...LIKE THAT?
THAT'S WHAT I THINK...
...WHEN I SEE HIM AT HOME.
BUT...
BUT?
HE REALLY IS...
...UN-CANNY.

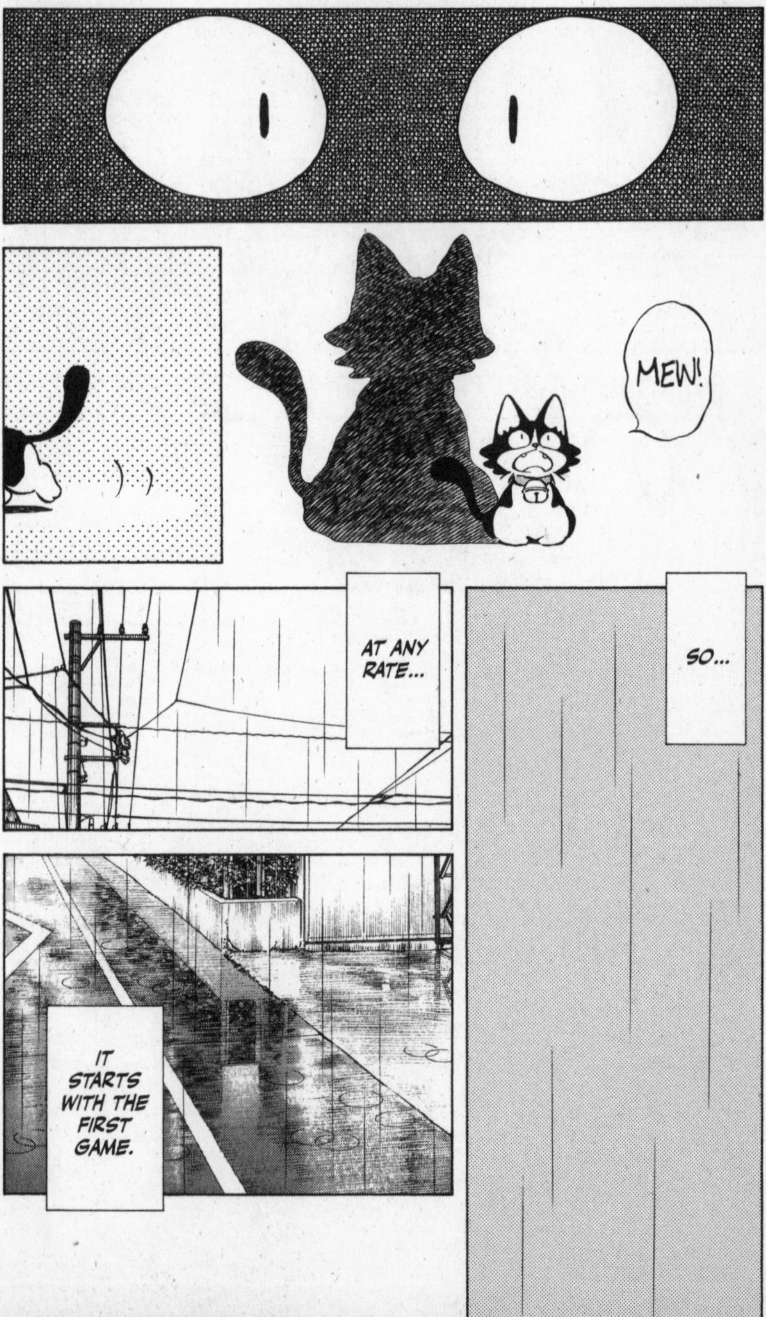
MEW!
SO...
AT ANY RATE...
IT STARTS WITH THE FIRST GAME.

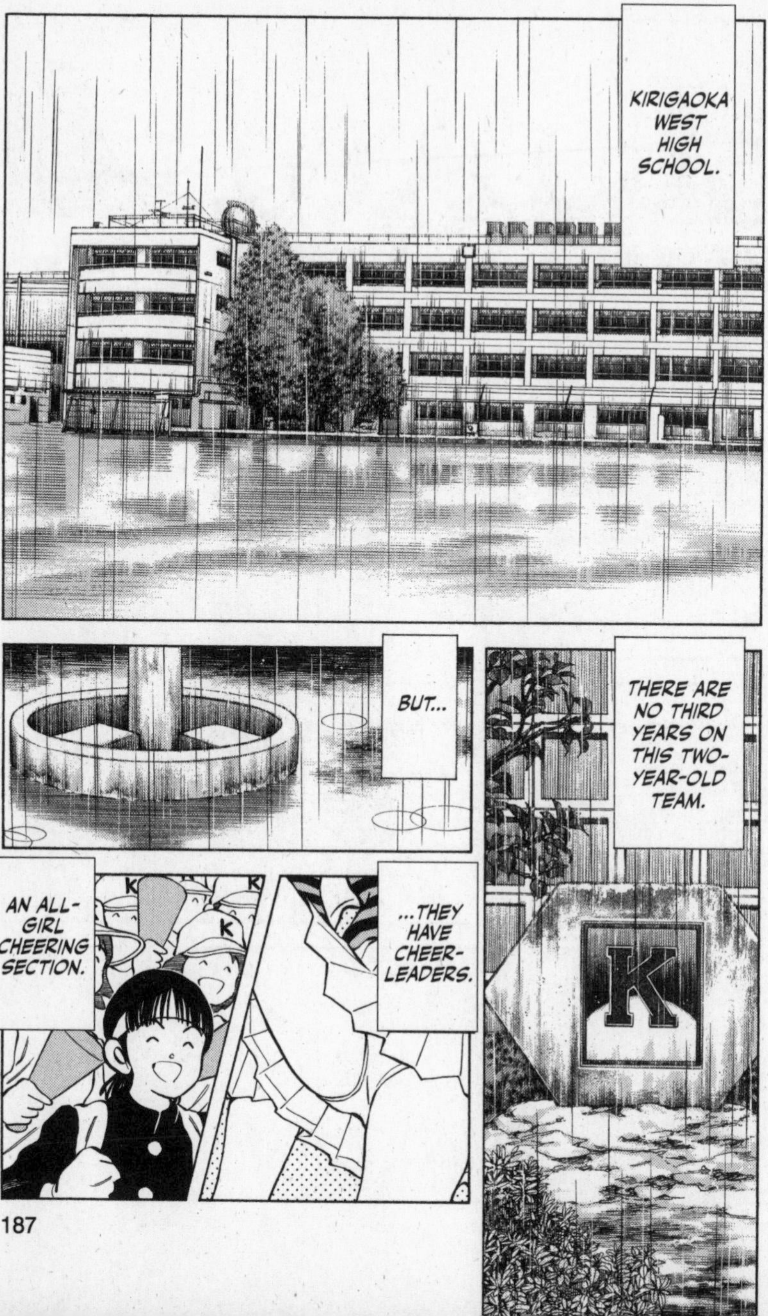
KIRIGAOKA WEST HIGH SCHOOL.
THERE ARE NO THIRD YEARS ON THIS TWO-YEAR-OLD TEAM.
BUT...
...THEY HAVE CHEER-LEADERS.
AN ALL-GIRL CHEERING SECTION.

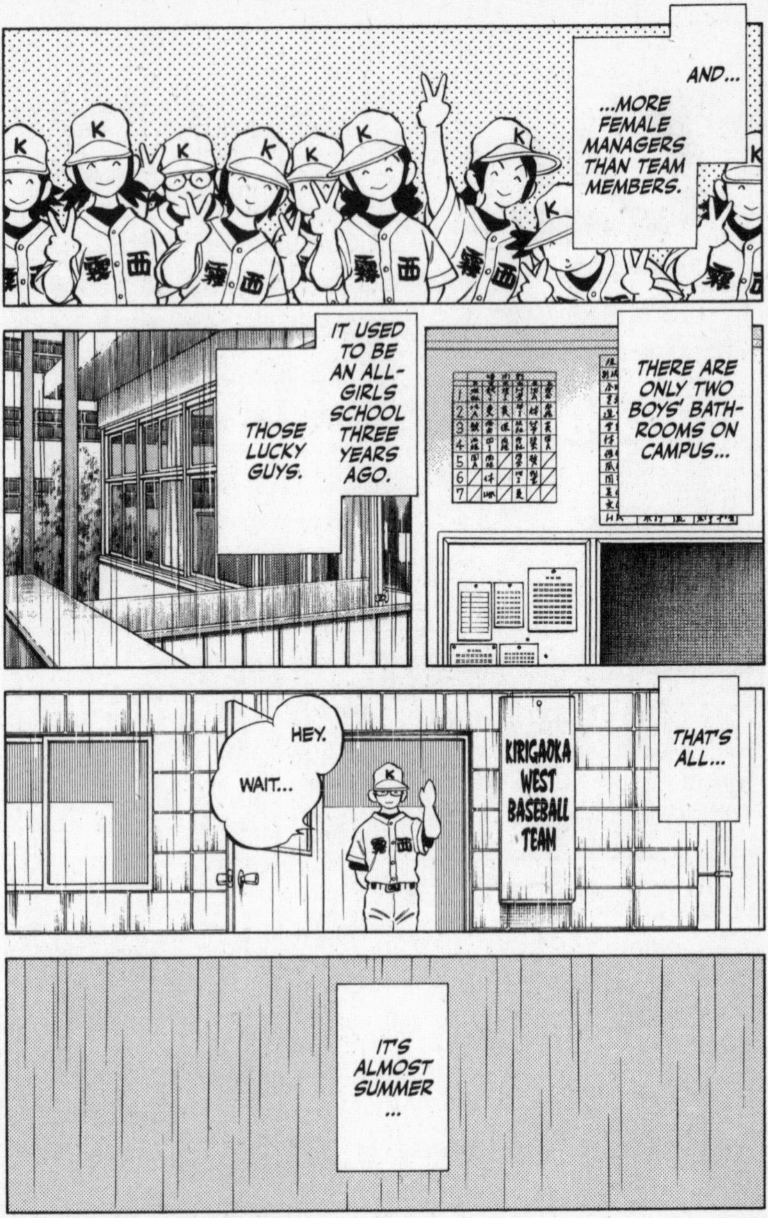
AND...
...MORE FEMALE MANAGERS THAN TEAM MEMBERS.
THERE ARE ONLY TWO BOYS' BATHROOMS ON CAMPUS...
IT USED TO BE AN ALL-GIRLS SCHOOL THREE YEARS AGO.
THOSE LUCKY GUYS.
THAT'S ALL...
KIRIGAOKA WEST BASEBALL TEAM
HEY.
WAIT...
IT'S ALMOST SUMMER ...

# Cross❤Game

## 9

## Story & Art by
## Mitsuru Adachi

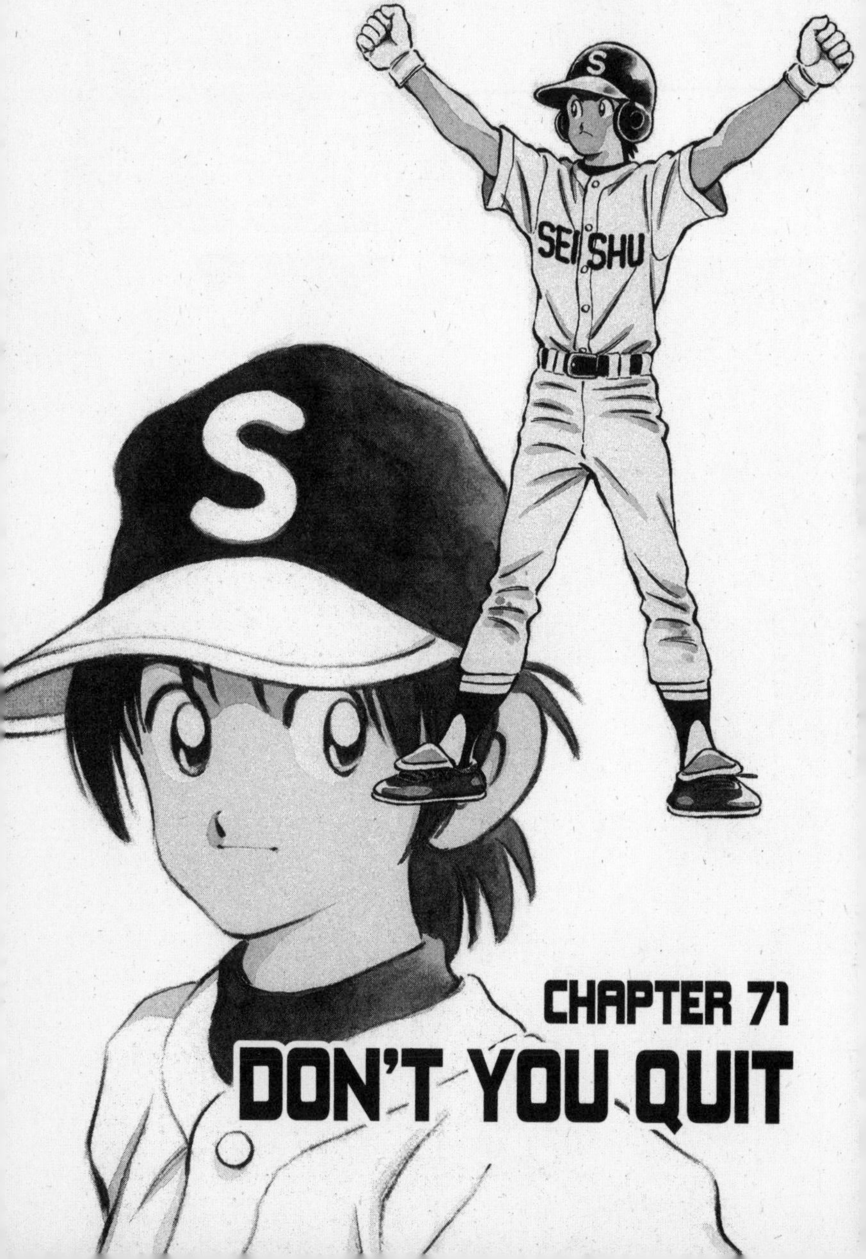
SEISHU

## CHAPTER 71

# DON'T YOU QUIT

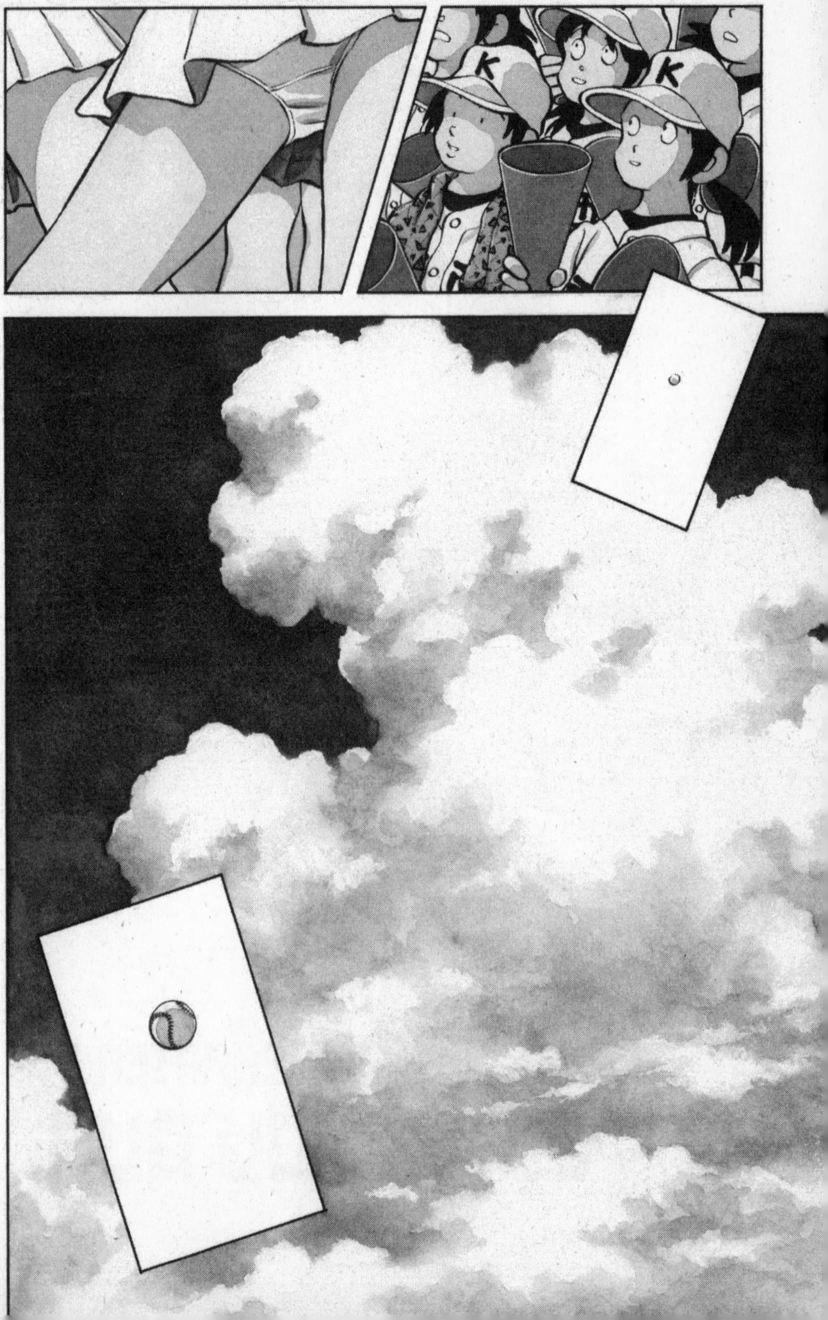

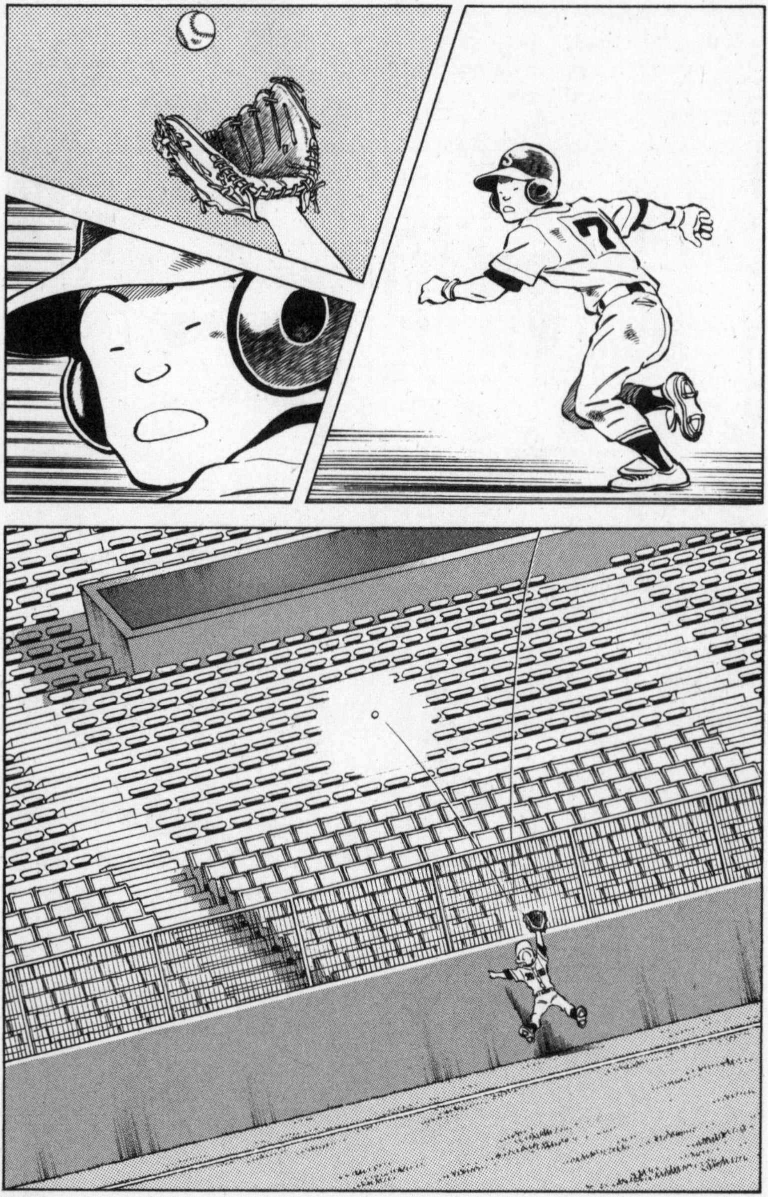

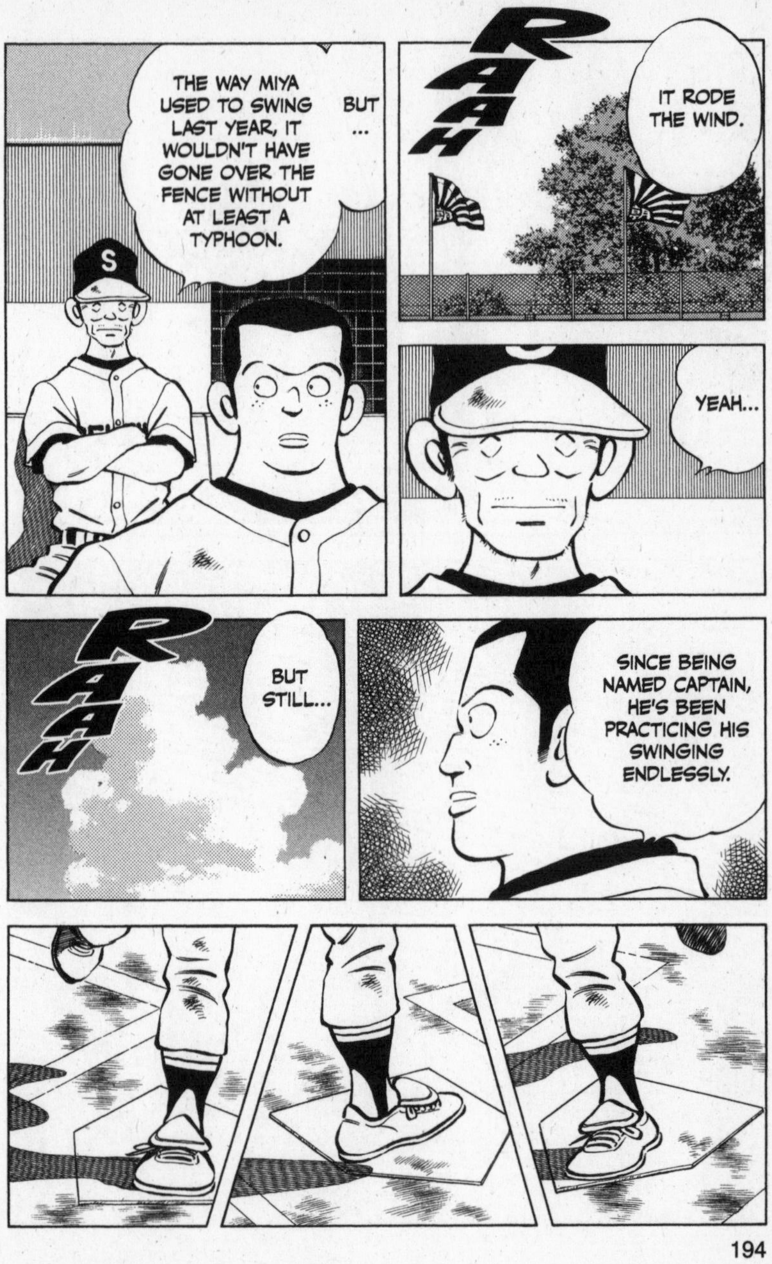
RAAAH
IT RODE THE WIND.
YEAH...
THE WAY MIYA USED TO SWING LAST YEAR, IT WOULDN'T HAVE GONE OVER THE FENCE WITHOUT AT LEAST A TYPHOON.
BUT ...
SINCE BEING NAMED CAPTAIN, HE'S BEEN PRACTICING HIS SWINGING ENDLESSLY.
RAAAH
BUT STILL...

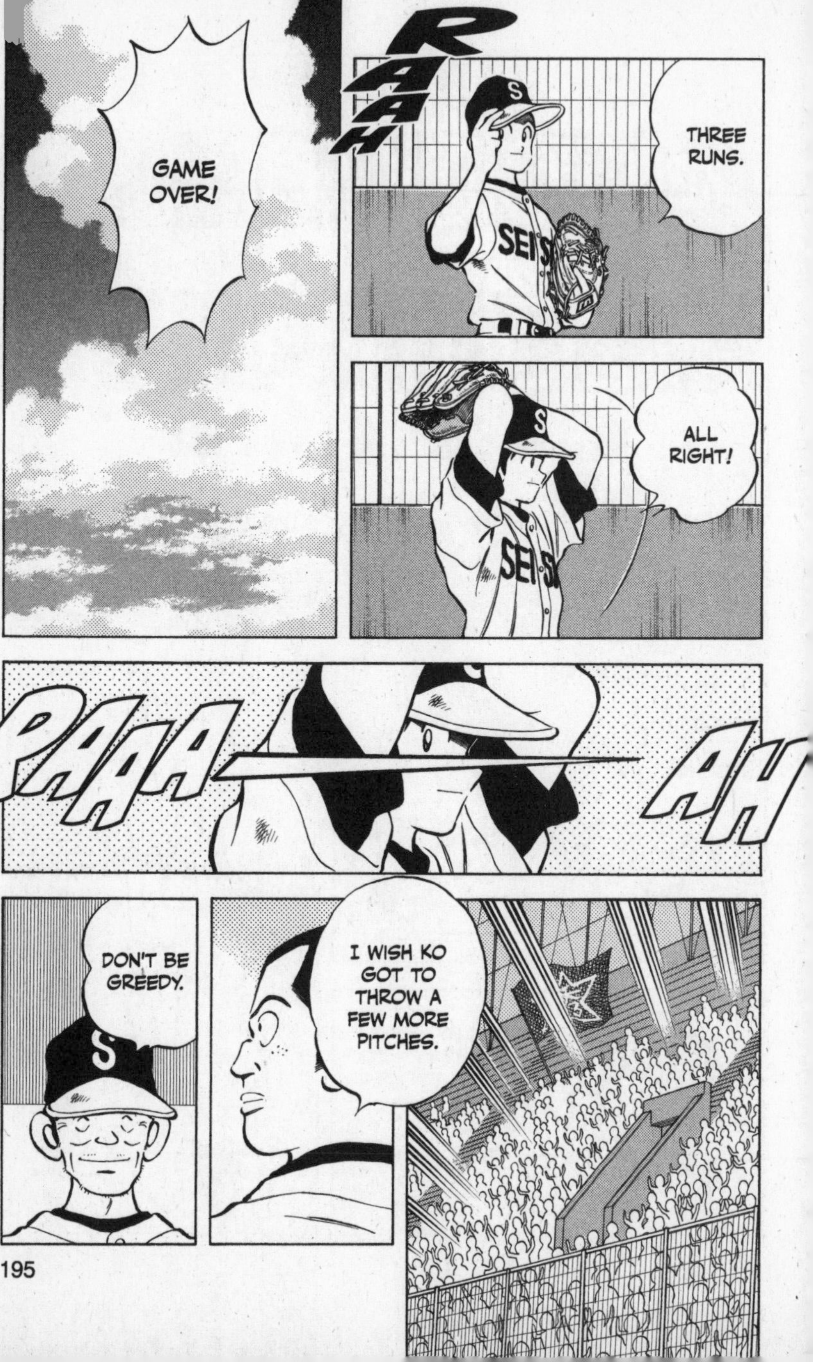
RAAAH
THREE RUNS.
ALL RIGHT!
GAME OVER!
RAAAAH
I WISH KO GOT TO THROW A FEW MORE PITCHES.
DON'T BE GREEDY.

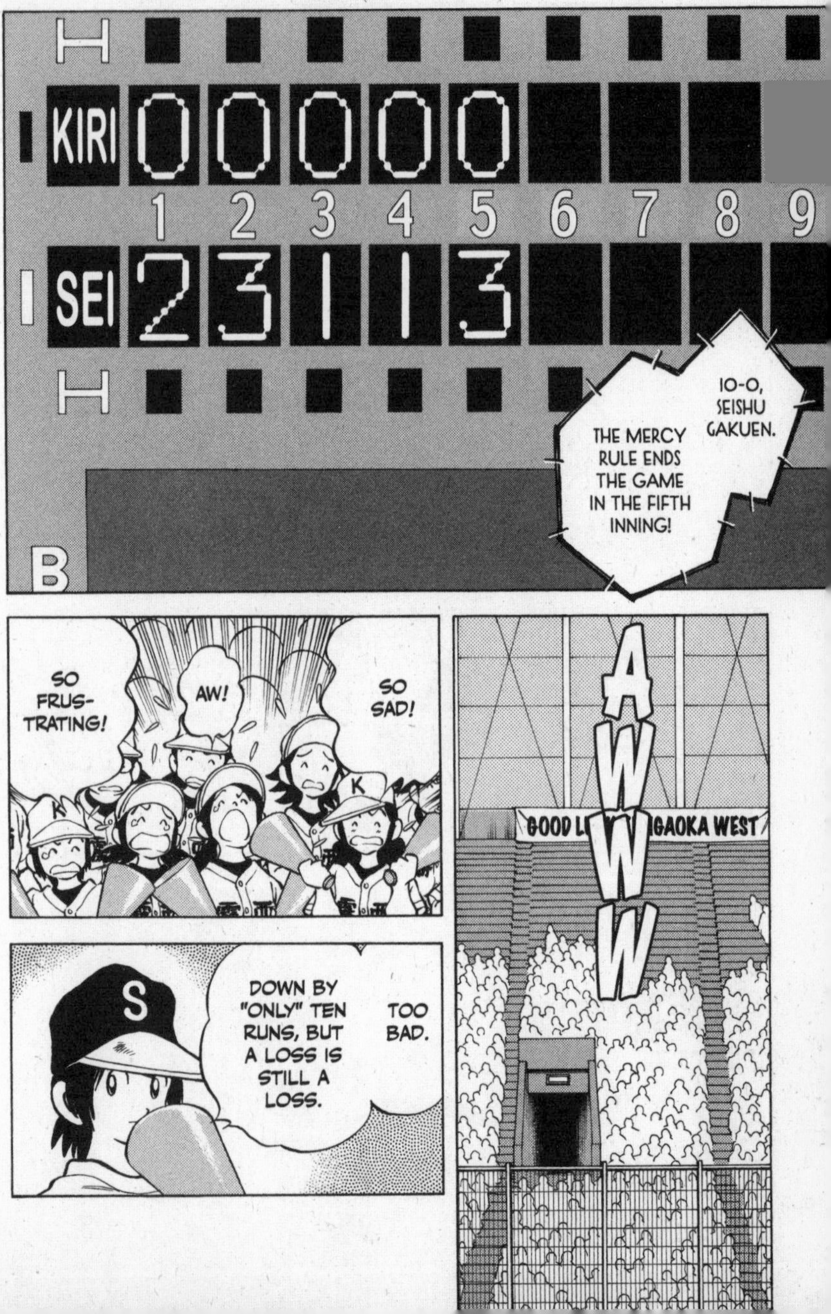
KIRI 0 0 0 0 0
1 2 3 4 5 6 7 8 9
SEI 2 3 1 1 3
10-0, SEISHU GAKUEN.
THE MERCY RULE ENDS THE GAME IN THE FIFTH INNING!
AWWWW
SO SAD!
AW!
SO FRUS-TRATING!
TOO BAD.
DOWN BY "ONLY" TEN RUNS, BUT A LOSS IS STILL A LOSS.

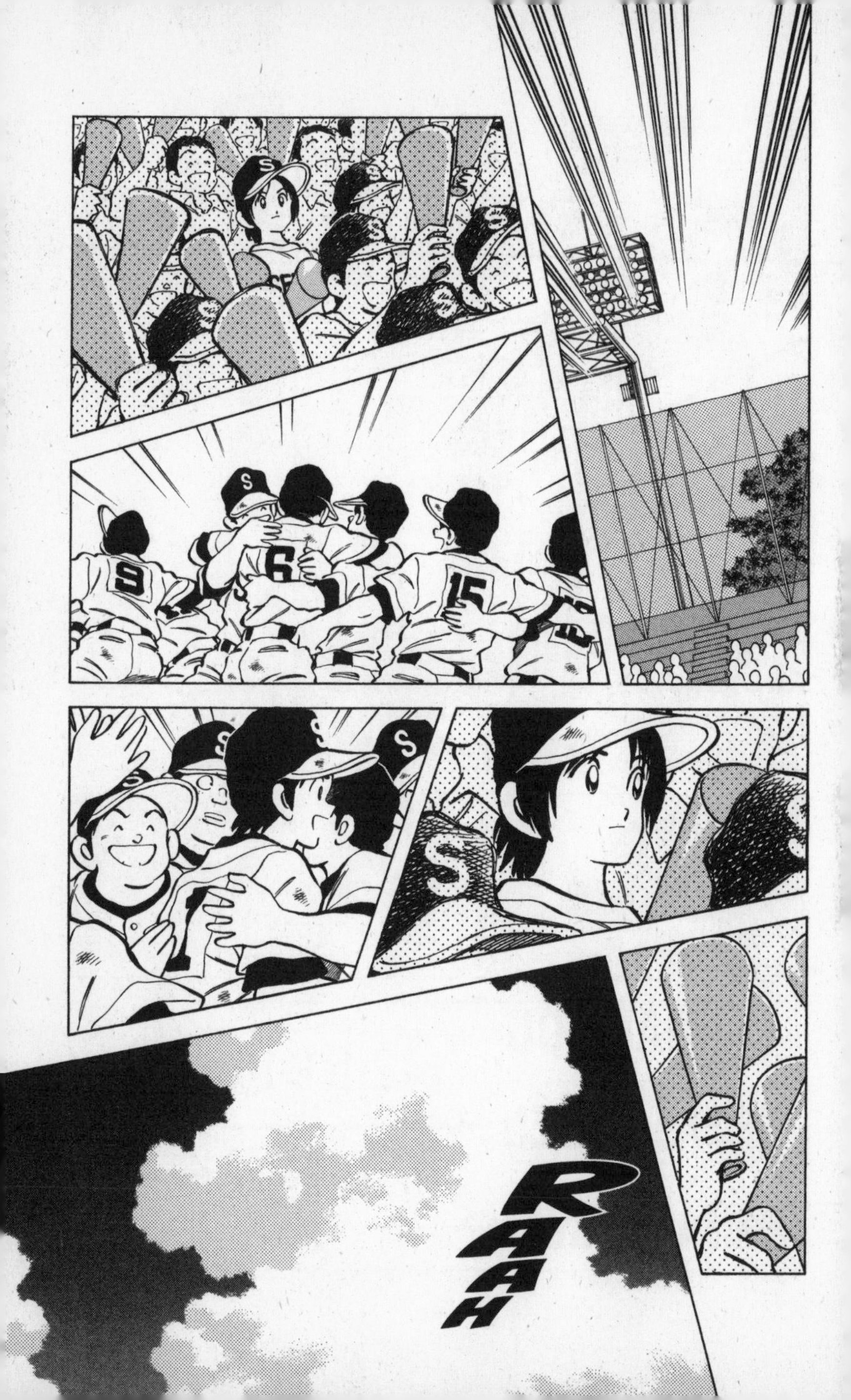
RAAAH

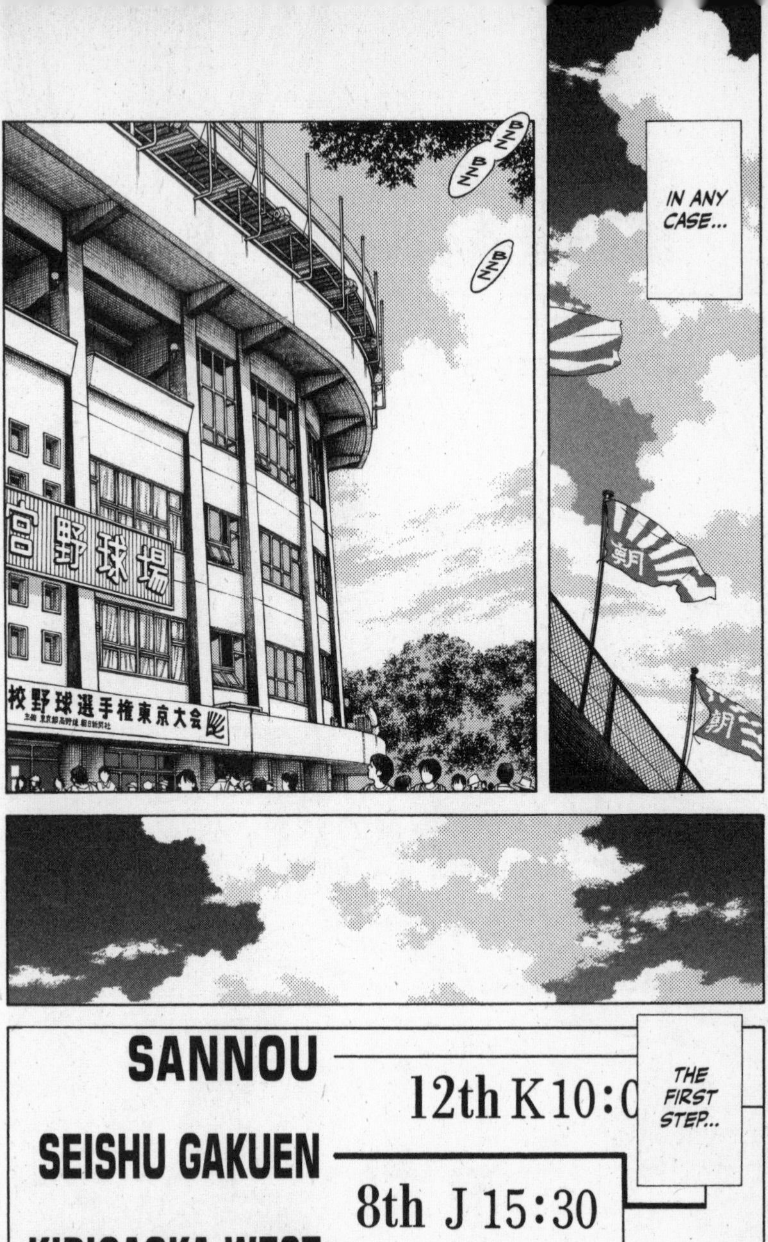
IN ANY CASE...
BZZ
BZZ
BZZ
宮野球場
校野球選手権東京大会
THE FIRST STEP...
SANNOU
12th K 10:0
SEISHU GAKUEN
8th J 15:30
KIRIGAOKA WEST

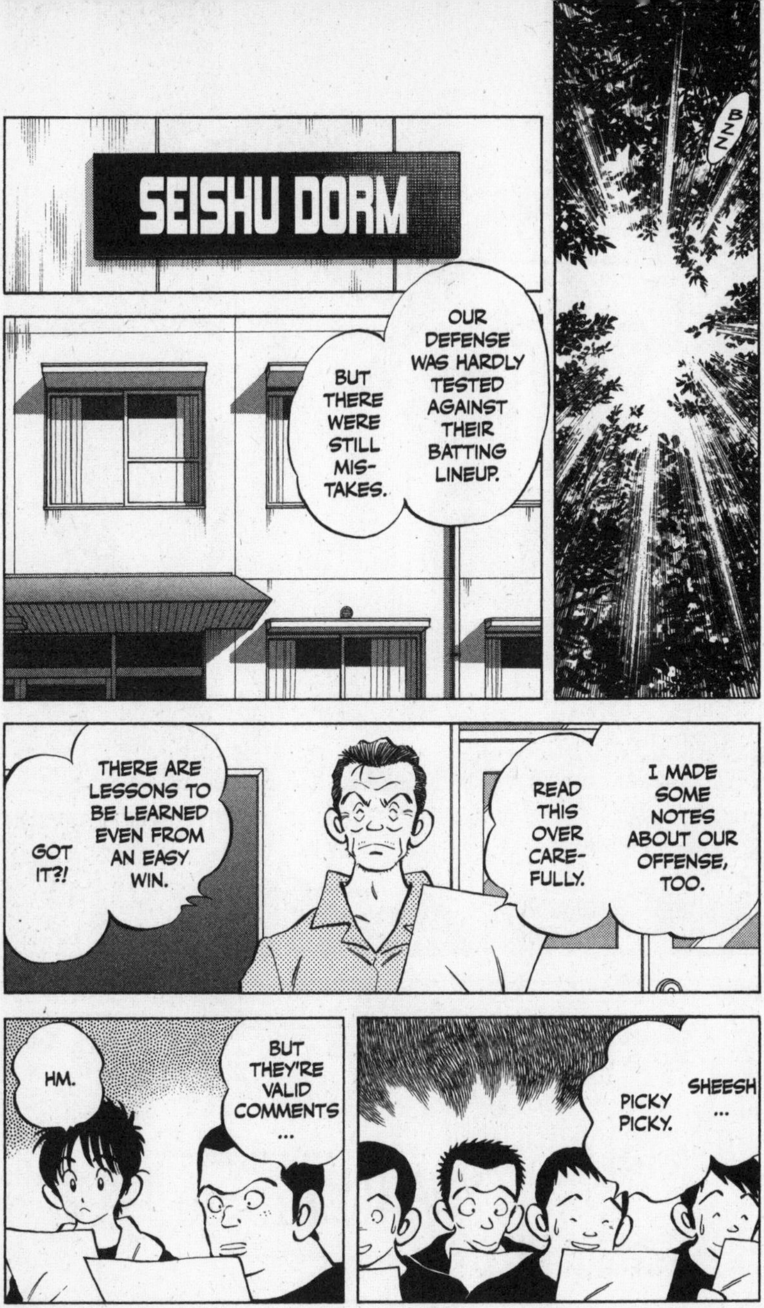
BZZ
SEISHU DORM
OUR DEFENSE WAS HARDLY TESTED AGAINST THEIR BATTING LINEUP.
BUT THERE WERE STILL MIS-TAKES.
I MADE SOME NOTES ABOUT OUR OFFENSE, TOO.
READ THIS OVER CARE-FULLY.
THERE ARE LESSONS TO BE LEARNED EVEN FROM AN EASY WIN.
GOT IT?!
SHEESH...
PICKY PICKY.
BUT THEY'RE VALID COMMENTS...
HM.

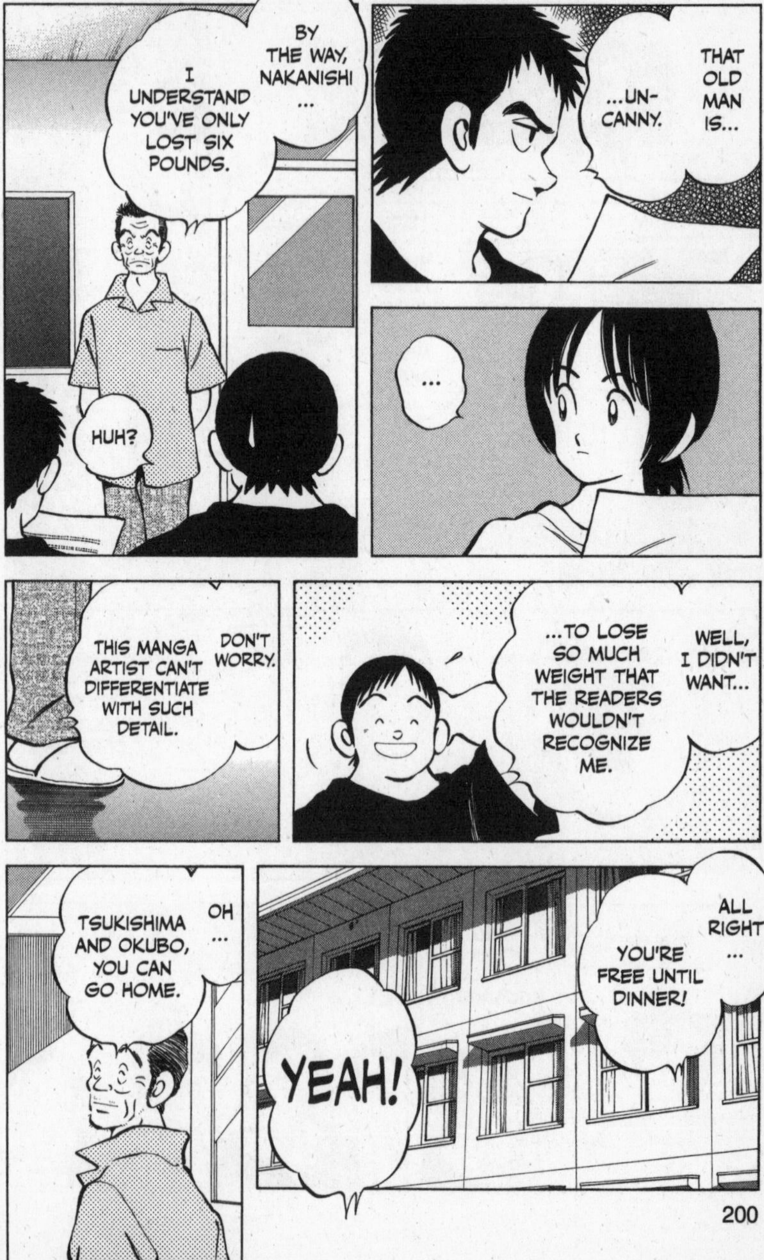
THAT OLD MAN IS...
...UN-CANNY.
...
BY THE WAY, NAKANISHI...
I UNDERSTAND YOU'VE ONLY LOST SIX POUNDS.
HUH?
WELL, I DIDN'T WANT...
...TO LOSE SO MUCH WEIGHT THAT THE READERS WOULDN'T RECOGNIZE ME.
DON'T WORRY.
THIS MANGA ARTIST CAN'T DIFFERENTIATE WITH SUCH DETAIL.
ALL RIGHT...
YOU'RE FREE UNTIL DINNER!
YEAH!
OH...
TSUKISHIMA AND OKUBO, YOU CAN GO HOME.

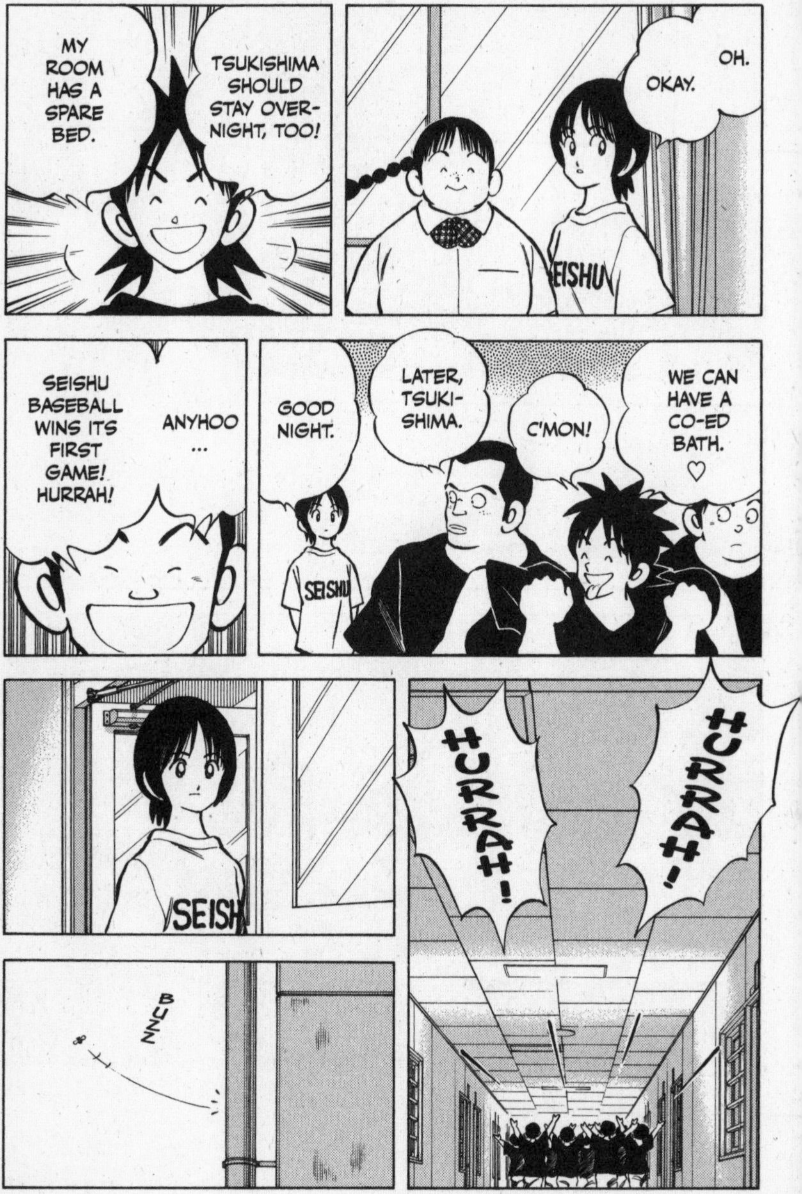
OH.
OKAY.
TSUKISHIMA SHOULD STAY OVER-NIGHT, TOO!
MY ROOM HAS A SPARE BED.
WE CAN HAVE A CO-ED BATH. ♡
C'MON!
LATER, TSUKI-SHIMA.
GOOD NIGHT.
ANYHOO ...
SEISHU BASEBALL WINS ITS FIRST GAME! HURRAH!
HURRAH!
HURRAH!
BUZZ

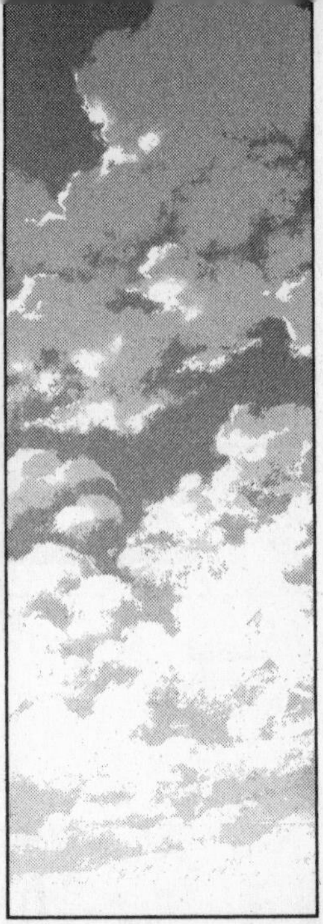
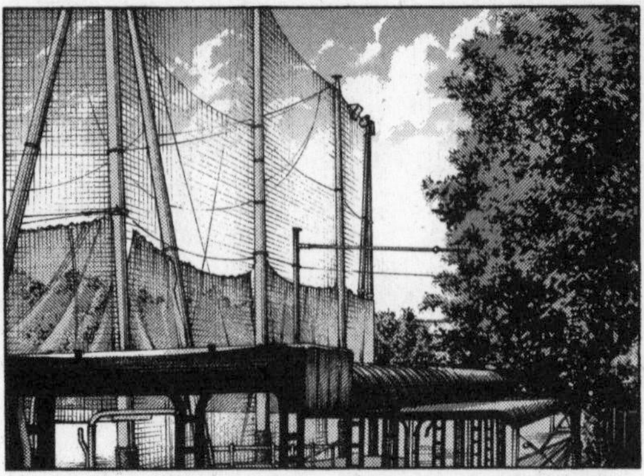
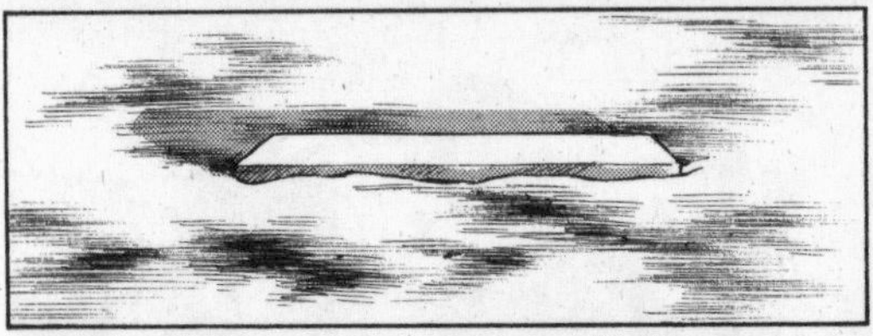
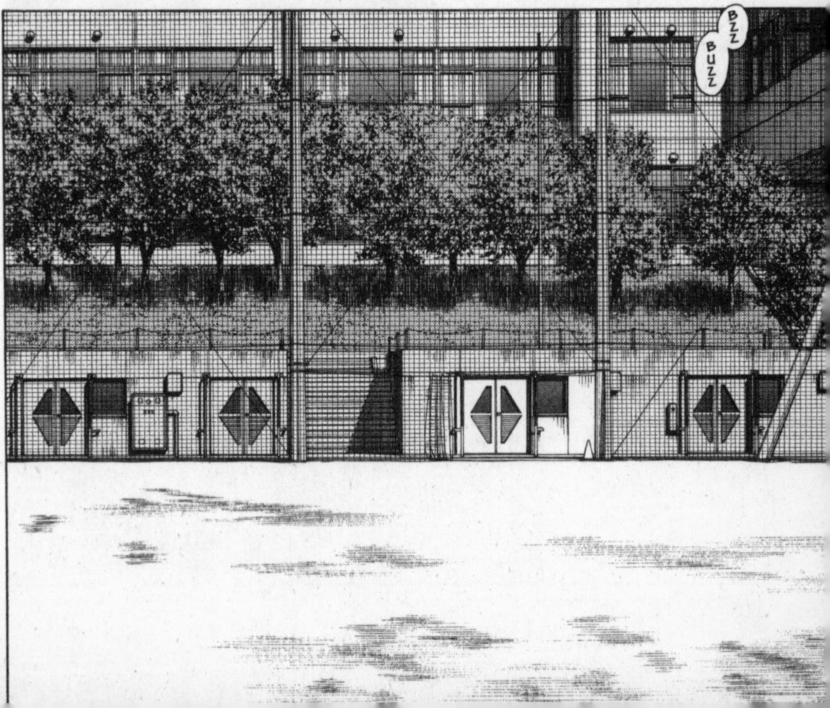
BZZ
BUZZ

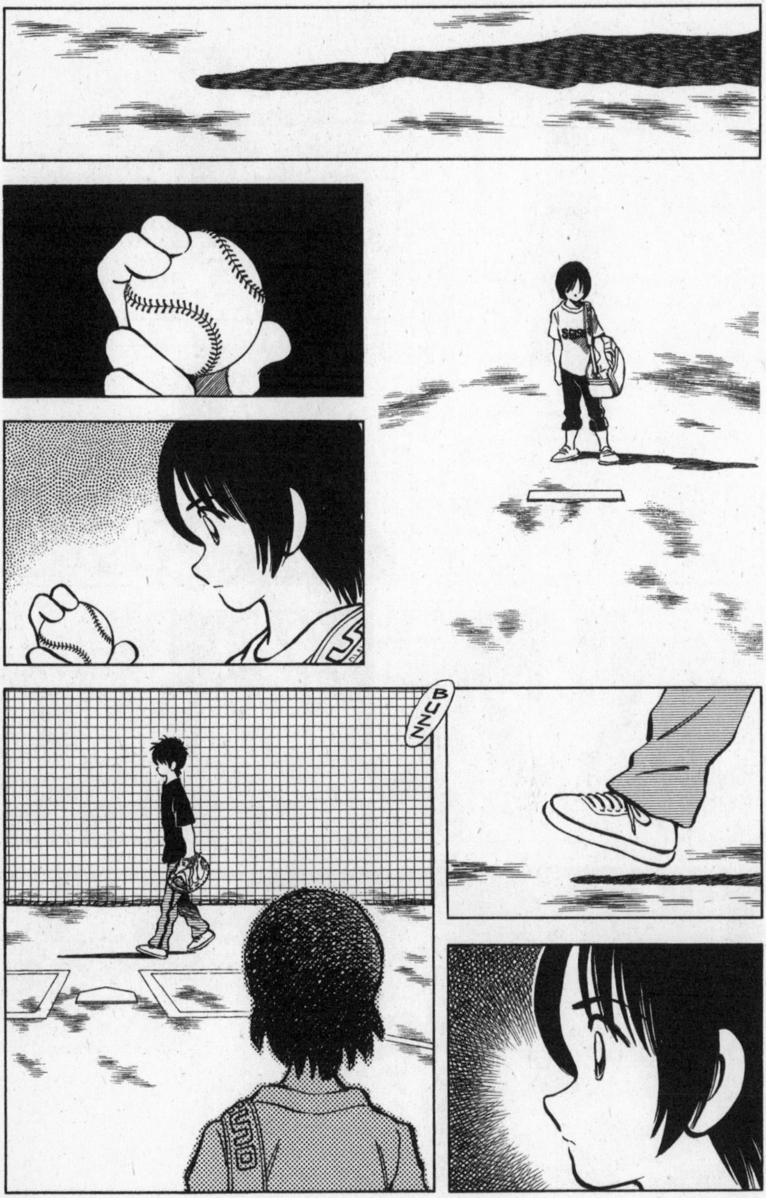
BUZZ

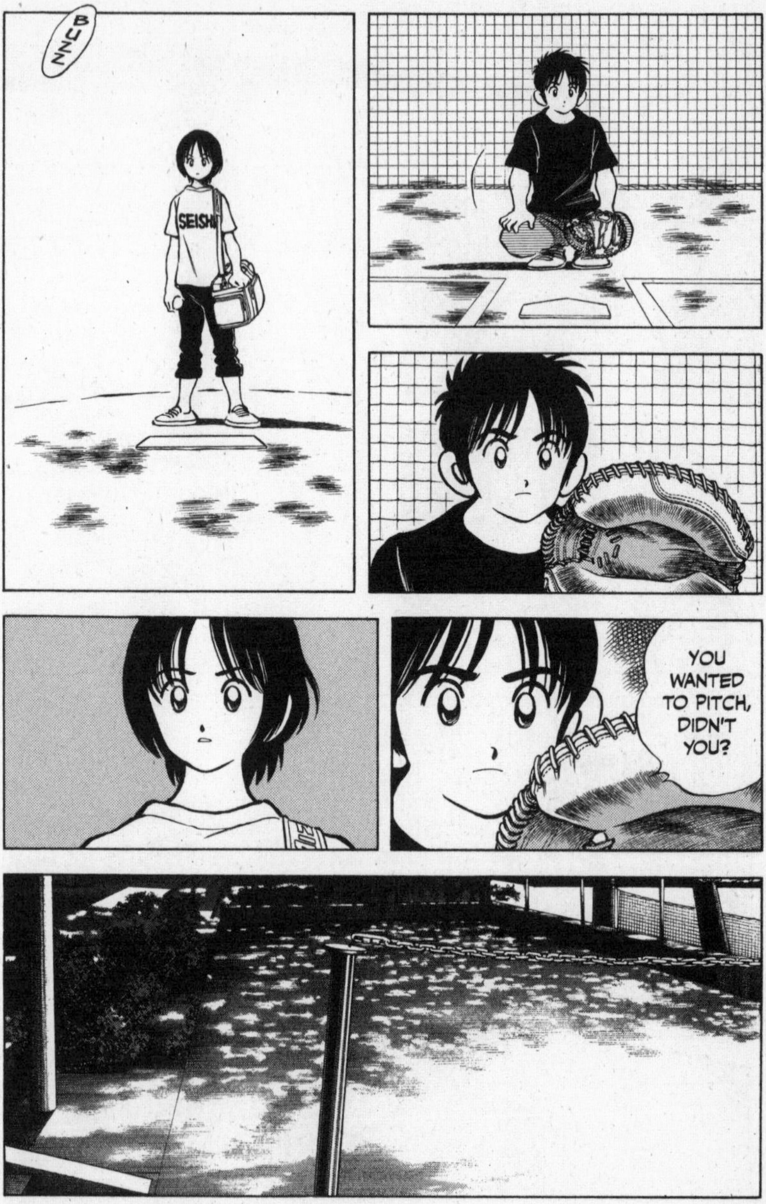
BUZZ
SEISHU
YOU WANTED TO PITCH, DIDN'T YOU?

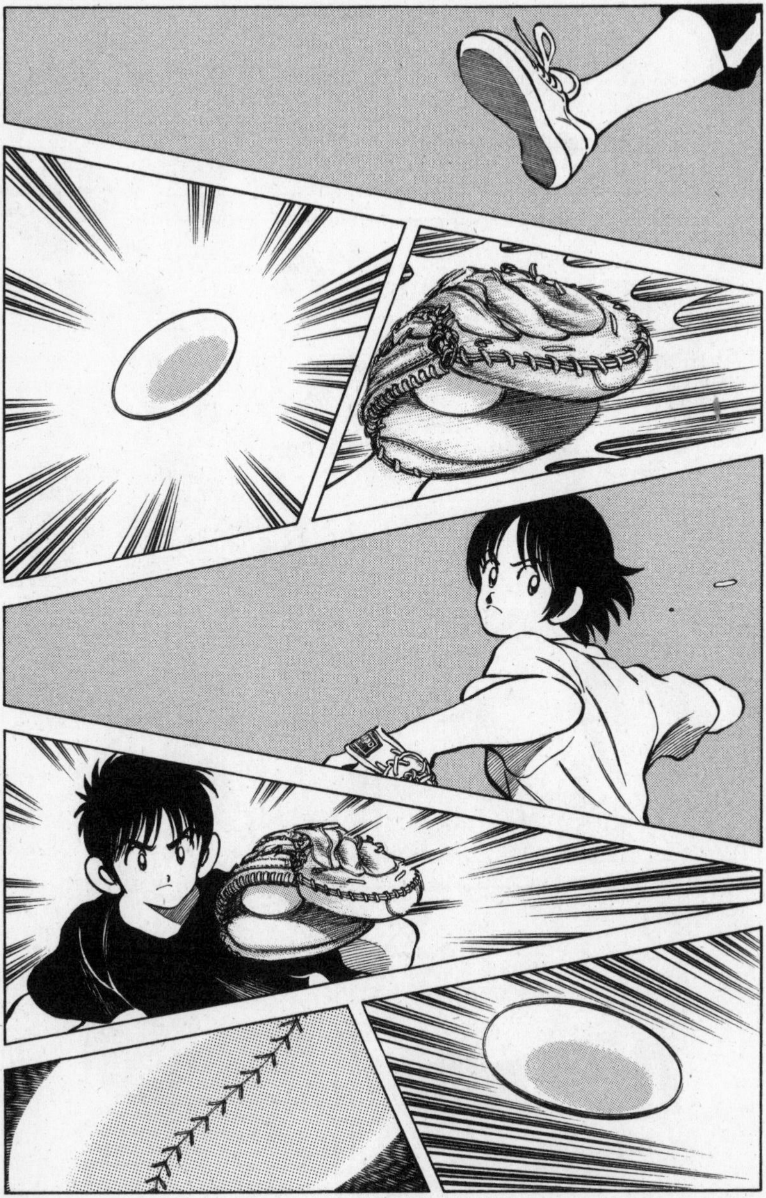

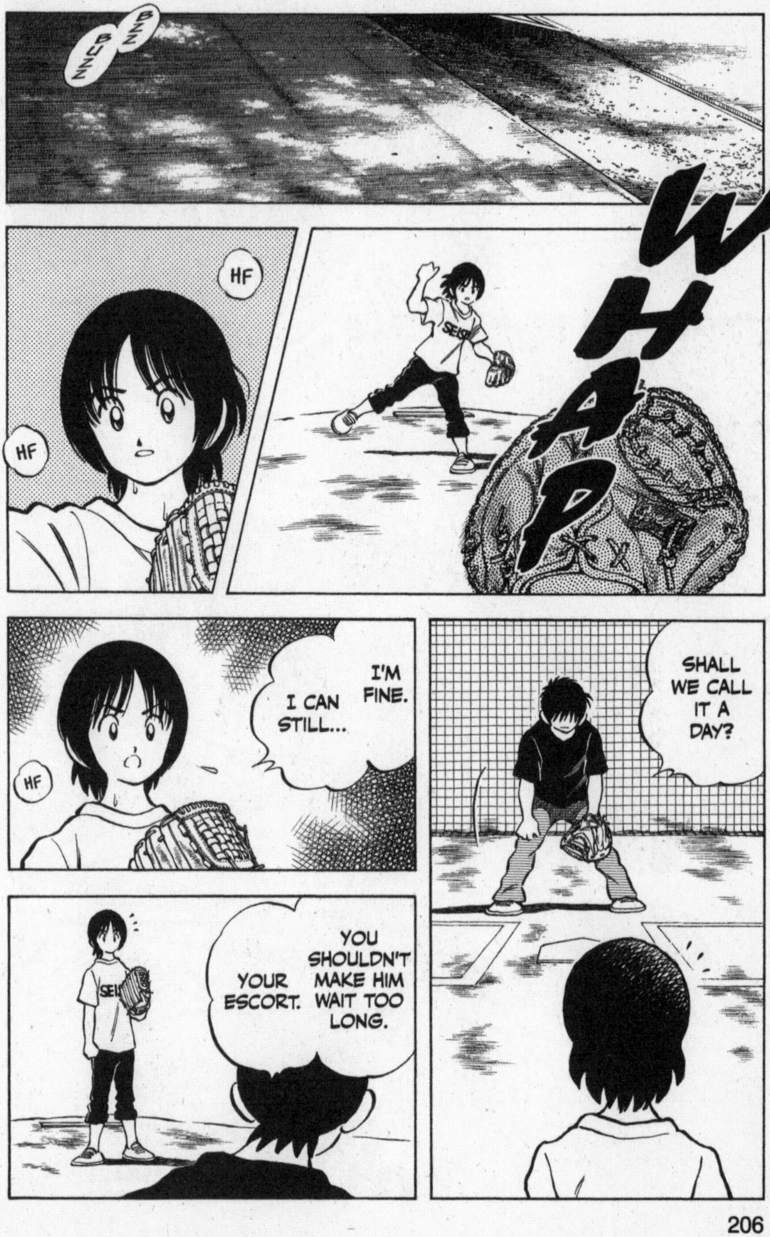
BUZZ BZZ
WHAP
HF
HF
SHALL WE CALL IT A DAY?
I'M FINE.
I CAN STILL...
HF
YOU SHOULDN'T MAKE HIM WAIT TOO LONG.
YOUR ESCORT.

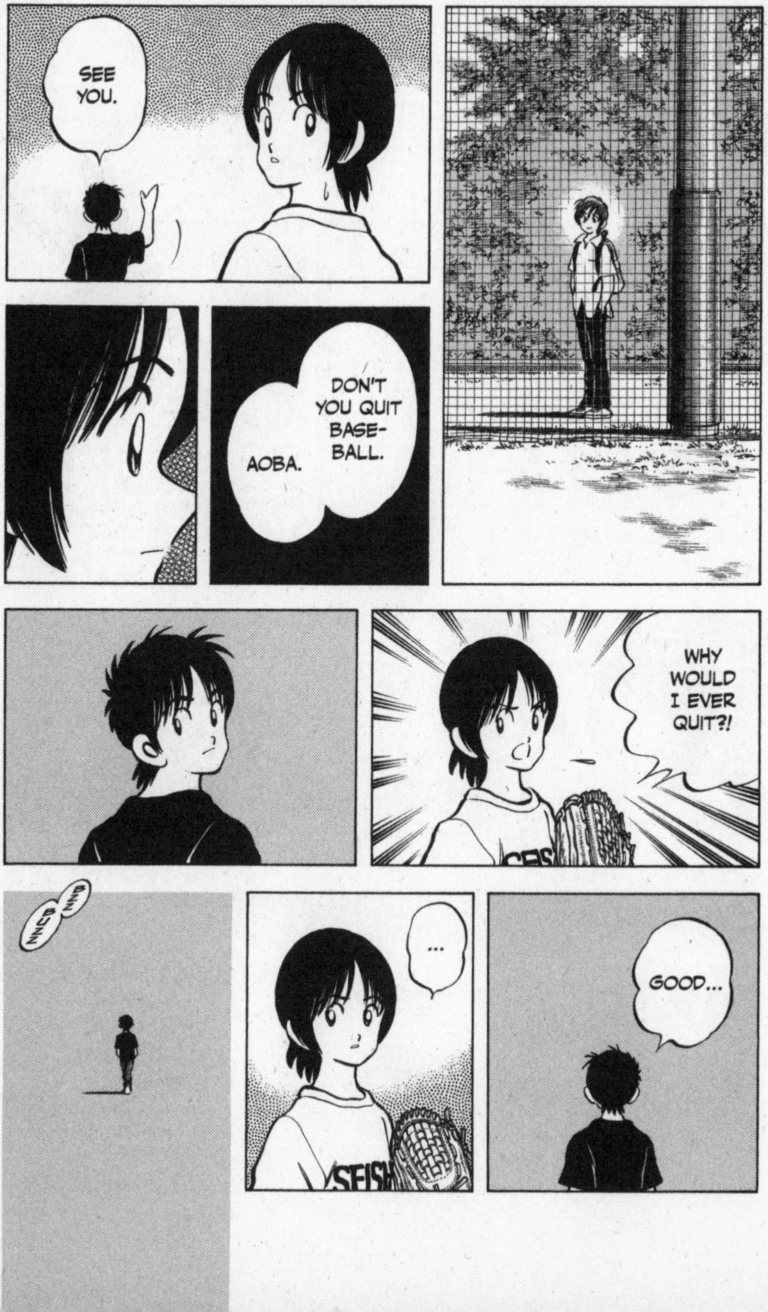
SEE YOU.
DON'T YOU QUIT BASE-BALL.
AOBA.
WHY WOULD I EVER QUIT?!
GOOD...
...
BZZ
BUZZ

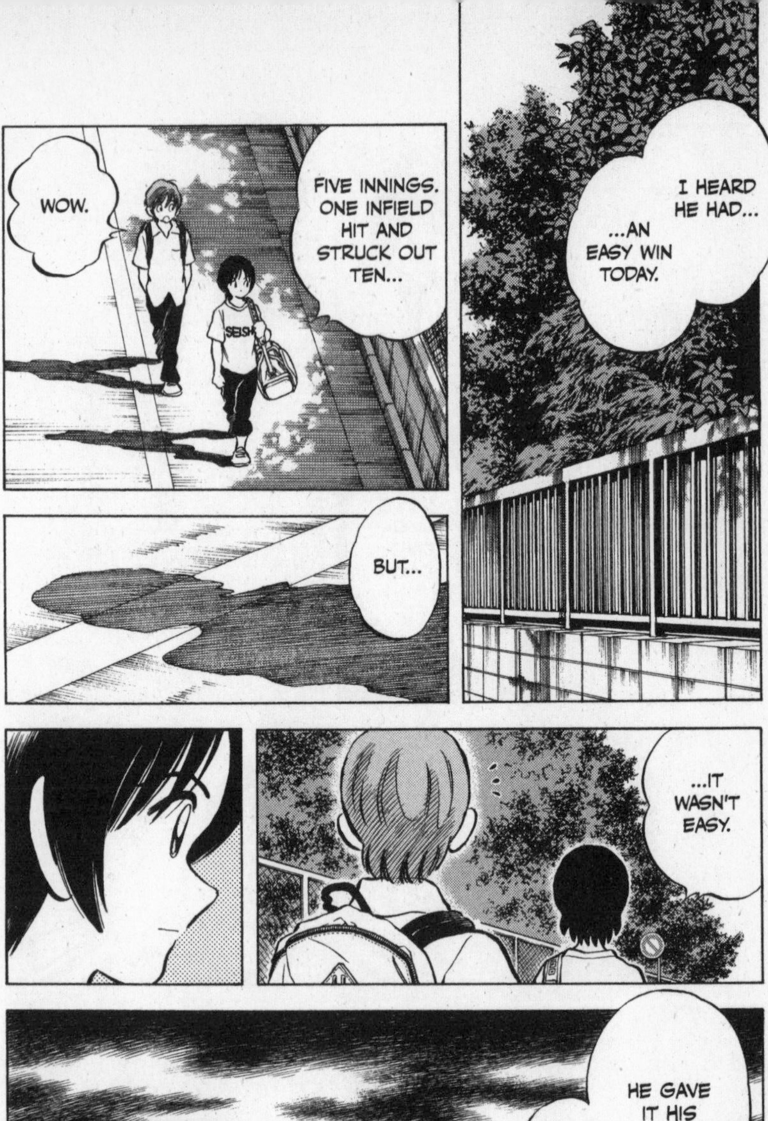
I HEARD HE HAD...
...AN EASY WIN TODAY.
FIVE INNINGS. ONE INFIELD HIT AND STRUCK OUT TEN...
WOW.
BUT...
...IT WASN'T EASY.
HE GAVE IT HIS ALL...
AGAINST EVERY BATTER.
BZZ

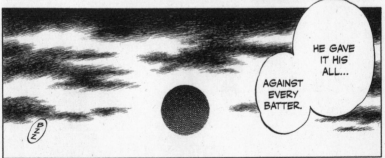

# CHAPTER 72
# IT'S AN HONOR

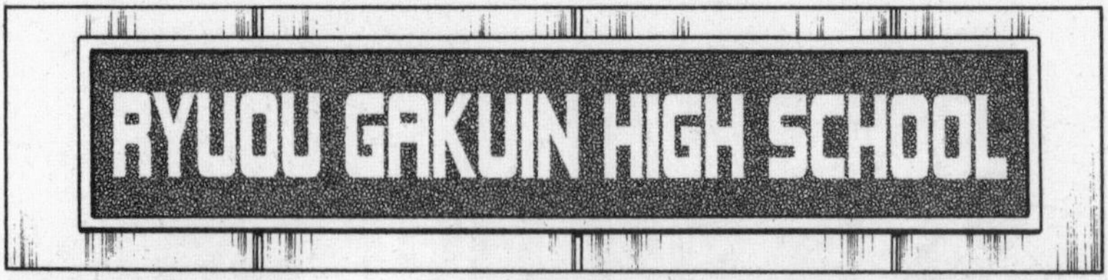
RYUOU GAKUIN HIGH SCHOOL

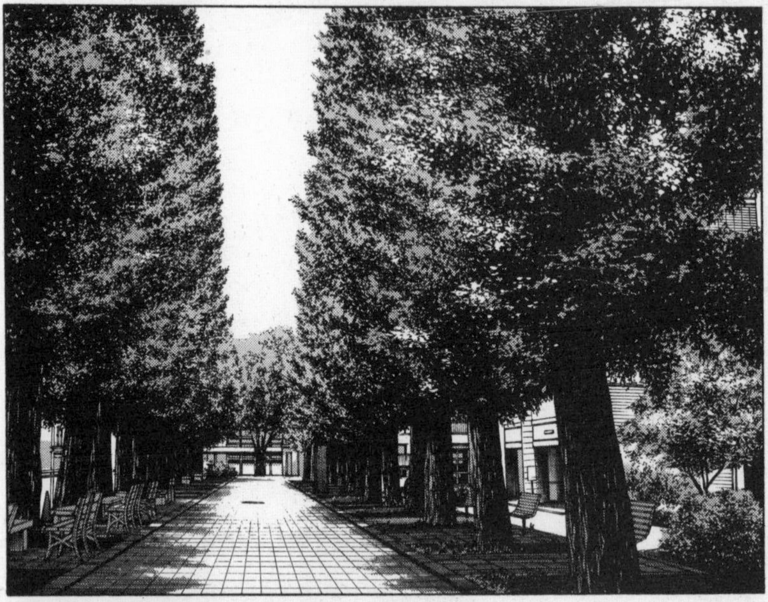

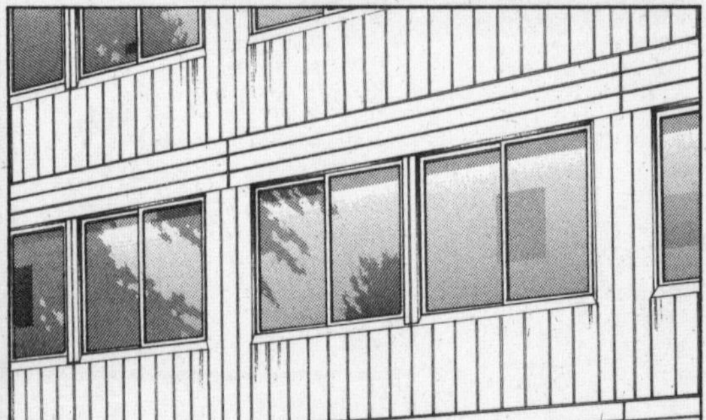

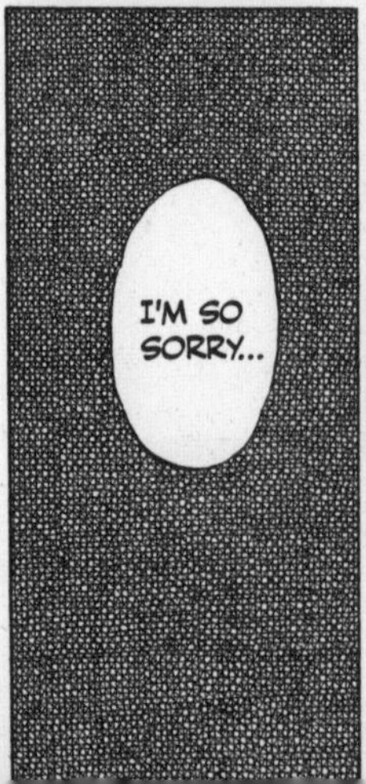
I'M SO SORRY...

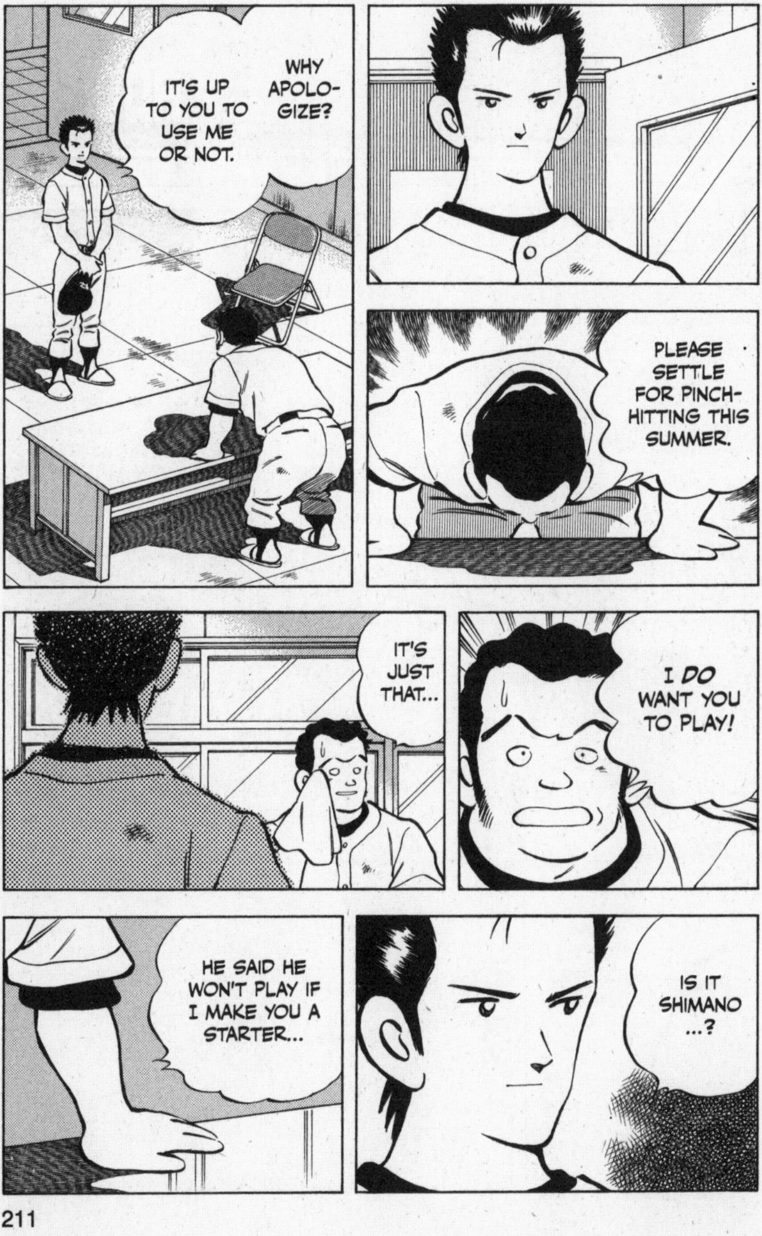
PLEASE SETTLE FOR PINCH-HITTING THIS SUMMER.
WHY APOLO-GIZE?
IT'S UP TO YOU TO USE ME OR NOT.
I *DO* WANT YOU TO PLAY!
IT'S JUST THAT...
IS IT SHIMANO ...?
HE SAID HE WON'T PLAY IF I MAKE YOU A STARTER...

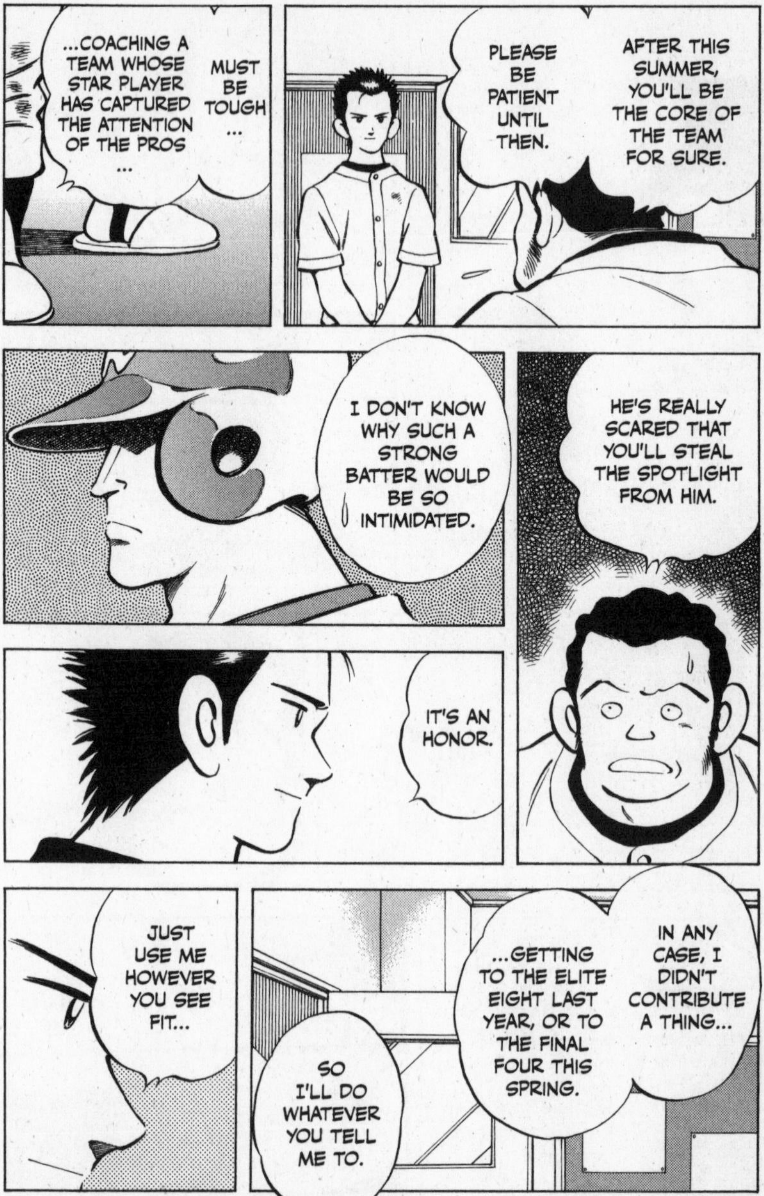
AFTER THIS SUMMER, YOU'LL BE THE CORE OF THE TEAM FOR SURE.
PLEASE BE PATIENT UNTIL THEN.
...COACHING A TEAM WHOSE STAR PLAYER HAS CAPTURED THE ATTENTION OF THE PROS ...
MUST BE TOUGH ...
HE'S REALLY SCARED THAT YOU'LL STEAL THE SPOTLIGHT FROM HIM.
I DON'T KNOW WHY SUCH A STRONG BATTER WOULD BE SO INTIMIDATED.
IT'S AN HONOR.
IN ANY CASE, I DIDN'T CONTRIBUTE A THING...
...GETTING TO THE ELITE EIGHT LAST YEAR, OR TO THE FINAL FOUR THIS SPRING.
SO I'LL DO WHATEVER YOU TELL ME TO.
JUST USE ME HOWEVER YOU SEE FIT...

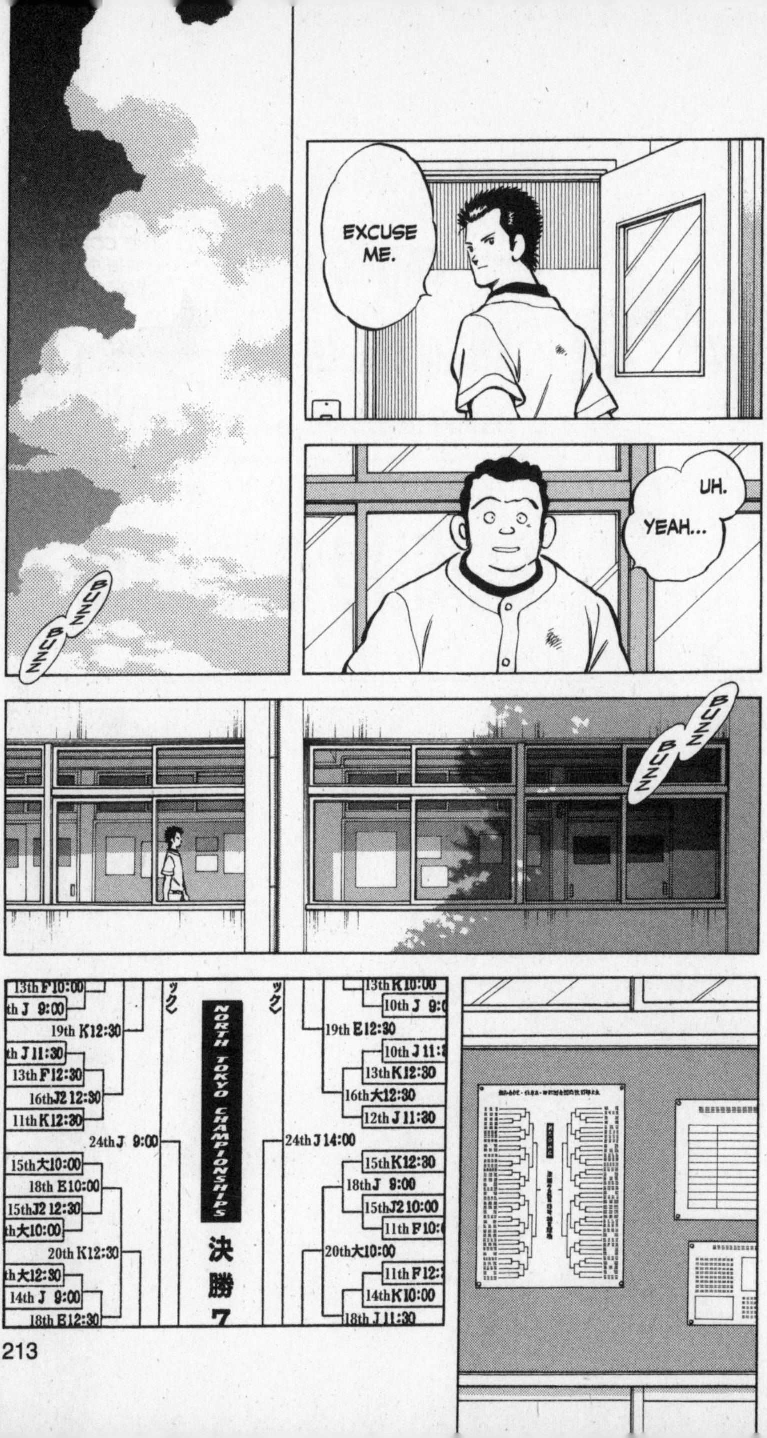
EXCUSE ME.
UH. YEAH...
BUZZ BUZZ
BUZZ BUZZ
NORTH TOKYO CHAMPIONSHIPS
決勝
7

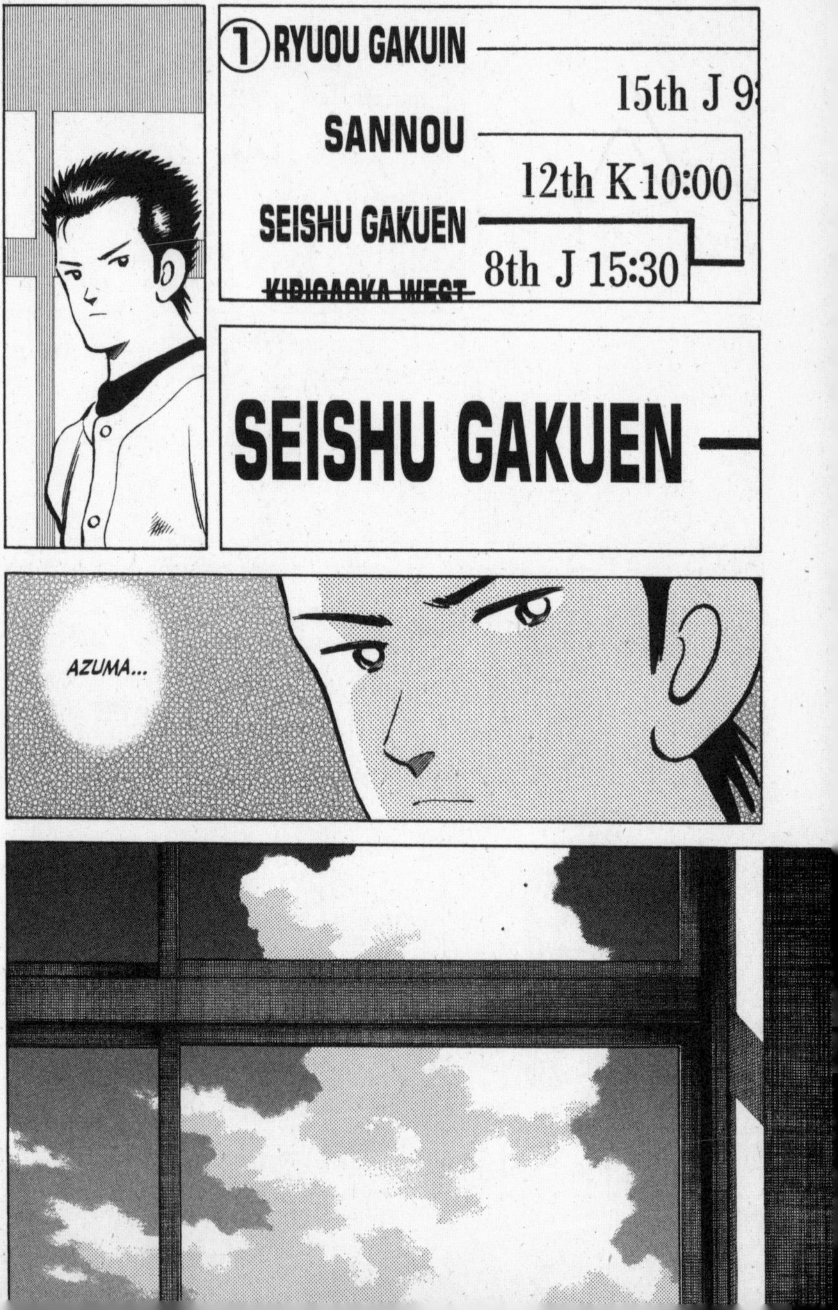
1 RYUOU GAKUIN
15th J 9
SANNOU
12th K10:00
SEISHU GAKUEN
8th J 15:30
SEISHU GAKUEN
AZUMA...

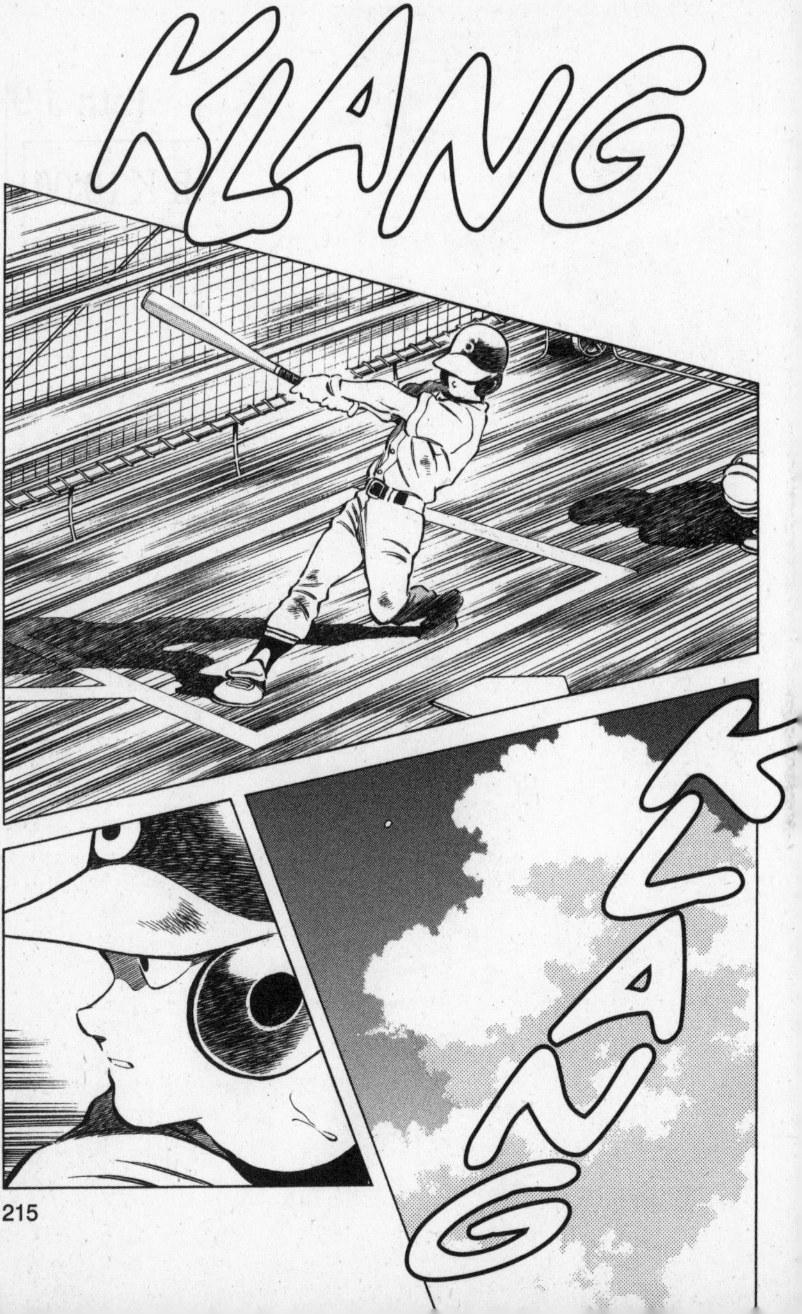
KLANG
KLANG

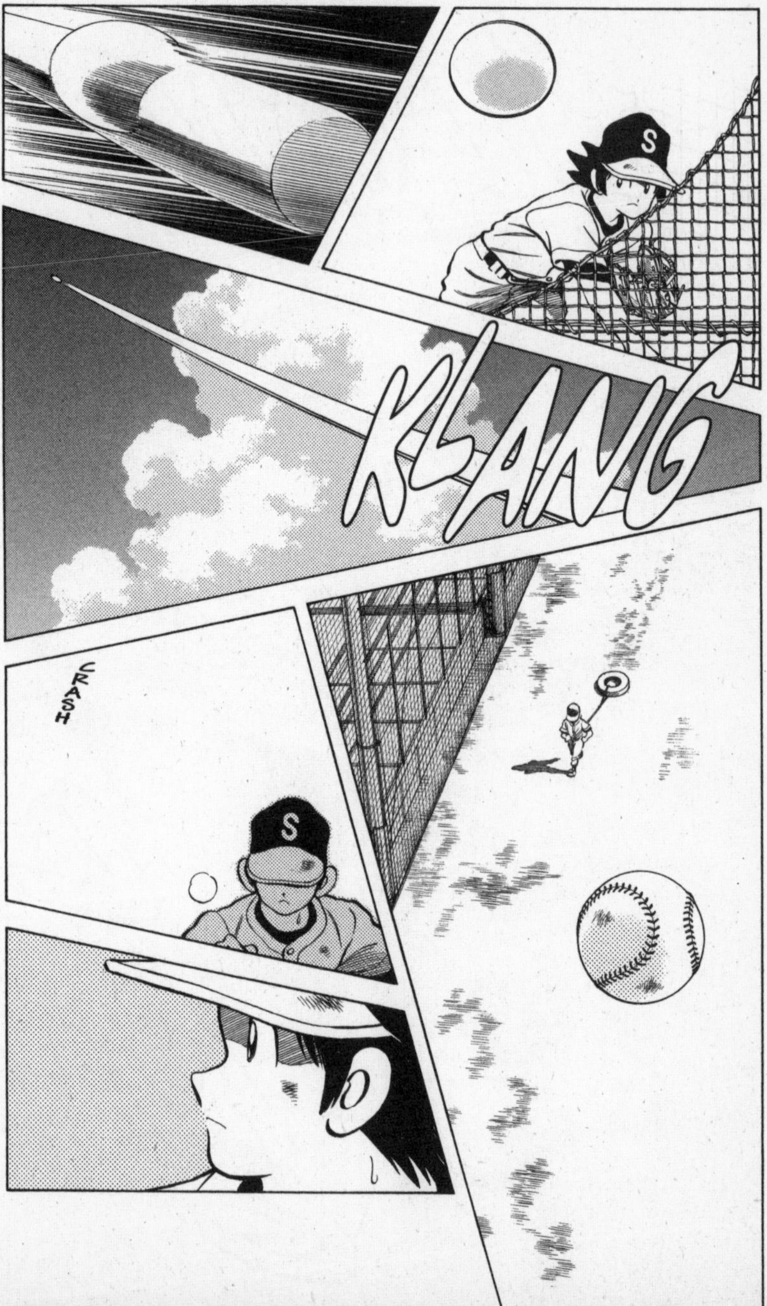
KLANG
CRASH

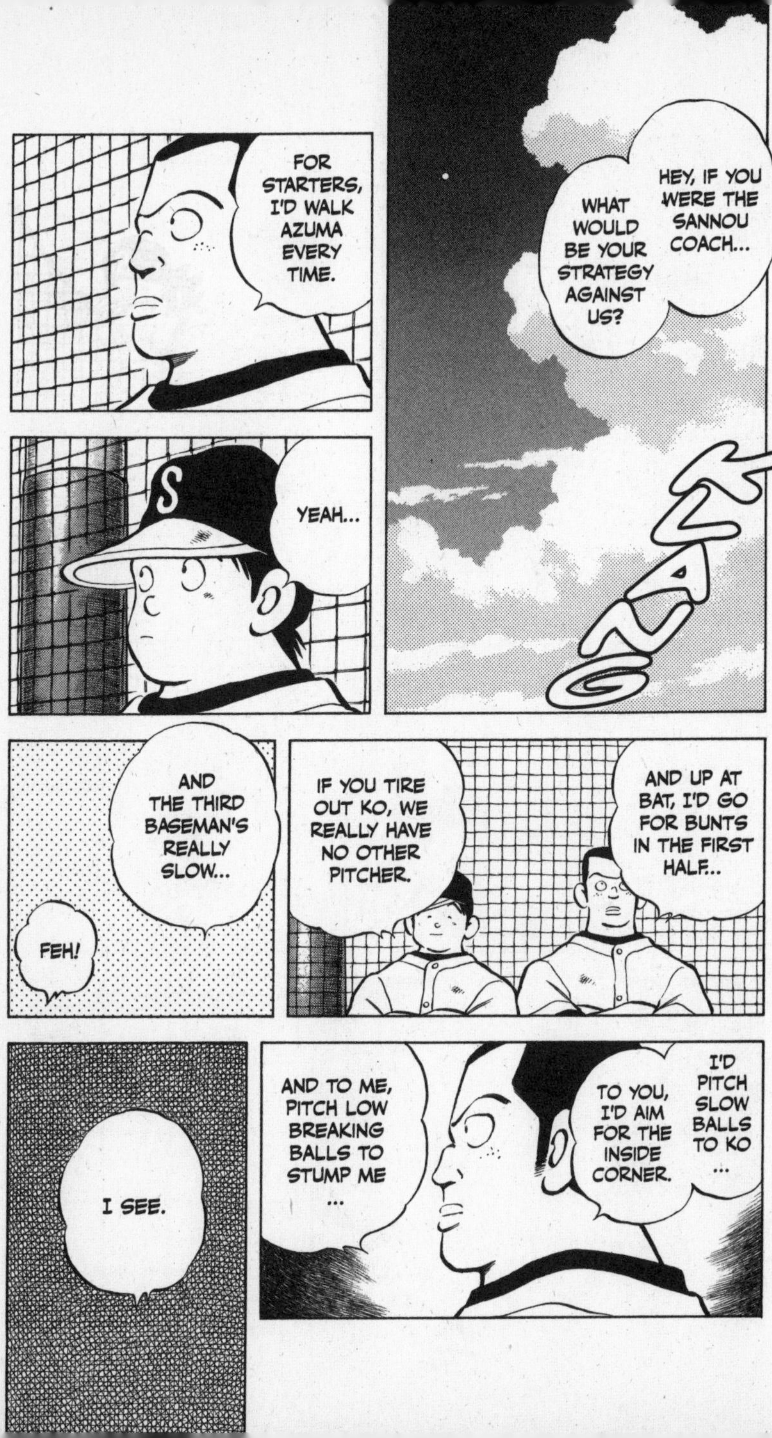
HEY, IF YOU WERE THE SANNOU COACH...
WHAT WOULD BE YOUR STRATEGY AGAINST US?
KANG
FOR STARTERS, I'D WALK AZUMA EVERY TIME.
YEAH...
AND UP AT BAT, I'D GO FOR BUNTS IN THE FIRST HALF...
IF YOU TIRE OUT KO, WE REALLY HAVE NO OTHER PITCHER.
AND THE THIRD BASEMAN'S REALLY SLOW...
FEH!
I'D PITCH SLOW BALLS TO KO ...
TO YOU, I'D AIM FOR THE INSIDE CORNER.
AND TO ME, PITCH LOW BREAKING BALLS TO STUMP ME ...
I SEE.

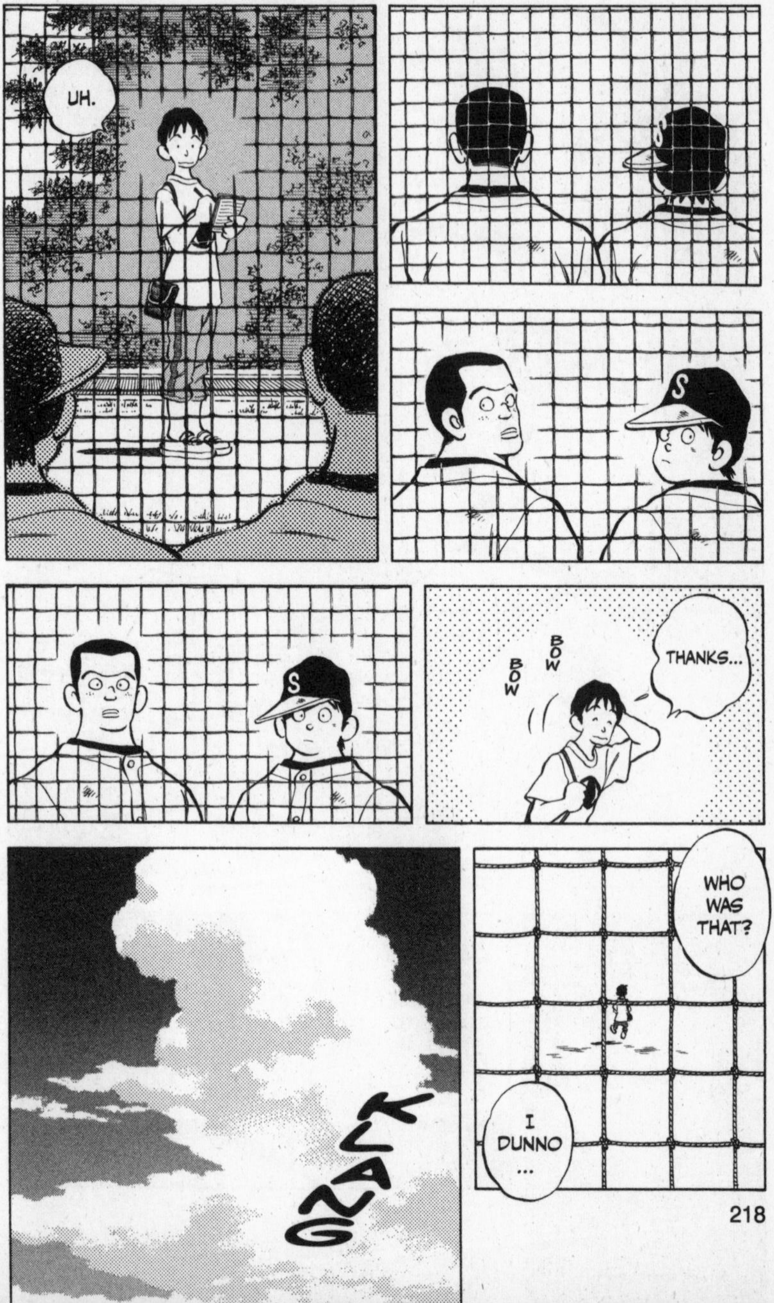
UH.
BOW BOW
THANKS...
WHO WAS THAT?
I DUNNO...
KLANG

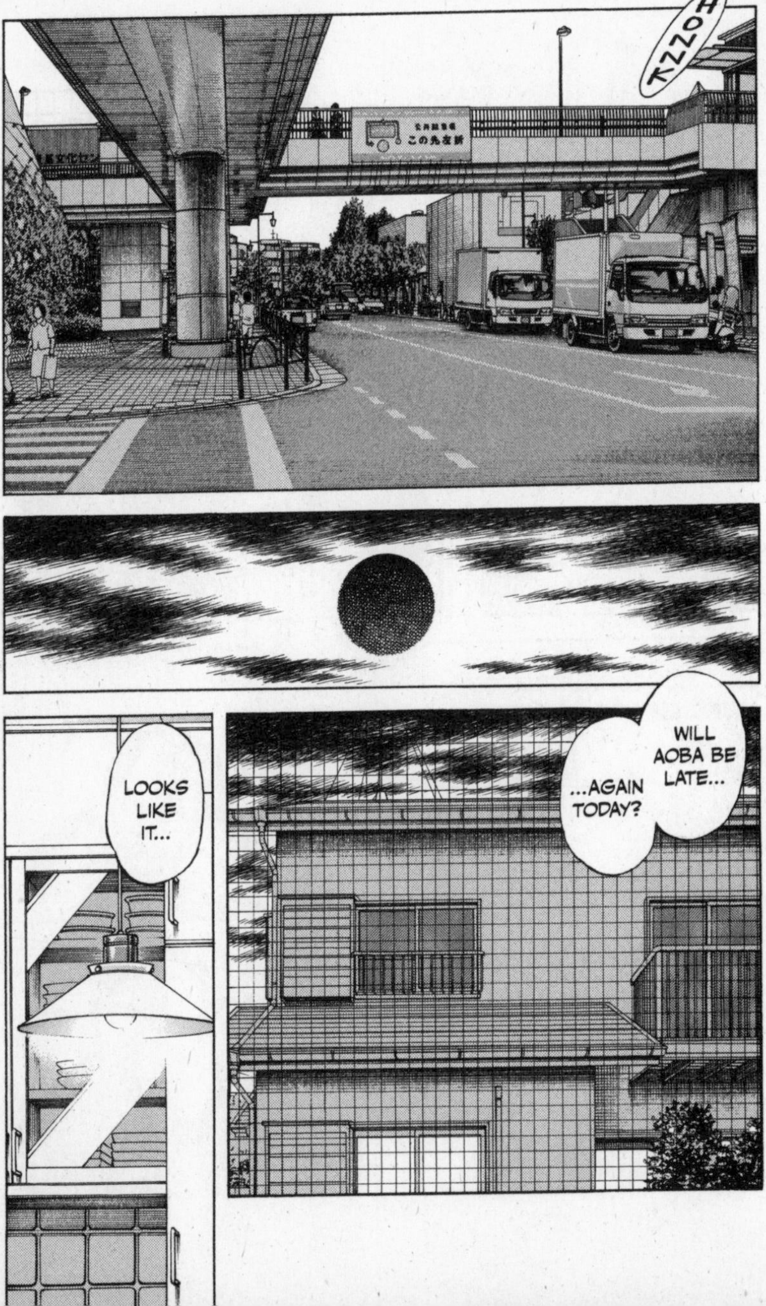
HONNK
この先左折
WILL AOBA BE LATE...
...AGAIN TODAY?
LOOKS LIKE IT...

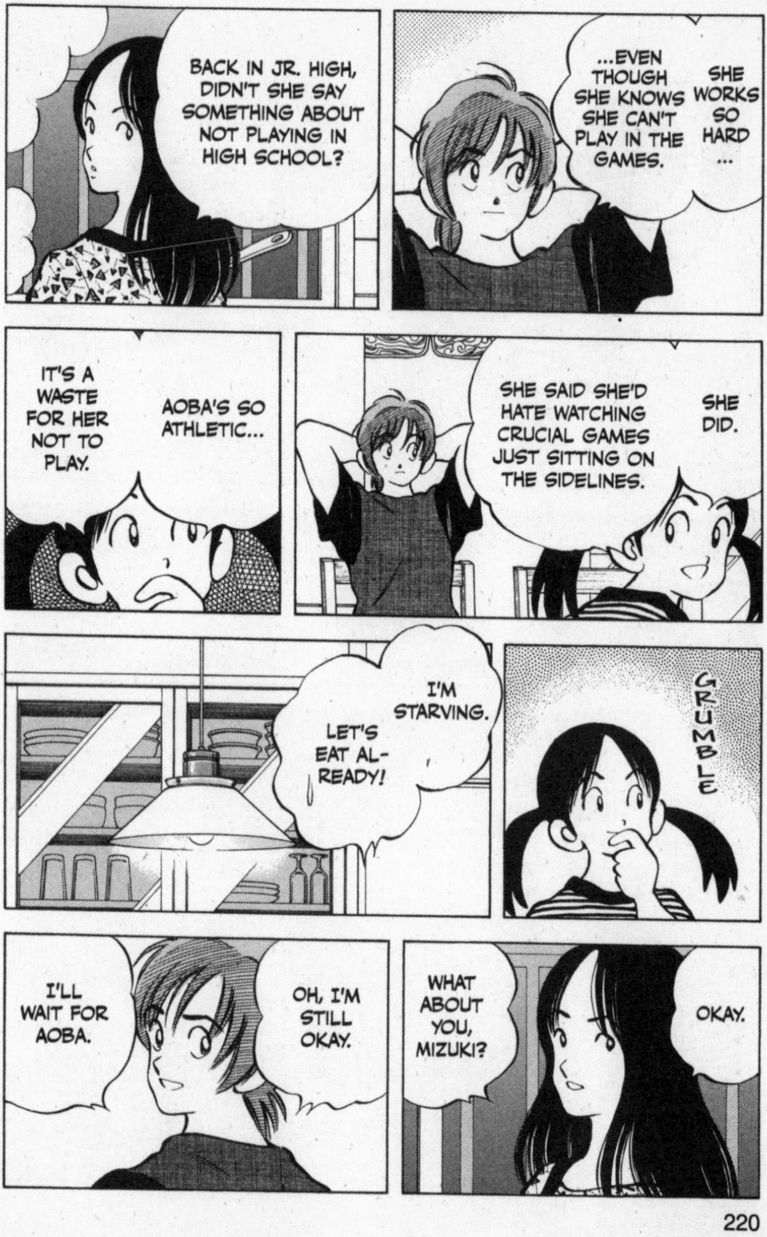

SHE WORKS SO HARD...
...EVEN THOUGH SHE KNOWS SHE CAN'T PLAY IN THE GAMES.
BACK IN JR. HIGH, DIDN'T SHE SAY SOMETHING ABOUT NOT PLAYING IN HIGH SCHOOL?
SHE DID.
SHE SAID SHE'D HATE WATCHING CRUCIAL GAMES JUST SITTING ON THE SIDELINES.
AOBA'S SO ATHLETIC...
IT'S A WASTE FOR HER NOT TO PLAY.
GRUMBLE
I'M STARVING.
LET'S EAT AL-READY!
OKAY.
WHAT ABOUT YOU, MIZUKI?
OH, I'M STILL OKAY.
I'LL WAIT FOR AOBA.

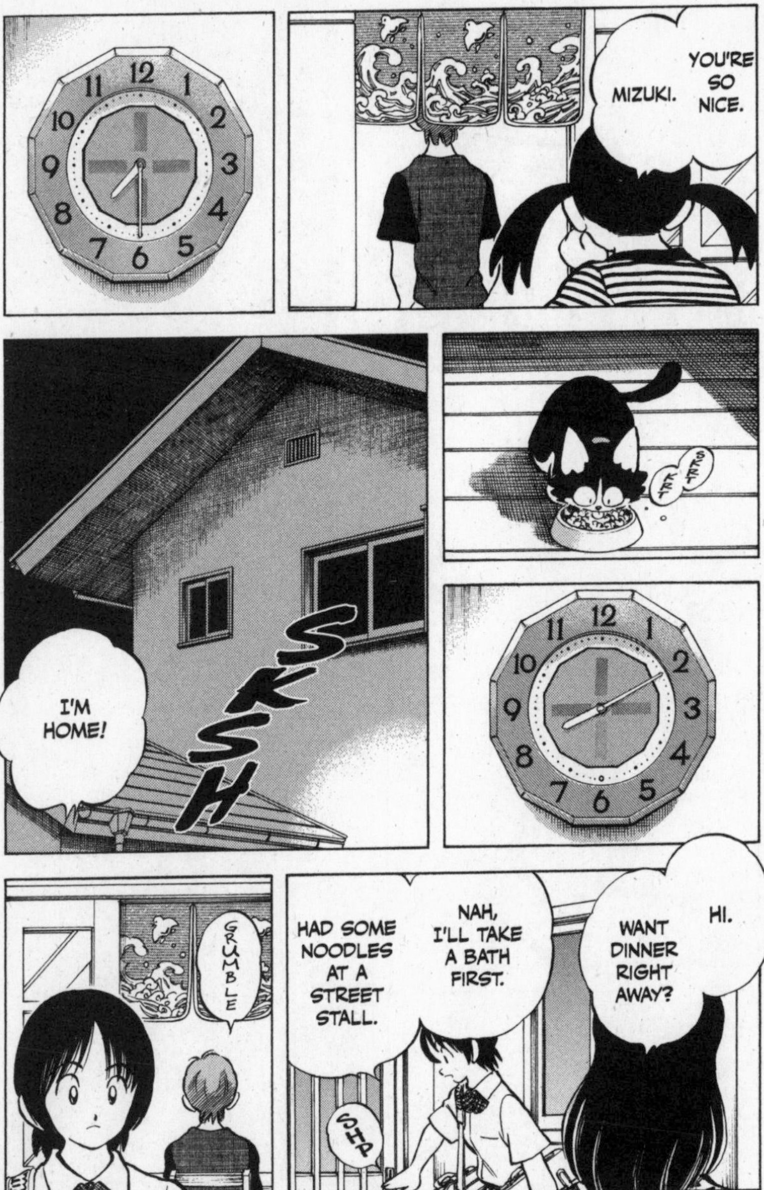
YOU'RE SO NICE.
MIZUKI.
SKRT
KRT
SKSH
I'M HOME!
HI.
WANT DINNER RIGHT AWAY?
NAH, I'LL TAKE A BATH FIRST.
HAD SOME NOODLES AT A STREET STALL.
SHP
GRUMBLE

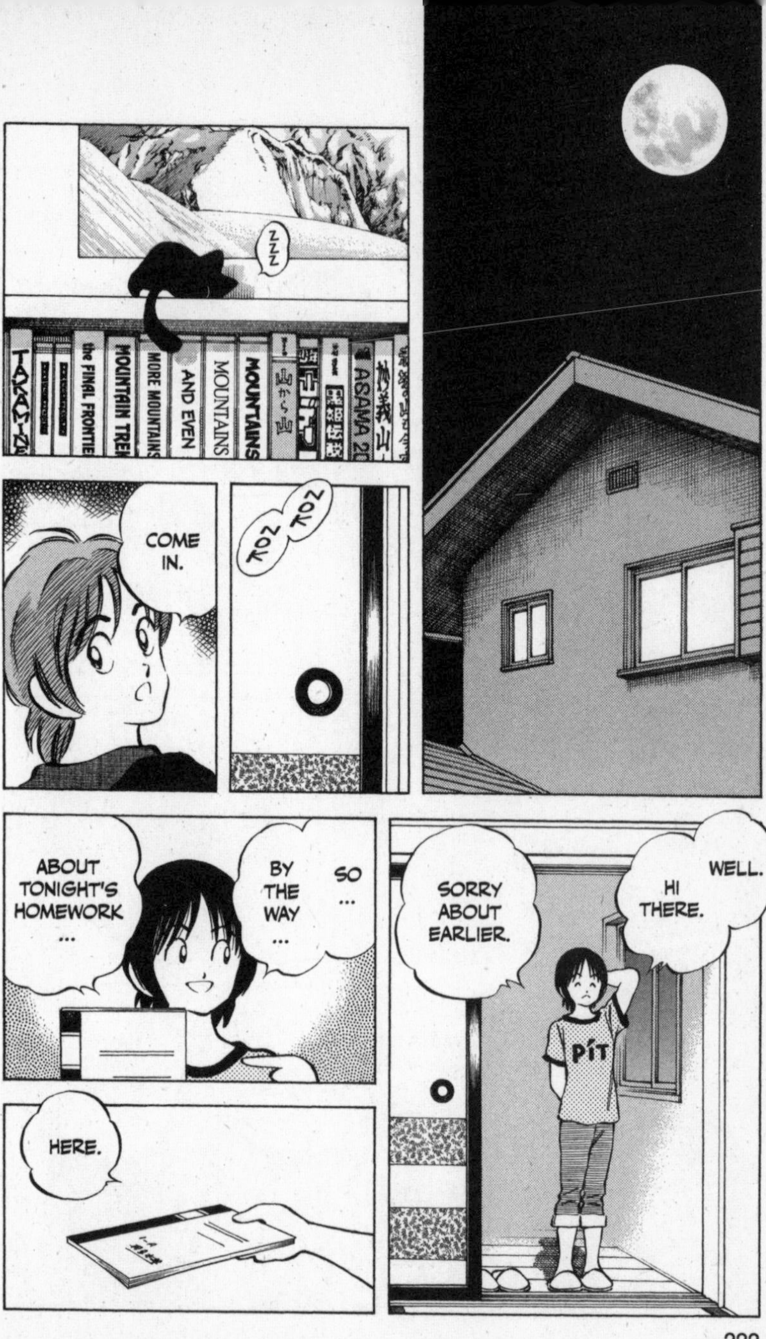
ZZZ
TAKAMINE
MORE MOUNTAINS
AND EVEN
MOUNTAINS
MOUNTAINS
山から山
NOK NOK
COME IN.
WELL.
HI THERE.
SORRY ABOUT EARLIER.
SO ...
BY THE WAY ...
ABOUT TONIGHT'S HOMEWORK ...
HERE.

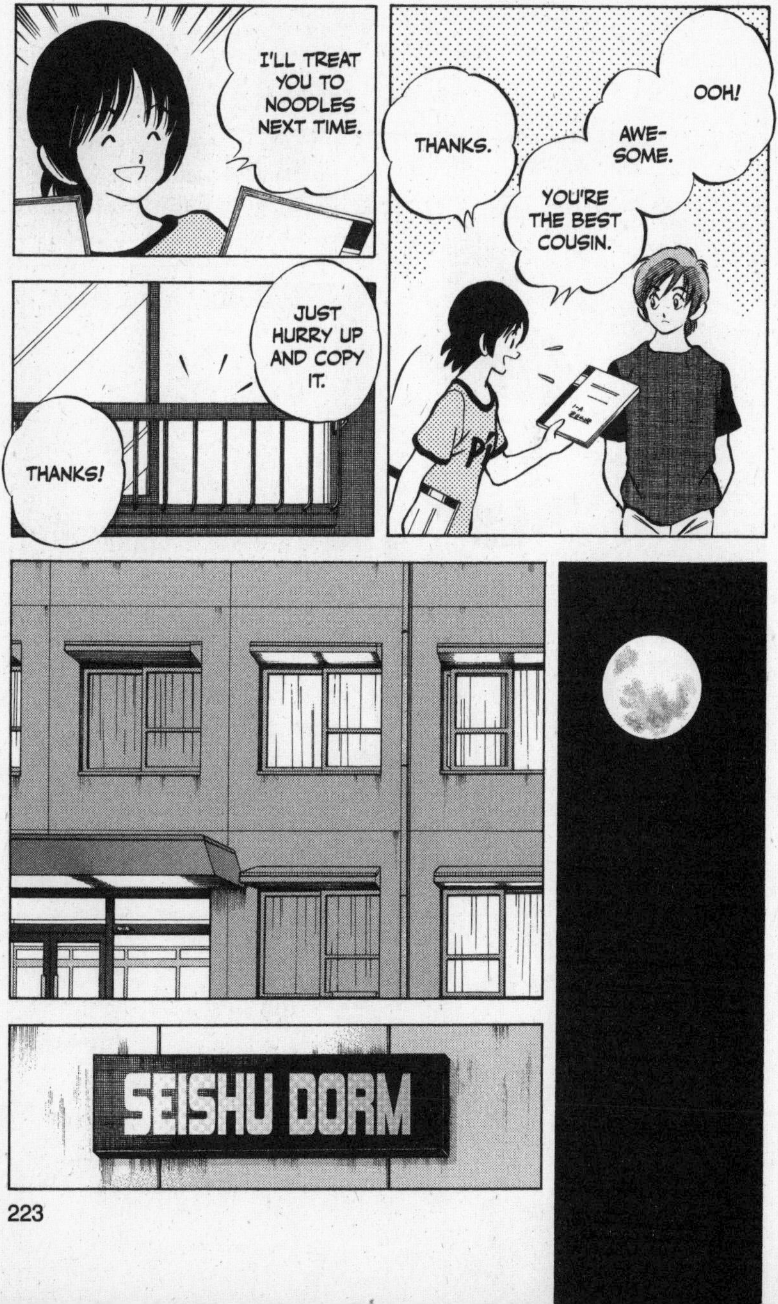
OOH!
AWE-SOME.
YOU'RE THE BEST COUSIN.
THANKS.
I'LL TREAT YOU TO NOODLES NEXT TIME.
JUST HURRY UP AND COPY IT.
THANKS!
SEISHU DORM

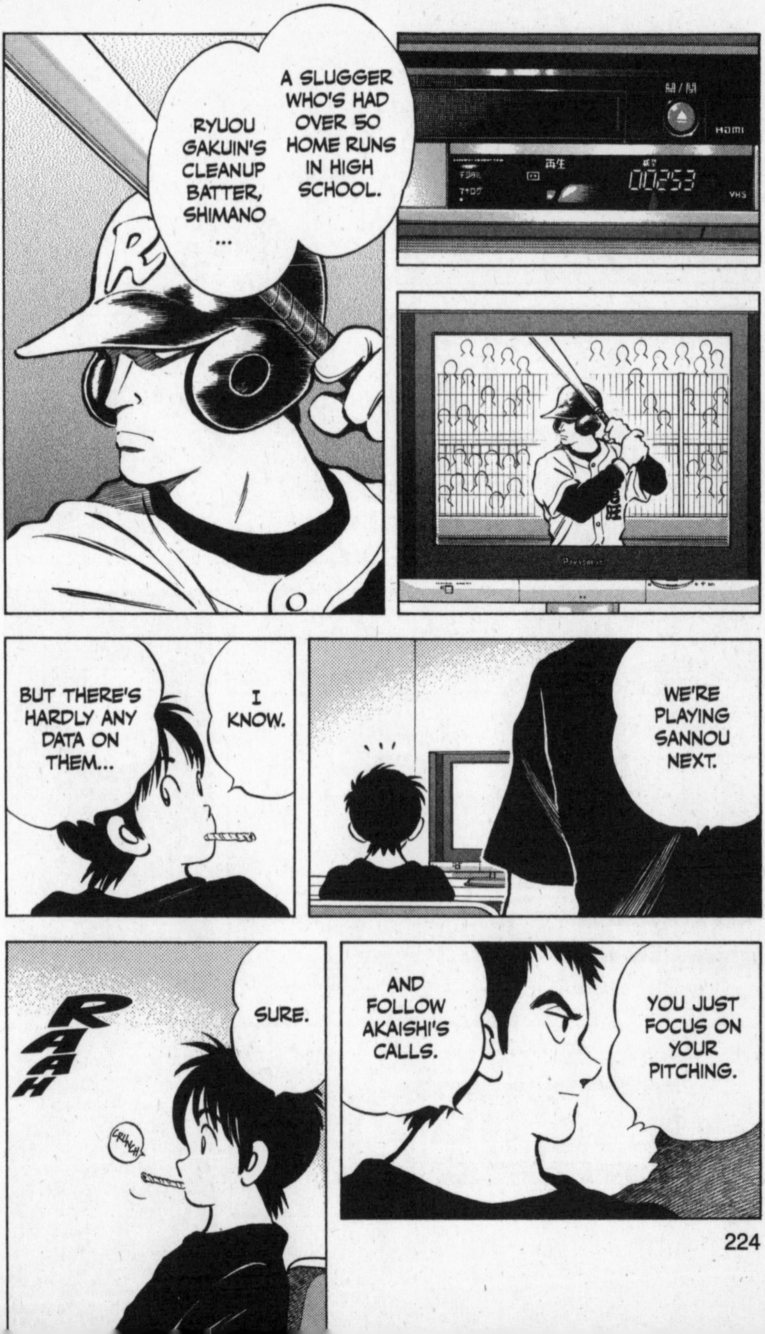
RYUOU GAKUIN'S CLEANUP BATTER, SHIMANO ...
A SLUGGER WHO'S HAD OVER 50 HOME RUNS IN HIGH SCHOOL.
WE'RE PLAYING SANNOU NEXT.
I KNOW.
BUT THERE'S HARDLY ANY DATA ON THEM...
YOU JUST FOCUS ON YOUR PITCHING.
AND FOLLOW AKAISHI'S CALLS.
SURE.
RAAAH
CRUNCH

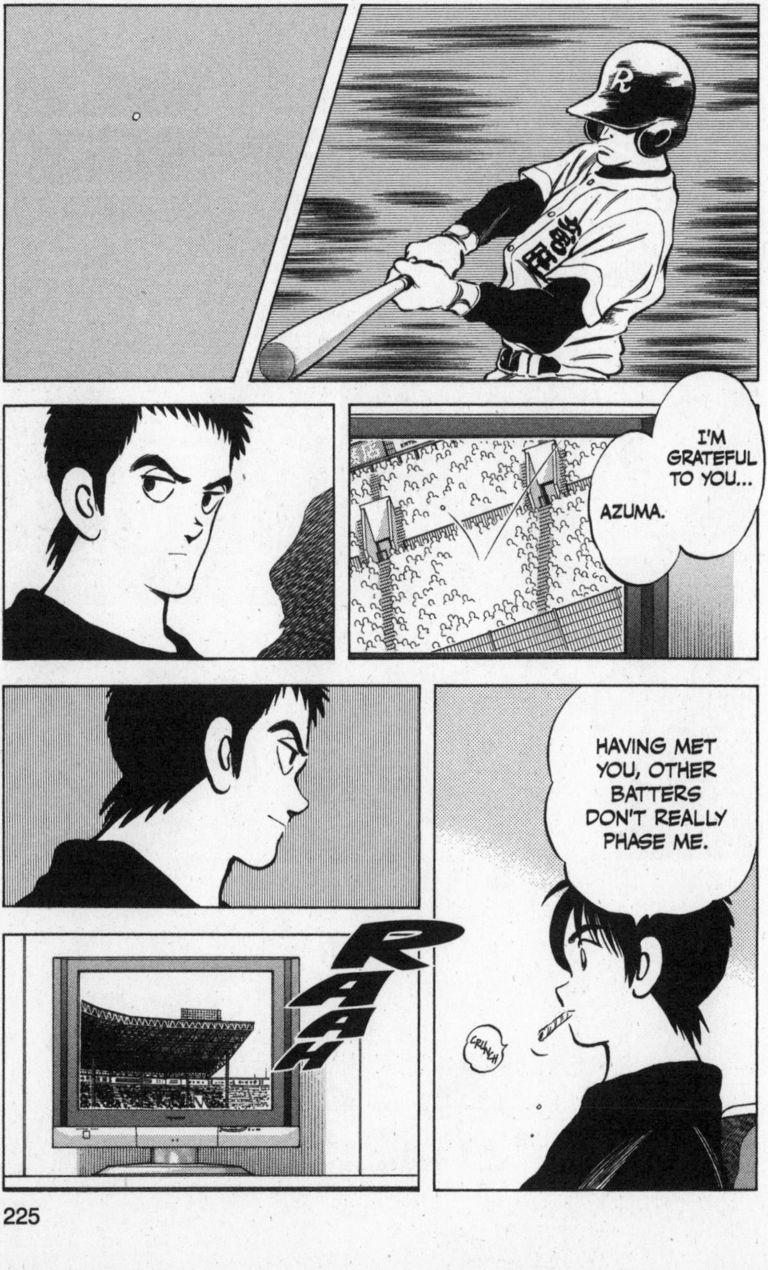
I'M GRATEFUL TO YOU...
AZUMA.
HAVING MET YOU, OTHER BATTERS DON'T REALLY PHASE ME.
CRUNCH
RAAH

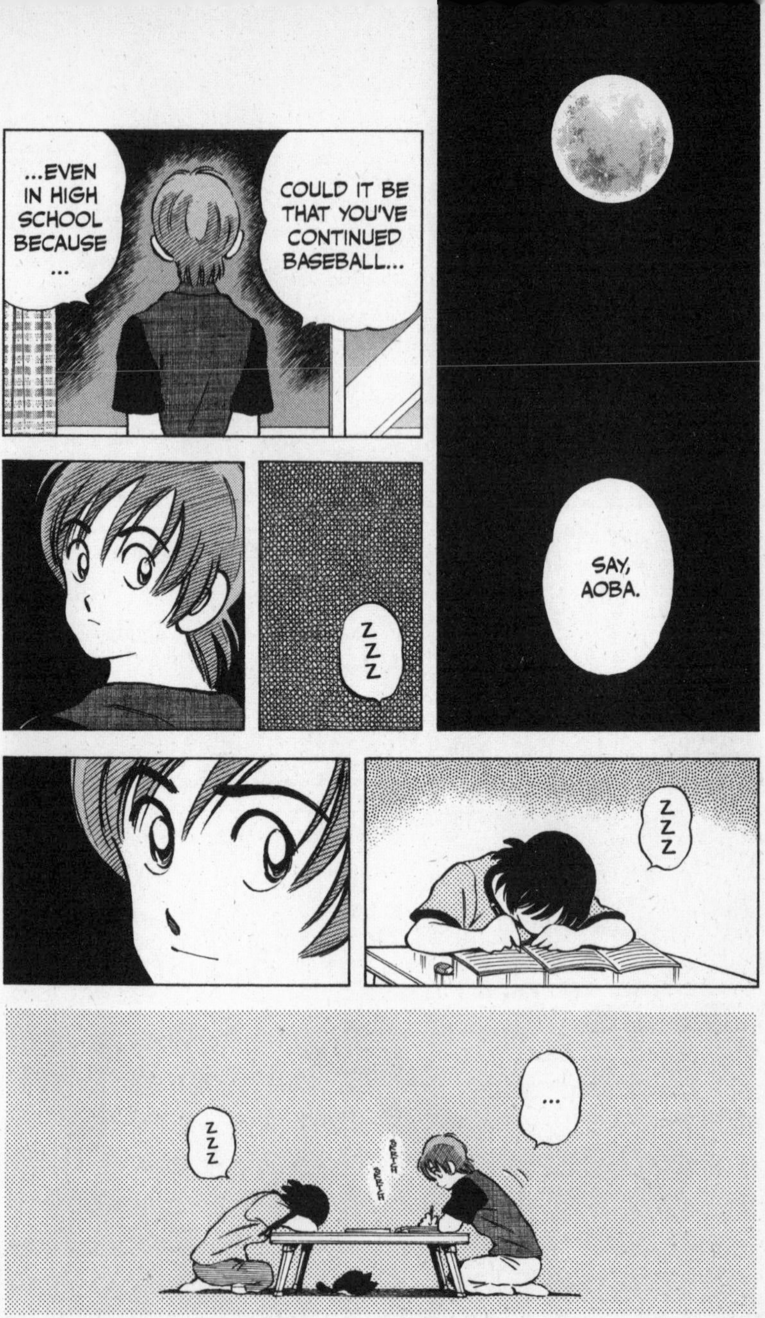
SAY, AOBA.
COULD IT BE THAT YOU'VE CONTINUED BASEBALL...
...EVEN IN HIGH SCHOOL BECAUSE ...
ZZZ
ZZZ
...
ZZZ

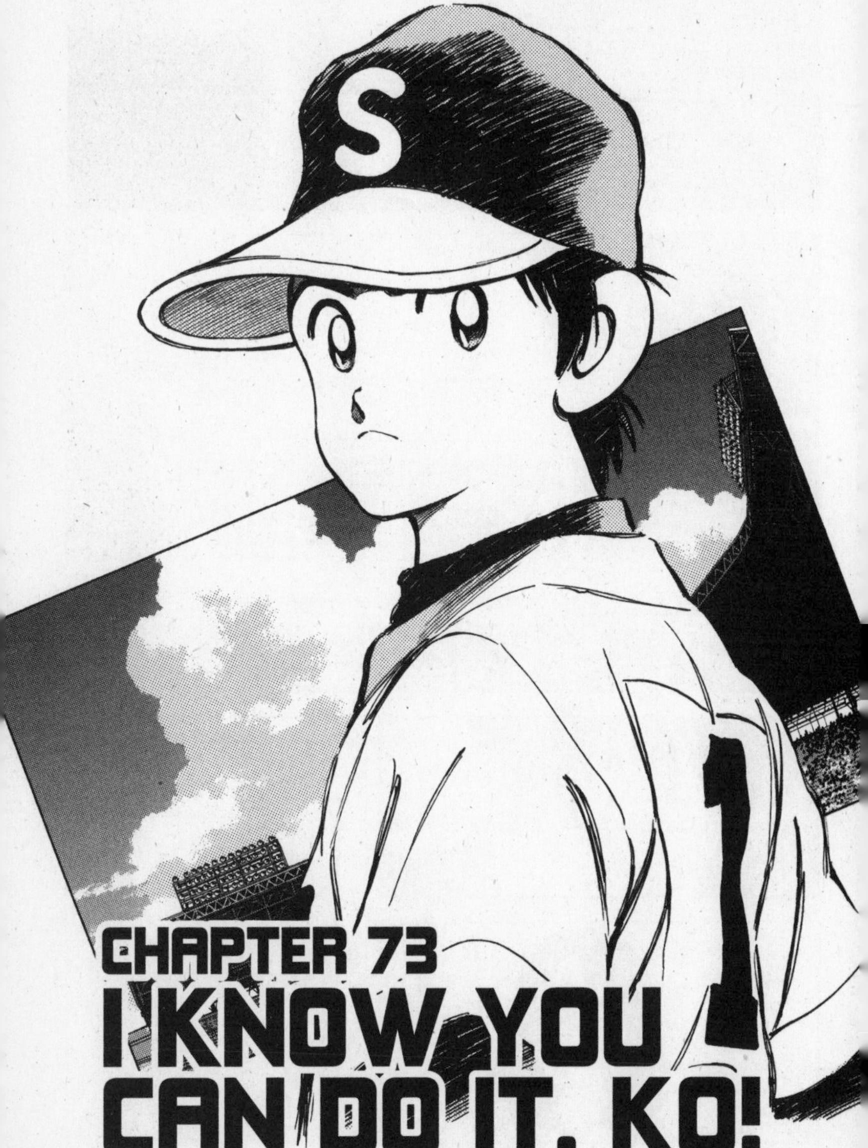
CHAPTER 73
I KNOW YOU CAN DO IT, KO!

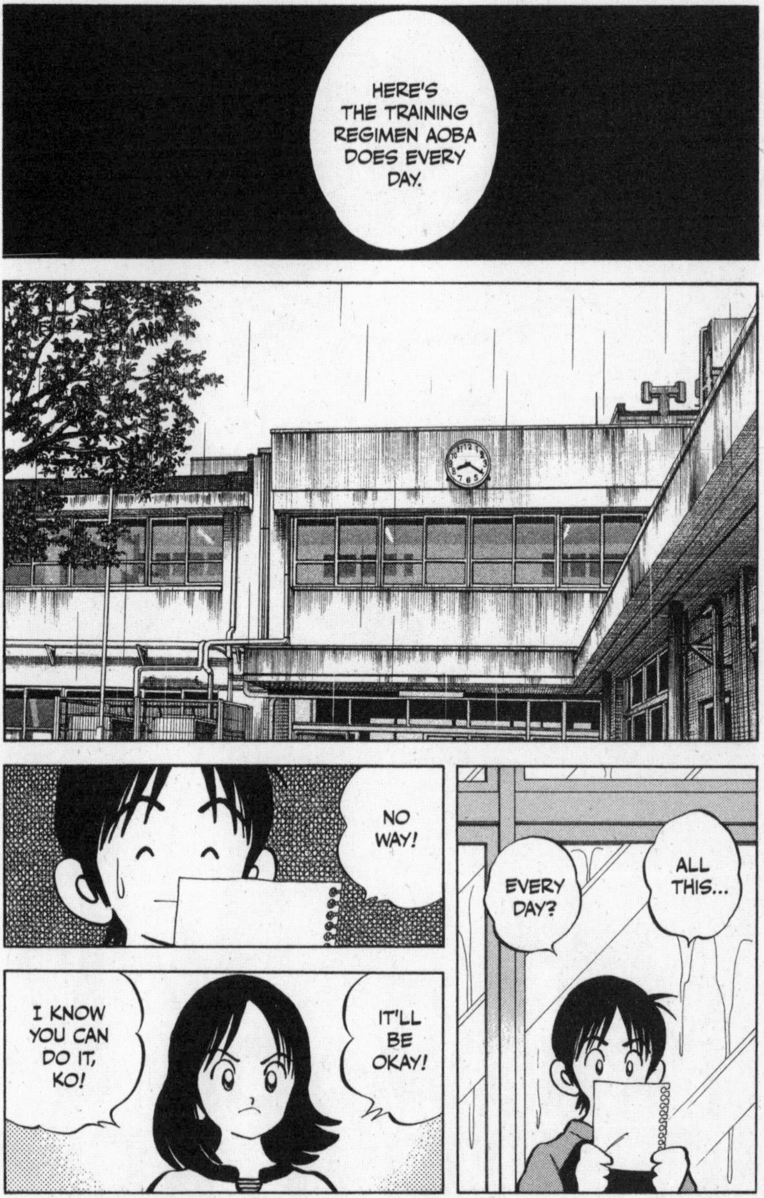
HERE'S THE TRAINING REGIMEN AOBA DOES EVERY DAY.
ALL THIS...
EVERY DAY?
NO WAY!
IT'LL BE OKAY!
I KNOW YOU CAN DO IT, KO!

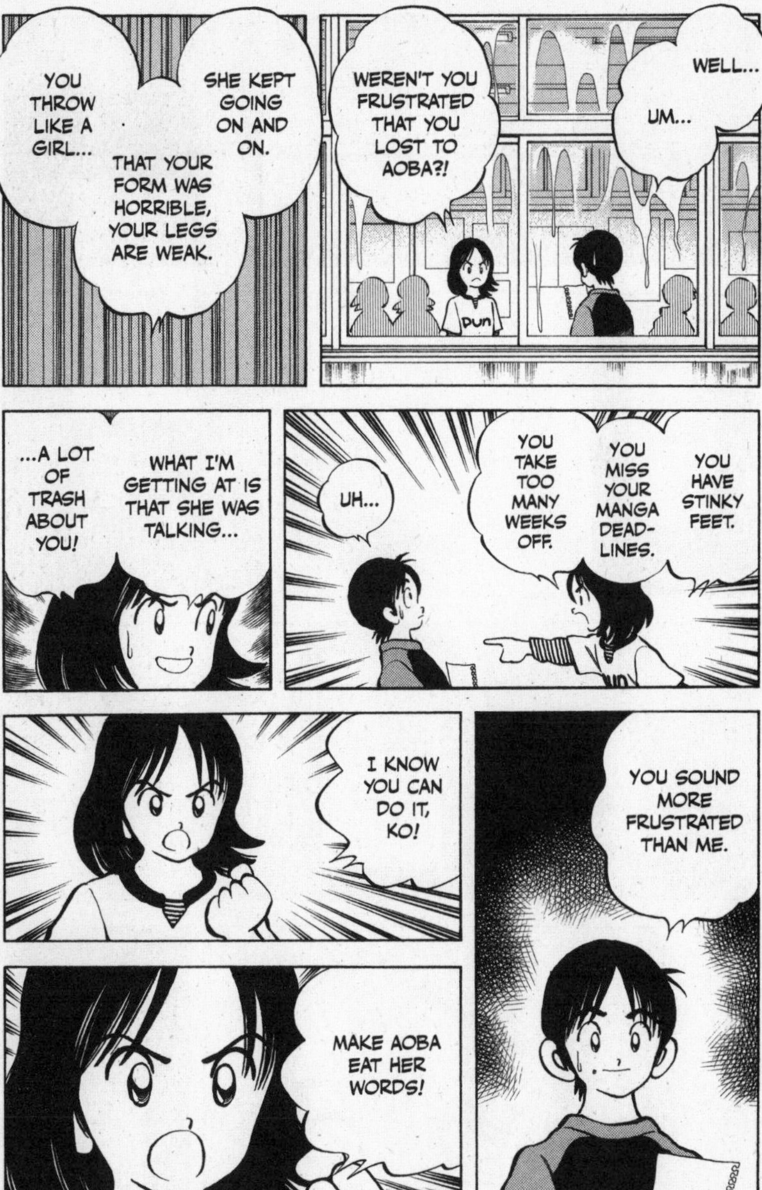
WELL...
UM...
WEREN'T YOU FRUSTRATED THAT YOU LOST TO AOBA?!
PUN
SHE KEPT GOING ON AND ON.
THAT YOUR FORM WAS HORRIBLE, YOUR LEGS ARE WEAK.
YOU THROW LIKE A GIRL...
YOU HAVE STINKY FEET.
YOU MISS YOUR MANGA DEAD-LINES.
YOU TAKE TOO MANY WEEKS OFF.
UH...
WHAT I'M GETTING AT IS THAT SHE WAS TALKING...
...A LOT OF TRASH ABOUT YOU!
YOU SOUND MORE FRUSTRATED THAN ME.
I KNOW YOU CAN DO IT, KO!
MAKE AOBA EAT HER WORDS!

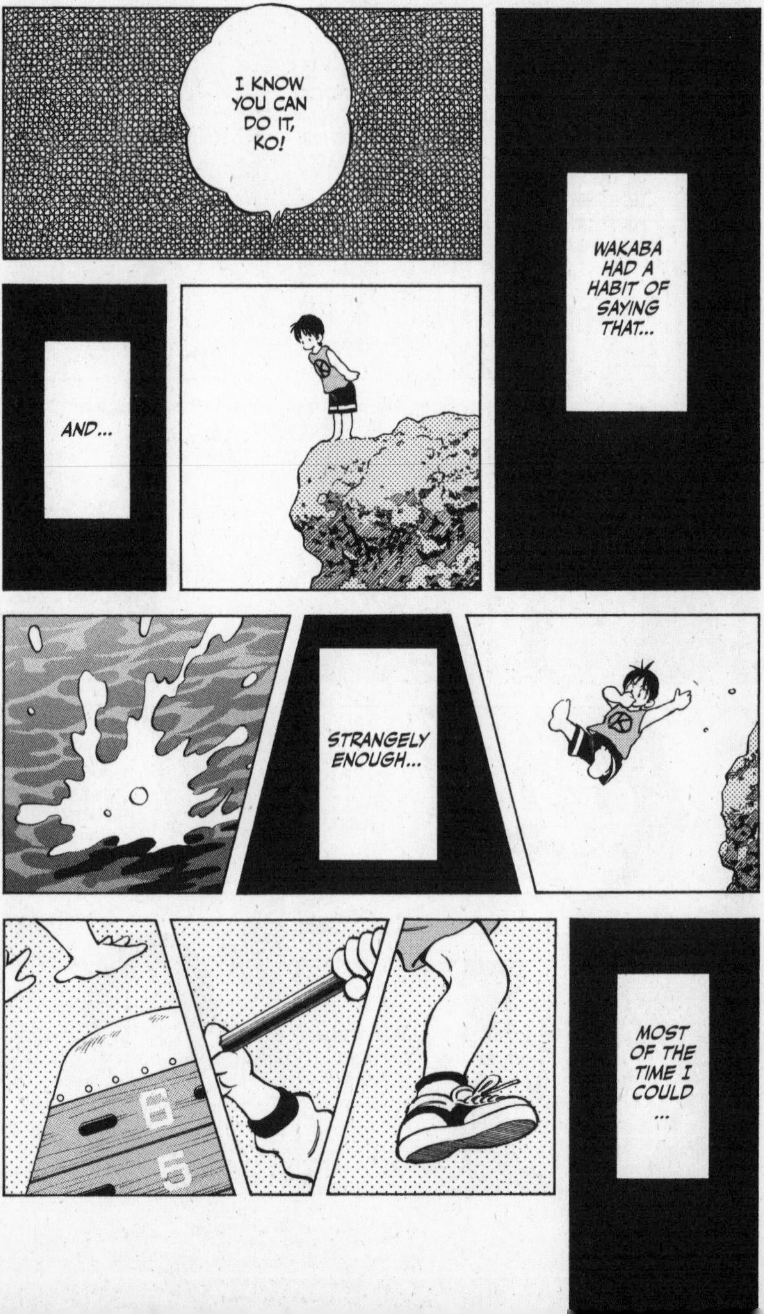
WAKABA HAD A HABIT OF SAYING THAT...
I KNOW YOU CAN DO IT, KO!
AND...
STRANGELY ENOUGH...
MOST OF THE TIME I COULD ...

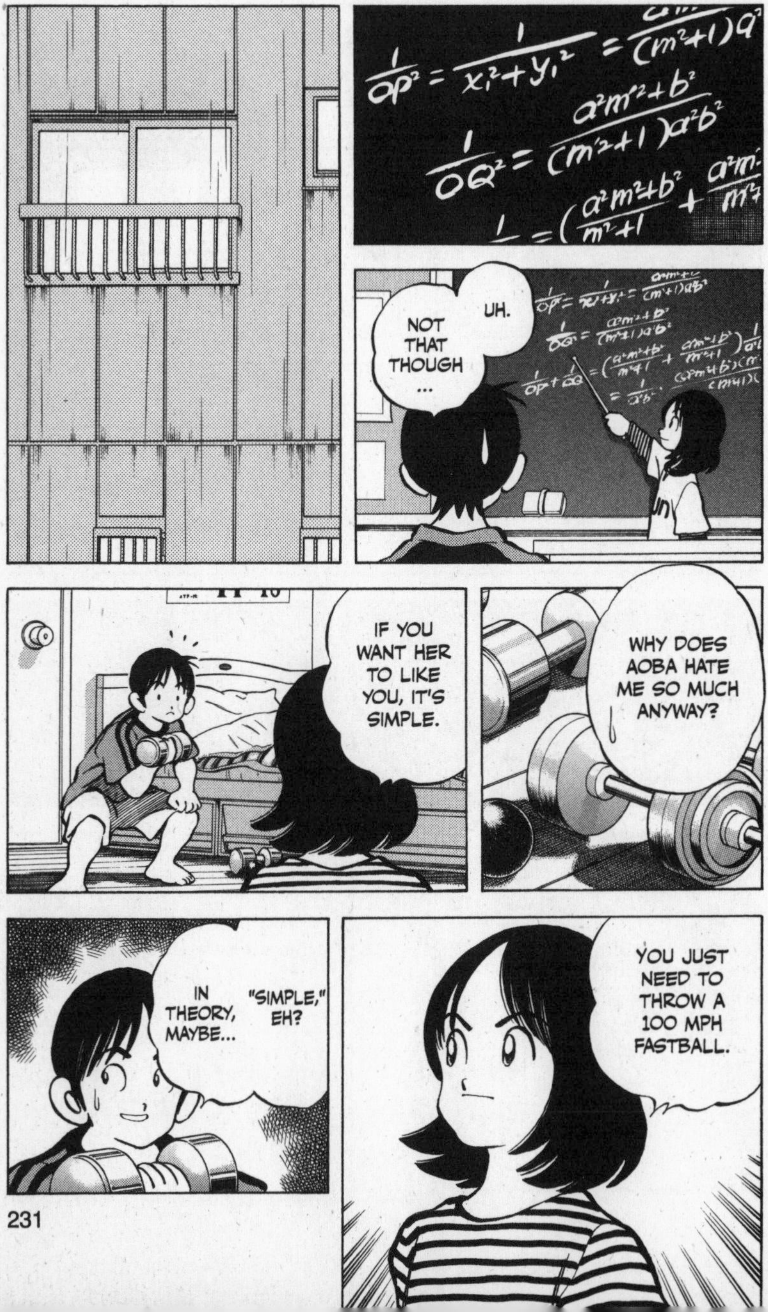
UH.
NOT THAT THOUGH ...
WHY DOES AOBA HATE ME SO MUCH ANYWAY?
IF YOU WANT HER TO LIKE YOU, IT'S SIMPLE.
YOU JUST NEED TO THROW A 100 MPH FASTBALL.
"SIMPLE," EH?
IN THEORY, MAYBE...

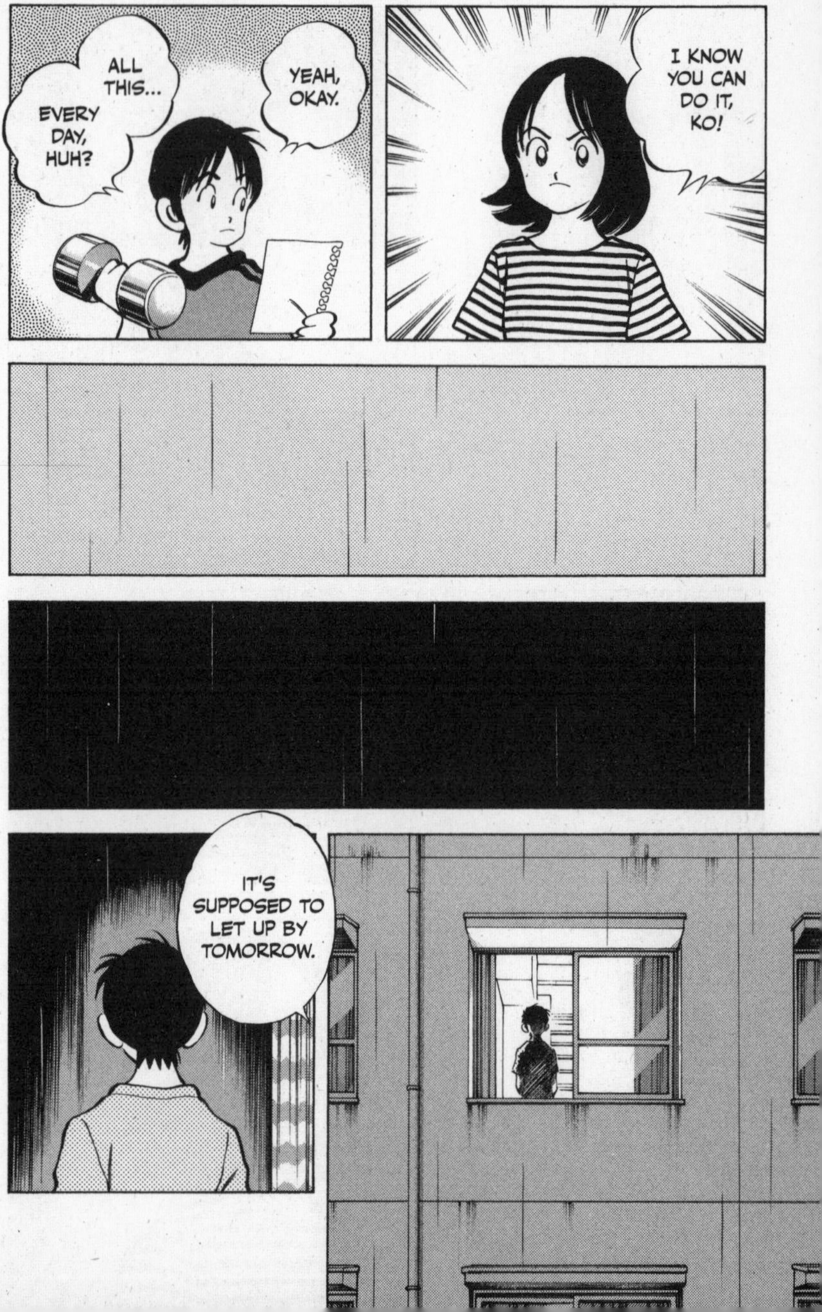
I KNOW YOU CAN DO IT, KO!
YEAH, OKAY.
ALL THIS...
EVERY DAY, HUH?
IT'S SUPPOSED TO LET UP BY TOMORROW.

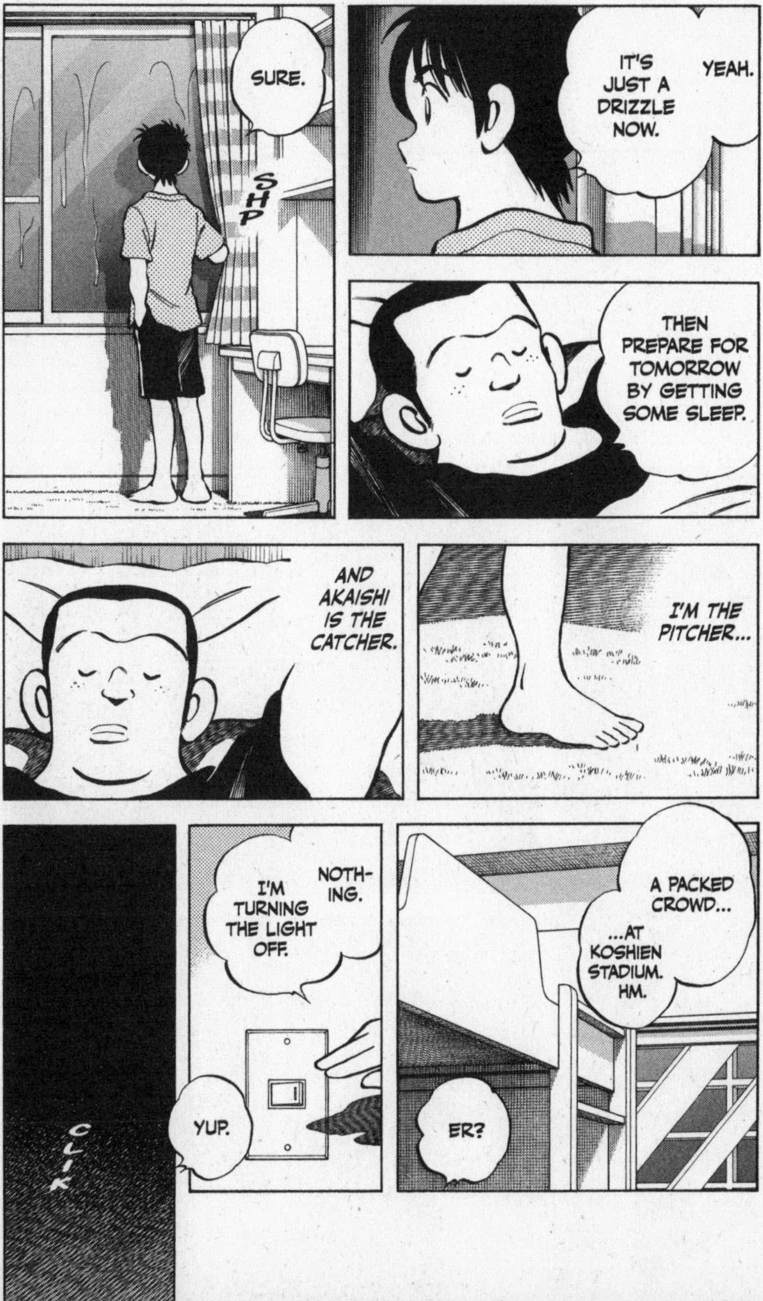
YEAH.
IT'S JUST A DRIZZLE NOW.
THEN PREPARE FOR TOMORROW BY GETTING SOME SLEEP.
SURE.
SHP
I'M THE PITCHER...
AND AKAISHI IS THE CATCHER.
A PACKED CROWD...
...AT KOSHIEN STADIUM. HM.
ER?
NOTHING.
I'M TURNING THE LIGHT OFF.
YUP.
CLIK

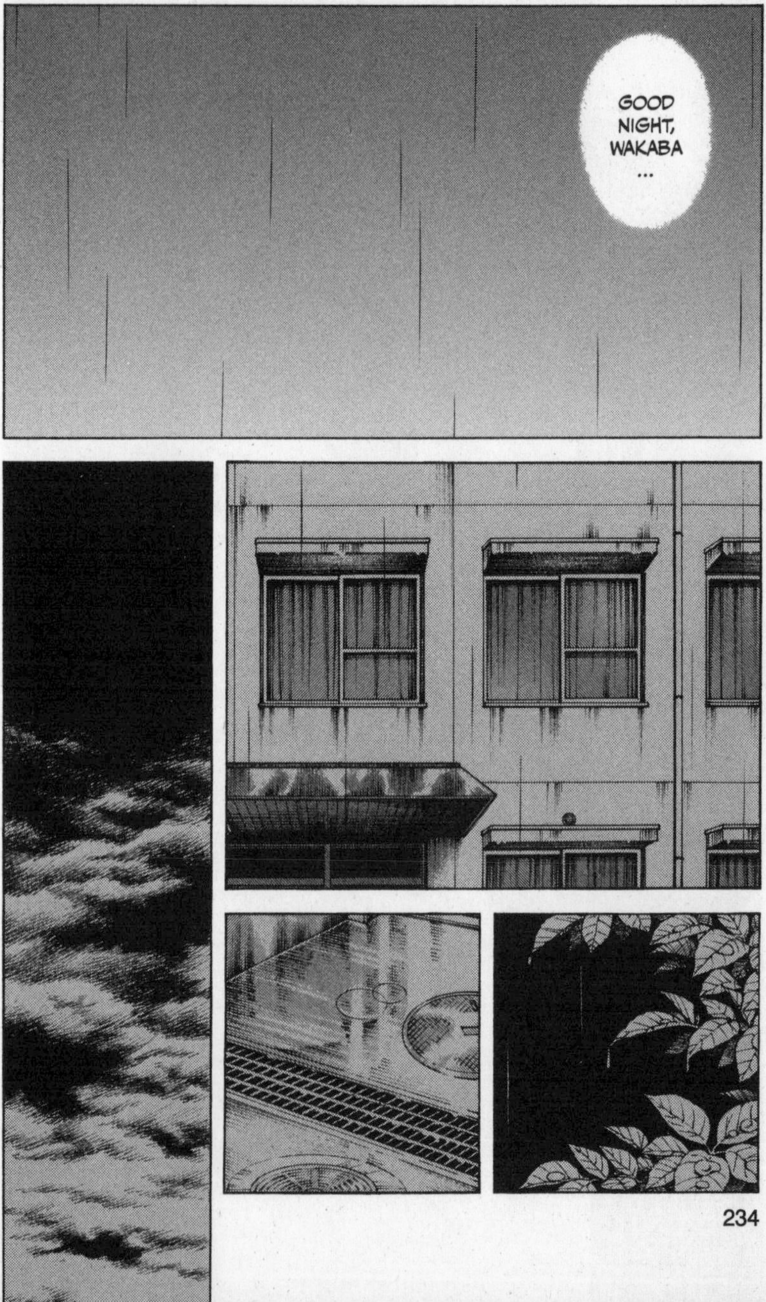
GOOD NIGHT, WAKABA ...

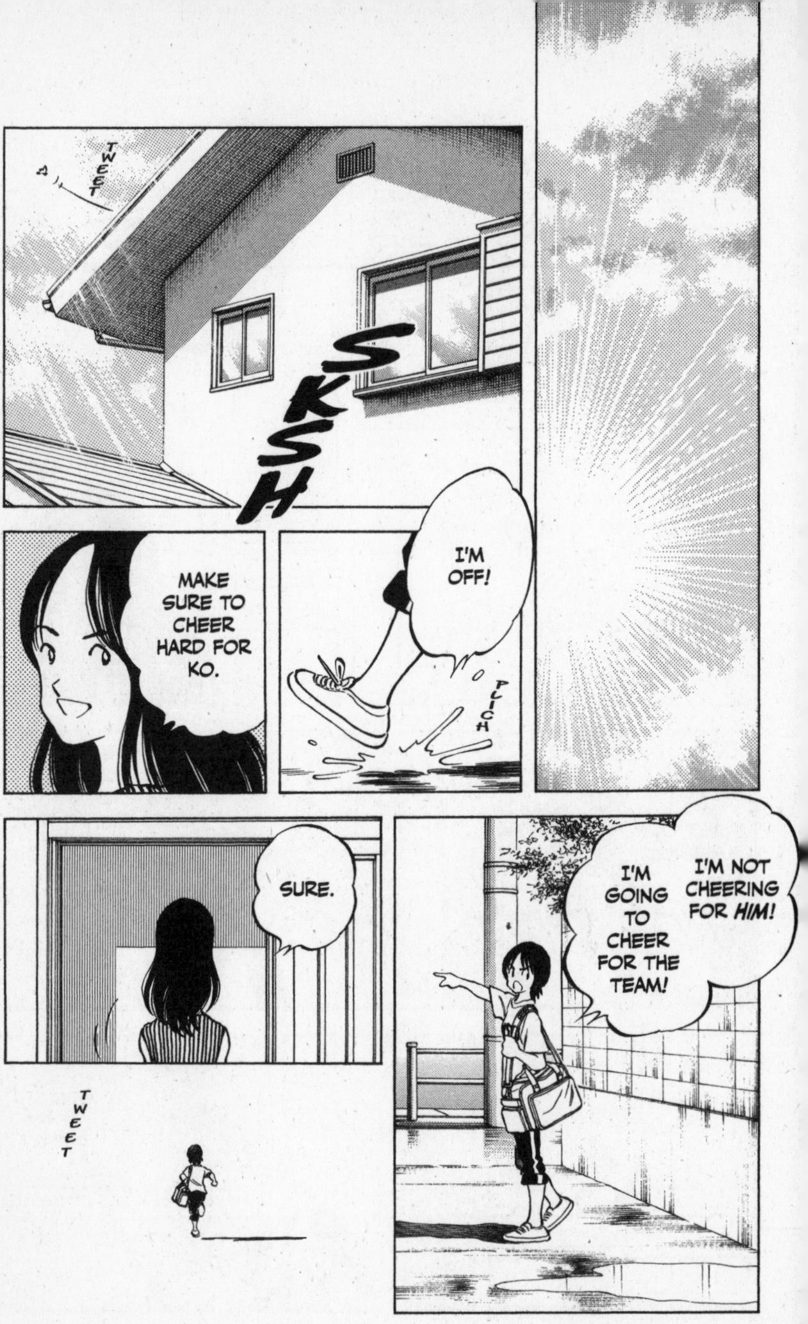
TWEET TWEET
SKSH
I'M OFF!
PLICH
MAKE SURE TO CHEER HARD FOR KO.
I'M NOT CHEERING FOR *HIM*!
I'M GOING TO CHEER FOR THE TEAM!
SURE.
TWEET

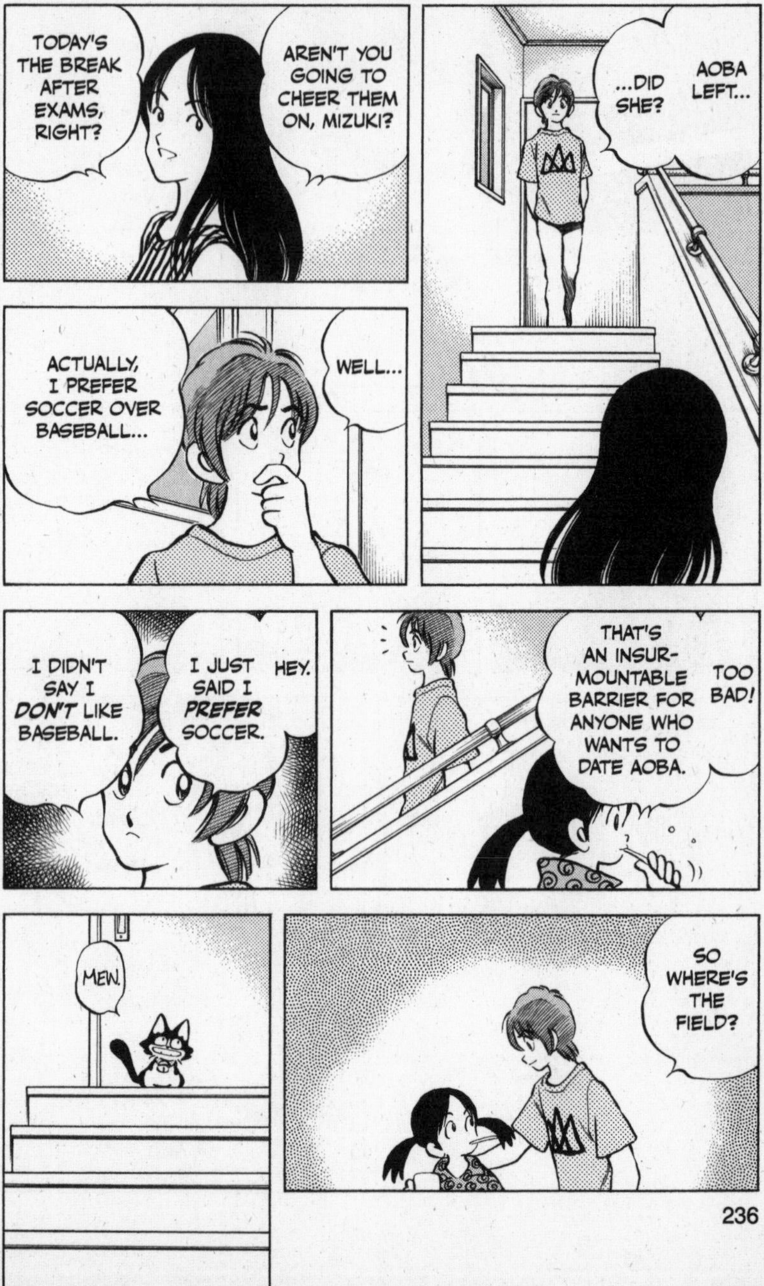
AOBA LEFT...
...DID SHE?
AREN'T YOU GOING TO CHEER THEM ON, MIZUKI?
TODAY'S THE BREAK AFTER EXAMS, RIGHT?
WELL...
ACTUALLY, I PREFER SOCCER OVER BASEBALL...
TOO BAD!
THAT'S AN INSUR-MOUNTABLE BARRIER FOR ANYONE WHO WANTS TO DATE AOBA.
HEY.
I JUST SAID I *PREFER* SOCCER.
I DIDN'T SAY I *DON'T* LIKE BASEBALL.
SO WHERE'S THE FIELD?
MEW.

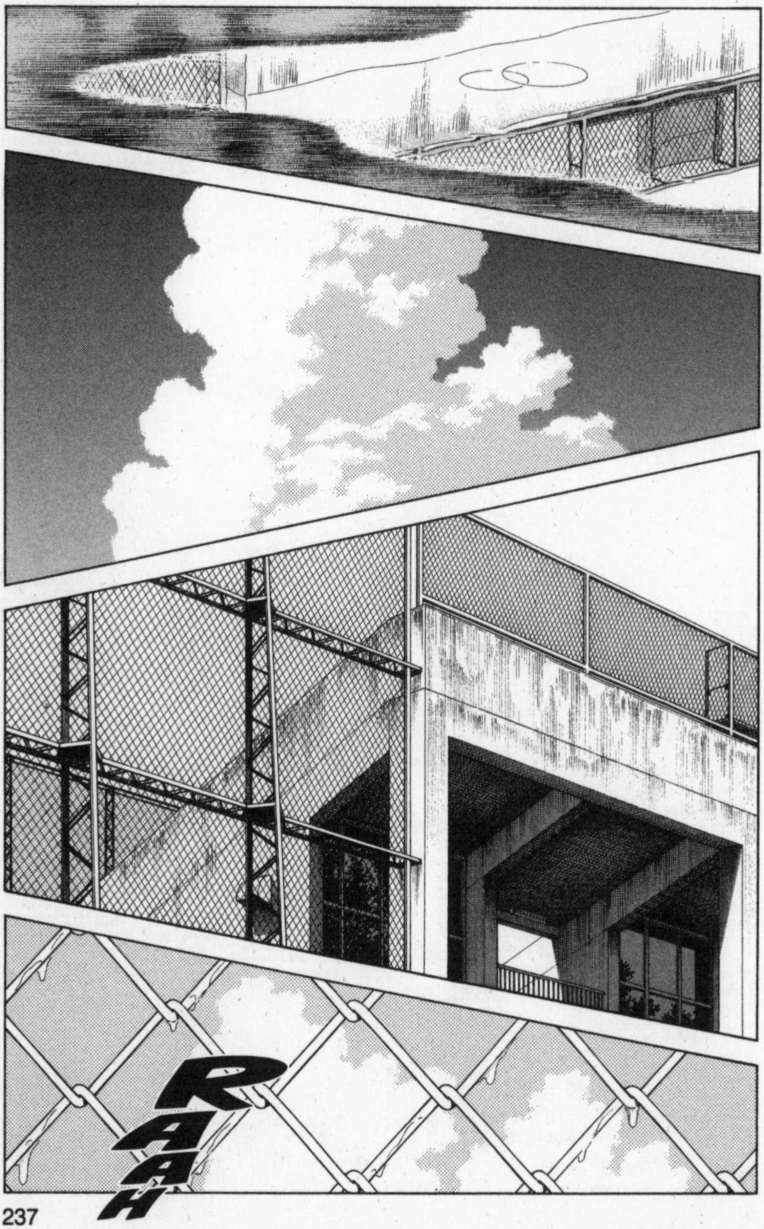
RAAAH

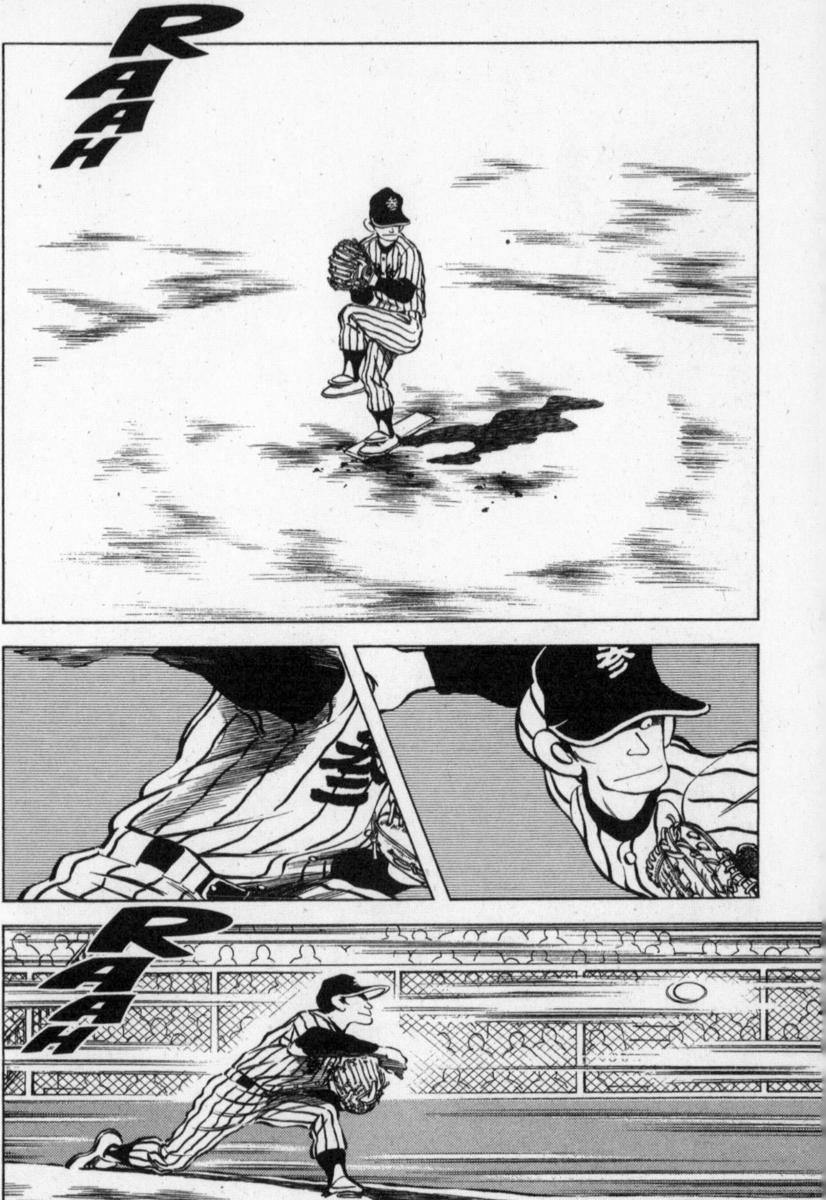
RAAH
RAAH

BATTING FIRST, SHORT-STOP SENDA (SECOND YEAR)

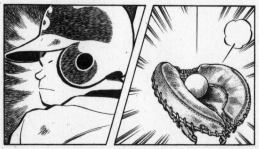

BATTING SECOND, LEFT FIELDER MIYA (THIRD YEAR)

THIRD
AND THIRD
BASEMAN,
NAKANISHI
(SECOND
YEAR)

RAAH

| TEAM | 1 | 2 | 3 | 4 | 5 | 6 | 7 | 8 | 9 |
|---|---|---|---|---|---|---|---|---|---|
| SEISHU | 0 | | | | | | | | |
| SANNOU | | | | | | | | | |

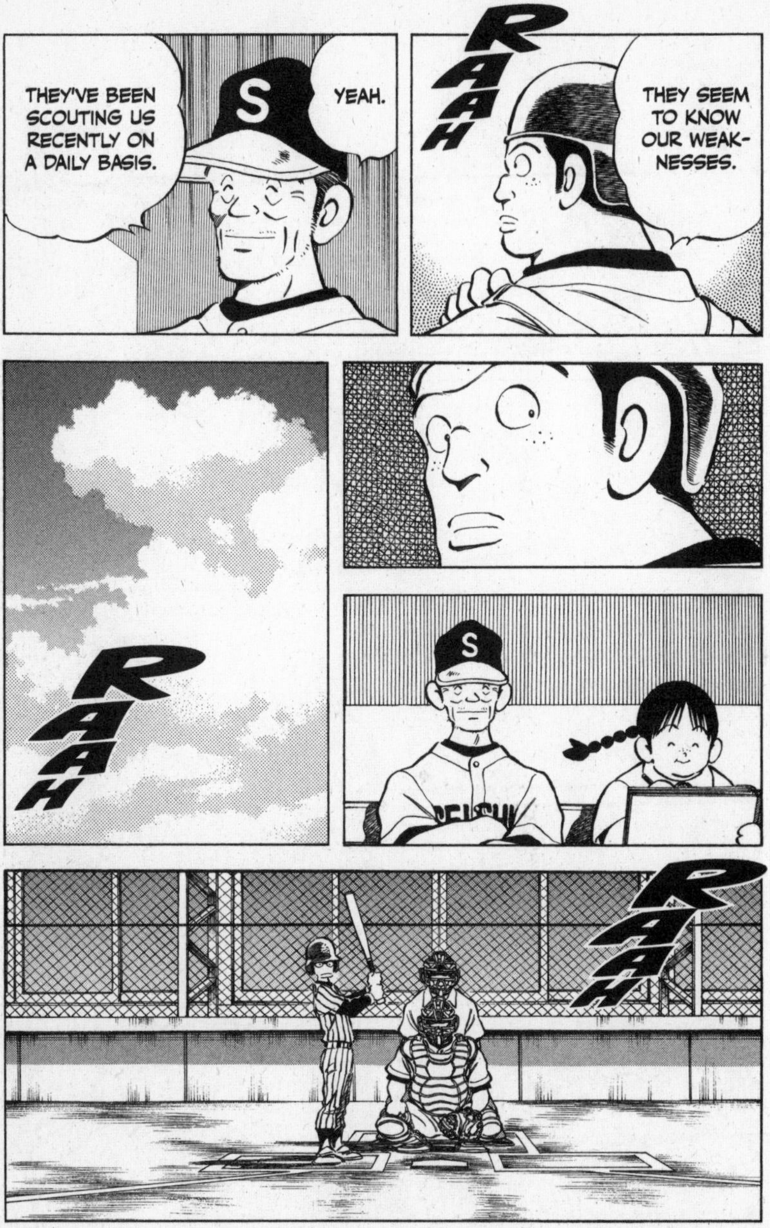
RAAH
THEY SEEM TO KNOW OUR WEAKNESSES.
YEAH.
THEY'VE BEEN SCOUTING US RECENTLY ON A DAILY BASIS.
RAAH
RAAH

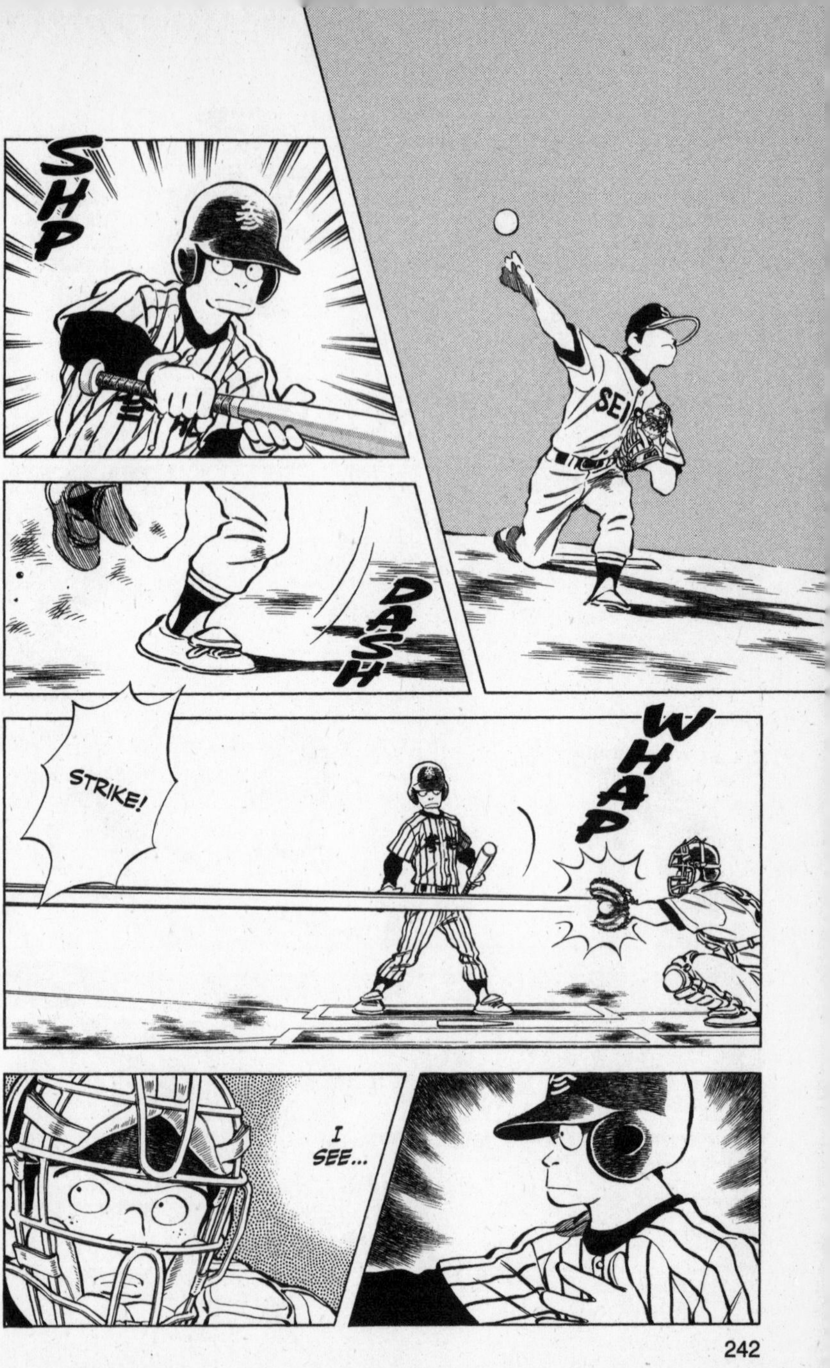
SHP
DASH
WHAP
STRIKE!
I SEE...

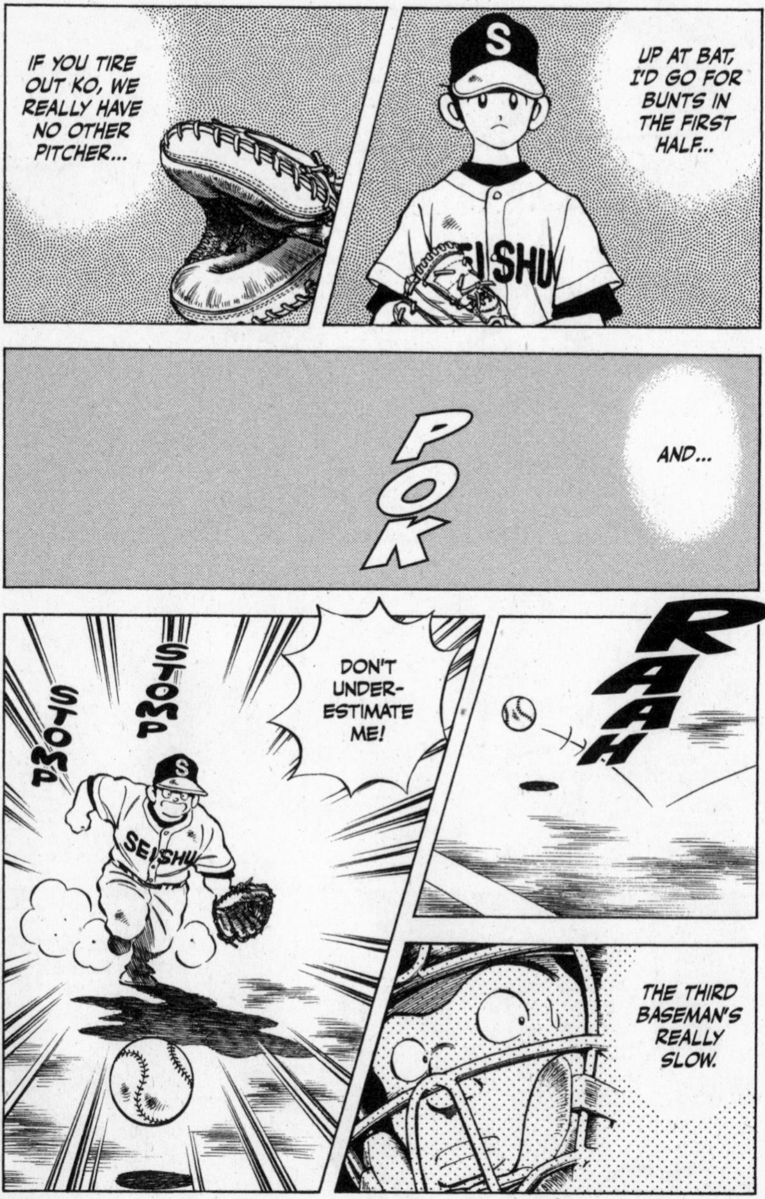
UP AT BAT, I'D GO FOR BUNTS IN THE FIRST HALF...
IF YOU TIRE OUT KO, WE REALLY HAVE NO OTHER PITCHER...
AND...
POK
RAAAH
THE THIRD BASEMAN'S REALLY SLOW.
DON'T UNDER-ESTIMATE ME!
STOMP
STOMP

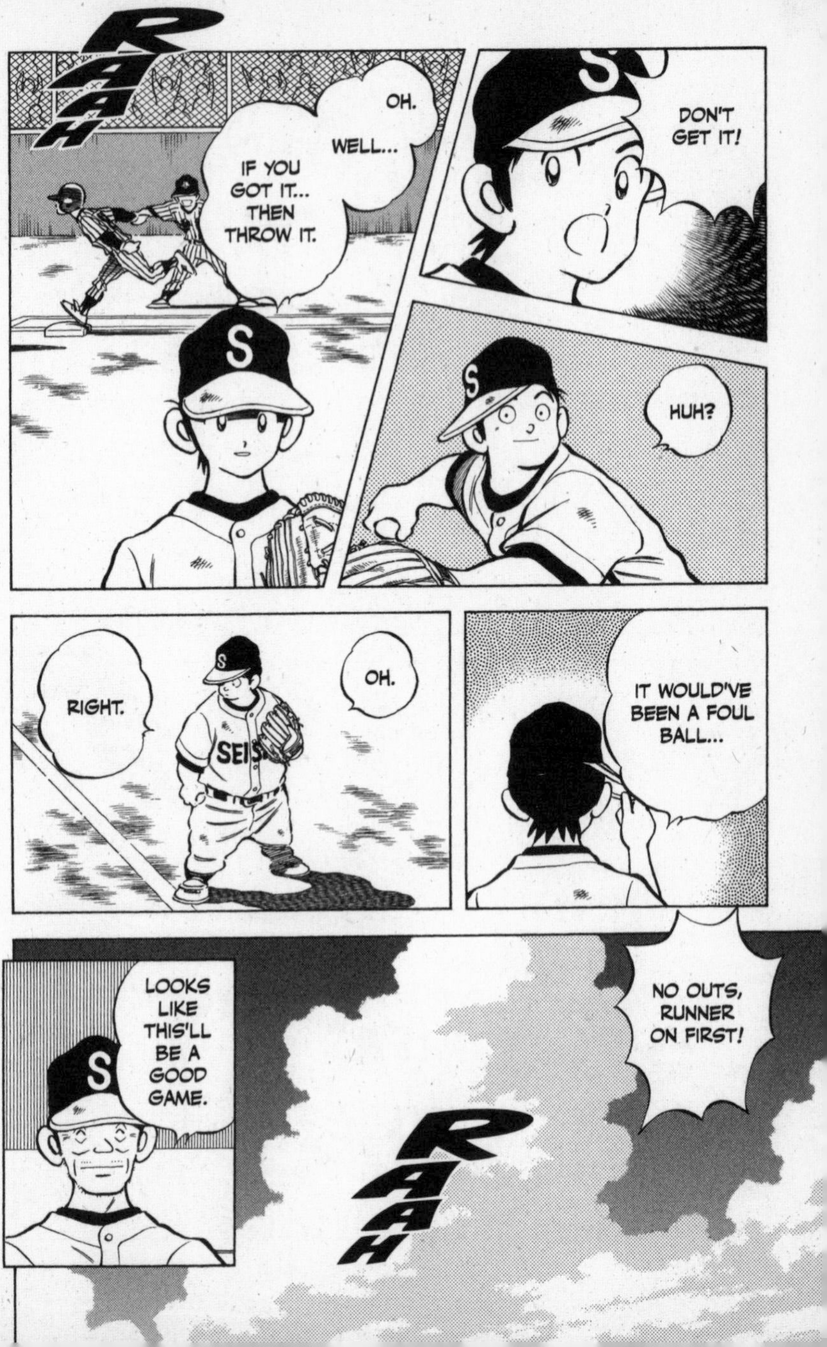
DON'T GET IT!
HUH?
OH. WELL... IF YOU GOT IT... THEN THROW IT.
RAAH
IT WOULD'VE BEEN A FOUL BALL...
OH.
RIGHT.
SEIS
NO OUTS, RUNNER ON FIRST!
RAAH
LOOKS LIKE THIS'LL BE A GOOD GAME.

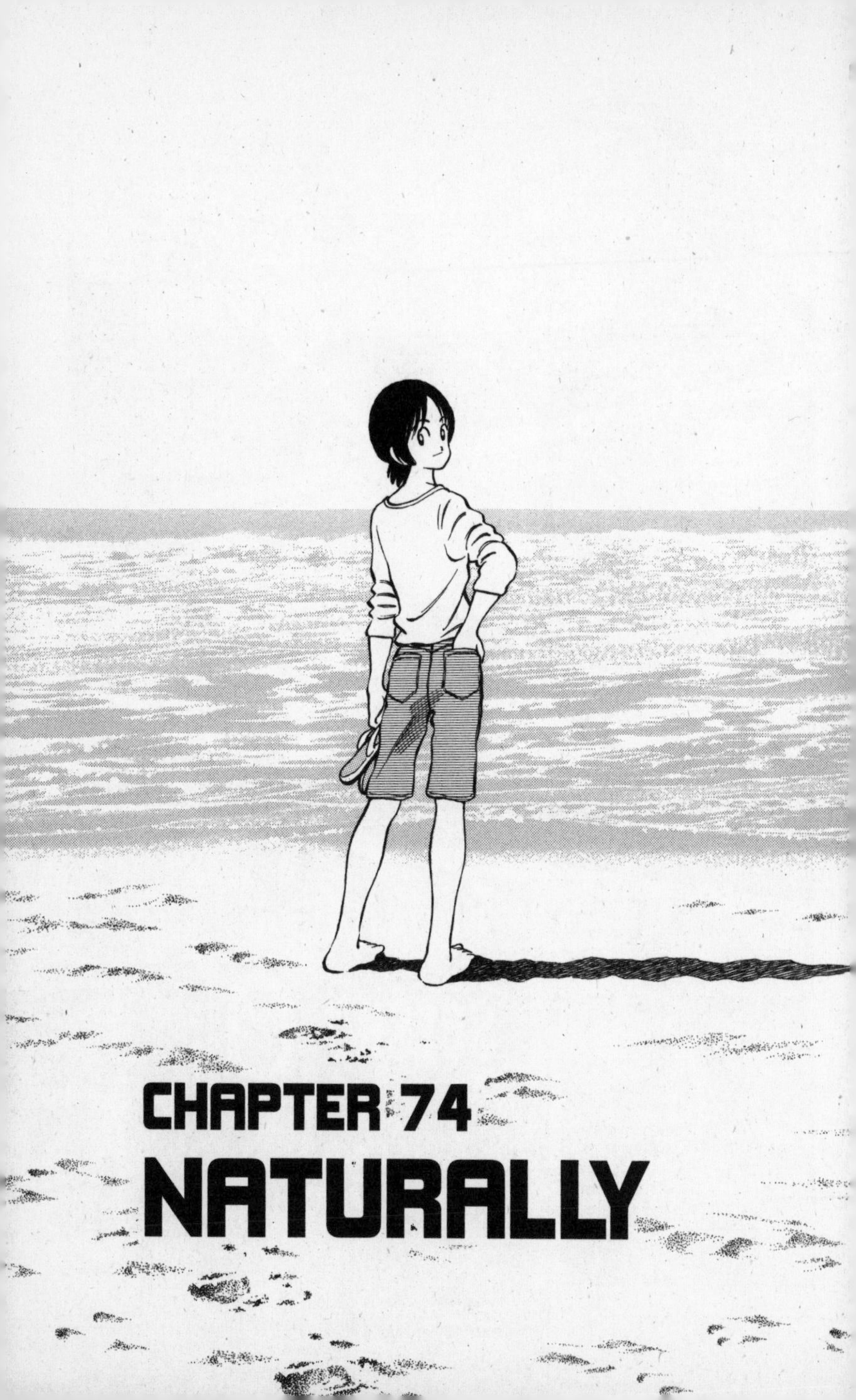
CHAPTER 74
NATURALLY

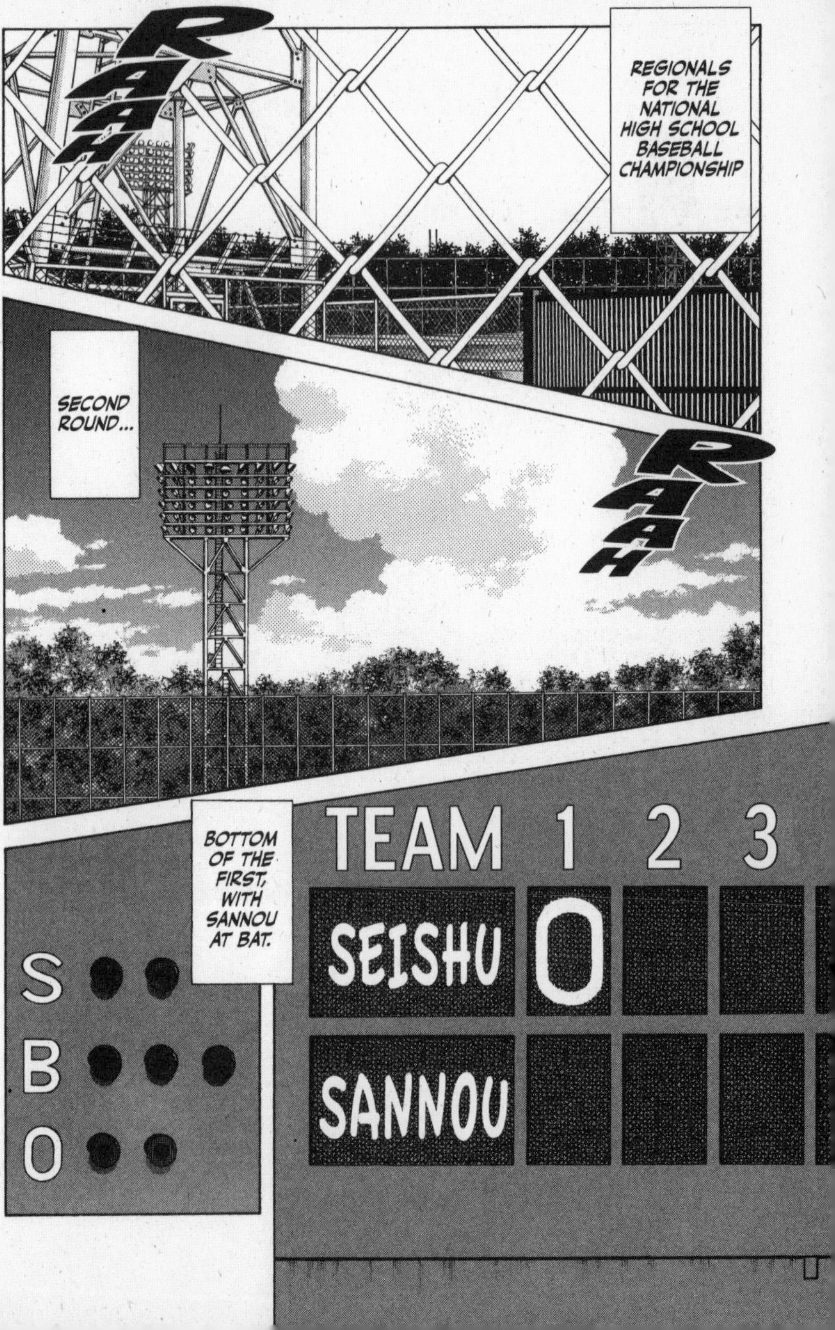
REGIONALS FOR THE NATIONAL HIGH SCHOOL BASEBALL CHAMPIONSHIP
RAAAH
RAAAH
SECOND ROUND...
BOTTOM OF THE FIRST, WITH SANNOU AT BAT.
TEAM 1 2 3
SEISHU 0
SANNOU
S
B
O

NO OUTS, RUNNER ON FIRST ...

SACRIFICE BUNT.

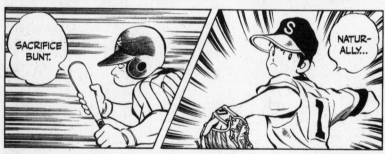

NATURALLY...

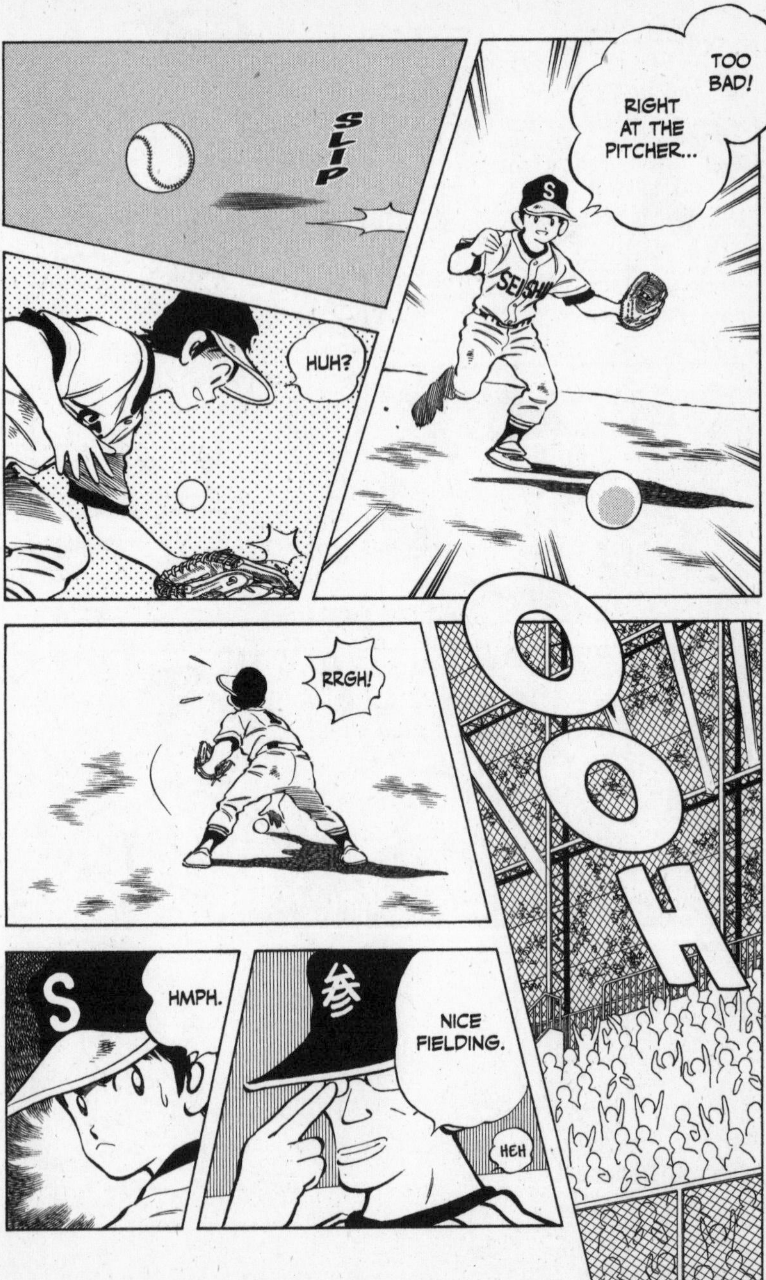
TOO BAD!
RIGHT AT THE PITCHER...
SLIP
HUH?
OOH
RRGH!
NICE FIELDING.
HEH
HMPH.

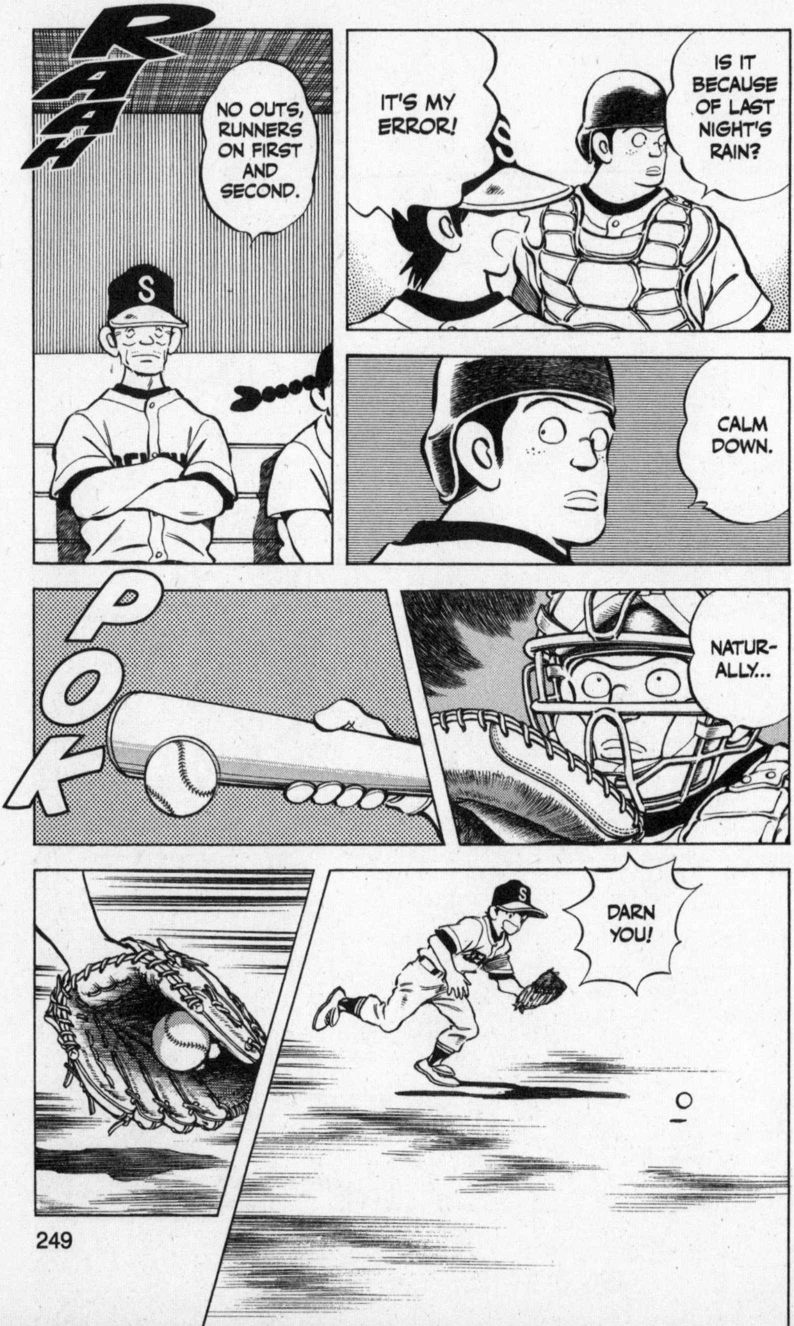
IS IT BECAUSE OF LAST NIGHT'S RAIN?
IT'S MY ERROR!
CALM DOWN.
RAAAH
NO OUTS, RUNNERS ON FIRST AND SECOND.
NATUR-ALLY...
POK
DARN YOU!

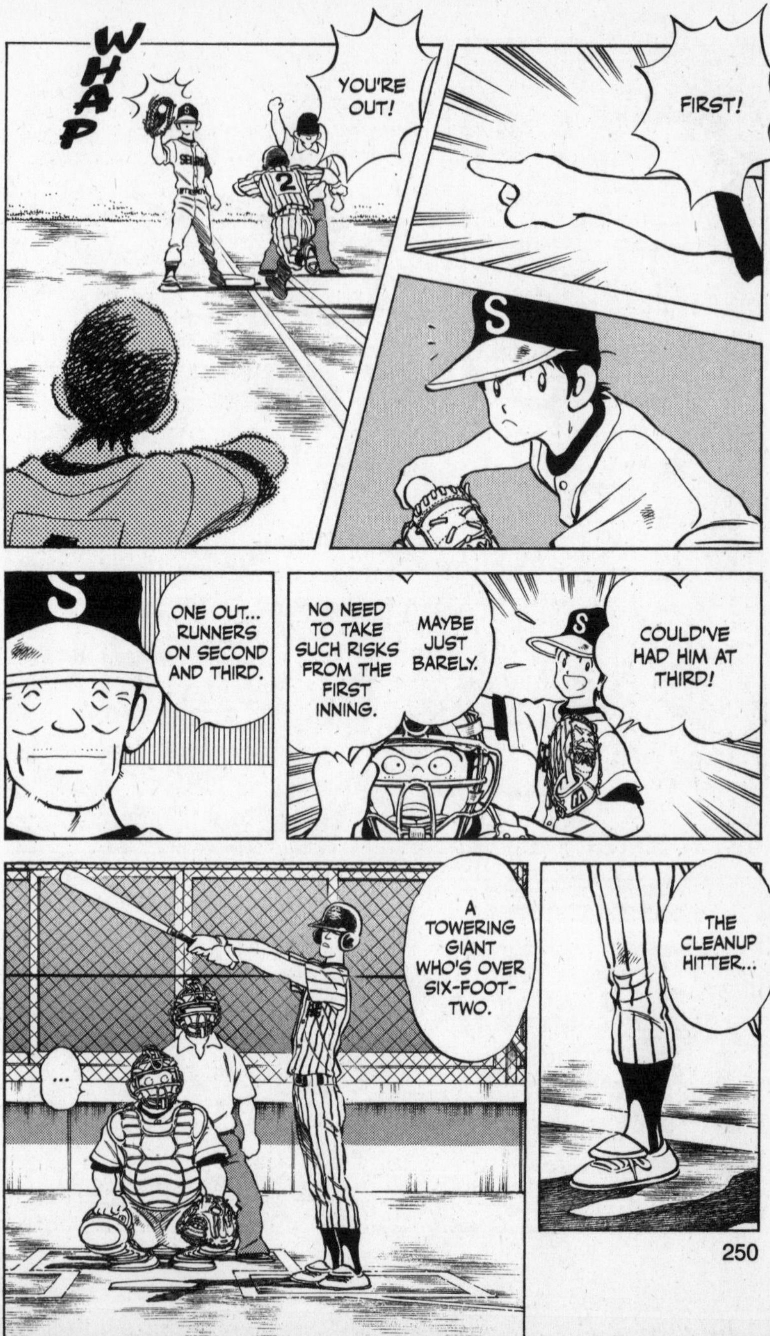
FIRST!
WHAP
YOU'RE OUT!
COULD'VE HAD HIM AT THIRD!
MAYBE JUST BARELY.
NO NEED TO TAKE SUCH RISKS FROM THE FIRST INNING.
ONE OUT... RUNNERS ON SECOND AND THIRD.
THE CLEANUP HITTER...
A TOWERING GIANT WHO'S OVER SIX-FOOT-TWO.
...

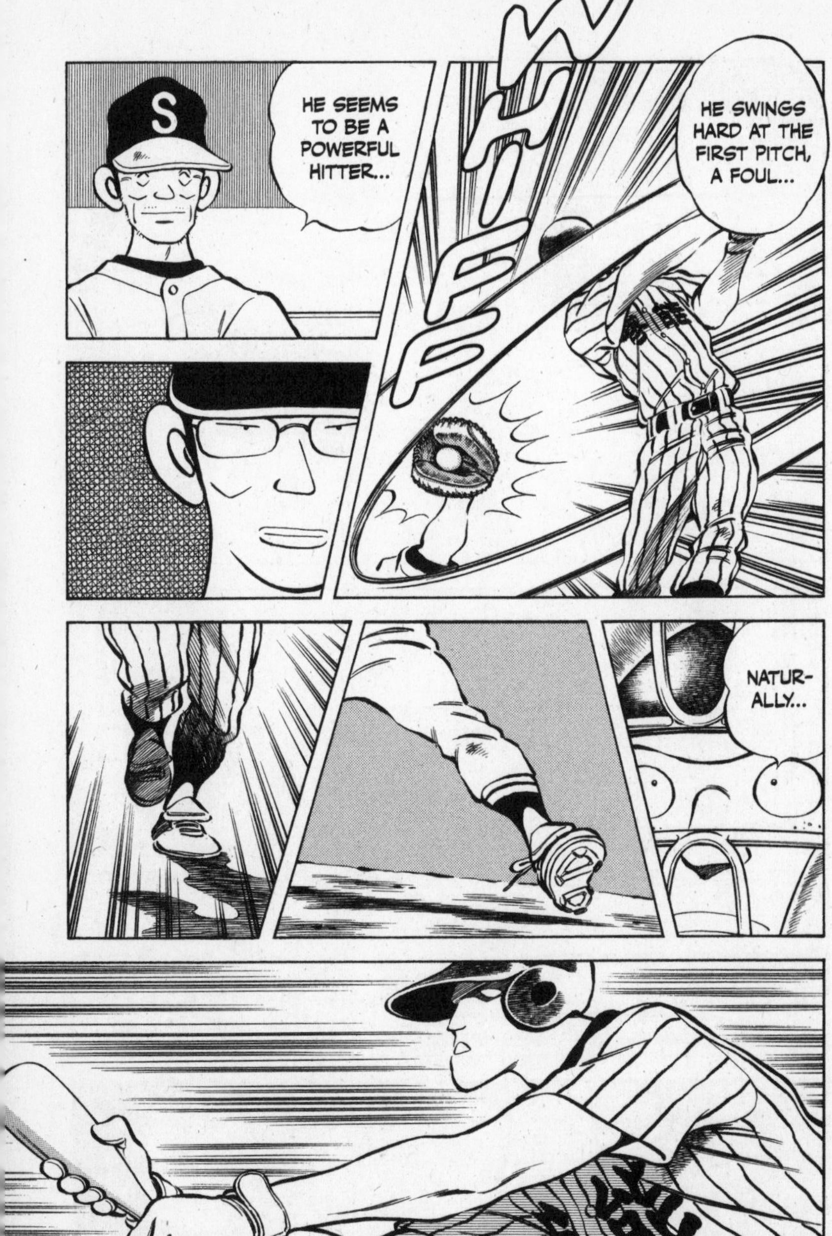
HE SWINGS HARD AT THE FIRST PITCH, A FOUL...
HE SEEMS TO BE A POWERFUL HITTER...
NATUR-ALLY...

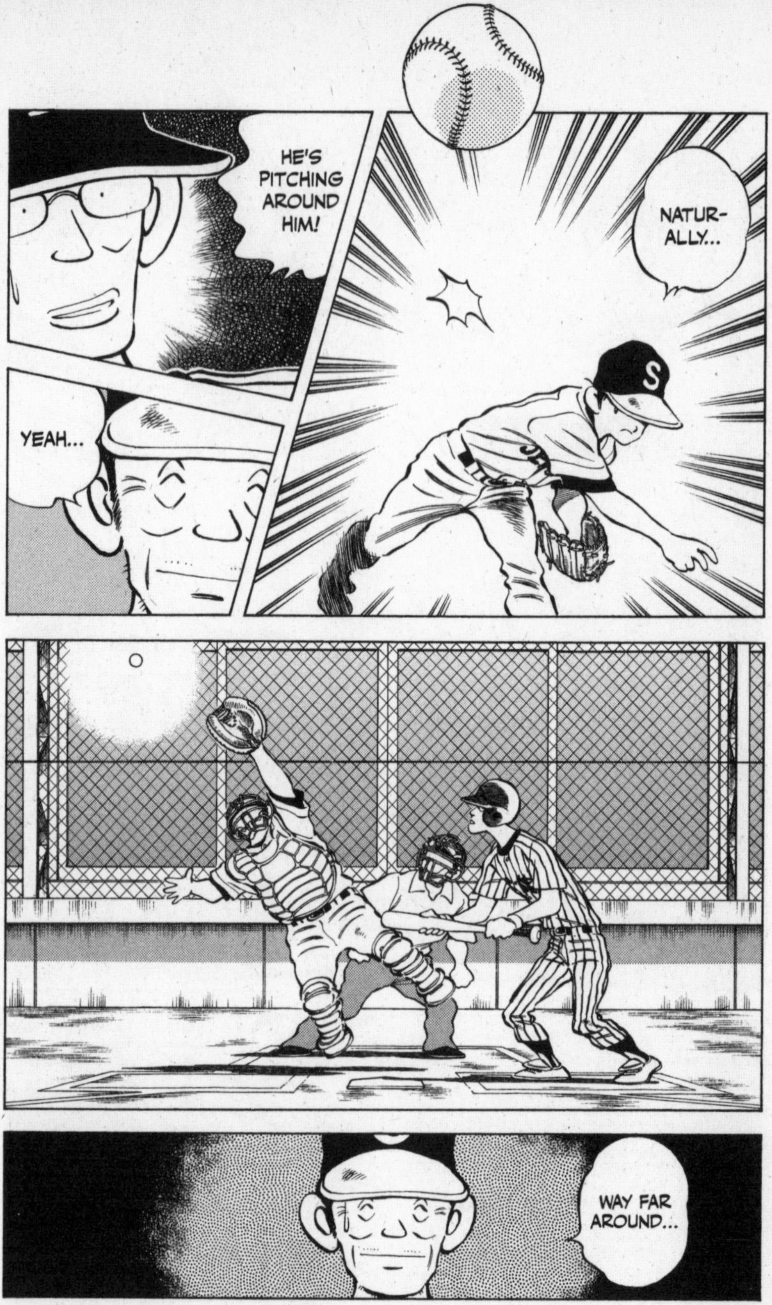
NATUR-
ALLY...
HE'S PITCHING AROUND HIM!
YEAH...
WAY FAR AROUND...

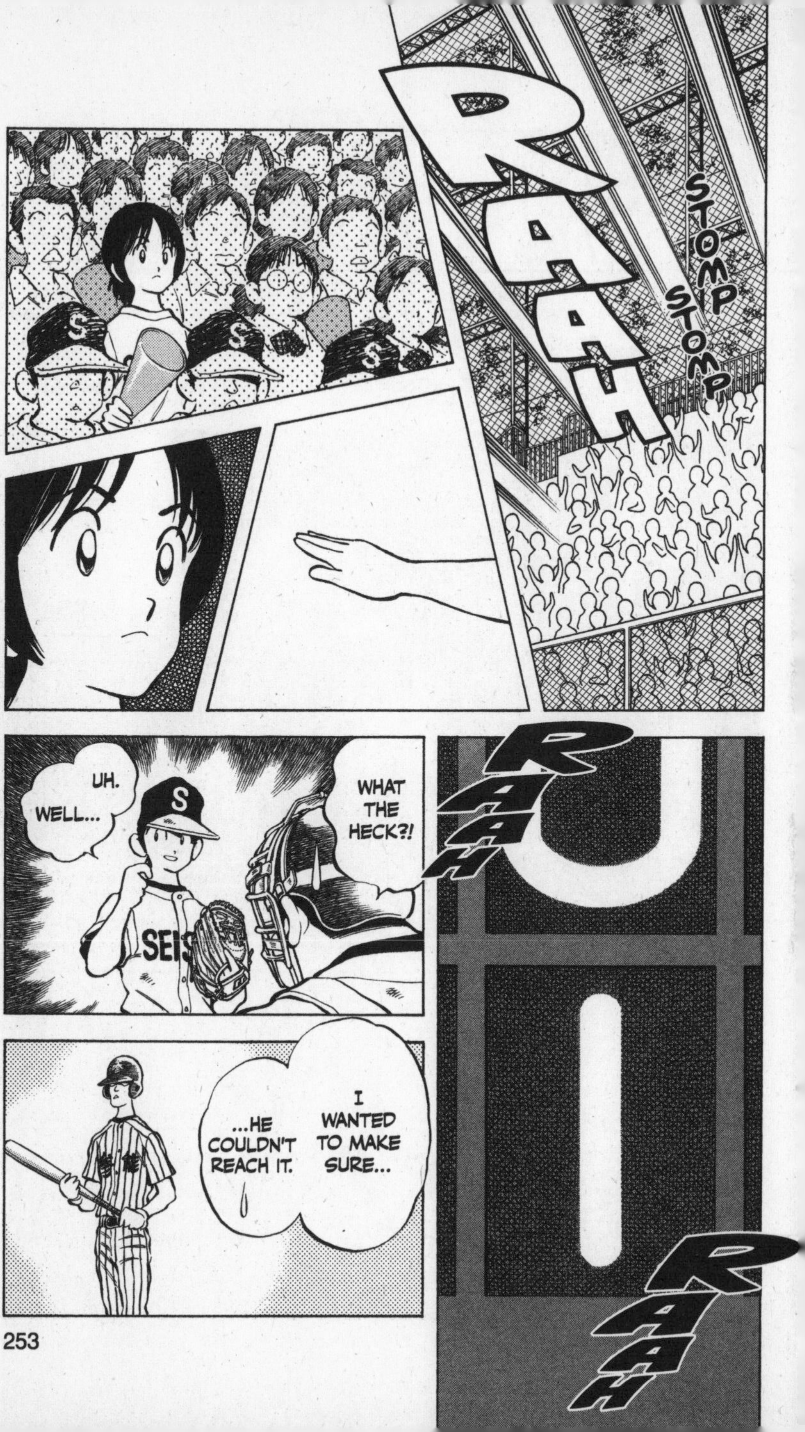
RAAH
STOMP STOMP
RAAH
RAAH
WHAT THE HECK?!
UH. WELL...
I WANTED TO MAKE SURE...
...HE COULDN'T REACH IT.

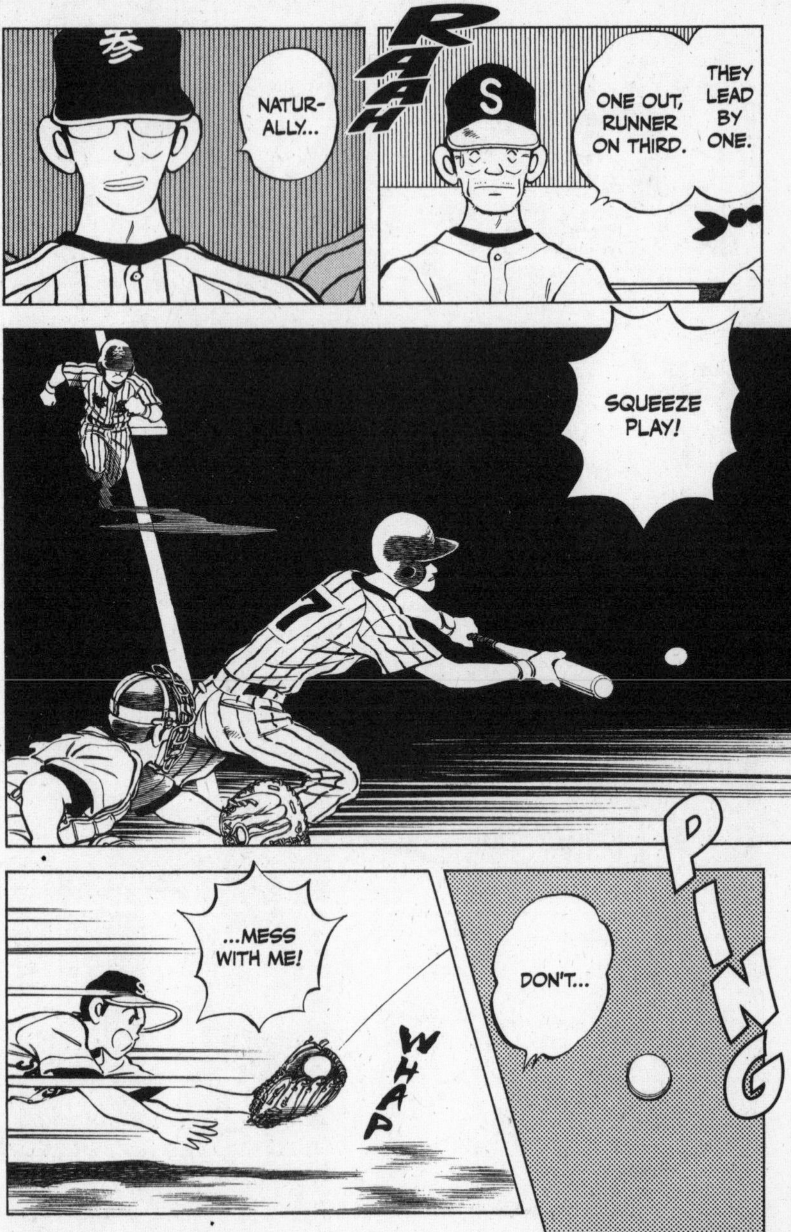
ONE OUT, RUNNER ON THIRD. THEY LEAD BY ONE.
RAAAH
NATUR-ALLY...
SQUEEZE PLAY!
PING
DON'T...
...MESS WITH ME!
WHAP

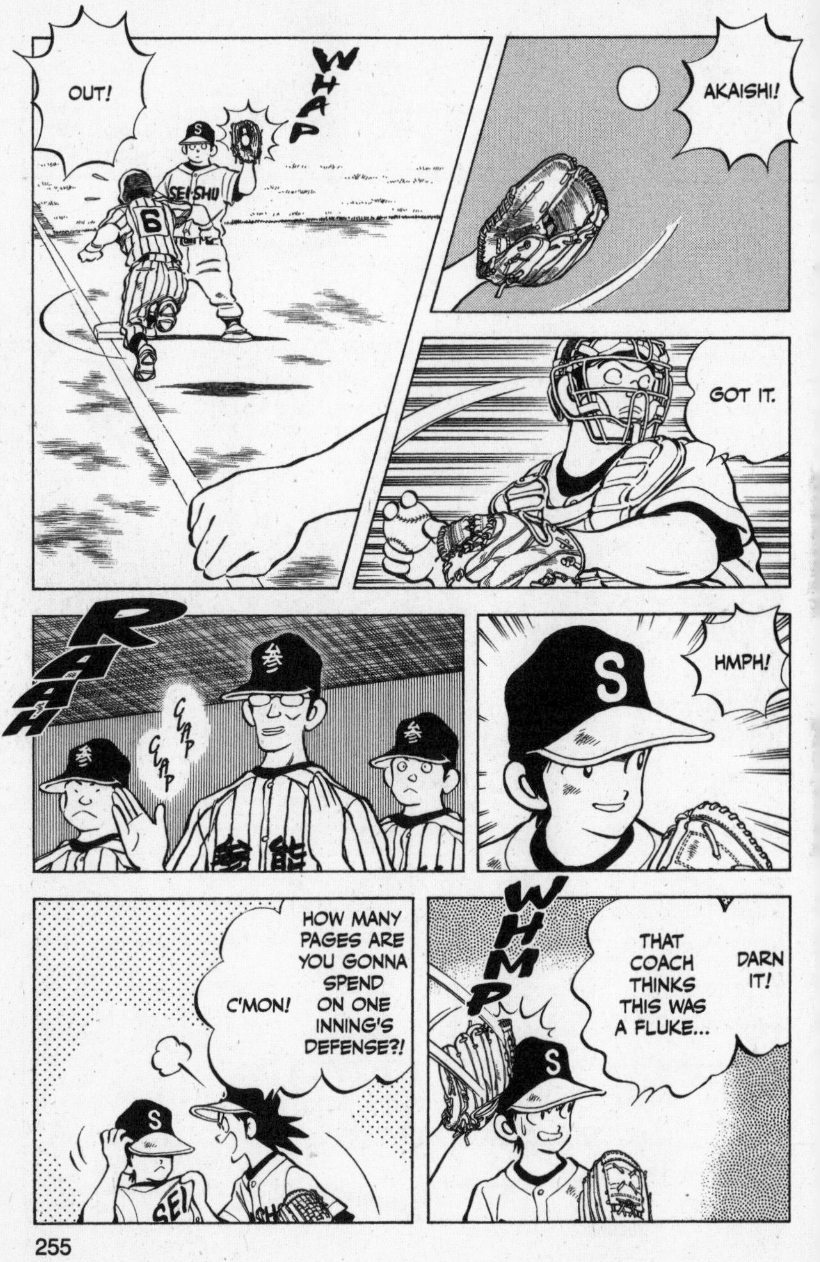
AKAISHI!
GOT IT.
WHAP
OUT!
HMPH!
RAAAH
CLAP CLAP
DARN IT!
THAT COACH THINKS THIS WAS A FLUKE...
WHMP
HOW MANY PAGES ARE YOU GONNA SPEND ON ONE INNING'S DEFENSE?!
C'MON!

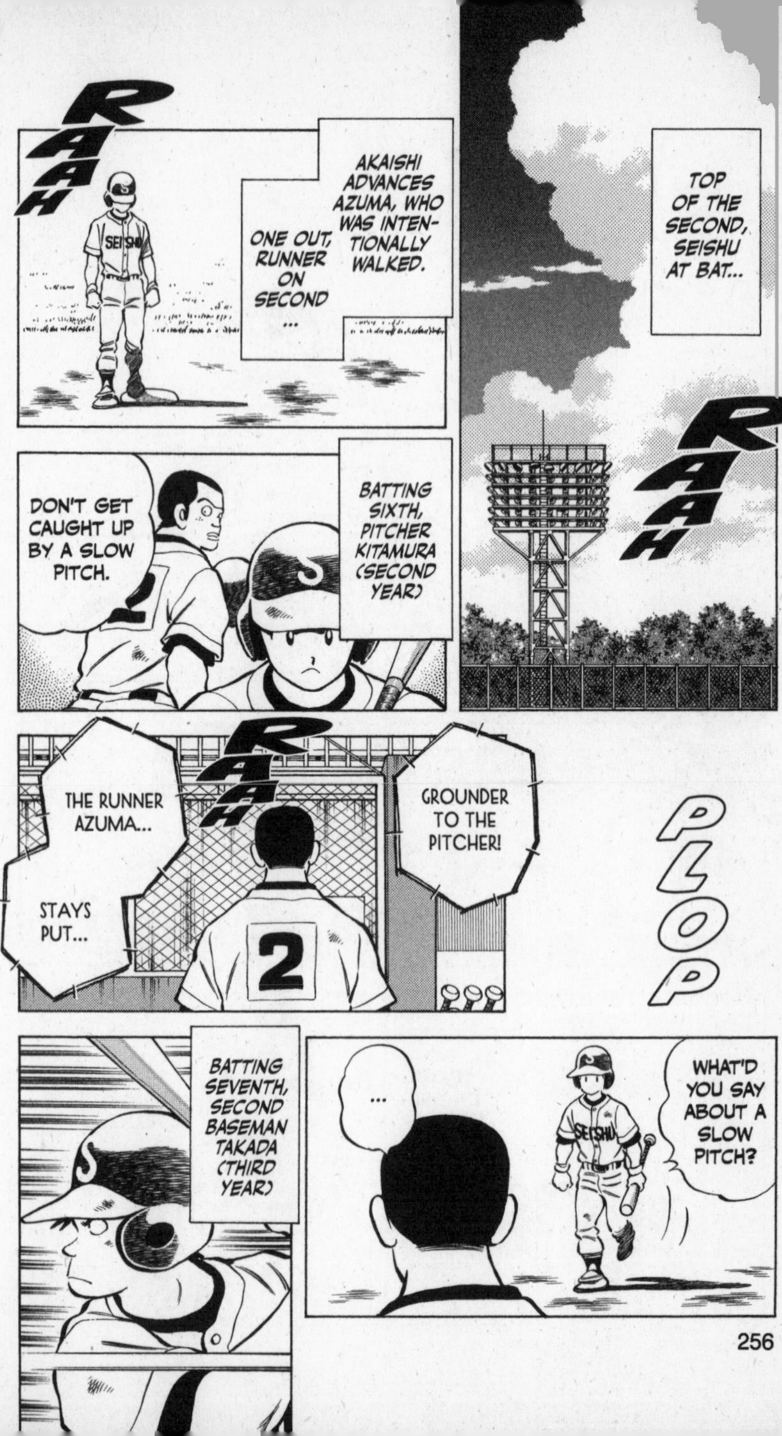
TOP OF THE SECOND, SEISHU AT BAT...
RAAH
RAAH
AKAISHI ADVANCES AZUMA, WHO WAS INTENTIONALLY WALKED.
ONE OUT, RUNNER ON SECOND ...
BATTING SIXTH, PITCHER KITAMURA (SECOND YEAR)
DON'T GET CAUGHT UP BY A SLOW PITCH.
PLOP
GROUNDER TO THE PITCHER!
RAAH
THE RUNNER AZUMA...
STAYS PUT...
WHAT'D YOU SAY ABOUT A SLOW PITCH?
...
BATTING SEVENTH, SECOND BASEMAN TAKADA (THIRD YEAR)

CHANGE SIDES!

RAAH

| TEAM | 1 | 2 |
|------|---|---|
| SEISHU | 0 | 0 |
| SANNOU | 1 | |

ALREADY ?!

KLANG

THIS IS THE CHEERING SECTION, RIGHT?

ALREADY DOWN ONE RUN?

WHAT'S THIS?

WHAT DO YOU THINK...?

WHAT ARE YOU DOING HERE?

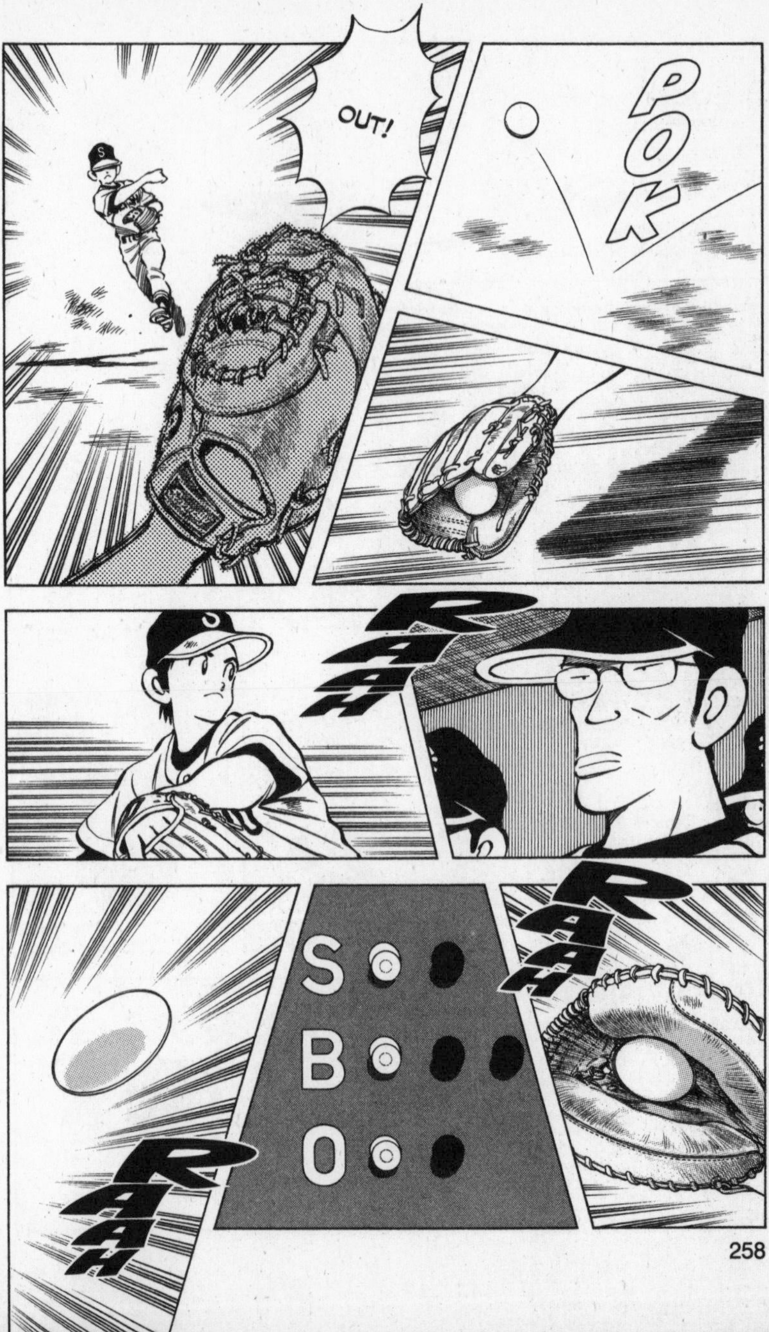
POK
OUT!
RAAH
RAAH
S
B
O
RAAH

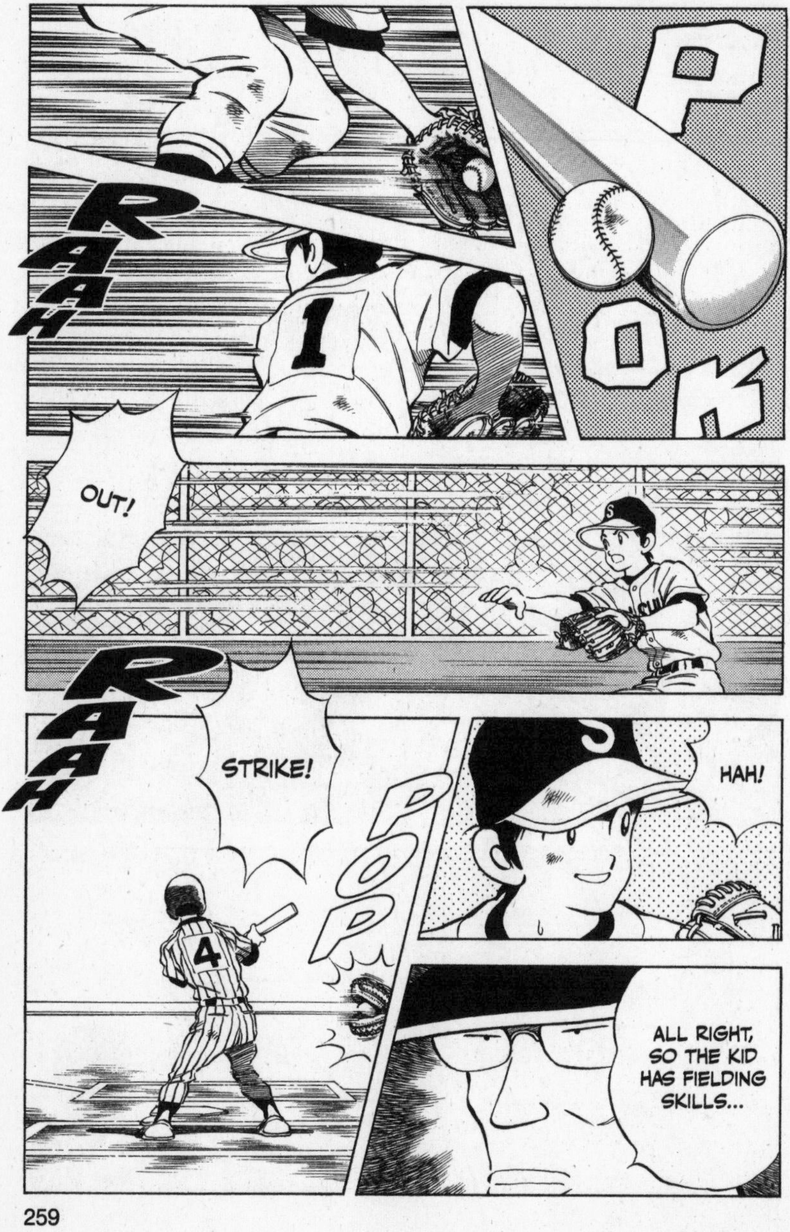
POK
RAAAH
OUT!
RAAAH
HAH!
ALL RIGHT, SO THE KID HAS FIELDING SKILLS...
STRIKE!
POP

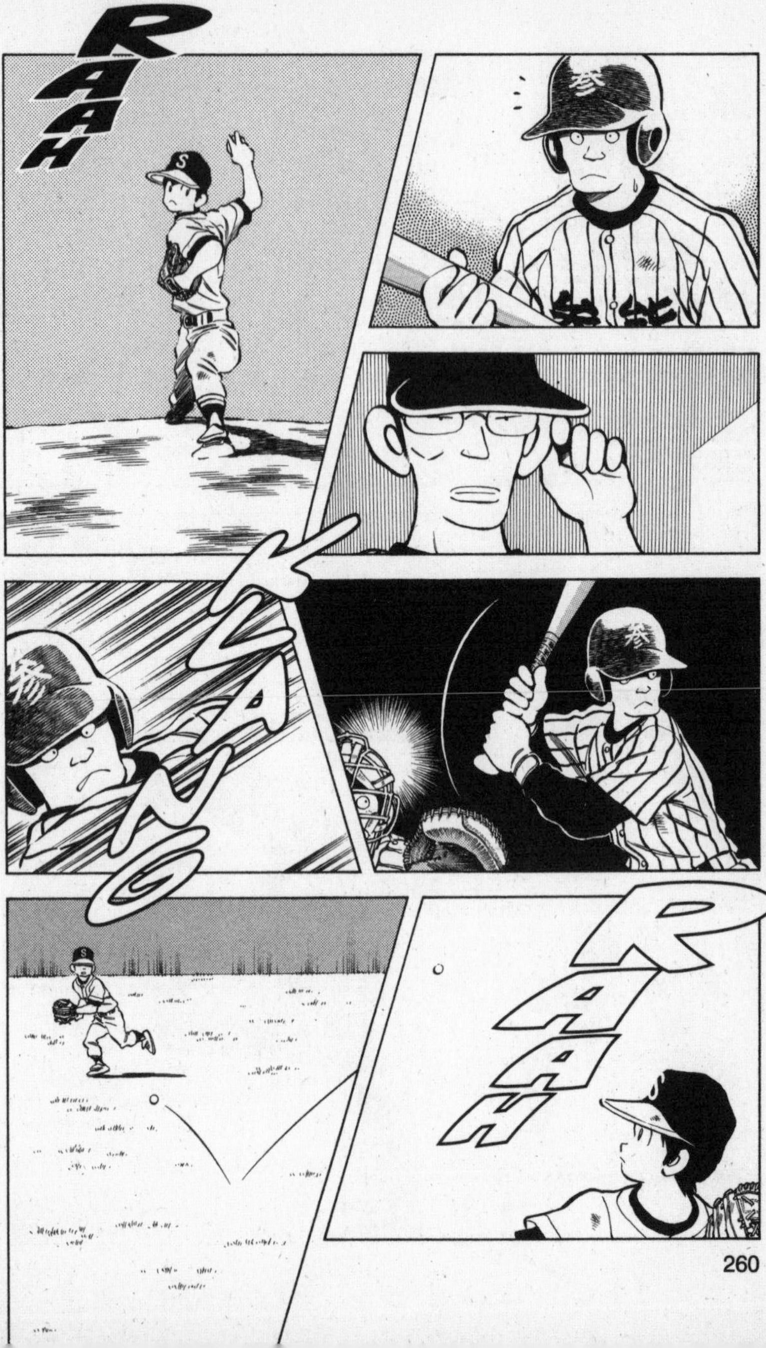
RAAH
KWANG
RAAH

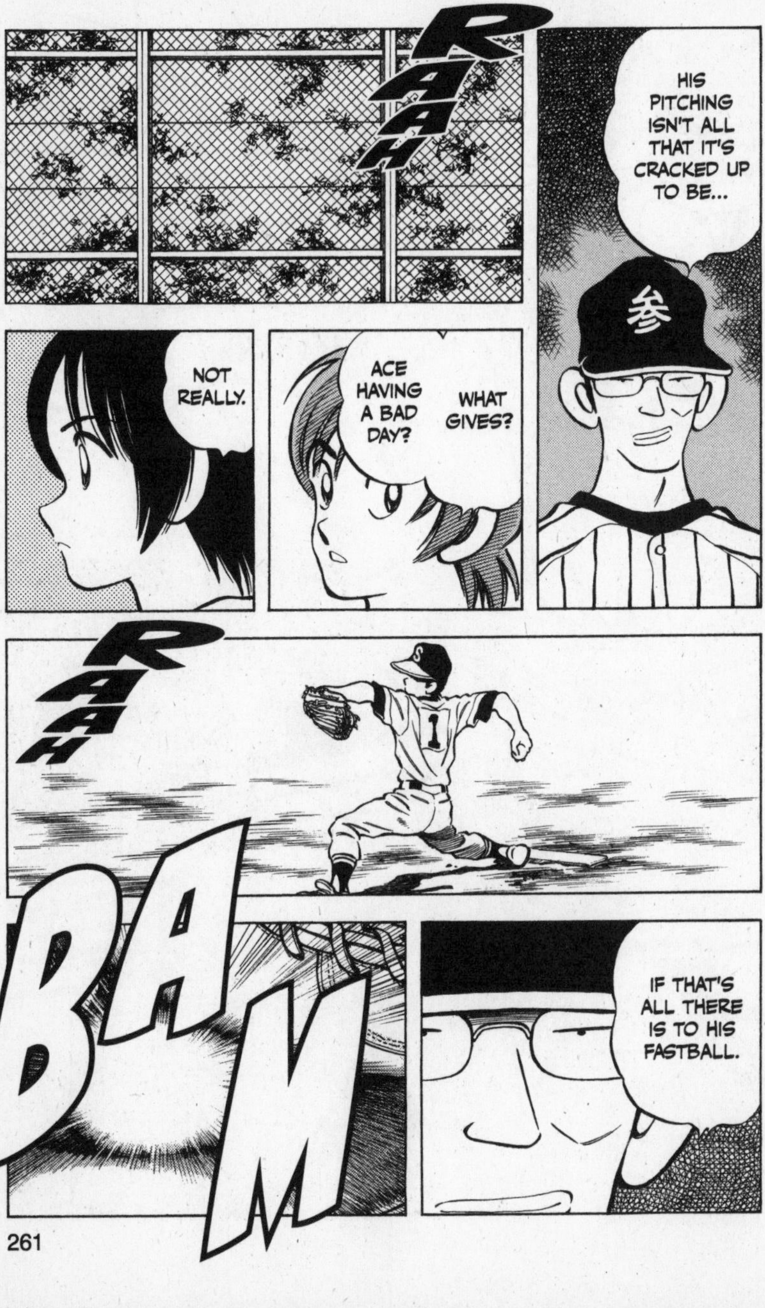
HIS PITCHING ISN'T ALL THAT IT'S CRACKED UP TO BE...
RAAH
WHAT GIVES?
ACE HAVING A BAD DAY?
NOT REALLY.
RAAH
IF THAT'S ALL THERE IS TO HIS FASTBALL.
BAM

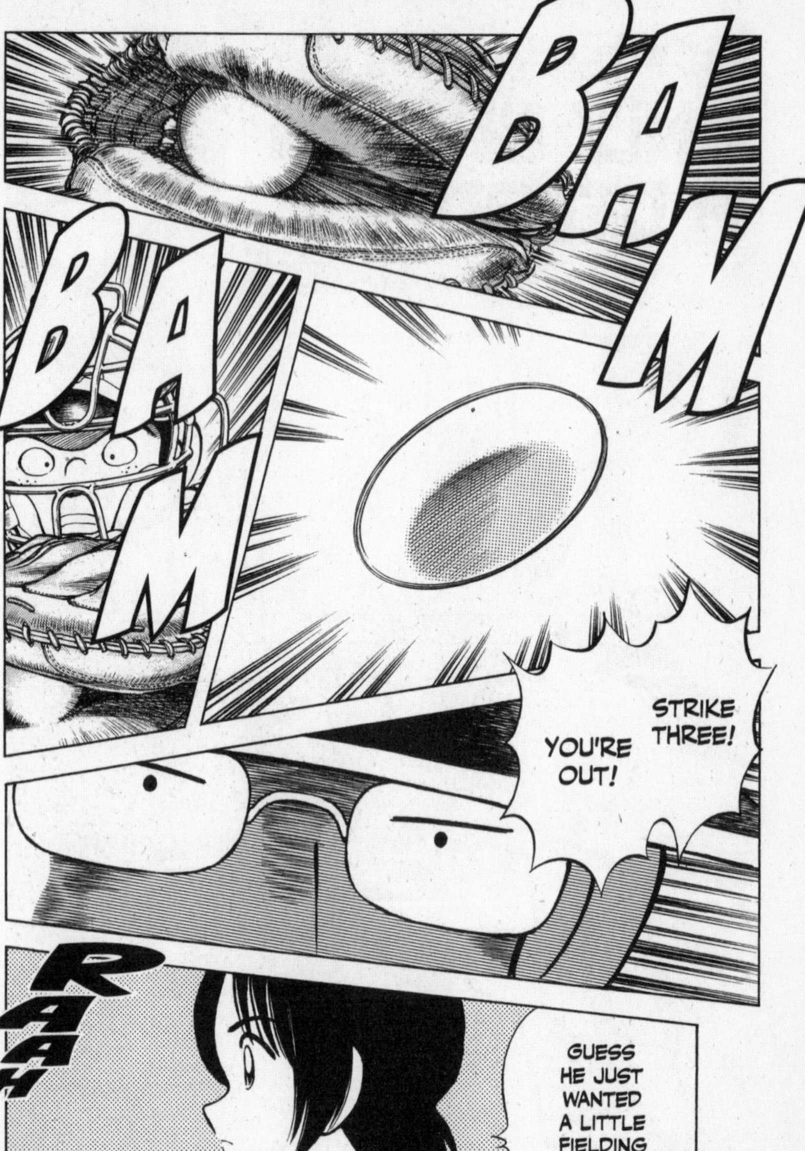
BAM
BAM
STRIKE THREE! YOU'RE OUT!
GUESS HE JUST WANTED A LITTLE FIELDING PRACTICE.
RAAAH

# CHAPTER 75
# ONLY ONCE IN A DECADE

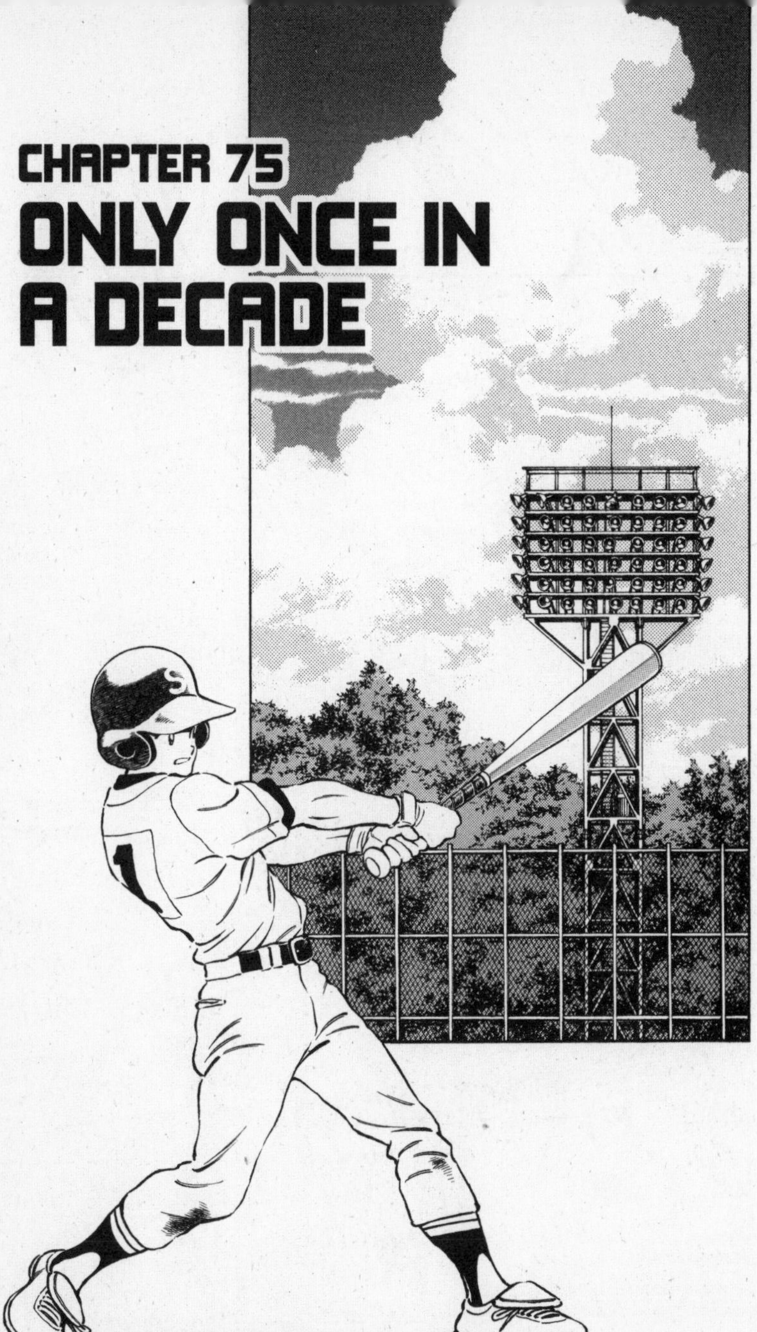

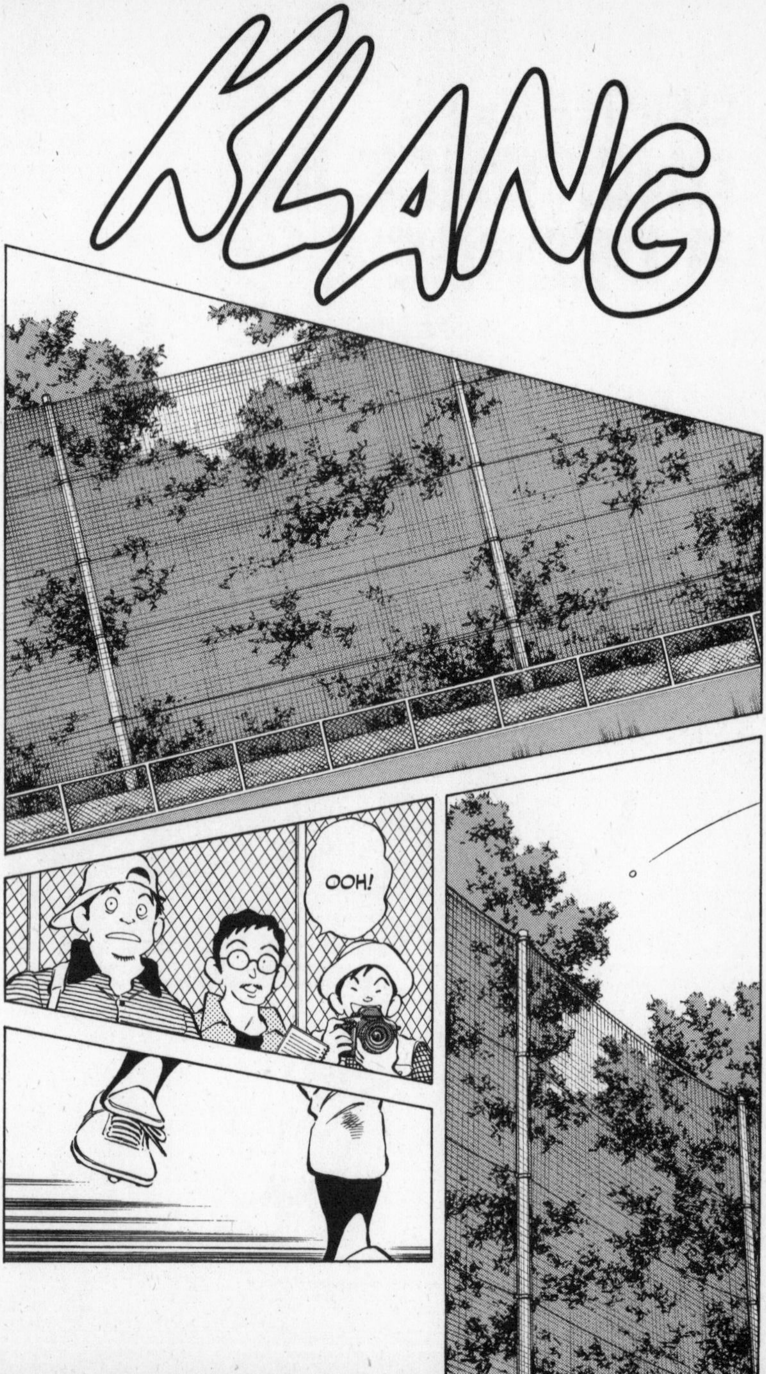
KLANG
OOH!

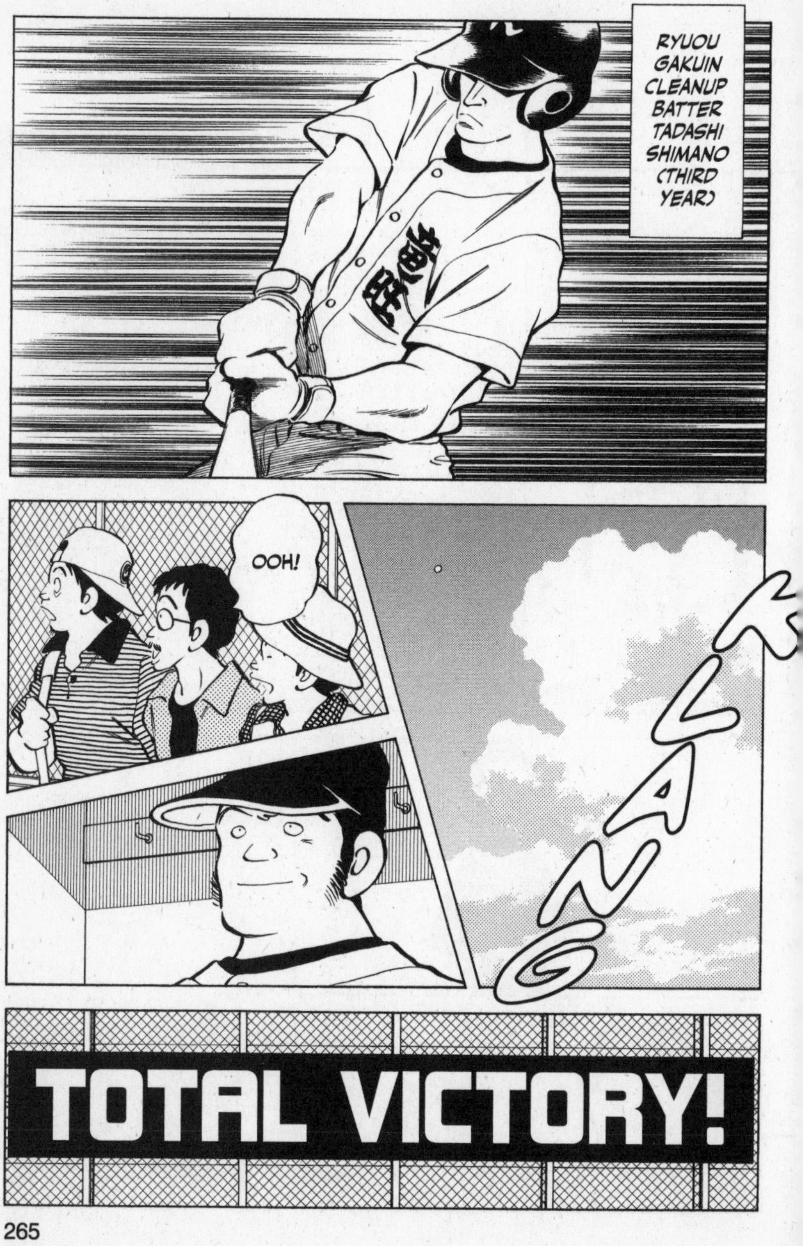
RYUOU GAKUIN CLEANUP BATTER TADASHI SHIMANO (THIRD YEAR)
KLANG
OOH!
TOTAL VICTORY!

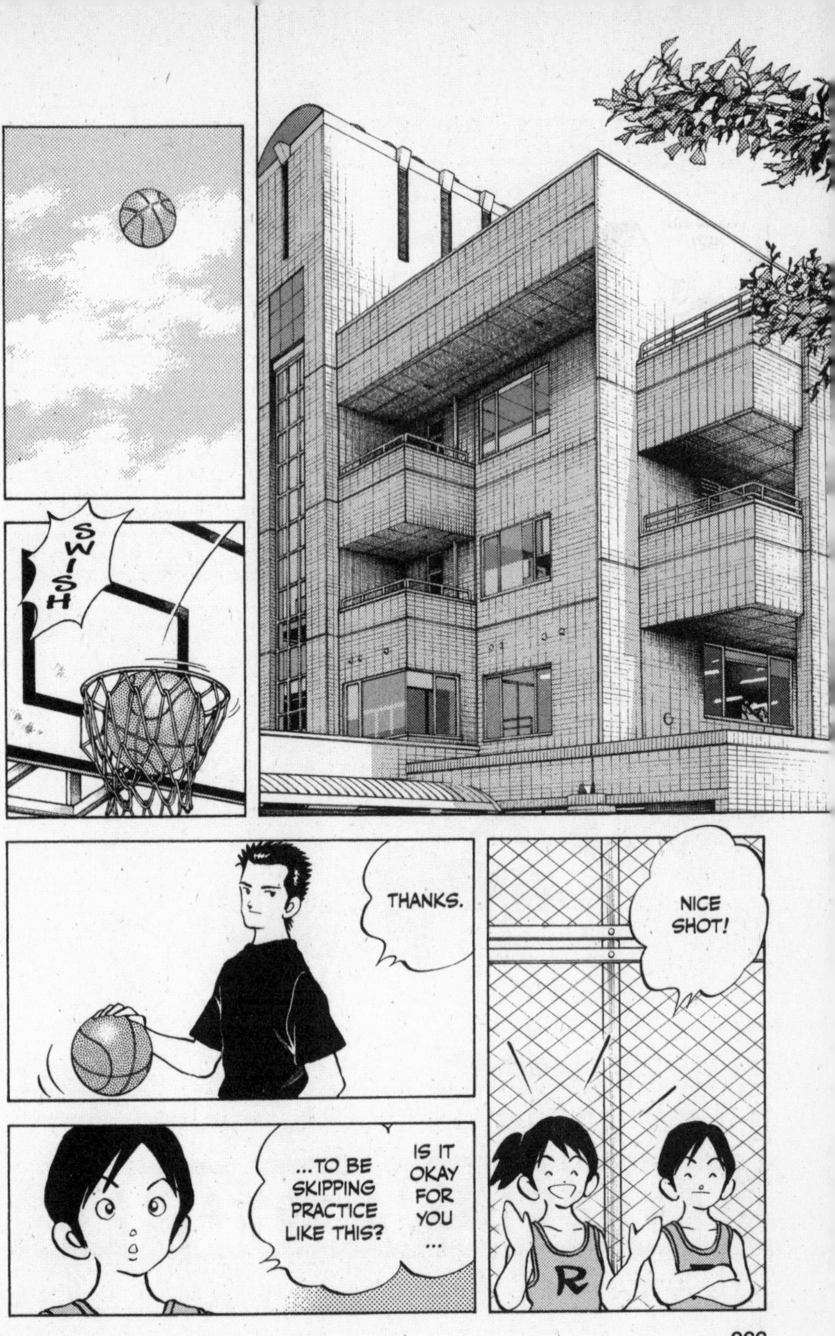
SWISH
NICE SHOT!
THANKS.
IS IT OKAY FOR YOU ...
...TO BE SKIPPING PRACTICE LIKE THIS?

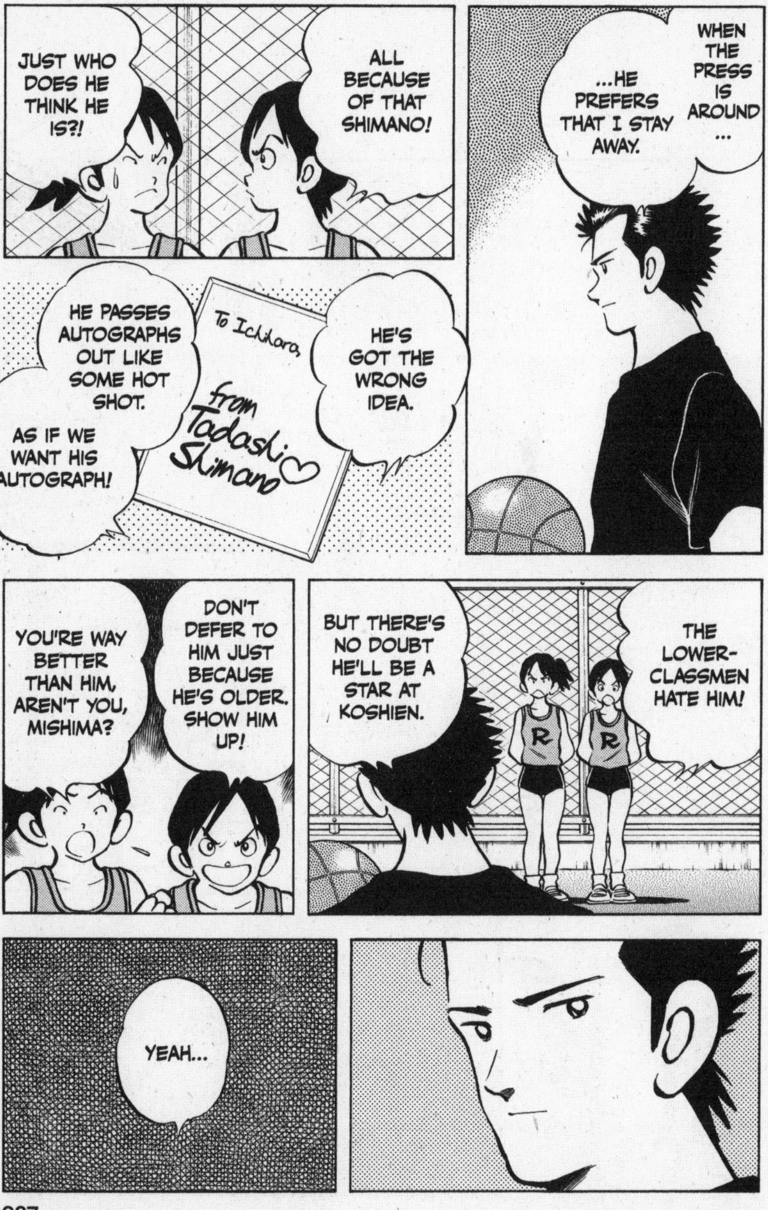
WHEN THE PRESS IS AROUND...
...HE PREFERS THAT I STAY AWAY.
ALL BECAUSE OF THAT SHIMANO!
JUST WHO DOES HE THINK HE IS?!
HE'S GOT THE WRONG IDEA.
To Ichihara, from Tadashi Shimano
HE PASSES AUTOGRAPHS OUT LIKE SOME HOT SHOT.
AS IF WE WANT HIS AUTOGRAPH!
THE LOWER-CLASSMEN HATE HIM!
BUT THERE'S NO DOUBT HE'LL BE A STAR AT KOSHIEN.
DON'T DEFER TO HIM JUST BECAUSE HE'S OLDER. SHOW HIM UP!
YOU'RE WAY BETTER THAN HIM, AREN'T YOU, MISHIMA?
YEAH...

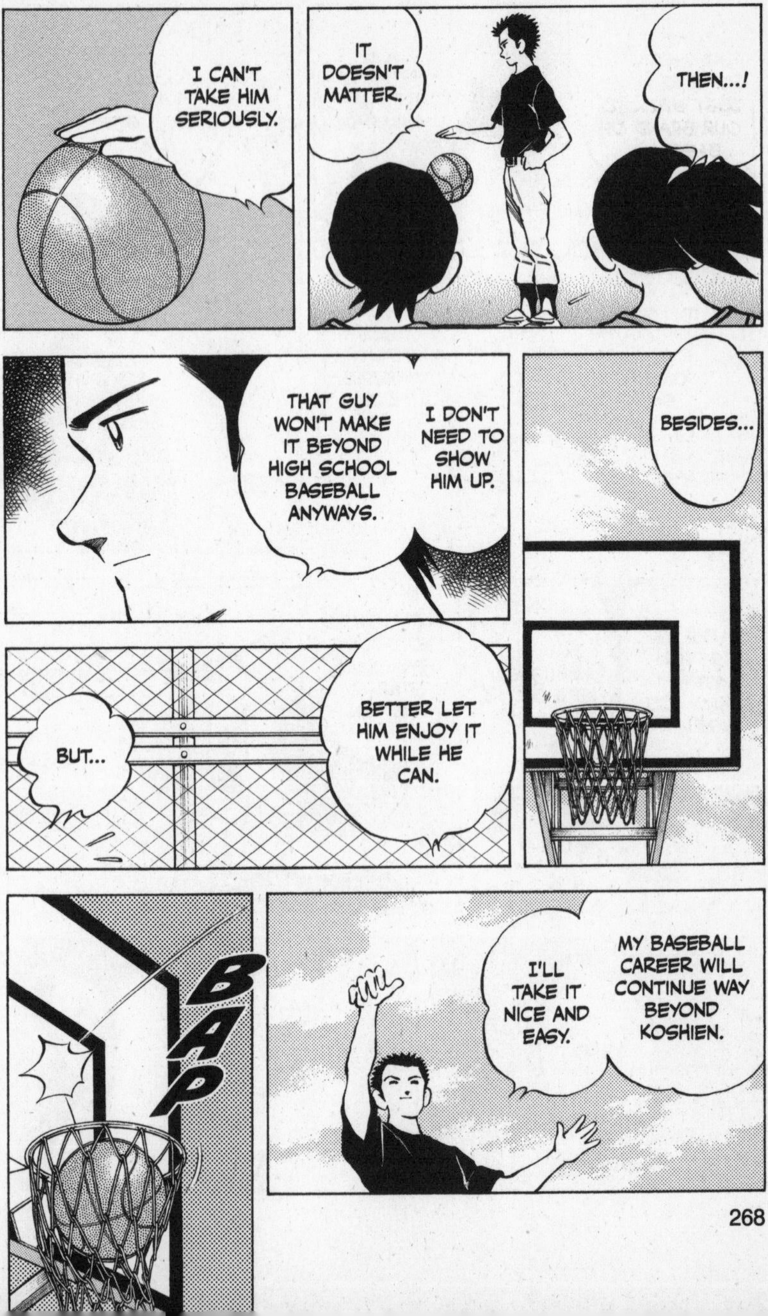
THEN...!
IT DOESN'T MATTER.
I CAN'T TAKE HIM SERIOUSLY.
BESIDES...
I DON'T NEED TO SHOW HIM UP.
THAT GUY WON'T MAKE IT BEYOND HIGH SCHOOL BASEBALL ANYWAYS.
BETTER LET HIM ENJOY IT WHILE HE CAN.
BUT...
MY BASEBALL CAREER WILL CONTINUE WAY BEYOND KOSHIEN.
I'LL TAKE IT NICE AND EASY.
BAP

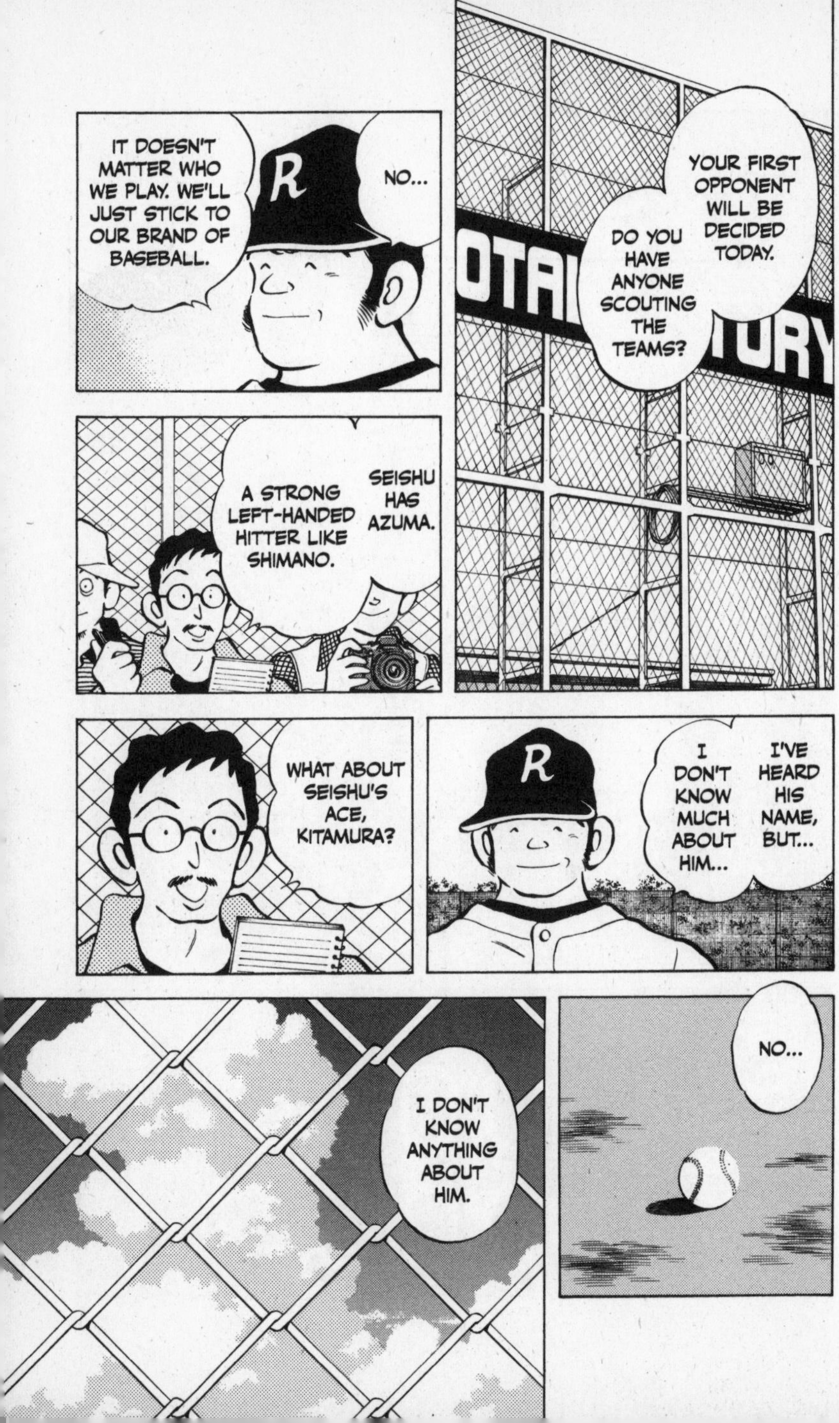
YOUR FIRST OPPONENT WILL BE DECIDED TODAY.
DO YOU HAVE ANYONE SCOUTING THE TEAMS?
NO...
IT DOESN'T MATTER WHO WE PLAY. WE'LL JUST STICK TO OUR BRAND OF BASEBALL.
SEISHU HAS AZUMA.
A STRONG LEFT-HANDED HITTER LIKE SHIMANO.
I'VE HEARD HIS NAME, BUT...
I DON'T KNOW MUCH ABOUT HIM...
WHAT ABOUT SEISHU'S ACE, KITAMURA?
NO...
I DON'T KNOW ANYTHING ABOUT HIM.

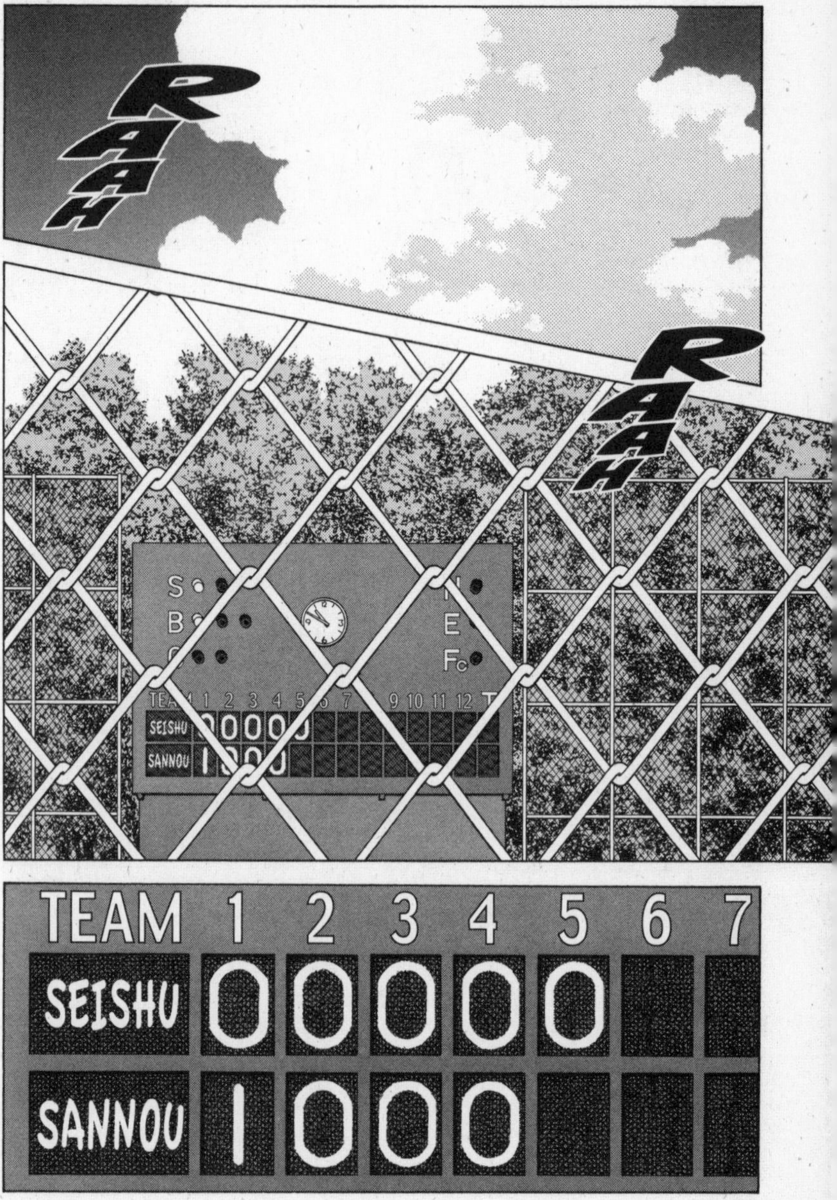
RAAAH
RAAAH
TEAM 1 2 3 4 5 6 7
SEISHU 0 0 0 0 0
SANNOU 1 0 0 0

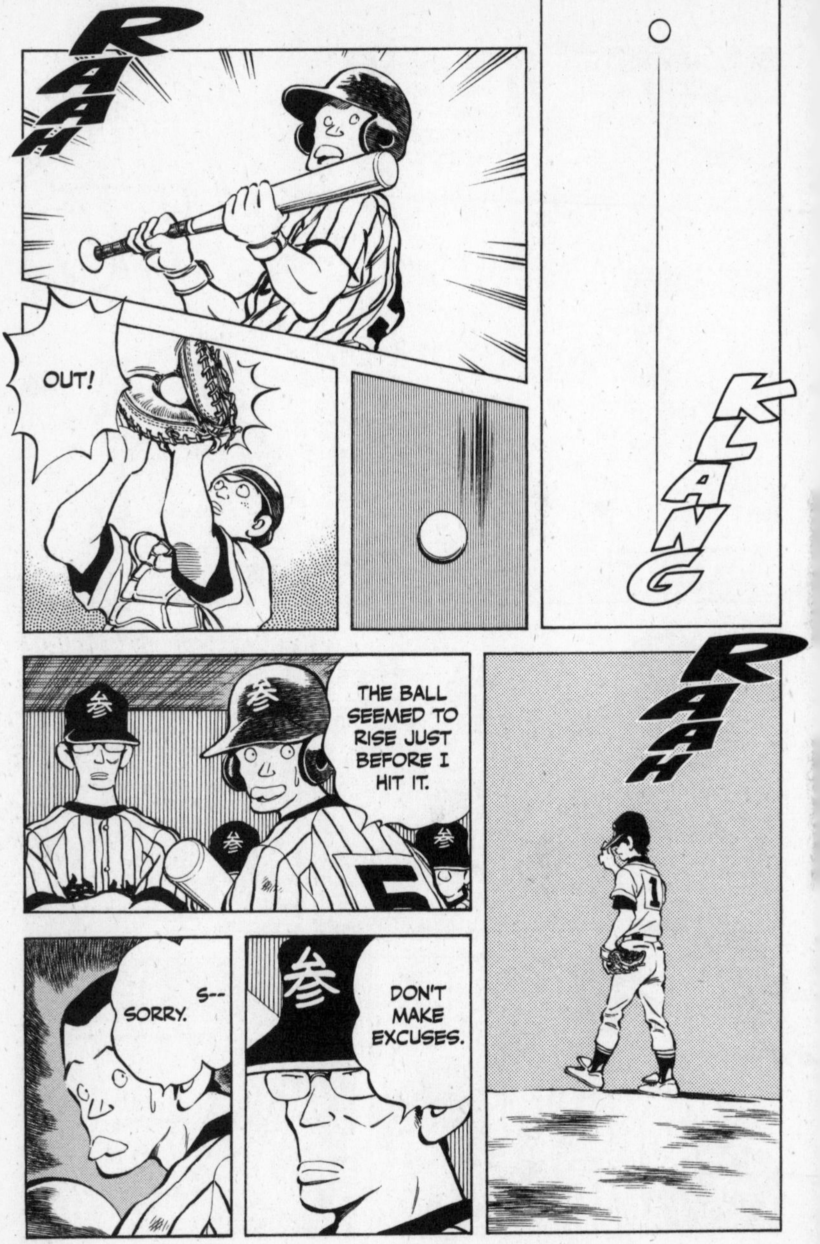
KLANG
RAAAH
OUT!
RAAAH
THE BALL SEEMED TO RISE JUST BEFORE I HIT IT.
DON'T MAKE EXCUSES.
S-- SORRY.

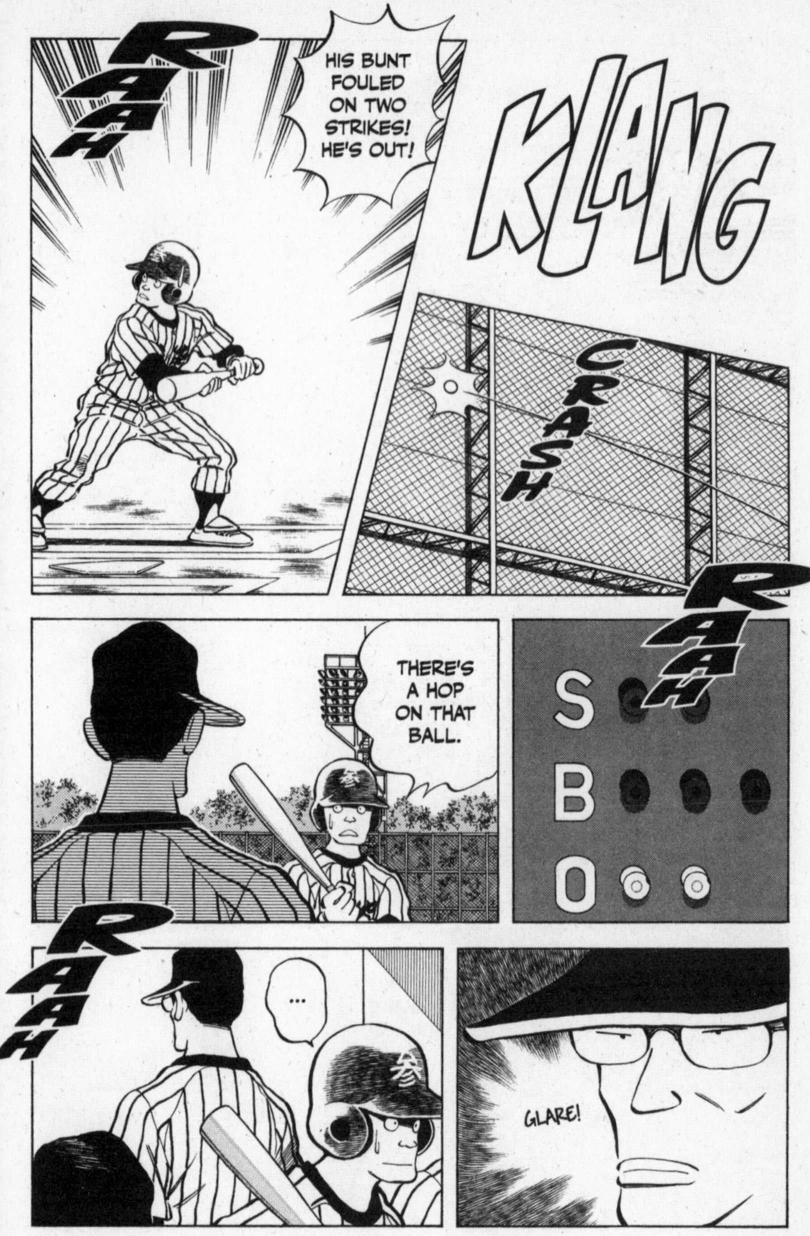
KLANG
CRASH
RAAAH
HIS BUNT FOULED ON TWO STRIKES! HE'S OUT!
RAAAH
S
B
O
THERE'S A HOP ON THAT BALL.
GLARE!
RAAAH
...

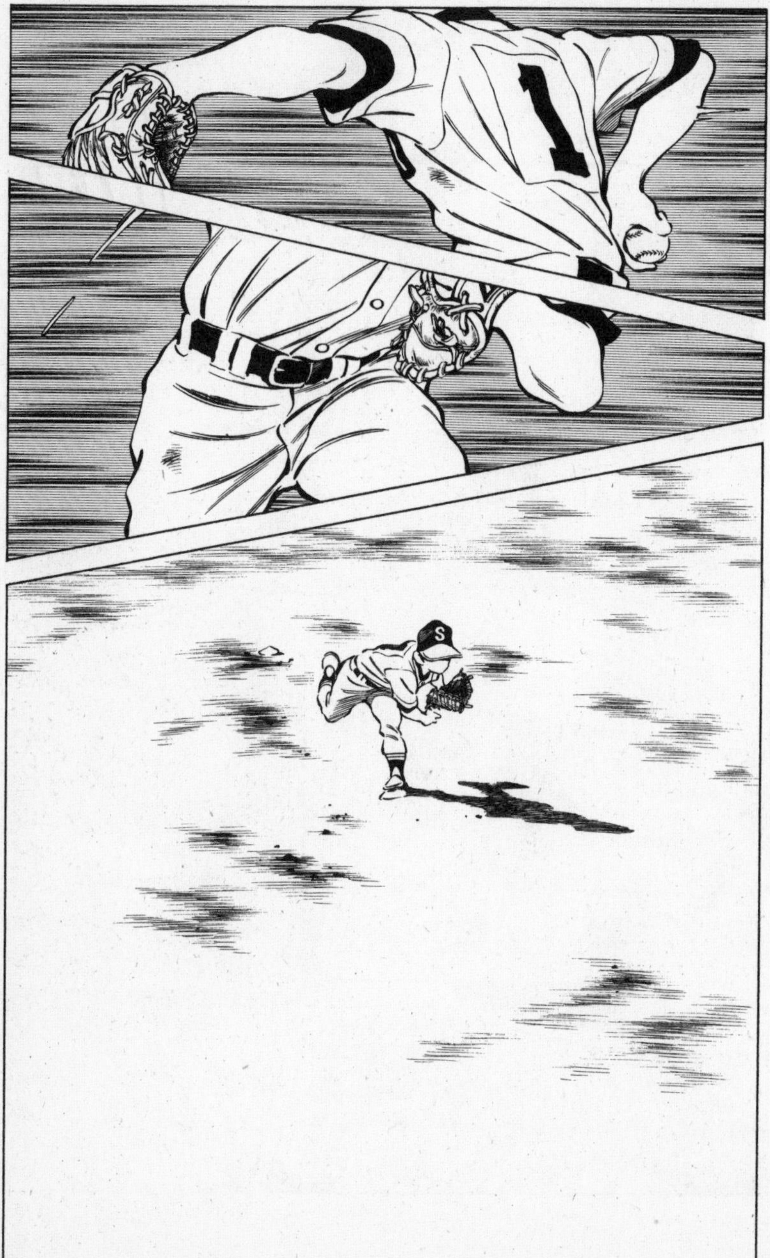

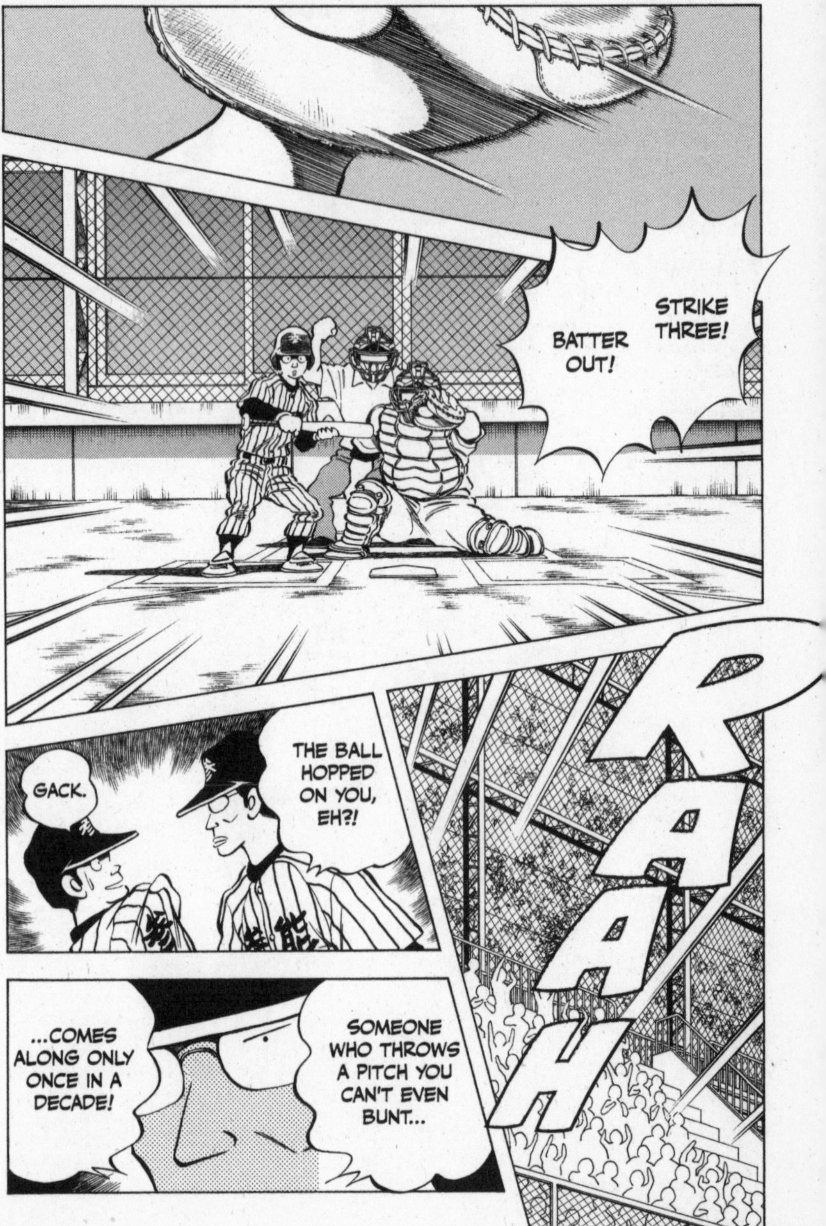
STRIKE THREE!
BATTER OUT!
RAAH
THE BALL HOPPED ON YOU, EH?!
GACK.
SOMEONE WHO THROWS A PITCH YOU CAN'T EVEN BUNT...
...COMES ALONG ONLY ONCE IN A DECADE!

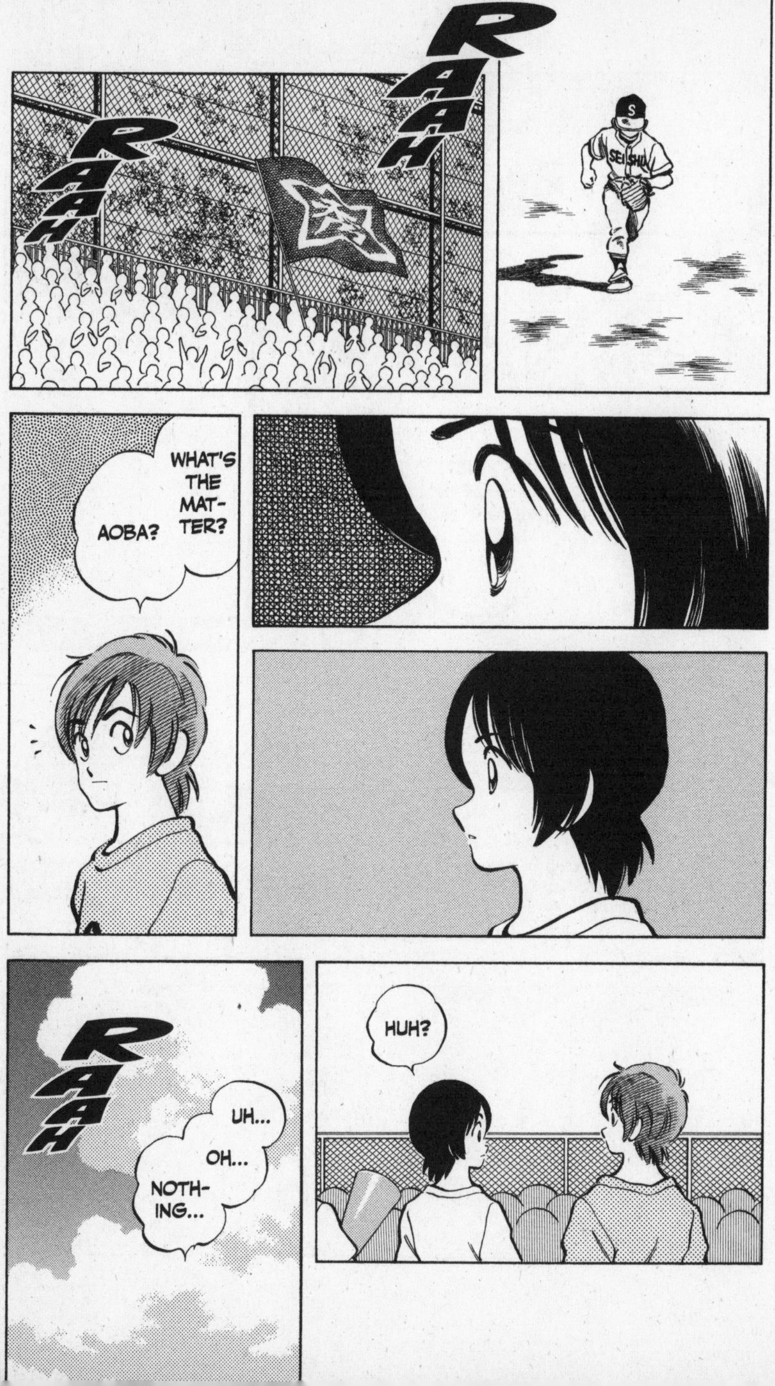
RAAAH
RAAAH
WHAT'S THE MAT-TER? AOBA?
HUH?
RAAAH
UH... OH... NOTH-ING...

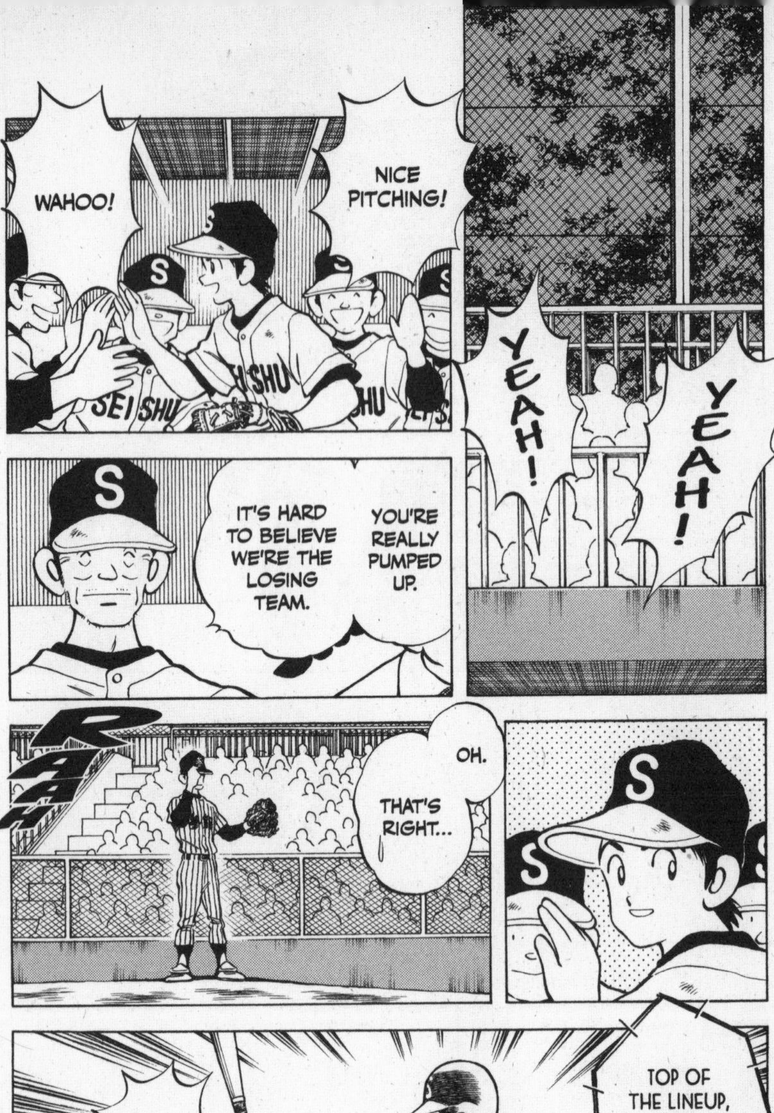
YEAH!
YEAH!
NICE PITCHING!
WAHOO!
YOU'RE REALLY PUMPED UP.
IT'S HARD TO BELIEVE WE'RE THE LOSING TEAM.
OH.
THAT'S RIGHT...
RAAAH
TOP OF THE LINEUP, SHORTSTOP SENDA!
YEAH!

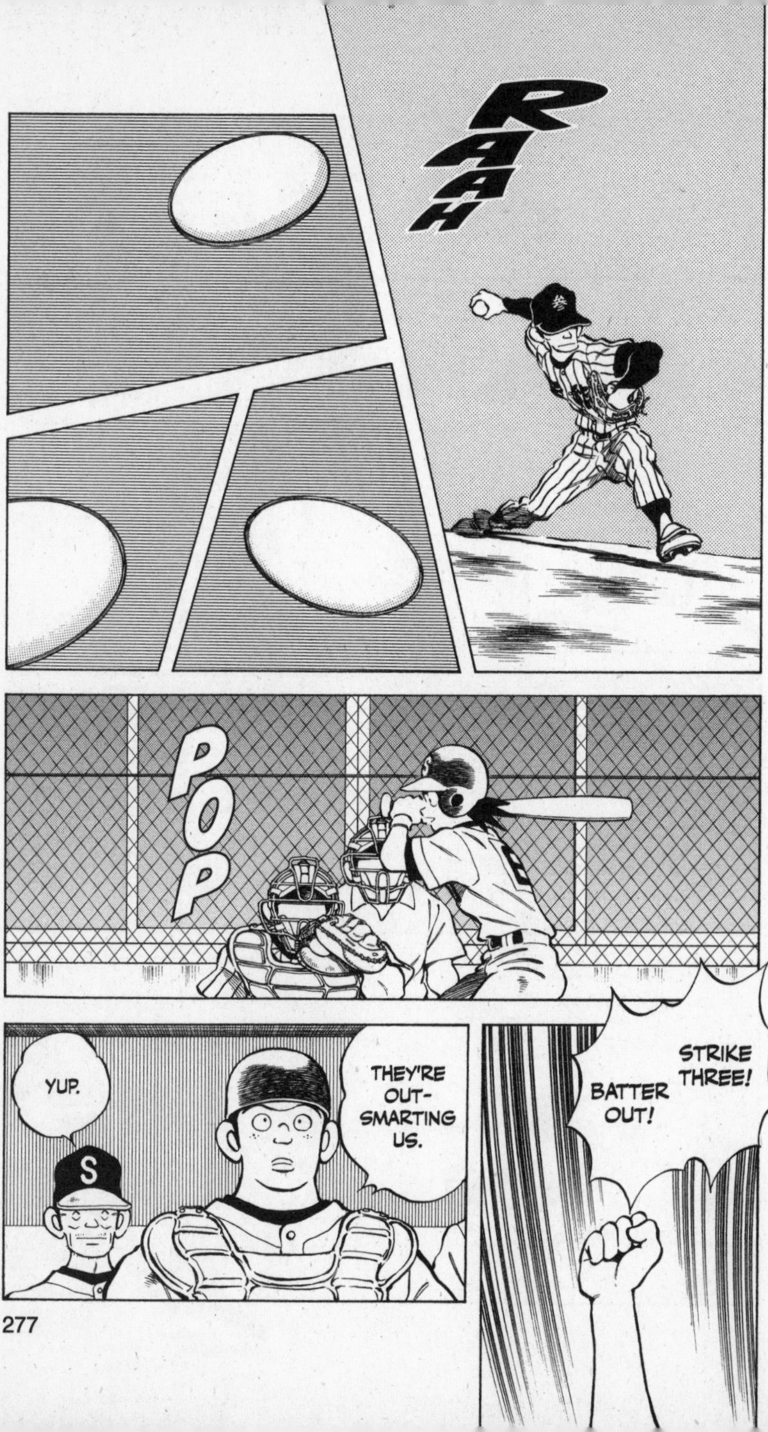
RAAAH
POP
STRIKE THREE!
BATTER OUT!
THEY'RE OUT-SMARTING US.
YUP.
S

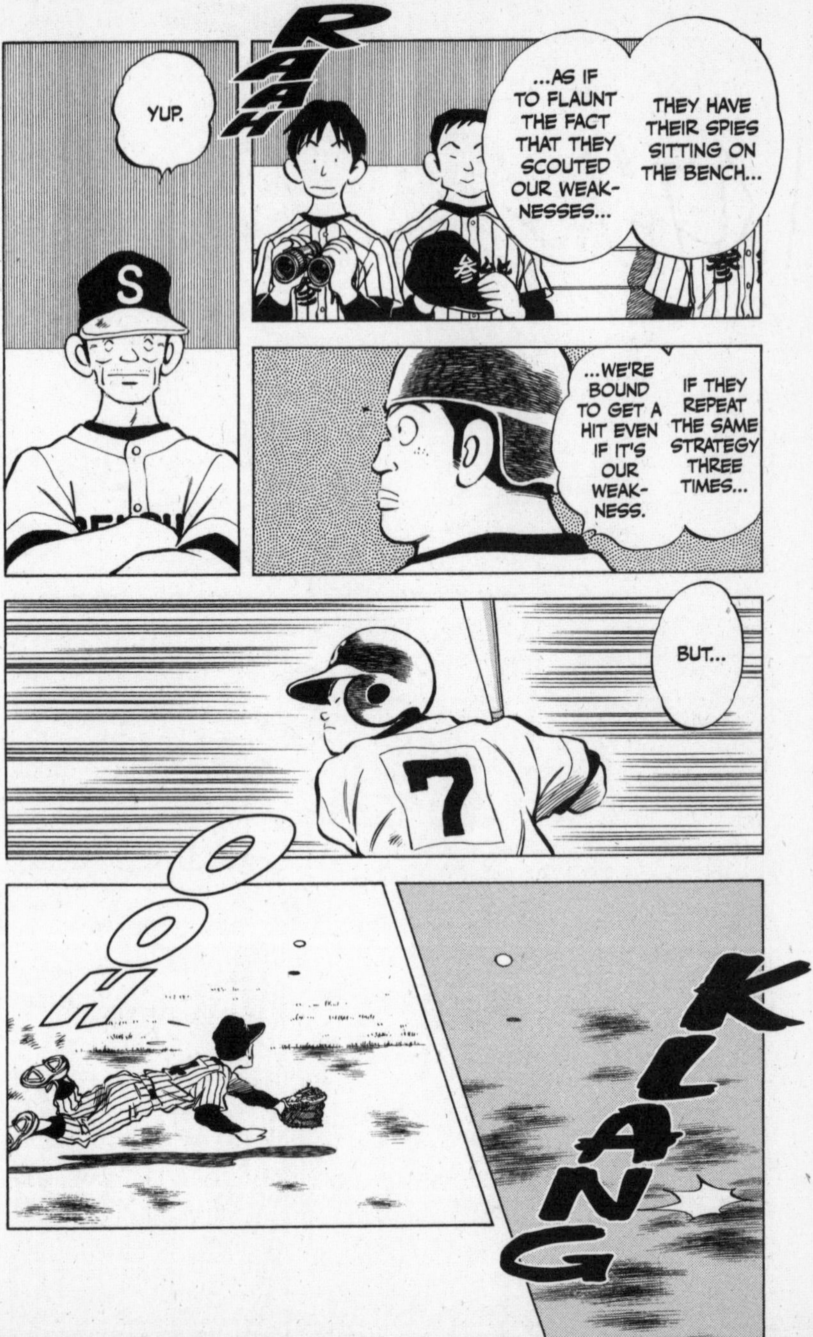
THEY HAVE THEIR SPIES SITTING ON THE BENCH...
...AS IF TO FLAUNT THE FACT THAT THEY SCOUTED OUR WEAK-NESSES...
RAAH
IF THEY REPEAT THE SAME STRATEGY THREE TIMES...
...WE'RE BOUND TO GET A HIT EVEN IF IT'S OUR WEAK-NESS.
YUP.
BUT...
KLANG
OOH

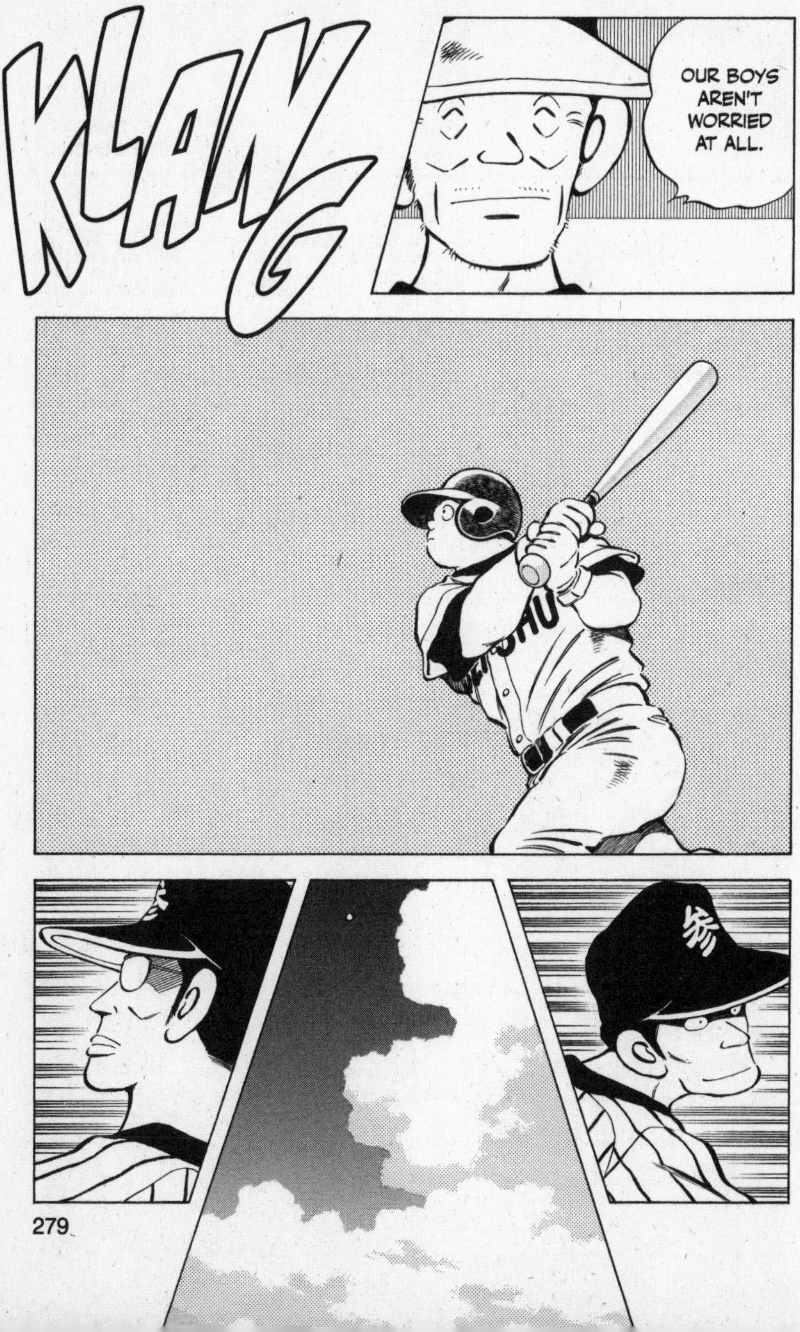
OUR BOYS AREN'T WORRIED AT ALL.
KLANG

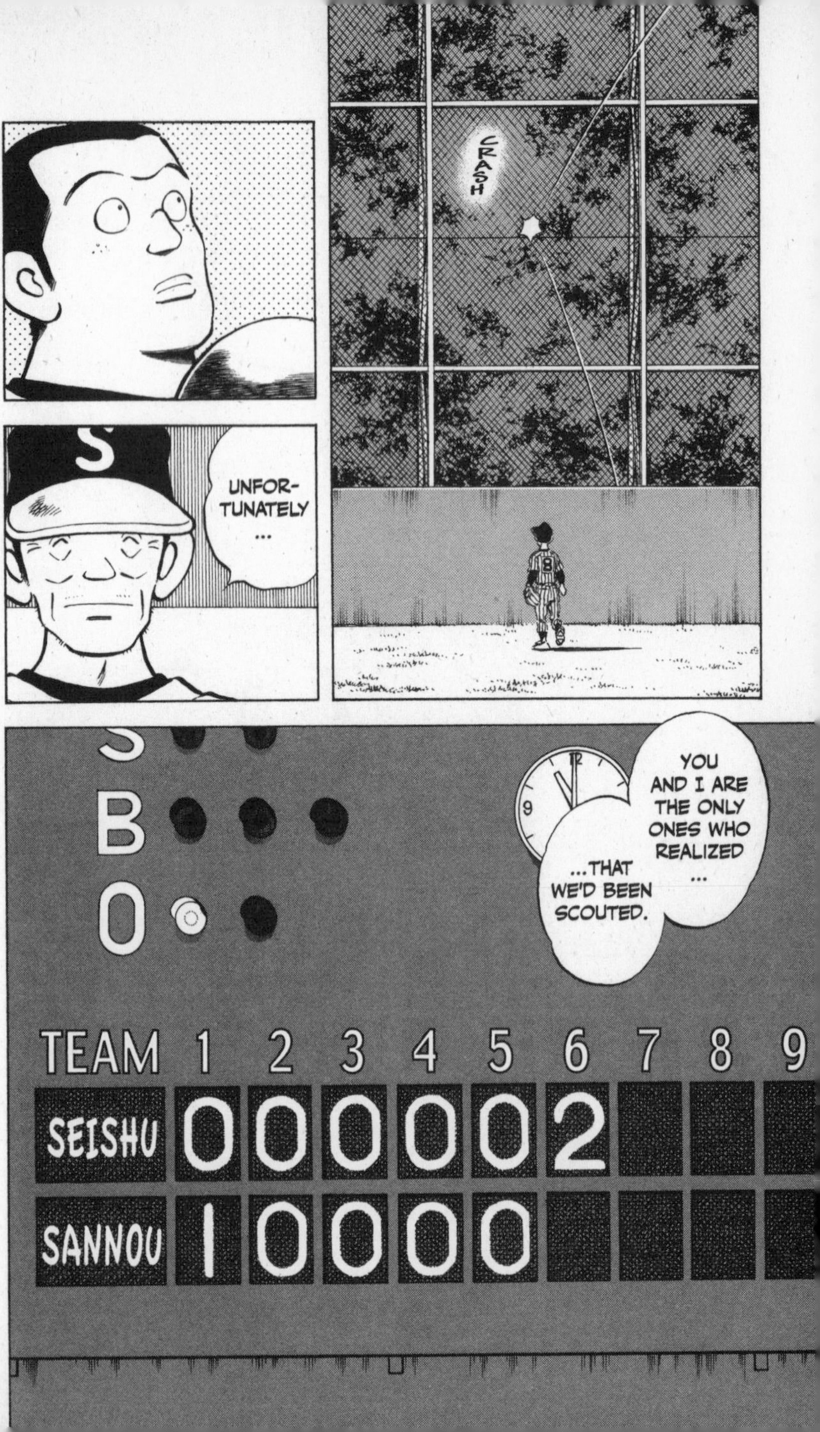

CRASH

UNFOR-TUNATELY...

S

B

0

YOU AND I ARE THE ONLY ONES WHO REALIZED...

...THAT WE'D BEEN SCOUTED.

| TEAM | 1 | 2 | 3 | 4 | 5 | 6 | 7 | 8 | 9 |
|------|---|---|---|---|---|---|---|---|---|
| SEISHU | 0 | 0 | 0 | 0 | 0 | 2 | | | |
| SANNOU | 1 | 0 | 0 | 0 | 0 | | | | |

# CHAPTER 76
# WHERE DO YOU WANT IT?

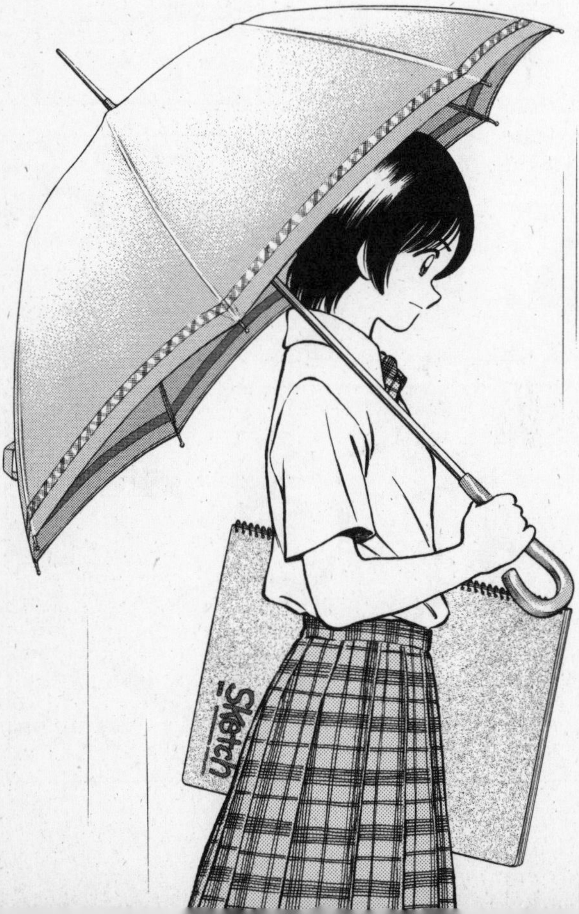
Sketch

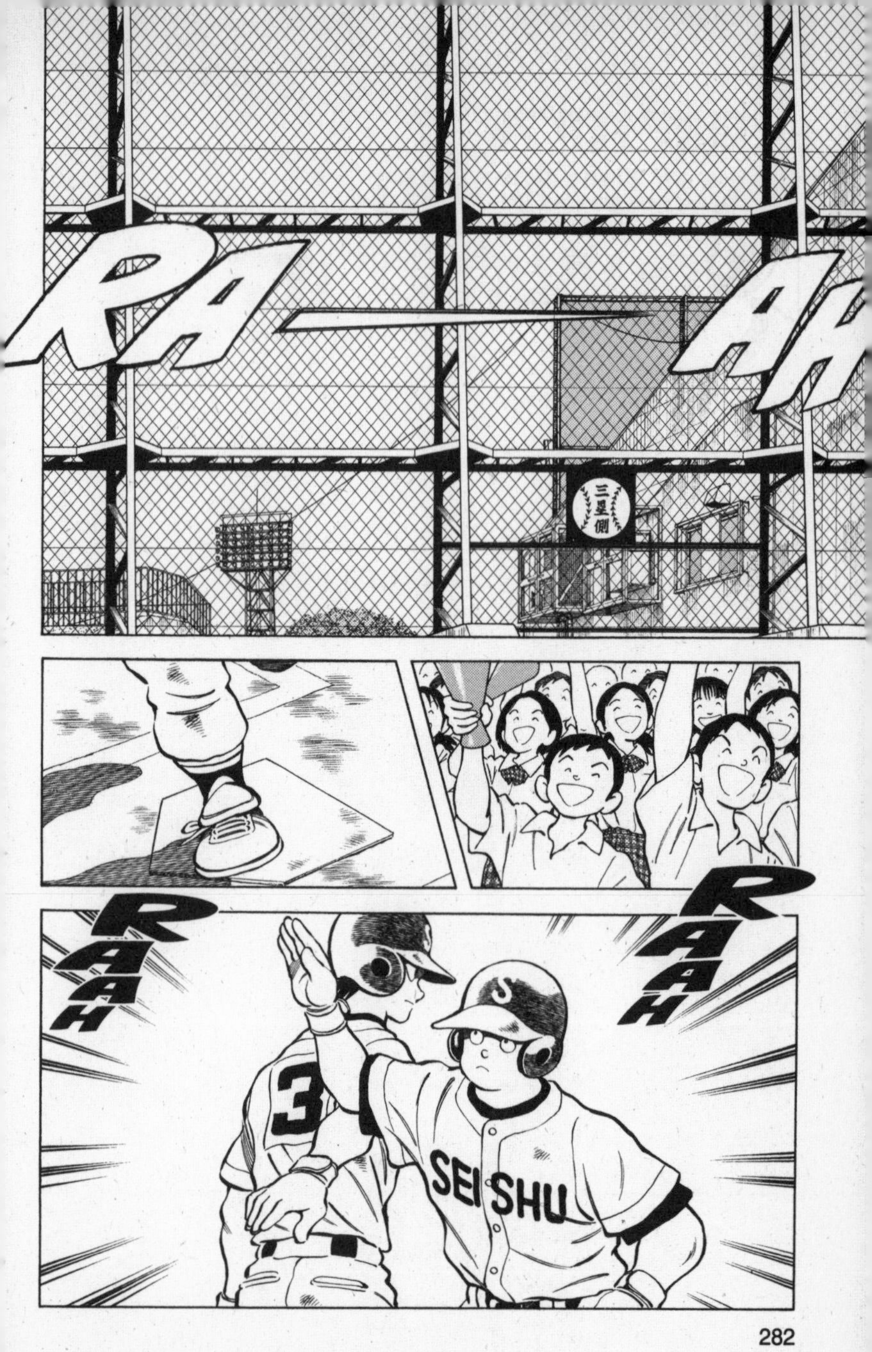
RA—AH
三塁側
RAAAH
RAAAH
3
SEISHU

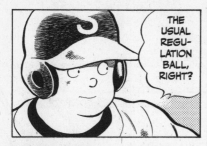

RAAAH
WHAT KIND OF BALL WAS IT?
THE USUAL REGULATION BALL, RIGHT?
HIGH OR LOW?
INSIDE OR OUTSIDE?
STRAIGHT, OR BREAKING BALL?
OH. RIGHT.
HMM.
LET'S SEE...
NEVER MIND.
WHAP

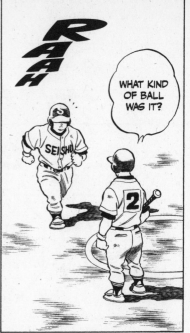

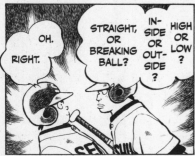

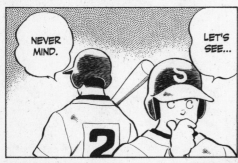

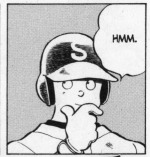

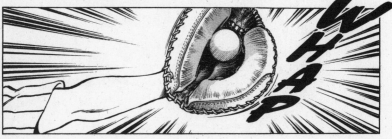

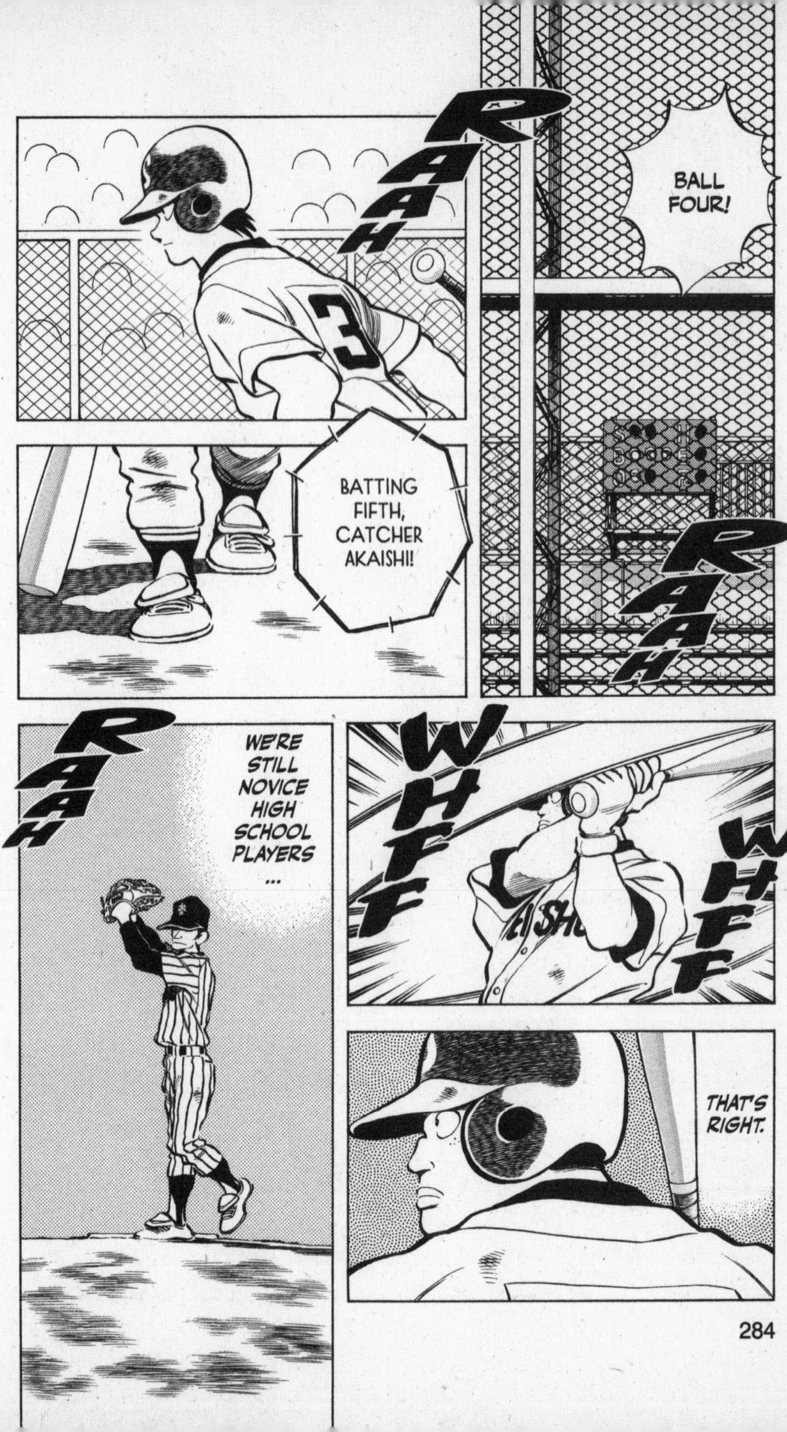
BALL FOUR!
RAAAH
RAAAH
BATTING FIFTH, CATCHER AKAISHI!
WHFF
WHFF
THAT'S RIGHT.
RAAAH
WE'RE STILL NOVICE HIGH SCHOOL PLAYERS ...

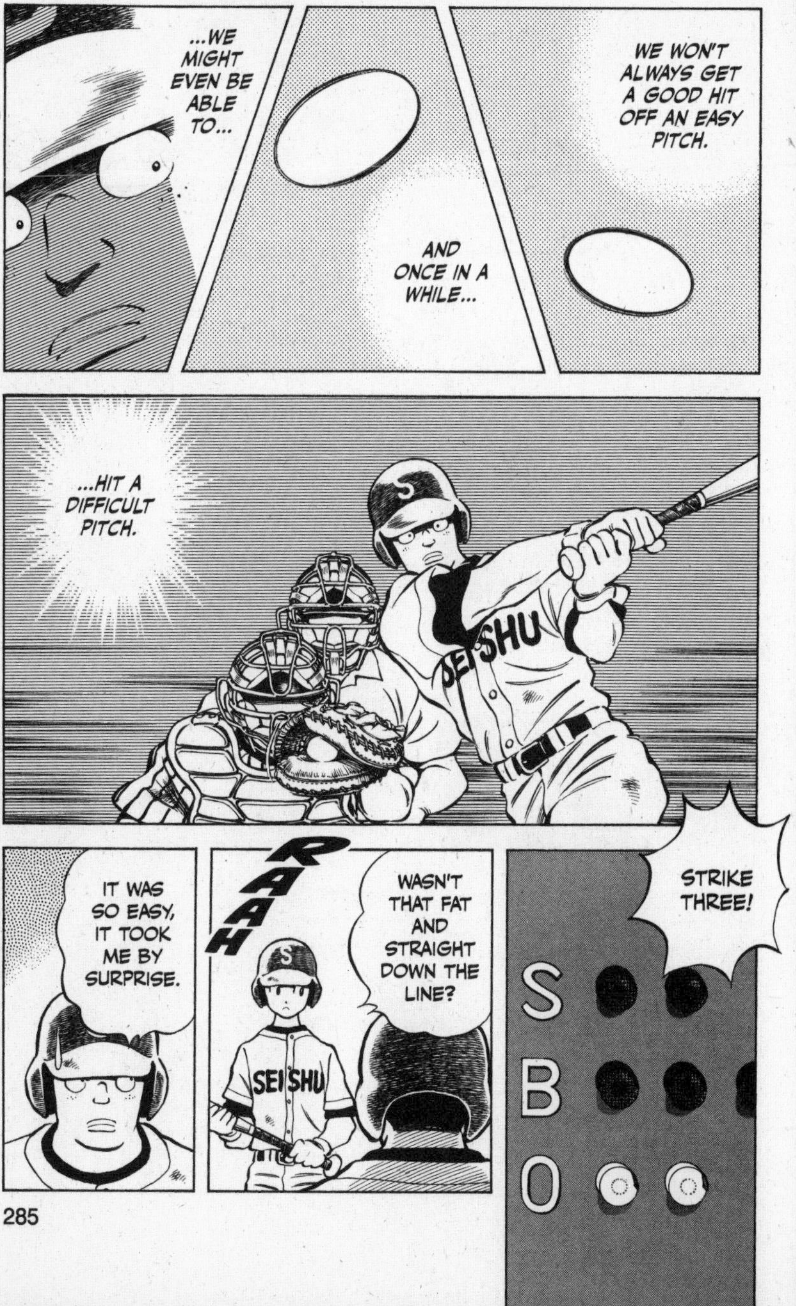
WE WON'T ALWAYS GET A GOOD HIT OFF AN EASY PITCH.
AND ONCE IN A WHILE...
...WE MIGHT EVEN BE ABLE TO...
...HIT A DIFFICULT PITCH.
SEISHU
STRIKE THREE!
S
B
O
RAAAH
WASN'T THAT FAT AND STRAIGHT DOWN THE LINE?
SEISHU
IT WAS SO EASY, IT TOOK ME BY SURPRISE.

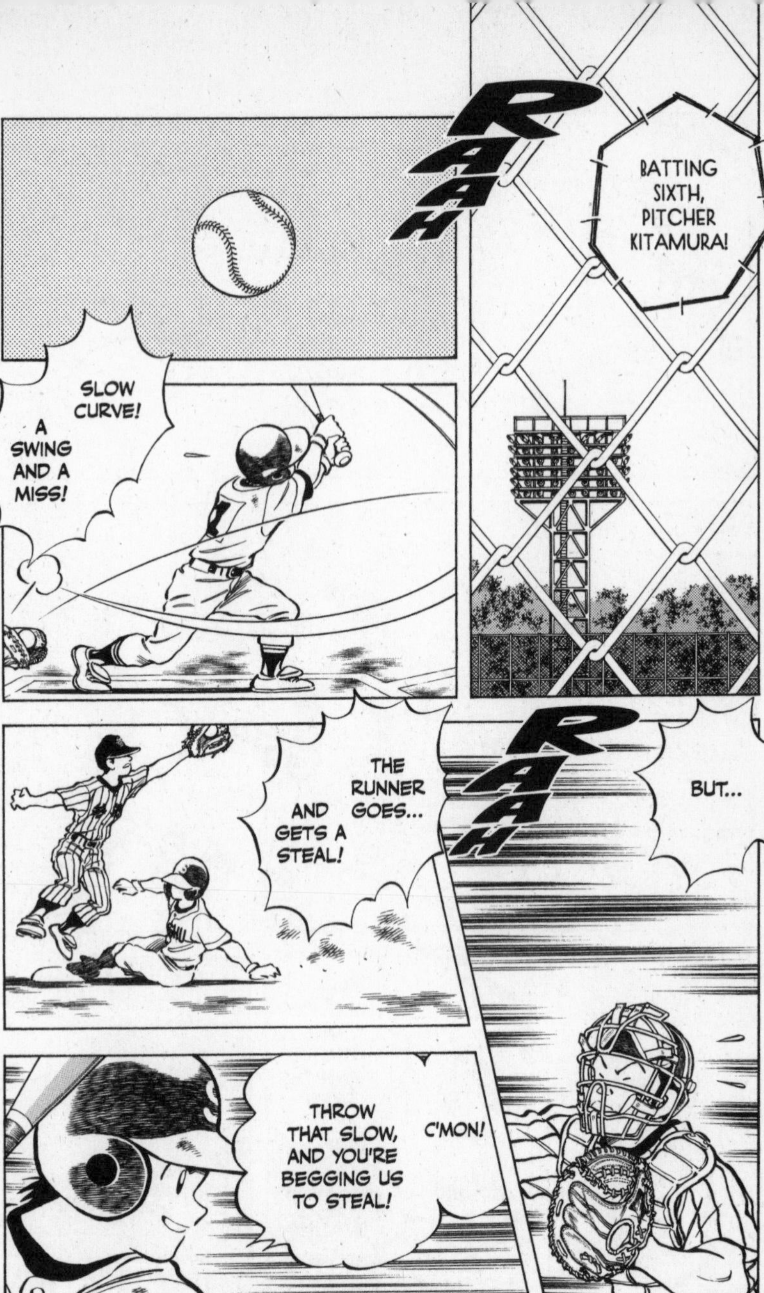
RAAAH
BATTING SIXTH, PITCHER KITAMURA!
SLOW CURVE!
A SWING AND A MISS!
RAAAH
BUT...
THE RUNNER GOES...
AND GETS A STEAL!
C'MON!
THROW THAT SLOW, AND YOU'RE BEGGING US TO STEAL!

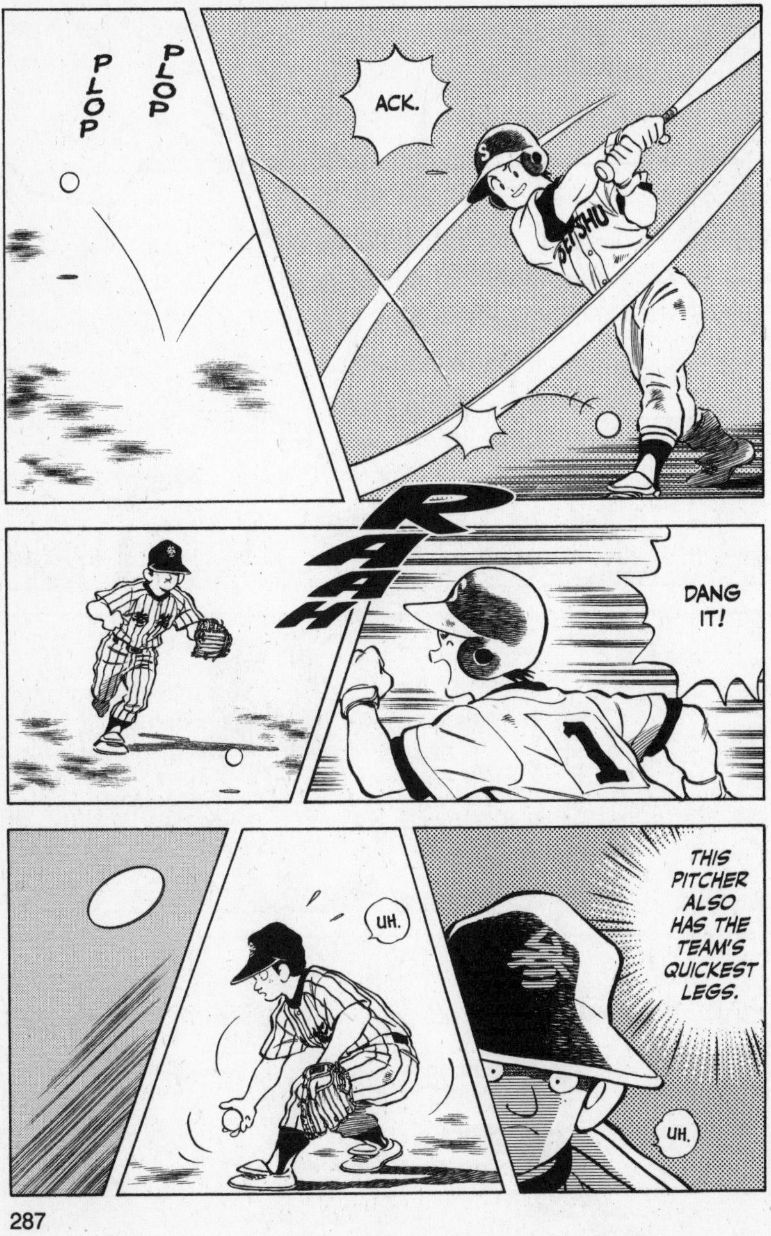
ACK.
PLOP PLOP
RAAH
DANG IT!
THIS PITCHER ALSO HAS THE TEAM'S QUICKEST LEGS.
UH.
UH.

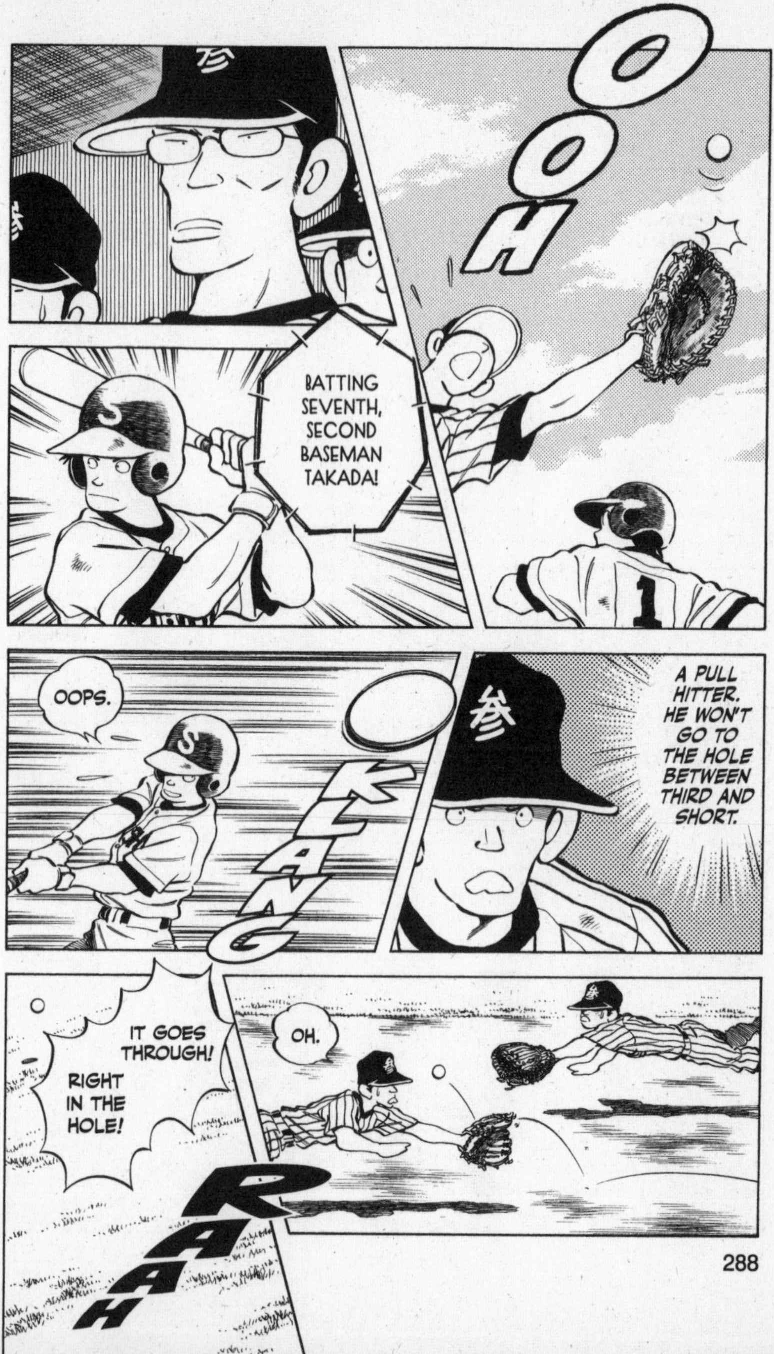
OOOH
BATTING SEVENTH, SECOND BASEMAN TAKADA!
A PULL HITTER. HE WON'T GO TO THE HOLE BETWEEN THIRD AND SHORT.
OOPS.
KLANG
OH.
IT GOES THROUGH!
RIGHT IN THE HOLE!
RAAH

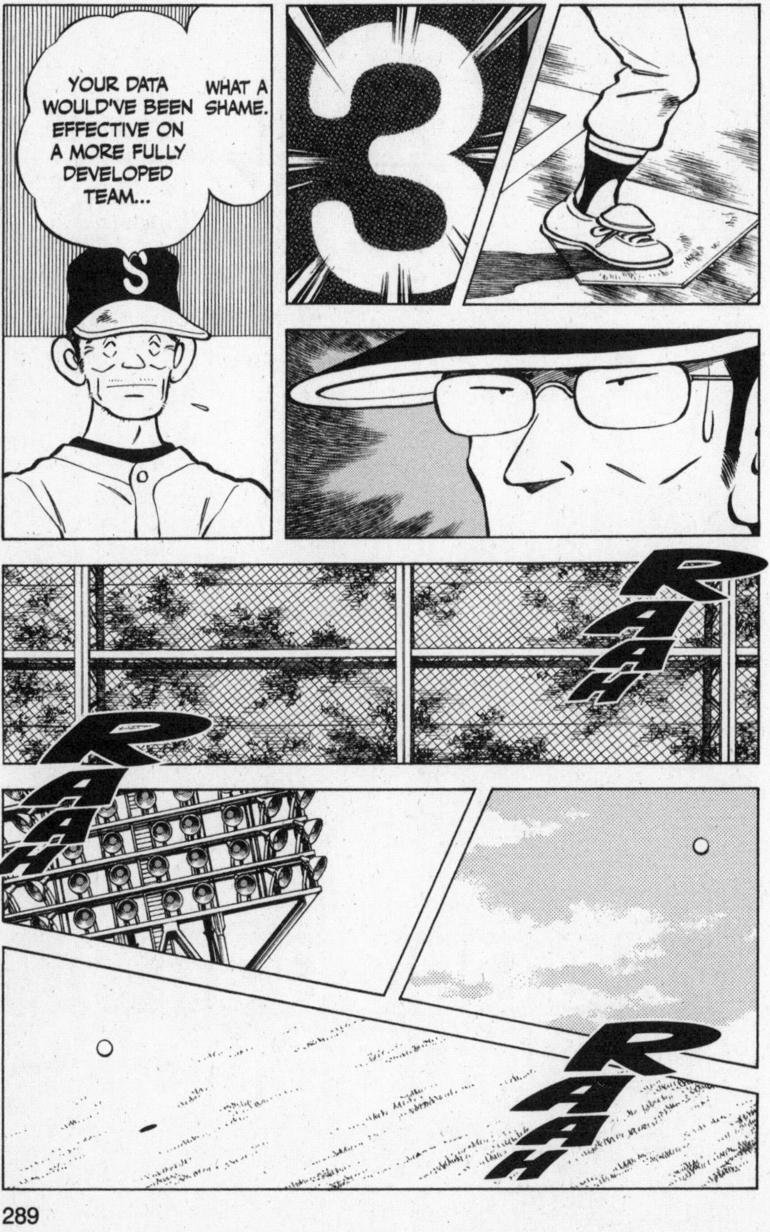
3
WHAT A SHAME.
YOUR DATA WOULD'VE BEEN EFFECTIVE ON A MORE FULLY DEVELOPED TEAM...
RAAH
RAAH
RAAH

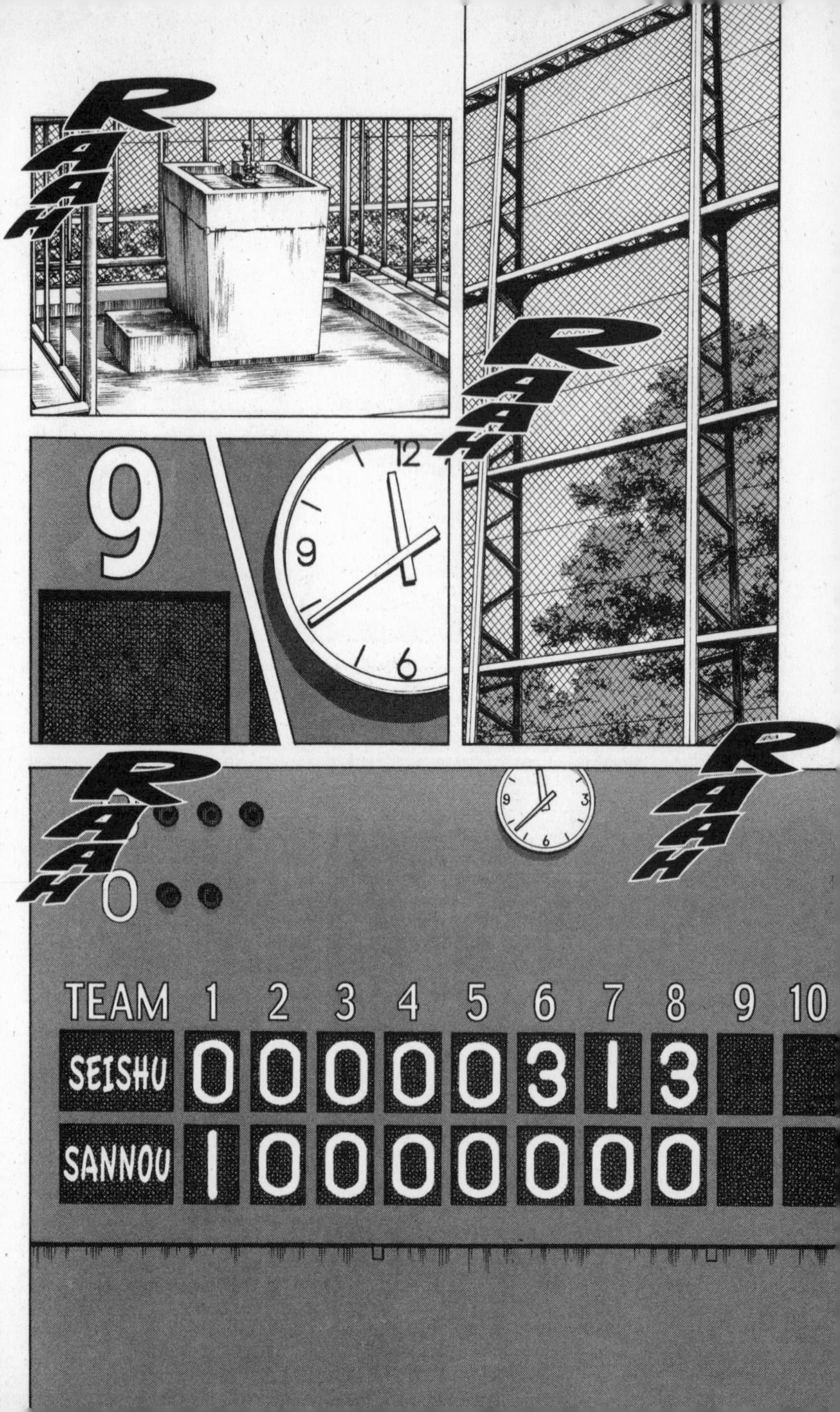
RAAAH
RAAAH
9
RAAAH
RAAAH
0
TEAM 1 2 3 4 5 6 7 8 9 10
SEISHU 0 0 0 0 0 3 1 3
SANNOU 1 0 0 0 0 0 0 0

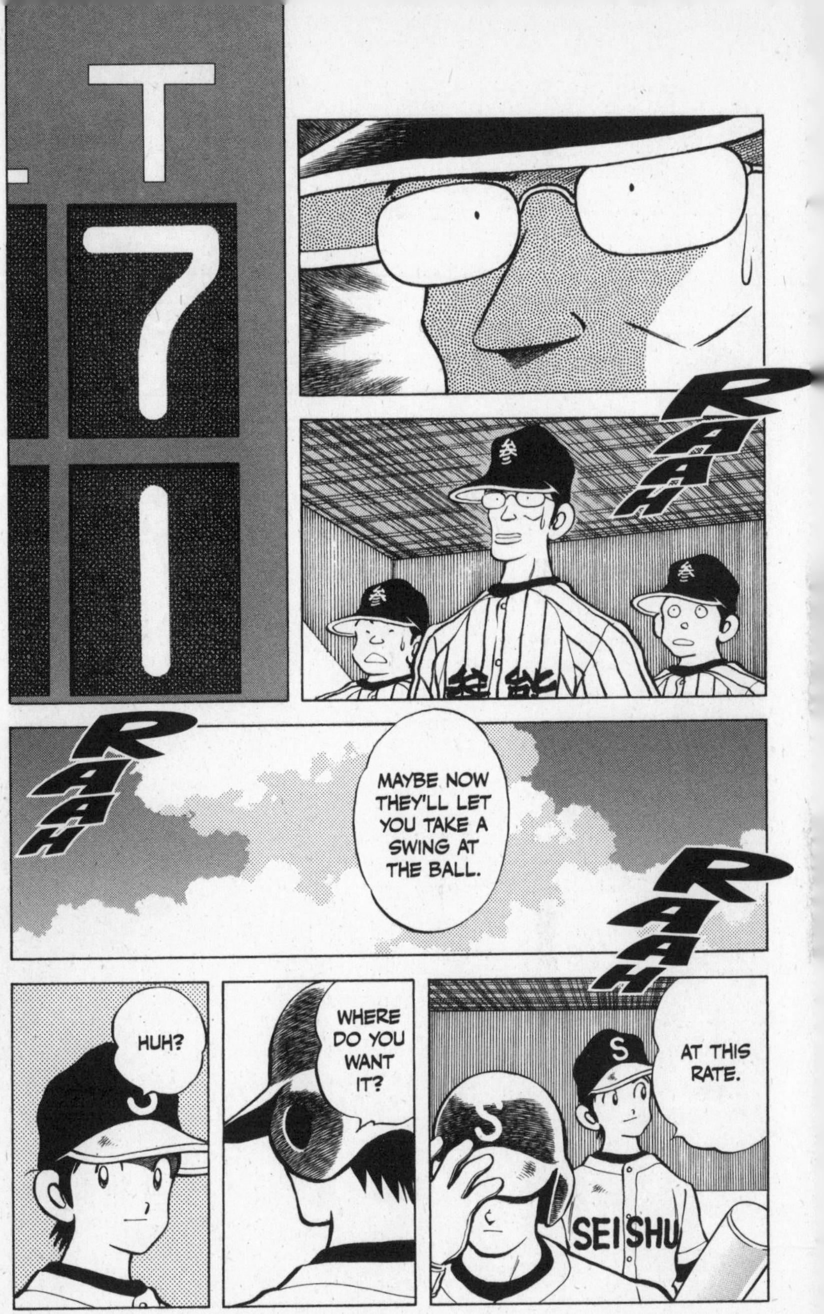
RAAH
T
7
1
RAAH
MAYBE NOW THEY'LL LET YOU TAKE A SWING AT THE BALL.
RAAH
AT THIS RATE.
WHERE DO YOU WANT IT?
HUH?
SEISHU

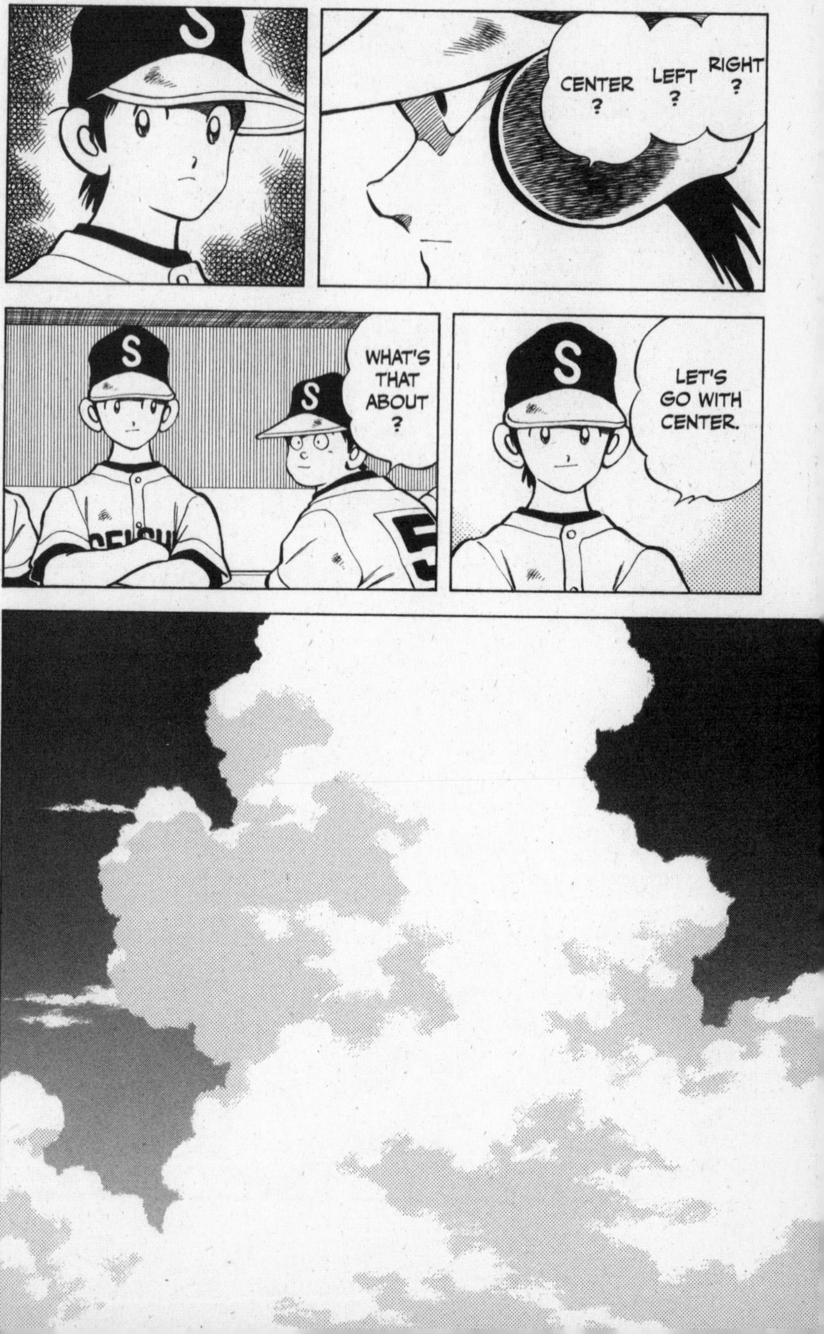
CENTER? LEFT? RIGHT?
LET'S GO WITH CENTER.
WHAT'S THAT ABOUT?

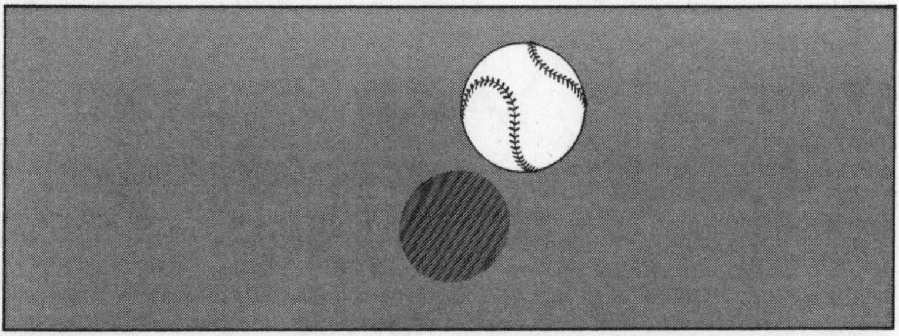

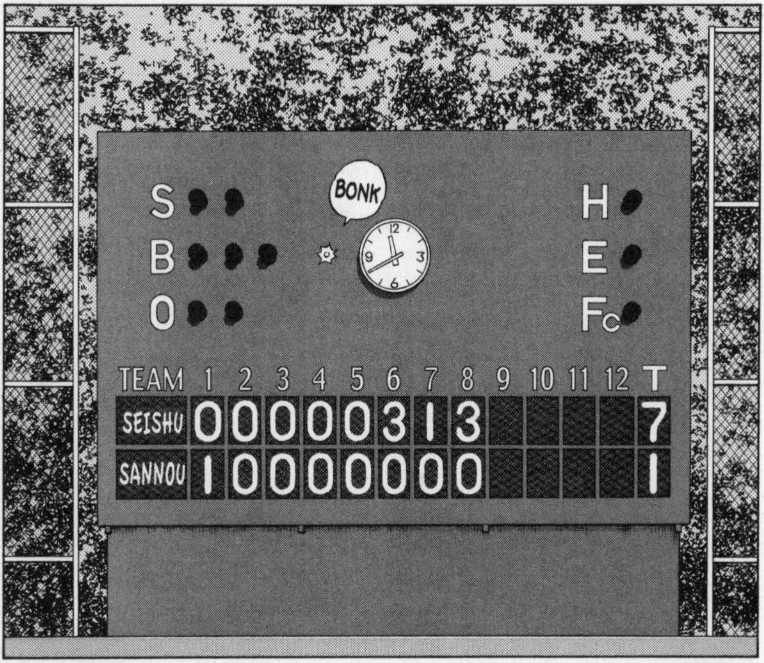
BONK
S
B
O
H
E
Fc
TEAM 1 2 3 4 5 6 7 8 9 10 11 12 T
SEISHU 0 0 0 0 0 3 1 3 7
SANNOU 1 0 0 0 0 0 0 0 1

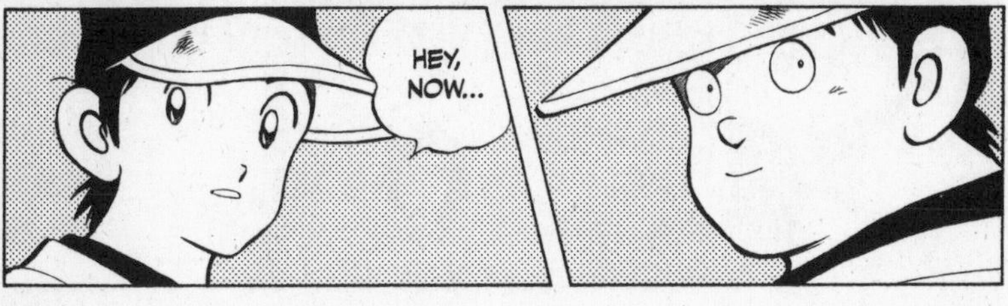
HEY, NOW...

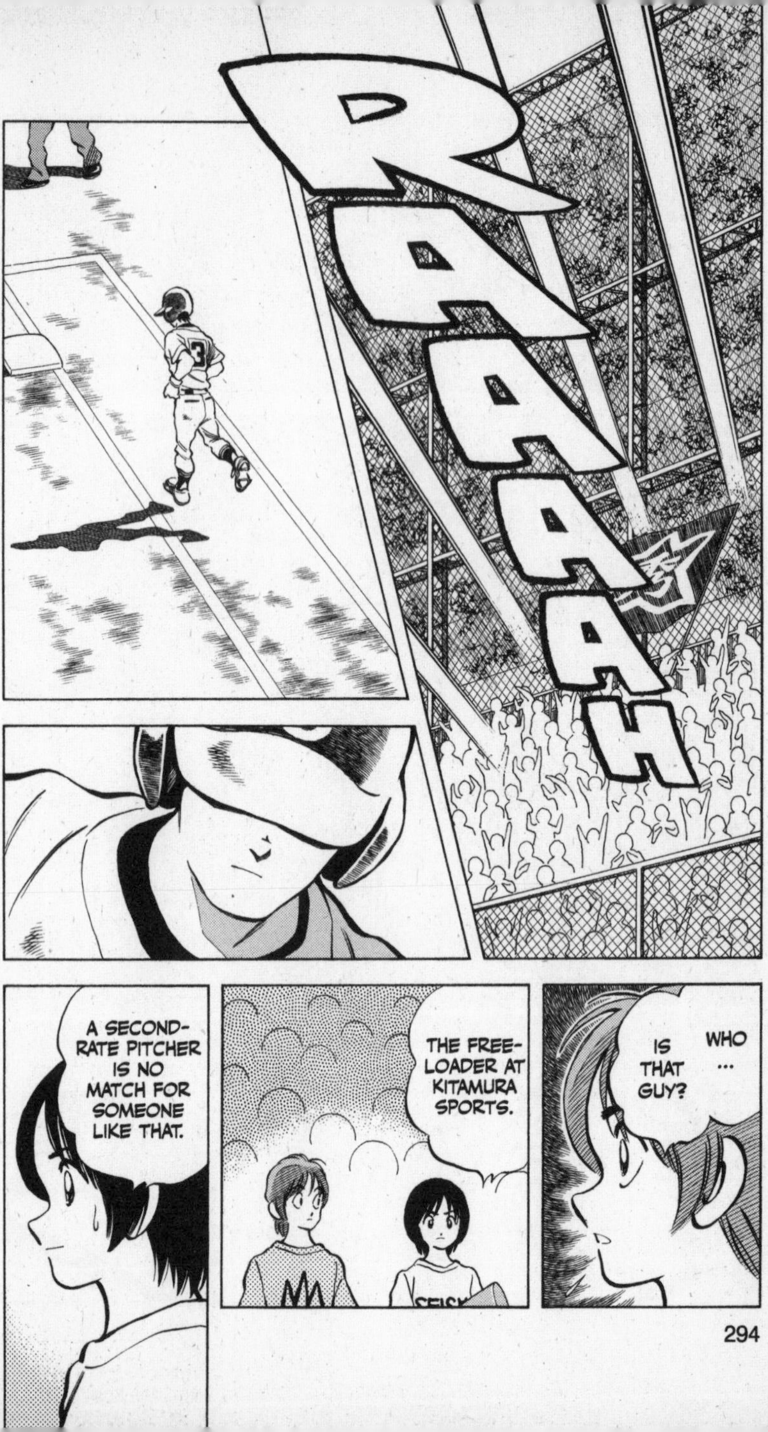
RAAAAH
WHO... IS THAT GUY?
THE FREE-LOADER AT KITAMURA SPORTS.
A SECOND-RATE PITCHER IS NO MATCH FOR SOMEONE LIKE THAT.

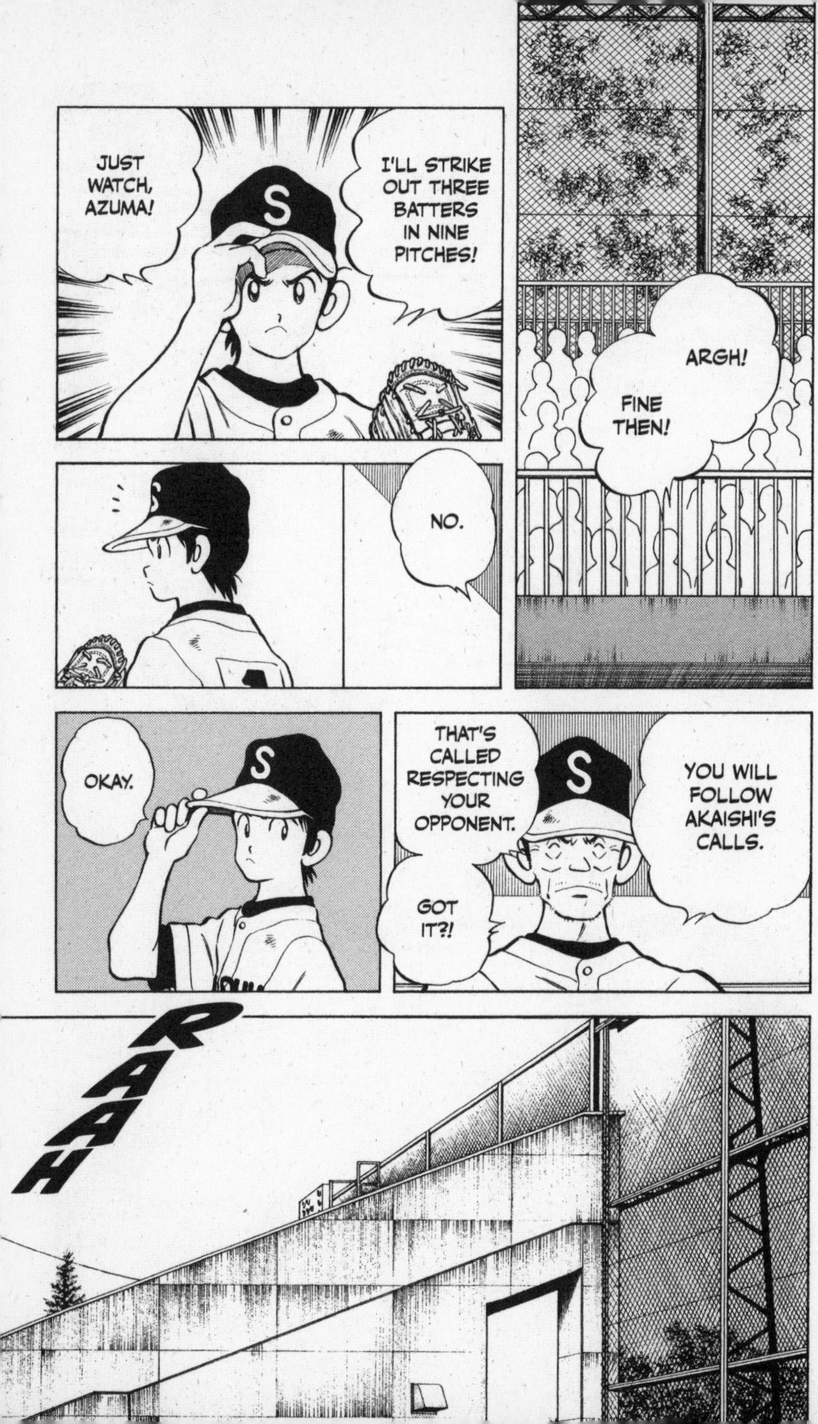
ARGH!
FINE THEN!
I'LL STRIKE OUT THREE BATTERS IN NINE PITCHES!
JUST WATCH, AZUMA!
NO.
YOU WILL FOLLOW AKAISHI'S CALLS.
THAT'S CALLED RESPECTING YOUR OPPONENT.
GOT IT?!
OKAY.
RAAAH

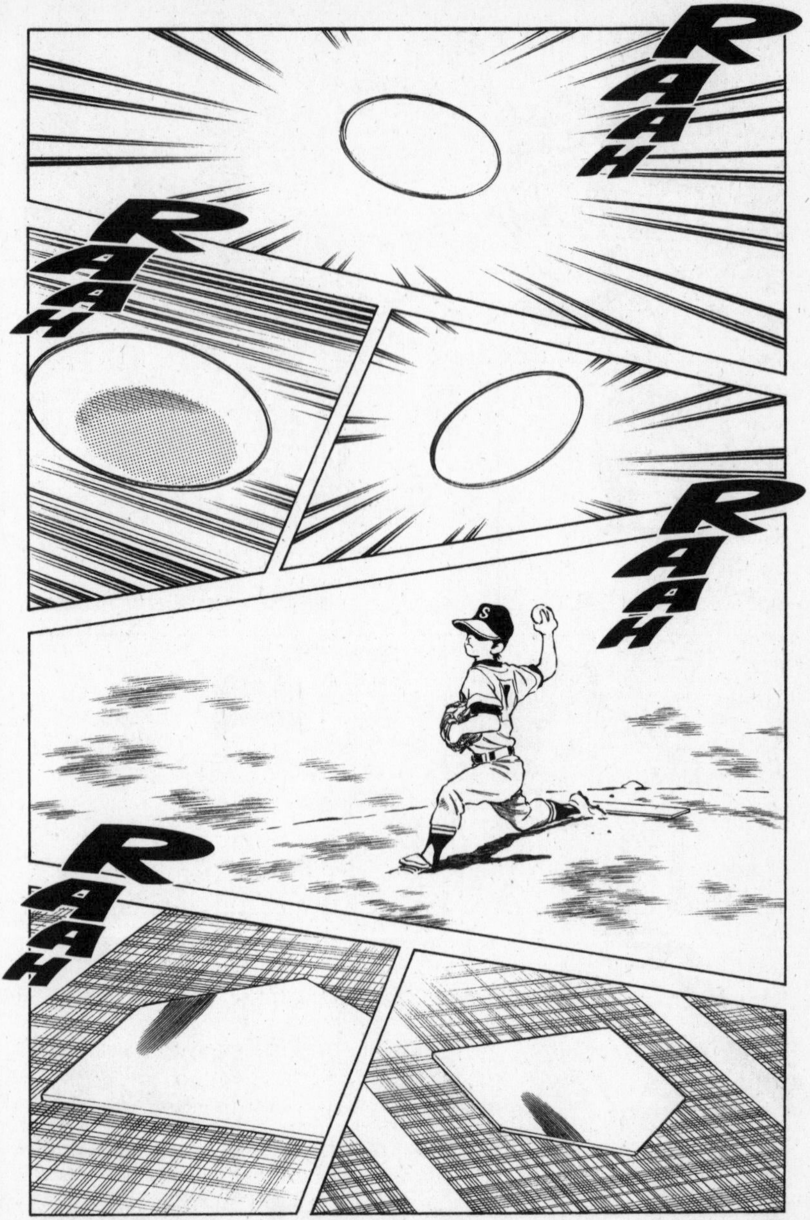
RAAH
RAAH
RAAH
RAAH

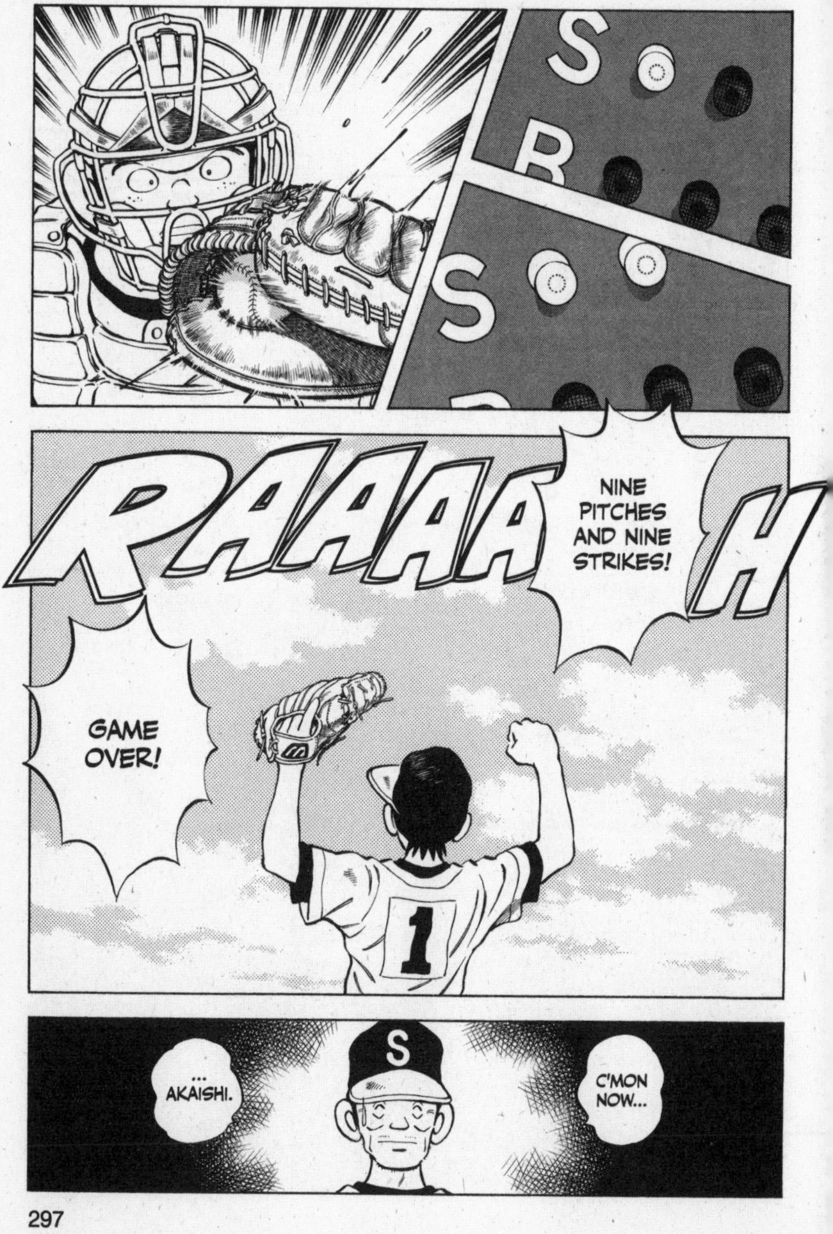
NINE PITCHES AND NINE STRIKES!
RAAAAH
GAME OVER!
C'MON NOW...
...AKAISHI.

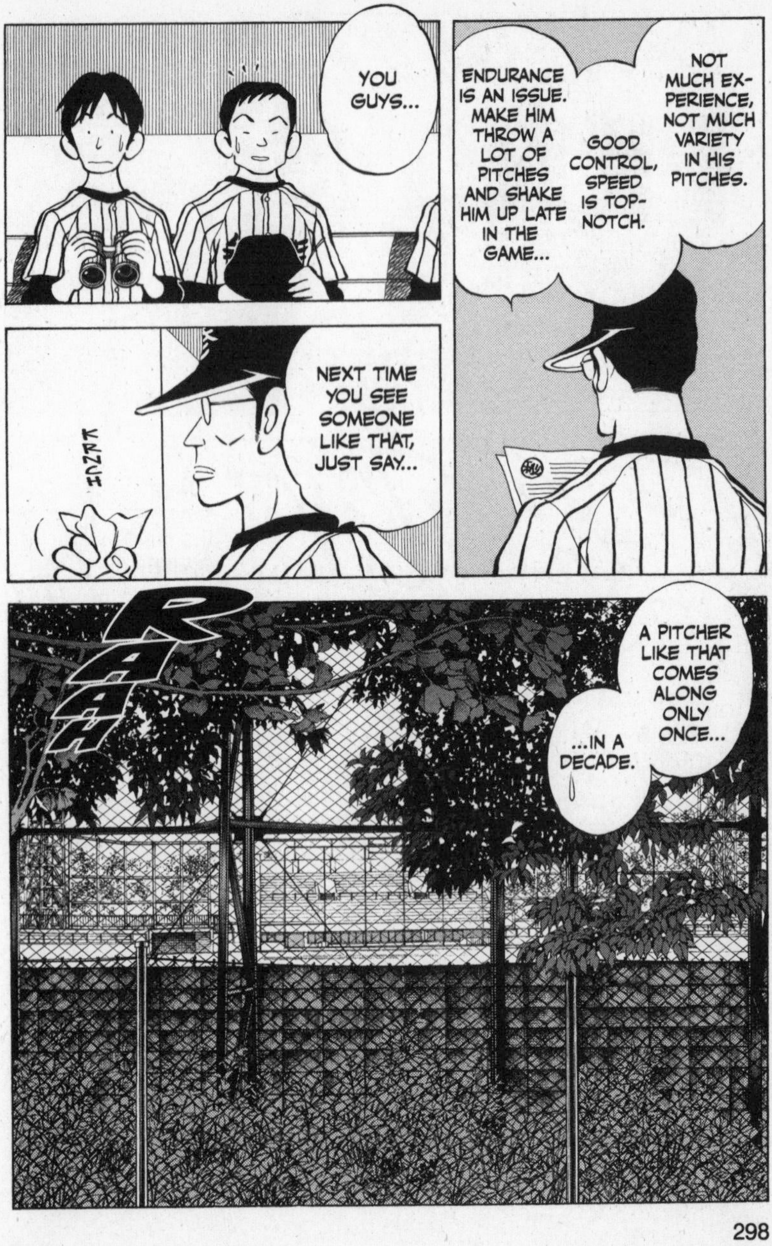
NOT MUCH EX-PERIENCE, NOT MUCH VARIETY IN HIS PITCHES.
GOOD CONTROL, SPEED IS TOP-NOTCH.
ENDURANCE IS AN ISSUE. MAKE HIM THROW A LOT OF PITCHES AND SHAKE HIM UP LATE IN THE GAME...
YOU GUYS...
NEXT TIME YOU SEE SOMEONE LIKE THAT, JUST SAY...
KRNCH
RAAAA
A PITCHER LIKE THAT COMES ALONG ONLY ONCE...
...IN A DECADE.

# CHAPTER 77
# I KNOW...

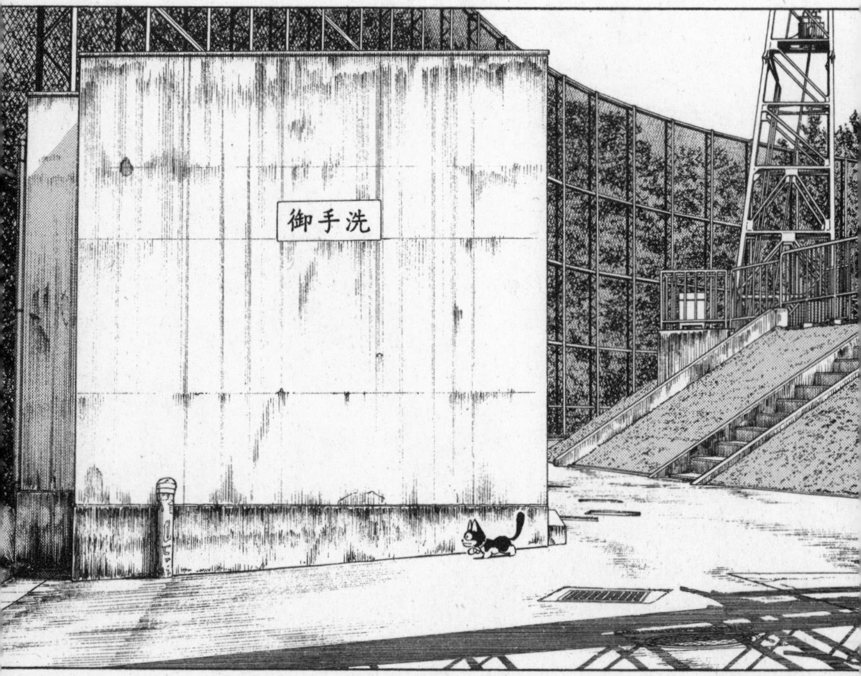
御手洗

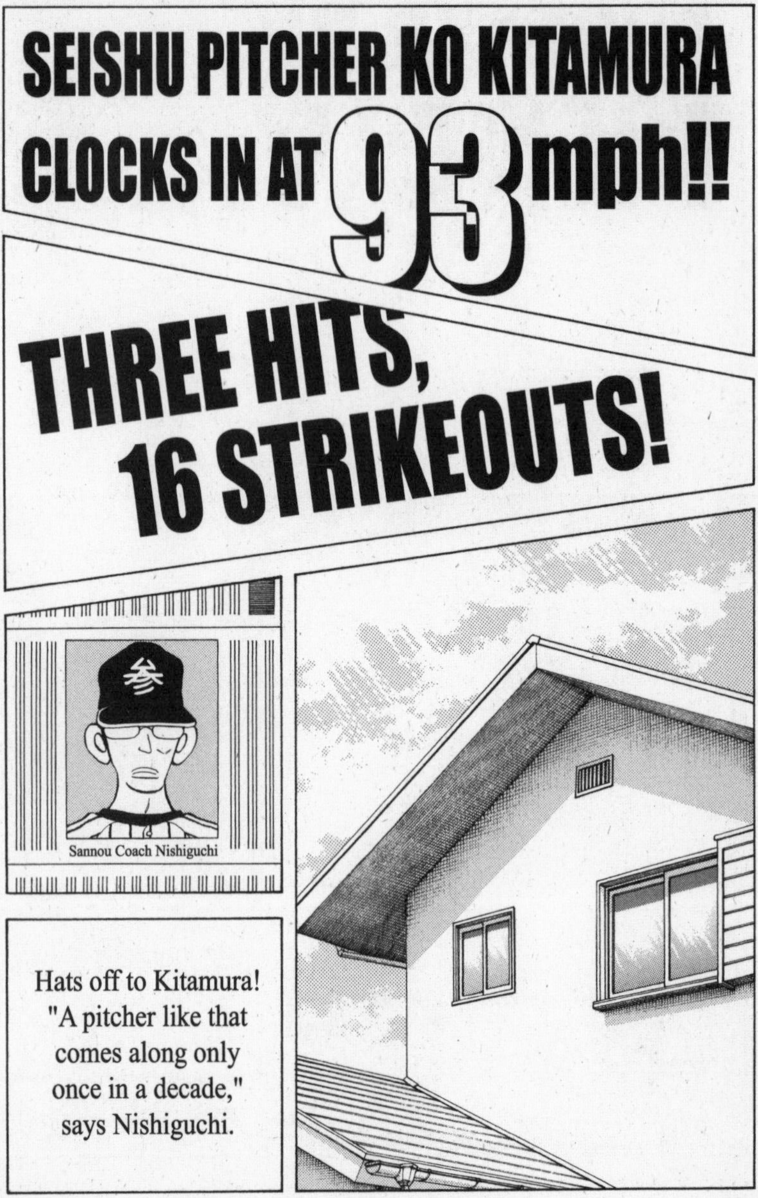
SEISHU PITCHER KO KITAMURA CLOCKS IN AT 93 mph!!
THREE HITS, 16 STRIKEOUTS!
Sannou Coach Nishiguchi
Hats off to Kitamura! "A pitcher like that comes along only once in a decade," says Nishiguchi.

93 MPH...

THANK GOOD- NESS.

RIGHT ?

STILL ONLY 93 MPH...

WHAT?

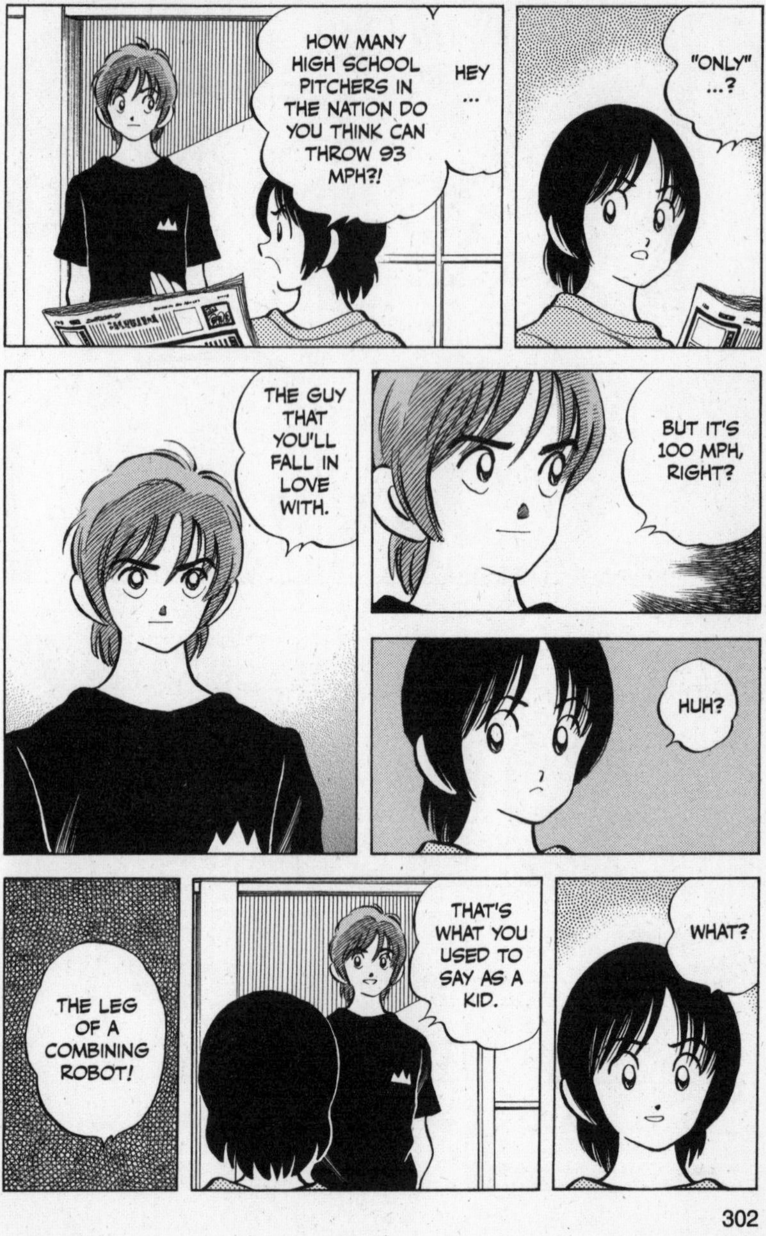
"ONLY" ...?
HEY ...
HOW MANY HIGH SCHOOL PITCHERS IN THE NATION DO YOU THINK CAN THROW 93 MPH?!
BUT IT'S 100 MPH, RIGHT?
HUH?
THE GUY THAT YOU'LL FALL IN LOVE WITH.
WHAT?
THAT'S WHAT YOU USED TO SAY AS A KID.
THE LEG OF A COMBINING ROBOT!

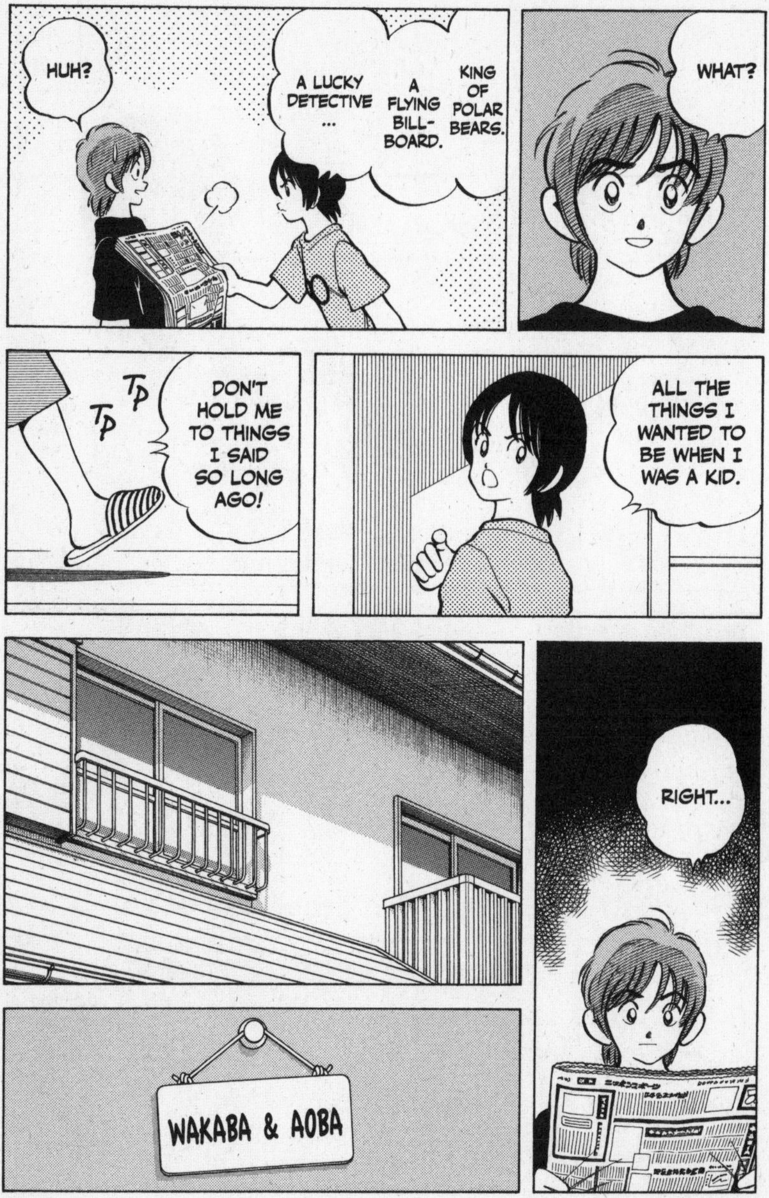
WHAT?
KING OF POLAR BEARS.
A FLYING BILL-BOARD.
A LUCKY DETECTIVE ...
HUH?
ALL THE THINGS I WANTED TO BE WHEN I WAS A KID.
DON'T HOLD ME TO THINGS I SAID SO LONG AGO!
TP
TP
RIGHT...
WAKABA & AOBA

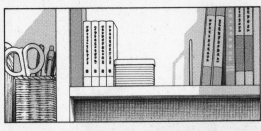

IT'S THE LAST DREAM WAKABA HAD.
I ALREADY KNEW...
KO WAS THE PITCHER ...
AKAISHI WAS THE CATCHER.
THE STAGE WAS A CAPACITY CROWD AT KOSHIEN STADIUM...

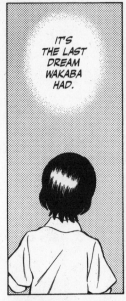

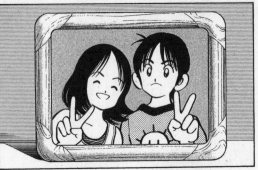

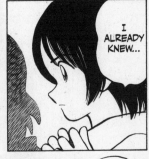

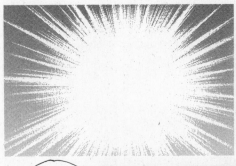

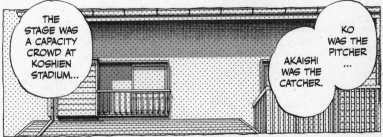

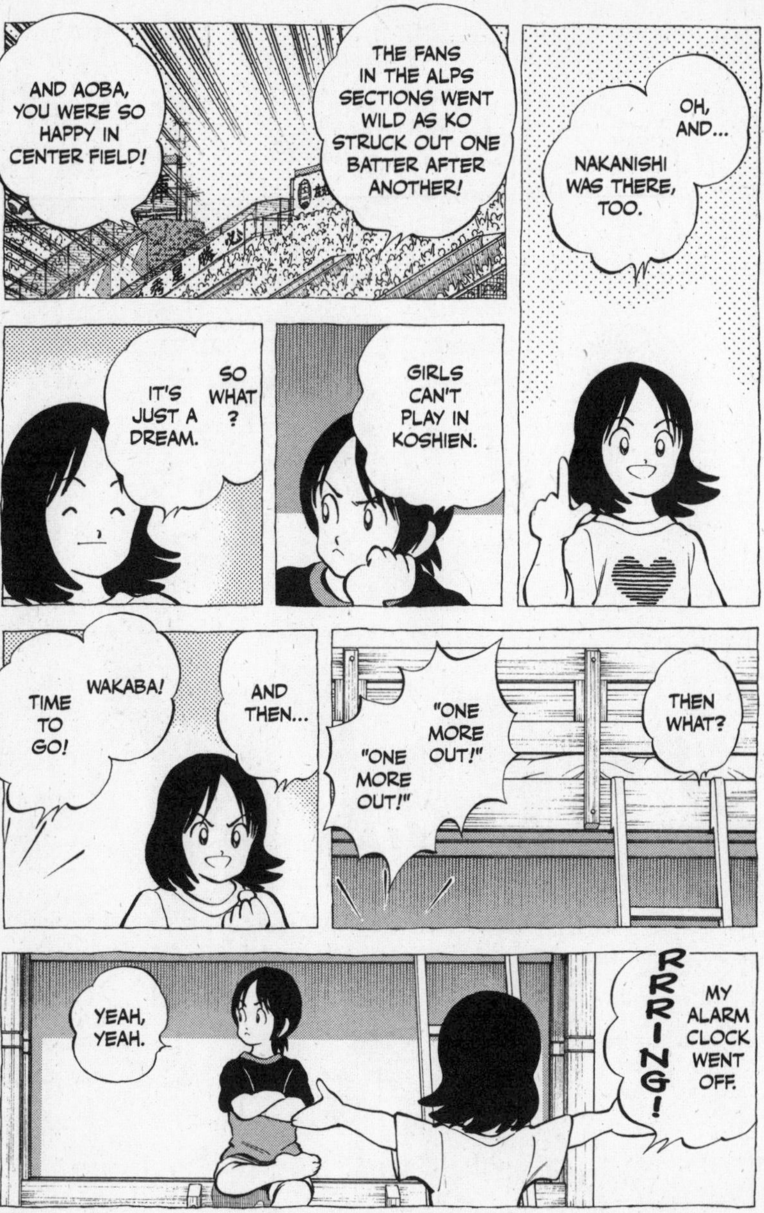
OH, AND...
NAKANISHI WAS THERE, TOO.
THE FANS IN THE ALPS SECTIONS WENT WILD AS KO STRUCK OUT ONE BATTER AFTER ANOTHER!
AND AOBA, YOU WERE SO HAPPY IN CENTER FIELD!
GIRLS CAN'T PLAY IN KOSHIEN.
SO WHAT?
IT'S JUST A DREAM.
THEN WHAT?
"ONE MORE OUT!"
"ONE MORE OUT!"
AND THEN...
WAKABA!
TIME TO GO!
MY ALARM CLOCK WENT OFF.
RRRING!
YEAH, YEAH.

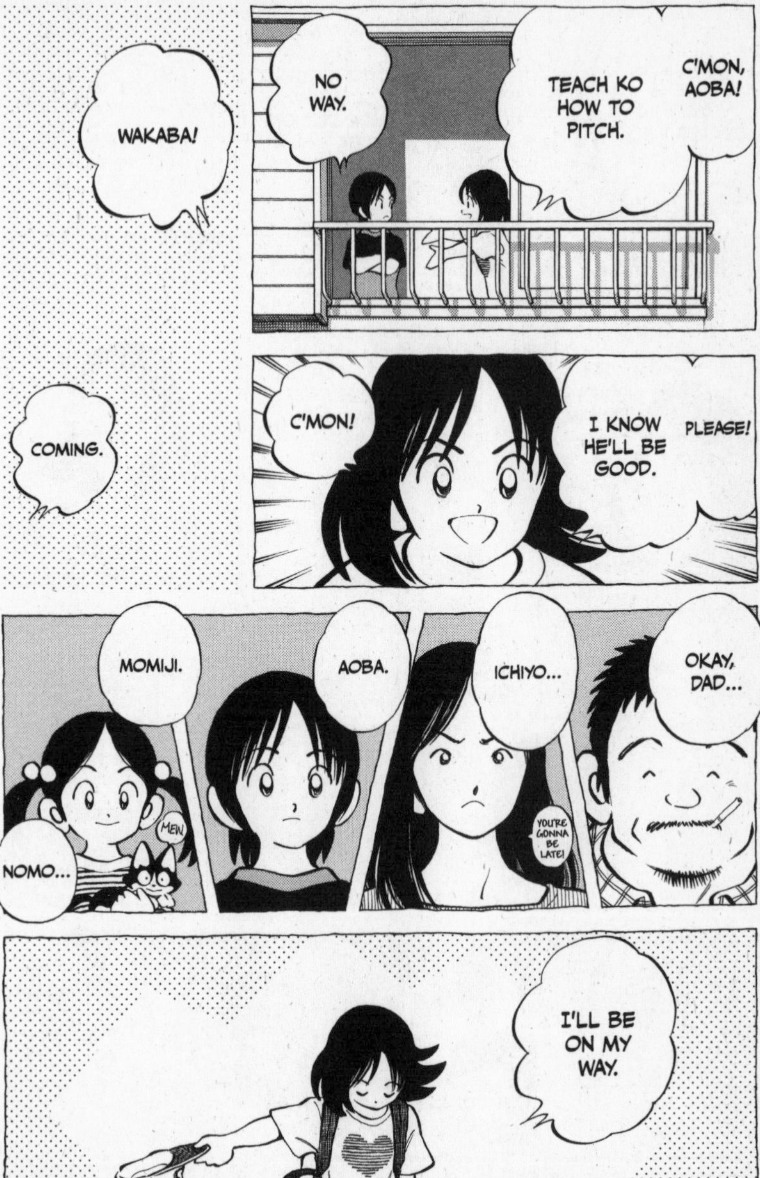
C'MON, AOBA!
TEACH KO HOW TO PITCH.
NO WAY.
PLEASE!
I KNOW HE'LL BE GOOD.
C'MON!
WAKABA!
COMING.
OKAY, DAD...
ICHIYO...
YOU'RE GONNA BE LATE!
AOBA.
MOMIJI.
MEW.
NOMO...
I'LL BE ON MY WAY.

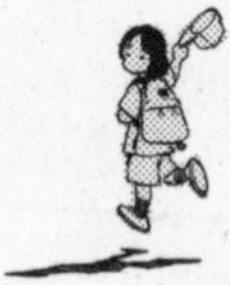

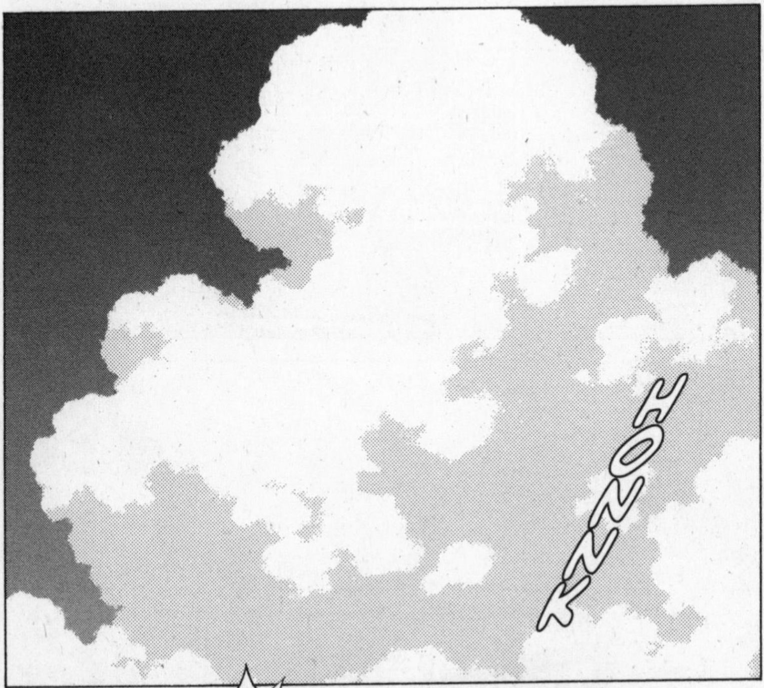
HONK

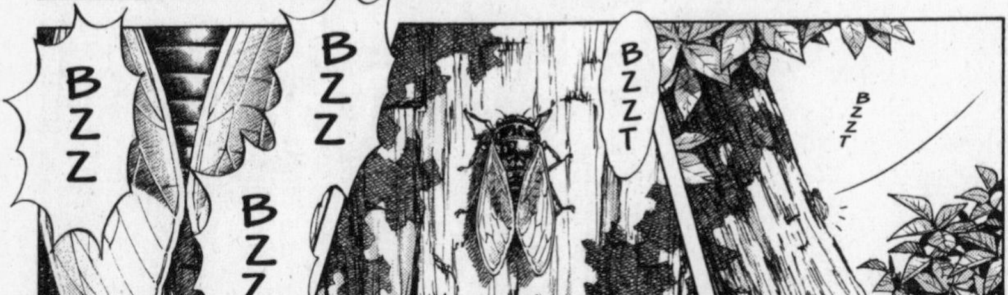
BZZT
BZZT
BZZ
BZZ
BZZ

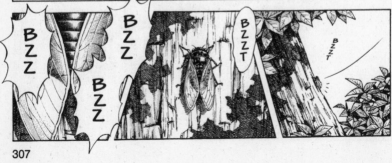

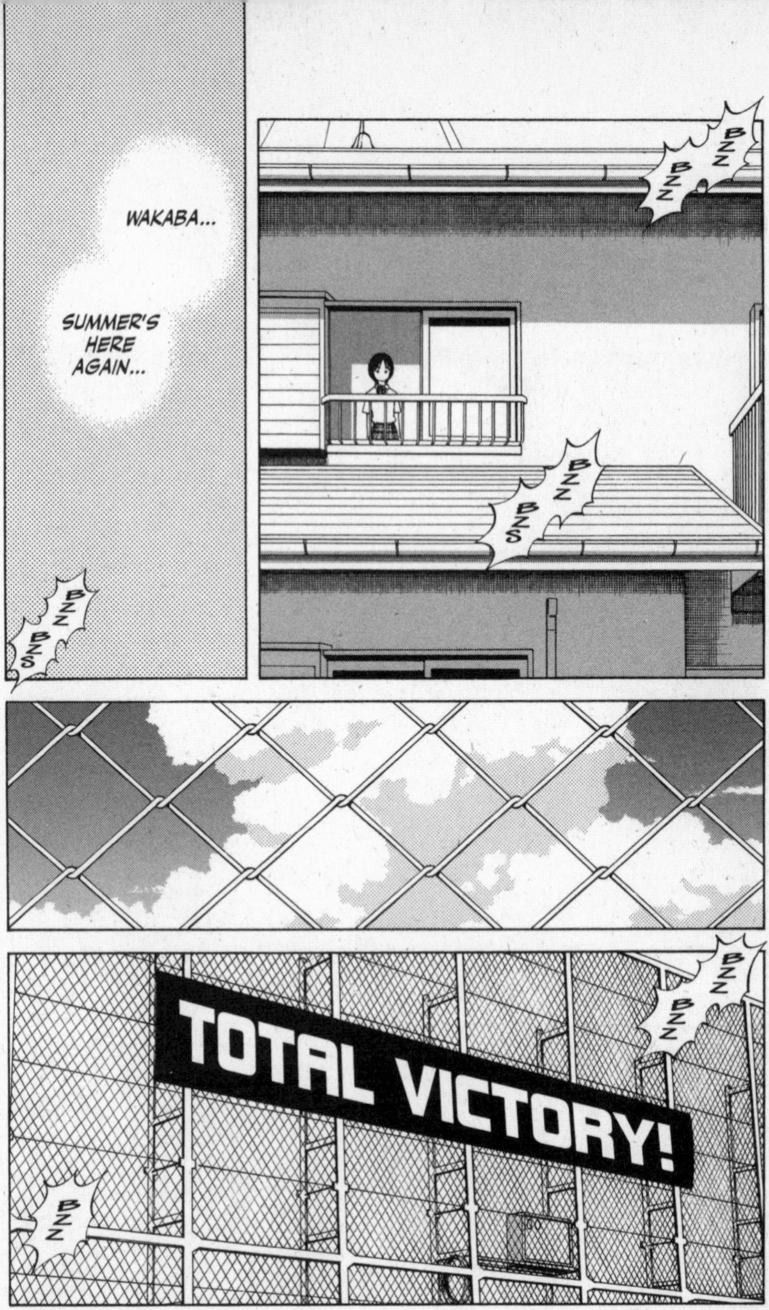
BZZ BZZ
BZZ BZS
WAKABA...
SUMMER'S HERE AGAIN...
BZZ BZS
TOTAL VICTORY!
BZZ BZZ
BZZ

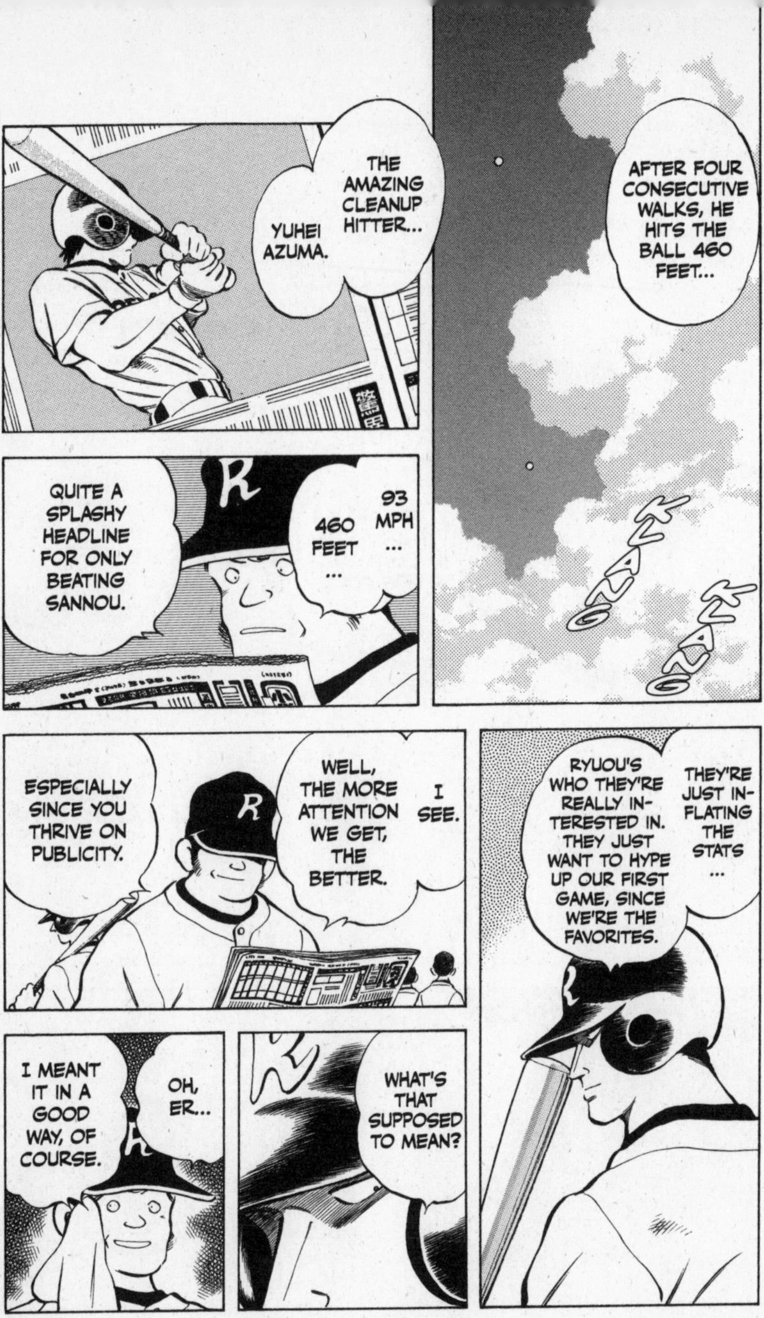
AFTER FOUR CONSECUTIVE WALKS, HE HITS THE BALL 460 FEET...
KLANG
KLANG
THE AMAZING CLEANUP HITTER...
YUHEI AZUMA.
93 MPH...
460 FEET...
QUITE A SPLASHY HEADLINE FOR ONLY BEATING SANNOU.
THEY'RE JUST INFLATING THE STATS...
RYUOU'S WHO THEY'RE REALLY INTERESTED IN. THEY JUST WANT TO HYPE UP OUR FIRST GAME, SINCE WE'RE THE FAVORITES.
I SEE.
WELL, THE MORE ATTENTION WE GET, THE BETTER.
ESPECIALLY SINCE YOU THRIVE ON PUBLICITY.
WHAT'S THAT SUPPOSED TO MEAN?
OH, ER...
I MEANT IT IN A GOOD WAY, OF COURSE.

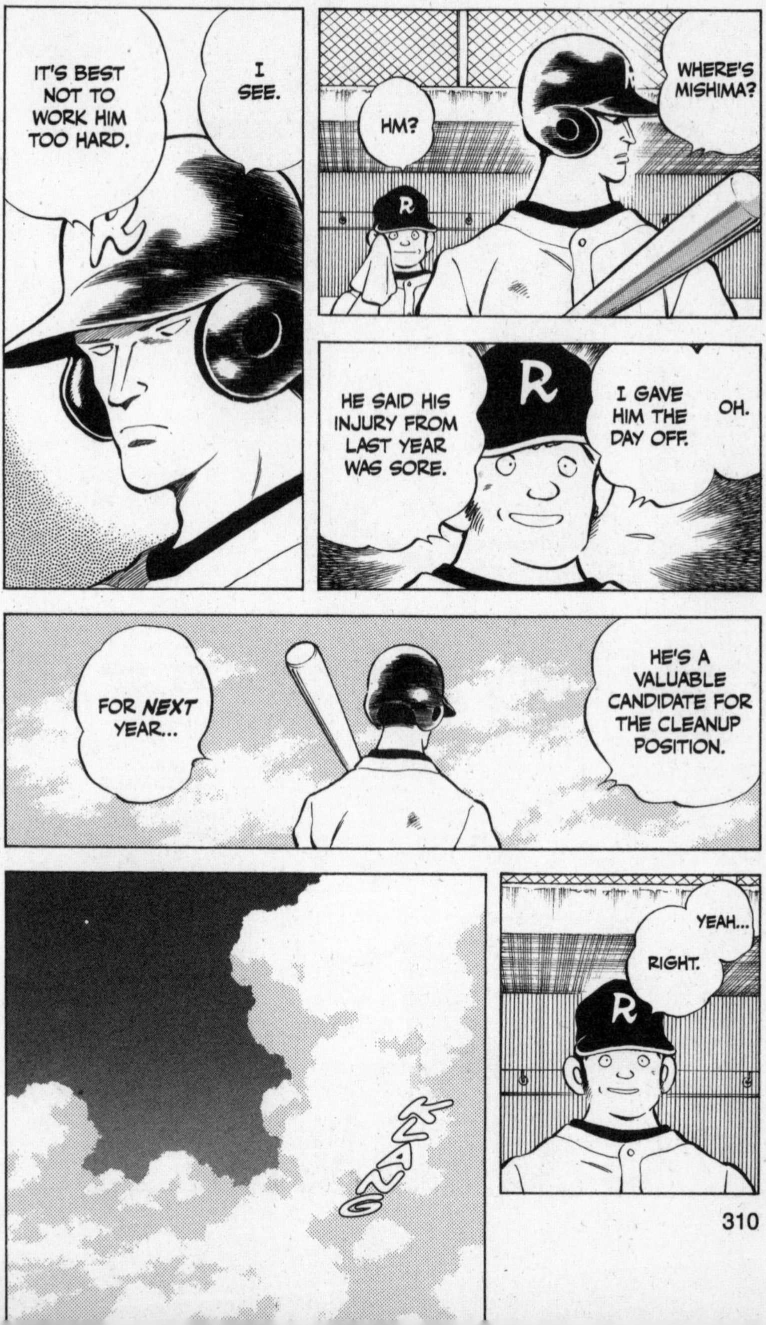
WHERE'S MISHIMA?
HM?
OH.
I GAVE HIM THE DAY OFF.
HE SAID HIS INJURY FROM LAST YEAR WAS SORE.
I SEE.
IT'S BEST NOT TO WORK HIM TOO HARD.
HE'S A VALUABLE CANDIDATE FOR THE CLEANUP POSITION.
FOR *NEXT* YEAR...
YEAH...
RIGHT.
KLANG

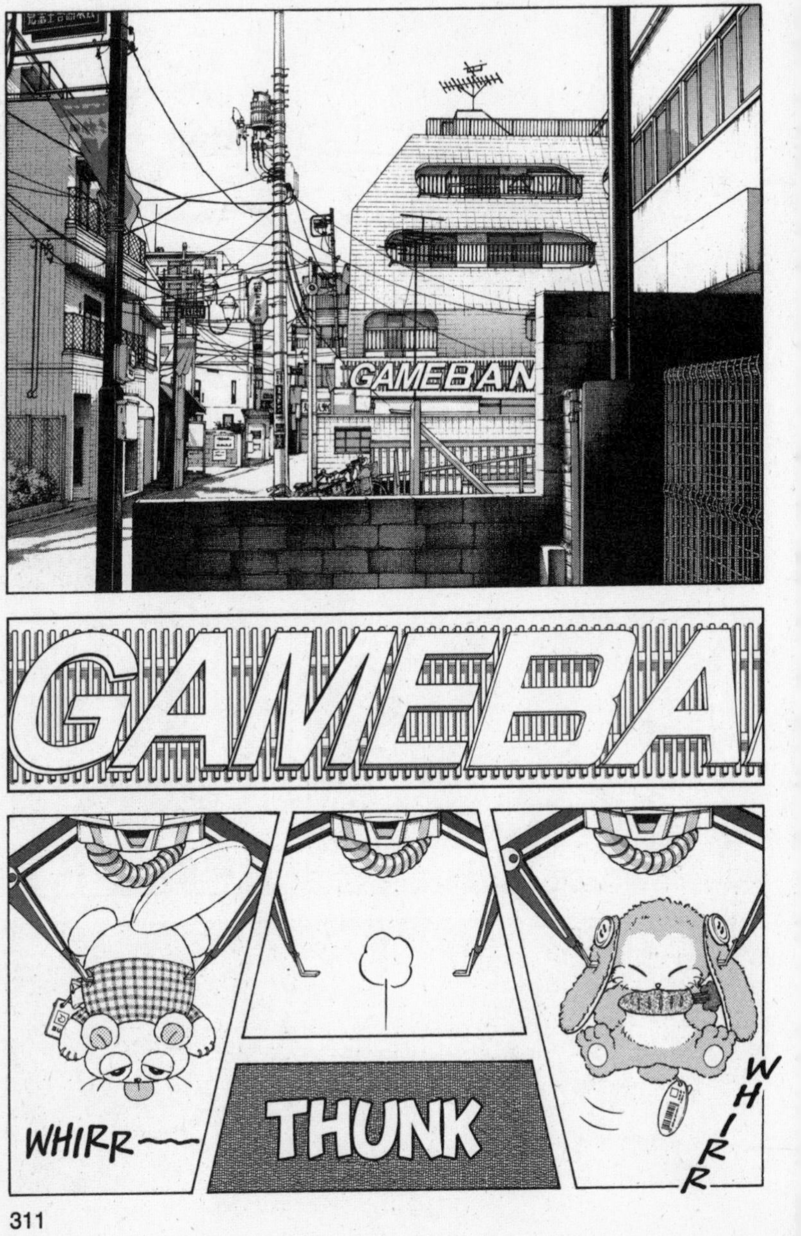
GAMEBAN
GAMEBA
WHIRR
THUNK
WHIRR——

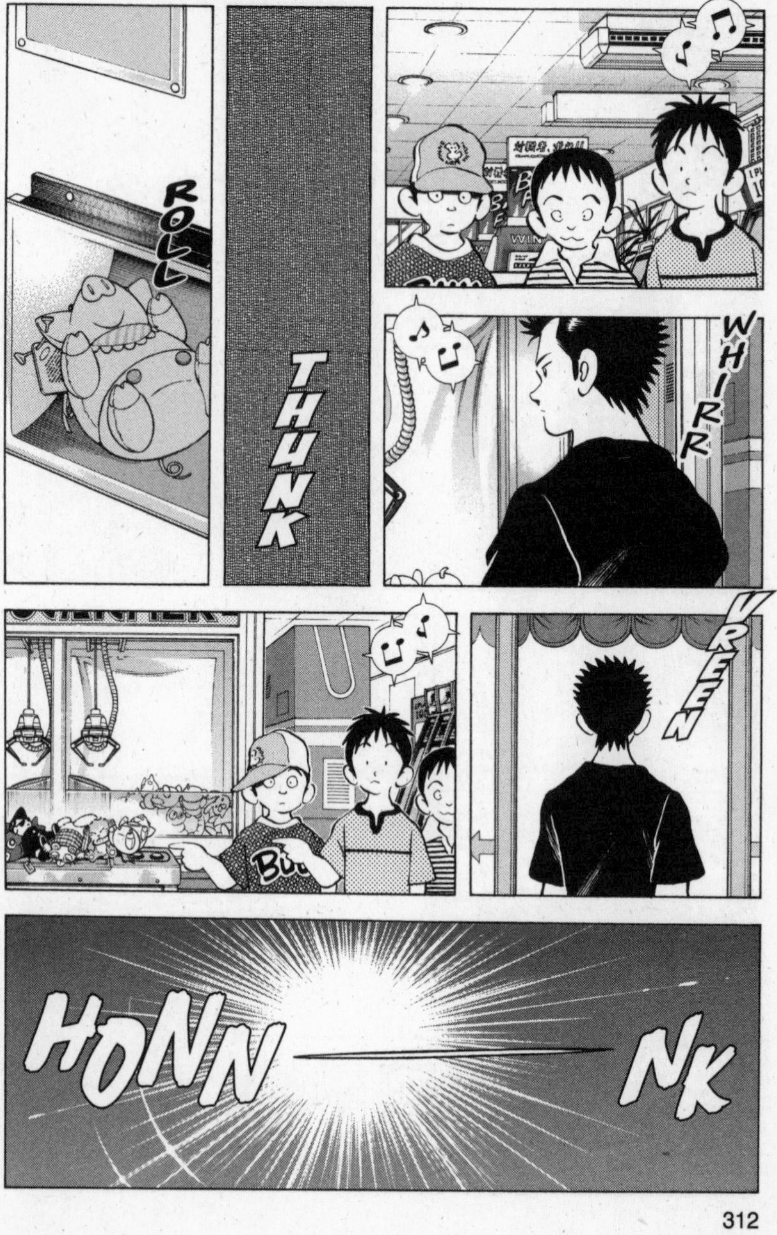
WHIRR
THUNK
ROLL
VREEN
HONNN—NK

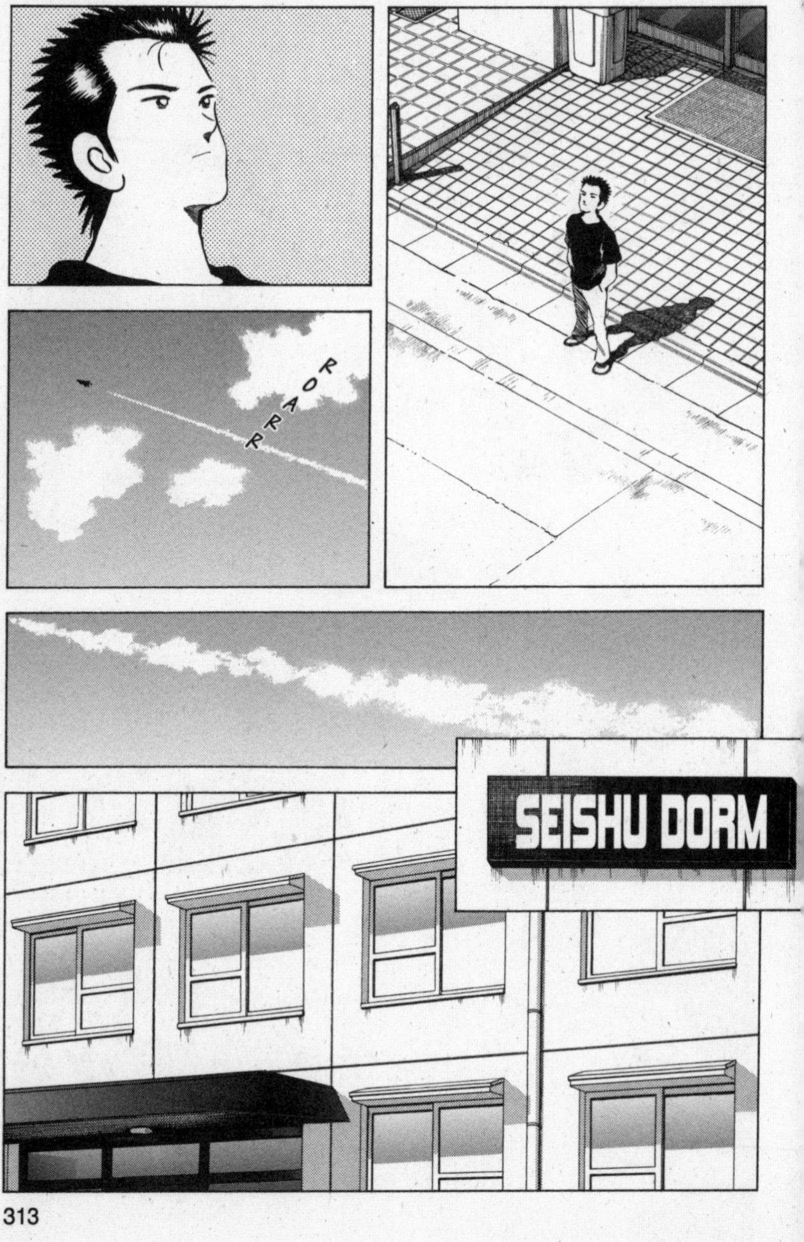
ROARR
SEISHU DORM

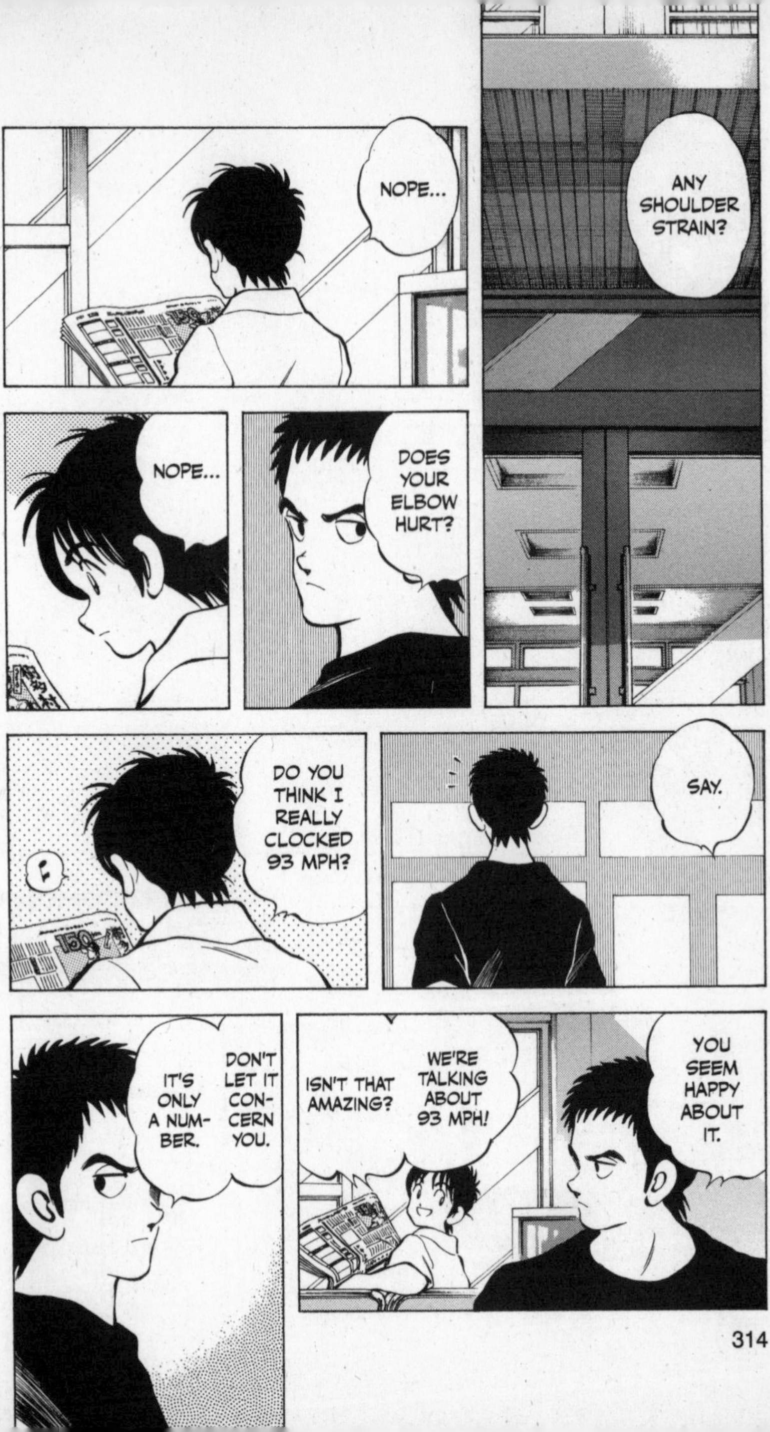
ANY SHOULDER STRAIN?
NOPE...
DOES YOUR ELBOW HURT?
NOPE...
SAY.
DO YOU THINK I REALLY CLOCKED 93 MPH?
YOU SEEM HAPPY ABOUT IT.
WE'RE TALKING ABOUT 93 MPH!
ISN'T THAT AMAZING?
DON'T LET IT CON-CERN YOU.
IT'S ONLY A NUM-BER.

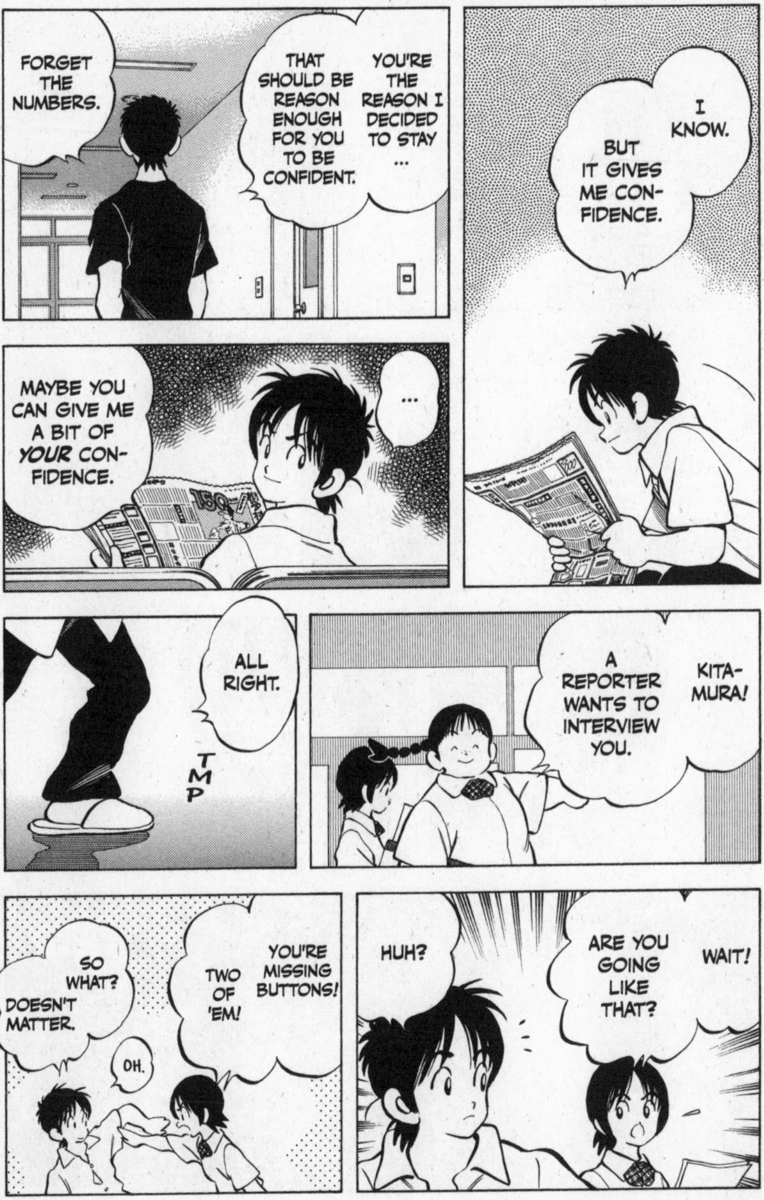
I KNOW.
BUT IT GIVES ME CONFIDENCE.
YOU'RE THE REASON I DECIDED TO STAY ...
THAT SHOULD BE REASON ENOUGH FOR YOU TO BE CONFIDENT.
FORGET THE NUMBERS.
...
MAYBE YOU CAN GIVE ME A BIT OF *YOUR* CONFIDENCE.
KITA-MURA!
A REPORTER WANTS TO INTERVIEW YOU.
ALL RIGHT.
TMP
WAIT!
ARE YOU GOING LIKE THAT?
HUH?
YOU'RE MISSING BUTTONS!
TWO OF 'EM!
OH.
SO WHAT?
DOESN'T MATTER.

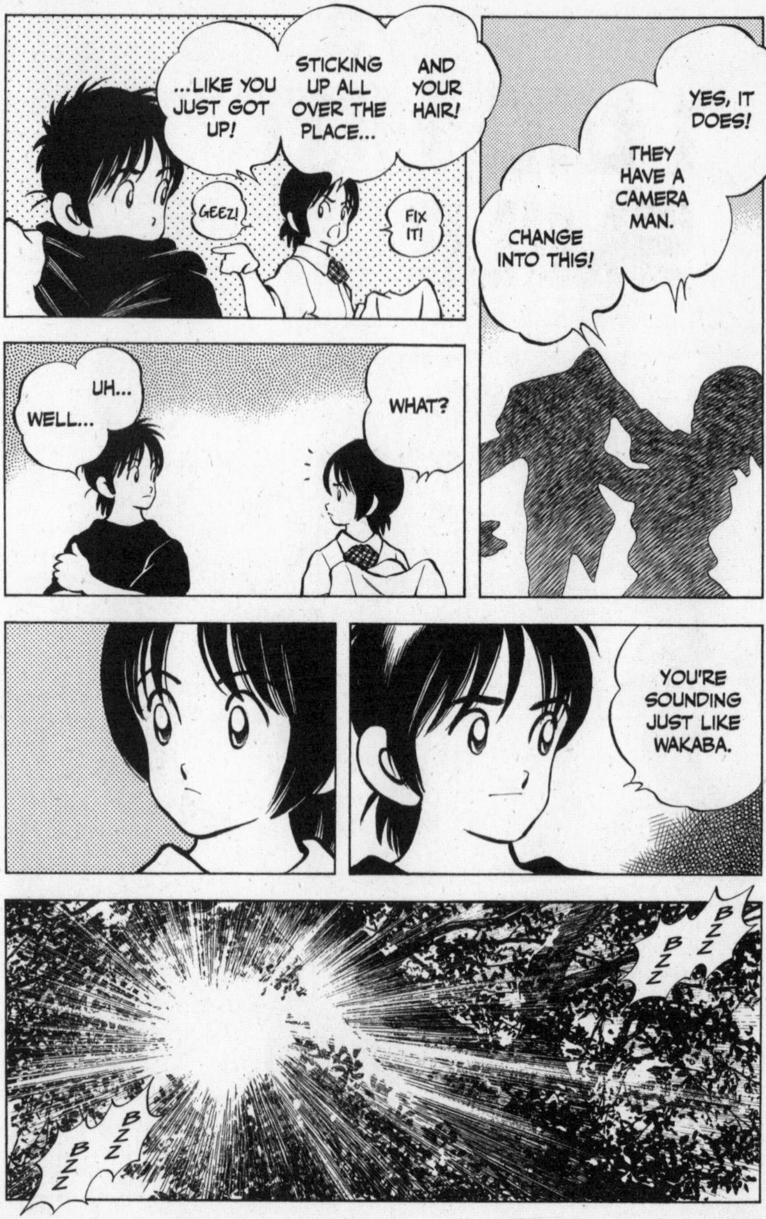
YES, IT DOES!
THEY HAVE A CAMERA MAN.
CHANGE INTO THIS!
AND YOUR HAIR!
STICKING UP ALL OVER THE PLACE...
...LIKE YOU JUST GOT UP!
FIX IT!
GEEZ!
WHAT?
UH... WELL...
YOU'RE SOUNDING JUST LIKE WAKABA.
BZZ BZZ
BZZ BZZ

# CHAPTER 78
# I DID NOT SMILE

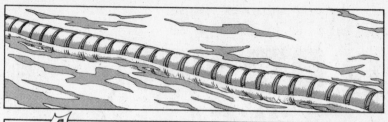

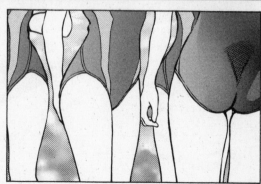

YOU'RE ASKING ABOUT ...

KITAMURA FROM SEISHU GAKUEN?

YEAH.
A TOUGH FIRST OPPONENT.
TAL VICTORY!
I MEAN, 93 MPH IS INCREDIBLE.
COME ON...
IN SPRING KOSHIEN, YOU KNOCKED MINESHIMA'S 94 MPH PITCH CLEAR INTO THE STANDS.
AND HE'S BEEN SCOUTED BY THE PROS.
I JUST GOT LUCKY.
REALLY.
YOU SAY THAT, BUT YOU LOOK PRETTY CONFIDENT.
HA HA HA
PLEASE...

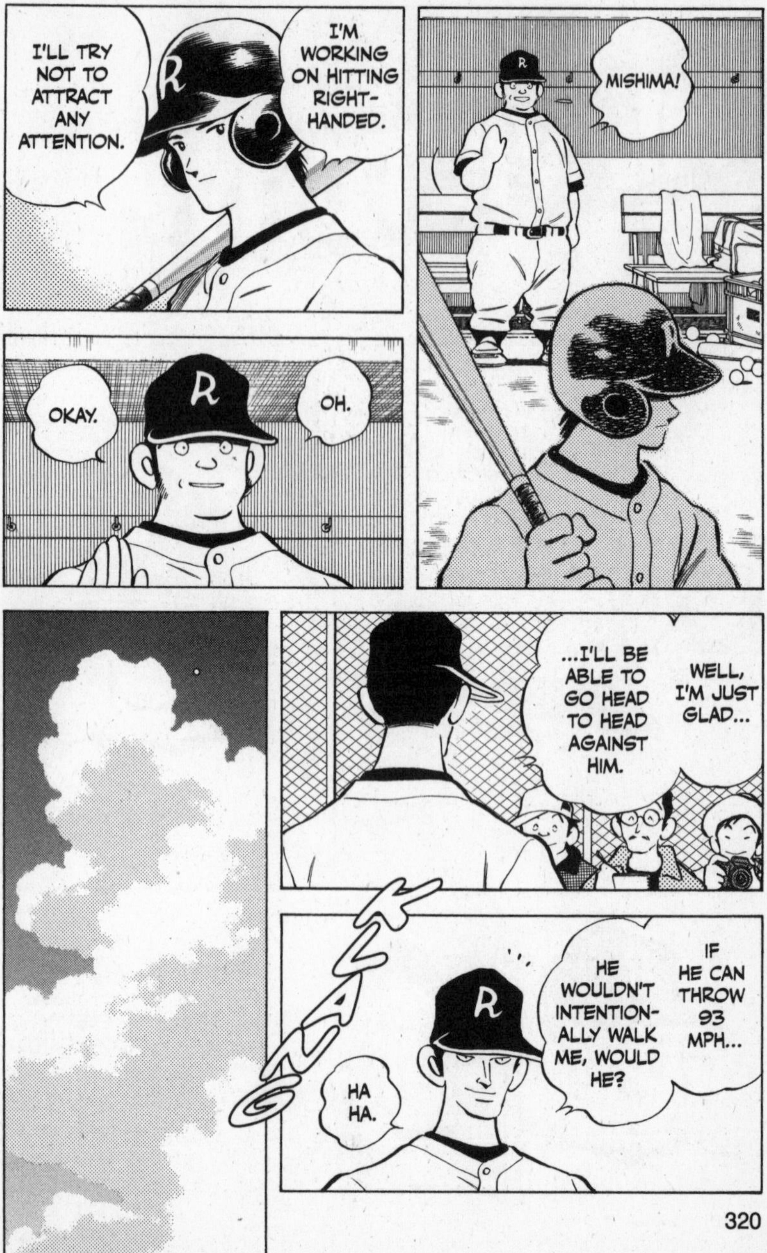
MISHIMA!
I'M WORKING ON HITTING RIGHT-HANDED.
I'LL TRY NOT TO ATTRACT ANY ATTENTION.
OH.
OKAY.
WELL, I'M JUST GLAD...
...I'LL BE ABLE TO GO HEAD TO HEAD AGAINST HIM.
IF HE CAN THROW 93 MPH...
HE WOULDN'T INTENTION-ALLY WALK ME, WOULD HE?
HA HA.
KLANG

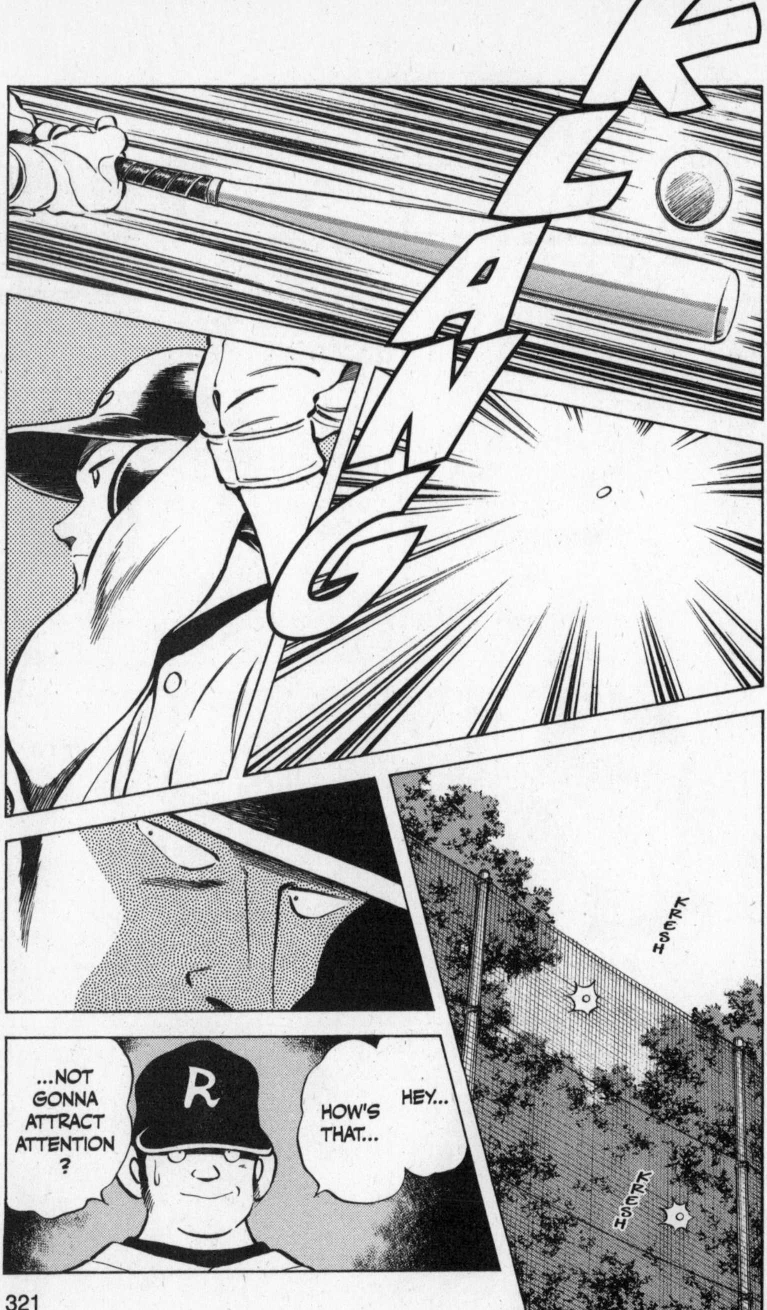
KLANG
KRESH
KRESH
HEY...
HOW'S THAT...
...NOT GONNA ATTRACT ATTENTION?

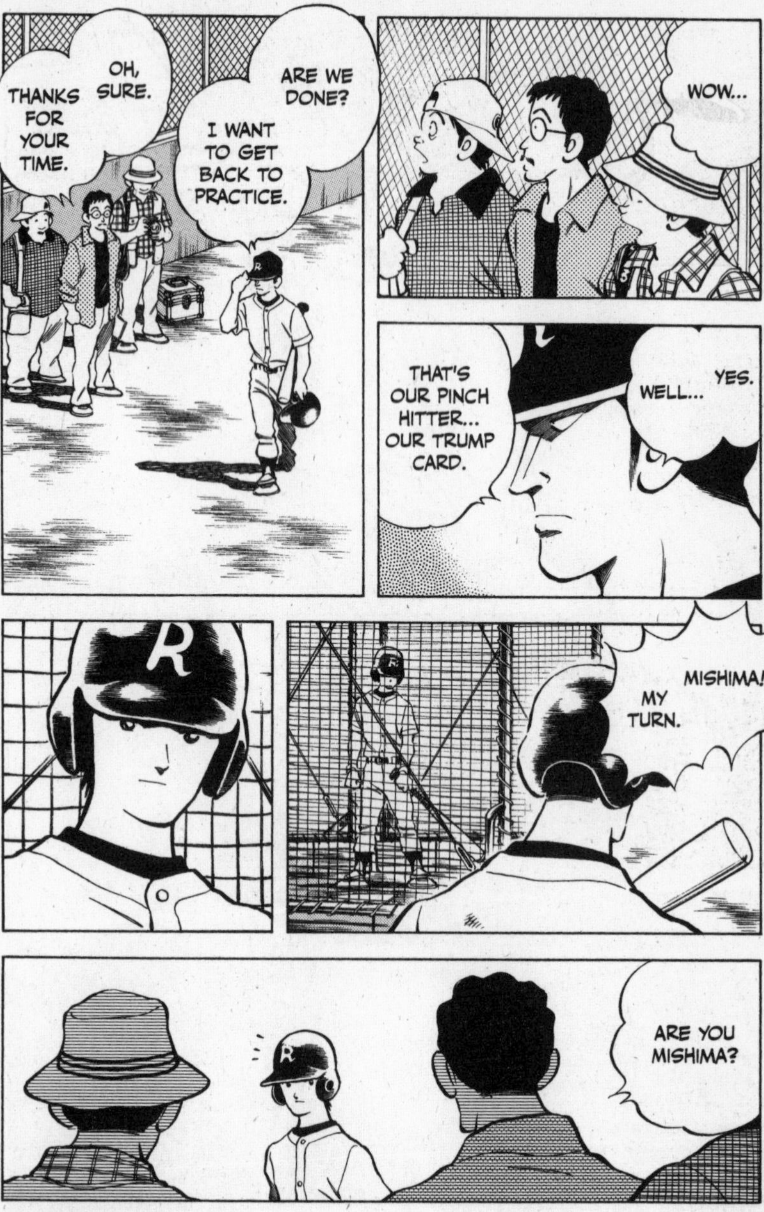
WOW...
YES.
WELL...
THAT'S OUR PINCH HITTER... OUR TRUMP CARD.
ARE WE DONE?
I WANT TO GET BACK TO PRACTICE.
OH, SURE.
THANKS FOR YOUR TIME.
MISHIMA!
MY TURN.
ARE YOU MISHIMA?

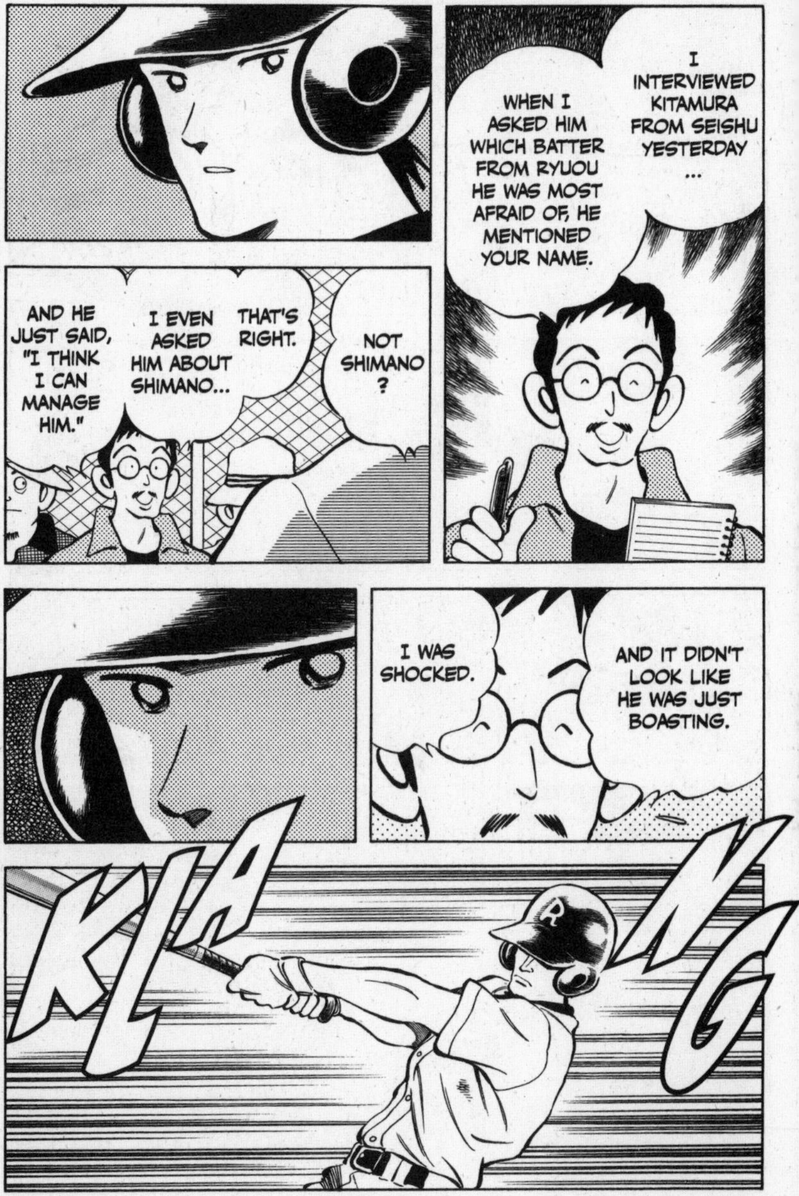
I INTERVIEWED KITAMURA FROM SEISHU YESTERDAY...
WHEN I ASKED HIM WHICH BATTER FROM RYUOU HE WAS MOST AFRAID OF, HE MENTIONED YOUR NAME.
NOT SHIMANO?
THAT'S RIGHT.
I EVEN ASKED HIM ABOUT SHIMANO...
AND HE JUST SAID, "I THINK I CAN MANAGE HIM."
AND IT DIDN'T LOOK LIKE HE WAS JUST BOASTING.
I WAS SHOCKED.
KLANG

THAT'S...

...QUITE A SHOCK...

...TO ME, TOO.

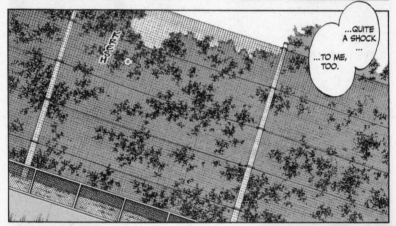

KKSH

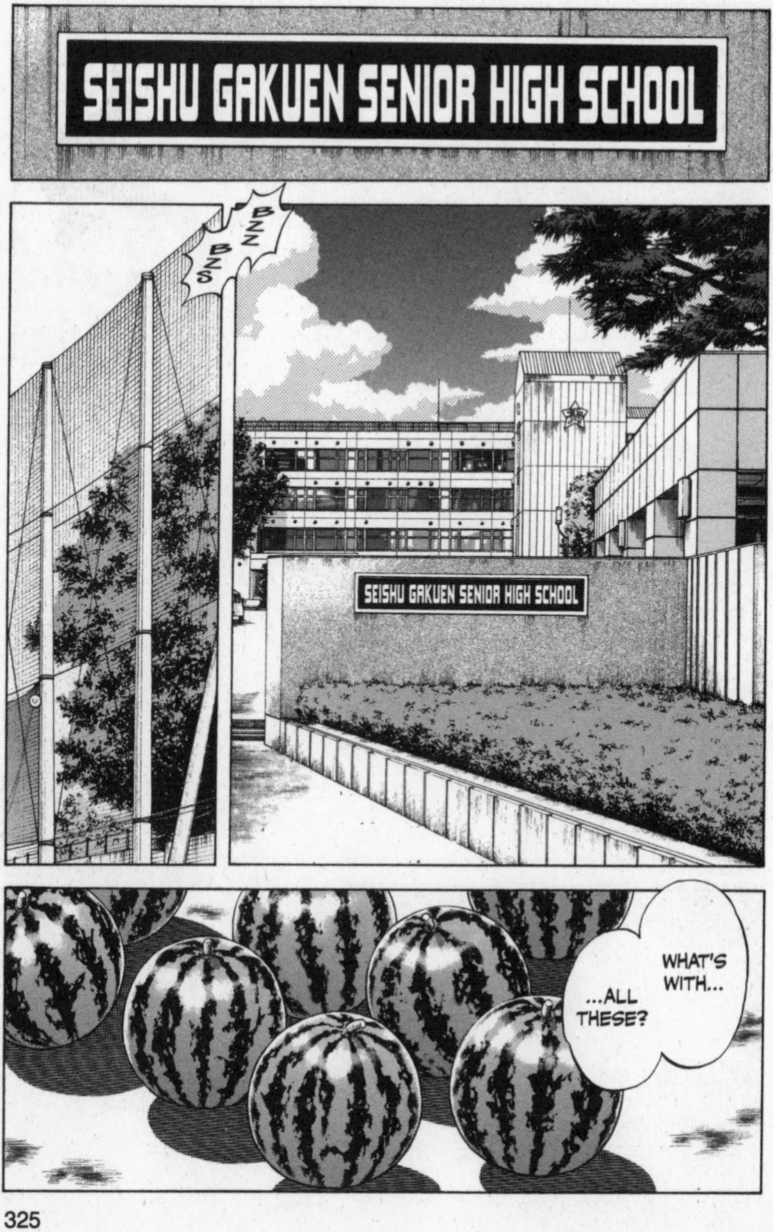
SEISHU GAKUEN SENIOR HIGH SCHOOL
SEISHU GAKUEN SENIOR HIGH SCHOOL
BZZ BZZ
WHAT'S WITH...
...ALL THESE?

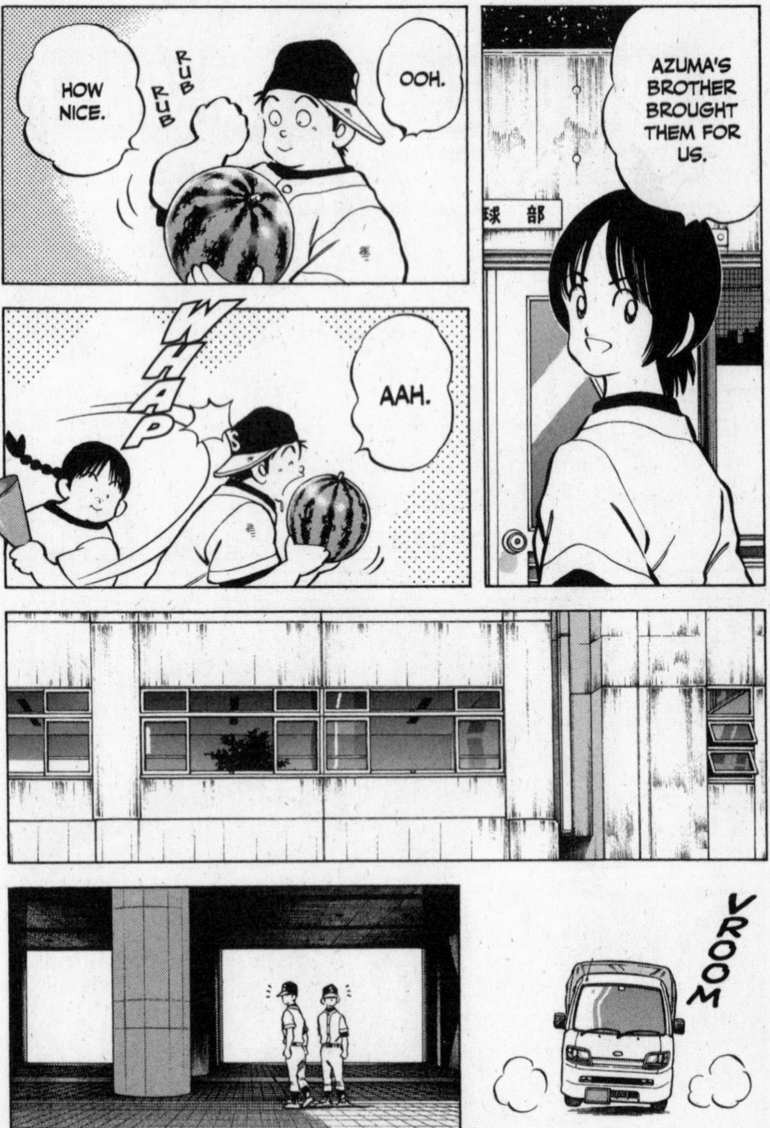
AZUMA'S BROTHER BROUGHT THEM FOR US.
球 部
OOH.
RUB RUB
HOW NICE.
AAH.
WHAP
VROOM

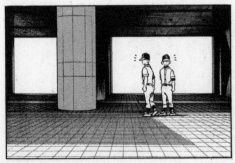

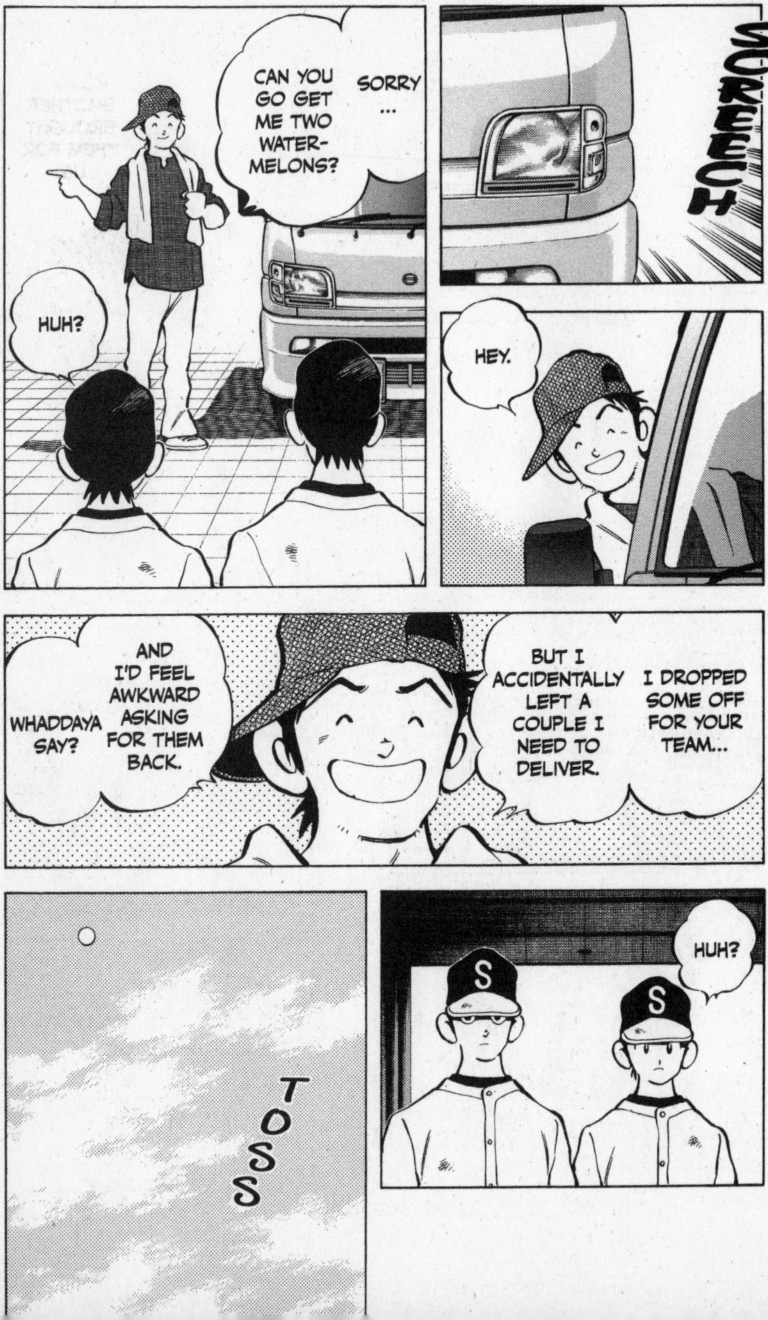
SCREECH
HEY.
SORRY ...
CAN YOU GO GET ME TWO WATER-MELONS?
HUH?
I DROPPED SOME OFF FOR YOUR TEAM...
BUT I ACCIDENTALLY LEFT A COUPLE I NEED TO DELIVER.
AND I'D FEEL AWKWARD ASKING FOR THEM BACK.
WHADDAYA SAY?
HUH?
TOSS

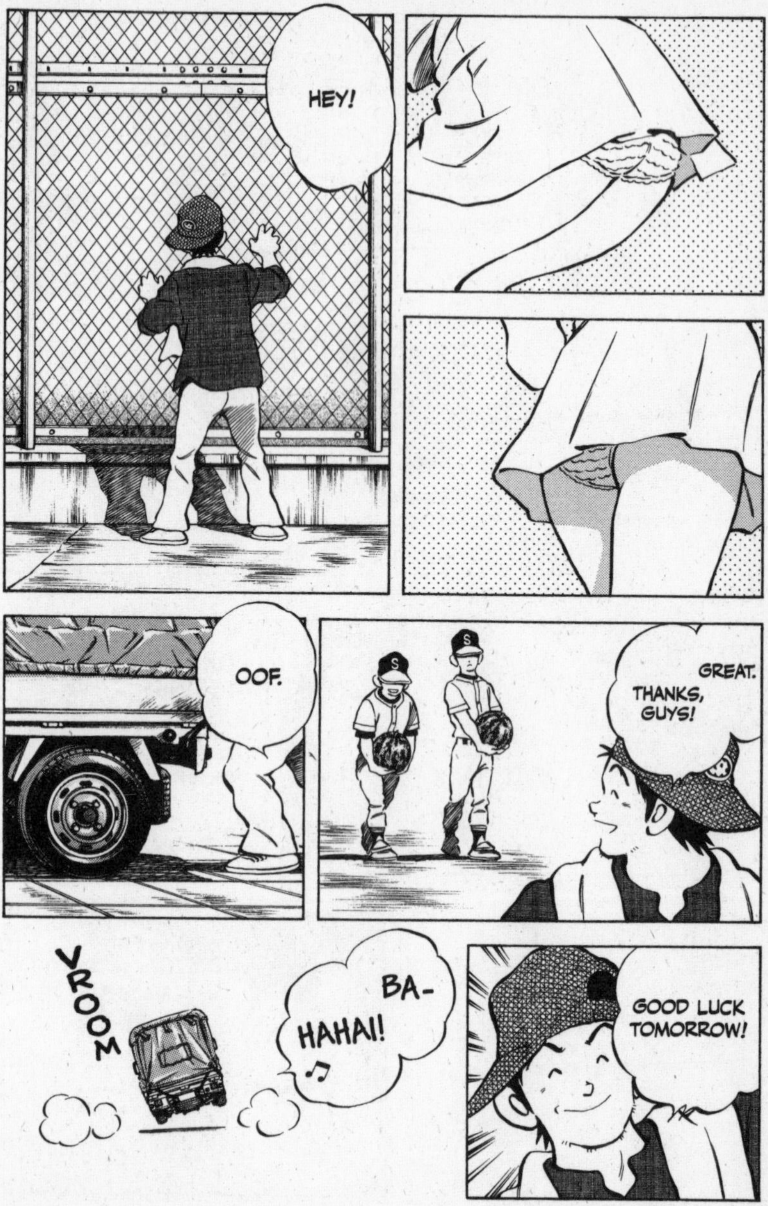
HEY!
GREAT.
THANKS, GUYS!
OOF.
GOOD LUCK TOMORROW!
BA-HAHA! ♪
VROOM

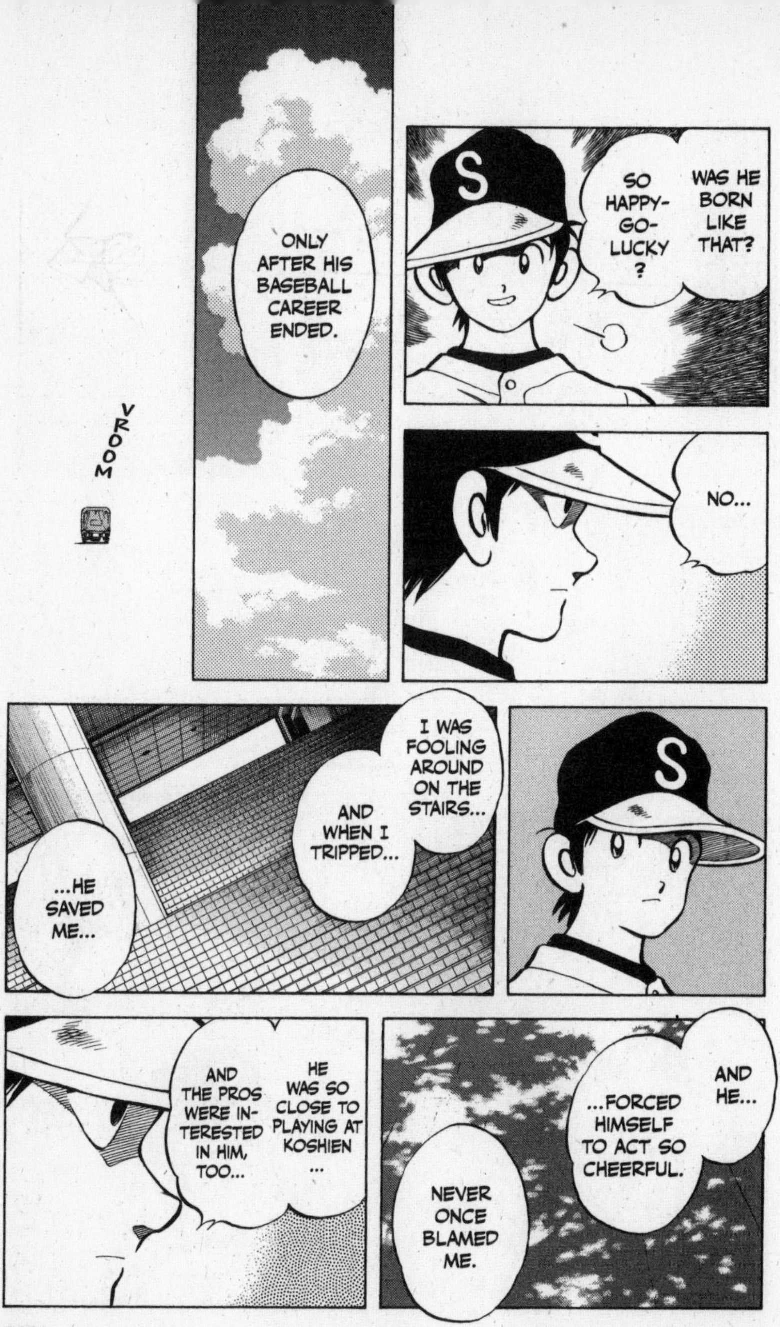
WAS HE BORN LIKE THAT?
SO HAPPY-GO-LUCKY?
NO...
ONLY AFTER HIS BASEBALL CAREER ENDED.
VROOM
I WAS FOOLING AROUND ON THE STAIRS...
AND WHEN I TRIPPED...
...HE SAVED ME...
AND HE...
...FORCED HIMSELF TO ACT SO CHEERFUL.
NEVER ONCE BLAMED ME.
HE WAS SO CLOSE TO PLAYING AT KOSHIEN...
AND THE PROS WERE INTERESTED IN HIM, TOO...

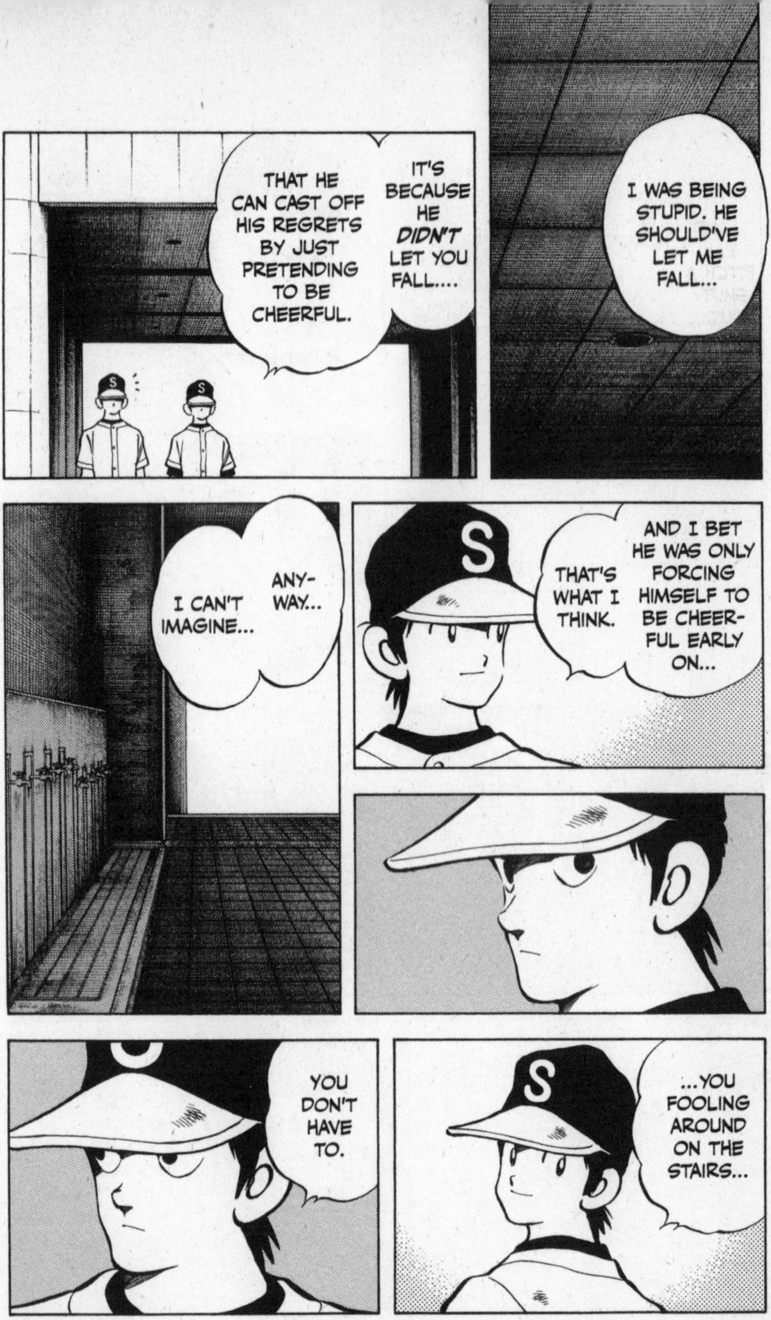
I WAS BEING STUPID. HE SHOULD'VE LET ME FALL...
IT'S BECAUSE HE DIDN'T LET YOU FALL....
THAT HE CAN CAST OFF HIS REGRETS BY JUST PRETENDING TO BE CHEERFUL.
AND I BET HE WAS ONLY FORCING HIMSELF TO BE CHEERFUL EARLY ON...
THAT'S WHAT I THINK.
ANY-WAY...
I CAN'T IMAGINE...
...YOU FOOLING AROUND ON THE STAIRS...
YOU DON'T HAVE TO.

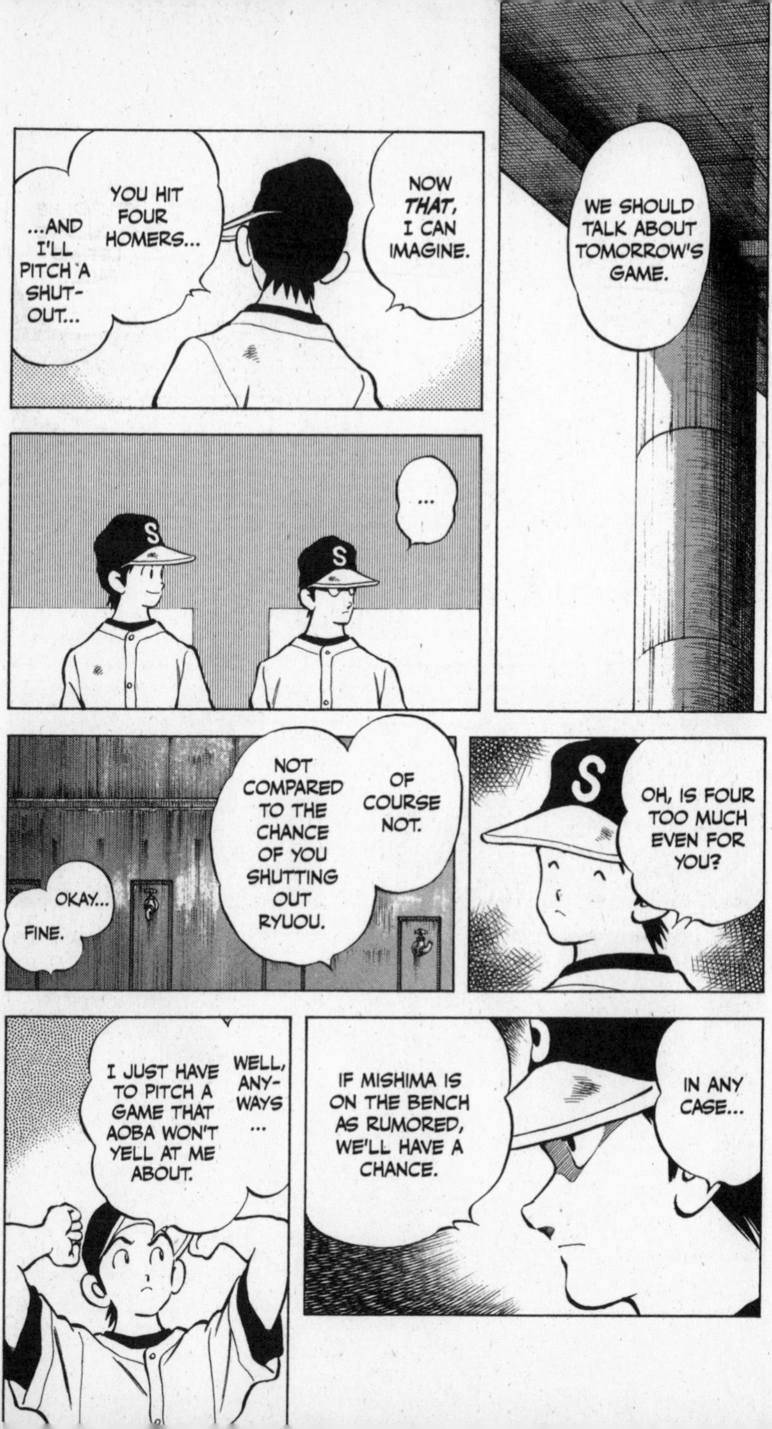
WE SHOULD TALK ABOUT TOMORROW'S GAME.
NOW *THAT*, I CAN IMAGINE.
YOU HIT FOUR HOMERS...
...AND I'LL PITCH A SHUT-OUT...
...
OH, IS FOUR TOO MUCH EVEN FOR YOU?
OF COURSE NOT.
NOT COMPARED TO THE CHANCE OF YOU SHUTTING OUT RYUOU.
OKAY... FINE.
IN ANY CASE...
IF MISHIMA IS ON THE BENCH AS RUMORED, WE'LL HAVE A CHANCE.
WELL, ANY-WAYS...
I JUST HAVE TO PITCH A GAME THAT AOBA WON'T YELL AT ME ABOUT.

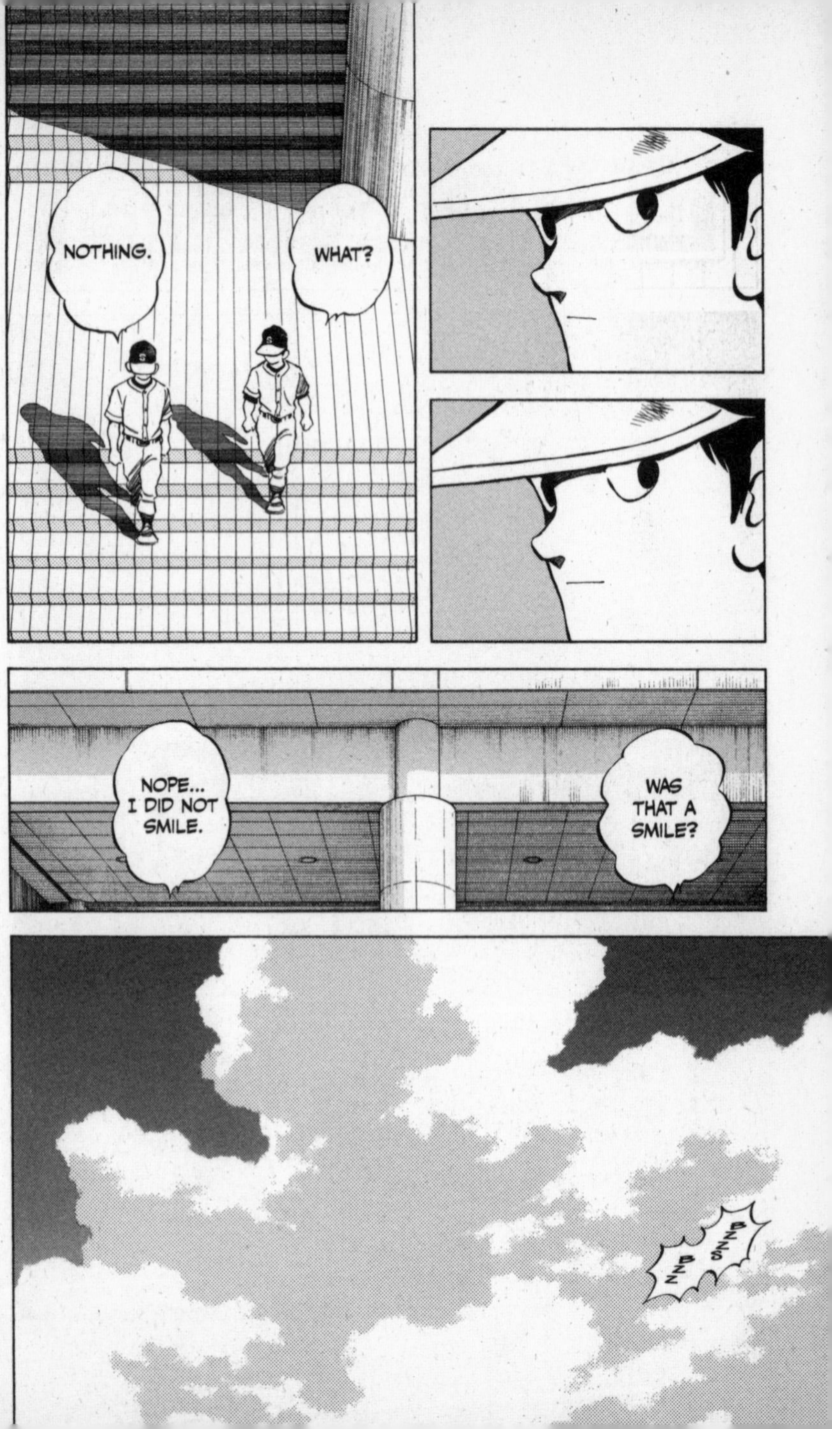
WHAT?
NOTHING.
WAS THAT A SMILE?
NOPE... I DID NOT SMILE.
BZZS
BZZ

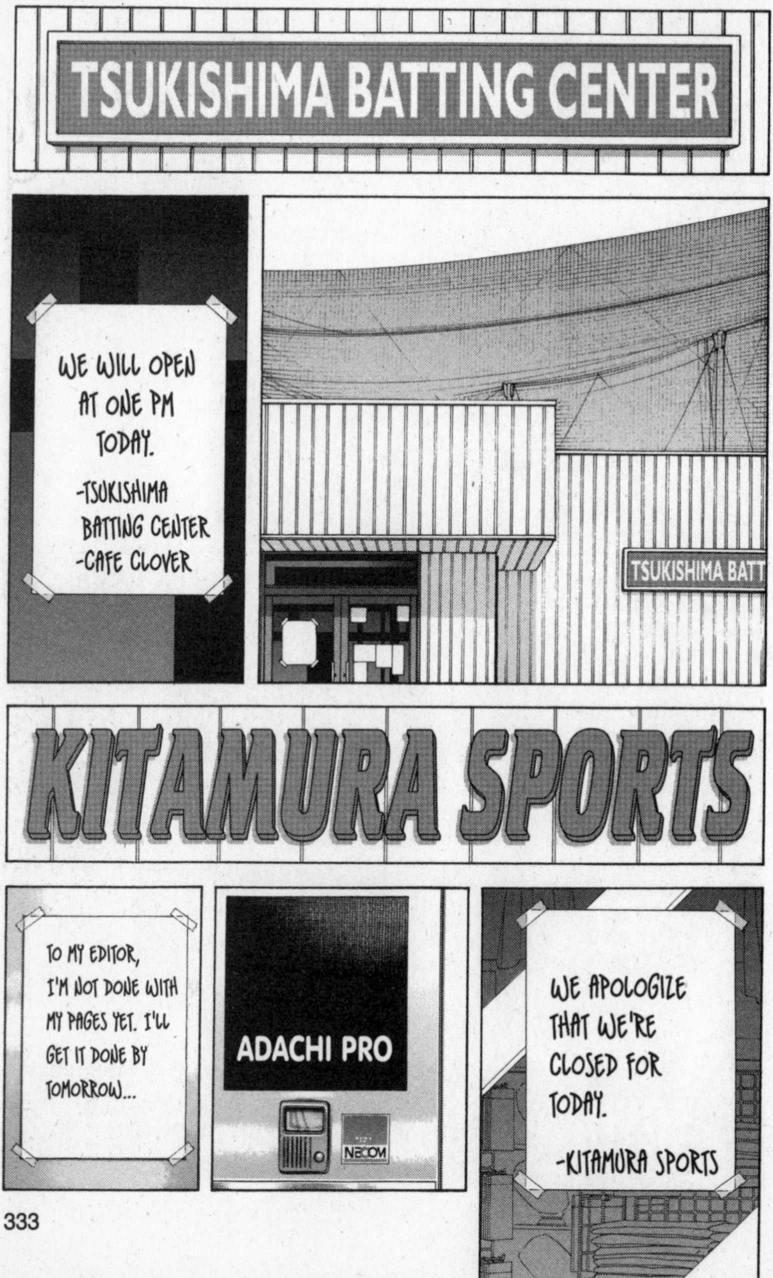
TSUKISHIMA BATTING CENTER
TSUKISHIMA BATT
WE WILL OPEN AT ONE PM TODAY.
-TSUKISHIMA BATTING CENTER
-CAFE CLOVER
KITAMURA SPORTS
WE APOLOGIZE THAT WE'RE CLOSED FOR TODAY.
-KITAMURA SPORTS
ADACHI PRO
NECOM
TO MY EDITOR,
I'M NOT DONE WITH MY PAGES YET. I'LL GET IT DONE BY TOMORROW...

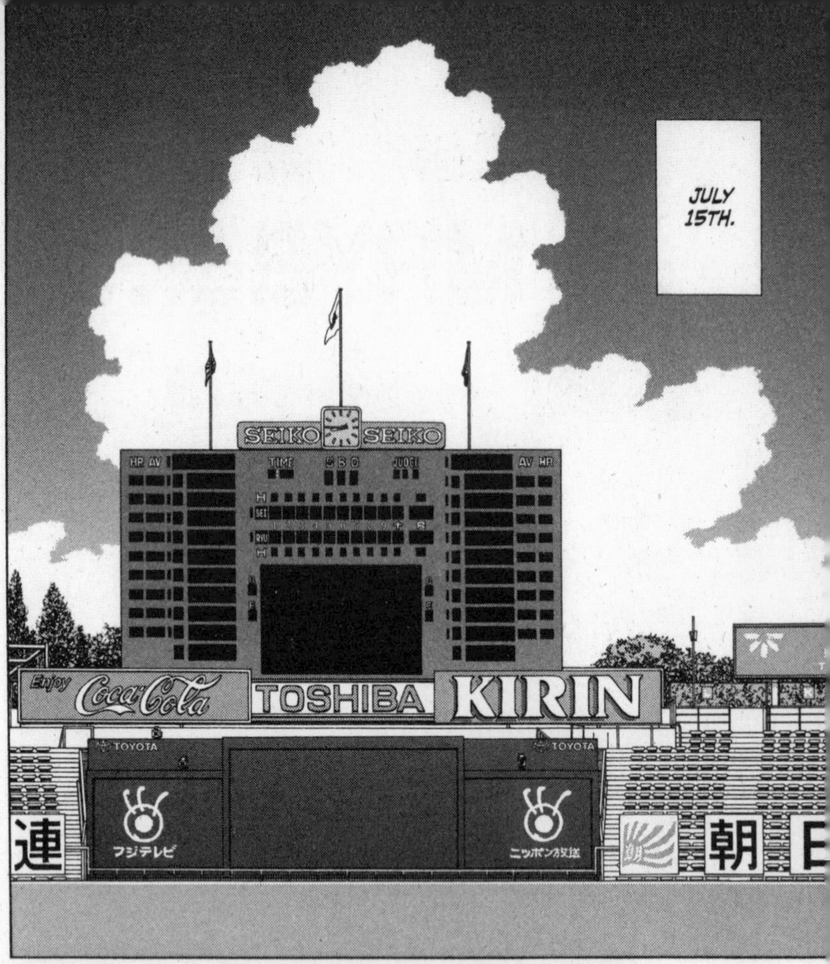
JULY 15TH.
SEIKO SEIKO
Enjoy Coca-Cola
TOSHIBA
KIRIN
TOYOTA
TOYOTA
フジテレビ
ニッポン放送
連
朝
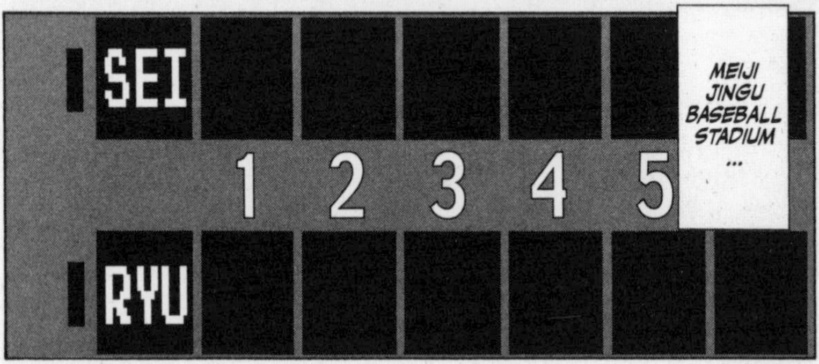
SEI
1 2 3 4 5
RYU
MEIJI JINGU BASEBALL STADIUM ...

# CHAPTER 79
# MAYBE...

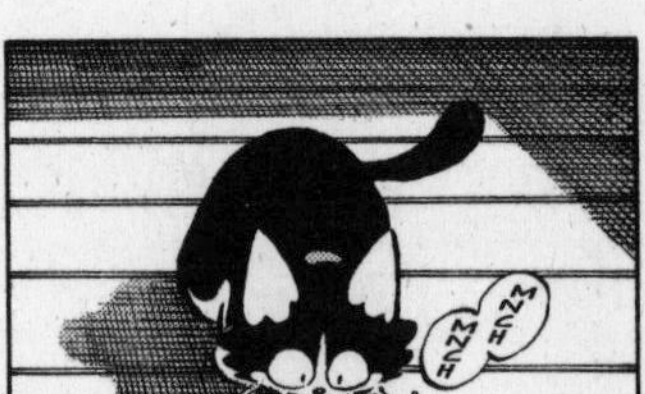
MNCH
MNCH

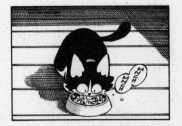

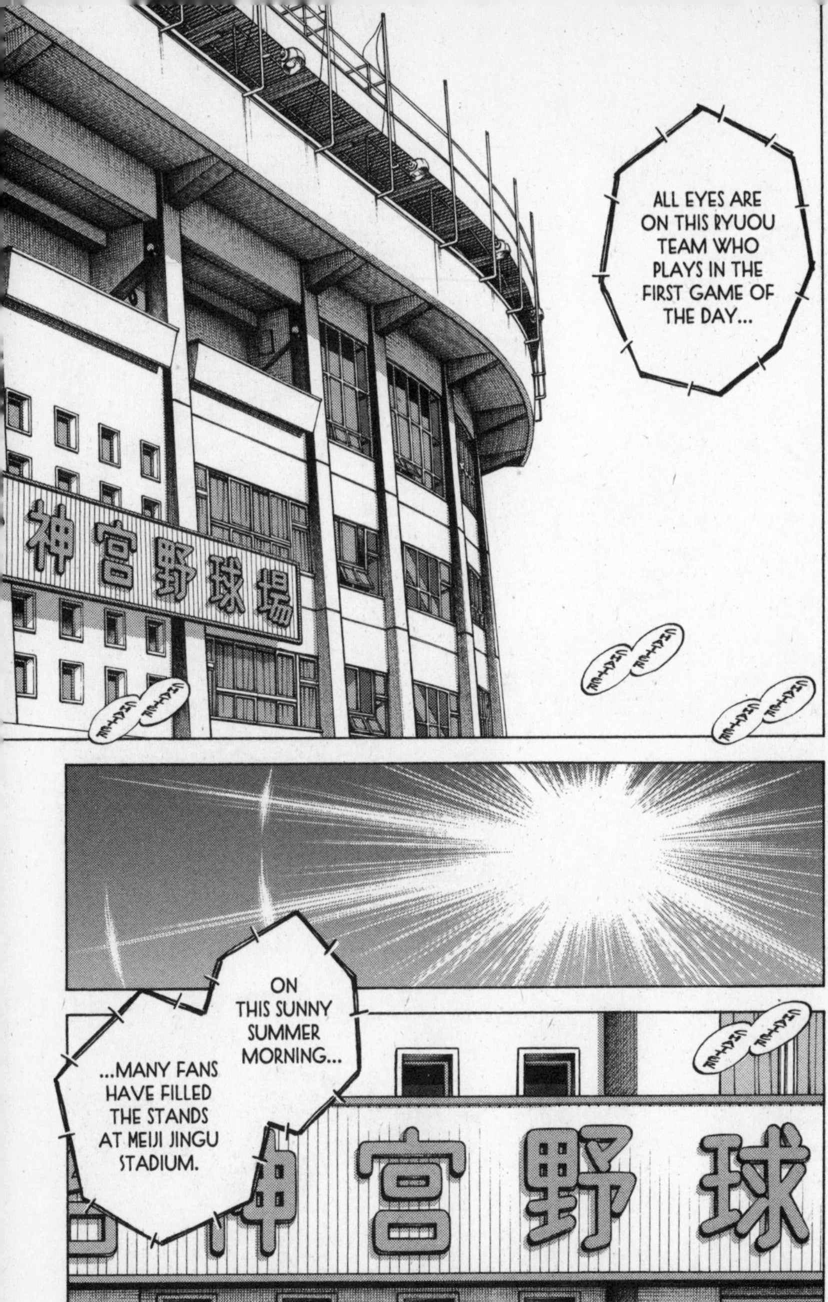
ALL EYES ARE ON THIS RYUOU TEAM WHO PLAYS IN THE FIRST GAME OF THE DAY...
神宮野球場
ON THIS SUNNY SUMMER MORNING...
...MANY FANS HAVE FILLED THE STANDS AT MEIJI JINGU STADIUM.

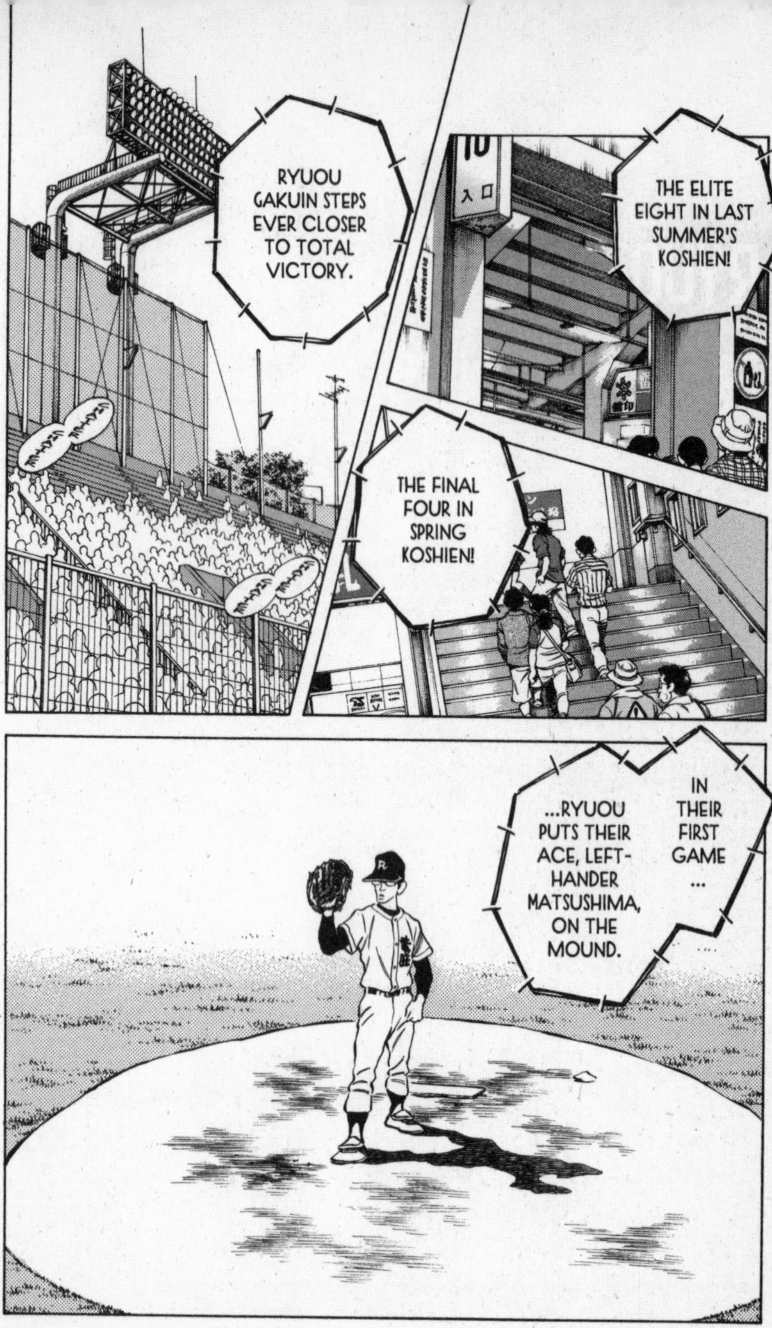
THE ELITE EIGHT IN LAST SUMMER'S KOSHIEN!
THE FINAL FOUR IN SPRING KOSHIEN!
RYUOU GAKUIN STEPS EVER CLOSER TO TOTAL VICTORY.
IN THEIR FIRST GAME...
...RYUOU PUTS THEIR ACE, LEFT-HANDER MATSUSHIMA, ON THE MOUND.

| RYUOU | |
|:---:|:---|
| 8 | NAKAGAWA |
| 4 | SAITO |
| 7 | MORI |
| 3 | SHIMANO |
| 5 | YAGUCHI |
| 2 | ONO |
| 6 | OZAWA |
| 9 | NISHIYAMA |
| 1 | MATSUSHIMA |
| | |

THIS IS RYUOU GAKUIN HIGH SCHOOL'S LINEUP!

AT FIRST BASE IS THEIR BIG GUN, TADASHI SHIMANO.

FOR THE REST OF THE FIELD...

...WE SEE THE REGULARS.

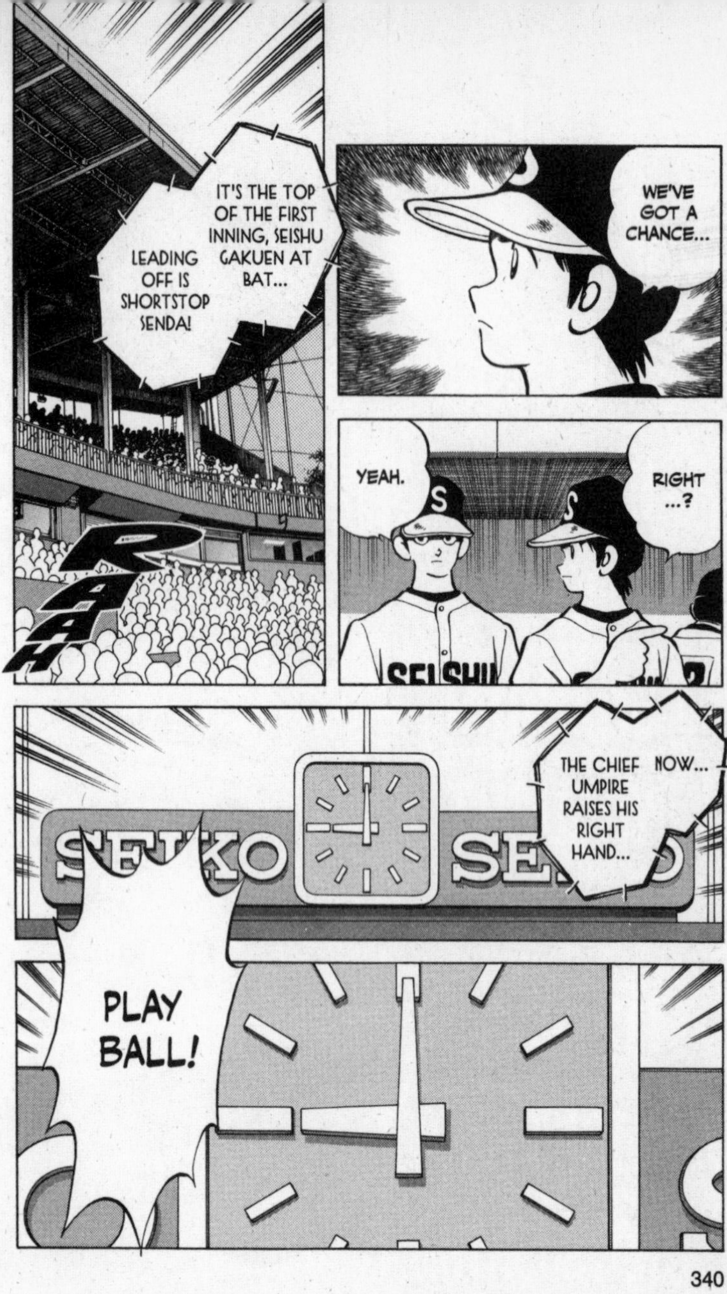
WE'VE GOT A CHANCE...
RIGHT ...?
YEAH.
IT'S THE TOP OF THE FIRST INNING, SEISHU GAKUEN AT BAT...
LEADING OFF IS SHORTSTOP SENDA!
RAAAH
NOW...
THE CHIEF UMPIRE RAISES HIS RIGHT HAND...
PLAY BALL!

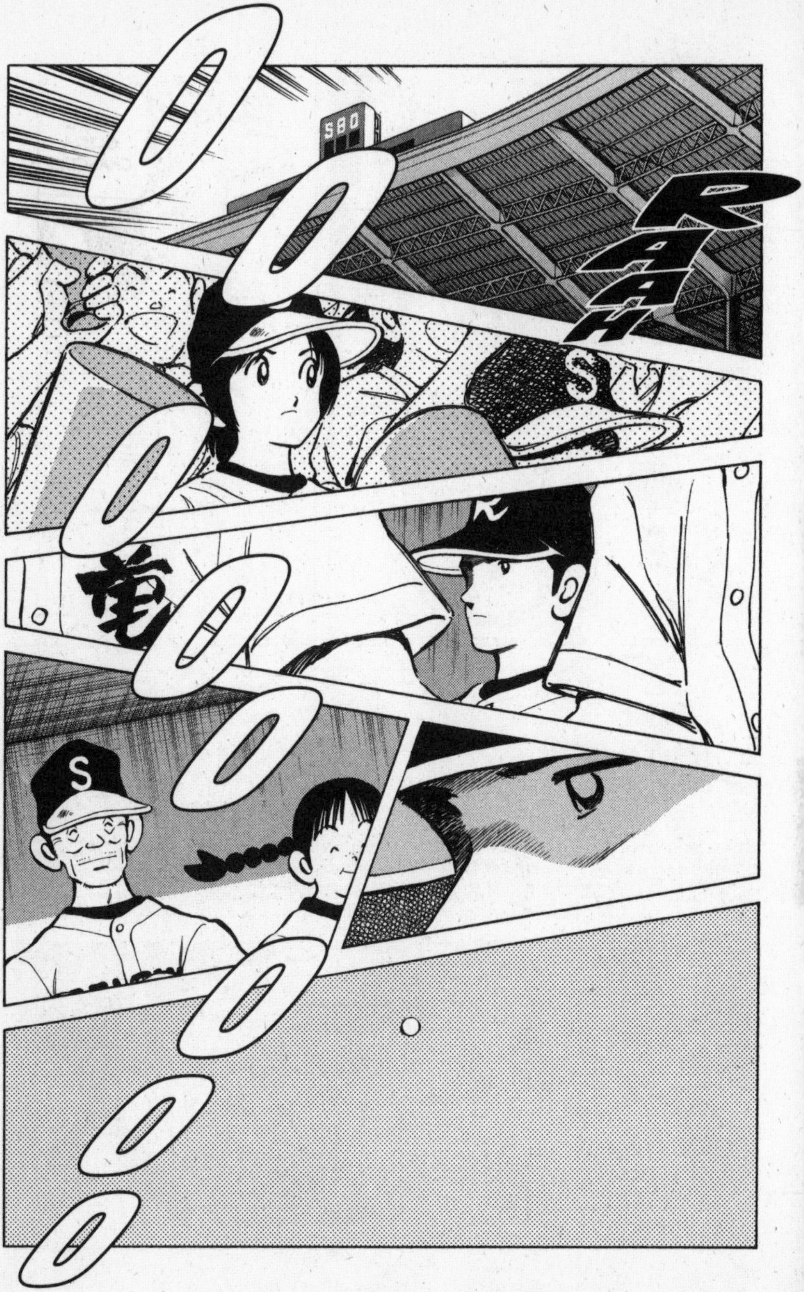
RAAH
SBO
OOOOOOOOO

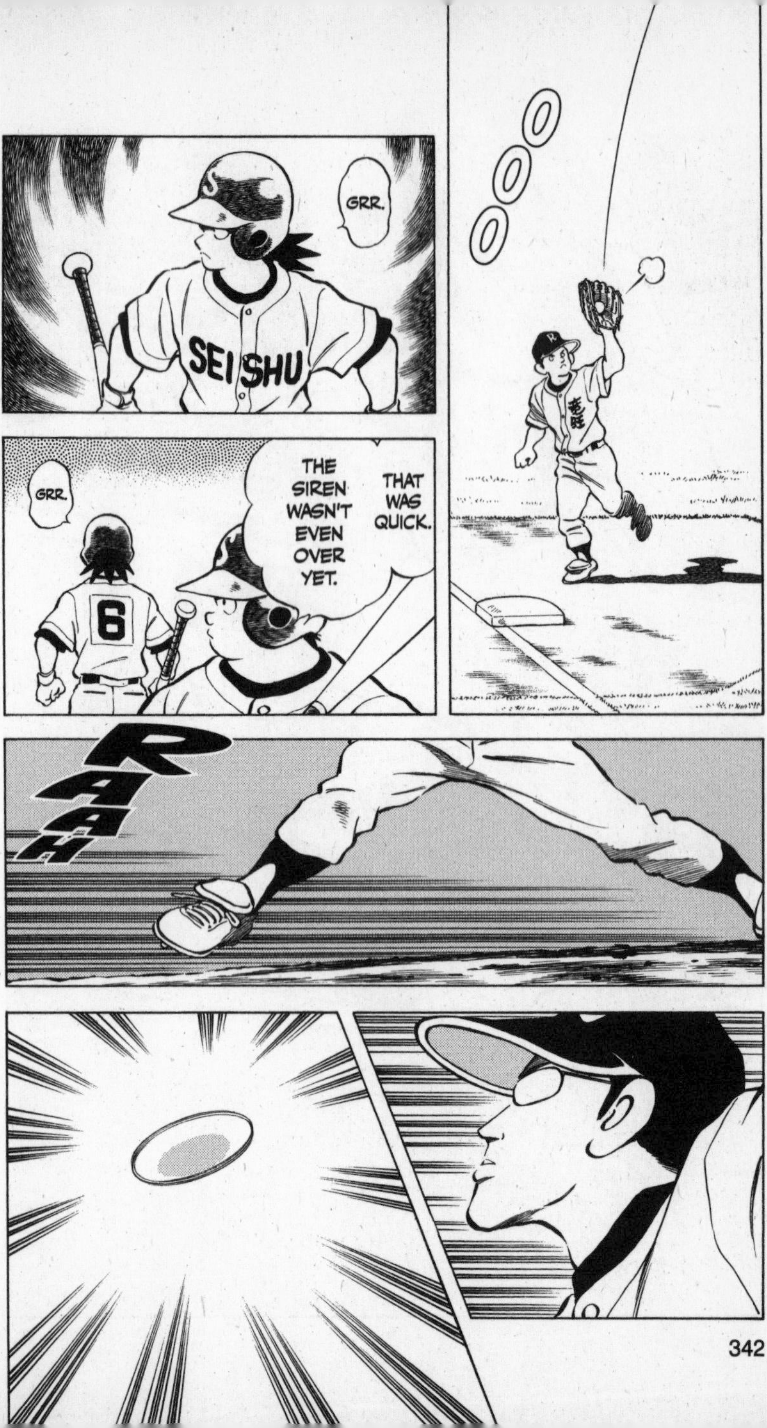
GRR.
THAT WAS QUICK.
THE SIREN WASN'T EVEN OVER YET.
GRR.
RAAAH

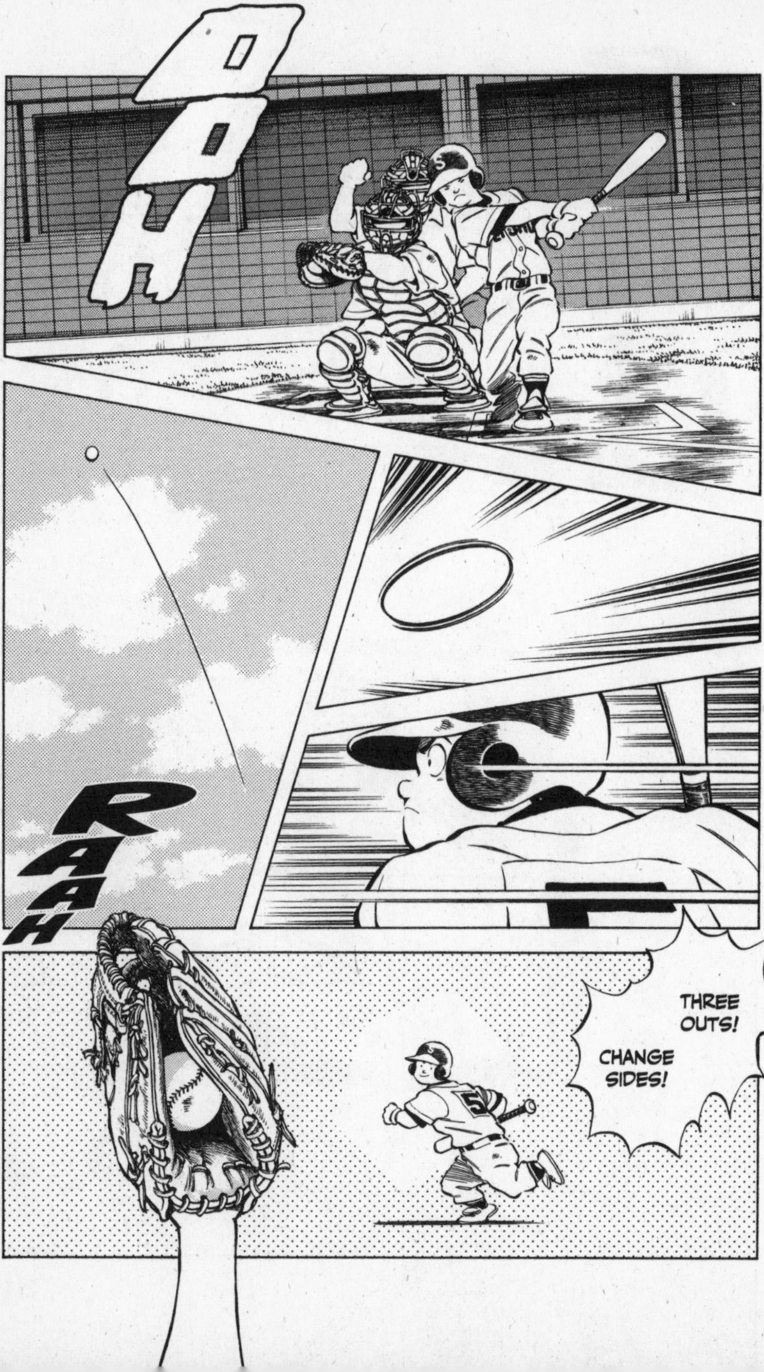
OOOH
RAAAH
THREE OUTS!
CHANGE SIDES!

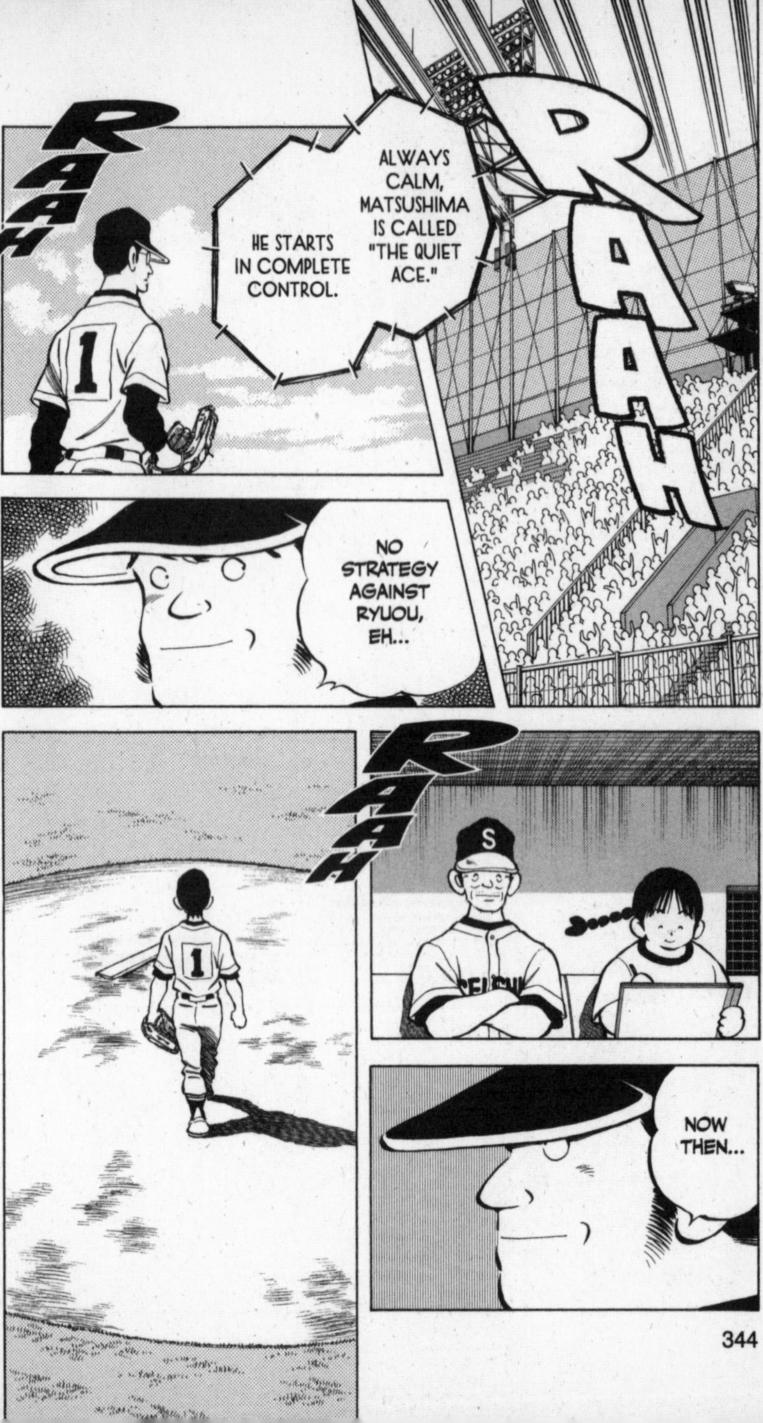
RAAAH
RAAAH
ALWAYS CALM, MATSUSHIMA IS CALLED "THE QUIET ACE."
HE STARTS IN COMPLETE CONTROL.
NO STRATEGY AGAINST RYUOU, EH...
RAAAH
NOW THEN...

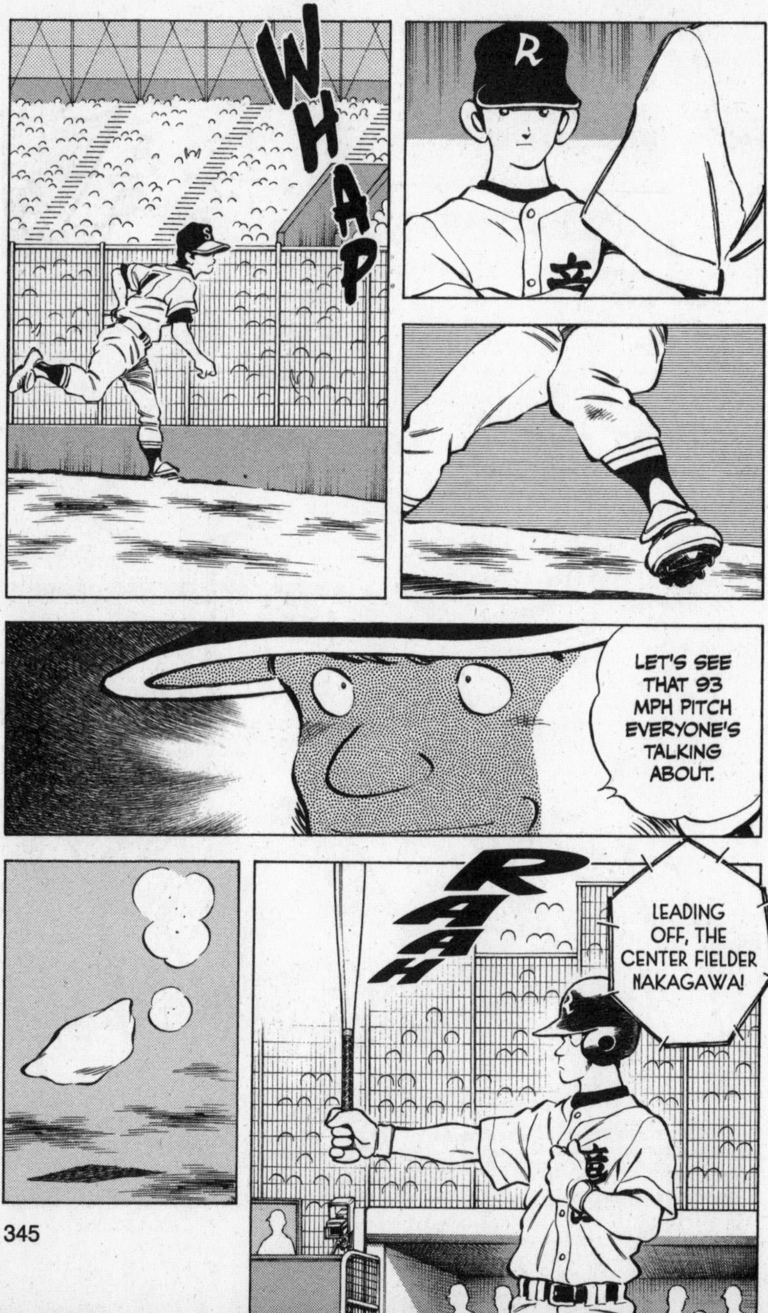
WHAP
LET'S SEE THAT 93 MPH PITCH EVERYONE'S TALKING ABOUT.
RAAH
LEADING OFF, THE CENTER FIELDER NAKAGAWA!

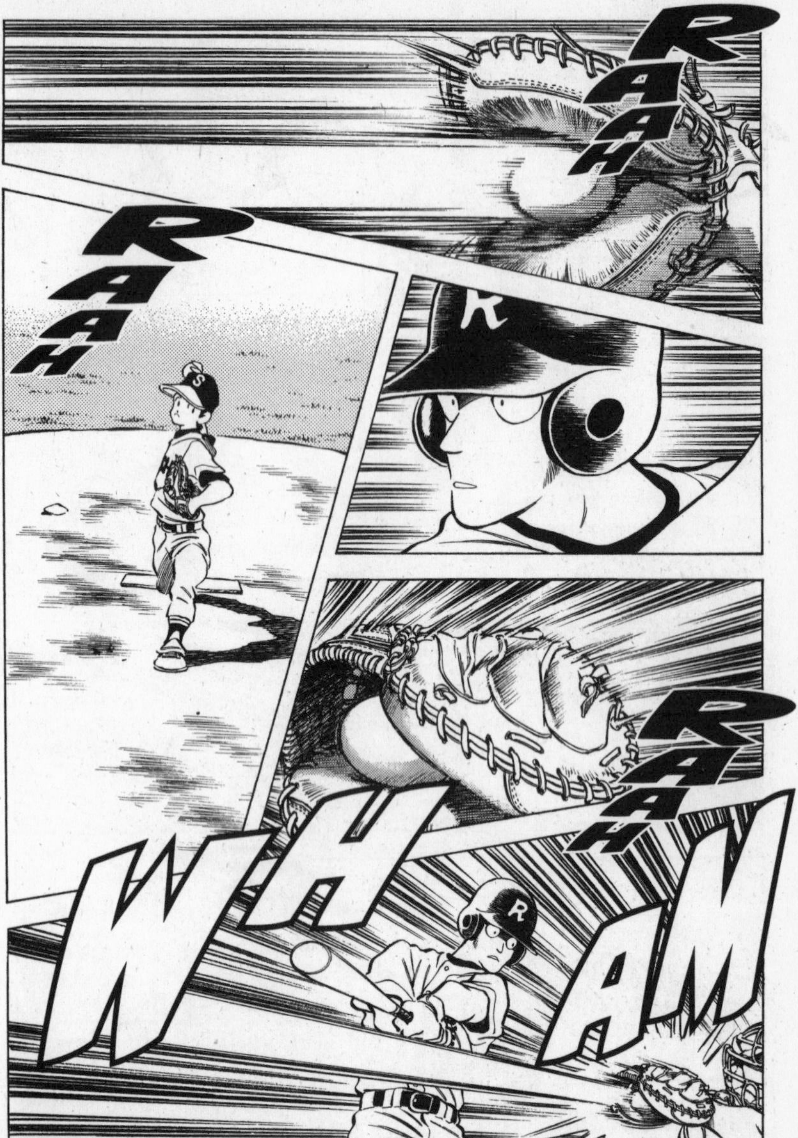
RAAAH
RAAAH
RAAAH
WHAM

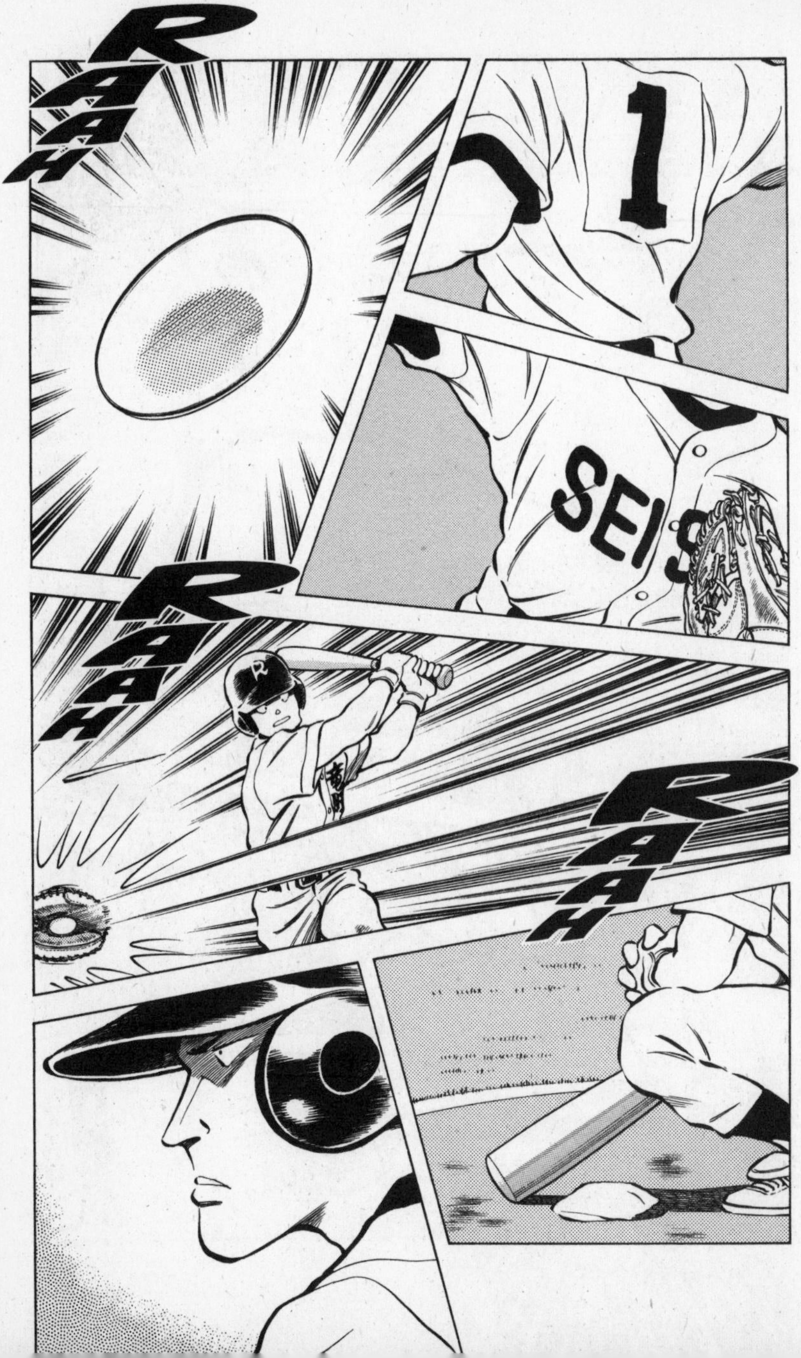
RAAAH
RAAAH
RAAAH

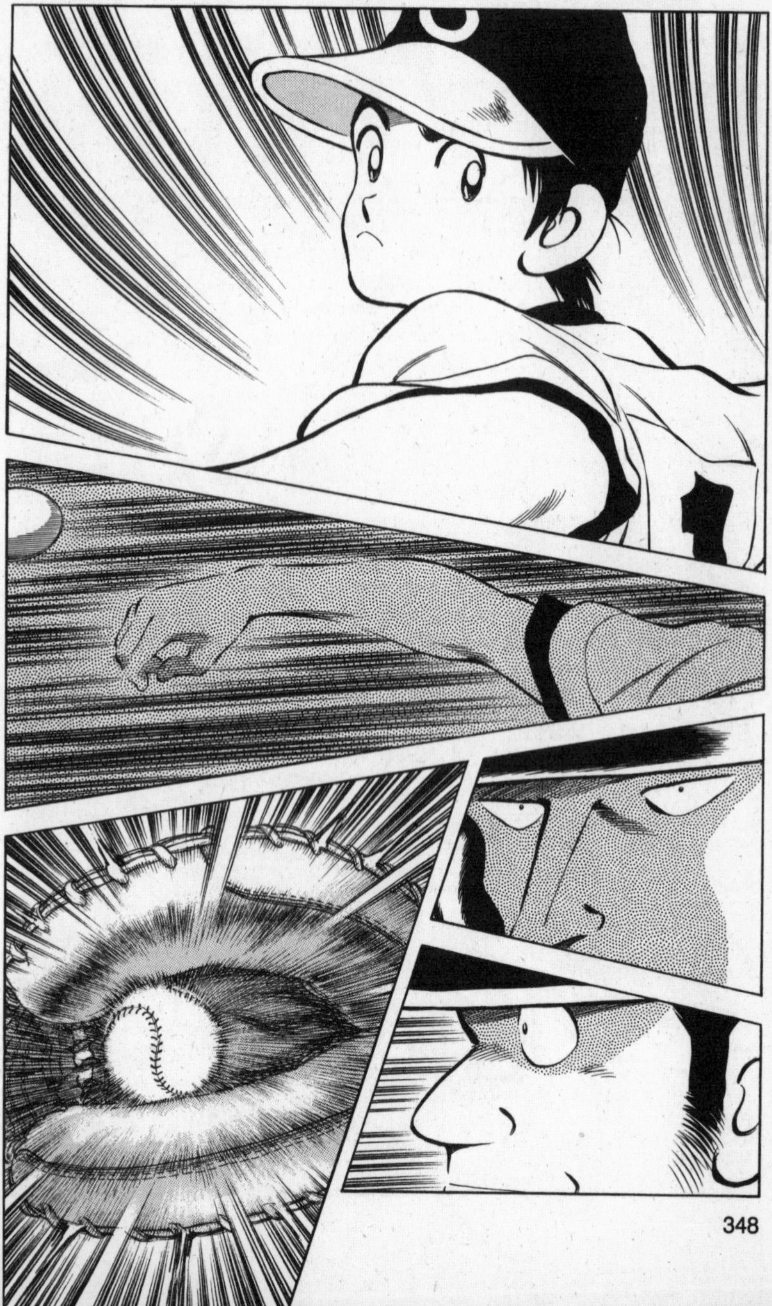

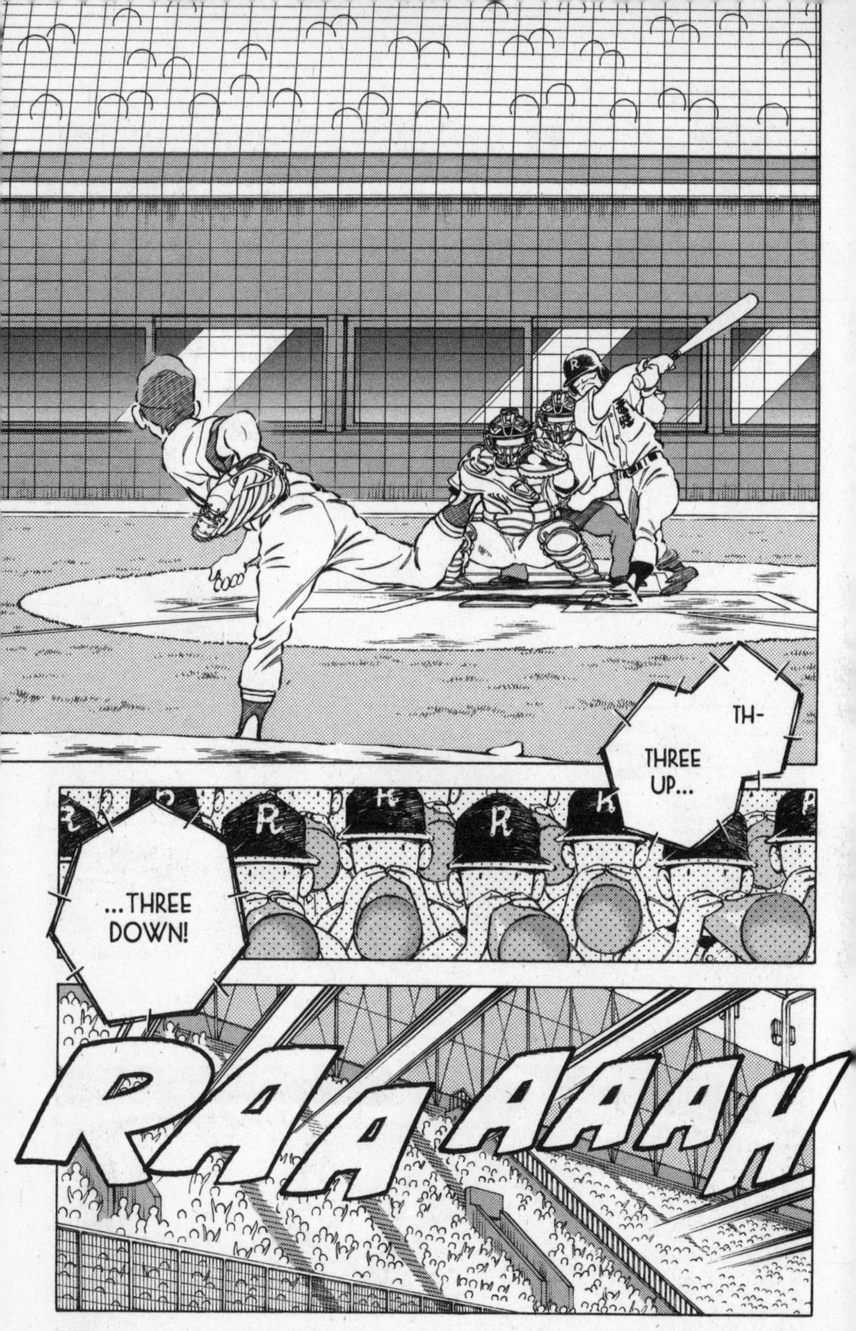
TH- THREE UP...
...THREE DOWN!
RAAAAAH

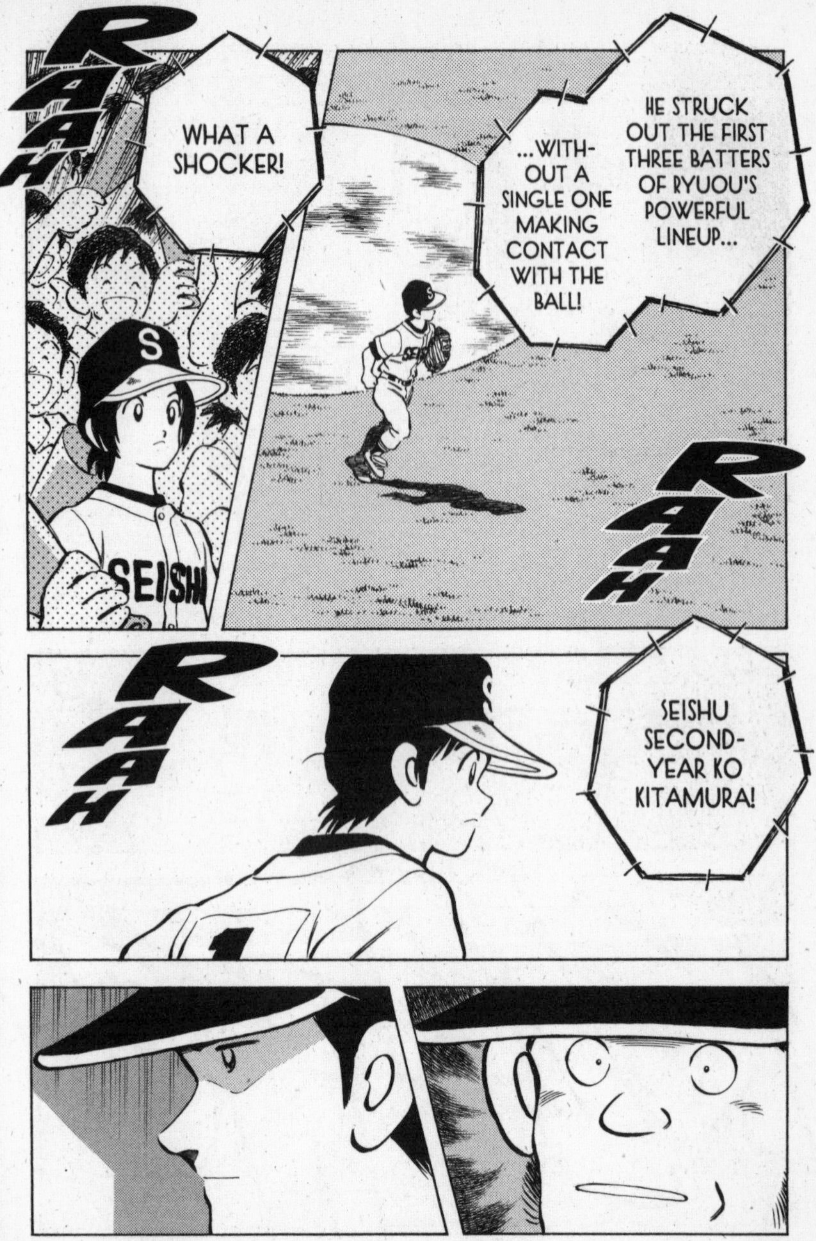
HE STRUCK OUT THE FIRST THREE BATTERS OF RYUOU'S POWERFUL LINEUP...
...WITHOUT A SINGLE ONE MAKING CONTACT WITH THE BALL!
RAAH
RAAH
WHAT A SHOCKER!
SEISHU SECOND-YEAR KO KITAMURA!
RAAH

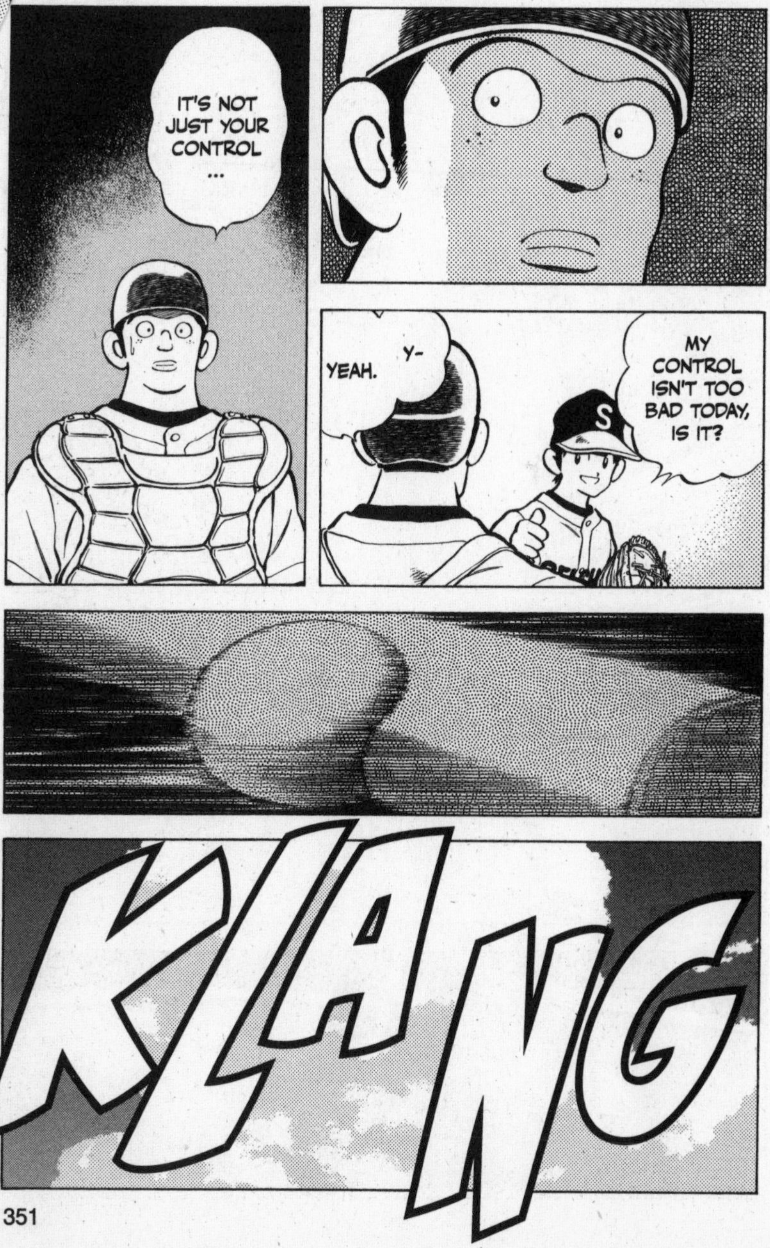
MY CONTROL ISN'T TOO BAD TODAY, IS IT?
Y- YEAH.
IT'S NOT JUST YOUR CONTROL ...
KLANG

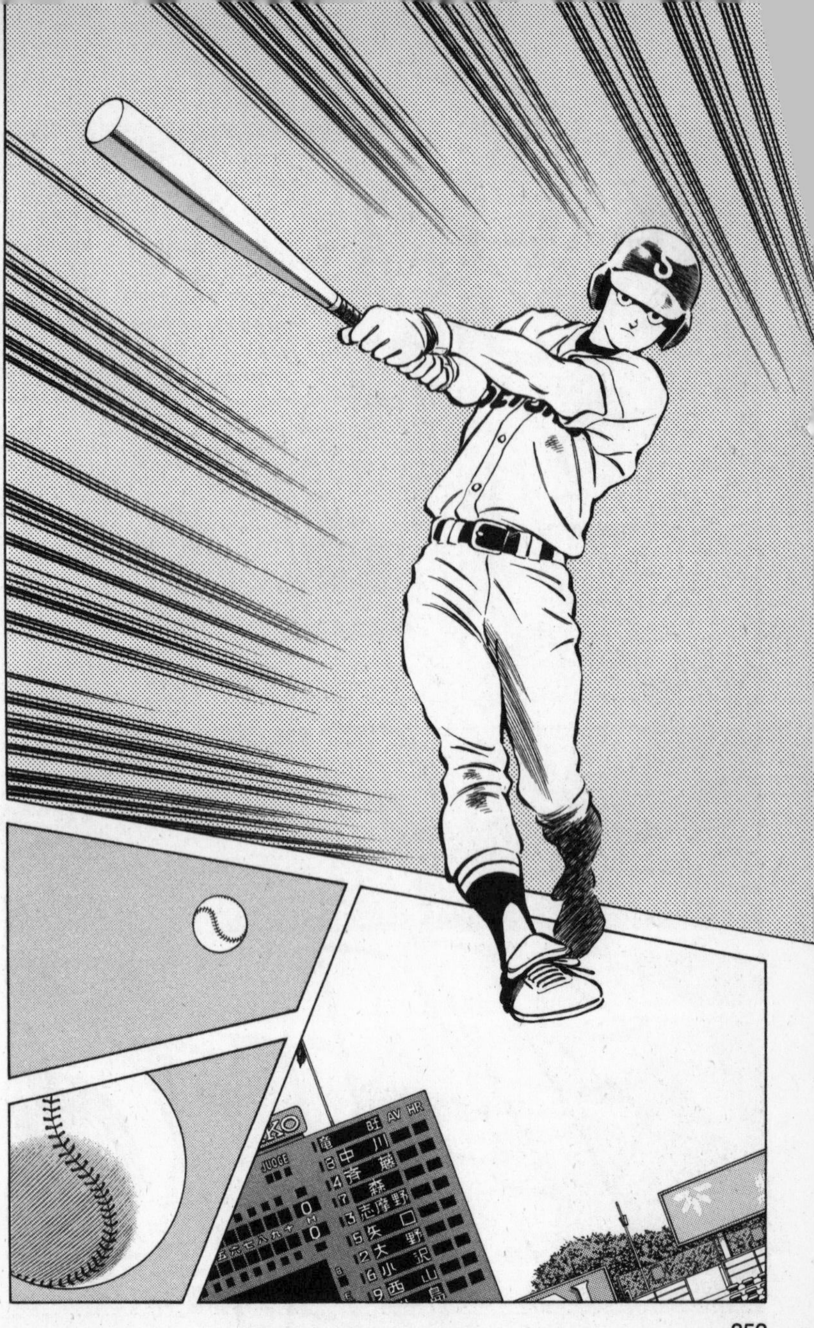

KO
AV HR
JUDGE
8 中川
4 斎藤
7 森
3 志摩野
5 矢口
2 大野
6 小沢
9 西山

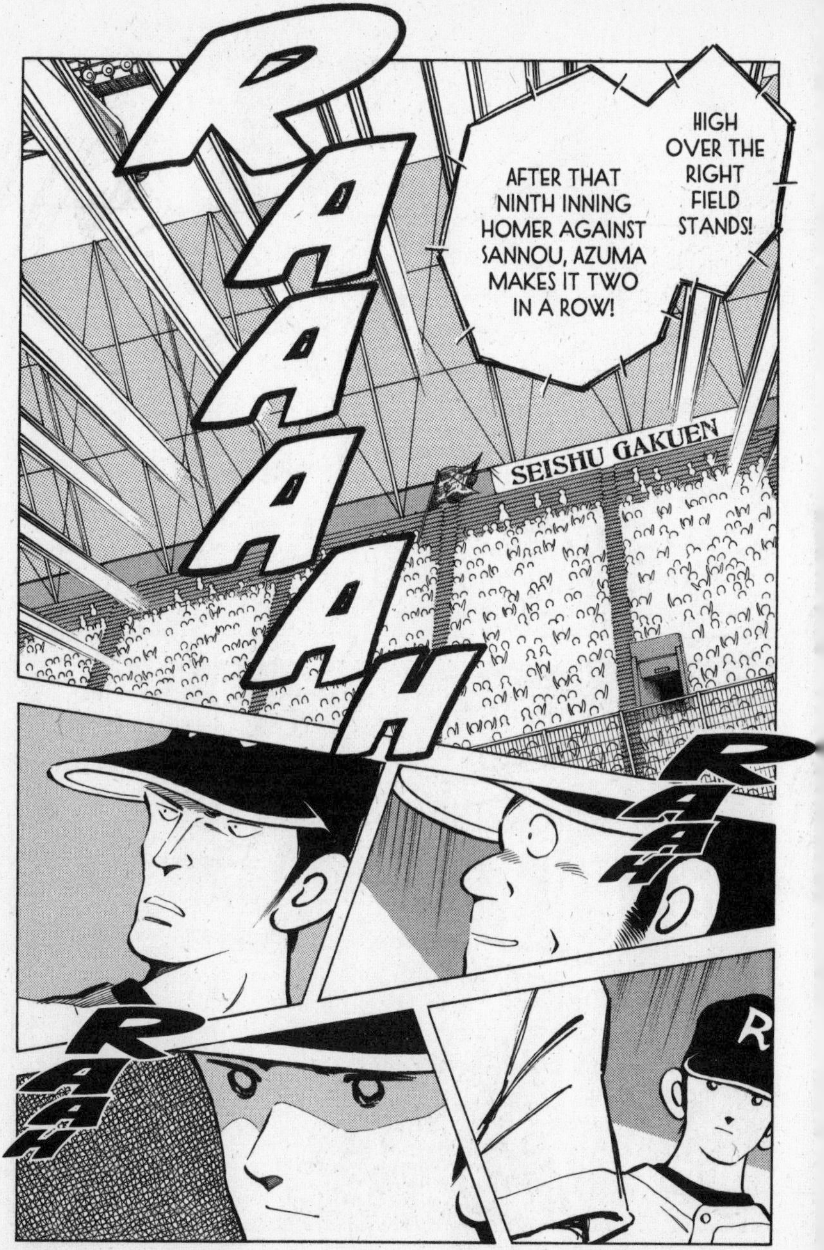

HIGH OVER THE RIGHT FIELD STANDS!
AFTER THAT NINTH INNING HOMER AGAINST SANNOU, AZUMA MAKES IT TWO IN A ROW!
RAAAAAH
SEISHU GAKUEN
RAAAH
RAAAH

RAAH

...THEN YOU GUYS ARE TO BLAME.

WITH ME AND KITAMURA ON THE TEAM, IF WE DON'T GET TO KOSHIEN...

THAT MIGHT BE RIGHT...

| H | | | | | | | | |
|---|---|---|---|---|---|---|---|---|
| SEI 0 | 1 | | | | | | | |
| | 1 | 2 | 3 | 4 | 5 | 6 | 7 | 8 |
| RYU 0 | | | | | | | | |
| H | | | | | | | | |

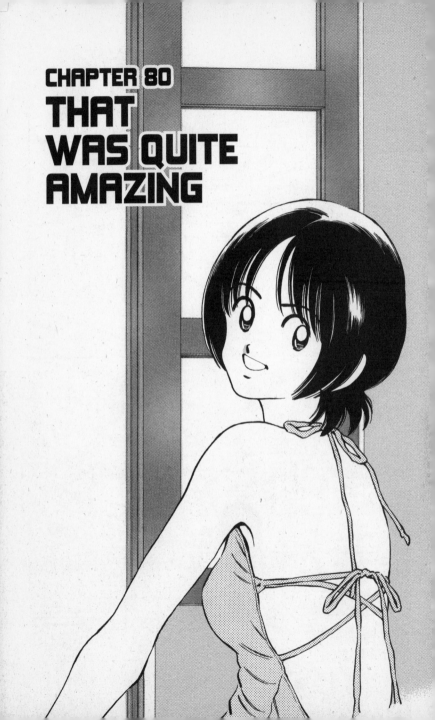

## CHAPTER 80
# THAT WAS QUITE AMAZING

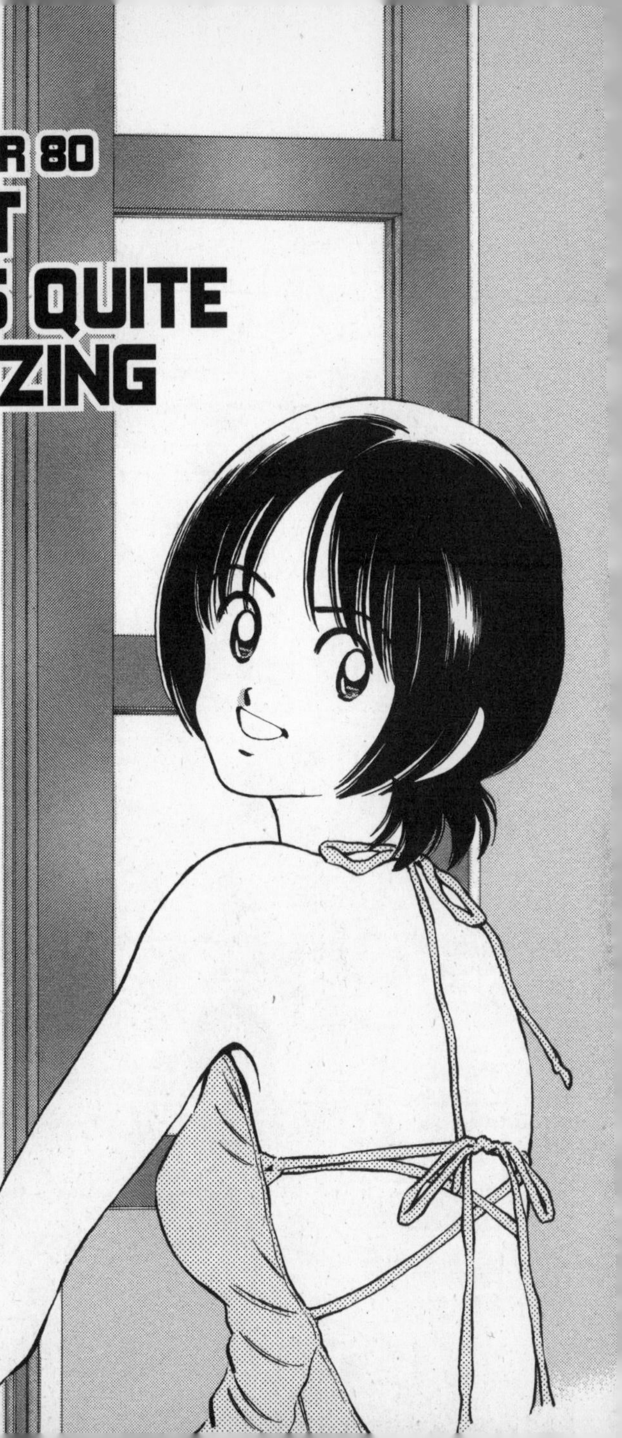

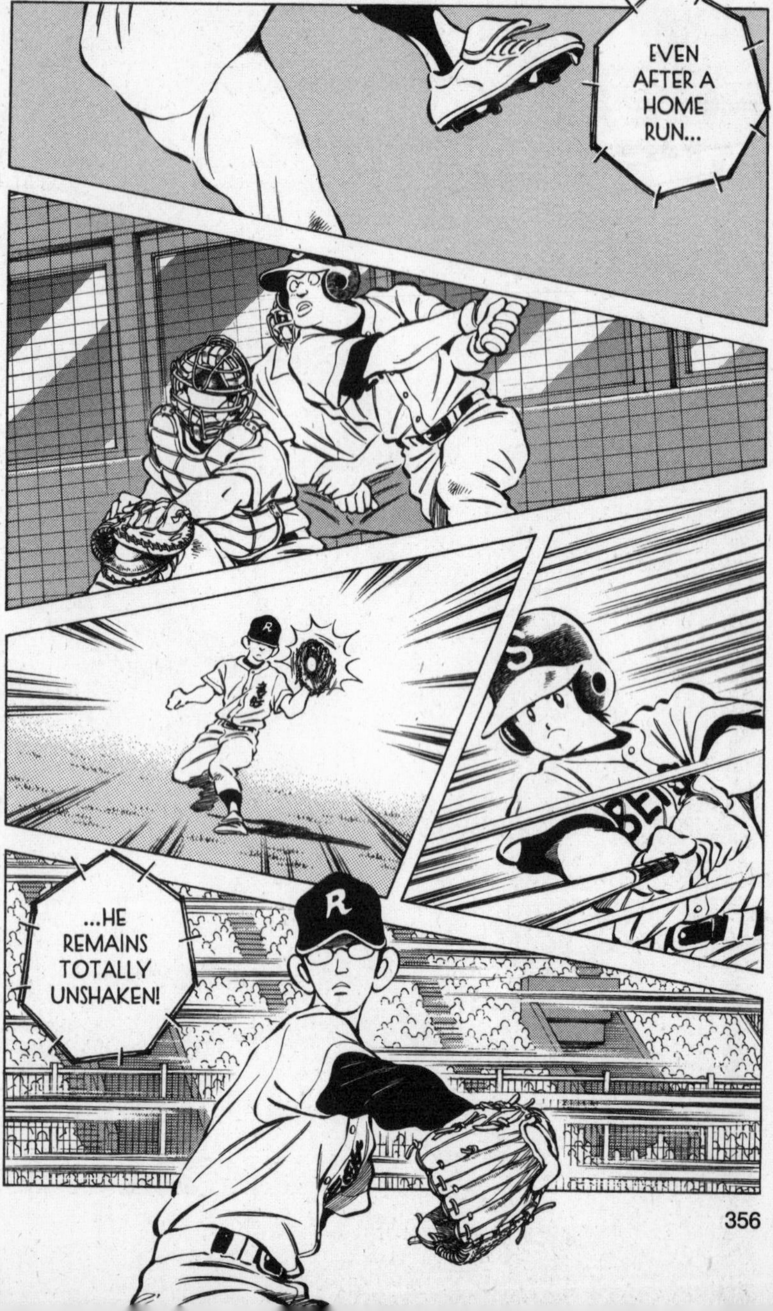
EVEN AFTER A HOME RUN...
...HE REMAINS TOTALLY UNSHAKEN!

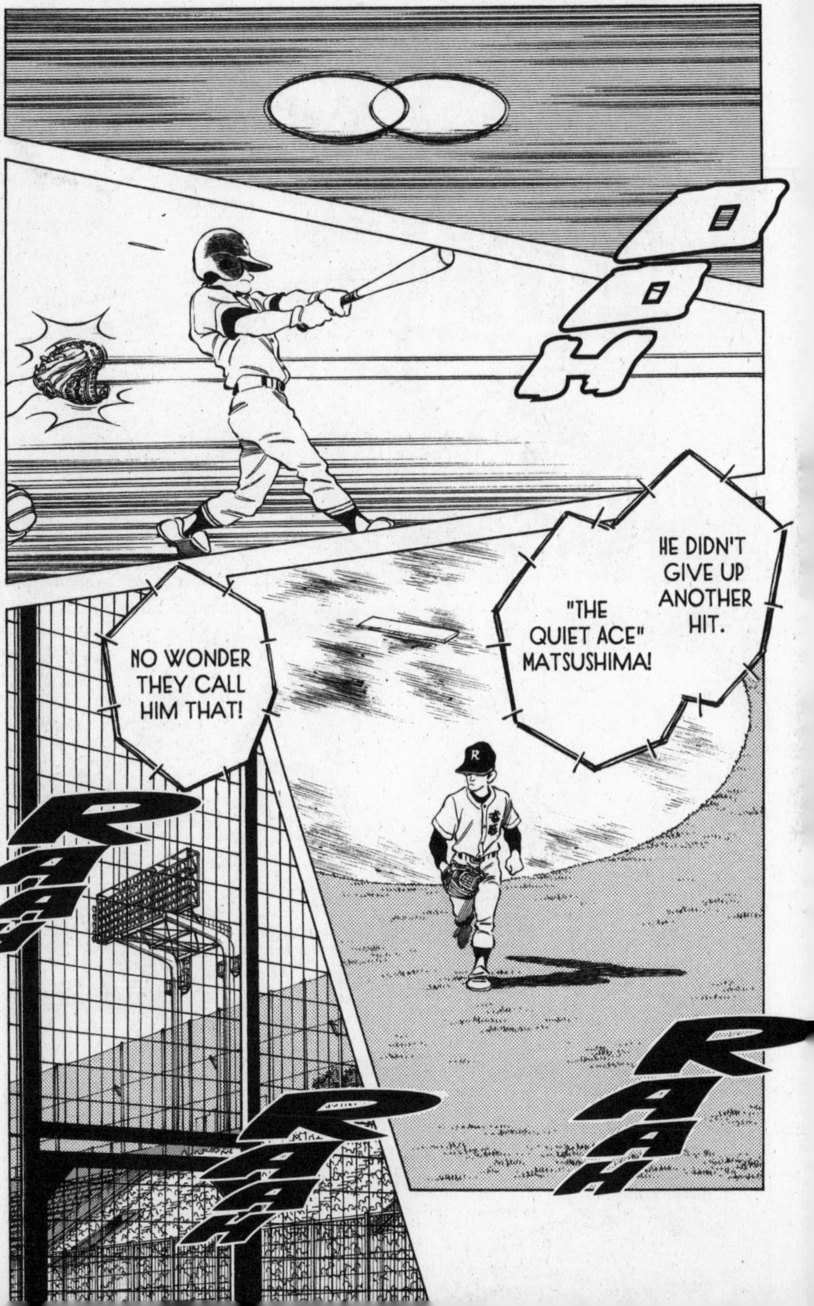
OOH
HE DIDN'T GIVE UP ANOTHER HIT.
"THE QUIET ACE" MATSUSHIMA!
NO WONDER THEY CALL HIM THAT!
RAAH
RAAH
RAAH

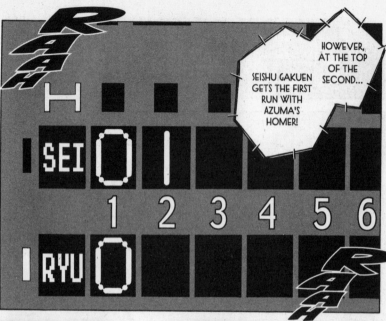

RAAH

HOWEVER, AT THE TOP OF THE SECOND...

SEISHU GAKUEN GETS THE FIRST RUN WITH AZUMA'S HOMER!

| | H | | | | | | | |
|---|---|---|---|---|---|---|---|---|
| SEI | 0 | 1 | | | | | | |
| | 1 | 2 | 3 | 4 | 5 | 6 | | |
| RYU | 0 | | | | | | | |

RAAH

THE BOTTOM OF THE SECOND...

RYUOU GAKUIN ALSO STARTS WITH THEIR FOURTH BATTER!

DON'T WORRY, MATSU-SHIMA.

I'LL GET US CAUGHT UP.

RAAH

COUNT-ING ON IT.

YEAH.

# 13 SHIMANO

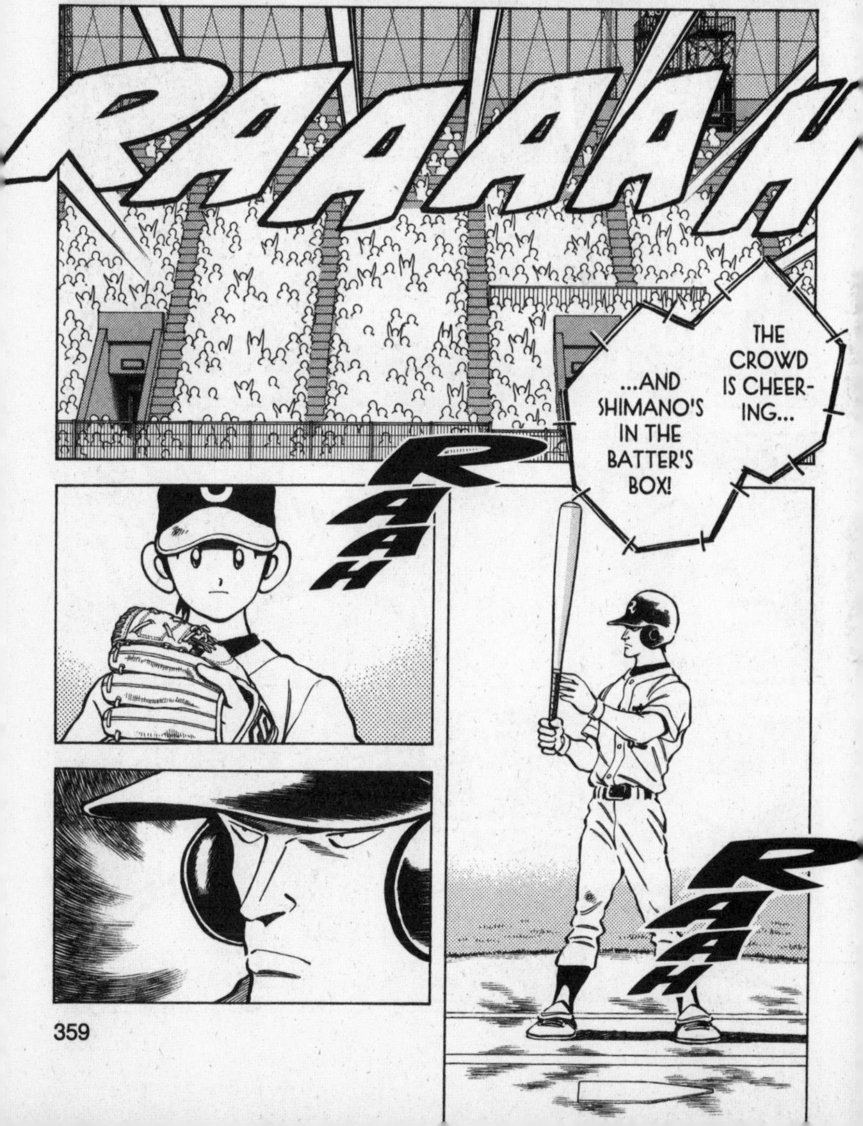
RAAAAH
THE CROWD IS CHEER-ING...
...AND SHIMANO'S IN THE BATTER'S BOX!
RAAAH
RAAAH

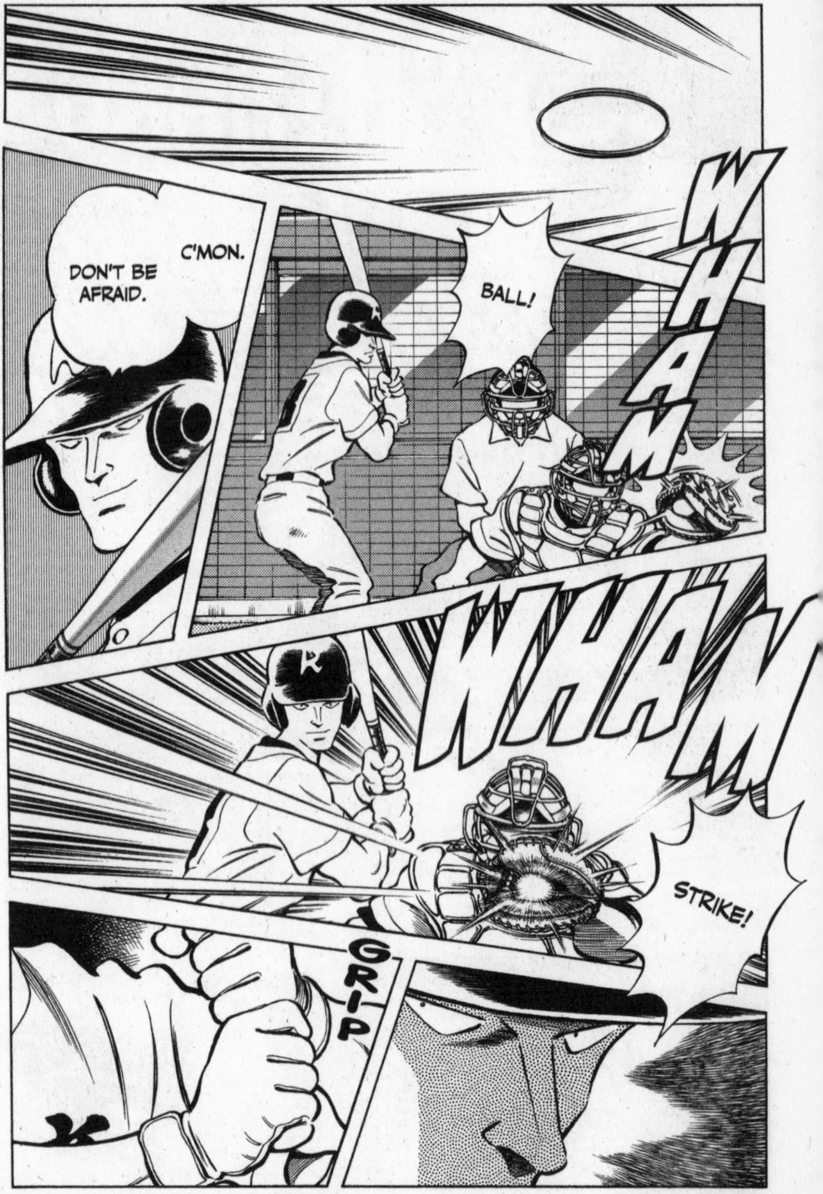
BALL!
WHAM
C'MON.
DON'T BE AFRAID.
WHAM
STRIKE!
GRIP

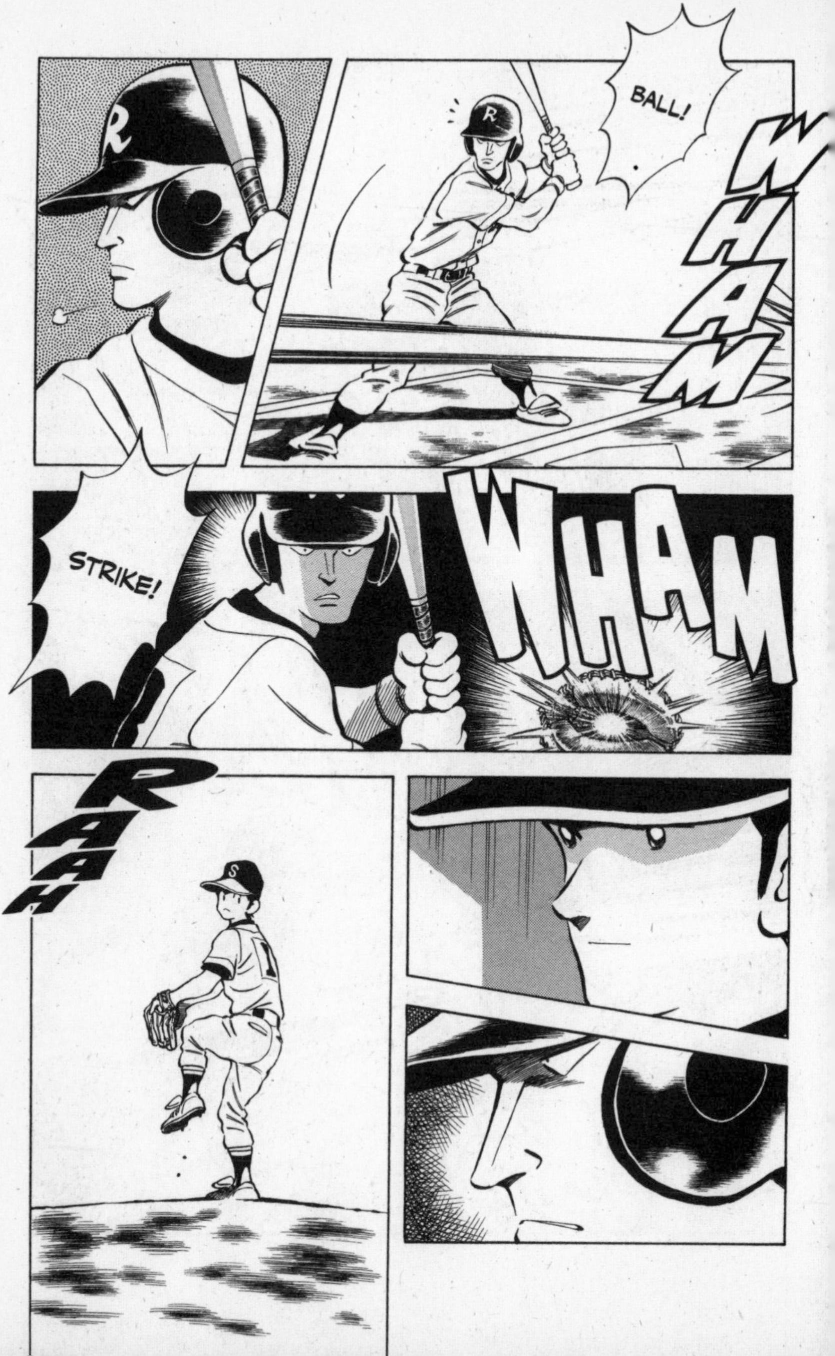
BALL!
WHAM
WHAM
STRIKE!
RAAAH

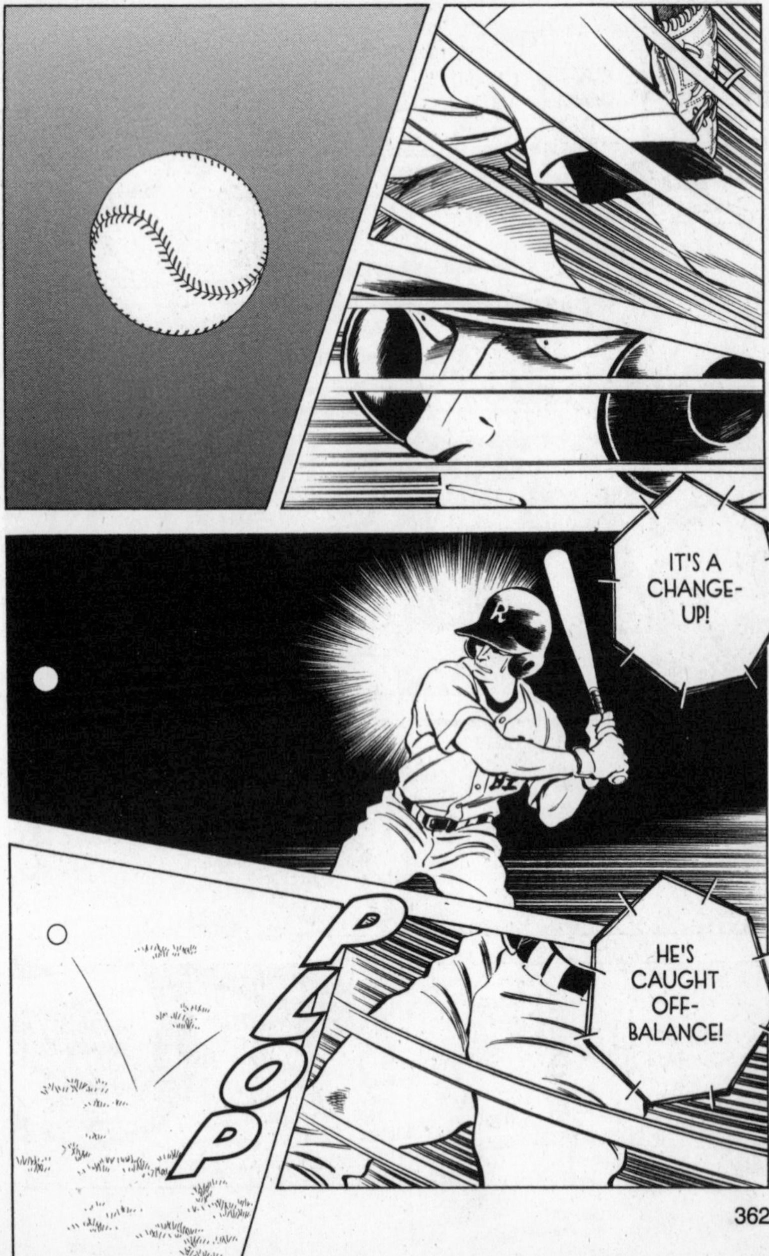
IT'S A CHANGE-UP!
HE'S CAUGHT OFF-BALANCE!
PLOP

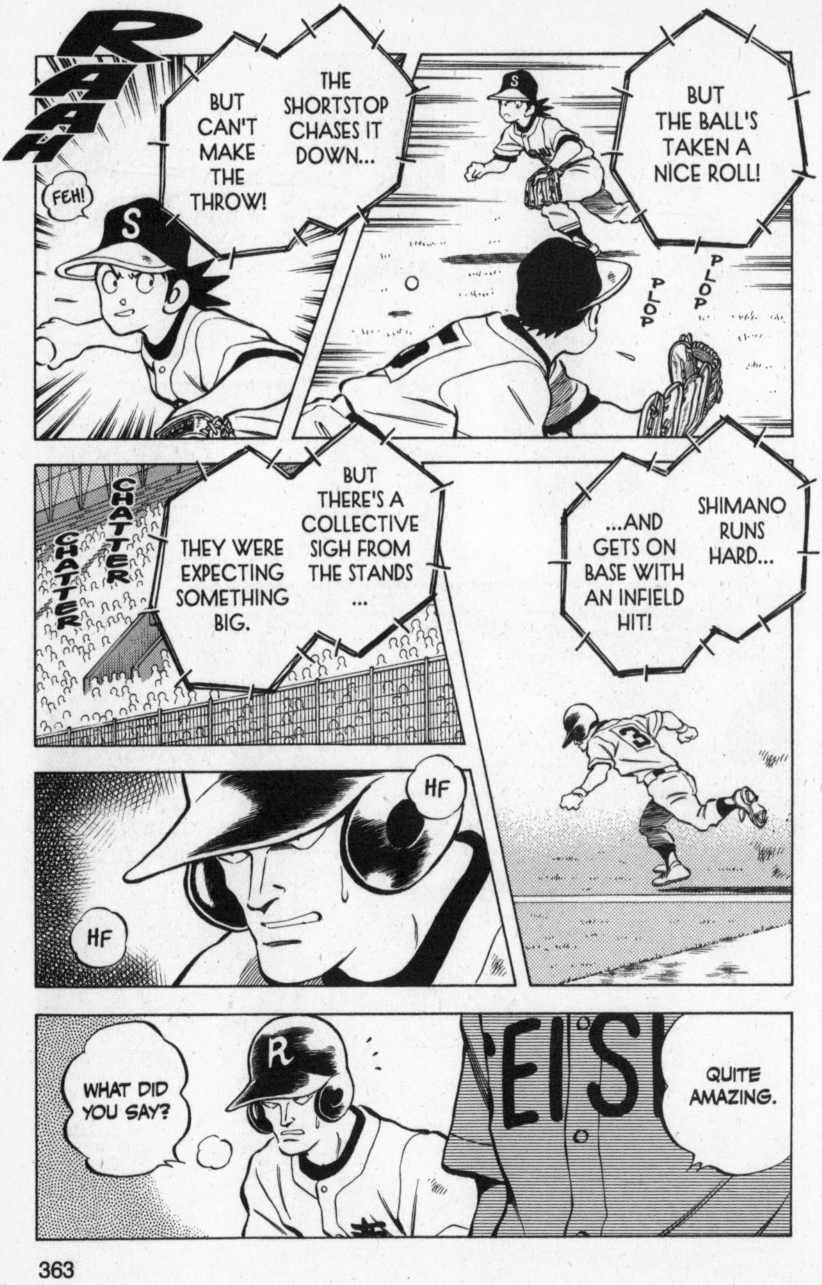
BUT THE BALL'S TAKEN A NICE ROLL!
PLOP PLOP
RAAAH
THE SHORTSTOP CHASES IT DOWN...
BUT CAN'T MAKE THE THROW!
FEH!
SHIMANO RUNS HARD...
...AND GETS ON BASE WITH AN INFIELD HIT!
BUT THERE'S A COLLECTIVE SIGH FROM THE STANDS ...
THEY WERE EXPECTING SOMETHING BIG.
CHATTER CHATTER
HF
HF
QUITE AMAZING.
WHAT DID YOU SAY?

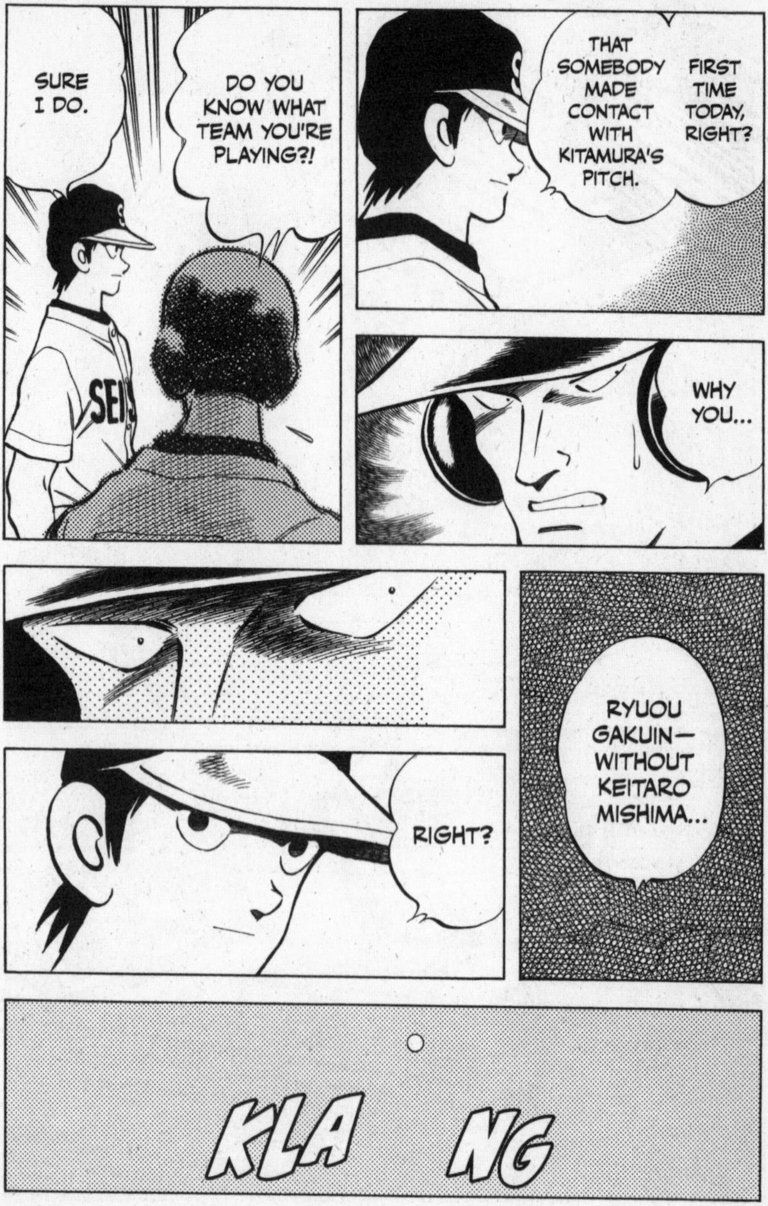
FIRST TIME TODAY, RIGHT?
THAT SOMEBODY MADE CONTACT WITH KITAMURA'S PITCH.
WHY YOU...
DO YOU KNOW WHAT TEAM YOU'RE PLAYING?!
SURE I DO.
RYUOU GAKUIN— WITHOUT KEITARO MISHIMA...
RIGHT?
KLA NG

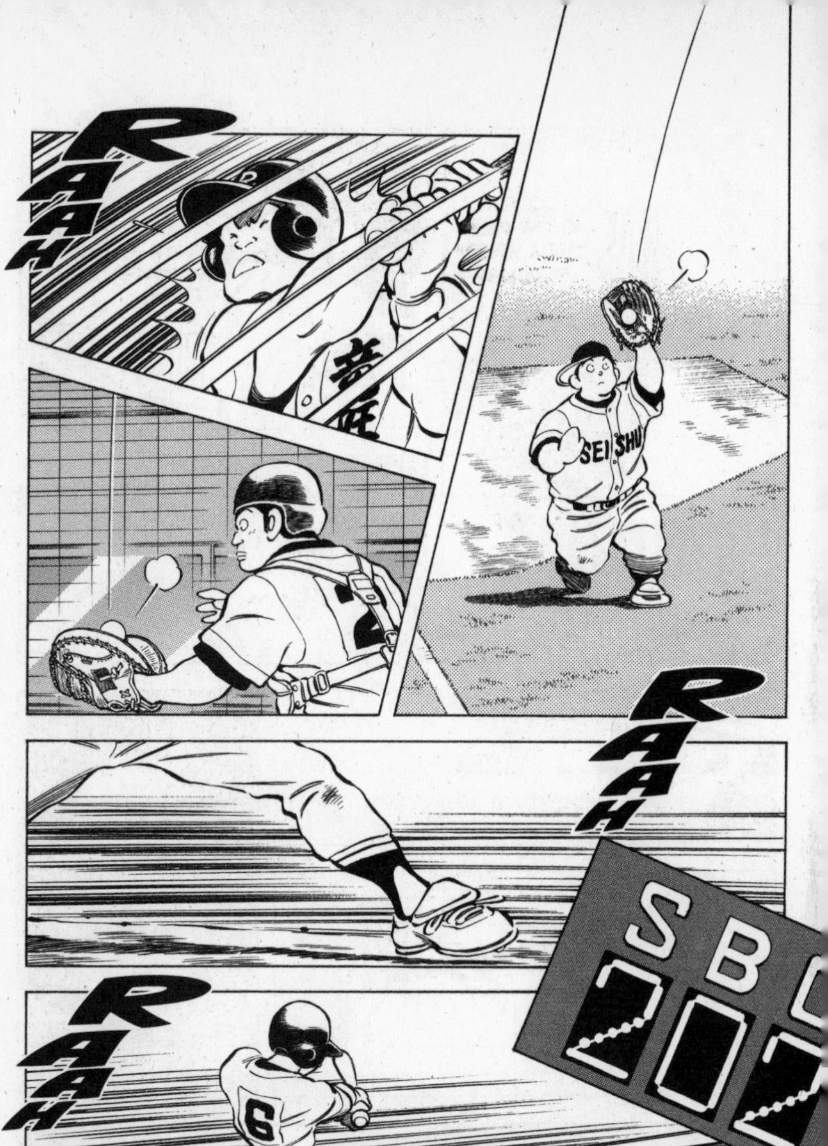

SEISHU
RAAAH
RAAAH
S B O
2 0 2
RAAAH

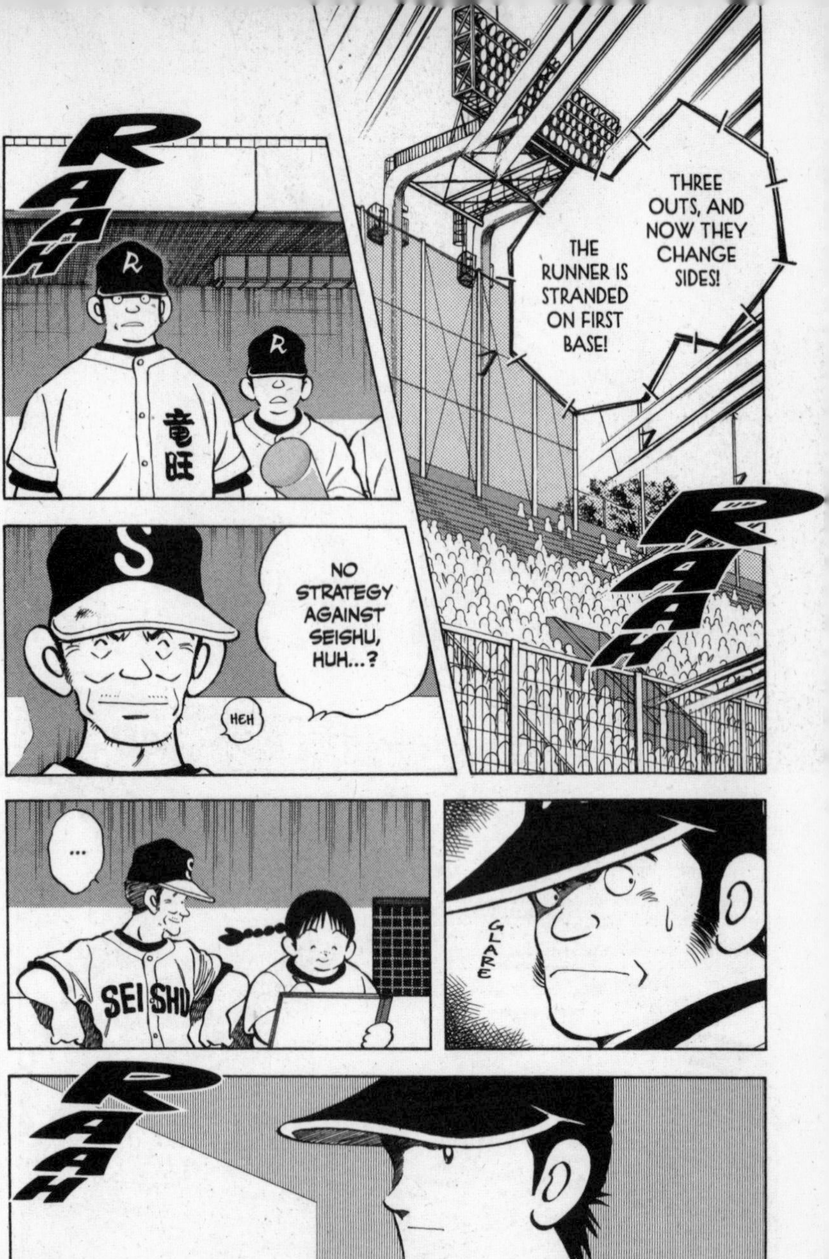
THE RUNNER IS STRANDED ON FIRST BASE!
THREE OUTS, AND NOW THEY CHANGE SIDES!
RAAH
RAAH
竜旺
NO STRATEGY AGAINST SEISHU, HUH...?
HEH
GLARE
...
SEISHU
RAAH

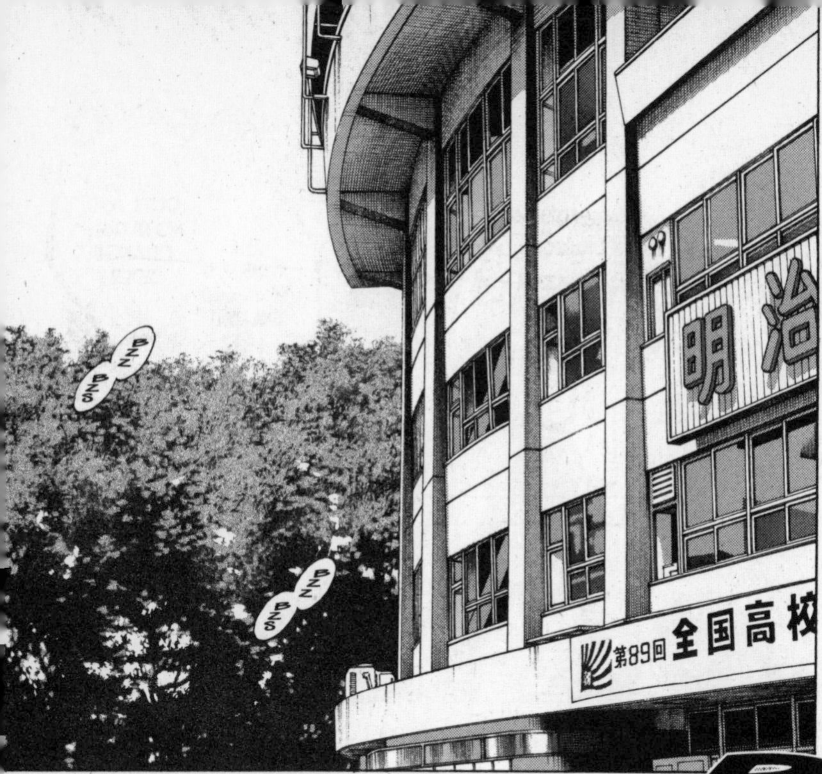
BZZ BZZ
BZZ BZZ
明治
第89回
全国高校

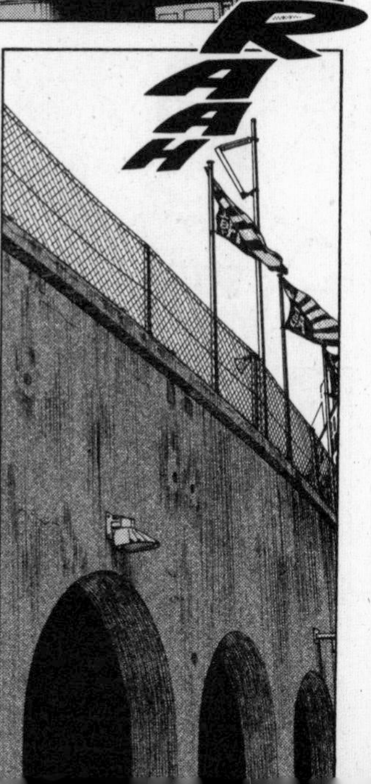
RAAH

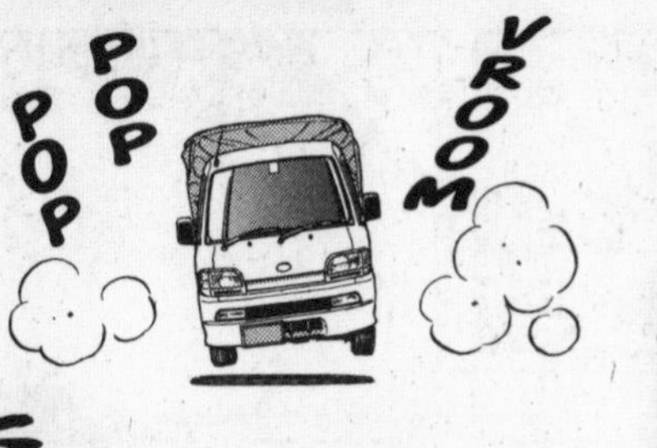
VROOM
POP POP

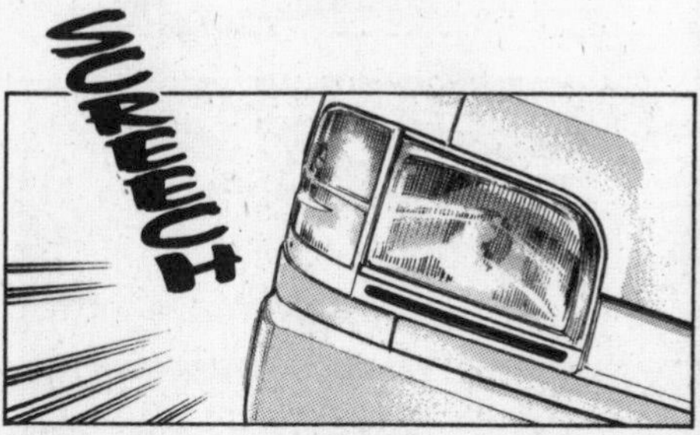
SCREECH

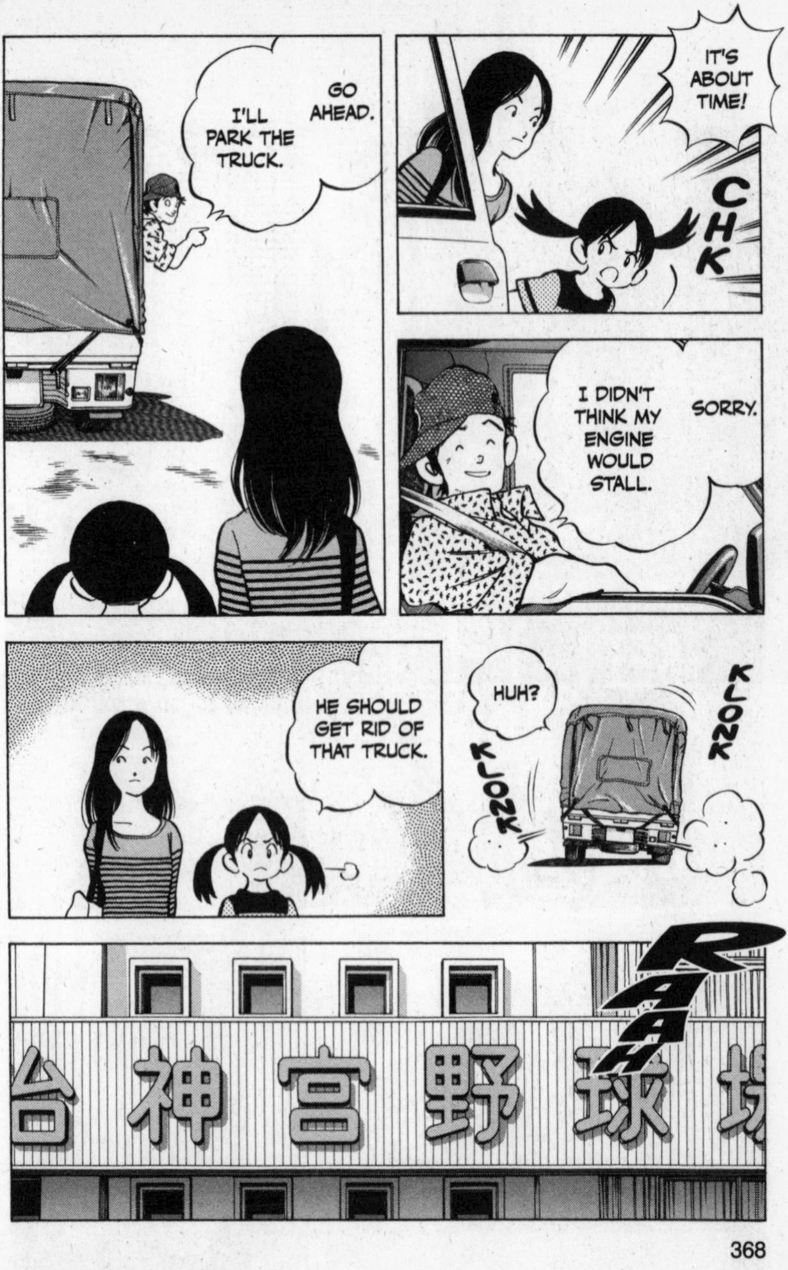
IT'S ABOUT TIME!
CHK
SORRY.
I DIDN'T THINK MY ENGINE WOULD STALL.
GO AHEAD.
I'LL PARK THE TRUCK.
KLONK
HUH?
KLONK
HE SHOULD GET RID OF THAT TRUCK.
RAAH
台神宮野球

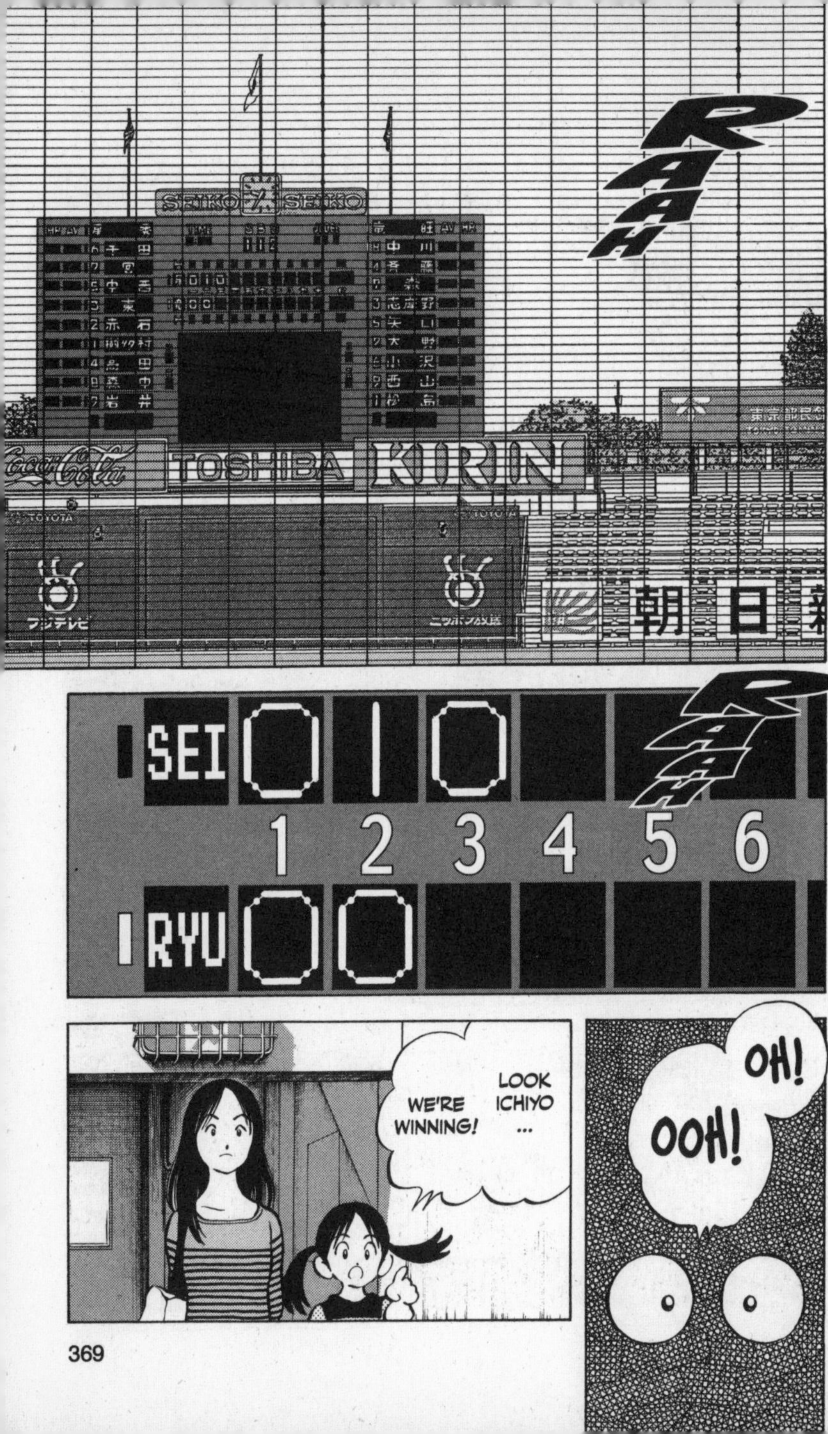
RAAH
SEIKO SEIKO
Coca-Cola
TOSHIBA
KIRIN
RAAH
SEI
1 2 3 4 5 6
RYU
OH!
OOH!
LOOK ICHIYO ...
WE'RE WINNING!

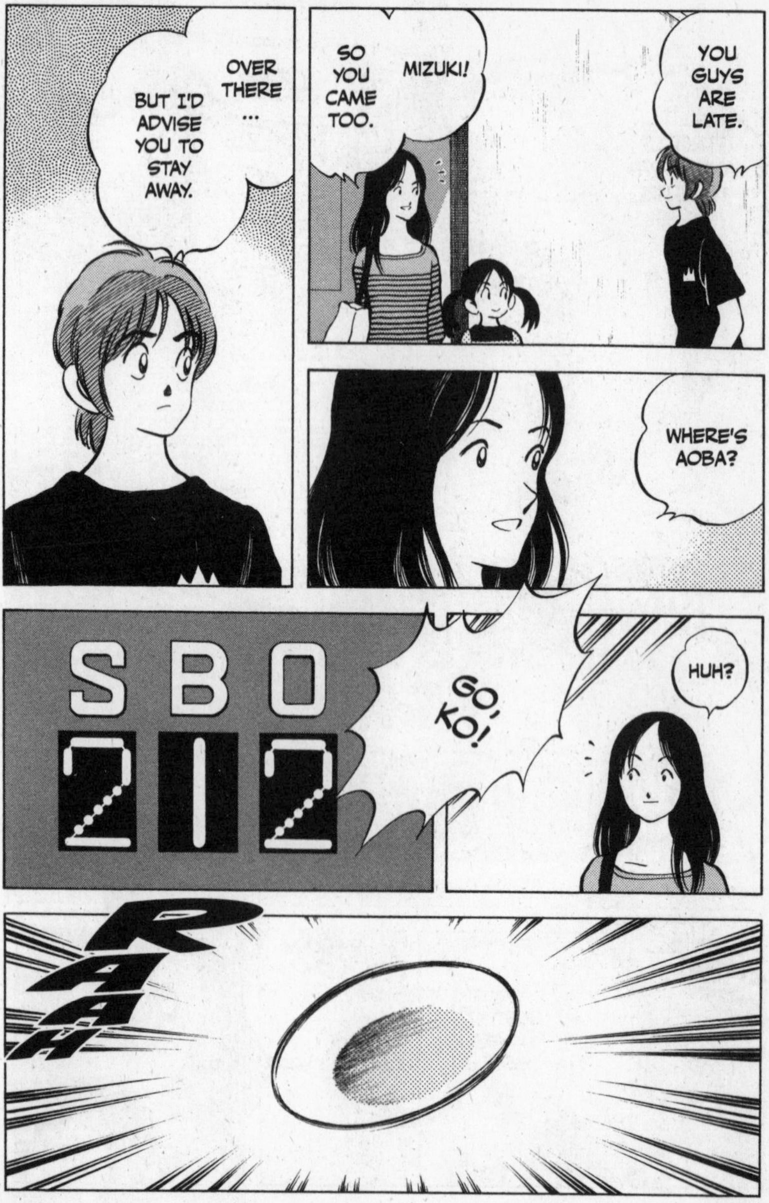

YOU GUYS ARE LATE.
MIZUKI!
SO YOU CAME TOO.
WHERE'S AOBA?
OVER THERE ...
BUT I'D ADVISE YOU TO STAY AWAY.
HUH?
GO, KO!
S B O
2 1 2
RAAAH

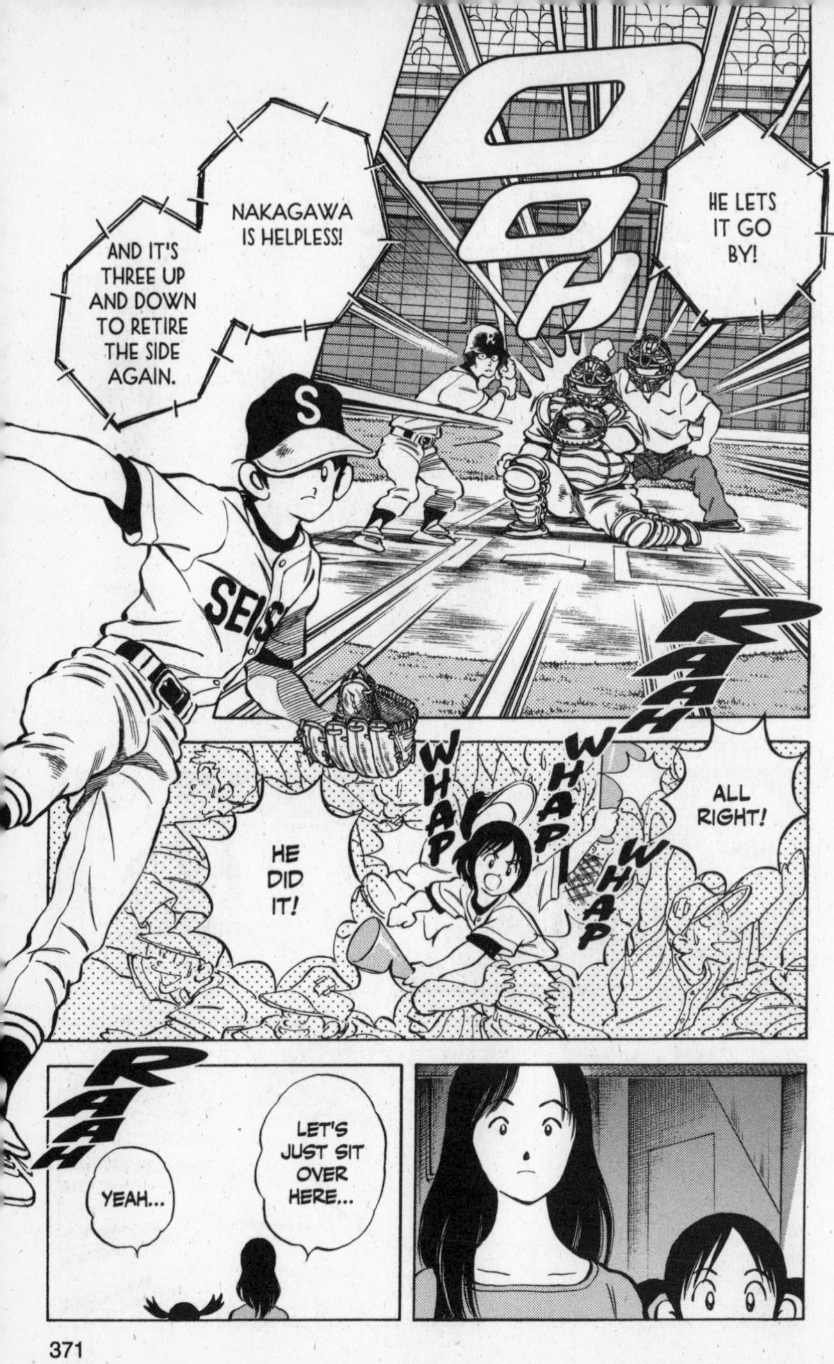
HE LETS IT GO BY!
OOH
NAKAGAWA IS HELPLESS!
AND IT'S THREE UP AND DOWN TO RETIRE THE SIDE AGAIN.
RAAH
ALL RIGHT!
WHAP
WHAP
WHAP
HE DID IT!
LET'S JUST SIT OVER HERE...
YEAH...
RAAH

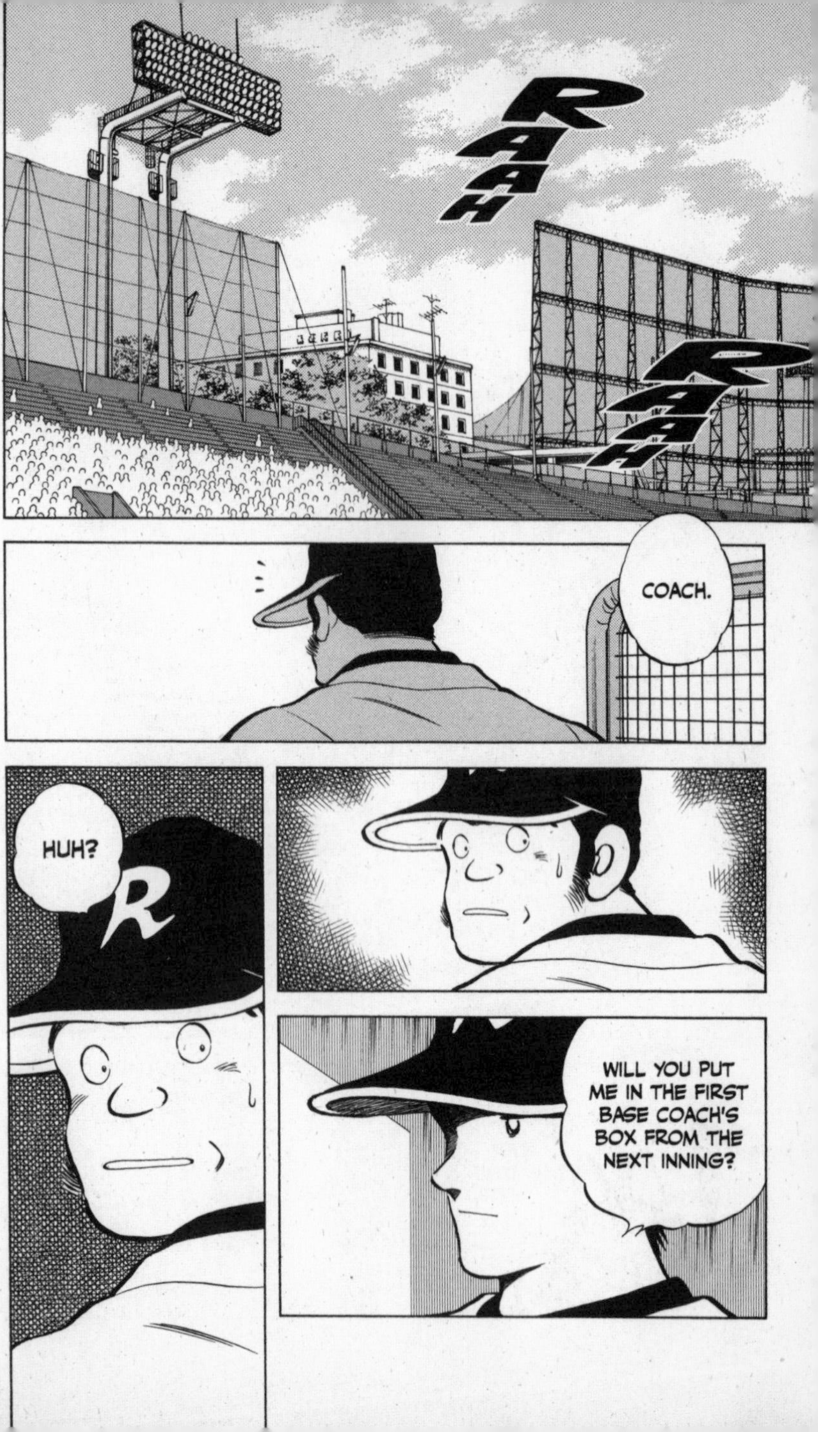
RAAAH
RAAAH
COACH.
WILL YOU PUT ME IN THE FIRST BASE COACH'S BOX FROM THE NEXT INNING?
HUH?

One of the biggest names in the manga industry today, Mitsuru Adachi made his debut in 1970 with *Kieta Bakuon* in the pages of *Deluxe Shonen Sunday*. The creator of numerous mega-hits such as *Touch*, *Miyuki* and *Cross Game*, Adachi Sensei received the Shogakukan Manga Award for all three of the aforementioned series. Truly in the top echelon of the manga industry, his cumulative works have seen over 200 million copies sold, and many of his series have been adapted into anime, live-action TV series and film. A master of his medium, Adachi has come to be known for his genious handling of dramatic elements skillfully combined with romance, comedy and sports. He, along with Rumiko Takahashi, has become synonymous with the phenomenal success of *Shonen Sunday* in Japan.

12-11
15⁰⁰

# CROSS GAME
## VOLUME 4
### Shonen Sunday Edition

STORY AND ART BY
# MITSURU ADACHI

© 2005 Mitsuru ADACHI/Shogakukan
All rights reserved.
Original Japanese edition "CROSS GAME" published by SHOGAKUKAN Inc.

Translation/Lillian Olsen
Touch-up Art & Lettering/Mark McMurray
Cover Design/John Kim, Yukiko Whitley
Interior Design/Yukiko Whitley
Editor/Andy Nakatani

The stories, characters and incidents mentioned in this publication are
entirely fictional.

Printed in Canada

Published by VIZ Media, LLC
P.O. Box 77010
San Francisco, CA 94107

10 9 8 7 6 5 4 3 2 1
First printing, July 2011

www.viz.com     WWW.SHONENSUNDAY.COM

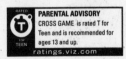